Injustice *on* Trial

Fitz John Porter

INJUSTICE *on* TRIAL

Second Bull Run, General Fitz John Porter's Court-Martial, and the Schofield Board Investigation That Restored His Good Name

CURT ANDERS

GUILD PRESS
EMMIS PUBLISHING LP

Guild Press Emmis Publishing, LP
10665 Andrade Drive
Zionsville, IN 46077
Phone: 317-773-4175

ISBN 1-57860-110-X
Library of Congress Control Number 2002115139

Interior and text design by Sheila G. Samson
Cover design by Karen J. Kennedy, Major Productions, Inc.

The photograph of Fitz John Porter on the front cover is courtesy of the National Archives.

Credits for the photographs in this book are as follows:

Library of Congress: Fitz John Porter, frontespiece; Edwin Stanton, page 13; John Pope, page 75; Irvin McDowell, page 104; David Hunter, page 113; Rutherford B. Hayes, page 275; and Joseph Choate, page 285. National Archives: Benjamin Wade, page 8; and Reverdy Johnson, page 96. National Archives at College Park: Joseph Holt, page 99. Massachusetts Commandery Military Order of the Loyal Legion and the U.S. Army Military History Institute: Asa B. Gardner, page 290. The image of John Schofield on page 280 is from a photograph by Falk.

Contents

The maps seen on pages 9, 11, 24, 32, 41, 48, 66, and 74 are by Joan Pennington, based on sketches by the author.

Preface and Acknowledgments

THIS book is the first on the subject to have been published since 1950 when Otto Eisenschiml's *The Celebrated Case of Fitz John Porter* appeared. What do these pages provide that his did not?

Roughly half of *Injustice on Trial* is devoted to day-to-day sessions of the Presidentially appointed Schofield Board which spent nearly seven months in 1878–1879 (mostly at West Point) taking testimony from almost a hundred and fifty witnesses—many of them former Confederates—leading to the report to President Rutherford B. Hayes that Fitz John Porter was not guilty of the crimes for which he had been convicted by the 1863 court-martial, and never had been, and that the destruction of his reputation as a soldier and as a man had been the result of studied injustice directed toward him before and during the trial and thereafter.

In short, the Schofield Board did exactly what Porter had been trying valiantly but in vain for nearly sixteen years to get some President to appoint qualified officers to do: It *tried the 1862–1863 Court-Martial* and found it guilty of gross errors.

Hence, the primary title of this book: *Injustice on Trial.* No other study of the celebrated case could have used it unless it spotlighted the Schofield Board's sessions to the extent that this one does. None has.

Justice Delayed, Justice Denied was the original title of this study. It correctly described General Porter's experience; in no way could he possibly have been made whole after nearly a quarter of a century of unjustified disgrace.

Yet of vastly greater importance even than the eventual good fortune of a wronged soldier is the story of how three generals and three brilliant lawyers—and one too zealous for his own good—developed a record that eventually overturned Porter's conviction *but also* demolished the precedents that had long held beyond challenge the findings of general courts-martial once approved by a President.

So, *Injustice on Trial* is the appropriate title for this study, even though many of these pages are devoted to matters such as how Fitz John Porter and George Brinton McClellan came to be kindred spirits, how the Union Army of Virginia under John Pope was mauled by General Lee in Second Bull Run, and how politics drove the Union's scapegoating during the next quarter of a century.

Only by establishing such a background can the Schofield Board's contributions to jurisprudence's enhancement be viewed in perspective, which is why this book is so long. Since Eisenschiml, the preferred art form for telling Porter's story has been the sidebar, or short essay, or appendix. These summaries saved Porter from oblivion, but the authors lacked the space in which to convey more than a sharply limited number of facts. And this has led to some rather harsh judgments of his conduct. Three examples:

Kenneth P. Williams suggested that it was Porter's "habitual caution, not accurate knowledge of the enemy's strength, that controlled his action at Second Bull Run."[1] Fletcher Pratt, a biographer of Secretary of War Edwin M. Stanton, concluded a damning essay by declaring: "Porter simply did not want to attack (he never did in any other battle), and found excuses for not doing so, and he obtained his 'vindication' less through justice than through longevity."[2] And Stephen W. Sears has written recently that "An example had to be made, and General Porter was the not entirely undeserving victim. When everything about that time and place [Second Bull Run] is considered, the judgment of Allan Nevins seems a just one: With his frame of mind, Fitz John Porter 'was better out of the army.' "[3]

Might they have found General Porter more sinned against than sinner if they had read the 1,869 pages of *Proceedings and Report of the Board of Officers in the Case of Fitz John Porter*?

The Schofield dimension is all-important.

Consider Ulysses Grant's experience. As acting secretary of war and later President, he had rejected Porter's appeals because he considered the findings of the court-martial just and final. But when he read the proceedings of the Schofield Board's investigation, it quickly became apparent to him that a great injustice had been done to Fitz John Porter and he used all of the influence he had to correct it.

❋ ❋ ❋

But copies of the Schofield Board's *Proceedings* have long been scarce and Otto Eisenschiml's brief summary missed too many significant points. Accordingly, I have devoted six of this book's seventeen chapters and two appendices to the hearings conducted by the Schofield Board, with the two volumes of *Proceedings* as the primary source.

Why have the proceedings of the Schofield Board not earlier won the attention given, for example, the details of Porter's trial and conviction that have been available in full for more than a hundred years in the *Official Records*?

Unlike the *Official Records*, it is difficult to gain access to the few extant copies of *Proceedings*. I was able to borrow those precious books from the New York State Library through an inter-library loan secured by the Desmond/Fish Library here in Garrison. But Volume One had not aged well in its 121 years of existence. Its format was the same as *O.R.* volumes, except that it had no table of contents or index. Scanning and photocopying were out of the question. The only way to find out what was inside was to turn 1,011 extremely fragile pages—first to make an abstract of what they revealed, then to revisit the passages of greatest significance and copy them, in the manner of monks in the Middle Ages, into my computer.

To prevent harm to the volume, I padded a meat rack with paper towels and cradled the book in it, blanketing the pages left open at the end of each abstracting and extracting session with more towels. I took the same care with equally fragile Volume Two, which moved the proceedings from page 1,020 to 1,869.

The results are Chapters Twelve through Sixteen and Appendices VI and VII, herein. I believe that they fairly present, for the first time, the long-neglected day-by-day story of how the Schofield Board restored to Fitz John Porter the evidence that led to his vindication—absent which a full understanding of the general's ordeal is incomplete.

❋ ❋ ❋

"My object is to add my feeble note toward the establishment of truth, the vindication of honor, and the upholding of the sublime principles of justice."

So Alabama's former Confederate Major General Joseph Wheeler—the cavalry leader who at the age of twenty-six called himself the "War Child"—declared in early 1883 in a speech urging his colleagues in the House of Representatives to pass legislation to restore Fitz John Porter to the United States Army.

Honor *needed* vindicating. Along with reputation, honor is one of those forces that drive the present narrative. The moral of this many-paged tale may as well be: Character Counts—*Always!*

Finally, I did not undertake this project to grind an ax for or against General Porter. I hold with General Lee that Porter might "do well enough with someone to tell him [what to do]."[4] It was Porter's misfortune, however (as had been William Franklin's and Charles Stone's) to have come under the influence of George McClellan instead of—well, Henry Halleck, whose lieutenants included William Tecumseh Sherman and U. S. Grant and, by the way, John M. Schofield, but also, alas, John Pope.

Neither is this book an attempted biography. It is merely a contribution of some neglected chapters to a story that is a long way from having been fully and finally told.

Professor Hans L. Trefousse very graciously read an earlier version of the text and I am deeply grateful for his comments. Carol Donick and her associates at the Desmond/Fish Library in Garrison played critically important roles by obtaining the rare *Proceedings* volumes and also Henry Gabler's great but unfortunately unpublished dissertation for me through interlibrary loans, and I owe very special thanks to the New York State Library for allowing me to make use of those two volumes of the Schofield Board's *Proceedings* for the four months my abstracting and extracting required.

Alan Aimone, Chief of Special Collections at the United States Military Academy Library at West Point, gave me access to the rare pamphlets in which Judge Advocate Joseph Holt and Porter's counsel Reverdy Johnson continued to argue the case after the court-martial ended. Researcher Ceceily Kay Richter in Washington provided me with information regarding the availability of documents and some of the rare images of men such as lawyer Joseph Choate who were vitally important in General Porter's case. Joan Pennington converted my rough sketches into maps that are unusual because of their simplicity and the use of what we call story boxes instead of the usual unhelpful captions. And editor and text designer Sheila Samson has brought all of these elements together with skill and patience that are much admired and sincerely appreciated.

Finally, Guild Press's Nancy Baxter acted as readers' advocate and reminded me repeatedly to stick to story-telling, to keep answering "And then what happened?" Her guidance and encouragement were needed often and given graciously, and for her patience, as well as her wit and wisdom, I will always be deeply grateful.

C. A.
Garrison, New York
October 1, 2002

Prologue — 1878

Good name in man and woman, dear my lord,
Is the immediate jewel of their souls.
Who steals my purse steals trash; 'tis something, nothing;
'Twas mine, 'tis his, and has been slave to thousands;
But he that filches from me my good name
Robs me of that which not enriches him,
And makes me poor indeed.

—Soldier Iago to Soldier Othello

By early 1878, practically every American who could read a newspaper had a rough idea of who Fitz John Porter was: a Civil War veteran, an ex-Union army general who raised a fuss in the national press and the Congress every few years trying to get back the good reputation a court-martial had taken away from him back in 1863 in the wake of the battle of Second Bull Run.

Each flurry of activity had the same pattern. Either because there had been a change in presidents or some new evidence had turned up, Porter would file a request for a fresh review of his case; arguments pro and con would fill the newspapers' columns; and then, after a while, his appeal would be denied.

This had happened during the presidencies of Abraham Lincoln, Andrew Johnson, and Ulysses S. Grant. Now, with Rutherford B. Hayes in the White House, another cycle was beginning.

To some observers, Porter's quest for vindication seemed quaint. He reminded them of the fictional old Spaniard Don Quixote, foolishly lowering his lance and, mistaking windmills for enemy knights, charging them: pursuing the impossible dream of restoring his personal honor in an age that placed far higher values on gaining wealth and investing it to earn more.

There was much truth in such comparisons.

Prologue

To the generation coming of age thirteen years after Appomattox, any man of fifty-six would seem almost ancient, the times of his prime gone beyond relevance. Congress, Porter's periodic target, did bear some resemblance to a field of windmills. But, so far, none of Porter's thrusts had done anything more than roil empty air.

In his letter to President Hayes dated March 9, 1878, Porter spoke of justice and truth as though his high evaluations of those concepts—and of honor—were shared by the politicians who would consider his appeal and determine its outcome. However, the powers of lofty words and long-cherished beliefs had faded in the fifteen years separating January 1863 and March 1878. Cynics were more inclined to ask, what did *honor* ever buy? And what would Porter do with his, even if the Government ever restored it to him?

No longer did it make much here-and-now difference what good or evil things particular soldiers on either side had or had not done at any point during the long war. With half a million or more dead, or wounded, or simply gone and already duly mourned, who cared about anything but the future?

Also, early in 1878 it could have been argued that Fitz John Porter's loss of his reputation had not really harmed him. Instead of killing him as a traitor by hanging or putting him in jail for the rest of his life, Abraham Lincoln had approved a court-martial's finding of guilty as charged and the relatively moderate sentence of cashiering. Indeed, being expelled from the army might well have saved Porter's life. And although he was to be "forever disqualified from holding any office of trust or profit under the Government of the United States,"[1] within thirteen months of his disgrace he was in Colorado investigating mining properties on behalf of financiers in New York.[2] At the time of Porter's latest appeal he was employed as receiver of the bankrupt Central Railroad of New Jersey.[3]

So why did Fitz John Porter keep trying again after each request for review was denied, or simply ignored? Was he doomed to suffer the fate of Sisyphus, who was condemned by the gods to roll a huge rock to the top of a mountain, only to watch the heavy stone fall of its own weight, and then follow it down to begin to trip upward again, throughout eternity?

So it may well have seemed.

Fitz John Porter kept filing appeals because *he knew he was not guilty* of the gravest of military offenses and that his suffering from the loss of his reputation was *utterly unwarranted.* To President Hayes he wrote:

> I most respectfully, but most urgently, renew my oft-repeated appeal to have you review my case. I ask it as a matter of long-delayed justice to myself. I renew it upon the ground heretofore stated, that public justice cannot be satisfied so long as my appeal remains unheard.
>
> My sentence is a continuing sentence, and made to follow my daily life. For this reason if for no other, my case is ever within the reach of executive as well as legislative interference.
>
> I beg to present copies of papers heretofore presented, bearing upon my case, and trust that you will deem it a proper one for your prompt and favorable consideration.
>
> If I do not make it plain that I have been wronged, I alone am the sufferer. If I do make it plain that great injustice has been done me, then I am sure that you, and all others who love truth and justice, will be glad that the opportunity for my vindication has not been denied.[4]

So began another of Porter's pushes of his rock up the mountain of bureaucracy, prejudice, ignorance, and growing indifference. None of his earlier Quixotic attempts to right wrong having succeeded, he had no idea of how heavy the burden of proof of innocence might become.

Part I: Advance to Contact

CHAPTER ONE

How Did Fitz John Porter Get Into Such Serious Trouble?

Disgraced Fitz John Porter, in 1878 President Rutherford B. Hayes' petitioner, came from a family long and widely known as the "Fighting Porters." David Porter, serving in the American Revolution as captain of a gunboat, escaped from a British prison ship in an empty water cask and promptly took command of another Yankee warship.

One of his sons won more fame for the family as a commodore during the War of 1812. Five of *his* six sons also served in the United States Navy.

Among them during that war was John Porter, an officer on the U.S.S. *Congress.* His third son Fitz John was born on August 31, 1822. But he died when the boy was only nine, causing Mrs. Porter to remark: "The life of a public officer is beset with more pains and penalties than the highest renown can ever atone for." Even so, she sought to extend and enhance the reputations of the "Fighting Porters" by obtaining an appointment to a service academy for Fitz John—but, in a break with the family's strong historic ties to the navy, to West Point.[1]

Of the 104 cadets who entered the military academy in 1841 only 41 survived the four-year ordeal. Porter finished eighth in the Class of 1845.[2]

Lieutenant Porter, serving in the 4th Artillery, was in every battle General-in-Chief Winfield Scott's forces fought from Vera Cruz to the southwestern edge of Mexico City. After Molino del Rey and Chapultepec had been captured, the Americans seemed stalled by the defenders of a strong point known as La Garita de Belen (Bethlehem Gate). Beyond it was a fortress called the Cuidadela. Historian K. Jack Bauer described the fight:

> Although the defenders loosed a withering stream of musket and cannon shot at the advancing Americans, the attackers kept coming. [Captain Simon H.] Drum and Lieutenant Calvin Benjamin brought up an 18-pounder and a 24-pounder howitzer on either side of the causeway. Their fire caused extensive damage, showering the Mexican gunners with shell fragments and masonry splinters. . . . [After the garita was taken it] was exposed to heavy fire from the Cuidadela. Drum was killed and his successor, Lieutenant Fitz John Porter, had twenty-seven of his thirty men injured.[3]

"Thereupon Porter," wrote Otto Eisenschiml, "moved a single eight-inch howitzer in front of the infantry and, although painfully injured by a spent cannon ball, advanced to within 100 yards of the fortification, repulsing a Mexican sortie with canister and grapeshot. Following this brave act, Porter was breveted major, for 'Gallant and Meritorious Services.' "[4]

After the war Major Porter was stationed at West Point for several years as an instructor in artillery tactics. Among his friends were Captain George B. McClellan, who had been graduated a year behind him, and another Mexican War veteran, William Franklin.[5] In 1853 the academy's superintendent, Robert E. Lee, made Porter the post adjutant; Secretary of War Jefferson Davis assigned McClellan the task of leading a survey for extension of a railroad from St. Paul to Puget Sound.[6] Later in the decade McClellan, who had become Davis' protege, was sent with two other officers to observe the war in the Crimea.[7] By then Porter was in Utah as an adjutant serving with the expeditionary force led by Colonel Albert Sidney Johnston.[8]

General-in-Chief Scott had enabled Porter to serve under two of the most respected and promising officers in the regular army. With Southern secession looming after Lincoln's election, Scott began using Major Porter to carry out special, usually secret assignments. In November 1860, he inspected the federal military installations at Charleston—Castle Pinckney, Fort Moultrie, and unfinished Fort Sumter in the harbor—and, on his return, recommended to General Scott that Major Robert Anderson be placed in command. It is also possible that Porter and Scott worked on a plan for transferring Fort Moultrie's garrison out to Fort Sumter.[9]

Major Porter's next mission was to prevent the loss to secessionists of troops and weapons located along the lower Texas coast. According to a story published in 1880:

> Before Porter arrived at Indianola on March 4 [1861] with only a hundred and twenty recruits, [Brigadier General Robert] Twiggs had surrendered his troops and much property to the commissioners of Texas. Commanding a greatly superior force, [Twiggs] demanded surrender of Porter's ship, the *Webster*, with all and everything on board, including $40,000 in gold. Porter replied that he would defend the ship and, if necessary, throw the gold overboard. While the commissioners hesitated, Porter acquired the *Star of the West* for $13,000 and at night took on board what troops and batteries he could not accommodate on the *Webster*. In this way he rescued between four hundred and five hundred infantry and Stoneman's cavalry. . . .[10]

After Fort Sumter's surrender, Major Porter was sent to Harrisburg to organize and arm Pennsylvania's troops.[11] Recognizing that a commander of the state's forces was needed, Porter wrote his old friend George McClellan—by then, a railroad executive in Cincinnati.

But Ohio won the struggle over McClellan's services; he was commissioned a major general of volunteers, and not long afterward, as a major general in the regular army. Only General-in-Chief Scott outranked him.[12]

Pennsylvania Governor Andrew Curtin then turned to Brigadier General Robert Patterson, a veteran of the War of 1812 and the Mexican War, who agreed to serve for ninety days. Major Porter was assigned as assistant adjutant- general of Patterson's Department of Pennsylvania.[13]

Porter's contributions extended beyond his title. When Washington was isolated by the riots in Baltimore, he took some of Patterson's units and started in that direction—only to be stopped and told that by order of the President he was to return to Harrisburg. Afterward, journalist A. J. McClure described a meeting at which Curtin and Patterson were discussing the situation. McClure wrote:

> After all had spoken, Fitz John Porter, the youngest of the party, spoke with an earnestness that inspired everyone present. With his

> handsome face brightened by the enthusiasm of his patriotism, and his keen eyes flashing the fire of his courage, he said: "I would march the troops through Baltimore or its ashes to the defense of the capital."[14]

Absent telegraphic communication with Washington, a message from St. Louis requesting assistance in preventing a Confederate takeover arrived in Harrisburg. Porter's years as an adjutant enabled him to direct support to the distant threatened region. Later, ignoring the fact that Porter had acted without authority, Scott and Secretary of War Simon Cameron commended him.[15] More to the point, on May 14 they signed his commission as a colonel in the regular army. And three days later, Fitz John Porter was appointed to be a brigadier general of volunteers.[16]

Another indication that Porter's service was not all clerical was his participation in a skirmish that took place on July 2. Riding with Patterson's most advanced elements, he crossed the Potomac at Williamsport. Near a stream called Falling Waters, roughly eight miles into northern Virginia, the Union probe collided with a Confederate brigade commanded by Thomas J. Jackson, who had been graduated from West Point a year behind Porter, and rebel cavalry led by Colonel J. E. B. Stuart.

Porter ordered artillery fire placed on the enemy's blocking position, then gathered cavalry of his own and started to lead a charge aimed at Jackson's camp. But his horse failed to clear a fence, and Porter's collision with the ground ended his brief vacation from the boring duty of writing and responding to Patterson's messages, orders, and reports.[17]

After the surrender of Fort Sumter, the people of the North had responded admirably to Lincoln's call for troops. Anyone taking a carriage or horseback ride around the camps ringing the city and across the Potomac could see that a formidable army had been assembled to cope with the Confederate forces' presence as near to Washington as Manassas Junction on the Orange & Alexandria Railroad and Fairfax Court-House. And time was of the essence: if the ninety-day men were not used soon, their terms of service would expire without anything having been accomplished.

Many Northerners expected that for this new Union army, commanded by Major General Irvin McDowell, it would be merely a matter of marching thirty-odd miles, whipping the rebels, and then driving on to Richmond. However, General Lee, then directing Virginia Governor John Letcher's forces, had placed units down the Potomac, near Aquia Landing, and upstream from Washington at Harpers Ferry as well as near Manassas. Theoretically, he could move troops from any of these locations to another if reinforcements were needed to repel a Yankee attack.

General Scott was obliged to prevent Lee from shifting General Joseph E. Johnston's brigades from the Harpers Ferry area and the lower Shenandoah Valley via the Manassas Gap Railroad eastward to join General Pierre G. T. Beauregard's forces near Manassas Junction: McDowell's objective. In anticipation of such a situation, the general-in-chief had placed Patterson's units northwest of Washington on the Maryland banks of the Potomac and ordered them to "amuse" General Johnston—that is, to show enough belligerence to keep his troops where they were.

Another Confederate force was in western Virginia. With Winfield Scott's approval, some of General McClellan's troops skirmished with it in mid-June—then in early July the federal campaign in that region began in earnest. Before leaving Cincinnati, however, the general commanding made certain that his headquarters was bringing along a portable printing press. Subsequently, Northern newspapers were amply provided with news describing the victory of "the Young Napoleon" at Rich Mountain on July 11—a fight won, actually, by Brigadier General William S. Rosecrans.[18]

But the summer's main event was supposed to be the great whipping the Union's divisions were to administer to Beauregard's Confederates at Manassas. General McDowell's nigh-uncontested advance was a fiasco, a series of blunders that consumed five days instead of two. By Saturday, July 20, Joe Johnston had slipped his brigades away from old General Patterson's ineffective demonstrations and moved them in rail cars from the Shenandoah Valley eastward to reinforce Beauregard. Sunday's battle was actually a meeting engagement, a collision of combatants followed by build-ups on both sides until a brigade just arrived by the Manassas Gap Railroad hit the Yankees in the flank.

Surprise and shock begat fear that degenerated into panic and rout. But the Confederates were almost as unstrung by victory as the federal units were by defeat. Even so, Thomas J. Jackson wanted to pursue them. No, decided Commander-in-Chief Jefferson Davis, who had arrived from Richmond just as the battle was ending.[19]

Commander-in-Chief Lincoln stayed up all that night, listening to first-hand reports brought to the Executive Mansion by people who had been at

Manassas.[20] On the next day he sent a telegram to General McClellan out in western Virginia: "Circumstances make your presence here necessary. Charge Rosecrans or some other general with your present department and come hither without delay."[21]

2

For a time after Bull Run, General George McClellan seemed the answer to Washingtonians' most earnest prayers. Shortly after his arrival, soldiers who had been littering the streets were back in camps north of the city and across the Potomac. Troop movements—militia units heading home, volunteer regiments arriving—imparted the impression that strength was returning. One look at the handsome, vigorous, dashing Young Napoleon was about all it took to replace memories of recent chaos and despair with confidence and hope.

General McClellan was excited by the excitement he was generating. To his wife, Mary Ellen Marcy McClellan, he wrote on July 27:

> I find myself in a new & strange position here—Presdt, Cabinet, Genl Scott, all deferring to me—by some strange operation of magic I seem to have become *the* power of the land. I almost think that were I to win some small success now I could become Dictator or anything else that might please me—but nothing of that kind would please me—*therefore I won't* be Dictator! Admirable self-denial![22]

What the newly arrived general found, of course, was that his troops needed discipline, which meant intensive training. Among his first acts was to send for officers he deemed capable of turning a recently whipped rabble into a first-rate fighting field army: among them, Fitz John Porter.

Earlier, back in Ohio, McClellan had asked General-in-Chief Scott to assign Porter to his staff—in vain, for Patterson was in greater need of him. In Bull Run's wake, however, Porter found himself back where real soldiers always prefer to be: commanding troops.[23]

Brigadier General Porter was relatively fortunate. He could concentrate on motivating and inspiring company commanders to make their troops the best in their regiments, and colonels their regiments the best in his brigades.

McClellan, by contrast, was wearing himself out riding (usually, galloping) to inspect progress being made at one camp and fortification after another along the thirty-seven-mile circumference of Washington's combined training centers and defensive strong points—*and then* attending dinners and other social gatherings.

Much of what General McClellan learned during his visits to the capital he found disturbing. Some of it he shared with Fitz Porter.

Certain Radical Republicans in Congress, according to reports, were locked in a struggle with the President for control of the war's military operations. These men—called Jacobins by John Hay, one of Mr. Lincoln's secretaries—were said to be expecting great victories from the restored and renamed Army of the Potomac under the command of General McClellan. Accordingly, it behooved McClellan, Porter, and other newcomers among his division commanders to find out more about the Radicals.

Fervent desire for abolition united this faction of Lincoln's Republican Party.[24] The first gun fired at Fort Sumter provided the Radicals with hopes of success never dreamed of earlier. "What we could not have done in many lifetimes," gloated Carl Schurz, "the madness and folly of the South has accomplished for us."[25] Lest the opportunity be lost, the Radicals became the North's most strident advocates of relentless warfare. If the war "continues for thirty years and bankrupts the whole nation," declared Senator Benjamin Franklin Wade of Ohio, "I hope to God there will be no peace until we can say there is not a slave in this land."[26] And Wade's colleague, Charles Sumner of Massachusetts, confessed: "I fear our victories more than our defeats."[27]

Restoration of the Union had become the North's war aim only after acrimonious debate; even so, the Radicals behaved as though abolition had been included as an agreed-upon goal. Moreover, apparently they defined war as the continuation of political efforts *not* through purely military means, but through politics—specifically, through appointment of field army and corps commanders whose beliefs coincided with their own, generals who would take direction from Radicals in the legislative branch.

However, according to the Constitution, Abraham Lincoln was Commander-in-Chief of the Army and Navy. The executive branch was primarily responsible for the conduct of the war, supported by the Congress. And although Lincoln agreed with the Radicals that slavery was abhorrent and should be eliminated somehow, he began the task of quelling the rebellion by making the most of the resources available to him—among them, the counsel of Brevet Lieutenant General Scott, a soldier for almost fifty of his seventy-four years, a general officer since the War of 1812, and for the past two decades general-in-chief of the United States Army.

Radicals found Scott particularly obnoxious because of his admiration for graduates of the United States Military Academy, an institution they detested in the belief that it was "elitist." Worse, in the Radical Republicans' view, was the fact that up to eight out of ten of the senior officers who remained in the Union army were *Democrats*.[28]

Well, McClellan and Porter were West Point graduates, veterans of Scott's Mexico City campaign, and Democrats. So were Brigadier Generals Charles Stone and William Franklin. Irvin McDowell was a Radical. There were "Old Army" generals among the twelve commanders of the Army of the Potomac's divisions, and there was, so far, little congeniality between that group and the one centering on the Young Napoleon.

No good could ensue from the politicians fighting among themselves—not with a Confederate army commanded by the unusually able Joe Johnston almost within sight of the capitol's unfinished dome. It was devoutly to be hoped, therefore, but not very likely, that the civilian authorities would leave the Army of the Potomac alone.

BENJAMIN F. WADE, U.S. SENATOR FROM OHIO

A leader of the Radical Republican faction and Chairman of the Joint Congressional Committee on the Conduct of the War, Wade and his followers sought George McClellan's replacement by John Pope and—after Second Bull Run—Fitz John Porter's conviction.

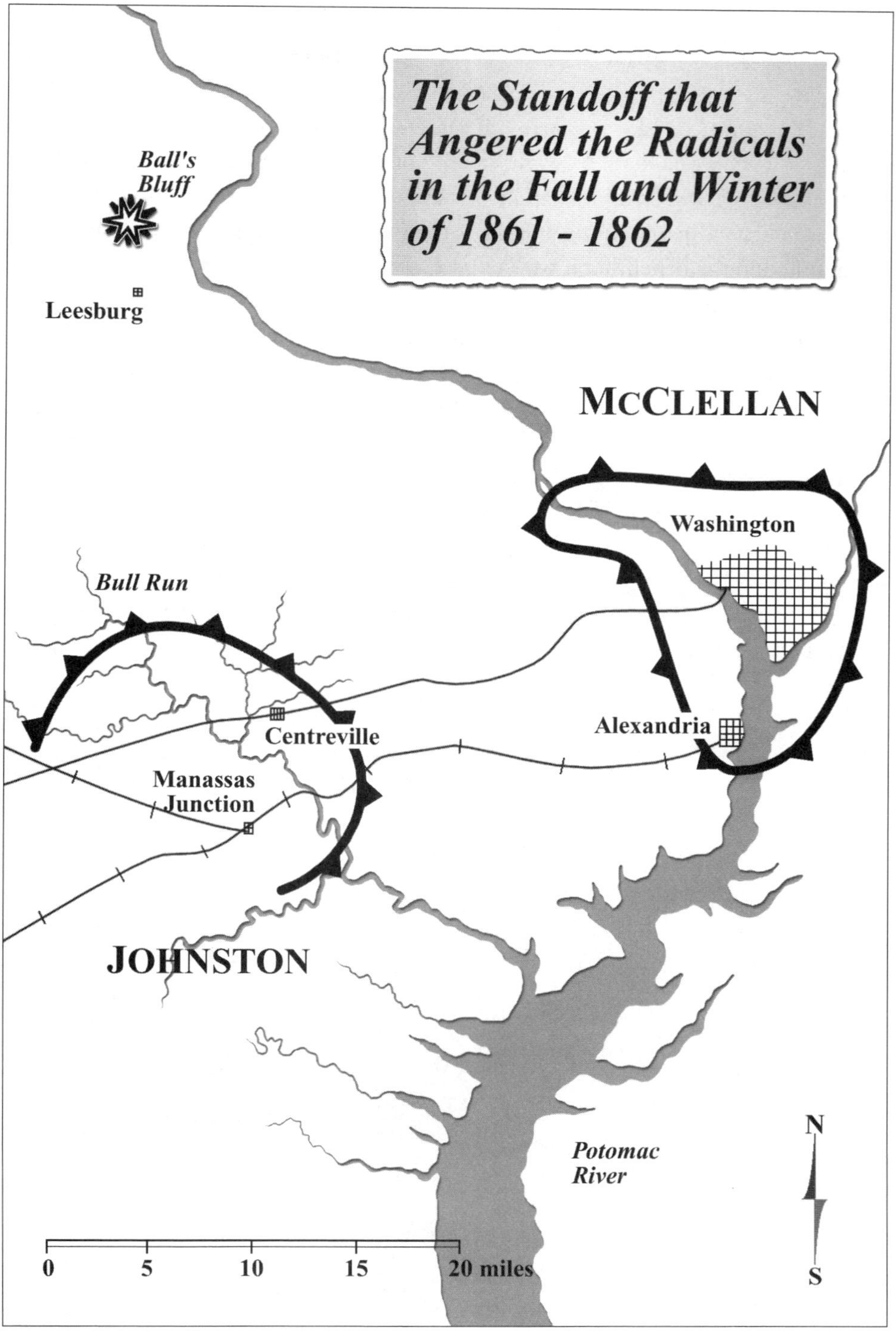

The Standoff that Angered the Radicals in the Fall and Winter of 1861 - 1862
Ball's Bluff
Leesburg
McCLELLAN
Washington
Bull Run
Centreville
Alexandria
Manassas Junction
JOHNSTON
Potomac River
N
S
0
5
10
15
20 miles

3

By summer's end, the Army of the Potomac seemed ready to drive Joe Johnston's Confederates away from nearby Manassas. The Radical Republicans in Congress applied heavy pressure on Lincoln to have McClellan do precisely that or indeed *anything* other than to stage larger and larger parades. In October's third week the Young Napoleon did take a division from Washington northwestward up the Virginia side of the Potomac to see if the Confederates had abandoned Leesburg. That reconnaissance was a wasted effort. But McClellan had given vague instructions to General Stone to have elements of his division along the Potomac's Maryland bank make a demonstration, and the result of subsequent skirmishing was a humiliating Union defeat known as Ball's Bluff in which Stone lost 921 men, including Colonel Edward D. Baker, one of Lincoln's closest friends and a United States Senator from Oregon.[29]

Although Porter had not been involved in the botched operation, it was only natural for him to have supported both his superior and Stone, who had graduated from West Point in 1845 one file ahead of him, when outraged senators blamed McClellan and especially Porter's classmate for Ball's Bluff. In December, Radical fury would lead to creation of the Joint Congressional Committee on the Conduct of the War. And by early February, Stone would be a prisoner in solitary confinement in Fort Lafayette on an island in New York harbor although no charges had been filed against him and none of the rights available to common thieves had been accorded him.[30]

Porter must have perceived that the Stone-McClellan relationship had made Stone so vulnerable. The Radicals could not remove McClellan, so through the Wade- and Chandler-dominated Committee on the Conduct of the War they took out his loyal subordinate. It was a blunt demonstration of what their power could do to anyone with a close relationship to the Young Napoleon who became controversial.

Of course, Stone and Porter had long known that in the army no one can *choose* relationships. All subordinates had to take the bad along with the good and concentrate on *duty*.

Another thing that Porter must have found troubling about "Little Mac" was the studied insubordination that McClellan had been showing all fall to old General Scott, who had advanced both their careers during the

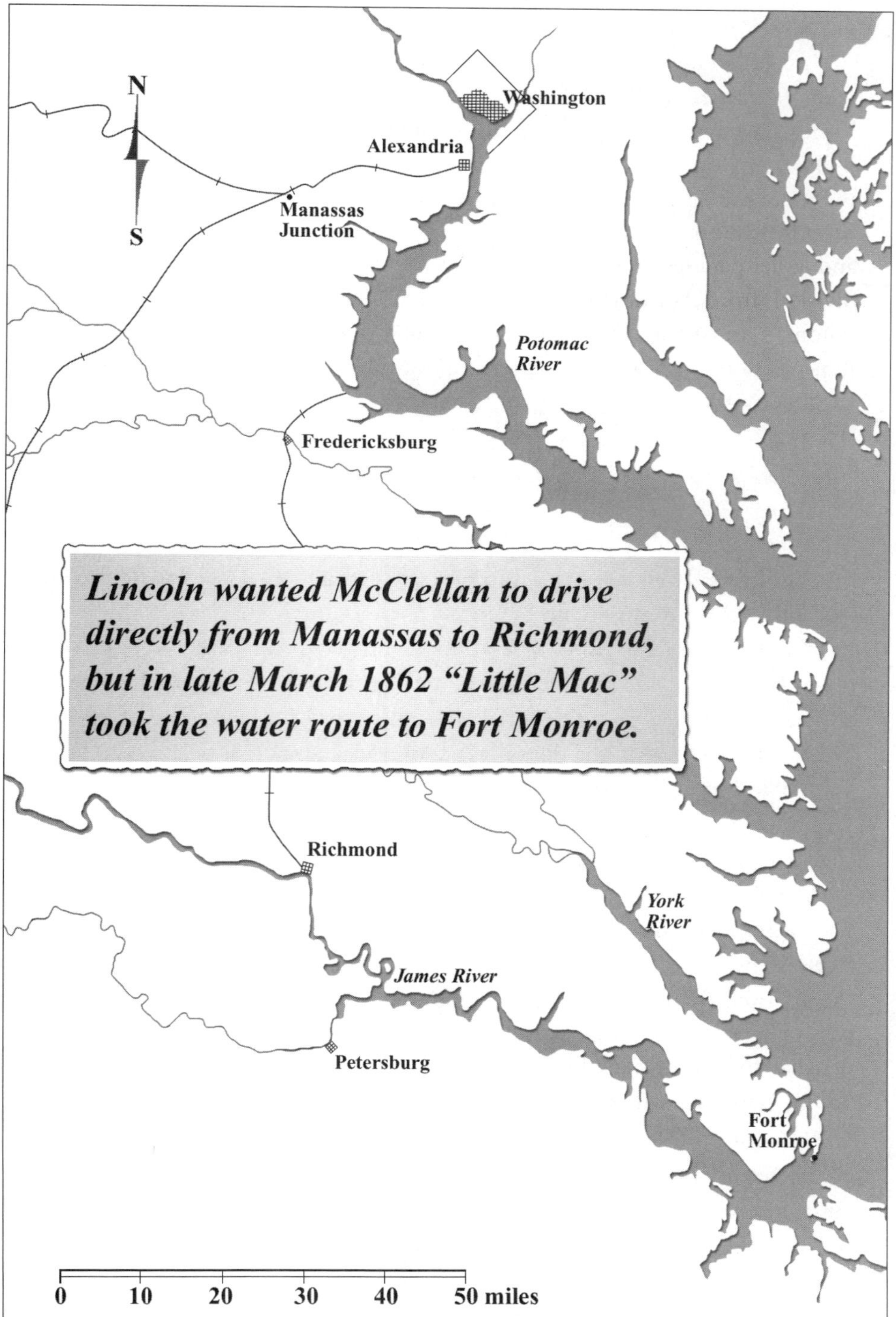
N
S
Washington
Alexandria
Manassas Junction
Potomac River
Fredericksburg
Lincoln wanted McClellan to drive directly from Manassas to Richmond, but in late March 1862 "Little Mac" took the water route to Fort Monroe.
Richmond
York River
James River
Petersburg
Fort Monroe
0
10
20
30
40
50 miles

Mexican War and ever since. Worse, the Army of the Potomac's commander had persuaded the Radicals that Scott was blocking him from attacking Johnston out at Manassas, and the Jacobins had joined his effort to force "Old Fuss and Feathers" into retirement. Success came in early November when Scott departed and Lincoln replaced him as general-in-chief with McClellan, half Scott's age.[31]

Might he be overloading McClellan? the President asked. "I can do it all," McClellan assured him.[32]

By early March 1862, however, McClellan and the Commander-in-Chief were locked in argument over the general's plan to move the Army of the Potomac down its namesake river to Chesapeake Bay and make a landing, then advance to Richmond—flanking Johnson out of the fortifications at nearby Manassas. Lincoln, concluding that McClellan could not "do it all," relieved him as general-in-chief and took the job himself; but he allowed Little Mac to make his waterborne envelopment *provided* enough troops were left behind to protect Washington. Then Joe Johnston humiliated his former friend by simply abandoning Manassas.[33]

McClellan's "Peninsula" operation would go forward with Union-held Fort Monroe as the landing point, but he and the President had new differences. Lincoln and the Radicals advocated the adoption of corps within the Army of the Potomac; Little Mac opposed the move. The squabble was really over which group of senior generals would be made corps commanders—Irvin McDowell and older officers Edwin Sumner, Erasmus Keyes, and Samuel Heintzelman, or McClellan's "pets" including William Franklin and Fitz John Porter. Predictably, Lincoln won.[34]

Presidential decisions continued to go against McClellan. Usually they were transmitted by Secretary of War Edwin McMasters Stanton, formerly a professed friend of the general, more recently a convert to Radicalism. This raised the question: How much did "Lincoln's" orders reflect pressures imposed by his poitical enemies?

Events soon amplified such concerns. After assuring McClellan that he would not transfer a 10,000-man division to Radical Major General John C. Fremont's command in the Allegheny Mountains, Lincoln did precisely that. Offsetting McClellan's disappointment, however, had been the understanding that Fort Monroe would be under his control and that he was authorized to form and add to the Army of the Potomac a division consisting of 10,000 troops stationed there. Moreover, according to the general, the President had "assured me that he would allow no other troops to be withdrawn from my command." But on April 3, the day after he reached Fort Monroe, from the War Department came a telegram revoking the agreement. "I was thus not only deprived of 10,000 more troops," General McClellan recalled years later, "but also of the control of my immediate base of operations and supplies."[35]

Next, Stanton telegraphed McClellan on April 4: "By direction of the President, General McDowell's army corps has been detached from the forces under your immediate command. . . ."[36] This amounted to an accusation that he had disobeyed a President's General War Order by not having left enough troops behind to protect Washington. Stanton declared this to be negligence or worse on McClellan's part. Ben Wade's Committee on the Conduct of the War demanded that the President hold back one of the two Army of the Potomac corps then about to embark for Fort Monroe. Lincoln approved retention of either Sumner's corps or McDowell's. Stanton designated McDowell's.[37]

On April 6, from near Yorktown on the Peninsula, McClellan wrote his wife, Mary Ellen:

While listening this P.M. to the sound of the guns, I received the

EDWIN M. STANTON, LINCOLN'S SECRETARY OF WAR

Although lawyer Stanton was ruthlessly efficient as an administrator, he was also the Radicals' agent within the Cabinet for carrying out their programs to destroy McClellan, Porter, and other conservatives in the Army.

> order detaching McDowell's Corps from my command—it is the most infamous thing that history has recorded. . . . The idea of depriving a General of 35,000 troops when actually under fire![38]

On April 9, the President sent McClellan a long message that was partly a rebuke and partly an explanation. He closed with an admonishment:

> The country will not fail to note, is now noting, that the present hesitation to move upon an intrenched enemy is but the story of Manassas repeated. I beg to assure you that I have never written you or spoken to you in greater kindness of feeling than now, nor with a fuller purpose to sustain you, so far as, in my most anxious judgment, I consistently can. *But you must act.*[39]

4

Counting heads, especially those in Confederate units opposing him, was not among George McClellan's skills. He had declared Joe Johnston's forces at Manassas to be twice as numerous as they had actually been. Operating now on the peninsula formed by Virginia's James and York rivers, he was crediting Brigadier General John B. Magruder with five times as many men as "Prince John" had deployed west of Yorktown.

On the Young Napoleon's fourth day ashore, Magruder and roughly half of his 11,000 troops had bluffed him into halting the Army of the Potomac's advance and ordering preparation of siege operations. By pausing so soon after he reached the Peninsula, he gave his enemies in the rear aid and comfort by seeming to have been intimidated by the foes to his front.

"*But you must act,*" Lincoln had warned McClellan, hoping no doubt that he would drop the notion of waiting for siege guns to arrive and drive rapidly up the Peninsula before the Radicals inflicted even more damage to his campaign. As it was, Little Mac's changes in plans—necessitated by the Confederates' surprises early in March—had been made in haste and had not allowed for terrain that was definitely on the rebels' side.

Water—the Warwick River, its many tributaries, and swamps—provided most of the protection to Magruder's line, which ran roughly southward from Yorktown to the James River. Confederates had converted the twelve-mile river into a lethal moat, flooding its boggy stretches and five fords by building dams and covering them with artillery batteries. And on the flat ground near Yorktown, fortifications (some surviving from the Revolutionary War) and fire from river batteries across the York blocked the federal advance.[40]

To direct the Army of the Potomac's siege operation McClellan selected Fitz John Porter. Earlier, over the initial objections of the President, he had created two new army corps and recognized Porter's steadfast loyalty as well as his abilities by assigning command of the one designated the Fifth to him.

McClellan's high regard for Porter was also reflected in a letter to Mary Ellen McClellan on April 11, 1862:

> I am just recovering from a terrible scare. Early this morning I was awakened by a dispatch from Fitz John's headquarters stating that Fitz had made an ascension in the balloon this morning, and that the balloon had broken away and come to the ground some three miles southwest, which would be within the enemy's lines. You can imagine how I felt. I at once set off to the various pickets to find out what they knew and try to do something to save him, but the order had no sooner gone than in walks Mr. Fitz just as cool as usual. He had luckily come down near my own camp after actually passing over that of the enemy. You may rest assured of one thing: you won't catch me in the confounded balloon, nor will I allow my other generals to go up in it.[41]

A reporter for the *New York Herald* contributed some details and an opinion:

> The rope was only nine hundred yards long, and only gave a limited view; but the accident of its snapping caused the balloon to ascend to an immense height, while, at the same time, it was moved by the wind right over the enemy. This, however, was an inconvenient point at which to effect a descent, and, as good luck would have it, when the balloon ascended a little higher it struck a counter current, which bore it eastward and over the Union camp, where he descended, highly delighted at the trip, and laughing and joking at his adventure, so coolly did he take his perilous journey.
>
> This is the right sort of man to lead our troops into battle. We

> have no doubt that, one of these days, he will give a good account of himself.[42]

On the night before Porter's siege guns were to open fire, however, Joe Johnston withdrew the Confederate forces. McClellan advanced up the peninsula against light opposition until by mid-May his army was less than ten miles east of Richmond. He deployed Porter's corps and two others north of the Chickahominy River, two more south of the stream, in anticipation of the promised arrival of McDowell's corps from Fredericksburg. Near the end of May he even sent Porter's corps westward and north of Richmond to Hanover Court House on a quick and well-executed raid that removed a Confederate force that might have interfered with McDowell's southward march. "Stonewall" Jackson's sudden appearance "out of the mountains" at Front Royal, however, caused Lincoln to divert McDowell's corps to the Shenandoah Valley.

General Porter and his troops were back north of the Chickahominy on May 31 when Johnston attacked the two federal corps south of the river. This fight would be called Fair Oaks in the North. Like Bull Run, Ball's Bluff, and out West, Shiloh, it settled nothing. No, not quite: Johnston was wounded seriously, and President Jefferson Davis replaced him with Robert E. Lee—who quickly renamed his new command the Army of Northern Virginia.[43]

"I prefer Lee to Johnston," wrote McClellan to Lincoln. "[Lee] is too cautious & weak under grave responsibility—personally brave & energetic to a fault, he yet is wanting in moral firmness when pressed by heavy responsibility & is likely to be timid & irresolute in action."[44]

Curiously, Little Mac might have said the reverse about his most reliable lieutenant, Fitz John Porter. From the days of the Army of the Potomac's reconstruction after Bull Run through the Hanover Court House raid, Porter's conduct and moral firmness under heavy responsibility had made him the corps commander most likely to excel as the war entered a phase that would call for more boldness and resolution in action than anyone could have foreseen.

CHAPTER TWO

Reputations' Crucible: The Seven Days

In the weeks following George McClellan's near-defeat at Fair Oaks, the Army of the Potomac's commanding general kept his forces astride the Chickahominy. Fitz John Porter's Fifth Corps remained on the north side; the others were south of the river, directly east of Richmond, preparing for siege operations. Ignoring the timid and irresolute Lee, Little Mac concentrated on obtaining reinforcements.

"I shall be very glad when we are really ready to open fire & then finish this confounded affair," George McClellan had written his wife from near Yorktown on April 30.[1] Clearly he was fully aware of the Radical Republicans' enmity and of their malign influence on Lincoln, yet in most of his letters to Mary Ellen he accused only the President and Edwin Stanton of desiring and indeed working toward the failure of his Peninsula Campaign. Considering the sources of the chain of nasty surprises that had stripped him of power, especially of combat manpower, his selection of his ordained superiors as targets for his condemnations was understandable. But the general's disputes—personal and official—with "Washington" raised at least two complex and therefore vexing questions:

One: To what extent was McClellan's military judgment impaired by his resentment of his civilian war managers' incompetence and their weather-vaning in decision-making, given turbulent gusts from the Radicals in Congress and the Jacobin press?

Two: To what extent did General McClellan's antipathies toward politicians affect the thinking and performances of his subordinates? This question would be particularly pertinent when asked with Fitz John Porter in mind.

Clues toward convincing answers began to emerge in Fair Oaks' wake. On June 5, Secretary of War Stanton telegraphed McClellan: "I intend sending you a part of McDowell's force as soon as it can return from its trip to Front Royal."[2] This was possible now that Stonewall Jackson had finished giving the forces directed from Washington by Acting General-in-Chief Lincoln a humiliating whipping out in the Shenandoah Valley.

By June 11 it appeared that George McCall's division would soon reach Fort Monroe. And that relations between the Secretary and the general might be reverting to their earlier cordiality was suggested by the paragraph with which Stanton closed a message that day:

> Be assured, general, that there never has been a moment when my desire has been otherwise than to aid you with my whole heart, mind, and strength since the hour we first met; and whatever others may say for their own purposes, you have never had, and never can have, any one more truly your friend, or more anxious to support you or more joyful than I shall be at the success which I have no doubt will soon be achieved by your arms.[3]

Stanton's conciliatory effusion was surprising, given the drastic change in their relationship that occurred in January when McClellan's then-close friend was being considered for appointment as secretary of war. Privately, Stanton advised Ben Wade and other Radicals that he had no use for a general-in-chief who would neither fight nor tell his civilian superiors what his plans were.[4] Edwin Stanton was a chameleon, an oleaginous manipulator who tried to be all things to all men. Yet he was tireless, incorruptible, a ruthless administrator. He recognized the power of the Radicals; Wade and his associates saw the new secretary of war as a person who could and would take action based on their promptings.

General McClellan did not refer to Stanton's olive branch in the message he sent the secretary on June 12, one in which he argued at considerable length that "Genl McDowell with the residue of his command" should be sent by water, definitely *not* overland.[5] He did not say that he preferred waterborne movement because twice it had proved so easy for the Radicals in Washington to cancel McDowell's scheduled marches.

Suspicion was reflected again in the remarkably extreme position McClellan took in a message to Stanton dated June 14 and sent at midnight:

> It ought to be distinctly understood that McDowell and his troops are completely under my control. I received a telegram from him requesting that McCall's division might be placed so as to join him immediately on his arrival. That request does not breathe the proper spirit. Whatever troops come to me must be disposed of so as to do the most good. . . . *If I cannot fully control all his troops I want none of them, but would prefer to fight the battle with what I have, and let others be responsible for the results.*
>
> The department lines should not be allowed to interfere with me, but General McDowell and all other troops sent to me should be placed completely at my disposal, to do with them as I think best. In no other way can they be of assistance to me. *[Crossed out: I doubt if he will ever reach me by land & I shall not count upon his aid, but if he does come]* I therefore request that I may have entire and full control. The stake at issue is too great to allow personal considerations to be entertained. You know that I have none.
>
> The indications are, from our balloon reconnaissances and from all other sources, that the enemy are intrenching, daily increasing in numbers, and determined to fight desperately.[6]

Fitz John Porter had not taken any more balloon rides, but he had emerged as the corps commander to whom McClellan gave the most demanding missions. How near Porter and McClellan were to being kindred spirits was indicated by a letter Porter wrote on June 20, 1862, to his friend Manton Marble, editor of the *New York World*, warning that the Army of the Potomac was in danger of "a defeat or serious check."

Stanton and Lincoln, Porter charged, were ignoring all of McClellan's calls for reinforcements. "I wish you would put the question," the soldier told the newspaperman, "Does the President (controlled by an incompetent Secy) design to cause defeat here for the purpose of prolonging the war?"[7]

Marble may well have been astonished both by the implications of Porter's words and the inordinate risk to his reputation the commander of the Fifth Corps had incurred by writing them. How close to treason was it to suggest that the Union's two most senior war managers might themselves be guilty of treason?

Concurrently, there was an abrupt change of subject in the middle of a report General McClellan was preparing to send Lincoln. "I am forced to [construct defensive works] by my inferiority in numbers so that I may bring the greatest possible numbers into action & secure the Army against unforeseen disaster," he had just written when—as though he expected to be restored as general-in-chief—he continued:

> I would be glad to have permission to lay before your Excellency by letter or telegram my views as to the present state of military affairs throughout the whole country. In the mean time I would be pleased to learn the dispositions as to numbers & positions of troops not under my command in Virginia and elsewhere.[8]

In replying, the President cited the risks inherent in using the mails. "I would be very glad to talk to you," he added, "but you cannot leave your camp, and I cannot well leave here."[9]

In fact, on June 23 Lincoln did leave—but for West Point, New York where during a secret conference he obtained retired Brevet Lieutenant General Winfield Scott's views as to the present state of military affairs throughout the whole country. Most of what they discussed as they sat on a bench that afforded a magnificent view of the Hudson River and the highlands confining it could be inferred only from subsequent events.

Several of the President's decisions that General Scott's counsel may have prompted—for example, sending for Henry Halleck and turning over to him the duties of general-in-chief of the Union armies—would have consequences that shaped the duration and outcome of the war. Near term, however, *only in theory* would Scott's advice prove correct regarding proper recommitment of the 35,000 or more exhausted, whipped, "out at the toes" (Lincoln's words) troops remaining in the Shenandoah Valley but scattered throughout it.

Excruciatingly obvious was the required course of action: corral all of those soldiers, get rid of the incompetent commanders—especially, Irvin McDowell and professional politicians Nathaniel Banks and John Charles Fremont, who had wasted the valiant efforts of their men—and *rebuild.* That much done, this new field army should be placed under the leadership of a general who was a proven *fighter*.

But who among the Union armies' available general officers had established a reputation for tearing into the rebels? Not Henry Halleck; from St. Louis he had merely managed "Unconditional Surrender" Grant's impressive recoveries of western Kentucky and Tennessee. And not General Grant, given the lingering history of his having been a four-finger whiskey drinker in the "Old Army."

Enter, from the West, Major General John Pope—summoned to Washington during June's third week.

Born in Kentucky but raised in Illinois, Pope entered West Point at sixteen and was graduated in 1842. He returned from the Mexican War as a brevet captain. In 1861 he was one of three officers—the other two were Colonel E. V. Sumner and Major David Hunter—who were Abraham Lincoln's military escorts during his train ride from Springfield, Illinois, to Washington for his inauguration; Captain Pope's father had been one of the President-elect's associates, and his father-in-law was a stalwart Republican congressman from Ohio. As a protege of Salmon Chase, Pope was an ardent opponent of slavery. But on his own, he had made a start toward a good military reputation while serving under Halleck in Missouri, in capturing New Madrid and Island No. 10 on the Mississippi, and during the Corinth Campaign.[10]

Lincoln's—actually, Edwin Stanton's—ordering of General Pope to Washington followed intensification of Jacobin pressure to replace McClellan.[11] And only three days after the President returned from his conference with Scott at West Point, Lincoln issued a general order that would cast some very long shadows.

First, the Commander-in-Chief consolidated the forces he had been directing in the futile effort to bag Jackson into what he called the Army of Virginia and assigned General Pope as its commander. Next, he gave Pope the mission of "protecting the national capital from danger or insult" and of rendering "the most effective aid to relieve [sic] General McClellan and capture Richmond."[12]

Lincoln and Stanton were thoughtful enough to telegraph the order to Generals Fremont, Banks, and McDowell but not to McClellan. Had the Young Napoleon been informed regarding this development, he would have been struck by the fact that *for the third time,* "Washington" had promised him McDowell's corps and then suddenly—as he seemed to have suspected, correctly—had yanked irretrievably away, at the worst possible moment for him as it turned out, the one possibly decisive resource he had been craving all along.

2

On June 23, 1862, while Lincoln was en route to West Point, in the Dabbs House east of Richmond General Lee was presenting his plan for destroying McClellan's Army of the Potomac to Major Generals James Longstreet, D. H. Hill, A. P. Hill, and Stonewall Jackson. Gambling that his opponent would leave Fitz John Porter's corps north of the Chickahominy to facilitate McDowell's march southward from Fredericksburg, Lee intended to bring Jackson's Valley army eastward and throw the forces of the four commanders present against the isolated Porter—relying upon divisions led by "Prince John" Magruder and Benjamin Huger, deployed south of the Chickahominy, to "amuse" three or four times their number in the four Army of the Potomac corps facing them roughly six miles east of Richmond's fringe.[13]

George McClellan, too, was thinking about launching an offensive—or, rather, an advance by his corps south of the Chickahominy to gain ground favorable for besieging and ultimately capturing the Confederate capital. From the vicinity of Old Tavern, his heavy guns could pound Richmond until not one brick rested upon another. His army's work on Thursday, June 26, however, would not be seizure of Old Tavern, as a message McClellan sent Stanton from Camp Lincoln at 6:15 on Wednesday afternoon foreshadowed:

> Several contrabands just in give information confirming the supposition that Jackson's advance is at or near Hanover Court-House, and that Beauregard arrived, with strong re-enforcements, in Richmond yesterday.
>
> I incline to think that Jackson will attack my right and rear. The rebel force is stated at 200,000, including Jackson and Beauregard. I shall have to contend against vastly superior odds if these reports be true; but this army will do all in the power of men to hold their position and repulse any attack.

McClellan went on to declare that he was in no way responsible if "the splendid army I have the honor to command is destroyed by overwhelming numbers;" he could "at least die with it and share its fate."[14] Earlier, he had complained that General McDowell's desire to control McCall's division did not "breathe the proper spirit." What, then, were Stanton and Lincoln—and through Stanton, the Radicals—to think of an army commander who wrote nigh-hysterically of disasters and dying and blame *merely on suspicion*?

However, the Young Napoleon was correct in expecting that Jackson would arrive from the northwest. This meant that it would be up to Fitz John Porter's Fifth Corps *alone* to deal with this threat.

General Lee had made no changes in the orders he had issued on Monday. His attack would open as soon as Powell Hill's division, waiting near the Meadow Bridges to cross the Chickahominy, gained indications that Jackson's forces were arriving and making contact with Porter's cavalry and pickets northwest of Beaver Dam Creek's headwaters.

General Lee had made a dreadful mistake by leaving the *timing* of Hill's division's moving-out dependent on whatever progress Jackson's forces from the distant Shenandoah Valley may have made in their long march toward the Mechanicsville battle area. The real Napoleon had declared that the most difficult operation in combat, and therefore one definitely to be avoided, is combining one's separated forces on a field of battle in the presence of the enemy. Here, inadvertently, Stonewall proved the Corsican's point. Jackson was late. Lee had no information regarding where his main maneuvering element was. But Fitz John Porter knew—thanks to reports from his cavalry—that Jackson was too far away and moving too slowly to threaten his northern flank, much less his rear.

Accordingly, all Porter had to do was await any assaults Lee might throw at him and repel them. His men were in carefully prepared defensive positions, many of them concealed, from which they could inflict maximum casualties on the Confederates with minimum risk to themselves. And supporting their defense of the east bank of Beaver Dam Creek were artillery and reserves of infantry.[15]

What General McClellan did not seem to have realized early on that Thursday, however, was that Lee had left only 21,000 men to protect Richmond. Assuming Lee attacked Porter and that Porter held, what if McClellan ordered the 74,300 troops in his four corps south of the Chickahominy to charge into the rebels' capital through Magruder's and Huger's thin lines?

Such was the magnitude of the risk General Lee had assumed and *continued* to assume hour after hour on that Thursday afternoon as he stood on a bluff overlooking the Chickahominy Valley and Mechanicsville waiting

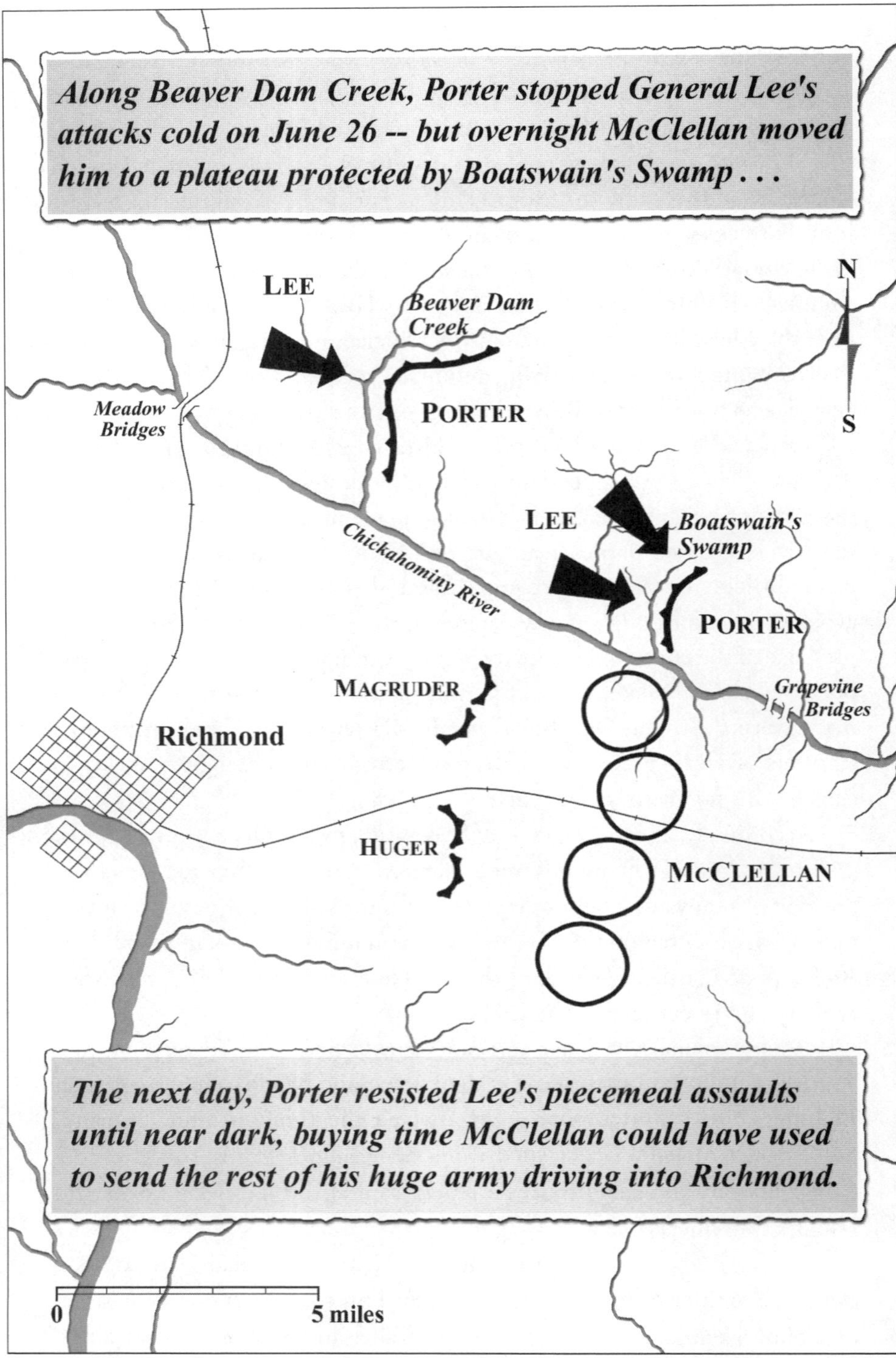
Along Beaver Dam Creek, Porter stopped General Lee's attacks cold on June 26 -- but overnight McClellan moved him to a plateau protected by Boatswain's Swamp . . .
LEE
Beaver Dam Creek
N
S
Meadow Bridges
PORTER
LEE
Boatswain's Swamp
Chickahominy River
PORTER
MAGRUDER
Grapevine Bridges
Richmond
HUGER
MCCLELLAN
The next day, Porter resisted Lee's piecemeal assaults until near dark, buying time McClellan could have used to send the rest of his huge army driving into Richmond.
0
5 miles

patiently for the sounds of firing to reach him from the north. Not so patient had been Powell Hill. At three o'clock he led his troops across the Meadow Bridges. They swept eastward, driving Porter's skirmishers back toward Beaver Dam Creek.

Powell Hill had taken control of the operation away from the Army of Northern Virginia's commander. All that General Lee, still ignorant of Jackson's whereabouts, could do was order Harvey Hill's division and Longstreet's to cross the river and ride across himself. Not surprisingly, and despite much gallantry, by sundown a series of Confederate errors and federal firepower had enabled Porter's men to thin the rebels' ranks considerably and to stop Lee's drive short of Beaver Dam Creek's west bank.[16]

In large part this was the result of General Lee's having set aside Napoleon's admonition regarding combining forces on a battlefield in the presence of an enemy. But this had been the first time that he had ever *commanded* troops in combat. For that matter, Mechanicsville was the first major battle the Young Napoleon had ever fought—*supervised* is more accurate, since the critical decision had been made by Fitz John Porter who stood and slugged it out with Lee rather than allow himself to be bluffed into abandoning his fortified creekline by reports of the dreaded Stonewall's approach.

3

Mechanicsville was neither the complete victory George McClellan proclaimed it to be nor the result of R. E. Lee's deficiencies as a combat commander that some Confederate historians professed shock at having discovered. Fitz John Porter had displayed skill in preparing and conducting his defense, but he was fortunate in that only a small fraction of the attackers present actually came within range.

More important than allocations of praise and blame were the contrasts in how Thursday afternoon's fight affected the thinking of each army's commander. General Lee listened to his subordinates' reports, ordered continuation of the advance in the morning, and went to bed. McClellan and the Army of the Potomac's chief of engineers Brigadier General John G. Barnard lingered at Porter's headquarters long after the guns had cooled discussing various courses of action.

That afternoon, McClellan had told Barnard to go on a reconnaissance to see if it were feasible to keep any forces on the Chickahominy's north bank. Soon after he rode out, Barnard recalled, an aide arrived and called his attention to some interesting real estate five or six miles east of Beaver Dam Creek and east also of property owned by a Doctor Gaines.

"I had been obliged to ride fast," Barnard wrote. He rode fast enough to inspect some splendid terrain for defending bridges over the Chickahominy. Porter could be supported by McClellan from south of the river—*or* McClellan could add Porter's to the four corps already poised to smash through Richmond's defenders and win the war.

By sunrise on Friday, most of Porter's troops were on the way to a natural fortress protected by a moat called Boatswain's Swamp. General Lee launched a pursuit but he assumed that Porter's destination was Powhite Creek, a tributary of the Chickahominy between Beaver Dam Creek and Boatswain's Swamp. With contact with Jackson restored, Lee ordered him to sweep north of Powhite Creek and flank Porter out of his presumed new line; Boatswain's Swamp was not shown on Lee's map.

Confederate confusion lasted long enough for General Porter to deploy his corps' divisions and artillery along his moat's eastern trace from near the Chickahominy on his left to south of Old Cold Harbor on the right, with the Grapevine Bridges in his rear connecting him to the rest of McClellan's army. Although Porter had roughly 35,000 men, gaps in his three-mile front remained. In his report he wrote: "Believing my force too small to defend successfully this long line, I asked of General Barnard . . . to represent to the major-general commanding the necessity of re-enforcement, and he was to send me felling axes for defensive purposes."[17] Upon reaching Camp Lincoln, Barnard was told that the army commander was asleep. Not wishing to disturb him, Barnard went to his tent and followed McClellan's example.[18]

Axes borrowed from artillery batteries enabled Porter's infantrymen to fortify. Nature assisted; briars, thickets, and underbrush slowed Confederates descending into the eroded ravines where they had to wade through neck-high water in the creek before having to help each other to scale the federals' bank. From noon onward, Porter's main advantage was Lee's piecemeal commitment and his units' losses of cohesion as they groped their way toward enemies they could not see. But despite the effectiveness of federal firepower, by around two o'clock on Friday afternoon Porter was obliged to ask McClellan for reinforcements.[19]

Anomalies in atmospheric acoustics prevented most of the sounds of heavy firing along Boatswain's Swamp from reaching Camp Lincoln. Moreover, McClellan seemed to have placed considerable weight on reports from his four corps commanders facing Magruder's and Huger's demonstrators to the effect that the Confederates were uncommonly active. A check of those generals' willingness to send units to Porter if needed produced discouraging responses. But William Franklin released Brigadier General Henry W. Slocum's division, and for a time it seemed that Porter might hit Lee with a counterattack.[20]

Gaines's Mill, the name by which this battle would be remembered, had developed into the war's most vicious and bloody fight east of the Alleghenies. General McClellan had seen none of it, yet from Camp Lincoln he was diligent in telegraphing messages to Secretary of War Stanton.

This stream began flowing, apparently, at 10:00 A.M.:

> The night passed quietly. During it we brought all wagons, heavy guns, &c., to this side, and at daybreak drew in McCall's division about 3 miles. This change of position was beautifully executed under a sharp fire, with but little loss. The troops on the other side are now well in hand, and the whole army so concentrated that it can take advantage of the first mistake made by the enemy. White House [supply base north of the Chickahominy] yet undisturbed. Success of yesterday complete.[21]

At noon, before Powell Hill was really hitting Porter's defenses and while Jackson was nowhere near making contact: "My change of position on other [north] side just in time. Heavy attack now being made by Jackson and two other divisions. Expect attack also on this side."[22]

One hour later:

> We are contending at several points against superior numbers. The enemy evince much desperation, but as we have no choice but to win, you may be sure that we will do all that can be expected. Thus far we have been successful, but I think the most severe struggle is to come. The enemy neglect White House thus far and bestow his whole attention on us.
>
> If I am forced to concentrate between the Chickahominy and

James, I will at once endeavor to open communication with you. . . . It is absolutely certain that Jackson, Ewell, and Whiting are here. This may be the last dispatch I send you for some time. . . . Goodby, and present my respects to the President.[23]

Brigadier General Randolph Marcy, McClellan's chief of staff and father-in-law, signed the 3:00 P.M. message to Stanton but the text had a familiar ring to it:

> We have been fighting nearly all day against greatly superior numbers. We shall endeavor to hold our own, and if compelled to fall back, shall do it in good order, upon James River, if possible. Our men fight like veterans, and will do all that men can do. If we have to fall back on James River, supplies should be passed up to us under protection of the gunboats as rapidly as possible.
>
> McClellan has telegraphed you several times to-day. You may rely upon it the rebels are concentrating their greatest efforts at this juncture.[24]

McClellan to Fitz John Porter, at 4:30:

> Send word to all your troops that their general thanks them for their heroism, and says to them that he is now sure that nothing can resist them. Their conduct and your own has been magnificent, and another name is added to their banners. Give my regulars a good chance. I look upon to-day as decisive of the war. Try to drive the rascals and take some prisoners and guns. What more assistance do you require?[25]

Half an hour later, Porter replied: "I am pressed hard, very hard. About every Regiment I have is in action. [Without assistance] I am afraid I shall be driven from my position."[26]

"Hold your own," McClellan replied half an hour later. Certain outfits were on the way to him, he said, then added: "You must beat them if I [must] move the whole Army to do it & transfer all on this side."[27]

Confederate soldiers in the 4th Texas, led by Brigadier General John Hood, spared McClellan that trouble by fixing bayonets, advancing at trail arms, and following Hood across Porter's moat and—when they opened fire—driving the first tier of fought-out Yankees up the slope and blocking those in the second tier from firing, thus inspiring panic in the third and final tier.

Hood's Texan's breakthrough demoralized enough other Fifth Corps units to produce chaos on the plateau Porter's men had defended all Friday afternoon. A desperate federal cavalry charge blocked Porter's artillery from blasting the rampaging rebels—who were turning captured Yankee guns against their former owners.[28] Darkness "& two fresh brigades," wrote Confederate E. Porter Alexander, "enabled Porter to make an excellent retreat & with wonderfully little loss."[29]

At eight o'clock that evening, from Camp Lincoln, where he had spent the entire day, General McClellan told the Secretary of War:

> Have had a terrible contest. Attacked by greatly superior numbers in all directions on this [south] side; we still hold our own, though a very heavy fire is still kept up on the left bank of Chickahominy. The odds have been immense. We hold our own very nearly. I may be forced to give up my position during the night, but will not if it is possible to avoid it. Had I 20,000 fresh and good troops we would be sure of a splendid victory to-morrow.
>
> My men have fought magnificently.[30]

"On the [North] side of the Chickahominy," McClellan telegraphed General Heintzelman, "the day is lost. You must hold your position at all costs."[31] Actually, Heintzelman's corps had not been in any more danger than Camp Lincoln. Porter's stand on the plateau protected by Boatswain's Creek had bought the Young Napoleon time in which to get the army's supply wagons and his headquarters moving southward, the old White House base stripped and abandoned, and Flag Officer Goldsborough alerted to have his gunboats ready to cover the retreating army's left flank.[32]

George McClellan, who had done no fighting, was whipped; Fitz John Porter, weary from two struggles with Lee in as many days, was not. A major on Porter's staff recalled that throughout Friday, the belief at Fifth Corps headquarters was that they were fighting for time to enable the rest of the army to smash its way into Richmond.[33] Why should McClellan not have taken advantage of Lee's army's disorganization and of its being so badly out of position and drive straight westward? Did not withdrawing make in vain the sacrifices of more than 7,000 of Porter's men?[34]

That opportunity to win the war had existed—yet it would float away with the battlesmoke.

From Savage's Station on the Richmond & York River Railroad, lately the army's line of communications, shortly after midnight General McClellan wrote Edwin Stanton a long message that began:

> I now know the full history of the day. On this side of the river (the [south] right bank) we repulsed several strong attacks. On the left bank our men did all that men could do, all that soldiers could accomplish, but they were overwhelmed by vastly superior numbers, even after I brought my last reserves into action.
>
> I again repeat that I am not responsible for this, and I say it with the earnestness of a general who feels in his heart the loss of every brave man who has been needlessly sacrificed to-day. I still hope to retrieve our fortunes, but to do this the Government must view the matter in the same earnest light that I do. . . . As it is, the Government must not and cannot hold me responsible for the result.
>
> I feel too earnestly to-night. I have seen too many dead and wounded comrades to feel otherwise than that the Government has not sustained this army. If you do not do so now the game is lost.
>
> If I save this army now, I tell you plainly that I owe no thanks to you or to any other persons in Washington.
>
> You have done your best to sacrifice this army.[35]

Actually, McClellan had not left Camp Lincoln all day. He had seen no dead and wounded comrades. These were facts the real Napoleon would have concealed at all costs, had he stayed in the rear and left all of the conduct of a major battle to a subordinate, however able. How could Lincoln leave any general in command who was so foolish as to write such a letter to his superiors?

4

From Saturday, June 28, onward, McClellan devoted most of his attentions to completion of his change of bases. General Lee applied no immediate pressure, for he needed a day in which to regroup, gather all the weapons and accoutrements the Yankees had donated in their haste to cross the Chickahominy, and learn from cavalryman Jeb Stuart and others what Little Mac was most likely to do next.

Soon after dark on Friday, McClellan told his corps commanders that their mission was now to prevent Lee from spoiling their withdrawal—"change of base," he termed it—southward through White Oak Swamp to the James River. Erasmus Keyes' corps, southernmost of the four facing Richmond, would lead the column; Porter's would follow. The other three would protect the movement of the wagon trains and act as a rear guard to block Lee while Keyes and Porter, down near Malvern Hill and the river, kept the Confederates from doing anything nasty on the army's flanks.[36]

Mostly, these operations were carried out absent much direction from the Army of the Potomac's commanding general. On Saturday and subsequently he spent most of his time down on the north bank of the James River showing far more interest in arrangements for his new base than in what Lee was doing or was about to do.

In fact, from Sunday onward the Confederates were striking the western flanks of McClellan's corps as they moved southward from Savage's Station to near Glendale. Porter, meanwhile, had been planning and directing the conversion of Malvern Hill into a defensive position too formidable for Lee's forces to capture.[37]

Malvern Hill would be General Porter's third challenge in less than a week to conduct a critically important defense. At Beaver Dam Creek he had stopped part of Powell Hill's division. With only nominal reinforcement, for hours his Fifth Corps' lines along Boatswain's Swamp had withstood assaults hurled at them by all the units in Lee's maneuvering force. Now, on Tuesday morning, Porter had to be ready to hold the rolling high ground only slightly north of the James against every man in the Army of Northern Virginia.

Ultimately, Porter would have available all of the Army of the Potomac's divisions. But his use of artillery would be the distinguishing feature of Malvern Hill. Artillery had been Lieutenant Porter's choice of branches; he had fought as an artilleryman in Mexico; and he had taught artillery tactics at West Point after that war. Moreover, present with Porter was Colonel Henry Hunt, an artilleryman from his graduation at West Point in 1839

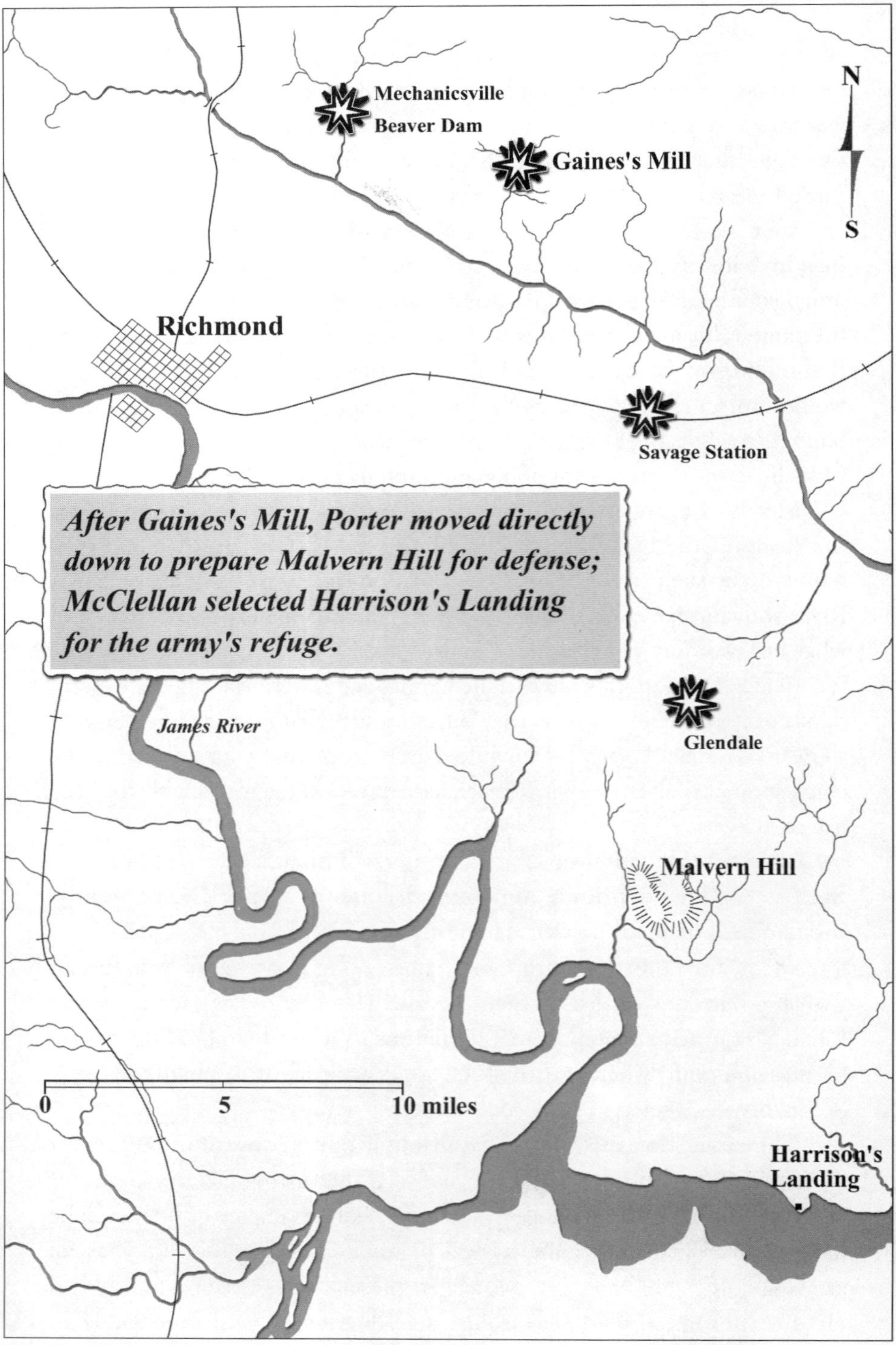
Mechanicsville
Beaver Dam
Gaines's Mill
N
S
Richmond
Savage Station
After Gaines's Mill, Porter moved directly down to prepare Malvern Hill for defense; McClellan selected Harrison's Landing for the army's refuge.
James River
Glendale
Malvern Hill
0
5
10 miles
Harrison's Landing

onward. Combining their talents and experience, across the half-mile front Porter and Hunt built line after line of rifled Parrott guns, batteries of bronzed Napoleons for antipersonnel fire, some 32-pounder Howitzers, even siege guns—4 1/2-inch Rodman rifles, 8-inch Howitzers, 30-pounder Parrotts, and two of the long-ranged 10-pounder Whitworths.[38]

The infantry's main mission was to protect those guns, more than a hundred in all, many parked hub-to-hub. But when the Confederates attacked late on that Tuesday, Porter's and Hunt's artillery fire proved devastating. With many troops in Harvey Hill's brigades dead or dying in the wheatfield, and others hugging the hillside or running for the rear, the guns shifted to blast away new arrivers. "It was not war, it was murder," Hill said later.[39]

Earlier on that Tuesday, July 1, Hill—warned by a resident of the region—had said to Lee, "If General McClellan is there in strength, we had better let him alone."[40] Fitz John Porter, not the Young Napoleon, proved Hill right. McClellan had appeared briefly on Malvern Hill's edges a few times, but during a significant part of the day he had been a passenger on Captain John Rodgers' gunboat U.S.S. *Galena* out on the James.[41]

After dark, when General Lee's men finally quit assaulting the artillery positions on Malvern Hill, Porter telegraphed McClellan that if he could be reinforced and have his ammunition replenished, "we will hold our own and advance if you wish."[42] A determined attack, he urged, would throw Lee into retreat through the streets of Richmond.[43]

However, General McClellan's primary concern since Mechanicsville had been saving his army. So it remained after the firing ceased on Tuesday night. Years afterward he wrote:

> Although the result of the battle of Malvern was a complete victory, it was nevertheless necessary to fall back still farther, in order to reach a point where our supplies could be brought to us with certainty. . . . I selected Harrison's Bar as the new position of the army. The exhaustion of our supplies of food, forage, and ammunition made it imperative to reach the transports immediately. . . . The order for the movement of the troops was at once issued upon the final repulse of the enemy at Malvern Hill. The order prescribed a movement by the left and rear, General Keyes' corps to cover the maneuver.[44]

That order drew vehement expressions of outrage from the commanders who had done the fighting. A sample: "I, Philip Kearny, an old soldier, enter my solemn protest against this order for retreat. We ought instead of retreating to follow up the enemy and take Richmond. And in full view of the responsibility of such a declaration, I say to you all, such an order can be prompted only by cowardice or treason."[45]

Harrison's Landing, actually a plantation known as Berkeley on the north bank of the James, provided adequate sanctuary for the Army of the Potomac. From there, Little Mac and his subordinates wrote their reports and took care of other army paperwork while the troops rested and units refitted. Among other documents emanating from the army's haven on July 7 was a message to Secretary of War Stanton:

> The energy, ability, gallantry, and good conduct displayed throughout the eventful period of this campaign through which we have just passed by Brig Genl F. J. Porter deserves [sic] the marked notice of the Executive of the Nation.
>
> From the very commencement his unwearied assiduity in various duties, the intelligent and efficacious assistance he has rendered me under all circumstances, his skillful management of his command on the march, in the siege, and on the field of battle and his chivalric and soldierly bearing under fire, have combined to render him conspicuous among the many faithful and gallant spirits of the army.
>
> I respectfully therefore recommend that Brig Genl Fitz-John Porter receive the brevet of Brigadier General in the regular Army for Hanover Court-House and the brevet of Major General in the regular Army for the battle of Gaines Mills.
>
> If there were another grade to add I would ask it for the battle of Malvern. The latter eclipses in its results any other engagement in the campaign, and too much credit cannot be given to Genl Porter for his skill, gallantry, and conduct on the occasion.
>
> If there be any vacancies among the General Officers in the regular Army I ask one for him. I saw myself the dispositions he made and the gallantry he displayed. I do not speak from hearsay, but from personal observation; would that the country had more General Officers like him.[46]

By direction of Abraham Lincoln, Porter had been already been promoted to brigadier general by brevet in the regular army to date from June 27 and to major general of volunteers to date from July 4.[47]

Virtually all the other communications McClellan sent northward ignited fresh controversy. His declaration that he had merely changed his base met with widespread disbelief, as did his assertion that he had not been defeated but had only failed to win. Wrote historian Margaret Leech: "Marking the places on the big war maps, the people of the Union could plainly see that Harrison's Landing was nearly twenty-five miles from Richmond; and, at last, after the strong hope that had survived the delays, and the terrible waste of men, despondency spread throughout the country like a sickness."[48]

There was much irony worth noting.

General Lee had won only one battle in a campaign that had ended in a distinct victory for the Confederacy. He made a number of serious mistakes—this was his first opportunity to command a field army in combat—but he emerged with his reputation enhanced. None of Lee's lieutenants had distinguished themselves; Stonewall Jackson, in particular, had been a great disappointment.

So far in this war the Seven Days Battles were the first of real consequence also for George McClellan and Fitz John Porter. Little Mac had proved—as he had said of Lee—"too cautious & weak under grave responsibility." In no way, at any time, had he grasped any of the openings available to him to seize Richmond, which suggested fundamental incompetence as a fighter. His moral breakdown after Gaines's Mill was shameless. Cruising on a gunboat during Malvern Hill bordered on cowardice.

If any one person had saved the Army of the Potomac, that man had been Fitz John Porter. Three times he had blocked General Lee, extracting a fearful price while adding to his reputation for "cool"—composure while employing skill under severest challenge. What other corps commanders had done anything worth mentioning during General McClellan's entire Peninsula Campaign?

In early July 1862, Fitz John Porter had every reason to feel enormous loyalty to the Army of the Potomac and to the controversial commander of it who had given him, from Yorktown onward, so many extraordinary opportunities to be of service. But what of the future of their relationship?

How long could the Young Napoleon endure further rise in Porter's reputation if his own remained in a steep decline?

5

Pressed by the political extremists and public opinion, Lincoln moved toward replacing McClellan. On Monday, July 7, he boarded the U.S.S. *Ariel* for a cruise down the Potomac. After a brief stop at Fort Monroe on Wednesday morning, he reached Harrison's Landing at around six and reviewed the troops, which he found to be in much better condition than he had expected.

Lincoln's visit became famous for McClellan's having presented him with a long letter in which the general presumed to advise him on political questions and all but nominated himself to be restored as general-in-chief.[49] But the Commander-in-Chief spent most of his time at Harrison's Landing soliciting the views of Little Mac's corps commanders as to what the Army of the Potomac's next mission ought to be and if they believed it could be removed successfully if ordered.[50] He made another stop at Fort Monroe on the way back to Washington. Before docking, though, the little steamer *Ariel* ran aground. Lincoln and his aides enjoyed the delay swimming.[51]

Those stops at Fort Monroe might have been for the purpose of evaluating Major General Ambrose E. Burnside as a potential conservative alternative to Radical-sponsored John Pope as a replacement for McClellan. Whether the Young Napoleon suspected as much or was referring to the interest Lincoln had shown in removing the Army of the Potomac from its captivity was not clear in two letters he wrote Mary Ellen. In the first, on Wednesday night: "I do not know to what extent he has profited by his visit—not much, I fear, for he really seems quite incapable of rising to the height of the merits of the question & the magnitude of the crisis."[52] And then to Nell early on Thursday morning, July10:

> I do not know what paltry trick the administration will play next—I did not like the Presdt's manner—it seemed that of a man about to do something of which he was much ashamed. A few days will however show, I do not much care what the result will be. I feel that I have already done enough to prove in history that I am a General

> & that the causes of my want of success are so apparent that no one except the [Radical Zach] Chandler tribe can blame me hereafter."[53]

General McClellan was somewhat prescient in that his visitor *was* about to do something. On Friday, July 11, the day after his return to Washington, President Lincoln issued a peremptory order directing Major General Henry W. Halleck to "repair" to the capital forthwith to become general-in-chief of the Union armies.[54]

Earlier, John Pope had been appointed to head the new Army of Virginia. While the Seven Days battles were in progress Stanton had a visit from newcomer from the West John Pope, who recalled:

> [During our first visit] Mr. Stanton made it clear without unfriendly criticism that the government had been greatly discontented with the lame results accomplished by the great army under McClellan's command and also that McClellan's personal and official conduct toward the authorities had taxed the President's forbearance to the last degree. He said enough—and it was his purpose, he told me, to do so—to enable me to realize the *uncertainty* of vigorous and harmonious co-operation of the various forces in front of Washington and on the Peninsula, . . .[55]

General Pope's presence in Washington in early July led to his standing aside while Secretary of War Stanton dictated the language contained in the message signed by Pope and addressed to the "Officers and Soldiers of the Army of Virginia" on July 14. "By special assignment of the President of the United States I have assumed the command of this army," this harangue began. Quickly, though, Pope and Stanton injected slurs obviously directed toward the Young Napoleon:

> I have come to you from the West, where we have always seen the backs of our enemies; from an army whose business it has been to seek the adversary and to beat him when he was found; whose policy has been attack and not defense. . . . I desire you to dismiss from your minds certain phrases, which I am sorry to find so much

> in vogue amongst you. I hear constantly of "taking strong positions and holding them," of "lines of retreat," and of "bases of supplies."
>
> Let us discard such ideas. . . . Let us look before us, and not behind. Success and glory are in the advance, disaster and shame lurk in the rear. . . .[56]

Many editors throughout the North were quick to note and applaud the anti-McClellan jabs. Pope's own troops, however, resented the newcomer's scolding tone regarding the Eastern army.

Fitz John Porter wrote to a friend:

> I regret that Genl Pope has not improved since his youth and has now written himself down what the military world has long known, [as] an ass. His address to his troops will make him ridiculous in the eyes of military men . . . and will reflect no credit on Mr Lincoln who has just promoted him. If the theory he proclaims is practiced you may look for disaster.[57]

Four days after issuing his bombastic address to his troops, John Pope confirmed the correctness of Fitz John Porter's low opinion of him by circulating certain orders that clearly had a Stantonian ring. This provoked General Lee into condemning Pope as "a miscreant who ought to be suppressed."[58]

An indication of George McClellan's discouragement, given Lincoln's having allowed Pope's harsh orders to stand, was a letter he wrote on July 19, 1862, to his fellow Democrat William H. Aspinwall, a business associate in the years between the wars:

> It is my opinion that I will be removed from the command of this Army in a short time. The present policy is, I think, merely a continuation of the inveterate persecution that has pursued me since I landed on the Peninsula—weakening my command so as to render it inadequate to accomplish the end in view, & then to hold me responsible for the results. I am quite weary of this.
>
> If I am superseded in the command of the Army of the Potomac I shall resign my commission in the service—feeling that I can no longer be of use—on the contrary, only in the way.

> Looking forward to that event, my main object in writing to you is to ask you to be kind enough to cast your eyes about you to see whether there is something I can do in New York to earn a respectable support for my family. . . .[59]

No seasoned veteran would blame him for wanting out. His letter to Aspinwall was a *cri de coeur*. Surely, in the circumstances, Aspinwall's reply was discouraging. "Your sphere while the war lasts is the Army," he wrote, adding: "you have no right to entertain any idea of return to civil life just now; . . . weigh well the political bearing of [Radicals'] advice which may be given you to the contrary."[60]

George McClellan would heed Aspinwall's admonition; the Jacobins had left him no honorable alternative. But from the Seven Days onward, almost every word he wrote in his messages and letters both to his superiors in Washington and to Mary Ellen reflected concern for his own future, and at times for that of the army he had rebuilt and commanded. On occasions when he did refer to General Lee's Army of Northern Virginia, his comments were peculiar. "I see that the Pope bubble is likely to be suddenly collapsed," McClellan wrote his wife on July 22. "Stonewall Jackson is after him & the paltry young man who wanted to teach me the art of war will in less than a week either be in full retreat or badly whipped."[61]

Regarding Halleck's appointment as general-in-chief, Little Mac's ire was directed mainly at Lincoln. On July 27, to Nell he complained:

> I was never informed of [the President's] views or intentions & even now have not been officially informed of the appt. I only know it through the newspapers. In all these things the Presdt & those around him have acted so as to make the matter as offensive as possible—he has not shown the slightest gentlemanly or friendly feeling & I cannot regard him as in any respect my friend—I am confident that he would relieve me tomorrow if he dared. His cowardice alone prevents it. I can never regard him with other feelings than those of thorough contempt—for his mind, heart & morality.[62]

In the same letter, McClellan rendered some other interesting judgments:

> McDowell is morally dead—he has no longer one particle of influence & is despised by all alike. Fitz Porter has, on the contrary, stuck through it all most nobly—he is all that I thought him & more. Nothing has depressed him; he is always cheerful, active & ready, & is much more efficient than all put together.[63]

Then, on August 1, McClellan sent General-in-Chief Halleck a long proposal that they work together to "save this unhappy country and bring this war to a comparatively early end," adding that "the doubt in my mind is whether the selfish politicians will allow us to do so. I fear the results of the civil policy inaugurated by recent Acts of Congress and practically enunciated by General Pope in his series of orders to the Army of Virginia."[64] Lest "Old Brains" miss his point, McClellan wrote:

> I and the Army under my command are fighting to restore the Union and the supremacy of its laws, not for revenge; I therefore deprecate, and view with infinite dread, any policy which tends to render impossible the reconstruction of the Union and to make this contest simply a useless effusion of blood.[65]

By August 8, the defiant Young Napoleon had received secret orders from the general-in-chief to move the Army of the Potomac to Aquia Creek on its namesake river, and he had already lodged his protest with Halleck.[66] Mary Ellen's husband revealed his reaction to the directive ending his Peninsular Campaign in this letter:

> [Halleck's orders] are as bad as they can be, & I regard them as almost fatal to our cause. . . . My only hope now is that I can induce the enemy to attack me. I shall of course obey the orders unless the enemy gives me a very good opening—which I should at once avail myself of.[67]

McClellan seemed to deem General Lee's Army of Northern Virginia worthy of mention only as a means of bringing about some consummation he—for reasons of his own—devoutly wished. Ironically, however, on that ninth day of August, Jackson had indeed fought elements of one of Pope's

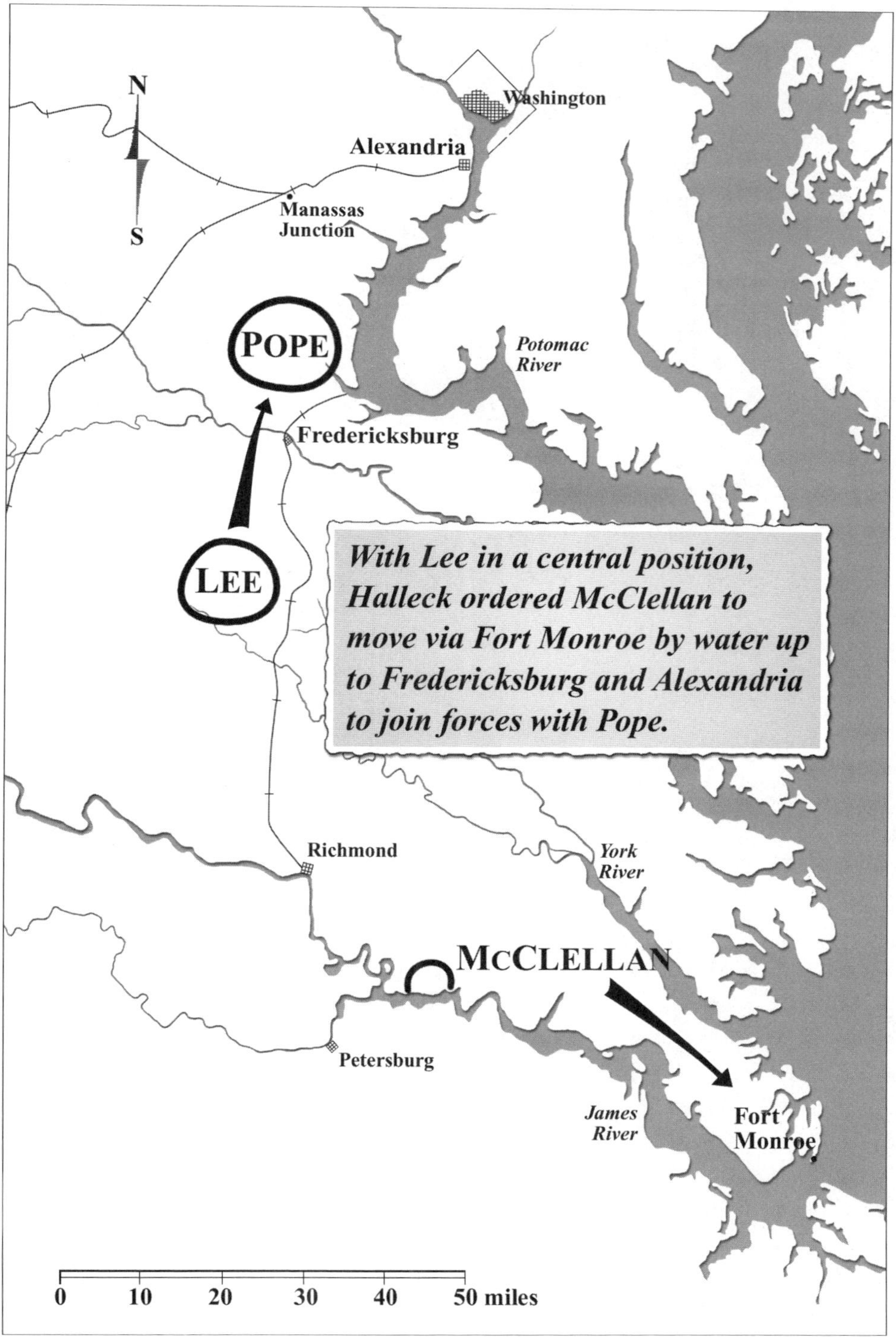
N
S
Washington
Alexandria
Manassas Junction
POPE
Potomac River
Fredericksburg
LEE
With Lee in a central position, Halleck ordered McClellan to move via Fort Monroe by water up to Fredericksburg and Alexandria to join forces with Pope.
Richmond
York River
MCCLELLAN
Petersburg
James River
Fort Monroe
0
10
20
30
40
50 miles

corps at Cedar Mountain. That action had the effect of heightening the importance and indeed the urgency of McClellan's obedience to Halleck's order to move the Army of the Potomac northward forthwith, for it marked the true opening of Second Bull Run—a campaign blighted by discord and tragedy whose consequences would be felt well beyond the end of the war.

CHAPTER THREE

Racing to Bull Run

PROTECTING the national capital from "danger or insult" had been one of the missions Commander-in-Chief Lincoln had assigned the Army of Virginia in the order creating it.[1] Washington itself was of no military value whatsoever. Government of the Union, including conduct of the war, could have continued with equal or possibly greater effectiveness from Philadelphia or New York or even Boston.

However, by the end of the Seven Days Battles twenty-odd miles east of Richmond, Lincoln had obliged Pope to operate in a region that enabled General Lee to take advantage of a central position. By so doing, Lincoln had given Lee his choice of which Union army to attack and destroy first, then turn and wipe out the other one.

R. E. Lee, correctly appraising George McClellan as too cautious and weak under grave responsibility, boldly—almost contemptuously—had left alone the Young Napoleon's whipped Yankees on former President William Henry Harrison's plantation and sent Stonewall Jackson north of nigh-undefended Richmond to begin mauling the approaching elements of Pope's army.

Indeed, General Lee's decision to ignore McClellan and to concentrate on wrecking Pope's army had been foreseen by the Union's new general-in-chief, Henry Halleck. On August 6, three days *before* Jackson whipped Banks for the second time in recent months, Halleck sent the Young Napoleon a long letter in which he answered, with precision and patience, the protests McClellan had registered when he received orders to return the Army of the Potomac to northern Virginia. The text reflected the kind of thinking that had been much needed in Washington since the war began. Some excerpts:

> You are 30 miles from Richmond, and General Pope 80 or 90, with the enemy directly between you, ready to fall with his superior numbers upon one or the other, as he may elect. Neither can re-enforce the other in case of such an attack.
>
> If General Pope's army be diminished to re-enforce you, Washington, Maryland, and Pennsylvania would be left uncovered and exposed. If your force be reduced to strengthen Pope, you would be too weak to even hold the position you now occupy should the enemy turn round and attack you in full force.
>
> In other words, the old Army of the Potomac is split into two parts, with the entire force of the enemy directly between them. They cannot be united on land without exposing both to destruction, and yet they must be united.
>
> To send Pope's forces by water to the Peninsula is, under present circumstances, a military impossibility.
>
> The only alternative is to send the forces on the Peninsula to some point by water, say Fredericksburg, where the two armies can be united. . . .
>
> I have not inquired, and do not wish to know, by whose advice or for what reasons the Army of the Potomac was separated into two parts, with the enemy between them. I must take things as I find them. I find the forces divided, and I wish to unite them. Only one feasible plan has been presented for doing this. If you or any one else had presented a better plan I certainly should have adopted it. But all of your plans require re-enforcements, which it is impossible to give you. It is very easy to ask for re-enforcements, but it is not so easy to give them when you have no disposable troops at your command.[2]

In all, General Halleck had used 1,097 words instead of just three: *Obey my orders!* In so doing, he had taken the case out of politics and restated it in purely military terms—where, of course, it had belonged from the beginning. This was not surprising to anyone who knew that Henry Halleck had been the most prominent and respected lawyer in California between the wars, or that he was author of the highly regarded *Elements of Military Art and Science.*

In his long letter to McClellan, Halleck had written, "The political effect of the withdrawal may at first be unfavorable; but I think the public are beginning to understand its necessity, and that they will have much more confidence in a united army than in its separated fragments."[3] This indicated that he was aware of political concerns, yet by confining himself to this one sentence he called attention to the great weight he was placing on military principles. Political extremists could take comfort from his decision to reinforce Pope; Lincoln would escape criticism from War Democrats; and if McClellan proved prompt in complying with the order, he might recover some of the esteem he had lost in "merely changing his base."

On August 8, Halleck had told General Pope: "Do not advance so as to expose yourself to any disaster . . . until we can get more troops [McClellan's] up the Rappahannock."[4] But Pope, in the field finally, had sent Major General Nathaniel Banks' corps into harm's way—and on the next day, Stonewall Jackson had shredded the former Speaker of the House of Representatives' troops at Cedar Mountain, a battle destined to become more accurately known in the South as Slaughter Mountain.[5] Subsequently, the very circumstance General Halleck had tried to preclude locked Pope's belatedly massed forces and General Lee's entire Army of Northern Virginia together in movements marked by heavy but inconclusive skirmishing steadily northward on opposite sides of the upper Rappahannock River.[6]

"Halleck is turning out just like the rest of the herd," McClellan wrote his wife on the morning of August 10. He continued:

> I have a strong idea that Pope will be thrashed during the coming week—& very badly whipped he will be & ought to be—such a villain as he is ought to bring defeat upon any cause that employs him. . . The absurdity of Halleck's course in ordering the army away from here is that it cannot possibly reach Washn in time to do any good, but will necessarily be too late—I am sorry to say that I am forced to the conclusion that H. is very dull & very incompetent—alas poor country! I hope to be ready tomorrow afternoon to move forward in the direction of Richmond—I will try to catch or thrash Longstreet & then if the chance offers follow in to Richmond while they are lamming away at Pope.

> I half apprehend that they will be too quick for me in Washn & relieve me before I have the chance to make the dash. If so—well & good. I am satisfied that the dolts in Washn are bent on my destruction if it is possible for them to accomplish it—but I believe that Providence is just enough to bring their own sins upon their heads & that they will before they get through taste the dregs of the cup of bitterness. The more I hear of their wickedness the more I am surprised that such a wretched set are permitted to live much less to occupy the positions they do.
>
> The next few days will probably be decisive. If I succeed in my coup everything will be changed in this country so far as we are concerned & my enemies will be at my feet. It may go hard with some of them in that event, for I look upon them as the enemies of the country & of the human race. . . .[7]

Such was the quality of George Brinton McClellan's thinking. There would be no haste in complying with Halleck's orders. Moreover, his comments to subordinates such as Fitz John Porter and William Franklin were likely to have been much closer in substance to what he had written Mary Ellen than the assurances he was giving General Halleck that "Everything [is] being done to carry out your orders."[8]

Overstatement aside, on August 15 McClellan reported that "two of my army corps marched last night and this morning en route for Yorktown."[9] One was Fitz John Porter's Fifth Corps. By August 16 it had reached Williamsburg. Later, McClellan wrote:

> I had directed him to halt until the entire army was across the Chickahominy. On his arrival at Williamsburg, however, he received an intercepted letter, which led to the belief that General Pope would have to contend against a very heavy force then in his front. General Porter therefore very properly took the responsibility of continuing his march directly on to Newport News, which place he reached on the morning of the 18th of August, having marched his corps 60 miles in the short period of three days and one night, halting one day at the crossing of the Chickahominy.
>
> The embarkation of this corps commenced as soon as transports were ready, and on the 20th it had all sailed for Aquia Creek.[10]

In no other corps commander had General McClellan reposed so much trust. Now, given Little Mac's expressed opinion that "Pope will be thrashed during the coming week—& very badly whipped he will be & ought to be—such a villain as he is ought to bring defeat upon any cause that employs him," it seemed inconsistent for him to have advanced his army's most valuable corps and the seasoned soldier commanding it toward assisting the Radical general he had so roundly damned.

2

On Monday, August 25, although still skirmishing with John Pope along the upper Rappahannock, General Lee had granted Jackson's request that he be allowed to take his divisions on an extended flank march—first around to the northwest toward the Shenandoah Valley, and then northeastward behind Thoroughfare Gap in the Blue Ridge to sweep down and cut Pope's Orange & Alexandria Railroad supply lifeline. On Wednesday, August 27, Confederates were helping themselves to the luxuries as well as the longed-for necessities they found in the Army of Virginia's vast supply depot at Manassas Junction. After sundown, having burned what they could not carry away, Stonewall's divisions simply vanished.

By then, General McClellan had followed his army up from Harrison's Landing and was operating from Alexandria, down the Potomac a dozen or so miles from Washington, the disembarkation point for units that had not (like Porter's) off-loaded at Aquia Landing. "I shall do all I can to help [Halleck] loyally," he wrote Nell, "& will trouble him as little as possible, but render all the assistance in my power without regard to myself or my own position. . . . Our affairs here are much tangled up & I opine that in a day or two your old husband will be called upon to unsnarl them."[11]

During that Wednesday, however, the Young Napoleon sent no less than seven messages to the general-in-chief. In the second, he raised the question of whether some of his units might "do better service in front of Washington" than by joining Pope.[12] The third was a petty complaint; in the fourth, he wondered if the capital's defenses should be placed in "efficient condition," if Burnside should "at once take steps to evacuate Falmouth & Aquia at the same time covering the retreat of any of Pope's troops who may fall back in that direction," and he closed with: "I do not see that we have force enough in hand to form a connection with Pope, whose exact position

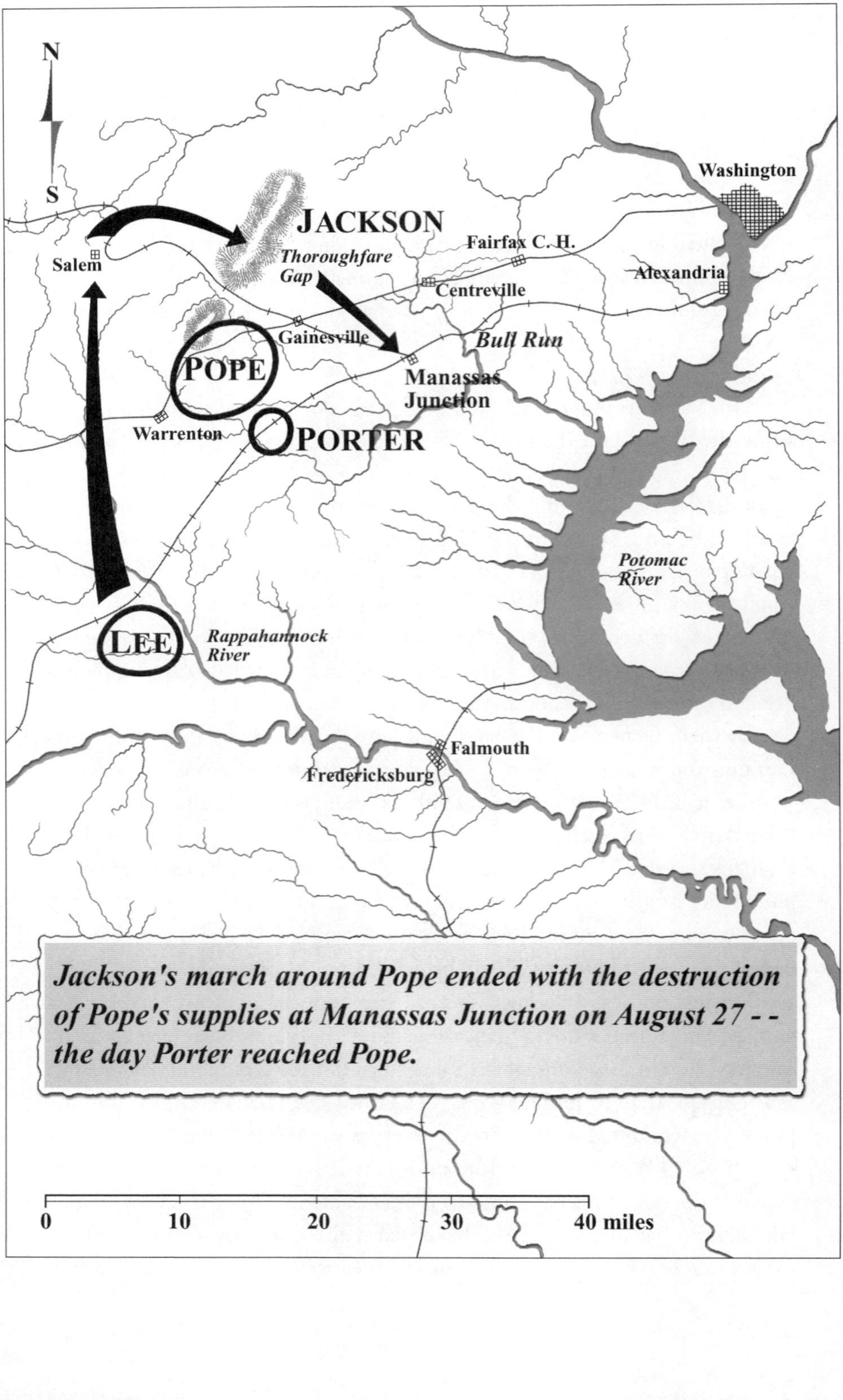

Jackson's march around Pope ended with the destruction of Pope's supplies at Manassas Junction on August 27 - - the day Porter reached Pope.

we do not know. Are we safe in the direction of the [Shenandoah] Valley?"[13] And in the sixth of seven messages that day:

> I still think that we should first provide for the immediate defense of Washington on both sides of the Potomac. I am not responsible for the past and cannot be for the future, unless I receive authority to dispose of the available troops according to my judgment. Please inform me at once what my position is. I do not wish to act in the dark.[14]

Back in July, General Halleck had written his wife that he wanted no part of the quarrel between McClellan and Stanton. As August neared its end, however, he was caught in precisely that trap. In a message to McClellan dated August 7 Halleck had written:

> It is my intention that you shall command all the troops in Virginia as soon as we can get them together; and with the army thus concentrated I am certain that you can take Richmond. I must beg of you, general, to hurry along this movement . . .
>
> I cannot regard Pope and Burnside as safe until you re-enforce them. Moreover, I wish them to be under your immediate command for reasons which it is not necessary to specify. As things now are, with separate commands, there will be no concert of action, and we daily risk being attacked and defeated in detail.[15]

Twenty days later, on August 27, General McClellan was presenting this promissory note for redemption. Halleck was not ready to honor it for at least two reasons: McClellan had not yet—as ordered—combined his forces with Pope's, and by then newcomer Halleck may well have discovered that only over the dead body of his immediate superior—Secretary of War Stanton—would John Pope *ever* be placed under the command of General McClellan.

Consequently, General McClellan—who had so recently assured Mary Ellen that he would "trouble [Halleck] as little as possible, but render all the assistance in my power without regard to myself or my own position"—proceeded to badger the general-in-chief regarding defending Washington, to offer excuse after labored excuse for not obeying peremptory orders (among other things) to rush William Franklin's and Edwin Sumner's corps out toward Manassas to reinforce Pope, and then to *whine* because he had not been told *what* he commanded.

Earlier, General Pope had expected that at some point Halleck would assume battlefield command over his army *and* McClellan's.[16] Indeed Halleck was directing both generals, but of necessity from his desk in Washington; via telegraph Halleck was also fighting the war out in the West where the Confederates were invading Kentucky. Even so, the general-in-chief had issued timely orders to Pope and McClellan. What more might he have accomplished *outside* Washington, given that Pope and McClellan were twenty or more miles distant from each other?

Actually, no Union general anywhere near Washington could do anything more than react to whatever Generals Lee and Jackson did. Old Jack had caught Pope badly out of position, south of him, on Tuesday when he cut the O&A Railroad at Bristoe Station. Knowing that Longstreet's divisions were up near Thoroughfare Gap, Pope tried to move between Lee's lieutenants—hoping to whip one, then the other—but after Jackson stripped and wrecked the Union's supply depot at Manassas Junction on Wednesday and then that night created the impression that he had advanced to Centreville, Pope ordered his corps out of Longstreet's intended path in the hope he could "bag" the other Confederates who had in fact disappeared.

Having jerked Pope's troops all the way from the upper Rappahannock northward and then eastward, Jackson had hidden his 25,000 men in the woods screening a stretch of an unfinished railroad embankment that paralleled the Warrenton Turnpike near Groveton, several miles west of the old Bull Run battlefield. There the Confederates rested, confident that with Pope shifting his scattered units in the wrong direction, Lee and Longstreet would have no trouble reaching them in due course and in reuniting the Army of Northern Virginia.[17]

Such were the benefits General Lee enjoyed by operating from a central position. Moreover, it could be argued that Lincoln had made an egregious mistake by placing Pope's Army of Virginia in harm's way.

The contending armies' movements during August 1862 had amounted to a race between General-in-Chief Halleck and General Lee. Halleck sought to combine the two Union armies in defense of Washington before Lee could prevent it; Lee meant to draw Pope's army so far westward that he could suppress the "miscreant's" forces before McClellan's Army of the Potomac arrived.

As noted, Jackson won the race for Lee by sweeping down from Thoroughfare Gap and cutting Pope's supply line, the O&A Railroad, at Bristoe Station on the afternoon of Tuesday, August 26, 1862. He might have moved directly from the gap to Pope's massive supply depot at Manassas Junction. But at Bristoe, seven miles south of Manassas Junction, he was able to burn the O&A's bridge over Cedar Run and place Major General Richard Ewell's division in a strong position to keep Pope—near Warrenton—from interfering with the looting and burning Jackson meant to start at the base up the tracks the next morning.[18]

At the time, only a few of McClellan's divisions had reached Pope. Porter's Fifth Corps was approaching from Falmouth. But the bulk of the Army of the Potomac was at Alexandria or near there, roughly twenty miles or a day's easy march from Manassas Junction. Troops were in camp, controller of the eastern railroads Herman Haupt recalled, "demanding transportation by rail which could not be furnished." And, wryly, he added: "The trouble seemed to have been an indisposition on the part of McClellan to assist Pope in gaining a victory."[19]

3

"I saw General F. J. Porter at Warrenton Junction about 11 o'clock on the morning of [Wednesday] the 27th," General Pope wrote years afterward, noting:

> I had seen General Porter at West Point while we were both cadets, but I think I never had an acquaintance with him there, nor do I think I ever met him afterward in the service. . . . He had such a high reputation in the army and for services since the outbreak of the war, that I was not only curious to see him, but was exceedingly glad that he had joined the army under my command with a corps which I knew to be one of the most effective in the service.[20]

George Sykes' division of regulars was camped nearby, the Army of Virginia's commander recalled; George Morell's was expected shortly. Pope's account continued:

> [Porter] appeared to me a most gentlemanlike man, of a soldierly and striking appearance. I had but little conversation with him, as I was engaged, as he was, in writing telegrams. He seemed to me to exhibit a listlessness and indifference not quite natural under the circumstances, which, however, is not unusual for a man to assume in the midst of dangers and difficulties, merely to impress one with their superior coolness.[21]

At the time, General Pope was preparing orders for the movement of his units northeastward in order to be in a central position between Longstreet and Jackson. Porter was to remain at Warrenton Junction until Nathaniel Banks' corps arrived, then "immediately push forward with his corps in the direction of Greenwich and Gainesville, to assist in the operations on the right wing."[22]

General Porter's weary troops may well have hoped that Banks' units would move at the pace of a snail, for on August 27 the Fifth Corps' infantrymen were completing a journey that began when they left Harrison's Landing a day short of two weeks before. Total distance marched: 127 miles in eight days.

"Everything here is at sixes and sevens," General Porter wrote Ambrose Burnside at Fort Monroe in one of the telegrams Pope recalled having seen him prepare. "I find I am to take care of myself in every respect."[23] Later that day, around four P.M., Porter sent Burnside a longer message:

> No enemy in our original front. A letter of General Lee, seized when Stuart's assistant adjutant-general was taken, directs Stuart to leave a squadron only to watch in front of Hanover Junction, &c. Everything has moved up north.
>
> I find a vast difference between [Pope's] troops and ours, but I suppose they were new, as to-day they burnt their clothes, &c., when there was not the least cause. I hear that they are much demoralized, and needed some good troops to give them heart, and I think head.
>
> We are working now to get behind Bull Run, and I presume will be there in a few days, if strategy don't use us up. The strategy is magnificent, and tactics in the inverse proportion. . . . I would like to be ordered to return to Fredericksburg to push toward

> Hanover, or with a larger force to push toward Orange Court House. I wish Sumner was at Washington, and up near the Monocacy, with good batteries. I do not doubt the enemy have large amounts of supplies provided for them, and I believe they have a contempt for this Army of Virginia. I wish myself away from it, with all our old Army of the Potomac, and so do our companions.
>
> I was informed today, by the best authority, that, in opposition to General Pope's views, this army was pushed out to save the Army of the Potomac—an army that could take care of itself. Pope says he long since wanted to go behind the Occoquan.
>
> Most of this is private, but if you can get me away please do so. Make what use of this you choose, so it does good.
>
> Don't let the alarm here disturb you. If you had a good force you could go to Richmond. A force should at once be pushed on to Manassas to open the road.[24]

Up the O&A's tracks a few miles to the north, near Bristoe, Dick Ewell's Confederates were obliging Joseph Hooker's troops to expend nearly all their ammunition—in vain—in trying to get to Manassas Junction to halt the orgy of gleeful consumption and destruction that had been in progress nearly all day.

The O&A's vulnerability to just such a strike had been pointed out to General Pope five days earlier by Herman Haupt during a visit. "What is to prevent the enemy from going even as far north as Thoroughfare Gap," Haupt had asked, "and getting behind you?" Pope's reply: "There is no danger."[25]

But by 6:30 P.M. on that Wednesday afternoon General Pope was at Bristoe Station and he had learned enough about Jackson's whereabouts and undesirable activities to realize how badly out of position his own corps were: All of them except Banks' were—as ordered—a dozen or more miles northwest of Manassas Junction. Worse, Joe Hooker's men were fought-out. Accordingly, Pope had his chief of staff write an order and send it to Fitz John Porter, back at Warrenton Junction. Starting "at 1 o'clock tonight," it began, Porter was to advance to Bristoe Station "so as to be here at daylight to-morrow morning."[26] But General Porter did not receive it until 9:30 or later that night, and for various reasons he and his leading division's elements did not reach Bristoe Station until 10:30 the next morning, instead of at daybreak.[27]

Major General Jackson had rendered that lapse moot, however, by skedaddling from the thoroughly looted ruins even as Pope was writing orders to his distant subordinates to speed their several divisions southeastward to Manassas Junction.[28] Typical was the preamble to this directive to old soldier Phil Kearny, in Heintzelman's corps:

> At the very earliest blush of dawn push forward with your command with all speed to this place. You cannot be more than 3 or 4 miles distant. Jackson, A. P. Hill, and Ewell are in front of us. Hooker has had a severe fight with them to-day. McDowell marches upon Manassas Junction from Gainesville to-morrow at daybreak; [Jesse] Reno upon the same place at the same hour. I want you here at day-dawn, if possible, and we shall bag the whole crowd.[29]

From Wednesday onward, however, Jackson's men having cut the telegraph wires at Bristoe and Manassas Junction, Pope was obliged to operate without guidance from Halleck. Relaying messages through Ambrose Burnside at Fort Monroe proved an awkward, ineffective alternative. Consequently, Haupt's telegraphers at O&A stations north of Manassas Junction became Washington's sole sources of news regarding Jackson's astonishing interposition of his forces between Pope and McClellan.[30]

Worse, from the Union point of view, by ordering the forces to concentrate at Manassas Junction that might have detected and reported and even opposed the progress of the other half of General Lee's army toward joining Jackson, General Pope had all but blinded himself.

4

On the next day, Thursday, August 28, 1862, Secretary of War Stanton imposed a demanding task on General-in-Chief Halleck, who at the time was straining the capacity of the Union's telegraph wires to support defense against Confederate drives out in Tennessee and Kentucky, as well as to spur McClellan to obey orders he had issued back on August 3. Stanton wrote Halleck:

> I desire you to furnish me information upon the following points:
>
> 1st. At what date you first ordered the general commanding the Army of the Potomac to move from James River.
>
> 2d. Whether that order was or was not obeyed according to its purport with the promptness which, in your judgment, the national safety required, and at what date the movement commenced.
>
> 3d. What order has been given recently for the movement of Franklin's corps, and whether it was obeyed as promptly as the national safety required.
>
> 4th. You will furnish me copies of the orders referred to in the foregoing inquiries.[31]

McClellan added to the evidence even as Halleck was compiling it. Early on Thursday afternoon he telegraphed the general-in-chief:

> I suggest that you take into consideration the propriety of Pope falling back. . . . I do not think it now worth while to attempt to preserve the [O&A] railway. The great object is to collect the whole army in Washington, ready to defend the works and act upon the flank of any force crossing the Upper Potomac.[32]

Fitz John Porter's corps was already present for duty with John Pope's Army of Virginia, but the one commanded by General McClellan's other favorite, William B. Franklin, was still in the vicinity of Alexandria. "Not a moment must be lost," Halleck telegraphed the Young Napoleon, "in pushing as large a force as possible toward Manassas."[33]

McClellan replied: "Neither Franklin nor Sumner's corps is now in condition to move and fight a battle. It would be a sacrifice to send them out now. . . . I still think that a premature movement in small force will accomplish nothing but the destruction of the troops sent out."[34]

And General Halleck shot back:

> There must be no further delay in moving Franklin's corps toward Manassas. They must go to-morrow morning, ready or not ready. If we delay too long to get ready there will be no necessity to go at all, for Pope will either be defeated or be victorious without our aid.[35]

At about the same time on Thursday—"4 miles from Manassas"—Fitz John Porter was sending Ambrose Burnside at Fort Monroe another report:

> All [Pope's] talk of bagging Jackson, &c., was bosh. That enormous Gap (Manassas) was left open and the enemy jumped through, and the story of McDowell having cut off Longstreet had no good foundation. The enemy have destroyed all our bridges, burned trains &c., and made this army rush back to look after its line of communications and find our base of subsistence. There is a report that Jackson is at Centreville, which you can believe or not. The enemy destroyed an immense amount of property at Manassas—cars and supplies. I expect the next thing will be a raid on our rear by way of Warrenton by Longstreet, who was cut off.[36]

Worth noting here is that General Porter not only gave Burnside an astonishingly accurate appraisal of the situation but identified a threat to which his new commanding general seemed utterly oblivious. In fact, General Pope's orders on Thursday called for his forces to concentrate at *Centreville* to "bag" Jackson—who was not there, just as he had been long gone from Manassas Junction that morning when Pope had found nothing left but smoldering ruins of what had been his main supply point.[37]

On Thursday, while complying with the order to move to Manassas Junction, Irvin McDowell attempted to compensate for Pope's error by sending James Ricketts' division up to deny use of Thoroughfare Gap to Longstreet. But the Confederates already held the high ground, and they sent Ricketts' men scrambling to catch up with McDowell's other units bound for whatever was left of the Manassas Junction supply base.

While most of Pope's units were shifting east-southeastward, the general commanding was spending Thursday, August 28, near Blackwell's Ford on Bull Run, not far from Centreville. Porter had moved his Fifth Corps from Warrenton Junction to Bristoe Station, but he had started at 3 A.M. instead of—as Pope had specified—at one. Darkness and congestion on the road prevented his arrival at Bristoe Station before 10:30 Thursday morning, several hours later than "daylight," after Pope had moved on to Manassas Junction. Porter's having been late was not unique and it had no effect on the military situation, which Stonewall Jackson had removed from the control of anyone in the Union.

In truth, almost every element of John Pope's army had been out of position *continuously* since Jackson had swept down from Thoroughfare Gap on Tuesday. Pope's cavalry resources were scant, but he had kept none of them under his control nearby—hence, his prolonged inability to find out where Jackson was. Moreover, Pope had a tendency to act impulsively on scraps of information without taking the time to obtain corroboration or even to analyze, to think through, the consequences of what he proposed to do and what he was ordering his subordinates to do. These deficiencies were never more evident than they turned out to be on that Thursday.

Late that afternoon, with his Confederates hidden near Groveton, General Jackson watched two Union brigades march eastward along the Warrenton Turnpike, toward Centreville, almost as though they were passing in review in his honor. He ordered an attack that struck the Yankees in the flank.

Because the Union division's commander, Rufus King, was incapacitated by an epileptic seizure, Brigadier Generals John Gibbon and Abner Doubleday were obliged to fight the ensuing battle on their own. Their key decision was to stay and slug it out, appalling though their losses were, realizing that their calls for help were not being heeded.

Only darkness ended the fierce firefight. Neither side had given an inch. Jackson, however, had done what he could to attract John Pope's attention—his objective being to prevent Pope from occupying Centreville's fortifications to await the arrival of Franklin's and Sumner's corps from Alexandria.[38]

After dark, Gibbon and Doubleday took the question of what to do next back to General King's headquarters. By then he had recovered enough to listen to his valiant but weary subordinates' reports and recommendations and to make a decision. It was incorporated in a message to King's corps commander, Irvin McDowell: "From prisoners' reports to-night there is no doubt that Jackson's main force is in our immediate front. Our position is not tenable, and we shall fall back toward Manassas. . . .[39]

From high ground eight miles away, General Pope had heard the sound of the guns coming from the nasty scrap near Groveton, and he may have seen flashes of bursting shells, but for several hours he had no idea of what was happening.[40] From King's message he concluded that King had collided with Jackson while Jackson was retreating from Centreville and that King was between Jackson and Longstreet. In fact, King had slipped southeastward and Jackson had remained in his hiding place along the unfinished railroad embankment screened by woods.[41]

At 9:50 on that Thursday night General Pope sent this order to Phil Kearny at Centreville:

> General McDowell has intercepted the retreat of the enemy, and is now in his front.
>
> Unless [Jackson] can escape by passes leading to the north to-night he must be captured. I desire you to move forward at 1 o'clock to-night, even if you can carry with you no more than 2,000 men, though I trust you will carry the larger part of your division.
>
> Pursue the turnpike from Centreville to Warrenton. The enemy is not more than 3½ miles from you. Seize any of the people of the town to guide you. Advance cautiously and drive in the enemy's pickets to-night, and at early dawn attack him vigorously.
>
> Hooker shall be close behind you. Extend your right well in the attack. Be sure to march not later than 1 [o'clock] with all the men you can take.[42]

Old soldier Phil Kearny, who back on July 1 had declared that whoever had ordered the withdrawal from Malvern Hill was a either a coward or a traitor, read the order and then snapped to an aide, "Tell General Pope to go to Hell. We won't march before morning."[43]

Pope sent similar orders to Franz Sigel. Curiously, no one knew where Irvin McDowell was.[44]

Such was the background for some of the comments Fitz John Porter made in a message he sent to Ambrose Burnside at Fort Monroe from Bristoe Station on Friday morning, August 29:

> Shall be off in half an hour. . . . Heintzelman and Reno at Centreville, where they marched yesterday, and Pope went to Centreville with the last two as a body guard, at the time not knowing where was the enemy and when Sigel was fighting within 8 miles of him and in sight.
>
> Comment is unnecessary.
>
> The enormous trains are still rolling on, many animals not

> having been watered for fifty hours. I shall be out of provisions tomorrow night. Your train of 40 wagons cannot be found.
>
> I hope Mac is at work, and we will soon get ordered out of this.
>
> It would seem from proper statements of the enemy that he was wandering around loose; but I expect they know what they are doing, which is more than any one here or anywhere knows.
>
> Just received the following order:
>
> *General McDowell has anticipated the retreat of Jackson. . . . Major-General Pope directs you to move upon Centreville at the first dawn of day with your whole command, leaving your trains follow. It is very important that you should be here at a very early hour in the morning. A severe engagement is likely to take place and your presence is necessary.*[45]

General Porter's references to wagon train movements, unwatered horses, and low levels of provisions may well have made him glad to be heading for Centreville—and possibly reunion with the Army of the Potomac. But soon after he reached the ruins of Manassas Junction, where his men were able to replenish at least their ammunition, General John Gibbon arrived. He had come from Pope's headquarters with fresh orders for Porter: "Push forward with your corps and King's division, which you will take with you, upon Gainesville. I [Pope] am following the enemy down the Warrenton turnpike. Be expeditious or we will lose much."[46]

Somewhat before ten o'clock on that Friday morning, up rode General McDowell. After exchanges of news and views, McDowell told Porter that he regretted Pope's transfer of King's division from his own to Fifth Corps' control.[47]

Actually, Irvin McDowell had a lot more to regret than an army commander's understandable switch of a division from one out-of-position corps to another in a fluid combat environment. From March until June, McDowell had been the general most likely to replace George McClellan; now John Pope was commanding McDowell. And Porter, one of McClellan's pets, was about to march off with one of *his* divisions.

General McDowell, who in the circumstances ranked Porter, held him at Manassas Junction while he awaited a response to a protest he had sent Pope. Around 10 A.M., no reply having been forthcoming, he allowed Porter to move out.

Porter turned his corps' column around. With King's division following, he led his troops back toward Bristoe Station until he came to the road that would take him northwestward to Gainesville, and then turned right.[48]

In effect, General Pope was sending Porter to fill the vacuum between Longstreet and Jackson created when McDowell and later King had obeyed his earlier orders to move to Manassas Junction. At Gainesville, Porter's Fifth Corps could act as an anvil against which Pope's units moving westward might hammer Jackson to destruction—or block Stonewall from escaping—or prevent Longstreet from reaching Old Jack.

Pope's purpose not having been made clear raised the question of whether he knew what he was doing. He was not in telegraphic contact with anyone in Washington and had not been for the better part of three days. Confederates' devastations at Bristoe Station and Manassas Junction had denied him access both to General Halleck's military advice and such direction as Stanton might have offered him. Hence, he alone could be held responsible for his subsequent decisions and their consequences.

Hindsight suggests that on Friday morning, August 29, the situation General Pope had faced was roughly this: Lee and Longstreet were within easy marching distance of Jackson's divisions, which were deployed near Groveton; almost all of Pope's forces were near enough to Jackson to be concentrated against him; but with the Manassas Junction supply base taken out, and with food and fodder and ammunition and everything else running low, these necessities could be replenished only from Centreville.

Pope's available courses of action were at least these:

- Withdraw into Centreville's fortifications to resupply and await the arrival of Franklin's and Sumner's corps from nearby Alexandria, and then move out to destroy Lee's army
- Concentrate against Jackson at Groveton
- Confine Jackson to his positions near Groveton while preventing Lee and Longstreet from joining him

Taking the third course first, and considering that Lee and Longstreet had more troops and guns with them than Jackson, Pope would find it nigh-impossible to fight both elements of the Confederate army at once unless and until he had Franklin's and Sumner's corps—which, on Thursday night, were idle under McClellan's control in the Alexandria vicinity.

Pulling back into Centreville's defenses, collecting—indeed, *massing*—all the Union's resources in the area, and restoring communications with Washington and Alexandria made the most sense. But withdrawal even to Centreville would remind millions of militarily ignorant newspaper readers throughout the North of McClellan's shameful "change of base." As Franklin and Sumner and other assets of the Army of the Potomac reached Centreville, the Young Napoleon was certain to supercede Pope in command.

Obliged by Confederate telegraph wire-cutting to rely only upon his own resources, John Pope responded to his challenges and opportunities more as a political operative than as a soldier. By adopting the second course of action, concentrating against Jackson at Groveton, he might avoid all the threats to his reputation embedded in the Centreville alternative. Moreover, *what if he could*, with only two Army of the Potomac's five corps present with him, *whip* Jackson?

Where would such an outcome leave George McClellan? And how might Pope's powerful political friends in Washington react to *that*?

Concentrating against Jackson, the course of action that General Pope adopted, may very well have been the worst mistake he ever made in his life.[49] And the most tragic aspect of that error was his preference for the easier wrong instead of the harder right.

However, the central compelling fact driving that situation fewer than forty miles west of Washington was that R. E. Lee, more than any man then alive, was controlling developments. Much more to the point: politics had absolutely no weight whatsoever in the military decisions he made.

Yes, but inevitably personal considerations exerted some influence. Having failed to annihilate McClellan's Army of the Potomac during the Seven Days, he was determined to prevent its junction with Pope's Army of Virginia. So decisively had General Lee moved toward that objective that he had split his army in the face of the enemy.

By keeping Longstreet's divisions in contact with some of Pope's forces on the upper Rappahannock, Lee had confused the Yankee opposing him so thoroughly that Jackson was able to reach Bristoe Station and loot Manassas Junction virtually without being observed. Once Longstreet followed Old Jack, Lee—trusting Jackson to take care of his own, and trusting Pope to waste his opportunities—did not rush the movement. It had to be slow in any case because of the wagon trains, Jackson's as well as Longstreet's. But

General Lee had shown no anxiety late on Thursday afternoon when he heard the sounds of the sharp firefight Stonewall had picked with the two Yankee brigades passing his front. Even on Friday morning, when after a short and unmolested march Longstreet's troops were moving into concealed positions Jackson had selected south of the southern end of his line, General Lee restrained himself from attacking or even calling Pope's attention to Longstreet's presence. McClellan was capable of upsetting everything; it would be best, the Army of Northern Virginia's commander decided, to wait and see what mistakes the Yankees made.[50]

On Friday morning, August 29, General McClellan was still protesting Halleck's demand that Franklin, ready or not, march to reinforce Pope. "I do not think Franklin is in condition to accomplish much if he meets serious resistance," he telegraphed the general-in-chief from Alexandria. "I should not have moved him but for your prodding order of last night."[51]

Angered by McClellan's insolent badgering, starved for news, frustrated by having to depend on Ambrose Burnside down at Falmouth to relay messages, it may be that the Union's war managers placed undue weight on some documents that Burnside had forwarded. They were the ones Fitz John Porter had sent him on Wednesday and a few hours earlier, in which McClellan's "pet" had expressed his dim views of Pope's generalship and his hope that "Mac is at work, and that we will soon be ordered out of this."[52]

Mac was indeed at work, replying to a terse inquiry from A. Lincoln, "What news from direction of Manassas? What generally?"[53]

> The last news I received from the direction of Manassas was from stragglers, to the effect that the enemy were evacuating Centreville and retiring toward Thoroughfare Gap. This by no means reliable.
>
> I am clear that one of two courses should be adopted: First, to concentrate all our available forces to open communications with Pope; Second, to leave Pope to get out of his scrape, and at once use all our means to make the capital perfectly safe.
>
> No middle ground will now answer. Tell me what you wish me to do, and I will do all in my power to accomplish it. I wish to know what my orders and authority are. I ask for nothing, but will obey whatever orders you give. I only ask a prompt decision, that I may at once give the necessary orders. It will not do to delay longer.[54]

Concentrating to open communications with Pope made sense; indeed, Halleck had long since ordered it. To *leave Pope to get out of his scrape* smacked of treason.

McClellan's thinking was revealed in a letter to his wife, written within minutes of his astonishing reply to President Lincoln:

> I have a terrible task on my hands now—perfect imbecility to correct. No means to act with, no authority—yet determined if possible to save the country & the Capital. I find the soldiers all clinging to me—yet I am not permitted to go to the post of danger! Two of my Corps will either save that fool Pope or be sacrificed for the country. I do not know whether I will be permitted to save the Capital or not—I have just telegraphed very plainly to the Presdt & Halleck what I think ought to be done—I expect merely a contemptuous silence.[55]

On Friday, August 29, "that fool Pope" was trying hard to get out of his scrape, but he was laboring in ignorance. He was fortunate in that he had no way of finding out what Lincoln, Stanton, and Halleck were learning from Burnside and Little Mac. But the Army of Virginia's commander had not been well served by Irvin McDowell, who had been out of communication all night, then had protested the assignment of King's division to Porter, and finally had failed at 9:30 that morning to forward a message sent to him by cavalryman Brigadier General John Buford: "Seventeen [Confederate] regiments, one battery, and 500 cavalry passed through Gainesville three-quarters of an hour ago on the Centreville road."[56]

Put simply, at 8:45 or so Lee and Longstreet had been in possession of the objective General Pope had subsequently sent Porter's corps toward. Absent that knowledge, Pope responded to Irvin McDowell's mid-morning complaint from Manassas Junction by issuing to both McDowell and Porter an order from hell:

> You will please move forward with your joint commands toward Gainesville. I sent General Porter written orders to that effect an hour and a half ago. Heintzelman, Sigel, and Reno are moving on the Warrenton turnpike, and must now be not far from Gainesville.

> I desire that as soon as communication is established between this force and your own the whole command shall halt.
>
> It may be necessary to fall back behind Bull Run at Centreville to-night. I presume it will be so, on account of our supplies. I have sent no orders of any description to Ricketts, and none to interfere in any way with the movements of McDowell's troops, except what I sent by his aide-de-camp last night, which were to hold his position on the Warrenton pike until the troops from here should fall on the enemy's flank and rear. I do not even know Ricketts' position, as I have not been able to find out where General McDowell was until a late hour this morning. General McDowell will take immediate steps to communicate with General Ricketts, and instruct him to rejoin the other divisions of his corps as soon as practicable.
>
> If any considerable advantages are to be gained by departing from this order it will not be strictly carried out. One thing must be had in view, that the troops must occupy a position from which they can reach Bull Run to-night or by morning. The indications are that the whole force of the enemy is moving in this direction at a pace that will bring them here by to-morrow night or the next day. My own headquarters will be for the present with Heintzelman's corps or at this place.[57]

At around eleven o'clock that morning the men in Porter's point brigade, en route from Manassas Junction to Gainesville, collided with and skirmished briefly with some Confederates where the road to Gainesville crossed a stream called Dawkins' Branch. With his advance halted, Porter rode forward. He was deploying elements of George Morell's division when a messenger brought him a copy of General Pope's "joint" order. Soon General McDowell arrived; he had galloped up from Manassas Junction with the message from cavalryman John Buford that Ricketts had forwarded to him and his copy of the order Pope had addressed to both of them. Porter completed the change from advance to defense, then he and McDowell—his superior, given Pope's joint order—sought such guidance as they might obtain from the general commanding's nigh-incoherent text.[58]

Nowhere in General Pope's directive did the word *attack* appear, yet something would have to be done about those rebels blocking the road to Gainesville, given that Porter's mission was still moving "upon" that town. That mission was now also McDowell's. But Buford's message, now in McDowell's pocket where it would remain all day, suggested that in no way could his and Porter's corps reach Pope's proposed junction point—Gainesville—with the forces Pope was ordering to move westward on the Warrenton Turnpike unless General Porter blew the Confederates blocking him out of his, and McDowell's, way.

And even if Porter and McDowell *were* to fight their way through the Confederates blocking them beyond Dawkins' Branch *and* link up with westward-bound Heintzelman, Sigel, and Reno, what were they to do next?

"I desire that as soon as communication is established between this force and your own the whole command shall halt," General Pope had directed. "It may be necessary to fall back behind Bull Run at Centreville to-night. I presume it will be so, on account of our supplies."

And General Pope had added: "One thing must be had in view, that the troops must occupy a position from which they can reach Bull Run to-night or by morning." Why? He thought that "the whole force of the enemy" was moving toward Centreville at a pace that would bring them there by Saturday night or Sunday—not whenever General Lee chose, now that Longstreet had gone into position on Jackson's right.

The strangest part of the strange document, however, was, "If any considerable advantages are to be gained by departing from this order it will not be strictly carried out." What *did* the general commanding want?

Porter and McDowell could hear the sounds of artillery dueling off to their right: ahead, toward Gainesville, they could see clouds of dust rising in the hot August air.

"Porter, you are too far out already," the senior officer declared. "This is no place to fight a battle."[59] McDowell mounted and headed back to his divisions, intending to take them over to the fighting.

"What should I do?" Porter called after him. There was no reply.[60]

5

When General Lee reached Jackson and learned that the Yankees were probing Old Jack's center, his first impulse was to order Longstreet to attack.

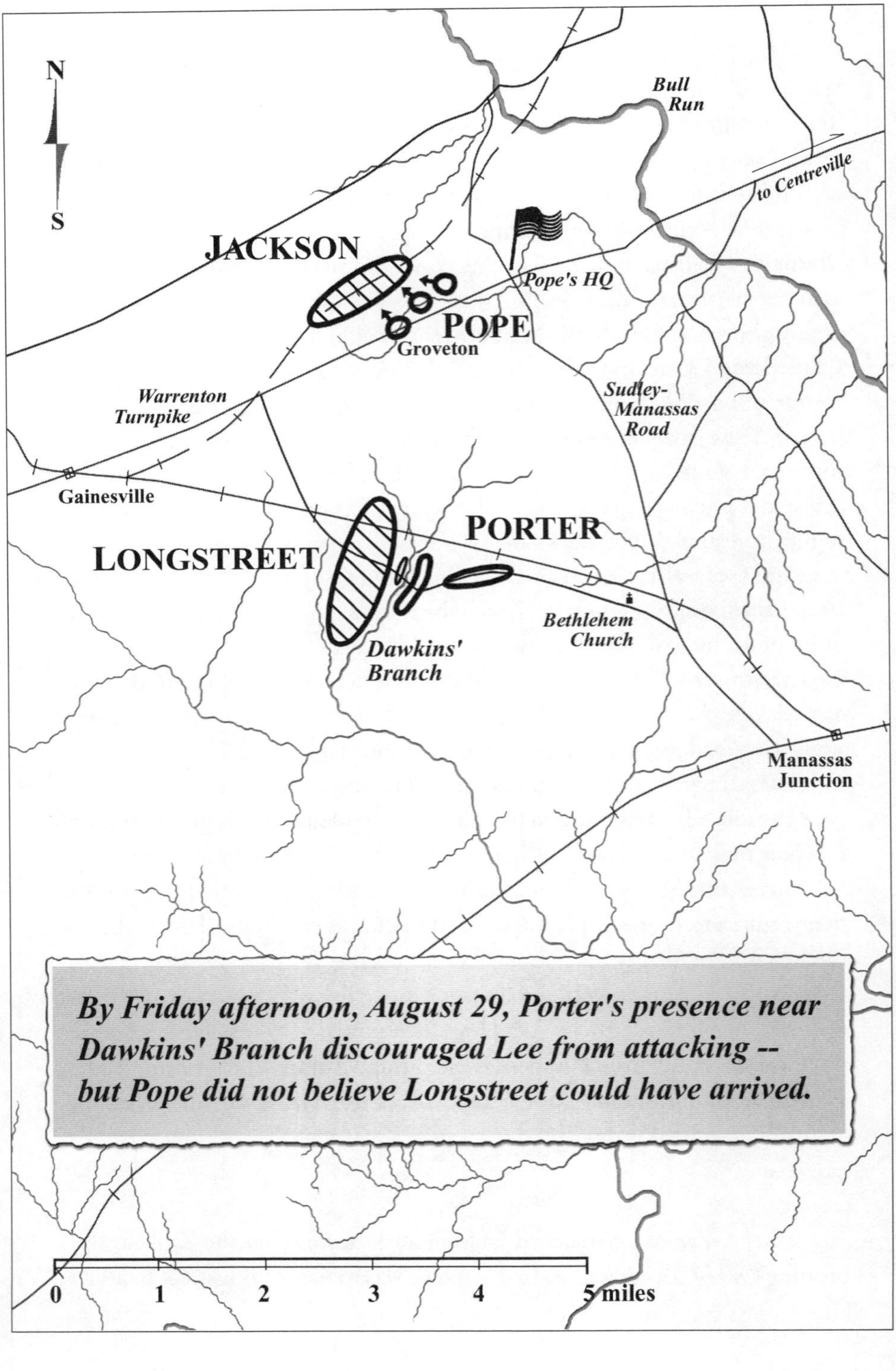

By Friday afternoon, August 29, Porter's presence near Dawkins' Branch discouraged Lee from attacking -- but Pope did not believe Longstreet could have arrived.

Longstreet, however, wanted to make a personal reconnaissance. Also, Stuart's cavalrymen were reporting Yankees in large force were off to the south, at Dawkins' Branch. If Longstreet attacked the federals in Jackson's front, his troops might be hit in the flank by the Yankees the cavalrymen had spotted. Accordingly, Lee decided to hold Longstreet where he was.

Stuart had too few riders to prevent the enemy—Porter—from advancing. "Jeb" sent for reinforcements, and while he waited he had his men cut brush and drag it up and down the Gainesville-Manassas road, thus creating the dust clouds Porter and McDowell had seen.[61]

By early Friday afternoon General Pope was with Franz Sigel's corps, the one attacking Jackson. He seemed utterly unaware that Longstreet had arrived and could be watching as he threw one piecemeal assault after another at the rebels defending the unfinished railroad embankment north of the Warrenton Turnpike.[62]

Indeed, Pope appeared to ignore the fact that Jackson was not behaving as he had expected. It was as though his recollection of the morning's joint order was that he had called for Porter and McDowell not only to march to Gainesville, but once there—presumably, in positions to strike Jackson's right flank and rear—to smash the Confederates. In fact, Pope had given neither Porter nor McDowell any such instructions; yet he seemed to have based his conduct of Friday afternoon's attacks against Jackson's railroad embankment as though he expected the two corps commanders he had ordered jointly to move up to Gainesville, and then halt, to have torn into Old Jack's rear.[63]

Friday afternoon's grim reality was that each time federal brigades broke a segment of Jackson's line, sharp counterattacks drove them back. Of valor there had been an abundance; of Yankee success, none. This oft-repeated cycle had extracted heavy casualties on both sides and had settled nothing at all.[64]

Curiously, by doing nothing, Fitz John Porter *was* accomplishing something important, though it was not perceived by anyone in a blue uniform; even he was unaware of it. His mere presence at Dawkins' Branch was keeping Generals Longstreet and Lee from attacking General Pope's corps hammering Jackson. Moreover, Porter's having *remained* where he was had suggested to the intimidated Confederates that he might well be awaiting reinforcements that would enable him to get around and behind Longstreet's southern flank.

Even so, as late as three o'clock on Friday afternoon, General Lee was still of a mind to strike out at Pope. Over to Longstreet's right to see what Porter was doing he rode. No, he concluded after a good look, the threat from this quarter was too great and the Confederate forces then blocking those Yankees were too scant; he ordered Longstreet to shift a division from his left to beef them up, even though this increased his risks by extending and changing the direction of his front.

Subsequently, Stuart's observers reported dust clouds rising from behind Porter's positions. Might the federals be pulling back?

Indeed, McDowell's divisions were on the move, having earlier left Porter isolated and unsupportable whether he decided to attack or had to defend. Absent any replies to any of the messages Porter had sent McDowell and Pope that afternoon describing his situation, requesting orders, warning that his troops were running low on water and food, and asking whether Pope still might want him to withdraw to Bull Run, he and his two divisions were standing fast.

Dust cloud sightings did not change General Lee's mind. He did permit some probing later by John Hood's Texans at the north end of Longstreet's line, but only to get ready for a massive assault in the morning.[65]

Apparently, General Pope's thinking remained tightly focused only on the wishful notion that sounds of battle from Gainesville's direction would cause Jackson's embattled line to crumble. By 4:30 on that Friday afternoon, however, he had misgivings—and he reflected them and his ignorance in an order he wrote and handed to his nephew and aide, Captain Douglass Pope, to deliver to General Porter:[66]

> Your line of march brings you in on the enemy's right flank. I desire you to push forward into action at once on the enemy's flank, and, if possible, on his rear, keeping your right in communication with General Reynolds.
>
> The enemy is massed in the woods in front of us, but can be shelled out as soon as you engage their flank.
>
> Keep heavy reserves, and use your batteries, keeping well closed to your right all the time. In case you are obliged to fall back, do so to your right and rear, so as to keep you in close communication with the right wing.[67]

Although the order was dated August 29, 4:30 P.M., General Porter did not receive it until after six.[68] The sun was setting; the task was not in line with reality; and he had no idea of where Jackson's flank might be. King's division, assigned to Porter by Pope that morning, had been reclaimed by McDowell and taken by him over to join the fighting near Groveton. Even so, Porter gave orders to advance. General Morell protested, as did other officers. Porter called off the attack.[69]

General Pope's futile and costly assaults finally ended at around 8:00 P.M. A little earlier, McDowell reported to him—the two generals had not met for four days. McDowell handed Pope cavalryman Buford's long-pocketed message, written at 9:30 that morning, and indicated that Lee and Longstreet must have been present near Jackson most of the afternoon. He also gave Pope a message Porter had sent but McDowell had not forwarded to Pope: "Please let me know your designs, whether to retire or not. . . . I cannot get water and am out of provisions. Have lost a few men from infantry fighting."[70]

General Pope's reaction, at about 8:50 P.M., was to start this message to Porter, still near Dawkins' Branch:[71]

> Immediately upon receipt of this order, the precise hour of receiving which you will acknowledge, you will march your command to the field of battle of to-day and report to me in person for orders. You are to understand that you are expected to comply strictly with this order, and to be present on the field within three hours after its reception or after daybreak to-morrow morning.[72]

General Porter received this order—actually a venting of spleen and an unmistakable rebuke—at 3:30 on the morning of Saturday, August 30, 1862.[73] It was peremptory. There was nothing he could do but obey, and obey he did.

Before sunrise on that Saturday, General Pope received a message from Major General William Franklin:

> I have been instructed by General McClellan to inform you that he will have all the available wagons at Alexandria loaded with rations for your troops, and all of the cars also, as soon as you will send in a cavalry escort to Alexandria as a guard to the trains.[74]

Regarding this, Pope would later write:

> All hope of being able to maintain my position, whether victorious or not, vanished with this letter. My cavalry was utterly broken down by long and constant service in the face of the enemy, and, bad as they were, could not be spared from the front, even [if] there had been time to go back 30 miles to Alexandria and await the loading of trains. At the time this letter was written Alexandria was swarming with troops and my whole army interposed between that place and the enemy. I at once understood that we must, if possible, finish what we had to do that day, as night must see us behind Bull Run if we wished to save men and animals from starvation.[75]

The general commanding was beginning to realize, in effect, that George McClellan was leaving him to get out of his scrape. "It was not until I received that letter," he recalled, "that I began to feel discouraged and nearly hopeless of any successful result."[76]

Even so, encouraged by reports that Jackson was retreating, General Pope called a meeting of his senior officers. After some discussion he ordered McDowell's, Porter's, and Heintzelman's corps to attack the eastern end of Jackson's line. But the order was verbal and vague, and at the time Porter's corps had not yet arrived from Dawkins' Branch.[77]

When Porter did report to Pope, he warned that the Confederates, present in strength back at Dawkins' Branch, could sweep eastward, south of the Warrenton Turnpike, and force Pope to retreat across Bull Run to Centreville. Major General John Reynolds joined the discussion, confirming Porter's information and opinion. But these were officers from McClellan's forces, an army Pope no longer trusted, and he dismissed them without giving them any orders.[78] Recalled a staff officer: "General Pope seemed wholly at a loss to know what to do and what to think."[79]

Saturday morning slipped away without the Army of Virginia's general commanding taking the one action he had recognized as inevitable but politically inexpedient: withdrawing beyond Bull Run to Centreville and supplies and reinforcements provided belatedly by General McClellan. General-in-Chief Halleck had admonished him, in nearly every message that had reached Pope since this phase of the campaign began, to maintain his communications with Alexandria. Centreville was critical, essential, the only link Pope could reach. But if he fell back behind those fortifications, would his political backers understand? And if those friends and supporters did not, what then?

Concurrently, General Lee both possessed and employed the luxury—very rare in combat—of being free to think and act *strategically*. His mind unencumbered by dread of politicians' retribution, he had decided what *he* ought to do no matter what Pope did.

If the Yankees did nothing, or withdrew to Centreville, Lee would send Jackson on another flank march north and east of there to cut Pope's lifeline to Alexandria at or near Fairfax Court-House; then Longstreet could either sweep eastward, over the ground Fitz John Porter had just been obliged to abandon, toward Alexandria itself, or turn northward, cross the Potomac, and invade Maryland.

But if Pope renewed his assaults along Jackson's railroad embankment line, General Lee could suppress him by pouring the fire of Longstreet's artillery batteries upon the blueclad attackers' flank and then release "Old Pete's" divisions, led by John Hood's Texans, to smash all of Pope's forces in their way as they drove south of the Warrenton Turnpike toward Centreville and possibly Washington—*and then* he could consider invading Maryland.[80]

More excruciating irony: General Lee was clearly the master in this strategic situation, yet he was allowing Pope to make the next move.

6

Fitz John Porter was stretching the outer limits of subordination in trying to persuade John Pope to listen to and be guided by precisely those things the general commanding did not want to hear. Concurrently, in nearby Washington Secretary of War Stanton was reading the report he had ordered General-in-Chief Halleck to prepare regarding suspicions that General McClellan had been less than prompt in obeying orders to move his Army of the Potomac from Harrison's Landing on the James River northward to operate between Washington and Richmond.

It had been a blatant abuse of power for Stanton to have taken General Halleck's attention away from how he could help hard-pressed Union armies' commanders in both eastern Tennessee and central Kentucky repel Confederate offensives and—concurrently—give maximum support to

John Pope less than forty miles away. Even so, Halleck answered the questions Stanton had posed by reproducing the paper trail of messages he had sent McClellan and to which McClellan had responded.

Halleck's report seemed to say, *Yes, there is a serious problem here*. He had included McClellan's excuses without commenting on their validity.[81] As any district attorney might before a grand jury, Halleck had simply presented the facts—then he reverted to his primary duty of telegraphing orders to officers everywhere within copper wires' reach to help stem those Confederate drives out in Tennessee and especially Kentucky and also the one within a single day's march of Edwin Stanton's War Department.[82]

Although in his brief lawyer Halleck had not charged McClellan with specific, actionable wrongdoing, prosecutor Stanton used the document as the starting point for a written remonstrance directed toward Abraham Lincoln. In the first draft, Stanton accused McClellan of incompetence and of imperiling General Pope's army through his inactivity and his documented disobedience of Halleck's peremptory orders. Among the dire consequences Stanton foresaw of the Young Napoleon's being continued in command were the war's protraction, waste of manpower and natural resources, even overthrow of the government.[83]

On that sultry Saturday afternoon, with a very nasty fight impending only forty miles or so southwest of them, Stanton and Salmon Chase promptly began soliciting concurring signatures from other members of Lincoln's cabinet. Concurrently, General Lee was making the most of the scraps of time allowed him by the Yankees' inactivity to write the orders for Jackson to execute a wide envelopment of Pope's positions and cut his communications with Alexandria.[84] Maryland was much on Lee's mind. But if Pope provoked more struggling before dark on that hot August Saturday afternoon, fine.

Indeed, as noonday passed, General Pope—despite the most earnest warnings of Fitz John Porter and John Reynolds of danger looming—was still inclined to act on his belief that Jackson was withdrawing. But Reynolds had encountered heavy resistance while testing enemy strength south of the Warrenton Turnpike. Rather than trust messengers, he galloped directly to the general commanding. "The enemy is turning our left," he reported.

General Pope's first response was, "Oh, I guess not." Reynolds was—like Porter—a newcomer from McClellan's army, so confirmation was required. But when it came, instead of reinforcing Reynolds, Pope ordered him to move his division eastward to a position on Chinn Ridge, one out of harm's way but otherwise seemingly useless.[85]

Around mid-day there was only one consistent thought embedded in the rest of the orders General Pope issued: that striking Jackson's force was the lone course of action he dared adopt and maintain. Having told Porter to do one thing toward that end, he directed a change in the thrust of the Fifth Corps' advance in a manner impossible for General Porter to comply with. In attempting to do so, however, Porter attacked the western end of Jackson's line.

Going into their assaults, the ranks of Porter's leading elements were thinned by sharp volleys from Jackson's infantry and concentrated fire from Longstreet's massed artillery. But the first wave of Porter's troops reached the unfinished railroad embankment and came so near to achieving a breakthrough that some of the Confederates, their ammunition gone, threw rocks at the Yankees.

At that point, any commander's instinct alone would have forced him to throw forward units, to exploit to the fullest the first wave's achievement. But an attempt to capture Longstreet's guns had failed, and this—together with recollection of the slaughter their withering fire had already inflicted—led Porter first to abstain from adding to his losses and in due course to order a withdrawal. Indeed, units that had made it to the Confederates' embankment found it more difficult, and more costly in casualties, to make tracks away from it than it had for them to get there.[86]

General Porter's withdrawal marked the end of his participation in the fight but the beginning of Longstreet's—actually, Hood's Texans'—sweep south of the Warrenton Turnpike that ended after sundown with Pope leading his thoroughly mauled Army of Virginia into Centreville.[87] But during that Saturday afternoon's last few daylight hours, as the army commander received one report after another of his brigades' having been flanked, or driven, or decimated, the soldier in John Pope seemed to have overridden all else; his calm, professional conduct of his whipped forces' retreat eastward over Bull Run denied General Lee and his gallant lieutenants and the men in his Army of Northern Virginia the satisfaction of having utterly annihilated the Yankee invaders of their soil.

As early as 6:00 P.M. Pope was concentrating on how best to cope with reality. From the battlefield, to Major General William Franklin, whose

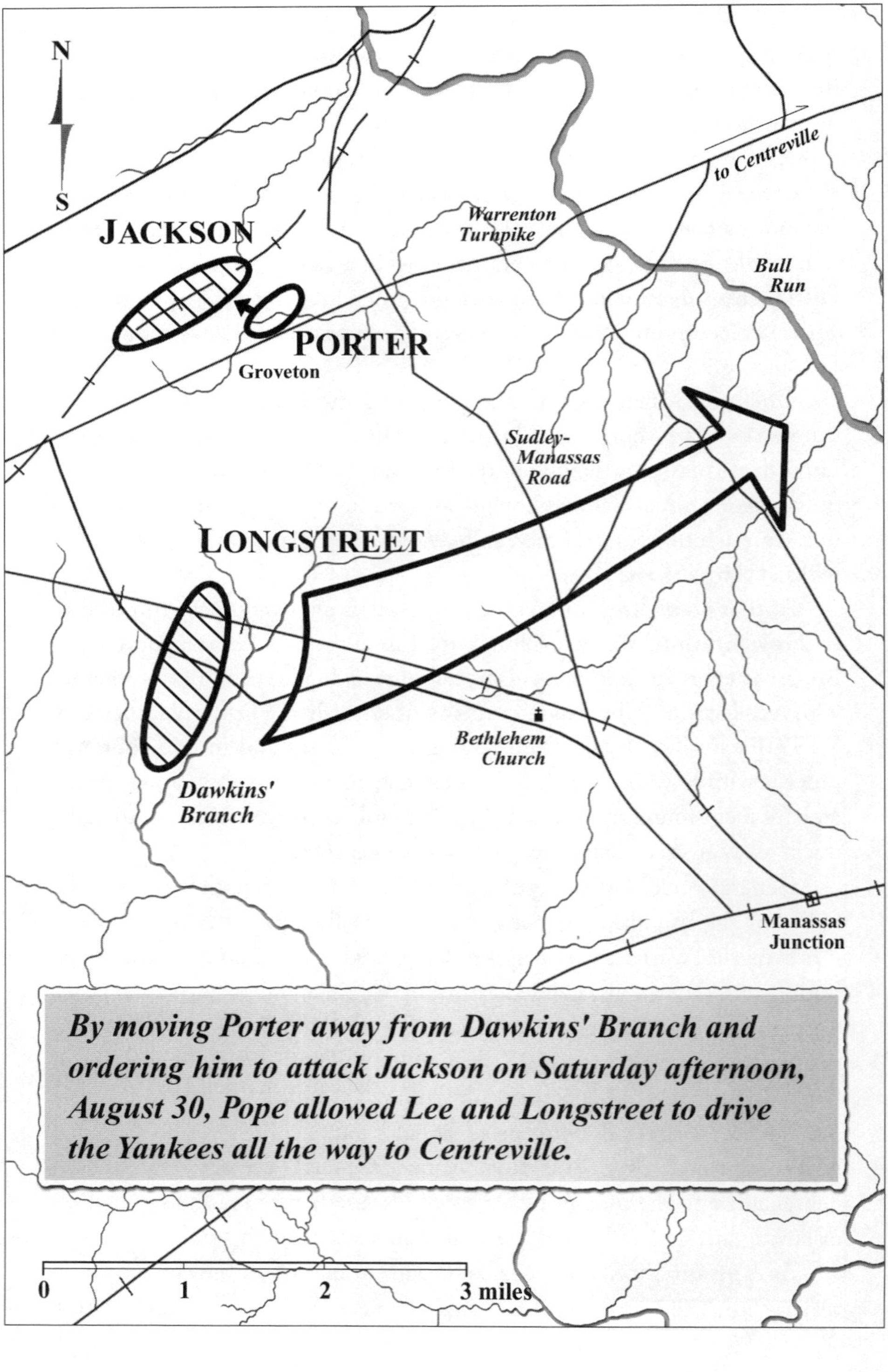
N
S
JACKSON
PORTER
Groveton
Warrenton Turnpike
to Centreville
Bull Run
Sudley-Manassas Road
LONGSTREET
Bethlehem Church
Dawkins' Branch
Manassas Junction
By moving Porter away from Dawkins' Branch and ordering him to attack Jackson on Saturday afternoon, August 30, Pope allowed Lee and Longstreet to drive the Yankees all the way to Centreville.
0
1
2
3 miles

corps—ironically—had finally, but too late, reached Centreville, he ordered: "Post your command and whatever other troops you can collect and put them in the fortifications and other strong positions around Centerville, and hold those positions to the last extremity."[88] Nor had Pope forgotten Nathaniel Banks and his depleted corps guarding the Army of Virginia's trains. "Destroy the public property at Bristoe and fall back upon Centreville at once," he directed. "Destroy all the railroad property."[89]

Three hours later, from Centreville, General Pope started a preliminary report on its way to General-in-Chief Halleck in Washington:

> We have had a terrific battle again to-day. The enemy, largely re-enforced, assaulted our position early to-day. We held our ground firmly until 6 P.M., when the enemy, massing very heavy forces on our left, forced back that wing about half a mile. At dark we held that position.
>
> Under all the circumstances, both horses and men having been two days without food; and the enemy greatly outnumbering us, I thought it best to draw back to this place at dark. The movement has been made, in perfect order and without loss. The troops are in

JOHN POPE, MAJOR GENERAL, U.S. ARMY

Decisively defeated by the Confederate Army of Northern Virginia in Second Bull Run, Radical-sponsored Pope made allegations regarding Porter's conduct during the battle that led to the court-martial. His testimony at the trial was an important factor in Porter's conviction. Pope and his associates blocked Porter's appeals for review for years afterward.

good heart, and marched off the field without the least hurry or confusion. Their conduct was very fine.

The battle was most furious for hours without cessation, and the losses on both sides very heavy. The enemy is badly crippled, and we shall do well enough. Do not be uneasy. We will hold our own here.

The labors and hardships of this army for two or three weeks have been beyond description. We have delayed the enemy as long as possible without losing the army. We have damaged him heavily, and I think the army entitled to the gratitude of the country. Be easy; everything will go well.[90]

CHAPTER FOUR
ORIGINAL SIN

SUNDAY, August 31, was one of those days on which officers and men in both armies carried out post-battle tasks such as reassembling units and counting heads, getting care for the walking wounded, cleaning weapons and restocking ammunition, and passing preliminary reports up the chain of command.

General Porter found the time in which to share his recollections and foreboding with the general commanding the Army of the Potomac in a letter carried by a messenger from Centreville to Washington. Porter wrote McClellan:

> I send you copies of some orders under which I have moved lately.
>
> [Yesterday] I advanced in pursuit of the enemy and struck the center of his line, especially under the direction of General Lee, and was whipped, as was the whole army, badly—that is, I was overpowered. Two of Morell's brigades were in action under Butterfield, and two of Sykes' (Buchanan and Chapman), and they did nobly. The latter lost by volunteers firing into them before passing through them. They were not sustained on the right, and had to retire. . . .
>
> We were driven from the field, and here we are, after marching all last night, strongly located in a position which, if the enemy shells, will cause slaughter; but I do not believe he will attack, but get in our rear, and compel us to attack him in a well-selected place. The men are without heart, but will fight when cornered.
>
> To-day General Pope asked the question of the Government if arrangements had been made to protect Washington in case the army met with a disaster. He said to us . . . that we were to fight

> wherever the enemy was—meaning we were not to return to Alexandria, &c., as all forces were coming to us. . . . However, we obey, and do what Halleck thinks is best. Pope says there are political considerations which control, not the safety of the army; but our men will not fight with heart when they know, if wounded (as we cannot retain the field against present odds), they are to be left to the care of the enemy. . . .
>
> Our wagons are gone, and our artillery and cavalry will not soon be movable. The latter is broken down, and, as Pope says, he has no cavalry, though he has regiments. . . .
>
> If we return [to Washington's defenses], I hope the forces will be directed to take different roads to the forts, and that they will be well manned and protected by us. I do not wish to see the army back if it can be helped; but I fear it may be kept here at the will of the enemy, to cripple it so that when it does get back it will be so crippled that it cannot defend the forts against the powerful enemy who will hold it here while they cross into Maryland. I may be in error as to their purpose.
>
> Lee is here; Jackson is not now here. Cadmus Wilcox commands Hill's division directly in front, and the enemy are massing to turn us.
>
> I expect to hear hourly of our rear being cut and our supplies and trains (scarcely guarded) at Fairfax Station being destroyed, as we are required to stay here and fight. . . .
>
> I understand the Secretary [of War] sent out some men to take care of our wounded, and they were much surprised to find that they were in the hands of the enemy. They return with a different impression from what they came. Good night. The bearer will tell you much.[1]

This long and candid letter was evidence of how strong the subordinate-commander relationship had grown during the past thirteen months. General Porter's report regarding the fighting on Saturday was preliminary but accurate, rendered in soldier-to soldier style. Some of his pessimistic speculations would indeed come to pass. Lee sent Jackson on a march intended to by-pass Centreville to the west and north, then to turn eastward and strike Pope's supply base at Fairfax Station; a force dispatched by Pope stopped the Confederate advance on Monday near Chantilly, whereupon Lee invaded Maryland. But Porter had made no references to Pope in his message to McClellan that were disrespectful or out of line with what might be expected, given that this subordinate-superior relationship had lasted all of four days.

Some reporting that General Pope did early on Monday morning, however, indicated clearly that the only kind of relationship he would ever have with Porter would be adversarial. Only about thirty-six hours after the firing ceased on Saturday, he began a telegram to General Halleck with six sentences covering routine matters, then he switched abruptly to what appeared to be uppermost in his mind: "I think it my duty to call your attention to the unsoldierly and dangerous conduct of . . . commanders of the forces sent here from the Peninsula." Specifically:

> One commander of a corps, who was ordered to march from Manassas Junction to join me near Groveton, although he was only 5 miles distant, failed to get up at all, and, worse still, fell back to Manassas without a fight, and in plain hearing, at less than 3 miles' distance, of a furious battle, which raged all day. It was only in consequence of peremptory orders that he joined me next day. One of his brigades, the brigadier-general of which professed to be looking for his division, absolutely remained all day at Centreville, in plain view of the battle, and made no attempt to join.
>
> What renders the whole matter worse, these are both officers of the Regular Army, who do not hold back from ignorance or fear. . . . When such example is set by officers of high rank the influence is very bad amongst those in subordinate stations.
>
> You have hardly an idea of the demoralization among officers of high rank in the Potomac Army, arising in all instances from personal feeling in relation to changes of commander-in-chief and others. These men are mere tools or parasites, but their example is producing, and must necessarily produce, very disastrous results.
>
> You should know these things, as you alone can stop it. . . . When there is no heart in their leaders, and every disposition to hang back, much cannot be expected from the men.[2]

General Halleck, noting the inordinate importance Pope had given the alleged "unsoldierly and dangerous conduct" of officers from the Army of the Potomac passed the message on to the President, who summoned General McClellan. Regarding the ensuing meeting, years afterward McClellan recalled:

> The President informed me that he had reason to believe that the Army of the Potomac was not cheerfully co-operating with and supporting General Pope; that he had "always been a friend of mine," and now asked me, as a special favor, to use my influence in correcting this state of things. I replied, substantially, that I was confident that he was misinformed; that I was sure, whatever estimate the Army of the Potomac might entertain of General Pope, that they would obey his orders, support him to the fullest extent, and do their whole duty. The President, who was much moved, asked me to telegraph to "Fitz John Porter, or some other of my friends," and try to do away with any feeling that might exist; adding that I could rectify the evil, and that no one else could. . . .
>
> I then wrote the following telegram to General Porter, which was sent to him by the General-in-Chief:
>
> > *I ask of you, for my sake, that of the country, and the old Army of the Potomac, that you and all my friends will lend the fullest and most cordial co-operation to General Pope in all the operations now going on. The destinies of our country, the honor of our arms, are at stake, and all depends now upon the cheerful co-operation of all in the field. This week is the crisis of our fate.*
> >
> > *Say the same thing to my friends in the Army of the Potomac, and that the last request I have to make of them is, that for their country's sake they will extend to General Pope the same support they ever have to me.*
> >
> > *I am in charge of the defenses of Washington, and am doing all I can to render your retreat safe, should that become necessary.*
>
> To which General Porter sent the following reply:
>
> > *You may rest assured that all your friends, as well as every*

> *lover of his country, will ever give, as they have given, to General Pope their cordial co-operation and constant support in the execution of all orders and plans. Our killed, wounded, and enfeebled troops attest our devoted duty.*
>
> Neither at the time I wrote the telegram nor at any other time did I think for one moment that General Porter had been or would be in any manner derelict in the performance of his duty to the nation and its cause. Such an impression never entered my mind. The dispatch in question was written purely at the request of the President.[3]

Eventually it would become apparent that the first week in September 1862 was the period in which malevolent forces were set in motion for the purpose of destroying the career, reputation, and if possible the life of Major General Fitz John Porter. And the origin of the lengthy paper trail—all of the records of proceedings, letters, and documents—that ensued was the telegram John Pope sent General-in-Chief Halleck on Monday after Saturday's humiliating defeat in the battle that would be known by the losers as Second Bull Run.

2

On the next day, Tuesday, September 2, in a message to the general-in-chief, General Pope reported: "The enemy is still in our front. It is his undoubted purpose to keep on slowly turning our position so as to come in on our right." Two paragraphs later, he returned to this subject. "The enemy from the beginning has been throwing his rear toward the north, and every movement shows that he means to make trouble in Maryland."[4]

In fact, R. E. Lee was already leading his Army of Northern Virginia across the Potomac near Ball's Bluff into Maryland because, as he explained afterward, simply, "My men had nothing to eat."[5]

General Halleck telegraphed Pope: "You will bring your forces as best you can within or near the line of fortification. General McClellan has charge of all defenses, and you will consider any direction given by him as coming from me."[6]

Stanton, aided by Treasury Secretary Salmon Chase, had prepared the case for sacking McClellan for presentation at Tuesday's cabinet meeting. But Lincoln stunned everyone present by announcing that Major General George B. McClellan would command the *combined* armies defending Washington.

"The President's decision caused the greatest anguish in the radical camp," wrote historian Hans L. Trefousse. "Extremist Cabinet members fumed; newspapermen complained; and members of Congress were outraged."[7] According to T. Harry Williams: "To the Jacobin politicos the sight of McNapoleon again in the saddle was the next to last straw, the sickening crash of their hard-won gains, and the end of a radical-run war."[8] Stanton was said to be so disgusted that he wrote out his resignation and would have given it to Lincoln but for the fervent pleadings of Senator Charles Sumner to spare the Radical cause another calamity.[9]

Pope seemed aware of the need to intensify his efforts to avoid becoming Second Bull Run's scapegoat. In a message to General Halleck on Wednesday he all but formally accused Fitz John Porter of military crimes actionable under the Articles of War:

> I have much to say and to report to you concerning the conduct of certain officers and their commands during these operations, which I will postpone for the present. There is no doubt in the mind of any man here that the battle of Groveton would have been a decisive and complete victory on the first day had General Porter advanced as I directed him. Why he did not is yet unexplained. The whole of the heavy re-enforcements which attacked us on Saturday passed down the road from Gainesville during the whole afternoon and night of Friday, while General Porter remained in full sight of them, on their flank, between Manassas Junction and Gainesville, although he had my positive written order to attack them in flank while I was urging the battle in front. He made no attack whatever, but retired a portion of his command, at least, to Manassas, which was not near enough the next day to take any part in the action.
>
> This is the second time since it has been with me that the delay of this same corps has hazarded the safety and success of our movements. The constant complaint is that the men are broken down, though what marching or other hard service they have done for a 1ong time I do not know.

I will state these facts officially within a day or two, or as soon as I can find a moment to make my report.[10]

Actually, General Pope found that moment on the *same day*, Wednesday, September 3. Some excerpts:

> To my surprise and disappointment I received late [Friday] afternoon from Porter a note saying that his advance had met the enemy on the flank in some force, and that he was retiring upon Manassas Junction, without attacking the enemy or coming to the assistance of our other forces, although they were engaged in a furious action only 2 miles distant and in full hearing of him. A portion of his force fell back toward Manassas, and he remained, as he afterward informed me, where he was, looking at the enemy during the whole of the afternoon of Friday and part of Friday night passing down in plain view to reenforce the troops under Jackson without an effort to prevent it or to assist us. . . .
>
> I do not hesitate to say that if the corps of Porter had attacked the enemy on the flank on the afternoon of Friday, as he had my written order (marked B) to do, we should have crushed Jackson before the forces under Lee could have reached him. Why he did not do so I cannot understand.[11]

And then on the next day Pope rode into Washington and read all that he had written regarding Porter to the President of the United States and Secretary of the Navy Gideon Welles.

Afterward, Welles recorded in his diary:

> [Pope's report was really] a manifesto, a narrative, tinged with wounded pride and a keen sense of injustice and wrong. . . . He declares all his misfortunes are owing to the persistent determination of McClellan, Franklin, and Porter . . . who were predetermined he should not be successful. They preferred, [Pope] said, that the country should be ruined than that he should triumph.[12]

Methinks the general doth protest overmuch, the canny, crusty former

Hartford newspaper editor might well have added. As secretary of the navy, Welles would have known how unusual it was for any commander to file even a preliminary report within less than a week after any battle. Usually, the higher the rank of the writer, the longer it would take, because he would have to wait until reports from his subordinates worked their way up the pyramid before he could possibly prepare his own.

Having made a maximum effort to have Porter declared Second Bull Run's scapegoat, Pope may well have expected support of some sort from the secretary of war. If so, he was mistaken. Lincoln's agreement with Halleck regarding McClellan had the effect of neutering Edwin Stanton.

Indeed, on Wednesday Lincoln and Halleck took steps toward giving McClellan the mission of following Lee's army into Maryland, removing the invaders therefrom, and destroying them when the enhanced Army of the Potomac was ready to take the field again.[13] Two days later, Halleck was able to measure McClellan's progress from a complaint lodged by John Pope:

> I have just received an order from General McClellan to have my command in readiness to march with three days' rations and further details of the march. What is my command, and where is it? McClellan has scattered it about in all directions, and has not informed me of the position of a single regiment. Am I to take the field and under McClellan's orders?[14]

The general-in-chief replied: "The armies of the Potomac and Virginia being consolidated, you will report for orders to the Secretary of War."[15] And to McClellan, Halleck telegraphed:

> The President has directed that General Pope be relieved and report to War Department; that Hooker be assigned to command of Porter's corps, and that Franklin's corps be temporarily attached to Heintzelman's. The orders will be issued this afternoon. Generals Porter and Franklin are to be relieved from duty till the charges against them are examined.
>
> I give you this memorandum in advance of the orders, so that you may act accordingly in putting forces in the field.[16]

Another message to McClellan from Halleck on that Friday indicated that the time had already come for part of his rapidly reconstituted army to move out:

> I think there can now be no doubt that the enemy are crossing the Potomac in force, and that you had better dispatch General Sumner and additional forces to follow. If you agree with me, let our troops move immediately.[17]

On Saturday, McClellan asked the general-in-chief to "suspend the operation of the order in regard to Franklin and Porter until I can see my way out of this difficulty."[18] Done, Halleck replied.

However, in lodging his request with both Halleck and Lincoln, McClellan had mentioned that Stanton had told him that "he would cheerfully agree with anything of this kind that met with your approval."[19] Even so, after Porter's Fifth Corps had made Washington's ring of fortifications safe against attack, Stanton replaced him with pro-Radical Nathaniel Banks. Porter wrote his wife:

> Mr. Stanton is represented as a scoundrel of the blackest sort. I hear much of him, know little, care less. I do not believe we have many men in power who are governed by love of country. Banks will now reap my labor.[20]

In the wake of Secretary Stanton's action, on Thursday, September 11, General Halleck telegraphed McClellan, by then in Maryland: "Why not order forward Porter's corps, or Sigel's? If the main force of the enemy is in your front, more troops can be spared from here."[21] McClellan's response was prompt: "Please send forward all the troops you can, . . . particularly Porter's, Heintzelmnan's, Sigel's, and all the other old troops."[22]

And so it was that General Porter and his Fifth Corps, under a deep shadow from Second Bull Run, were finally back with the Army of the Potomac for the battle that would become known as Antietam.

3

"We will make our stand," General Lee had declared soon after his arrival at Sharpsburg on Monday, September 15. Leading elements of

McClellan's army were moving into positions on the other (eastern) side of Antietam Creek. Both build-ups continued on Tuesday. On Wednesday morning Jackson's divisions wrecked the Yankees' opening assaults.[23] Heavy fighting continued, as McClellan indicated in a message to General Halleck early that afternoon:

> We are in the midst of the most terrible battle of the war—perhaps of history. Thus far it looks well, but I have great odds against me. Hurry up all the troops possible.
>
> Our loss has been terrific, but we have gained much ground. I have thrown the mass of the army on the left flank. Burnside is now attacking the right, and I hold my small reserve, consisting of Porter's (Fifth) corps, ready to attack the center as soon as the flank movements are developed. I hope that God will give us a glorious victory.[24]

Actually, McClellan was not giving God much help. After Jackson's troops shattered Joseph Hooker's corps, in went another—and another, piecemeal. "It is the most beautiful field I ever saw, and the grandest battle," McClellan declared to a staff officer. "If we whip them today it will wipe out Bull Run forever."[25]

Late in the afternoon Ambrose Burnside's forces crossed Antietam Creek, in part over a stone bridge, and prepared to destroy the village of Sharpsburg's reeling defenders—and also to deny General Lee access to the Potomac's last ford as an escape route. Suddenly, up the road from Harpers Ferry and charging across the Potomac into Burnside's flank came Ambrose Powell Hill's road-weary division.[26]

Wrote a reporter from the *New York Tribune*:

> McClellan's glass for the last half hour has seldom been turned away from the left. He sees clearly enough that Burnside is pressed—needs no messenger to tell him that. His face grows darker with anxious thought. Looking down into the valley where 15,000 troops are lying, he turns a half-questioning look on Fitz John Porter, who stands by his side, gravely scanning the field. They are Porter's troops below, are fresh and only impatient to share in the fight. But Porter slowly shakes his head, and one may believe that

the same thought is passing through the mind of both generals: "They are the only reserves of the army; they cannot be spared."[27]

"Tell General Burnside," said McClellan to an aide, "this is the battle of the war. He must hold his ground until dark at all cost. Tell him that if he cannot hold his ground, then the bridge, to the last man!—always the bridge! If the bridge is lost, all is lost!"[28]

Burnside's men held his bridge. Only sundown halted fighting that had taken or blighted the lives of an appalling 23,381 young Americans.[29] This had been the bloodiest day so far in the war and it had settled nothing.

R. E. Lee, master of audacious generalship when advancing, had demonstrated his proficiency in defense. He would hold his ground for another day, daring George McClellan to come and take it.

Early on Thursday morning, McClellan wrote his wife, Mary Ellen: "The spectacle yesterday was the grandest I could conceive of—nothing could have been more sublime. Those in whose judgment I rely tell me that I fought the battle splendidly & that it was a masterpiece of [military] art."[30]

Careful students of Antietam would suggest otherwise. Certainly at the top of any list of McClellan's mistakes had to be his failure to send Porter's corps crashing into Lee's center before Hill's arrival.

Antietam's indecisive ending left General Porter still vulnerable to the allegations of misconduct John Pope had made before Abraham Lincoln and his cabinet back on September 3. No offsetting glory had been forthcoming from the battle.

When his political opponents resumed their prosecution, Porter would need all of the defenders he could muster. And prominent among them, he had every right to expect, would be George B. McClellan. Even as the guns along Antietam Creek were cooling, however, the Young Napoleon was throwing away the soldier's gold General Halleck had enabled him to earn since the President had blocked Stanton's and Salmon Chase's attempt to remove him.

On October 1, more impatient than Halleck to learn what plans the Young Napoleon had for pursuing and destroying General Lee's army—by then, refitting in the lower Shenandoah Valley of Virginia, around Winchester—Commander-in-Chief Lincoln appeared suddenly at George McClellan's headquarters east of the Antietam battlefield. According to several reports, he mixed a tour of the killing grounds and reviews of troops with conversations held with McClellan and others—including at least one with Major General Fitz John Porter.

During lunch in Porter's tent, one account revealed, the President recalled the telegrams Porter had sent to Burnside before and during Second Bull Run—the ones in which he had reflected, among other things, his low regard for his new general commanding: John Pope.

Afterward, Porter wrote: "[Those telegrams'] value was acknowledged by the President to me. Lincoln gave me congratulations for the past, his warmest wishes for the future and thanks for having furnished those messages—the only correct information received at the time from [Pope's] army."

And an officer present in the tent later wrote Porter:

> Mr. Lincoln took your hand and walked aside and said to you, "General, I cannot sufficiently thank you for your total self-abnegation and attention to your duties. I have marked them, and your gallant service will ever be remembered. I have been your friend in the past, and, General, you can depend on me in the future."[31]

Nothing much came of Lincoln's brief stay, or so it seemed. However, on October 6—several days after Lincoln had returned from his trip—General Halleck gave McClellan a peremptory order: "The President directs that you cross the Potomac and give battle to the enemy or drive him south. Your army must move now while the roads are good."[32]

McClellan's response was disappointing.[33] His obstinance and use of requisitions to justify further stalling finally provoked the Commander-in-Chief into producing—with apparent help from General Halleck—a long letter, dated October 13, 1862, which emphatically set forth the case for moving the Army of the Potomac southward, east of the Blue Ridge, toward Richmond without delay. Unfortunately, however, at the close of it Lincoln added one sentence too many, one in which Halleck could not possibly have concurred: "This letter is in no sense an order."[34]

Even so, on October 22, McClellan telegraphed Halleck: "After full consultation, I have decided to move upon the line indicated by the President."[35] On October 26, McClellan's troops began moving southward across his army's namesake river. It would take the Young Napoleon nine days to carry out an operation that R. E. Lee had completed in only two.

By then, however, George McClellan's stock of soldier's gold had been depleted completely. After waiting until the fall elections were behind him, on November 5, 1862, Lincoln signed this order:

> By direction of the President, it is ordered that Major-General McClellan be relieved from the command of the Army of the Potomac, and that Major-General Burnside take the command of that army.
>
> Also . . . that Major-General Fitz John Porter be relieved from the command of the corps he now commands in said army, and that Major-General Hooker take command of said corps.[36]

4

In November 1862, military justice was being applied concurrently in several different ways:

- John Pope, banished to Minnesota as a department commander, claimed that he had been accorded no justice at all.[37] Radicals seemed to take the position that the less attention given Pope, the sooner the public would forget that they had ever sponsored him.
- Major General Don Carlos Buell, who failed to pursue Confederate Major Generals Braxton Bragg and Edmund Kirby Smith following the battle at Perryville, Kentucky, had been relieved of his command on October 24. His protests led to investigation by a military commission that cleared him but criticized him. Buell was given no more combat assignments and resigned from the army in 1864.[38]
- George McClellan had been parked in Trenton, New Jersey, to await orders. None would ever come.
- Irvin McDowell had to plant a letter in a New York newspaper to solicit charges entitling him to a court of inquiry.[39] Having lost two battles on the same ground, he was no longer important enough to harm anyone but Fitz John Porter.

Back on September 10, unaware that Stanton had secretly appointed a board of officers to review Pope's allegations, General Porter requested a court of inquiry in a letter to Lorenzo Thomas, adjutant-general of the United States Army. He would have done so earlier, Porter wrote, "had not Major-General Pope informed me at Fairfax Court-House that he had no cause to complain of me."[40]

However, General Porter had ample cause to complain regarding the publication of Pope's damning report in the New York newspapers. His reputation, and that of all the "Fighting Porters," was being blackened. His enemies were poisoning every public opinion well within reach with professed outrage over Pope's damaging allegations.

Senator Zach Chandler—who had told John Pope that his only mistake had been to allow Fitz John Porter to leave Second Bull Run's battlefield alive[41]—provided a good example of Radical expressions of wrath in a letter to a colleague on September 10:

> It is treason, rank treason, call it by what name you will, which has caused our late disasters. . . . Your president is unstable as water, if he has as I suspect been bullied by those traitor generals. How long will it be before he will by them be set aside & a military dictatorship be set up?[42]

From Saint Paul, General Pope wrote privately to General-in-Chief Halleck in October to complain that "my character and reputation as a soldier have been deeply, I may say irretrievably, injured" because the Lincoln administration had not acknowledged "that I did my duty bravely and skillfully in Virginia." Near the close, he asked:

> Why are McClellan, Porter, and Griffin retained in high commands with such charges of treachery and baseness hanging over them? Do you not believe these charges true? Are they not substantiated to your satisfaction by the papers attached to the report containing them? Did not both you and the President know before the battles at Manassas, from Porter's intercepted dispatches, that he was likely to do precisely what he did? . . .
>
> I would not care to press these charges if the Government would only do me the barest justice. . . .[43]

During the rest of October and early November, Pope divided his attention between putting down a Sioux uprising and supervising members of his staff, notably, Benjamin S. Roberts (formerly inspector-general of the Army of Virginia) and Thomas C. H. Smith, who were assembling messages, copies of orders, and other documents issued during Second Bull Run for use in a pamphlet advocating disciplinary action against Porter. By November 13, Roberts was in Washington distributing the product and filing charges and specifications he had prepared with the Adjutant General's office.[44] A week earlier, Edwin Stanton had been—in effect—enabled by the President's order isolating McClellan in Trenton, New Jersey, to apply military justice to Fitz John Porter whenever and in whatever way his Jacobin string-pullers jerked.

On November 17, General Porter was placed under arrest and confined first to his hotel room in Washington, then to the city limits. On the next day he asked both General-in-Chief Halleck and Judge-Advocate General Joseph Holt to tell him what charges had been lodged against him. Both subordinates of Stanton declined to do so.[45]

Not until a week later, on November 25, did Porter obtain any clue as to what was happening to him. What had been going on behind his back became clear in the text of an order issued that day:

> The military commission ordered to assemble on the 20th instant. by Special Orders, No. 350, November 17, 1862, from Headquarters of the Army, is hereby dissolved, and a general court-martial is hereby appointed, to meet in this city on the 27th instant, or as soon thereafter as practicable, for the trial of Maj. Gen. Fitz John Porter, U.S. Volunteers.[46]

After listing the nine officers detailed for the court, the order added: "No other officers than those named can be assembled without manifest injury to the service."[47]

Within this formal order, however, lurked manifest injury it professed the intention to avoid. Admittedly, in the latter part of November 1862, Ambrose Burnside's confrontation of R. E. Lee's Army of Northern Virginia along the Rappahannock at Fredericksburg had drawn away a great many general officers whose experience in military justice was superior to the left-behinds. But could it have been accidental that almost all of the members of the court detailed had reasons rooted in Secretary of War Stanton's power over their own futures for wishing the worst for Porter?

Consider, for example, the probable objectivity of the president of the court, Major General David Hunter.[48] Although he was a graduate of West Point, his military service had been undistinguished. Also, he was an ardent supporter of abolition and other Radical causes. In November 1862 he was in Washington seeking restoration to an active command following his relief in South Carolina for having proclaimed the emancipation of slaves, a prerogative President Lincoln reserved. Pending was Hunter's wish to return to duty with troops, a boon Stanton could grant.[49]

Next on the list of officers detailed to serve on the court-martial was Major General Ethan Allen Hitchcock. He was in Washington very much against his will, having been summoned back in March by Stanton to act as a military advisor shortly after Lincoln had removed McClellan as general-in-chief.

For ten years Hitchcock had been living in St. Louis, retired after forty years of service in a calling his family felt he was obliged to enter because he was the grandson and namesake of the Revolutionary War hero. Hitchcock had been graduated from West Point in 1817, five years earlier than David Hunter, but he considered himself "a scholar rather than a warrior" and he became the author of books on Swedenborg and alchemy and Jesus.

Despite Hitchcock's age (sixty-five), poor health, and desire to get back to St. Louis and his studies, Stanton and Lincoln both displayed their astonishing military naivete by trying to persuade him to replace the Young Napoleon (thirty-five) as commander of the Army of the Potomac. Correctly, the old student of hidden meanings in the poetry of Shakespeare and Edmund Spenser agreed to assist in matters that could be handled within the War Department. Now, those included serving on the Porter court-martial.[50]

Availability rather than politics may well have been the circumstance that led to the selection of Brigadier General Silas Casey.[51] In November 1862 he was in Washington to seek correction of damaging statements regarding his conduct at the battle of Fair Oaks that General McClellan had made. He was disturbed also because after the Seven Days General Porter appeared to have refused to give Casey command of a unit in his Fifth Corps, and because his promotion to the rank of major general seemed unduly delayed. Any officer embittered by acts attributed to McClellan and

Porter had to have been attractive to the Radicals. And Secretary of War Stanton controlled submission of general officers' promotions to confirmation by the Congress—Casey's, and also three other members of the Porter court-martial detail: Brigadier Generals N. B. Buford,[52] B. M. Prentiss,[53] and J. P. Slough,[54] who replaced W. W. Morris, who had questioned the legality of the trial.

Arguably, Rufus King and James B. Ricketts[55] should not have been appointed to the court. Both generals' performances during the Second Bull Run campaign had provoked controversy. Whether or not Secretary Stanton had selected them because of the precariousness of their reputations, he possessed the power to blight their careers.[56]

Finally, there was Stanton's selection of Brigadier General James A. Garfield.[57] Salmon Chase may have prompted it as a means of boosting his fellow Ohioan's political career, since Garfield's days as a soldier were over and he appeared to have a promising future as a Radical.

Such were the obstacles Lincoln's implacable foes had placed in the path of impartial justice. But John Pope had gone beyond Stanton's efforts by having Benjamin Roberts distribute copies of his anti-Porter pamphlet to each proposed member of the court and also, to guide their testimony, to prosecution witnesses.[58]

A stacked deck was seriously detrimental to General Porter among other reasons because members of courts-martial perform the functions of juries in civil courts. The accused, however, had the right to challenge any or all of the officers named in Special Order No. 362. According to Otto Eisenschiml, "Porter's friends behind the curtain warned him that when John Tucker, assistant secretary of war, was shown the list of officers Stanton had selected, he exclaimed, 'Why, Mr. Secretary, that detail is made up to convict!' and another employee of the War Department, John Sykes, was reported as having expressed the same opinion, and then added, 'The Secretary of War looked assent.' "[59] Also, Stanton appointed Colonel Joseph Holt judge-advocate for the court-martial.[60]

What more might he have done to make Fitz John Porter's conviction certain?

Part II: Crime and Punishment

CHAPTER FIVE

The Star Witness Shines in His Role

A STRIKING feature of the American military justice system has long been that it could be applied anywhere, at any time, without the participation of civilian lawyers. This reflected the assumption, embedded in common law, that a person accused ought to be judged by a jury of his peers.

Fine, but how effective was the system in balancing the rights of a defendant to able defense counsel and the duties of enforcers of Army Regulations, especially of the Articles of War? The capabilities of officers detailed to act as trial judge-advocates and defense counsel varied widely, of course. So did a host of other relevant circumstances and ultimately the degrees of justice apparent in outcomes. On the frontier, fort commanders had to do their best with such talent for adjudication as they had available within a stockade's walls. And even in Washington, girt by the ring of forts the Young Napoleon had established after First Bull Run, soldier Fitz John Porter's fate was now heavily dependent upon the quality of the performances of his defenders relative to that of the prosecutor.

Here, Porter could take considerable comfort from the presence on his behalf of two distinguished civilian lawyers. In a civil court their talent and experience and reputation would surely have had awesome effect on the minds of those whose decisions were to shape the outcome. Given the circumstances of this general court-martial, however, and especially the powerful influence of Stanton and through him of the Radicals, Reverdy Johnson and Charles Eames faced challenges that would call for extraordinarily effective responses.

Marylander and War Democrat Reverdy Johnson, sixty-five, Porter's chief counsel, was among the most highly regarded lawyers in the country. According to *Dictionary of American Biography*:

> He had an unusual memory, which served him especially well in the latter part of his life, when he became partially blind. His mental alertness made him a rare cross-examiner. He possessed a deep, oratorical voice that immediately commanded attention and was an important professional asset, as were also his tact, good nature, and unusual courtesy. . . . His chief legal fame rested upon his ability as a constitutional lawyer. He appeared as counsel in a number of very important suits and had as associates or opponents many of the most famous men of his time.[1]

In 1858 one of Johnson's opponents was Edwin Stanton, in the second McCormick Reaper case. A year earlier, Johnson had represented the defense before the Supreme Court in *Dred Scott v. Sanford*. He had been a United States Senator from Maryland from 1845 to 1849 and attorney general in President Zachary Taylor's brief administration. Before Fort Sumter's surrender he had urged conciliation. But he looked upon secession as treason and stood for preservation of the Union.[2] He was senator-elect from Maryland in November 1862.[3]

Assisting Johnson in defending Porter was Charles Eames, born in Massachusetts and educated at Harvard, who had alternated the practice of law and service as a diplomat. At the time of the trial, Eames was counsel to the Navy Department and on the way to prominence as an expert in admiralty law.[4]

Varied indeed were the backgrounds of the men who assembled on November 27, 1862, in a room in the building on the corner of Fourteenth Street and Pennsylvania Avenue in Washington to determine the future of Major General Fitz John Porter. On Day One, however, only four of the nine members of the Court were present, along with Judge-Advocate Joseph Holt and "the Accused." Nothing could be done.[5] Day Two was only slightly more productive. General Morris was replaced for cause as a member of the Court by General Slough. Judge-Advocate Holt stated that he was not ready to present anything to the Court and probably would not be until Monday next, whereupon the Court adjourned.[6]

On Monday next (December 1, Day Three), Holt told the Court that the formal charges had just been delivered to the Accused and wondered if Porter required time in which to examine them.

Be it remembered that General Pope had read his damning allegations to Lincoln and his cabinet back on September 3, and that at no time since then had Porter had more than his own suspicions on which to base his preparations of any sort of defense. Yet as late as on Trial Day Three, December 1, almost three months later, Colonel Holt had the effrontery to ask such a question.

General Porter told the Court that yes, he would need time in which to study the charges, which he had only then been given, and to "decide upon what witnesses he should want to be called," which he thought he could do by "Thursday next."

But Rufus King had not yet reported for duty on the Court. Holt presented the question of what to do about this to General Hunter, president of that body. According to the record, "the Court proceeded to deliberate within closed doors" which did not reopen on that Monday afternoon. Consequently, Porter's request for time was left unaddressed.[7]

How gross an affront to the Accused this negligence actually was may be

REVERDY JOHNSON, LAWYER,
U.S. SENATOR FROM MARYLAND

Johnson was Porter's main defense counsel during the court-martial. In a civil court his efforts were likely to have been more effective, for he was among the most respected lawyers of his generation. After Porter's conviction, Johnson published a pamphlet exposing the errors and distortions in the summary of the case Holt prepared for Lincoln, and for as long as he lived he encouraged Porter to keep fighting.

judged by considering the appalling gravity of the charges General Porter had so belatedly been told he faced.[8] The first was Violation of the Ninth Article of War, disobedience of orders; the second, Violation of the Fifty-Second Article of War, misbehavior in the presence of the enemy. Specifications under each charge cited orders issued by Major General John Pope, commander of the Army of Virginia during Second Bull Run, and General Porter's conduct in response to each as described by Brigadier General B. S. Roberts, inspector-general, Army of Virginia, who prepared and filed the charges. The events occurred on the night of August 27–28 near Warrenton Junction and during August 29 near Dawkins' Branch. One specification involving the fighting on August 30 was withdrawn.

Judge-Advocate Holt's duty was to present the witnesses whose testimony, together with documents and other evidence, would tend to prove to the members of the Court that Porter was guilty of the offenses set forth in the charges and specifications. The Accused—actually, Porter's counsel, Johnson and Eames—would cross-examine each of the government's witnesses in search of flaws in the body of adverse evidence being developed. Once Holt had presented his case, the Accused would present witnesses supporting Porter's innocence and Holt would cross-examine them. Members of the Court could question any witness at any time. After hearing closing arguments by each side, they would retire to consider the record, reach a verdict, and (if guilty) prescribe punishment. The outcome would be subject to the approval of President Lincoln.

In these circumstances, the Accused was obliged mainly to react to whatever Holt did and developed. The initiative was to be Holt's from the start. Not until he had done all he could to convince the members of the Court that Porter was guilty could the Accused counterattack. When that time came, Reverdy Johnson and Charles Eames needed to have men on hand to place in the witness chair who could refute damaging testimony and replace it with facts as Porter and his associates during the battle found facts embedded in his and their recollections and beliefs.

Accordingly, after Day Three's session was adjourned, only two courses of preparatory action were open to Porter and his lawyers: identify and list officers to call as witnesses, and study the charges and specifications in order to locate and isolate differences between General Roberts' version of events and the truth.

On Day Four, December 2, 1862, the absence of General King was the only matter considered.[9]

King was present on Day Five, Wednesday, December 3, and the trial proper began with the reading of the order establishing the Court, whereupon General Porter was asked if he had an objection to any member named in the detail. He replied that he had no objection.[10]

Was this prudent? Hindsight would reveal that it was an egregious blunder. As noted, the Court had been loaded with officers beholden to Stanton. But it seems doubtful that Porter and his counsel were aware of that circumstance. Moreover, because of the short notice "the Accused" had been given, it was unlikely that they could have developed—almost overnight—grounds for successful challenges.

Inadvertantly but profoundly, General Porter may well have contributed to the mistake of accepting a Court prejudiced heavily against him. Having dealt mostly with honorable fellow officers (notably, R. E. Lee, Albert Sidney Johnston, and Winfield Scott) for nearly two decades, it is arguable that he was unprepared to detect the depth of depravity in which he was now immersed.

After the Court was duly sworn, counsel for the Accused presented a letter signed by General Porter requesting that the proceedings be open to the public and representatives of the press. "Accusations of a most serious character are laid against me," he wrote. "My character has been assailed through the public press with charges of 'doubtful loyalty,' and my name stained with such epithets as 'traitor' or 'semi-traitor.' " The Court decided that it would sit with open doors, in accordance with the custom of the service.[11]

With that matter settled, Judge-Advocate Holt read General Roberts' charges into the record and then announced that he was withdrawing a specification under the second charge, misbehavior in the presence of the enemy, that General Porter's attack on Saturday, August 30, had been (in effect) too feeble. "It is my purpose," he said, "to offer no proof under it."[12] But a valid question remained and Reverdy Johnson asked it: "Is the withdrawn specification to be entered upon the record?"

Yes, Holt replied: "It is necessarily a part of the record, but I enter a formal withdrawal, and that is an end to that specification. There is, therefore, no plea necessary to it."[13]

Johnson then raised the question of whether the Court should proceed with the case in view of a provision in a statute of 1830 dealing with who had the power to convene a general court-martial. If General Pope as a field army commander was preferring the charges, even though his late army's inspector-general, Roberts, signed the submission, then the Court should have been ordered by the President and not General-in-Chief Halleck.[14]

"I wish to state distinctly that Major-General Pope is not the prosecutor in this case," Holt maintained, "nor has he preferred these charges, nor do I present them as being preferred by him."

Then it was time for Major General Porter to plead. "Not guilty," he declared, of any and all of the charges and specifications.[15] Yet—surely—there was much more he might have added if court procedure and military tradition had permitted.[16] *You are all soldiers,* he could have reminded his nine judges, *and you have all been in situations—as I was—where conditions made it impossible for you to obey orders sent from a distance by a commander ignorant of the facts you faced. Why, then, are you pressing these absurd allegations against me? Don't your experience and common sense compel you to drop them right now?*

But all that Porter could do next was stand over by the windows and watch and listen as the trial began.

JOSEPH HOLT,
JUDGE ADVOCATE GENERAL,
U.S. ARMY

Holt, a lawyer appointed by Stanton, conducted the prosecution of General Porter at the December 1862–January 1863 court-martial. He also prepared a summary of the case that may have misled Lincoln, and he was active for years afterward in resisting Porter's attempts to clear his reputation.

2

Day Six of Major General Fitz John Porter's trial, Thursday, December 4, 1862, opened as usual at 11:00 A.M., at the same site, with the nine members of the Court (seated on three sides of a large square table) approving the reading of the previous session's minutes. A few minutes earlier, Major General John Pope had been greeted more as an honored guest than as the prosecution's first witness; indeed, a rocking chair had been provided for him.[17]

Judge-Advocate Holt followed Pope's swearing-in with the usual questions establishing his rank and assignment on August 27, 1862. Then he asked, "Did you or not issue to General Porter an order in reference to the movements of his troops; and, if so, what was the character of that order?"

"I issued an order to General Porter late in the afternoon of the 27th, directing him to move with his command at 1 o'clock that night to the position I then occupied at Kettle Run."

"Will you explain to the Court the reasons for the urgency of the order, as indicated by the following words of the order: 'It is necessary on all accounts that you should be here by daylight. I send an officer with this dispatch, who will conduct you to this place'?"

Pope responded that General Hooker's division had had a severe fight along the railroad, commencing some four miles west of Bristoe Station, and had succeeded in driving the division of General Ewell back along the road, but without putting it to rout; so that at dark Ewell's forces still confronted Hooker's division along the banks of a small stream at Bristoe Station. Just at dark Hooker sent Pope word that he was almost entirely out of ammunition, having but five rounds to a man left, and that, if any action took place in the morning, he would, in consequence, be without the means of making any considerable defense.

"As it was known that Jackson, with his own and the division of A. P. Hill, was at or in the vicinity of Manassas Junction," Pope continued, " and near enough to advance to the support of Ewell, it was altogether probable that, if he should learn the weakness of our forces there, he would unite, and make an attack in the morning. It was for that purpose that I was so anxious that General Porter's corps should be present by daylight, the earliest moment at which it was likely the attack would be made."

"What distance," Holt asked, "would General Porter have had to march to have obeyed your order?"

"About 9 miles."[18]

"And within what time? From 1 o'clock until when?"

"He would have had until daylight. I do not remember exactly what time daylight was; perhaps 4 o'clock, perhaps a little earlier. I directed him to move at 1 o'clock, in order to give his command as much time to remain in their beds at night as possible, supposing that it would occupy him perhaps three hours to get upon the ground. I had expected him there certainly by 4 o'clock."

"Did General Porter obey that order?"

"He did not."

So John Pope testified under oath concerning the first charge and specification. But Holt developed additional substantiating detail. He asked Pope, "At what time on the 28th did he arrive at Bristoe Station, the point indicated in your order?"

"As the head of his column came to Bristoe Station, I took out my watch; it was 20 minutes past 10 o'clock in the morning."

"Did the Accused at that time, or at any time before his arrival, explain to you the reason why he did not obey the order?"

"He wrote me a note, which I received, I think, in the morning of the 28th; very early in the morning, perhaps a little before daylight. I am not quite sure about the time. The note I have mislaid."

Reverdy Johnson asked General Pope if he had looked for the note. "I looked for it," the witness replied, "but I have not been able to find it."

Holt continued his examination: "What was the character of the night? Was it starlight?"

"Yes, sir; as I remember, it was a clear night; that is my recollection."

"If there were any obstacles in the way of such a march as your order contemplated, either growing out of the night or the character of the road, will you please state them?"

"There was no difficulty in marching, so far as the night was concerned," said Pope. "There was some obstruction on the road in a wagon train that was stretched along the road, marching toward the Manassas Junction, in rear of Hooker's division; not sufficient, in my judgment, to have delayed for any considerable length of time the passage of artillery. But even had the roads been entirely blocked up, the railroad track was clear, and along that track had passed the larger portion of General Hooker's infantry. There was no obstruction to the advance of infantry."

"Whatever obstacles, in point of fact, may have existed to the execution of this order, I ask you, as a military man, was it, or not, the duty of General Porter, receiving this command from you as his superior officer, to have made efforts, and earnest efforts, to obey?"

"Undoubtedly. It was his duty."[19]

At this point, Judge-Advocate Holt switched from his development of testimony regarding events that occurred on Wednesday, August 27 and early on Thursday to questions about what happened on Friday. "Will you state what orders, if any," Holt asked, "you gave to General Porter, on the 29th of August, in reference to the movements of himself and his men, and the grounds upon which those orders were based?"

General Pope's response was lengthy, confirming the comments of those who had said that he was overly fond of words.[20] "In answer to that question," he began, "information from the front, upon which the dispositions of the army were made, varied at different periods of the day and night, and it was not until toward daylight in the morning of the 29th that I became thoroughly satisfied of the position of the enemy, and of the necessary movements of troops to be made in consequence."

General Pope gave the first of five orders to General Porter well before sunrise on August 29. Porter, then at Bristoe, was to move to Centreville because Stonewall Jackson's force was thought to be threatening that vital base. By daylight, however, it appeared that Jackson was in fact west of Centreville. Pope's second order directed Porter to move up the Manassas-Gainesville Road, taking King's division of McDowell's corps with him. That order reached Porter at or near Manassas; so did General McDowell, who had been separated from his units overnight and was unaware of the assignment of King's brigades to Porter.

General Pope continued: "I received a note from General McDowell requesting that King's division of his corps be not turned over to General Porter, but that he be allowed to conduct it himself. I then sent a joint order to Generals Porter and McDowell, directed to them at Manassas Junction, specifying in detail the movement that I wished to be made by the troops under their command." This message, Pope's third, became known as the "joint" order and it contained some unusual provisions.

"I did not desire to pursue Jackson beyond the town of Gainesville,"

Pope explained, "as we could not have done so on account of the want of supplies—rations for the men and forage for the horses. My order to Generals Porter and McDowell is, therefore, worded that they shall pursue the route to Gainesville until they effect a junction with the forces that are marching upon Gainesville from Centreville—the forces under Heintzelman, Sigel, and Reno—and that when that junction was formed, as I expected it would have been very near to Gainesville, the whole command should halt, it being, as I stated before, not feasible with my command in the condition it was in, on account of supplies, to pursue Jackson's forces farther."

During the morning the forces under Sigel and Heintzelman had kept up a skirmishing with the rear of Jackson's forces, General Pope testified. The Confederates were brought to a stand at the little town of Groveton, about eight miles, he estimated, from Centreville and perhaps five or six miles from Gainesville. "When I rode on to the field of battle," he recalled, "which was about noon, General Sigel reported to me that he needed re-enforcements in the front; that his line was weak, and that his troops required to be withdrawn from the action. I told him—as I did General Heintzelman, who was present on the ground—that I only wished them to maintain their positions, as the corps of McDowell and Porter were then on the march from Manassas Junction toward the enemy's right flank, and ought, in a very short time, to be in such position as to fall upon that portion of his line. I desired them, therefore, only to maintain the positions they occupied."

General Pope waited until "4 o'clock, or some little after that time, perhaps half-past 4 in the afternoon," and then—finding that neither McDowell nor Porter had made their appearance—"I sent an order to General Porter, informing him, generally, of the condition of things on the field, and stating to him that I desired him to push forward and attack the enemy in flank, and, if possible, in rear, without any delay. This order was sent to General Porter about half-past 4 in the afternoon." It would long be remembered as the "4:30" order.

"Finding that General Porter did not comply with this order," the witness continued, "and receiving a dispatch which he sent to Generals McDowell and King, stating to them that he was about to fall back, or was falling back, to Manassas Junction, and that he did so because he saw clouds of dust, showing that, in his judgment, the enemy was advancing on the road he was occupying, and stating that it appeared to him, from the fire of the battle that he had been listening to, that our forces were retreating and the enemy advancing, and he had determined to fall back to Manassas Junction, and recommended Generals McDowell and King to send back their trains also. Receiving this note, purporting to be from General Porter to Generals McDowell and King, I sent an order to General Porter, directing him, immediately upon the receipt of the order, to march his whole command to the field of battle, and to report to me in person for orders, stating to him that I expected him to comply strictly with that order. I put it in such form—perhaps not entirely courteous—because I had understood General Porter, upon two occasions, to have disobeyed the orders that I had sent him."[21]

Holt selected the joint order to Generals McDowell and Porter and

IRVIN MCDOWELL, MAJOR GENERAL, U.S. ARMY

A protege of Radical Republican Secretary of the Treasury Salmon P. Chase, McDowell survived being the loser in the 1861 battle of First Bull Run to command a corps in Pope's Army of Virginia during the mauling inflicted by Confederates led by Lee, Jackson, and Longstreet on the same ground a little over a year later. Conversations he had with Porter during Second Bull Run were central to Holt's case at the court martial and again to the outcome of the Schofield Board's investigation in 1878–1879.

asked his loquacious witness at what hour in the morning it had been sent.

"I do not remember distinctly," Pope replied. "I think it was somewhere between 8 and 9 o'clock in the morning."

"Was there an engagement then pending?"

"Fighting was then going on along the turnpike that led from Centreville to Warrenton—fighting was going on quite sharply."

"Did the march of General Porter's command, as indicated in that order, lead him toward that battle?"

"Yes, sir; it led him toward the flank of the enemy."

"Did General Porter obey the order addressed to him and General McDowell?"

"I do not know whether he obeyed it; he did not obey it fully; how far he obeyed it, I am not able to say; he certainly did not obey the order fully."

"If he had obeyed it, would it not have brought him up with the enemy before half-past 4 in the evening?"

"Yes, sir."

Holt was leading General Pope nearer and nearer to his goal, asking next: "On your arriving on the battlefield, where was [Porter] reported to you to be?"

"I arrived on the battlefield at 12 o'clock—about noon. At 4:30 o'clock nobody on the field knew where General Porter was."

"Did, or did not, General Porter obey the second order to which you refer, issued at 4:30 P.M. on the 29th of August, directing him to engage the enemy in flank, and, if possible, in rear?

"He did not, so far as my knowledge of the fact goes."

"You have no knowledge of his having made any attack then?"

"I should have known it if he had attacked."

"Will you state to the Court, and describe the condition of the battlefield at that hour, and the importance of Porter's obedience of that order to the success of your troops?"

General Pope replied that late in the afternoon, about the time that he had hoped that General Porter would be assaulting the enemy on the flank, General McDowell had arrived with his corps. "I directed an attack to be made on the left of the enemy's line," Pope continued, "which was handsomely done. The enemy was driven back in all directions, and left a large part of the ground with his dead and wounded upon it in our possession."

And then John Pope told the Court precisely what Judge-Advocate General Holt had been working toward having them hear: "Had General Porter fallen upon the flank of the enemy, as it was hoped, at any time up to 8 o'clock that night, it is my firm conviction that we should have destroyed the army of Jackson."

3

So far, Holt had enabled General Pope to establish his reasons for issuing the order of August 27 as he did and to maintain that General Porter did not obey it. And so it was as to the orders Pope issued on August 29; the testimony was longer but to the effort that Porter had violated all of them. However, Holt had allowed Pope to describe events in a manner favorable to himself, thus establishing background for further exploration.

So matters stood as counsel for the Accused took over the examination of the witness seated in the rocking chair.

As had Judge-Advocate Holt, Reverdy Johnson began with the first offense cited. "At what time after the order of the 27th of August," he asked, "and where, did you see the Accused?"

General Pope replied, "I saw him at Bristoe Station, where I had passed the night, and to which point he had been ordered."

"Had you any conversation with him in relation to the order of the 27th, and his having obeyed or disobeyed it; and, if so, what?"

"I do not remember having any conversation with him in reference to obeying or disobeying the order, although I had much conversation with him."

"Try to recollect if you complained to him then, at any time during that conversation, that he had not obeyed the order of the 27th, or whether he gave to you any explanation in relation to what he had done under that order."

"I should not be likely to complain to my subordinate officer of a disobedience to my orders. I am, therefore, very sure that I did not complain to General Porter. I am not sure that he gave me any explanations. I have a general recollection that he spoke to me of his march and the difficulties that he had in getting wagons out of the road; but the particulars I do not remember, as I was very much occupied, and the necessity which made his presence important had passed away."

"Recollect, if you can, whether, upon hearing his explanations, you did or did not express yourself satisfied."

"No, sir; I have no remembrance of that."

"Are you certain that you did not?"

"I cannot be positively certain that I did not, but I am sure that it is quite impossible that I could have been satisfied."

Reverdy Johnson applied more pressure. "Did you at any other time," he asked, "or on the day of the 28th, express yourself as having been satisfied with the manner in which he had carried out, or tried to carry out, your orders?"[22]

"No, sir," Pope replied, but he went on to reveal more than counsel for the Accused may have expected. "I had a conversation with General Porter at Fairfax Court-House [after the battle], in which I told him, as distinctly as I thought it was necessary to tell him, that I was not satisfied, and I did so in consequence of a question of General Porter, which he seemed to make a point of to me, in asking at Fairfax Court-House whether I had had any occasion to be dissatisfied with the manner in which he had discharged his duties. I replied to him that I had had occasion to be dissatisfied, and mentioned certain particulars, I think, in which I had had that occasion."

"Will you state the particulars in which at that period you expressed yourself dissatisfied?"

"I mentioned, as well as I recollect, the disobedience of orders at Bristoe Station, and his failure on the field of battle on the 29th. I also mentioned to him the absence of Griffin's command, and its remaining the whole day at Centreville, in sight of the battlefield, and not coming on the field, as being among the reasons I had for being dissatisfied."

"Did he give you any, and, if so, what, explanation in answer to your expressions of dissatisfaction?"

"I understood him to say in relation to Griffin that he did not know, did not understand exactly how Griffin had got to Centreville. In relation to the other matters, I do not know that he gave any explanation. It was no time for explanations. We were at Fairfax Court-House, in the midst of a great deal of confusion, troops passing backward and forward, and we were expecting to move at any moment. This conversation occurred in two or three minutes, I should think. He was in the room where I was. Perhaps three minutes covered the whole time we were talking."

John Pope's volunteered openings invited more probing by Johnson. He asked: "Are you sure it was not longer; say, about a half an hour?"

"I think not a half an hour. I should think five minutes would cover what conversation General Porter and I had there. It might, perhaps, have been more, but that is my recollection of it."

That answer was typical of many that followed. There were several persons in the room but Pope said he could not recollect who they were—then, a few questions later, he named four. He was not sure whether Colonel Ruggles was among them. Even so, Johnson asked: "Try and recollect if you had a conversation with Colonel Ruggles, after your final report of the battles, in relation to the charges and imputations against the Accused, and whether he did not tell you that he had heard you say to the Accused that you had no fault to find with him."

"I have no remembrance of any such conversation."[23]

"Are you certain that you had not?"

"I am not certain that I had not, but I am very certain that Colonel Ruggles never stated a thing of that kind to me; I feel quite sure of it, although I am not prepared to swear that he did not; I have no knowledge of it."

"State on what day, if you can remember, you had the conversation with the Accused at Fairfax Court-House."

"I think it was on Tuesday morning, the 2d of September."

"Say, if you can, what led to the conversation between the Accused and yourself on that occasion."

"I think what led to it was that General Porter came into the room and brought me a telegraphic dispatch, or a dispatch of some kind, from General McClellan, in which General McClellan urged General Porter to support me in the operations of the army. The exact character of that dispatch I do not remember, whether it was telegraphic or otherwise. I have repeated the substance of it."

"Is the paper now shown you, marked 'Accused, Exhibit No. 1,' that dispatch?"

"I think that is the dispatch. This is the substance of the impression made upon my mind by it. I did not read it very carefully; but it seems to me this is it."

The dispatch was then read.

Then Reverdy Johnson asked: "If, as you have stated, you were of the opinion that the army under your command had been defeated, and in danger of still greater defeat, and the capital of the country in danger of capture by the enemy, and you thought that these calamities could have been obviated if General Porter had obeyed your orders, why was it that you doubted, on the 2d of September, whether you would or would not take any action against him?"

Counsel for the Accused might have added: *Why did you not charge him with treason immediately?*

General Pope declined to answer the question Johnson had asked, claiming that it was not relevant to this investigation.

The room was cleared, and the Court proceeded to deliberate with closed doors. When the doors were reopened, the judge-advocate stated the decision of the Court to be that the question was irrelevant.

On behalf of the Accused, Reverdy Johnson submitted a protest in writing, and asked that it be entered upon the record. Again the room was cleared, and the Court deliberated. After some time the doors were reopened, and the judge-advocate stated that "the Court determined to hold the question as to the disposition to be made of this paper under advisement until tomorrow."[24]

Whereupon, the Court adjourned: Day Six had ended.

⁂

The text of the Accused's protest:

> The witness having, in his examination-in-chief, attributed the disasters of the army under his command in Virginia in August last to the failure of the Accused to obey all or some of his orders, and having stated that he was of the opinion that such orders might have been obeyed, and it being, so far as the prosecution has gone, upon his evidence that such disobedience occurred that the prosecution has endeavored to be maintained, the Accused is advised by his counsel that the question just ruled out by the Court is not only relevant and legal but most material, in order to show that the recollection of the witness in such his examination-in-chief is not to be relied upon; and that he for the first time afterward charged the alleged disobedience upon the Accused; because it was the duty of the witness, not only not to doubt whether he would take any action in relation to the matter, but to report the same as

> a grave offense on the part of the Accused; and his determination or doubt whether he would take such action, or make such report, are facts not only admissible but material evidence that at the time to which the question relates he did not believe there had been any such disobedience on the part of the Accused, and, therefore, respectfully request to have this protest entered on the proceedings of the Court against the exclusion of the question referred to.[25]

One sentence, 245 words in length. No wonder the Court decided to take the protest "under advisement" and adjourn; the members would need all of the overnight hours in order to comprehend the thrust of the turgid prose.[26]

Yet, it was remarkable that such a document could have been created in time to be submitted at that particular point. In effect, it was notice to the Court that the Accused was represented by lawyers who were extraordinarily alert, even perhaps prescient.

No matter how the Court ruled in the morning, clearly Reverdy Johnson had put John Pope on the defensive. Moreover, allowing the general to place such a profusion of words on the record would facilitate the efforts of Porter and his counsel to draw rings around passages in the session's minutes that—they suspected—contained lies.

4

Day Seven of Major General Fitz John Porter's Court-martial, Friday, December 5, 1862, opened with the reading into the record by Judge-Advocate Joseph Holt of the Accused's protest that had been filed the day before. As on Day Six, a rocking chair had been provided for General Pope.

The government's most prominent witness surprised all who had listened to that recitation by declaring that now he was perfectly willing to answer the question to which he had objected as being irrelevant and that had just been sustained by the Court as being irrelevant.[27] Why had, overnight, Pope changed his mind?

Pope's biographer Peter Cozzens has written:

> Retiring to his room at Willard's, Pope realized he had been out-

> witted. He implored Holt to put General Roberts on the stand the next morning, both to distance himself temporarily from Johnson's fire and so that Roberts should afterward be free to help Holt in Court. "Many little points important in a military view may escape your attention, while Roberts having been in action in all the scenes involved has the very details stored away in his mind," Pope told Holt. "He may be of much assistance to you by reminding you on occasion of small matters of this kind."[28]

But Judge-Advocate Holt had not agreed, and on Day Seven Counsel for the Accused resumed his cross-examination by restating the controversial question: "Why was it that you doubted, on the 2d of September, whether you would or would not take any action against General Porter?"

Again, John Pope's reply was so wordy that seasoned Court observers could detect intensive overnight coaching of this witness by Judge-Advocate Holt and his associates.[29] Toward the end, however, he said: "It was not until the campaign was closed, and I came to Washington City, on the 4th or 5th of September, that I was informed by the President of the United States that he had seen several dispatches or letters from General Porter to General Burnside, dated a day or two previous to these battles, which had occasioned him very grave apprehensions that General Porter would fail to do his duty.

"This communication of the President to me opened my eyes to many matters which I had before been loth to believe, and which I cannot bring myself now to believe.

"I will now proceed to answer the preface to this question which has been put to me. The question is prefaced by a representation that I have here given certain testimony and made certain statements which I have not made, and which will not be found upon the records of this Court. Why the question is put in that shape, when the record is before the Court and before the counsel for the Accused, I am not able to say. Certainly no such statements as those have been made by me.

"The reason why I did not put these charges against General Porter, and why I told him, at Fairfax Court-House, that I thought I should take no further action, was that I did not then believe that General Porter's conduct was deliberate and of purpose, but I was inclined to think that his action or want of action there was the result of mistake or blundering rather than of intention. But I never for a moment had an idea of withholding from the knowledge of the Government a full detail of facts, which, as every member of this Court must know, every officer commanding an army is required to give in his official report concerning every important transaction that takes place in his command.[30]

"I will say to the Court that I have answered this question, and only should have answered it, in consequence of the manner in which the protest of the Accused was presented to the Court, which protest sought to present me in a false light. I answer it with reluctance, and I respectfully submit to the Court that that sort of questions are not relevant to this case, and I would say to them respectfully that I shall decline, unless they insist upon it, to answer any such questions in future."

Had Reverdy Johnson's resort to the written protest boomeranged? At a minimum, introduction by Pope—at this time and in this manner—of General Porter's having made indiscreet statements in his letters to Ambrose Burnside, was an unintended consequence.

Reverdy Johnson's cross-examination of Pope continued: "Will you state by whom and when you were told or cautioned that the Accused would not obey your orders or cooperate with you?"

Pope's retort was tinged with insolence. "I would prefer the question to be put in the form in which I made my statement. I said that 'General Porter would fail me.' That was the statement I made. I do not like to have these questions put so as to seem to imply that I have made statements which I have not made."

"I will put it in that form," Johnson offered. "I understood it the other way. By whom were you told or cautioned that the Accused would fail you, and when were you so told?"

"I think on the 27th of August, and again, I think, on the 28th of August, by General Roberts, and on the night of the 28th of August by Lieutenant-Colonel Smith."

"Are those the only two officers from whom you got this information?"

"Those are the only two that I remember distinctly. I heard much talk of that kind from many others, but I do not remember who they are. I heard it on several occasions."

"Will you state whether you informed the Accused, in the conversation at Fairfax Court-House, or before or after, that it had been your purpose to put him under arrest?"

"I do not think I informed him at all on the subject."

"Will you state by whom you were advised not to put him under arrest?"

"By General McDowell, for one; by General Roberts, I think, for another; by General Hooker, I think, for a third, and, I think, by General Heintzelman."[31]

For a time counsel for the Accused continued to probe General Pope's recollections of events on the night of August 27, then he took the witness to what happened two days later: "Was not the purpose of the joint order of the 29th August to place the entire commands mentioned in that order under the command of Major-General McDowell?"

"It was not. General McDowell had the authority, as the senior officer, to command the two corps while acting together, and not under the immediate orders of the general commanding the army. I did not, however, intend at the time that he should do so, but that the two corps should act separately, though, when they were joined, of course, if General McDowell chose to assume the command, he had the right, for the time, to do so."[32]

At this stage of the examination, the Court adjourned.

David Hunter, Major General, U.S. Army

Hunter's zeal as an abolitionist made him the Radicals' choice to preside over Porter's court-martial. As was true of most of the court's members, he stood to benefit if he found as Stanton wished.

5

Saturday, December 6, 1862, was the trial's Day Eight and it would be the third on which the witness was Major General John Pope. Before the Accused's counsel Reverdy Johnson could continue his questioning, however, Judge-Advocate Joseph Holt called the Court's attention to "gross inaccuracies" in several newspapers' reports of General Pope's testimony. This led to closing and opening of doors and an admonition from Major General Hunter, the Court's president, to the reporters present that "the Court may find it necessary to take such action as will correct the abuse."[33]

The warning delivered and memories refreshed by the reading of the previous day's minutes, Reverdy Johnson picked up his interrogation of General Pope more or less where the expiration of time had obliged him to leave it on the previous afternoon: "Will you state, as accurately as you can, in what particular the Accused failed to carry out your joint order of the 29th of August?"

"I can only state the facts from the reports of others," General Pope replied, "as I did not myself see the Accused during the 29th of August, nor did I know of his exact position on that day until it was reported to me by my aide-de-camp [Captain Douglass Pope], quite late in the evening, when he returned from the delivery of the [4:30] order to him."

Johnson repeated the question: "Will you state in what particular or particulars the Accused failed to carry out that joint order?"[34]

"I have stated that the Accused had failed, in my opinion, to carry out that order, first, because I believed that if he had attacked the enemy on the flank, as he was directed, I should have known it, being myself on the field of battle and near to the front. In relation to the joint order of the 29th, I have General Porter's note to Generals McDowell and King, in which he himself states that he has not fully obeyed that joint order of the 29th of August."

Holt produced and read a paper as follows:

> Generals McDOWELL and KING:
>
> I found it impossible to communicate by crossing the woods to Groveton. The enemy are in strong force on this road, and, as they appear to have driven our forces back, the firing of enemy having

advanced and ours retired, I have determined to withdraw to Manassas. I have attempted to communicate with McDowell and Sigel, but my messengers have run into the enemy. They have gathered artillery and cavalry and infantry, and the advancing masses of dust show the enemy coming in force. I am now going to the head of the column to see what is passing and how affairs are going. Had you not better send your train back?

F. J. PORTER,
Major-General.

Holt asked Pope: "Is this the note of the Accused to which you refer?"

"That is the note."

Reverdy Johnson continued: "Will you state on what day, and at what hour of the day, you received the note just read?"

"I received it on the night of the 29th of August; I think between 7 and 8 o'clock in the evening."

"Did you, after that time, and after the receipt of that note, receive another note from the Accused; and, if so, have you that other note?"

"I do not remember to have received another note; I certainly have not got it anywhere amongst my papers."

"Have you any recollection now, without looking at the paper, that you admit in your official report the reception of that other note?"

"No, sir; I have not. The note to which I refer in my official report was the note to Generals McDowell and King which I received. That note, as I understand, was brought direct to me, and not delivered to General McDowell, and, so far as I understand, not to General King."

"If you did not receive another note, did you receive information from the Accused as to his position after the reception of the note which has been produced?"

"The only information that I remember to have received of the position of the Accused I received from General McDowell when he arrived on the field, and from my aide-de-camp, who reported his position when he returned from delivering him the order dated at half past 4 in the afternoon. I do not remember to have received any other information."

"Recollect, if you can, whether you received a note by the hands of one of your own aides, after the reception of the first note, stating that the

Accused was there in position, and could hold it, and perhaps attack, if strengthened by the division you had taken from him—King's division—or another?"

"I do not remember to have received a note; but I remember that my aide-de-camp told me that General Porter stated to him, or in his hearing, that if he had King's division, he could make a dash, or something of that kind."[35]

"If you have the note, will you produce it?"

"Certainly, if I have it. This suggestion of General Porter, whether oral or in writing, made no impression upon me, because King's division was at that time, or about that time, engaged in an action with the enemy in our immediate front, and there were no troops to spare that could be sent to General Porter. In fact, I thought he already had force sufficient to have accomplished during the day the purpose implied in the order of half-past 4 o'clock."

"Where, if you recollect, did you suppose the Accused with his command was when you issued your order to him of the 29th August, at 4:30 P.M.?"

"I supposed him to be somewhere on the road between Manassas Junction and Gainesville, and by that time far advanced toward Gainesville on that road."

"Would the Accused, by obeying the joint order of the 29th August, have been brought up in front of the enemy at 4:30 o'clock of that evening; and, if so, at what point of the enemy's line?"

"As I have stated in my testimony, when that joint order was issued, I was not certain at what point, if at any, of the Warrenton turnpike east of Gainesville, the enemy could be brought to a stand. The joint movement of McDowell and Porter was, therefore, made so as to intersect the Warrenton turnpike at Gainesville, and being on a road which constantly converges toward the Warrenton turnpike, those two corps would have been near enough to the turnpike, in case the enemy were brought to a stand at any point of it, to be brought on the field within a short time. I could not tell, of course, at the time that order was issued, not knowing where the enemy would be brought to a stand or whether he would be brought to a stand or not, whether the forces of McDowell and Porter would come up in his front or on his flank."

"Do you know now where, in point of fact, the Accused was with his command, in whole or in part, at 4:30 P.M. of the 29th August, and where the enemy nearest to him at that time were?"

"Of my own knowledge, I do not."

"Without knowing the relative position of the forces under the command of the Accused and of the enemy at 4:30 P.M. of the 29th of August, how could you have been certain, if you were, that it would be in the power of the Accused to turn the enemy's right flank?"

"I knew the position of the enemy, who occupied a line perpendicular to the Warrenton turnpike, and at or near the town of Groveton. I was sure, from the orders I had given him, that General Porter must be somewhere between Manassas Junction and Gainesville, on the road to Gainesville. So far, I knew within certain limits, though not exactly, the relative positions of General Porter and of the enemy. My belief was that the road from Manassas Junction to Gainesville either passed by the right flank or was occupied by that flank of the enemy, and that Porter's march, if pursued, conducted him either to the right flank of the enemy or past the right flank of the enemy, toward his rear."

"Will you point out upon the map produced by the prosecution, marked 'Government, Exhibit A,' the positions, as you now understand, held by the Accused with his command, and by the enemy, at 4:30 P.M. of the 29th of August?"[36]

"I have stated that I did not know the exact position of the Accused beyond the fact that I felt sure, from the orders I had given him, that he was somewhere between Manassas Junction and Gainesville, on the direct road to Gainesville. His exact position on that road, as I said before, I do not know."

"Then you cannot point it out?"

"I do not know exactly where it was; I can point out somewhere between Manassas Junction and Gainesville."

"Point out as accurately as you can."

"I can only say he was somewhere between these two points on that road; where, I cannot say. From my orders to General Porter, he ought to have been somewhere between Manassas Junction and the town of Gainesville, on the direct road. As I understand, the road runs along the railroad although I am not clear about that, as I have never been over it.

What I mean by the direct road is the main traveled road from Manassas Junction to Gainesville, which I understood to be along or very nearly along the railroad."

"State, generally, where you supposed the Accused to have been."

"I have no supposition about it, except that I suppose he was somewhere between Manassas Junction and Gainesville. The enemy in front of us; their left, as far as we could ascertain it, was in these woods here [referring to the map], extending along, perhaps, toward Sudley Springs. But they were massed in these woods, along an old railroad grade, and they had batteries which extended along a crest of hills, across the Warrenton turnpike, and their troops extended into the woods south of that road; how far their right extended, I do not know."

"Did you know at that time, or do you know now, whether at that time—4:30 P.M., August 29—or about that time, Longstreet's corps, in whole or in part, had joined or were joining Jackson's?"

"I had feared the junction of those corps at any moment, as I knew from information that Longstreet was pushing forward to join Jackson. I therefore expected that movement of Longstreet, certainly during the afternoon of the 29th. General Buford, with his cavalry, was in that direction, and I knew that he was watching for that movement, and expected him to report as soon as he could ascertain anything about it. At 4:30 o'clock I had not received any report from him. He (General Buford) was at that time under the command of General McDowell."

"Did you know then or do you now know what line of march Longstreet's corps was taking to unite with Jackson; and, if you do, state whether that would not have carried that corps to the right of Jackson's line, as you have marked it on the map?"

"I expected that Longstreet—and understand now that a part of Longstreet's corps, at least, passing through Gainesville, did so—would seek to join Jackson by the Warrenton turnpike. According to my understanding of his position then, that would have brought Longstreet to the center of Jackson's line, as we understood it; though it was easy, as I supposed, though I have not been over the ground at any point between Gainesville and Groveton, to have changed the course of his column, or a part of it, so as to have brought them in on the right or the left of Jackson, as they thought proper."

"If, in fact," Reverdy Johnson asked, "the corps of Longstreet formed on the right of Jackson, what distance of march would the Accused have been compelled to have made to carry out the order of 4:30 P.M. of the 29th of August, which was 'to push forward into action at once on the enemy's flank, and, if possible, on his rear'?"

"As I did not know the position of General Porter on the road from Manassas Junction to Gainesville at the time I wrote that order, it is impossible for me to state how far he would have had to go."[37]

"That perhaps is not an answer to the question. The Accused desires you to state, if you can, whether, assuming that Longstreet's corps had united on the right of Jackson's line, from what you now know or understand was the actual position of the Accused and his command at 4:30 P.M. on the 29th of August, what distance of march would he have had to have made in order to strike the enemy on the flank or in the rear?"

"In the first place," Pope replied, "I do not assume that at 4:30 o'clock Longstreet was on Jackson's right. The Accused requires me to assume certain facts."

"I assume them."

"Very well, then, I will say further that unless I could know how the command of Longstreet was termed, what disposition for battle he had made on Jackson's right, it is impossible for me to tell how much ground he would have occupied. Therefore I cannot say where his right would have rested, even if Longstreet had been there. I cannot say, therefore, how far General Porter would have been required to march. The distance certainly would have been much less than the distance from Manassas Junction to Gainesville."

Be it noted, here, that after two and a half days of questioning John Pope, Reverdy Johnson had hammered him into being unresponsive to most of his questions and—more to the point—into revealing how far out of control of his forces he actually had been.

Seasoned lawyer Reverdy Johnson must have relished it. His pressure continued: "Then, without knowing the facts which in your preceding answer you state you did not know at the time when the order of 4:30 P.M. of the 29th August was given, how could you then have known whether it would or would not be in the power of the Accused to strike the enemy in flank and rear?"

"If the Accused will state to the Court what facts he says I am ignorant of, I may be able to answer that question. The question sets out that I was ignorant of certain facts. I should like to know what they are. It is said that I have stated myself to be ignorant of certain facts. Who states those facts, and what are those facts? And I will state further that in my previous answer I declined to assume that Longstreet was then on Jackson's right at 4:30 P.M. I am giving an answer only on the assumption of the Accused that Longstreet was there, which is not a fact stated or proved."

"Without knowing that Longstreet's command was formed or would be formed," said Johnson, "or without knowing what disposition for battle he had made or might make on Jackson's right, how did you certainly know when you issued the order of 4:30 P.M. of the 29th of August, to attack the enemy in flank and rear, that that order could be carried out by the Accused?"

"The Accused was expected to attack, if possible—and as I understood to be practicable—the right flank of Jackson's forces, and, if possible, the rear of his forces, to prevent, if it were practicable, the junction of Longstreet's forces with Jackson's, and to crush Jackson's flank before Longstreet could effect a junction with him. I did not then believe, nor do I now believe, that at that time any considerable portion of Longstreet's corps had reached the vicinity of the field."

"How long did you suppose, when you issued the order of 4:30 P.M., it would take to place it in possession of the Accused?"

Pope replied: "I did not then know precisely, or even nearly, at what point of the road from Manassas Junction to Gainesville the Accused could be found. I could not tell, except within limits, how long it would take to deliver him the order. But I knew that an aide-de-camp, riding rapidly, could go from the field of battle to Manassas Junction, or to any point west of Manassas Junction on the Gainesville road, if he found General Porter in advance of Manassas Junction, within an hour, by going at speed."

"Do you know whether at 5:30 P.M., or between that hour and 7 o'clock, the Accused had the enemy immediately in his front?"

"I do not know it, except from the reports of others, though I would think it altogether likely that Jackson would have pushed out some force to observe the road between Gainesville and Manassas Junction. It is altogether likely, therefore, that some of Jackson's troops were in presence of General Porter's advance, though of my own knowledge I do not know that."

"Will you point out, if you can, upon the map, the position of each of the corps other than that of the one under command of the Accused, at 4:30 P.M., August 29?[38]

"There is no difficulty in telling the position of the other corps of the army, with the exception of McDowell's, which had not then reached the field, but was on the march from Manassas Junction. Our troops confronted the line of the enemy as represented there [pointing]."

"State, if you can," said Johnson, "whether the line of McDowell's march, that he made under the joint order of the 29th August, and which took him to Groveton, did not necessarily carry him to the rear of the column of the Accused, and make him march in that direction past the line of the Accused."

"I understood from General McDowell, subsequently, that General Porter, with his corps, was a little in advance toward Gainesville—a little west of the junction of the roads leading to Gainesville and Groveton; and that McDowell's corps had passed him whilst there, taking the Sudley Springs road instead of the Gainesville road, and passing, of course, in the rear of General Porter's column. That is what I understood from reports."

"If General McDowell's statement was accurate as to the position of the corps of the Accused, was not the Accused at that time on the road which he was directed to take by the joint order of the 29th August?"

"Certainly I so understood it; but that he was at a halt when McDowell passed him."

"Are you now unable to say that you were informed or knew at 7 o'clock P.M. on the 29th of August that Longstreet's corps was up with Jackson in force?"

Pope's reply: "By 7 o'clock in the evening I knew from the report of General Buford that a portion of Longstreet's force—numbering, perhaps, one-half the force under General Porter, certainly not more than two-thirds, as General Buford estimated it—had passed through Gainesville, and by that time, in all probability, had joined Jackson. The report of General Buford was in writing. He states the number of battalions, pieces of artillery, I think, and the cavalry which passed through Gainesville, according to his observation. That information came to me quite late in the evening; certainly by 7 o'clock, I think.

"The question put by the Accused seems to imply that I have previously stated somewhere in my testimony that I did not know at 7 o'clock in the evening that portions of Longstreet's force had joined Jackson. I have nowhere so stated."

"That was not the purpose of the question."

General Pope's fatigue was reflected in his reply: "The question, as I submit to the Court, is written as many other questions have been to which I have objected, on account of their making me appear to have made statements which I have not made. The question, after going on with a great deal of testimony is put in this way: 'Are you now unable to say,' as if I had previously stated differently."

Reverdy Johnson took Pope to another matter.

"State in what particular the Accused failed to obey the order of 8:50 P.M. of the 29th August, which order was: 'Major-General PORTER: *Immediately upon receipt of this order, the precise hour of which you will acknowledge, you will march your command to the field of battle of to-day, and report to me in person for orders. You are to understand that you are expected to comply strictly with this order, and to be present on the field within three hours after its reception, or after daybreak to-morrow morning.*' It is signed by the witness."[39]

"I thought that he failed to obey the order entirely, because two brigades of his command were not only not brought up with him, but by some means had either straggled or been permitted to straggle from the command, and were in Centreville."

"Do you mean to say that, because two brigades referred to were in Centreville, the Accused entirely neglected to obey the order?"

"I presume that is a matter for the Court to decide. My own answer to that would be a mere opinion upon the subject. That is exactly a question for the Court to decide."

"State in what, if to any, extent the Accused did obey that order or carry it out."

"The Accused appeared upon the field on Saturday morning, the 30th of August, with his command, excepting, so far as I am informed, the two brigades specified."

"At what hour of the morning did he appear with his command?

"I do not know at what hour of the morning precisely; but it was somewhere between 8 and 10 o'clock, I should think; perhaps earlier than 10 o'clock, perhaps 8 o'clock. I know I made no objections in consequence of the hour that he arrived there."

"State now, as a military man, if the two brigades belonging to the corps of the Accused had left his command without his knowledge, and had gone to Centreville in opposition to instructions, whether his failing to bring up those two brigades with the rest of his command, on the morning of the 30th of August, as you have stated he did, was, in your judgment, a disobedience of the order."[40]

Of all the questions Reverdy Johnson had put to the Radical witness in the rocking chair since Thursday, this one may well have been the most painful and unsettling so far in the trial for John Pope even to try to answer. Benjamin Roberts, Pope's ghost writer in drafting the charges, had included too many offenses. But a member of the Court saved Pope from possible perjury and certain embarrassment by entering an objection: the answer of the witness would be a mere opinion.

To Reverdy Johnson that may well have hardly mattered, for he pressed on. "At what time of the day on Saturday, the 30th of August," he asked John Pope, "did the battle of that day commence?"

"There was more or less skirmishing all the time. But the main battle commenced, I should think, about 12 o'clock; perhaps after that.

"Was the Accused with his command, so far as he had it on that morning, in that battle?"

"A portion of his command was in the battle under his orders. His position in reference to them I did not myself know."

"Will you state what was the extent of his force in that battle, if you can?"

"I cannot state it exactly; but I can state, I suppose, something like it."

"State it approximately."

"The brigade of Griffin and the brigade of Piatt were absent from the field, which I suppose reduced his force between 5,000 and 6,000 men; I presume, therefore, that he had in the battle not to exceed 7,000 men of his own corps with him on the ground. Perhaps he had not so many as that: but that is my estimate of the number. In addition to that he had, however, at that time, King's division operating with him, under his command."

"State, if you can, the number of his killed and wounded upon that occasion."

"I have not received any report of the killed and wounded from him. But a day or two ago, since my arrival here, there were lists of killed and wounded sent, I think, by Sykes and Morell, who commanded the divisions of his corps; I have not, however, yet examined them."[41]

So ended a Saturday that had been a long one for John Pope, the third day since he had seated himself in the rocking chair and lived up to his reputations of being both a master of using an outpouring of words and—as Fitz John Porter had once styled him—an ass.

Moreover, under Reverdy Johnson's expert questioning the Government's star witness had admitted several times that he had not known where Porter's corps and Longstreet's forces were—yet he had issued orders to the Accused anyway. General Pope's frequency of being unresponsive to questions and his displays of arrogant hostility to Johnson suggested also that he wished that Judge-Advocate Holt had not talked him out of his being replaced by Benjamin Roberts after his first day in the rocking chair.[42]

There would be no session on Sunday, a mercy given the complexities of the information already placed upon the record by sundown on December 6, 1862.

CHAPTER SIX

"General Porter will fail you."

Day Nine, December 8, 1862, opened with Reverdy Johnson continuing his cross-examination of General Pope. After a number of questions that seemed to have been put in the manner and for the purposes that the matador teases the wounded bull with *veronicas* and other *paseos* as the *hora de verdad* approaches, Johnson figuratively planted his boots in the sand, raised the red *muleta* in his left hand, and over it aimed the *espada*:

"Bearing in mind the terms and tenor of the order of 4:30 P.M. of the 29th of August, and its direction to the Accused to attack the enemy's flank, and, if possible, his rear, and at the same time to keep up communication with General Reynolds on the right of the Accused, *please inform the Court* whether, if it could have been foreseen at 4:30 P.M. that at the time when the Accused should receive that order he would find himself in front of the enemy in large force, in such a position that he could not outflank the enemy without severing his connection with General Reynolds on his right, *you would have expected or anticipated obedience from the Accused to the order according to its terms.*"

Lengthy though it was, this thrust touched sensitive nerves. Quickly a member of the Court objected, for it shifted attention to John Pope's competence.

The substance of Reverdy Johnson's response was that it was important for Porter to show that at the time he *received* the 4:30 order, circumstances made it impossible for him to execute it according to its terms and Pope's expectation of its being carried out. In addition, General Pope had already testified that on the 2d of September, he had not regarded General Porter as guilty of purposed and intentional criminality and delinquency. Obviously, a negative answer to Johnson's question would be most important fortification of that opinion. And finally, the Judge-Advocate, with the sanction of the Court, had repeatedly asked Pope whether he did or did not consider that certain actions of General Porter amounted to a disobedience of the 4:30 order. Precisely the same rule of examination, Johnson argued, would make this question admissible.[1]

Predictably, the Court deliberated behind closed doors. Equally unsurprising was the outcome: "The witness," Joseph Holt announced, "shall not answer the question."[2]

Although no carcass needed to be dragged from the arena—General Pope's testimony soon ended and he walked away from the rocking chair shortly thereafter—Johnson had in effect served notice that Fitz John Porter was not the only person whose conduct was under examination.[3]

True, in the same building a court of inquiry was taking testimony regarding the performance of Major General Irvin McDowell. And before returning to Minnesota, John Pope would say all that he could toward McDowell's exoneration. But Reverdy Johnson's steady stream of incisive, astute questions had made Pope increasingly uneasy. Accordingly, the general's trip back to Saint Paul and the Sioux uprisings must have seemed twice as long as the one to Washington during which it had seemed so certain that the charges Benjamin Roberts had filed on his behalf would result quickly in Fitz John Porter's conviction and the heaviest of punishments.

2

Following General Pope's departure from the courtroom on Day Nine, Judge-Advocate Holt called to the stand Captain Drake DeKay, the next prosecution witness. After DeKay had been sworn the judge-advocate focused on his having been the aide General Pope had sent on the night of August 27 to instruct General Porter to begin his corps' march to Bristoe Station at one o'clock on the morning of August 28. Joseph Holt began their colloquy: "At what hour of the 27th of August did you deliver the order to General Porter?"

"Between 9 o'clock and half-past 9 P.M.," DeKay replied. "I think about half-past 9; I could not say within a half an hour."

"Had you any conversation with General Porter at the time in relation to the order or the execution of the order by him?"

"Yes, sir; some conversation."

"Will you please state it, as far as you can recall it?"

"I arrived, as I have said, about half-past 9 o'clock, at his tent, and found General Porter and two or three generals there—General Sykes and General Morell, and, I think, General Butterfield. I handed General Porter the order, which he read, and then handed to one of the generals, saying as he did so, 'Gentlemen, there is something for you to sleep upon.' I then said that the last thing that General Pope said to me on leaving Bristoe Station was that I should remain with General Porter and guide the column to Bristoe Station, leaving at one o'clock, and that General Pope expected him certainly to be there by daylight or relied upon his being there by daylight, something of that nature; those may not be the exact words; I only give to the best of my recollection, of course.

"General Porter then asked me how the road was. I told him that the road was good, though I had had difficulty in getting down on horseback, owing to the number of wagons in the road; but I told him I had passed the last wagon a little beyond Catlett's Station from this direction, I told him that as they were moving slowly, he would probably be up with them by daylight. I also stated to him that his infantry could take the railroad track, as many small squads of men had gone up that way. These small squads, I would state here, though I did not state that to General Porter, were stragglers from Hooker's corps; I should think some 600 or 800 of them, which we passed in going down to Bristoe Station; they all took the railroad track as the shortest and easiest road."

Holt asked: "What remark, if any, did General Porter make, either to you or to the generals with him, in reply to this statement in reference to the road and the expectation of General Pope?"

"He stated—I do not think to me—he spoke generally to all who were in the tent—that his troops had just got into camp; that they had been marched hard that day; that they would be good for nothing if they were started at that time of night; that, if their rest was broken, they would be good for nothing in the morning on coming up with the enemy."

"Did he, or not, at the moment, announce any purpose either to obey the order or not to do so?"

"I do not recollect precisely."

"From the remarks made by General Porter, in your hearing, in reply to these statements of yours, was or was not the impression made upon your mind that it was not his purpose to march in obedience to the order?"

Reverdy Johnson objected. Holt explained that he was merely trying to find out if the witness knew what Porter had decided to do about the order. Johnson withdrew his objection.

Captain DeKay answered: "There was no order issued to my knowledge, of course, one way or the other. I can only say that I was aware of the determination not to start until daylight, inasmuch as I laid down and went to sleep."[4]

Prosecutor Holt then drew from Pope's aide some vague responses to questions regarding how tired he thought Porter's men may have been. Next, the judge-advocate turned to the weather—which Pope had recalled as having been clear: "What was the character of the night of the 27th of August?"

"To the best of my recollection," DeKay said, "it was a cloudy night, but not rainy."

Holt's next questions had to do with distances. Getting nowhere, he returned to reconstructing events: "Did you remain over night," he asked, "and wait until the march of General Porter's command the next day"?

"I did."

"At what hour, in point of fact, did he move from Warrenton Junction?"

"I should think the head of the column left about 4 o'clock in the morning; I am not positive about the hour."

"At what rate did the command march after it left Warrenton Junction?"

"I could not say at what rate. We started at or about 4 o'clock in the morning, and marched along quietly, without any apparent haste, meeting with no obstruction or detention, except that arising from the wagons we found in the road. The head of the column arrived at Bristoe Station about 10 o'clock, I should judge."

"Was, or was not, the march throughout at the usual rate at which troops move, or was it slower?"

"It was at the rate at which troops would move if there was no necessity for rapid movement."

"Could they, or could they not, in your judgment, have moved much faster than they did in point of fact?

"They could."

Judge-Advocate Holt's next questions regarding the wagons and Captain DeKay's *I do not recollect* answers moved the testimony hardly at all.

The prosecutor tried another line of interrogation:[5] "Did you see General Porter during the march?"

"I accompanied him after the first 3 miles. He came up to the head of the column about a quarter of a mile this side of Catlett's Station."

"Did, or did not, General Porter or any of the officers under him, during the march, make any unusual personal exertions to accelerate the march of the troops?"

"In drawing the wagons off the road, to enable the troops to pass, at one or two points, General Porter and also his staff used great exertions."

At that point, Holt passed Pope's aide on to counsel for the Accused. Reverdy Johnson opened his cross-examination by asking: "Will [you] please state what [your] going to sleep, or retiring to rest, at half-past. 9 o'clock, had to do with the question of the determination of General Porter to start or not to start at one o'clock in the morning?"

"I have not stated that it was half-past 9 when I went to sleep."

"Or 10 o'clock."

"Nor 10 nor 11 o'clock. I should judge, however, that it was about 11 o'clock when I laid down."

"We understood it to be immediately after the conversation."

"Very soon after the conversation. Had it not been the intention of the general not to move until daylight, I should not have lain down."

"Did you hear all the conversation that took place between General Porter and the generals who were with him, at the time of your arrival, touching his determination when to start?"

"I am not aware that I heard all of it, neither do I remember the conversation—merely the impression derived from it."

"Try and recollect whether you heard anything said of the determination to start as early as 3 o'clock."

"I think that 'daylight' was the expression used; not any hour."

"At what time did you hear the reveille?"

"I did not hear it. I was awakened, I think, by the servant of General Porter, in whose tent I was sleeping."

"Was it a dark night when you went to sleep?"

"I think it was a cloudy night, but not dark."[6]

"Was there a moon that night?"

"I do not think so, at any time that I was up."

"Was it a starlight night?"

"I think not."

"Was it still dark when you were aroused from your slumbers in the morning?"

"I think it was just at dawn."

"We mean to inquire whether the darkness of the night still continued so as to be at that time a serious impediment to the movement of troops?"

"I cannot say. When I was awakened up, it was, I think, just at dawn, the day just breaking. I was invited to breakfast. Whether at that time we used candles, or whether it was light enough to take breakfast without, I do not remember."

After having considered several aspects of the events of that late August night, Johnson began to pull those lines of questioning together. He asked: "Having passed at about half-past 8 o'clock, at or near Catlett's Station, the last of the train of wagons proceeding from Warrenton Junction to Bristoe Station, why did you conclude that if General Porter got under way at 1 o'clock, that is, nearly five hours thereafter, he would still overtake those wagons with his troops before daybreak? Were they necessarily proceeding so slowly as that?"

"Wagons always proceed slowly where they are in large numbers."

"You spoke of a park of wagons near Warrenton Junction. Was that park vacant when General Porter's column passed it on the way to Bristoe Station?"

"I think that it was. I think there were wagons still there; but the main body of the train had left."

"Those wagons, then, which had left the park were proceeding toward Bristoe Station?"

"They were."

"They were moving very slowly?"

"Moving at the same rate as the others."

"Would not that, then, have constituted a serious obstacle to a rapid advance of troops by that road?"

"No, sir."

"Referring to what you have stated, of the great exertions of General Porter and his staff after daybreak to get the wagons out of the way of the advancing column, do we understand you now to testify that these last wagons of which you speak, being in front of the advancing column, would not constitute an obstacle to its movement?"

Captain DeKay replied: "As a train of wagons they would not constitute a great obstacle—an obstacle to some degree, of course. I did not state that General Porter used great exertions throughout the march. I said that he did at one or two points; at one or two points where the wagons had been stalled, or a number of them jammed up."

Johnson persisted: "Would not the presence of wagons on a road during a dark, moonless, and starless night have constituted a most serious impediment to the rapid advance of troops, either infantry or artillery?"

"I do not consider that that night was a dark night. I have stated that it was a cloudy night, that is, the moon, if there was a moon, was clouded over. The sky was cloudy; but it was not a dark night."[7]

Recognizing, perhaps, that the prosecution witness seemed determined to be unresponsive, Johnson closed his cross-examination. However, members of the Court (unnamed in the trial's record) had some questions:

COURT: Were you awake so as to speak of the character of the night after 11 o'clock and before you arose in the morning?

DEKAY: No, sir.

COURT: Do you know how often the column halted in the march and how long those halts were?

DEKAY: No, sir.

COURT: How long a time elapsed from the time the head of the column started from Warrenton Junction till the head of the column arrived at Bristoe Station?

DEKAY: I should judge from five to six hours. I cannot say positively.

COURT: Was the column closed up, or can you say whether the mass of the troops of the column, substantially, arrived at Bristoe at that time?

DEKAY: I cannot say; I acted as guide of the troops, and was at the head of the column all the time. The road runs through the woods a part of the way, and part of the way through an undulating country of small hills and valleys, so that I could not tell whether the troops were closed up or not.

COURT: Did any portion of the infantry march along the railroad track?

DEKAY: I think not. I am not aware that they did. Occasionally, in crossing runs, they would take the railroad track to avoid getting wet.

COURT: Did the artillery march with the column?

DEKAY: I presume in the rear of the column. I do not know.

3

In nine working days, two witnesses had testified. General Pope had made a number of statements that might well be contradicted in due course. Captain DeKay's testimony related only to events on the night of August 27 and the early morning of the 28th. Anyone who found the trial's progress glacial had ample cause.

An offset, of course, was that from then onward it would be interesting to see in what ways and to what degrees the testimonies of persons yet to be called would differ from what Pope and his aide had placed in the record. But there were several other anti-Porter officers waiting, and as the prosecution's third witness on Tuesday, December 9, the trial's tenth day, Judge-Advocate Holt presented Brigadier General Benjamin S. Roberts.[8]

After establishing Roberts' rank and former position, Holt began his examination:[9] "Did, or did not, your duties bring you near the person of General Pope, and make you familiar with his plans of operations and his orders?"

Roberts replied: "As chief of cavalry, I had quarters and was near the person of General Pope. As his inspector-general, I was near his person at his headquarters, and made very familiar with his plans and his operations."

Omitted was the fact that Roberts had prepared and filed the charges and specifications against Fitz John Porter.

Holt continued: "What knowledge, if any, have you of an order issued by Major-General Pope, on the 27th of August last, to Major General Porter, in reference to his movements?"

"At [Manassas Junction] General Pope dictated an order in my presence, and sent that order by an officer of his staff to General Porter. My recollection is that Captain DeKay was the officer who carried the order; and I think he left about dark—I should think half-past 6 or 7 o'clock. The order was written about sundown; and the hour at that season of the year was, I should think, about half-past 5—between that and 6 o'clock."

"State what was the character of that order."

Reverdy Johnson conceded that the order referred to by the witness to be the same as the one set forth in specification first of charge first.

Holt then asked the witness to state what he knew, if anything, in regard to any order or orders issued by Major General Pope to General Porter on the 29th of August, in reference to his movements.

"On the morning of the 29th," Roberts answered, "an order was directed to General McDowell and General Porter, severally, requiring them to move their forces from Manassas Junction in the direction of Gainesville, and to continue on the road leading from Manassas Junction toward Gainesville to a point which I inferred to be near Gainesville, but I do not know how near, and there they were to halt their commands."

Judge-Advocate Holt pointed out that the order referred to by General Roberts was the joint order set forth in specification second of the first charge. The witness continued:

"In this order I remember they were instructed not to proceed so far as to be unable, in case of necessity, to fall back behind Bull Run that night. This order gave to these generals a discretion of departing from its strict letter, if any great advantages were to be derived from such a departure; but it pressed upon them the importance of keeping in a position where they could fall back behind Bull Run that night, as it was believed by General Pope that they would be obliged to do so to get back to rations and supplies."

"What do you know, if anything, in regard to the order issued by General Pope to General Porter, set forth in the third specification of the first charge, bearing date 4:30 P.M. of the 29th August?"

"About 4:30 P.M. of the 29th of August it was supposed by General Pope that General Porter was near the field of battle. The direction in which the first order required him to move would have brought him, as was supposed, near the field of battle before that hour; and I had noticed, in the direction where I knew General Porter was expected, the flash and the smoke from some pieces of artillery, and I inferred it to be artillery from General Porter, who was expected to attack there about that time. But it very soon ceased, and General Pope then wrote another order to General Porter, which, according to my recollection, stated that the direction of his movement would bring him on the enemy's right flank or rear, and that he wished him to press forward and attack immediately."

"Will you state what you know, if anything, in regard to General Porter's having either obeyed or disobeyed those orders?"

"I know that General Porter did not attack, as he was directed to attack in that order. I was on that part of the field several times, and was expecting every minute that the attack would be made, and was watching for it with a great deal of anxiety, but it was not made."

"Did you continue upon the field until the engagement closed?"

"I was on the field all day, and remained on the field all that night."[10]

"What were the results of the battle when the night closed in?

"General Pope's troops, when night closed in, occupied quite a portion of the field from which the enemy had been driven, and, in my opinion, although the battle was not a decisive one, the advantages of the day were in favor of General Pope's army."

"In view of what the army had accomplished during the battle of the day in the absence of General Porter's command, what do you suppose would have been the result upon the fortunes of the battle if General Porter had attacked, as ordered by the order of 4:30 P.M., either on the right flank or the rear of the enemy?"

Counsel for the Accused, recalling no doubt objections the prosecution had made to his questions thought to be calling for opinions, objected to Holt's question. Doors closed, the Court deliberated, and after the doors were opened the judge-advocate announced that the Court had decided that the question would be answered.

General Roberts declared: "I do not doubt at all that it would have resulted in the defeat, if not in the capture, of the main army of the Confederates that were on the field at that time."[11]

Holt continued: "What do you know, if anything, in regard to the order set forth in the fourth specification of the first charge, addressed by Major-General Pope to the Accused, which was as follows:

> HEADQUARTERS ARMY OF VIRGINIA,
> *In the Field, near Bull Run, August 29, 1862—8.50 p.m.*
>
> Maj. Gen. F. J. PORTER:
>
> GENERAL: Immediately upon receipt of this order, the precise hour of receiving which you will acknowledge, you will march your command to the field of battle of to-day, and report to me in person for orders. You are to understand that you are expected to comply strictly with this order, and to be present on the field within three hours after its reception, or after daybreak to-morrow morning.

Roberts replied: "I know that that order was dispatched to General Porter by an aide-de-camp or a staff officer of General Pope at about 8:30 o'clock in the evening of Friday, the 29th of August. I know that General Porter in person reported to General Pope on the field in obedience to that order, and that a part of his command was brought onto the field on the morning of the 30th."

"Do you know what part of his command he failed to bring upon the field under this order?"

"I do not know, of my own knowledge, what part of his command he failed to bring onto the field. I know that there were parts of his command that I did not see on the field during that day—the 30th August."

"Have you at any time had any conversation with the Accused in regard to these orders?"

"I have not."[12]

At this point, Judge-Advocate Holt handed the witness over to counsel for the Accused, who asked Roberts: "Will [you] state at about what hour the battle of the 29th of August ceased?"

"It was some time after dark; I should think quite as late as half-past 7 or 8 o'clock."

"Do [you] know at what hour General Porter, on the 29th of August, received the order bearing date of 4:30 P.M. of that day?"

"I do not know."

With preliminaries established, Reverdy Johnson's questioning took on added point. "[Given your] having spoken of [your] expectation of an attack to be made upon the enemy by General Porter, are we to understand that [you] expected such an attack to be made prior to the issue of the order of 4:30 P.M. August 29?"

"Yes, sir; that is what I intend the Court and the Accused to understand, and for the reason that I had supposed that any general within hearing of an important battle, in whose power it was to engage in it, would do so; and I had supposed that General Porter's line of march from Manassas Junction would have brought him onto the right of the enemy's lines before 4 o'clock, and I had supposed that he would attack on coming onto those lines."

Johnson pressed harder: "Under what order was General Porter acting on the 29th of August, prior to the issue of the order of 4:30 P.M. of that day?"

"I do not know that he was acting under any special order; but I supposed that the order that directed him to move in that direction was sufficient authority for General Porter to engage in the action."

Johnson, again: "Having described various specifications in that joint order in your testimony-in-chief, *no mention has been made of any specification directing an attack*, but, on the contrary, of a specification *directing a halt*, and a halt in such a position as to *reach Bull Run that night*; [do you consider] that joint order to have been in force up to the time when the order of 4:30 P.M. was issued?"

And Roberts' reply: "There was discretion in that order which, in my estimation, would have authorized General Porter to have joined, at any time during the fight of the afternoon of the 29th, in that fight when he could have done it to advantage. And, in my estimation, any general has the discretion, in the nature of things, when an important action is going on, to join in it, and he is bound to do it."

"Did not the joint order *specially exclude* from the discretion of Generals Porter and McDowell the necessity of their remaining in such position as to enable them to fall back behind Bull Run?"

A member of the Court objected, with the usual result when Reverdy Johnson was interrogating a prosecution witness: Roberts did not have to answer.

Johnson restated the question, encountered another objection, then tried again:

"It being, in your judgment, the plain duty of General Porter to have attacked prior to the reception of the order of 4:30 P.M. of the 29th of August, what explanation do you give of the fact that the order of 4:30 P.M. prescribed a single specified form of attack, with the positive condition that the attack should be made in such manner as not to sever connection with General Reynolds on the right?"[13]

"As I understood the relation of General Reynolds' Pennsylvania Reserves to the enemy's right, General Porter's having attacked the right of the enemy, would have brought him in closer connection with Reynolds' left."

"Will you inform the Court whether, at any time in the course of the day of the 29th of August, you saw the command of the Accused and the enemy in such a position as to make an attack by General Porter upon the flank or rear of the enemy possible?"

"I did not see General Porter's command on the field on Friday, the

29th of August. But I suppose that I know nearly the position where General Porter's command was between 4 and 5 o'clock, and I supposed that I had seen smoke from guns of his command. I know the direction of the road from Manassas Junction to the field of battle, and, in my opinion, General Porter was in a position where he could have moved forward and have attacked the right of the enemy; and I also believe that he could have turned the enemy's right flank and attacked their rear, from what I know of their relative positions and from what I know of the country."

"Between 4 and 5 o'clock P.M. of the 29th of August, did [you] know whether or not Longstreet's forces, in whole or in part, had made junction with Jackson, on Jackson's right?"

"I did not know; but I had reason to believe that they had not made junction, as I had been requested by General Pope, before going on to the field, while at Centreville in the morning, to take a position, and with a glass to observe whether troops were moving from the direction of Thoroughfare Gap to Gainesville; and having closely observed that country for a long time, I became convinced from the clouds of dust that arose above the Bull Run range beyond Thoroughfare Gap, toward a gap north of Thoroughfare Gap, the name of which I now forget, that Longstreet was moving very rapidly to get through that northern gap and to re-enforce Jackson. But, from the distance from the head of the column of dust to Gainesville, I did not believe that he would be able to effect a junction before late in the evening, and so reported to General Pope."

"Such having been [your] opinion during the day of the 29th of August, will [you] please state whether up to the present time [you] have become satisfied that Longstreet's forces, in whole or in part, did effect such junction with Jackson's right in the afternoon—say between 5 and 6 o'clock, or before that time—on the 29th of August?"

"I am convinced, by information that I have received since that day, that a part of Longstreet's forces effected a junction with Jackson in the evening of the 29th—I think about dark."

"Please state your judgment as to the number of troops of Longstreet thus effecting a junction."

"As I understand, about seventeen battalions."

"Numbering, in all, about how many men?"

"Between 4,000 and 5,000 men."

"From what you know of the position of General Porter's command and of Jackson's right, would that junction of Longstreet's troops bring the enemy in front of General Porter's force?"

"If General Porter's force was on the road leading from Manassas Junction to Gainesville, where I supposed it was, and they had moved toward the right of Jackson's forces, it would have brought him upon the leading column of Longstreet's forces that came in."

"In front of that column?"

"They would have met each other coming in opposite directions on the same road."[14]

Matador Johnson had brought another bull to *la hora de verdad.*

"Would it not, then," he asked, "in that state of facts, have been materially impossible for General Porter to have outflanked and attacked the enemy, and at the same time to have kept up his connection with Reynolds on his right?"

"I can give merely an *opinion* on that subject."

"I ask the *fact* as it would appear from the dispositions of the forces there."

"My opinion is, that the fact that [you] stated would not have been impossible; but that General Porter's force was sufficient to have defeated Longstreet's, and to have attacked the right of Jackson's forces, and to have turned their rear."

"From your knowledge of the position of the troops of the enemy and of General Porter's command, will you state what distance General Porter must have marched to have made such an attack on the right flank of the enemy?"

"If General Porter's troops were in the position where I saw the flash of cannon and the smoke on the road between Gainesville and Manassas Junction, he could have reached the right of the enemy and turned its rear in less than one hour, in my judgment."

"At half-past 6 or 7 o'clock P.M. on that day, at the time when [you] suppose the junction by Longstreet's forces to have been effected, was it not becoming dark?"

"It was."

"During the hour's march necessary to effect an attack in flank, the darkness, of course, would have increased; would such a march and such an attack at that hour and in such darkness as would then prevail have been possible?"

"[You] make a supposition which is not founded upon any fact which I have stated, and I cannot properly answer the question without a better understanding of its meaning."

"Please point out the supposition made in the question which you refer to."

"I have been supposing that at 5 o'clock, by which time I supposed this last order had reached General Porter, that he was within an hour's march of the enemy's right flank, which would have brought him on that flank by 6 o'clock, and it would not then have been too dark to have made the attack."

Johnson pressed: "Have we not understood [you] correctly in understanding [you] to say that [you] did not know at what hour the order of 4:30 P.M. reached General Porter?"

"I do not know, except by information. I meant to say that I did not know the fact; but, from information, I believe it to have reached him before 5 o'clock."

"[Were you] present with General Pope when General Pope issued the order of 4:30 P.M. of the 29th of August?"

"I was present with him when the order was issued."

"[Were you] then of the opinion that that order could reach General Porter in a half an hour after it was written?

"It could have reached him in less than that time as orders are generally carried on such occasions."

"Do [you] know the fact that at about 5 o'clock on that day a messenger, and aide-de-camp, I think, from General Porter, came to General Pope to ask for orders?"

"I do not."[15]

"[Do you] know whether, on the 29th of August, it was a leading part of General Pope's plan of operations to fall back behind Bull Run, or immediately before that day, on the 27th or 28th?"

A member of the Court observed that General Pope himself, when on the stand, would have been the best witness of whom to have asked that question. Reverdy Johnson waived the question; he had surprised Roberts, and while the witness was shaken Johnson added to his confusion by changing the thrust of his interrogation.

"Did it occur [to you]," Johnson asked, "that [you] at any time, on or about the 27th, 28th, or 29th of August, made statements to General Pope touching the probability that General Porter would fail him, or touching the fidelity of General Porter to his duty as an officer?"

"After General Porter failed to march at 1 o'clock on the morning of the 28th of August, in compliance with General Pope's orders, it occurred to me that General Porter might fail General Pope, for the reason that I had never conceived that an officer who failed to obey so plain an order would do his duty. And when General Porter failed to attack on Friday, the 29th, when I expected he would attack, and when I know General Pope expected he would attack, that impression of mine was made still stronger that he would not do his duty. I may have suggested to General Pope my impression that he better not rely on General Porter; but I do not now recollect that I did state that to him."

"Is it true, in any event, that prior to the action taken by General Porter under the order of the 27th of August, [you] made any such statements touching the fidelity of General Porter to General Pope?"

"I made none prior to that time, and prior to that time I had felt convinced that General Porter would not only do his duty, but I was of the impression that he would do it as well as any officer in the army could do it."

"Then the grounds, and all the grounds, of any such unfavorable suggestions [you] made, if any were made, are simply the judgment [you] formed of the events with which General Porter was connected on the 27th and on the 29th of August?"

"They were not the only grounds, as, on the 28th, while at Manassas Junction, an officer of the army, a major general whose name it is not necessary for me to mention, in a conversation that I had with him, in which I mentioned General Porter and the high estimation in which I had held him, told me that I did not know him, and told me that he would fail General Pope. The disobedience of the orders, and this conversation, led me up to the opinion that General Porter was not doing his duty in good faith to General Pope."

"Had you heard such unfavorable surmise or report concerning General Porter prior to the 28th of August?"

"I had not."

"Did you on that day hear it from any other person than the major general to whom you have referred?"

"I do not remember that I did."

"We must ask you, then, to give us the name of this major general with whom you had this conversation."

"It was Major General Philip Kearny."[16]

"Was anyone present at that conversation between yourself and General Kearny, or during any part of it?"

"There were several officers in the vicinity; but General Kearny and myself were withdrawn, I think, at the time, some little distance from the other officers."

"Do you suppose the conversation to have been loud enough to have been within the hearing of any one of the other officers?"

"It is possible that it was."[17]

"Can you tell us who those officers were, as nearly as you can recollect?"

"General Pope was near by, and several officers of his staff."

Johnson pressed again: "Try and recollect the names of any you can recollect."

"I do not know as I can mention any names. There were five or six officers of his staff with him."

Such an unresponsive answer invited sarcasm: "You know, of course, who were the officers of his staff?"

"Yes, sir."

"Who were they, at that time?"

"Colonel Ruggles was chief of his staff officers."

Not good enough. "State the names of such officers of the staff as, from their avocations and positions on the staff, would have been likely to have been with General Pope at that time."

"Colonel Ruggles, I think, was with General Pope at the time, and Captain Douglass Pope, I think, and Colonel Morgan and Colonel Welch; from their avocations they would have been most likely to have been there at that time. Several of the staff officers were absent—had been sent off."

Johnson asked a few more questions regarding the weather and other limiting conditions during the night of August 27–28, predictably drawing answers in line with those given to similar queries earlier by General Pope and Captain DeKay. Examination of General Roberts by Judge-Advocate

Holt resumed briefly, then members of the Court probed the Accuser of record mainly for clarification.

One inquiry, however, moved the testimony onto new ground. "Had, or had not," a member asked, "the fact of the retreat of General Porter on the evening of the 29th of August been communicated to General Pope previous to his order of 8:50 P.M. of that day?"

General Roberts replied. "I have reason to believe that it had not. I was with General Pope when he received the information, on a note or on a piece of paper, from General Porter that he was retreating back to Manassas, and stating the reasons why he was falling back; but previous to that time I do not believe that General Pope knew that he was falling back."

"What time was it when he received that note?"

"I think it was between 8 and 9 o'clock at night; probably half-past 8 o'clock."

"Did the note you have just referred to state whether General Porter was falling back, or had determined to do so, and was himself going to the front?"

"The substance of the note was this, that seeing clouds of dust advancing, and knowing that the enemy had massed in his front cavalry, artillery, and infantry, he had determined to fall back to Manassas."[18] The note, addressed to Generals McDowell and King, was then read.[19]

Just at the point where those present in the courtroom seeking entertainment might have expected some fireworks, the Court adjourned.

4

During Day Eleven, Wednesday, December 11, 1862, two men who had acted as messengers testified. The first was General Pope's nephew and aide, Captain Douglass Pope, who had delivered the 4:30 order to General Porter late on the afternoon of August 29. He was followed as a witness by Union army surgeon Robert A. Abbott, bearer of the joint order to McDowell and Porter earlier on that day.

Both were prosecution witnesses. Apparently, Judge-Advocate Holt's objective had been to establish times of orders' delivery to Porter, locations and existing conditions on those occasions, routes followed, distances to and from General Pope, and Porter's reactions as the messengers had perceived and now recalled them. Holt and even Reverdy Johnson derived little from their interrogations. Replies such as "I don't know" or "I don't recall" and variations thereupon predominated.

Members of the Court, all general officers, may well have been inclined to disregard the testimony rendered by young Douglass Pope, whose only distinction was the nepotism that had made him a participant, and also the availability of a surgeon whose mission at the time he was obliged to act as a message deliverer was to move medical supplies forward to Porter's Fifth Corps in an ambulance wagon in anticipation of fighting.

However, Abbott's participation in the early morning march of Porter's Fifth Corps from Warrenton Junction toward Bristoe Station on August 28 may well have caused Judge-Advocate Holt to wish he had not called this witness. The surgeon's recollection of road and weather conditions directly contradicted that of Major General John Pope.

Moreover, near the end of Surgeon Abbott's tenure in the witness chair, for the first time "the Accused" himself asked a few questions:

PORTER: I wish you to state what were my relations to you during our march, and whether they were of an intimate character or not.

ABBOTT: We were always on very friendly and free terms.

PORTER: If I ever manifested at that time during the march, either in conversation or in spirit, any disposition to trammel the movements of any portion of the army, or in any manner whatever to disobey any order, would you be likely to have known it?

ABBOTT: I think I should have known it.

PORTER: Did I ever manifest in any manner any other disposition than to do my duty fully?

ABBOTT: Never, as far as I saw or heard.[20]

On Day Twelve of the trial, Thursday, December 11, 1862, Judge-Advocate Holt opened the session by asking the usual establishing questions of the sworn witness *du jour*, Lieutenant Colonel Thomas C. H. Smith. Understandably, those queries did not develop certain circumstances—specifically, that Smith was a lawyer with no known qualifications for having been commissioned a field grade officer except that he may have been related to General Pope.[21]

With Thursday's session just beginning, Holt invited Colonel Smith to tell the Court about his first encounter with General Porter. "I had been sent back to the ammunition on the train at Bristoe," the witness began, "and charged with its distribution. General Porter wished over 400,000 rounds. About 2 or 3 o'clock I had sent forward to General Porter some 320,000 rounds. I went on to find General Pope. I found he had moved on, and, to inquire the road he had taken, I went to General Porter's headquarters, near the Manassas water station. I found General Porter in his tent, and asked him which road General Pope had taken, and he informed me. I had some ten minutes' conversation with him."

Judge-Advocate Holt asked Smith to state that conversation.

"After asking him about the road, I told General Porter the amount of ammunition that I had sent forward to him, and also that the balance would come immediately forward. I asked him if he had received it, or made some remark; I cannot remember the exact expression. General Porter said that he had not; that was the substance of his reply—either that he had received hardly any of it, or none of it, if I remember aright.

"I expressed some surprise, and said that it had been sent forward to the front, as ordered; and, either in reply to some question of mine or to some remark, or of himself, he said that he had no officers to take charge of it and distribute it, or look it up, or something of that kind. I remarked that he could hardly expect us at headquarters to be able to send officers to distribute it in his corps; that it had been sent forward on the road, in the direction where his corps was. He replied that it was going where it belonged; that it was on the road to Alexandria, where we were aligning.

"I do not know as it is evidence to give the spirit in which this was said—the way it impressed me. Those remarks were made in a sneering manner, and appeared to me to express a great indifference.

"There was then a pause for a moment. General Porter then spoke in regard to the removal of the sick and wounded from the field of Kettle Run. He said it would hurt Pope, leaving the wounded behind. I told him that they were not to be left behind; that I knew that a positive order—an imperative order—had been given to General Banks to bring all the wounded with him, and for that purpose to throw property out of the wagons if necessary.

"To this General Porter made no reply in words; but his manner to me expressed the same feeling that I had noticed before. This conversation, from General Porter's manner and look, made a strong impression on my mind. I left him, as I have said, after an interview of about ten minutes, and rode on, arriving at our headquarters on Bull Run just as we entered them and pitched our tents for the night.

"After my tent was pitched, and I had had something to eat, I went over to General Pope, and reported to him briefly what I had done in regard to the ammunition. I then said to him, 'General, I saw General Porter on my way here.' Said he, 'Well, sir?' I said, 'General, he will fail you.' 'Fail me?' said he; 'what do you mean? What did he say?'

"Said I, 'It is not so much what he said, though he said enough; he is going to fail you.' These expressions I repeat, I think I remember them with exactness, for I was excited at the time from the impression that had been made upon me.

"Said General Pope, 'How can he fail me? He will fight where I put him;' or, 'He must fight where I put him'—one of those expressions. This General Pope said with a great deal of feeling, and impetuously and perhaps overbearingly, and in an excited manner.

"I replied in the same way, saying that I was so certain that Fitz John Porter was a traitor, that I would shoot him that night, so far as any crime before God was concerned, if the law would allow me to do it.

"I speak of this to show the conviction that I received from General Porter's manner and expressions in that interview. I have only to add that my prepossessions of him were favorable, as it was at headquarters, up to that time. I never had entertained any impression against him until that conversation. I knew nothing with regard to his orders to move up to Kettle Run, and I knew nothing of any failure on his part to comply with any orders."

Holt asked: "In the conversation to which you refer, did, or did not, General Porter manifest any anxiety to get possession of, and have distributed in his corps, the ammunition of which you speak?"

"No, sir; I thought he showed an utter indifference upon the subject; showed it very plainly."[22]

"At what hour of the day did this conversation between you and General Porter take place?"

"I think it must have been about 4 o'clock in the afternoon; half-past 3 or 4 o'clock."

"In anything that was said in that conversation or in the manner of General Porter, was there evidenced any desire or any willingness on his part to support General Pope in the military operations in which he was then engaged?"

"Quite the contrary to that."

"Can you state whether the disinclination to support General Pope, which you thought he manifested, was the result of disgust with the immediate service in which he was then engaged, or of hostility to the commanding general, or upon what did it seem to rest?"

Joseph Holt had cast his net wide. But Smith narrowed the question, responding: "It seemed to me to rest on hostility. But I do not know that I could analyze the impression that was made upon me. I conveyed it to General Pope in the words that I have stated. I had one of those clear convictions that a man has a few times, perhaps, in his life, as to the character and purposes of a person whom he sees for the first time. No man can express altogether how such an impression is gained from looks and manner, but it is clear."[23]

Suddenly, Judge-Advocate Holt moved away from this fascinating line of questioning to geography: conditions of the road from Warrenton Junction to Bristoe Station. Then, in another switch, Holt asked whether or not a battle had been raging at 5 P.M. on August 29.

Smith's reply: "Yes, sir; severely."

Holt then asked, "Are you sufficiently acquainted with the disposition of the forces under General Pope, and of those of the enemy at that hour, to express an opinion as to what would have been the effect of an attack by General Porter's corps upon the right flank of the enemy at between 5 and 6 o'clock P.M. of that day?"[24]

Reverdy Johnson had not objected at several points of Colonel Smith's windy testimony, but Holt's last question was more than he could abide. Doors closed, then opened, and the judge-advocate announced that the decision of the Court—predictably—was that the witness shall answer the question.

"I do not know as I am sufficiently acquainted with the numbers and disposition of the enemy to give a conclusive answer in regard to that," Smith replied. "I can give my view of it, and give the reasons why I think a flank attack would have been successful. The enemy were fighting a defensive battle."

Reverdy Johnson suggested to the Court that in view of the doubts the witness had said regarding his knowledge of the number and disposition of the Confederates, it was improper for him to continue with his answer. Smith was told to proceed.

"Their right lay near the turnpike road between Warrenton and Centreville," the witness recalled. "The main force, from which they were detached for the time being, were off toward Thoroughfare Gap, or beyond it. [Jackson's] position was a strong one for defense in front, and in the direction in which the three corps of Sigel, Heintzelman, and Reno were fighting them.

"Far and back from the front they had a line of retreat toward Thoroughfare Gap, toward their main force. The direction of a flank attack moving on the road from Manassas to Gainesville, and then moving in upon their flank, was such as to cut off their line of retreat. We drove them off the ground as it was.

"I believe that if the attack had been made on their flank at that time, exhausted as they were by the fighting through the day, it would have made the defeat a rout, by striking them on their line of retreat toward their main forces, and rolling them up on Bull Run and the east of the Gum Spring road, and so on in that direction.

"In saying that I did not know their disposition sufficiently to give a conclusive answer, I meant, of course, that I did not know the amount of those on their right. But from the fact that all our attack had been directed with our left resting on that road, and their right apparently resting there, I supposed that if they had had a heavy force beyond that road they would have attempted a flank attack upon us.

"The appearance of the field was such as to lead one to suppose that the entire force of the enemy, except, perhaps, something thrown out to guard that flank, was right in front of us on those ridges. That was where all their artillery fire was, and there was where the fight continued daring the day. They were fighting in that position, with their backs toward their main force. Of course, though we might drive them off the field, we could accomplish not any great success, with their great force in the rear and off beyond Thoroughfare Gap.

"This [Porter's] flank attack was the main attack to decide the battle, by striking them quartering on the flank and cutting off their line of retreat, so that they could not unite with their main force in that direction."[25]

Judge-Advocate Holt asked: "You have no knowledge of General Porter's position with his command during the 29th of August?"

"I have not. I could mention one more fact, that of seeing clouds of dust, as indicating the march of some forces toward Centreville, as near as I could judge."

Holt drew from the witness some vague answers to questions that seemed crafted to suggest that the dust clouds were being raised by Porter's retreating troops. Having given the Court a great deal of well-rehearsed testimony to evaluate, Holt then turned the witness over to counsel for the Accused.

Reverdy Johnson's opening questions established that Thomas C. H. Smith was a volunteer officer with no prior military service or education prior to August 1861, whose only early battle experience had been as a lieutenant colonel of an Ohio regiment in John Pope's corps during Henry Halleck's nigh-bloodless Corinth Campaign back in May.[26]

Johnson linked Smith and Pope by asking the witness when he joined the force of General Pope during his campaign in Virginia. "Somewhere about the 9th of July last here in Washington," Smith replied.

"When for the first time," Johnson asked, "did you see the Accused?"

"On the day I speak of. I do not remember ever having seen him before that interview on the 28th of August."[27]

"Were you acquainted with the Accused [by reputation] when you saw him on the 28th, and did you know what his services had been in the army during this rebellion?"

"Nothing more than I had heard Colonel Marshall at our headquarters speak of him; and also other officers at our headquarters."

"Favorably or otherwise?"

"Favorably."

"Have you had any interview with the Accused since the 28th of August?"

"I do not remember of having had any interview with him. I have met him occasionally, and spoken to him, not to amount to anything, or to make any impression on my mind. I do not think I have exchanged a half a dozen words with him."

"When you have seen him since, and when, as you say, you have spoken to him occasionally, did you exchange the usual civilities between officers and gentlemen?"

"I believe I have. I may have omitted it from absent-mindedness. I believe I have always exchanged them."

"If you did it, *when you did it*, were you then under the impression that the Accused had been a traitor in the Pope campaign?"

"Yes, sir; and I have not changed that impression."

Reverdy Johnson devoted a number of questions to develop how and why Smith had visited General Porter's headquarters on August 28. The answers amounted to this: Smith's main purpose had been to inquire regarding the road General Pope had taken; he may also have intended to have asked Porter in regard to the ammunition.

Then Johnson asked, "Are you to be understood now to say that you were under the impression, when you afterward saw the Accused, that he was indifferent whether he had the ammunition or not?"

"Yes, sir."

"That opinion you derived exclusively from what you have termed his sneering manner, or was it from his manner in other particulars that were not sneering?"

"I do not wish to say that his manner was not gentlemanly and courteous, as it was throughout; but—and I stated so—there was his indifferent and sneering manner in regard to these matters of which I spoke. I do not know as I understood indifference in regard to the ammunition so much as his general indifference in regard to the success of General Pope in that campaign.

"I am speaking now, of course, of my impression from the whole interview. The first impression of that kind I received was from his reply in regard to the ammunition, which was also increased by the whole look and manner of the man."

"Do I understand you now to say that, from your present recollection, you do not remember that his manner was sneering?"

"No, sir, I do not say that. I am meaning to make a distinction from rudeness; his manner was not rude or insulting—nothing of that kind."

"In relation to what did you understand him as sneering at all—from anything that he said?"

"I do not know that a person can know to what a sneer is directed. All his expressions in regard to ammunition, and in regard to other matters, gave me the impression that his manner was sneering; that it was indifferent. If the object is to know about the impression that was made upon my mind, I will say that it was that of indifference and hostility to the success of General Pope. The sneers, among other things, gave me that impression."[28]

"If his answers and conversation with you during the whole interview were not only not rude, but polite and courteous, will you say *in what* there could have been any sneering according to your recollection?"

"By sneering, I refer to the manner."

"Can you describe the manner in words?"

"I do not know that I could describe it any better than to say that it was a sneering, indifferent manner and tone. As for the sneering, it was somewhat suppressed."

Reverdy Johnson had reached another of those questions that test a witness's nerves as well as his memory and cunning. "Without having ever before seen him," he asked, "and, of course, without knowing what his manner in conversation was habitually, how are you able to tell that his manner upon that occasion was not his usual manner?"

"I am able distinctly to tell," Smith replied, "because that manner and tone were whenever he spoke of anything connected with this matter of the ammunition, and the matter of General Pope's conduct in leaving the wounded; it was when he spoke of those matters connected with General Pope."

Smith's answer was unresponsive and Johnson pressed him: "You seem not to have understood the meaning of my question. I will repeat it: Without having ever before seen him, and without knowing what his manner in conversation was habitually, how are you able to tell that his manner upon that occasion was not his usual manner?"

"I thought I understood that question, and I have answered it. I would be glad to have my attention called to anything in that question that I have not answered."

Johnson accommodated the witness he had just shaken: "What the Accused wants to know is, how it was possible for you, who never before had seen him or conversed with him until this occasion, to have known that his manner of conversation then was not his usual manner?"

"I presume his manner and conversation then, when he spoke of other matters than in regard to those connected with our moving back to Alexandria, and with regard to the care of the wounded at Kettle Run, was his usual manner; but I have no means of knowing whether or not it was his usual manner. There was nothing in that connection that showed the tone I spoke of. While this tone and manner that I speak of was more distinct in regard to these two points I have mentioned, I do not wish to be understood as saying that I did not receive the same continuous impression all through the conversation, after the remarks about the ammunition, in regard to the character of the man. Of course, I cannot remember distinctly about that."

Utter gibberish: the predictable consequence for a witness whose coaches had not anticipated *everything* a lawyer of Reverdy Johnson's skill and experience might ask him. Counsel for the Accused then employed indirection and diversion, returning to the false issue of the ammunition and then Smith's awareness of the presence of Longstreet's forces and General Lee in Jackson's vicinity on the afternoon of August 29. Finally, matador Johnson had another occasion to raise his *muleta* and aim his *espada* over it—and then lunging.

"If Jackson's corps was the one immediately in front of our forces," he asked Smith, "and of that portion of our forces commanded by the Accused, and Longstreet's corps had united with Jackson's corps on his right, are you sufficiently acquainted with the character of the country, and the position in which the Accused was with his corps, to be enabled to say that he could have, after that junction, attacked the enemy's right in flank and in rear?"

"From the general character of the country there," Smith replied, hedging, "although I do not know the nature of the ground immediately between the Gainesville road and the right of the enemy, I infer that the corps of the Accused could have moved up, its right joining with the forces engaged, and have flanked the enemy. It is based, also, on the fact that that portion of the country over which, as I understand it, the corps of the Accused would have moved upon the enemy, was sufficiently practicable to enable the enemy, as they did, to make a similar movement upon our left on the next day."

Johnson asked Colonel Smith to designate upon the map the exact trace, as near as he could, along which the Confederates attacked General Pope's left on Saturday, August 30. Smith complied. He also answered a number of Johnson's questions regarding Porter's conduct, most of which Smith found admirable, during that day's disaster.

Then it was time for Reverdy Johnson to wrap something else that was unexpected around Smith's neck. He asked: "Do you know what distance the Accused would have had to have marched in order to carry out the order of 4:30 P.M. of the 29th, if he received it, and if he received it at 5 o'clock?"

"It would depend on where his corps was. I cannot tell what distance he would have had to have marched."

Ignoring Smith's unresponsive response, Johnson went directly for his jugular: "Having stated that you had no knowledge of the Accused personally until your interview with him on the 28th of August, and such as was obtained during that interview, which you say was some fifteen minutes long, are you to be understood now as thinking that you were justified in giving the opinion, and in now maintaining it—looking to the past history of the Accused during the present war—that he was a traitor to the cause of his country?"

Thomas C. H. Smith's answer was forthright: "I have as clear an opinion as I had at that time in regard to General Porter, although not as vivid. I think that General Porter was determined so far not to co-operate as to force us back to Washington—to compel us to give back. In using the expression that General Porter was a traitor, which I used to General Pope, I am not aware that I considered in my mind the term as meaning treason to the country, or whether I analyzed in my mind what his motives were, any more than I had gained, as I have said, the impression that he was indifferent to the fate of the campaign as regarded General Pope. In regard to the matter, I do not now remember that I then thought out or came to any conclusion as to whether it was general treason.

"The conviction on my mind was that he would fail General Pope. That failure had to do with his personal relations to General Pope, that is, that General Pope was to be made to fail in that campaign, because these expressions—this sneering, as I have termed it—were connected, as I have said, with these matters in regard to General Pope.

"I cannot say that I came at that time, or have now come, to any conviction that General Porter was a traitor to his country. That expression, as I used it at that time, must be taken with the context. In that point of view, I considered him a traitor; it was treason to fail to support the commanding general.

"I do not doubt that the expression *traitor* was a heated expression, used under excitement, and that the impression on my mind would have been expressed sufficiently by having said that he would fail General Pope."

Johnson then asked: "Was there anything in the words actually spoken by the Accused in your interview with him, independent of the manner in which they were spoken, to lead you to the conviction that he was a traitor, or would act traitorously to General Pope? If there was, state what the words were, as near as you can recollect."[29]

"The first words were his indifference in regard to the distribution of the ammunition, saying he had no officers to send. Then his expression, showing that he supposed it a settled matter that we were going back to Alexandria—were to be driven back—saying that it was just as well that the ammunition had gone where it belonged—in the direction where we were going. The expressions were of that kind.

"I cannot remember the exact words, but that was the substantial character of them. Those expressions, combined with the look and manner of the man, led me to that conviction; looked to me like those of a man with a crime on his mind. Those expressions attracted my attention, and probably led me to examine and look at the face and notice the eye and manner of the Accused."

"Are you able to say now whether those expressions alone, without regard to what you supposed to have been the manner of the Accused, would have led you to the opinion of the Accused that you have stated?"

"I think the tone would have led me to that conviction. I cannot answer the question more distinctly than I have. The impression is all one. I will endeavor to make any further explanation if it is of any use."

Very well, Johnson seemed to have assumed by asking: "Are you to be understood as having said seriously that, if there was no human law to prevent it, you would have killed the Accused, because of what had occurred at the interview of which you have spoken?"

"I am to be understood as having said that," Smith admitted. "That was the feeling I had at that time." And he added something new: "I did not ride away from the Accused with that feeling. I suppose it was aroused, perhaps, by the manner in which General Pope took my opinion in regard to the Accused; I became more vehement, perhaps, and took a stronger expression."

Johnson, lending emphasis to the witness's concession by turning beyond it, asked: "Will you state, as exactly as you can, what the Accused said to you in relation to the sick and wounded?"

"I think his first expression was, that 'it would hurt Pope, leaving the wounded behind.' I then told him that they were not left behind; that positive orders had been given to General Banks in regard to it; that I had seen the order."[30]

It would hurt General Pope, leaving the wounded behind. What a perfect point, Reverdy Johnson must have thought, at which to terminate for the time being the cross-examination of a man who had just shot himself in the foot! Why should Fitz John Porter have expressed any concern whatsoever for Pope's reputation if indeed he harbored any traitorous intent at all to *fail* the Army of Virginia's commander?

But the trial's twelfth day was not quite over. A member of the Court asked Colonel Smith a penetrating and acutely pertinent question: "In using the expression 'traitor' in connection with General Porter, did you bear in mind the character of a traitor in connection with the definition of treason in law?"

"No, sir; it was, as I have said, a vehement, excited expression, founded on my conviction that General Porter was going to fail us; that it was his purpose to do so."

"Supposing that General Porter's corps had been at the junction of the Manassas Railroad with the road from Sudley Springs south, on the 29th of August, at 5 P.M., how long would it have taken that corps to have reached the right flank of the enemy, had it been moved with promptness and rapidity?

"I have never been over the country at that point," Smith replied. "I only know the general character of the country. I should say that that was about 3 miles from the right flank of the enemy; and I think, from the nature of the country, as far as I saw it, it could have been accomplished, with activity, in an hour."[31]

Surely, Judge-Advocate Joseph Holt welcomed the sharp sound of Radical David Hunter's gavel ending the self-exposed Pope puppet's inept performance and the twelfth day's work. Yet Holt could be grateful for one thing: Reverdy Johnson had not drawn out the fact that Lieutenant Colonel Smith had been appointed a brigadier general on November 29, 1862[32]—Day Three of the Porter court-martial—and that consummation of this jump promotion depended upon the urgency Secretary of War Stanton and his good friends in Congress chose to devote to its confirmation.

CHAPTER SEVEN

THE TRUTH ACCORDING TO IRVIN MCDOWELL

MAJOR General John Pope's return to Saint Paul so early in the trial had been a sign of his assurance that Benjamin Roberts and Thomas C. H. Smith could and would assist Judge-Advocate Holt to their fullest extents in prosecuting Fitz John Porter. From Day Ten through Day Twelve, indeed they had. So had aides Drake DeKay and nephew Douglass Pope, or at least they had done the prosecution's case no great harm. Reverdy Johnson's cross-examinations of Smith and Roberts had called the Court's attention to the extraordinary mind-reading powers Smith professed to have. But Porter *had* failed General Pope, five witnesses had declared or implied, and now as Day Thirteen, December 12, 1862, had arrived, Holt was certain that the testimony of Major General Irvin McDowell would provide more than enough evidence to convince the Court that Porter was guilty and fully deserved the harshest of punishments.

As usual after swearing-in a new witness, Judge Advocate Holt asked Irvin McDowell to state his position in the military service of the United States. McDowell's reply was as much a matter of form as the question; he was a major-general of volunteers and a brigadier-general in the Regular Army, "so called." But he might have gone beyond such well-known facts and reminded the Court that he was the main scapegoat for the Union defeat at First Bull Run and that he and his corps had been caught in the crossfire between Edwin Stanton and George McClellan during the spring and summer that had led to the Army of the Potomac's involuntary residence on the Harrison plantation. Also, in late August General Pope had often relied on McDowell as *ex-officio* second in command of the Army of Virginia.

As if to encourage the outpouring of narrative honed during rehearsal sessions, Judge Advocate Holt asked McDowell to "state the nature of any order that you may have received from General Pope on the morning of the 29th, directed jointly and severally to yourself and General Porter, and the hour, so far as you remember it, of its receipt, and the position of your command at the time."

On cue, General McDowell took full advantage of the latitude Holt had granted him. Finally, he came to Pope's "joint order:"

"I have that order here," McDowell offered, "and will read it."[1]

"How did you regard that order—as placing General Porter in subordination to you, or as indicating that you were both to act independently of each other, and each of you in subordination to General Pope?"

McDowell replied, "I cannot say that at that time the order occupied my mind in connection with the question of subordination or otherwise. . . . At that time I conceived General Porter to be under me. When the joint order reached us, we were doing what it directed us to do. It found the troops in the position in which it directed them to be. It gave us discretion to the effect that, if any considerable advantages were to be gained by departing from that order, it was not to be strictly construed.

"I decided that considerable advantages were to be gained by departing from that order, and I did not strictly construe it, or strictly carry it out. That order contemplated a line being formed which was to be joined on to a line that was to come up from the east to the west, and have the troops on the Gainesville road to attack the flank and rear of the enemy, as I understood it, in moving along on the Gainesville road.

"This long line of troops—those who were ahead of me, General Porter's corps—coming to a halt, I rode to the head of the column. On the way I received a note from General Buford, addressed to General Ricketts, and to be forwarded to me. This note was addressed primarily to General Ricketts, and then to myself, for I do not think General Buford knew of General Porter's being there at the time he wrote it. I will read the note:

HEADQUARTERS CAVALRY BRIGADE—9:30 A.M.

General RICKETTS: *Seventeen regiments, one battery, 500 cavalry*

> *passed through Gainesville three-quarters of an hour ago, on the Centreville road. I think this division should join our forces now engaged at once.*
>
> JOHN BUFORD,
> *Brigadier-General.*
> *Please forward this.*[2]

"I do not know whether the message went to General Ricketts direct or came to me direct, or came to me from General Ricketts. I infer it had reference to that division. General Buford belonged to General Banks' corps, but had been temporarily under my orders the day before, and had gone up to Thoroughfare Gap with Ricketts' division at the time I expected a force of the enemy to come through that gap; and he had fallen back with Ricketts, and at that time, as I understood, occupied a position to our left and front."

"Did you, or not, communicate to General Porter the contents of the note from General Buford which you have read?"

"Yes, sir; I did communicate it to him."

"Where was General Porter's command at that time?"

"On this road leading from Manassas Junction, by way of Bethlehem Chapel or Church, toward Gainesville. The rear of his column had passed by Bethlehem Chapel, which is at the junction of the Sudley Springs road with the road from Manassas Junction to Gainesville."

"Bethlehem Church enables you to identify that position?"

"Yes, sir."

"Can you speak with any confidence as to the hour of the day at which you communicated to General Porter the contents of this note from General Buford?"

"It was somewhere before noon, I think. It is impossible for me to keep the hours of the day in my mind on such occasions. I have tried it several times, but have never succeeded except some important things, such as daylight and darkness. It was communicated a short time after it was received."

"Did you, or not, upon communicating this note, confer with General Porter in reference to his movements and your own?"

"I did."

"Will you state fully what occurred in that conference?"

"General Porter was in advance of the head of his column, I think, on a slight eminence or roll or rise of ground, with some of his staff near him. I rode up to him, and saw that he had the same order as myself—the joint order. Soon after, my attention was directed to some skirmishing, I think some dropping shots in front of us.

"The country in front of the position where General Porter was when I joined him was open for several hundred yards, and near, as I supposed by seeing the dust coming up above the trees, the Warrenton turnpike, which was covered from view by woods. How deep those woods were I do not know. It did not seem at that time to be a great distance to that road—the Warrenton turnpike. I had an impression at the time that these skirmishers were engaged with some of the enemy near that road.

"I rode with General Porter from the position he occupied eastward to the right, that is, the column being somewhat west of north, and I going east, made an angle with the line of troops on the road. The joint order of General Pope was discussed between us—the point to be held in view, of not going so far that we should not be able to get back beyond Bull Run that night. That was one point; others were that the road being blocked with General Porter's troops from where the head of his column was back to Bethlehem Church; the sound of battle, which seemed to be at its height on our right toward Groveton; the note of General Buford, indicating the force that had passed through Gainesville, and, as he said, was moving toward Groveton, where the battle was going on; and the dust ascending above the trees seeming to indicate that force to be not a great distance from the head of General Porter's column. I am speaking now of that force of the enemy referred to by General Buford as passing down the Warrenton turnpike toward Groveton.

"The question with me was how soonest, within the limit fixed by General Pope, this force of ours could be applied against the enemy. General Porter made a remark to me which showed me that he had no question but that the enemy was in his immediate front. I said to him, 'You put your force in here, and I will take mine up the Sudley Springs road, on the left of the troops engaged at that point with the enemy,' or words to that effect.

"I left General Porter with the belief and understanding that he would put his force in at that point. I moved back by the shortest road I could find to the head of my own troops, who were near Bethlehem Church, and immediately turned them up north on the Sudley Springs road, to join

Reynolds' division, which belonged to my command and which I had directed to co-operate with General Sigel in the movements Sigel was making at the time I left him in the morning.

"After seeing the larger part of my troops on the Sudley Springs road, I rode forward to the head of the column. I met a messenger from General Pope. I stopped him, and saw that he had an order addressed to General Porter alone. I do not recollect more than the general purport or tenor of that order. It was to the effect that he should throw his corps upon the right flank or rear of the enemy from the position he then occupied. When I say right flank, I do so merely because of my knowledge of the position of the forces, not from any recollection of what that order contained on that point."[3]

Might Reverdy Johnson have discerned that Holt had been in too much of a hurry here? The Judge-Advocate's colloquy had been dealing with events centering fore and aft of noon. Now, seamlessly, the prosecutor had taken the distinguished witness to an encounter that had in fact occurred several hours later.

"Was, or was not, the messenger to whom you refer, who bore that order, a staff officer—Captain Douglass Pope?"

"I do not recollect. I do not think it was."

"You did not meet on the way, or take from the hands of any other staff officer on that day, an order from General Pope to General Porter, except this one, did you?"

Was Joseph Holt leading his witness? Apparently Reverdy Johnson thought not, or that it did not matter.

"No, sir," General McDowell answered, "and I did not take the order from his hands in one sense. I examined it, gave it back to him, and he went on his way."

"Is Captain Pope personally known to you?"

"Yes, sir; he is. My impression is that it was not Captain Pope, but I will not be confident. I do not remember who it was."

Holt read the 4:30 order, then he asked McDowell: "Do you, or not, recognize that as the order which you saw and read?"

"I can only say that the order that I saw in passing was of that same import. Whether that was the order or not, I cannot say."

The Judge-Advocate shifted to another subject. "You have said that the Accused made an observation to you which showed that he was satisfied that the enemy was in his immediate front; will you state what that observation was?"

"I do not know that I can repeat it exactly, and I do not know that the Accused meant exactly what the remark might seem to imply. The observation was to this effect. Putting his hand in the direction of the dust rising above the tops of the trees [he said], "we cannot go in there anywhere without getting into a fight."

"What reply did you make to that remark?"

"I think to this effect: that is what we came here for."[4]

"What would probably have been the effect upon the fortunes of that battle if, between 5 and 6 o'clock in the afternoon, General Porter, with his whole force, had thrown himself upon the right wing of the enemy, as directed in this order of 4:30 P.M. of the 29th of August, which has been read to you?"

"I think it would have been decisive in our favor."

Here, the Judge-Advocate had the answer he had been seeking since the colloquy began. To follow up, he asked McDowell: "Did any considerable portion of the Confederate forces attack General Pope's left on Saturday, passing over the ground that General Porter would have passed over had he attacked the enemy's right on Friday?"

That had been bold, but Holt had reached too far. "I cannot say," the general replied. "They may have done so. I do not know."

2

Reverdy Johnson opened his cross-examination of Irvin McDowell by asking him if, when he found General Porter, "you told him that you found in his front a different state of affairs than you had expected to find."

McDowell replied that he did not recollect such a statement.

"Did you not say to him, in substance, that he was too far in the front, and that the position in which he was was not a position in which to fight a battle, or anything to that effect?"

"I do not recollect."

"Are you sure you did not?"

"I have no recollection of any question about that place not being the one to fight a battle. Something may have been said about not going farther toward Gainesville, with reference to falling behind Bull Run that night."

Johnson kept trying. "If anything was said in relation to the facility of getting back to Bull Run that night, do you remember whether it was that the Accused was too far in the front, or would be too far in the front if he moved farther on?"

"It was hardly a question of going farther on. It was more a question of turning to the right and going against the enemy, then passing down the Warrenton turnpike."

"When did you first see the order of which you have spoken in your testimony-in-chief, that of 4:30 P.M. of the 29th of August, which directed the Accused to turn the right flank and attack the enemy in the rear? You have been understood as saying that that was the effect of the joint order. That is not your meaning, is it?"

"It was the effect of the joint order as modified by me, when I left General Porter, so far as I had the power to modify that order, and so far as the understanding with which I left him at the time."

"Are you saying that before you saw the order to General Porter of 4:30 P.M. of the 29th of August, you—under the discretion you supposed was reposed in you by the joint order—had directed him to attack the enemy's right flank and rear?"

"To that effect, yes, sir; I knew I had that discretion; I did not suppose it." After a few more questions along the same line and answers that were mostly evasive, Johnson tried to move the witness in another direction. "Have you any recollection," he asked, "that, after you left the Accused on the 29th, and took with you King's division, the Accused sent a message to you, requesting that that division should be permitted to stay with his command?"

"I received no such message."

"Will you say whether, in consequence of a message, or otherwise, you sent a message to the Accused, with your compliments, telling him that you were going to the right and should take King with you, and that he—the Accused—should remain where he was for the present, and, if he had to fall back, to do so on your left?"

"I do not recollect."

"Are you able to say that you are certain that you did not send such a message?"

"That is my impression, that I did not."[5]

"When you left the Accused where you found him on the 29th of

August, were you at that time advised that Longstreet's corps, or any other corps of the Confederate army, was marching on to unite with the right of Jackson?"

"I did not know anything about Longstreet's corps or Jackson's corps. I have mentioned before that I received a note from General Buford that seventeen regiments, a battery, and 500 cavalry were marching from Gainesville upon Groveton. To whom they belonged, or to whom they were going, was not a matter of which I was informed."

"Do you know now whether the information given by General Buford in the note to which you have just referred was correct?"

"I know nothing more now than I knew then; I believed it then to be correct."

"If the force to which General Buford referred in his note actually passed through Gainesville at 30 minutes past 9 o'clock on the 29th of August, how long you suppose it would have taken it to have joined the force in front, which, as we have supposed, was commanded by Jackson?"

McDowell dodged: "It would depend upon how fast they marched."

"I know that."

"I do not know how fast they marched. so I cannot tell."

This unproductive sparring continued until Johnson asked a vitally important question: "How long had you left the Accused, on the 29th of August, when you saw the order dated at 4:30 P.M. of that day, which was handed you by some officer?"

"I cannot tell; I do not recollect. I cannot fix the time when I left General Porter, and, of course, cannot fix the time when I saw this messenger."[6]

Here, Johnson might have broken McDowell's resistance by pressing; the witness' answer seemed contrived to cover the uncomfortable truth, which was that he had seen the 4:30 order very late in the afternoon. But instead, counsel for the Accused shifted his line of interrogation again. "How often during this campaign of General Pope in Virginia," he asked, "had you seen the Accused before you saw him on the 29th of August?

"I had not seen him during that campaign before I saw him on the 29th of August."

Question: How long were you together during that interview of the 29th of August?

"I cannot fix the exact time. We rode together some distance, perhaps a mile; perhaps it may have been more; I do not recollect now."

"Was it five, ten, fifteen, or twenty minutes?"

"Yes, sir."

"Which?"

"You may put it at fifteen minutes, or at twenty minutes."

"During that conversation, that interview, did the Accused say anything, or do anything, from which you inferred disloyalty upon his part, or unwillingness to perform his duty under the command of General Pope?"

"No, sir; what he said was the reverse. He professed to have but one feeling, which was that for the success of his country. It was not a question with me about his loyalty or disloyalty; I never think of such things; what I mean is this: I assume everybody to be loyal; my suspicions do not run that way. The suspicion that persons who hold commissions as general officers in the army are disloyal does not occur to me."[7]

Reverdy Johnson strayed into irrelevant areas where the witness preferred to testify. Adjournment precluded Johnson from getting his cross-examination back under control.[8]

3

Members of the Court had some questions for General McDowell as Day Fourteen, December 13, opened:

COURT: Did, or did not, General Porter put his troops in action at the point indicated by you at the time he said he could not go in anywhere there without getting into a fight?

MCDOWELL: Of my own knowledge, I know nothing of what General Porter did after I left him.

COURT: Did you report to General Pope any change you had made?"

MCDOWELL: No further than by bringing my troops up, reporting to him that they were there, and receiving his orders. His [4:30] order to General Porter met me on my way to join the main army.

COURT: When you saw the order from General Pope to General Porter, the one subsequent to the joint order, did you give, or had you given, any order to General Porter which would interfere with his obedience to it?

MCDOWELL: None.

COURT: Could the Accused have engaged in the battle according to your order, and according to the subsequent order of General Pope, and still have fallen back to Bull Run within the time named in the joint order to yourself and the Accused?

MCDOWELL: Yes, sir.

COURT: From your knowledge of the nature of the country between General Porter's column and the forces engaged on the 29th of August, was there anything to have prevented the Accused from making an attack upon the enemy's right or rear, as directed by General Pope? If so, state what it was.

A simple *yes* or *no* would have sufficed, or an *I do not know*. Instead, General McDowell told the Court at great length about his travels elsewhere in the region, ending by saying: "That country is a mixture of woods, cleared ground, and hills, and it is easy for troops to march without being seen or seeing the enemy."

There was a note of exasperation in the next question posed by the member of the Court: "Does the country which you have just described include that over which General Porter was required to march in obeying the order of 4:30 P.M. from General Pope to attack the enemy?"

"Yes, sir," McDowell answered, adding: "I would say that I do not know that order by that hour."

The general's augmented response was curious; surely, everyone paying any attention at all to the trial was familiar with Pope's 4:30 order as such. Continuing:

COURT: Please state the ground on which you formed the opinion that if the Accused had attacked the right wing of the rebels, as he was ordered, the battle would have been decisive in our favor.

MCDOWELL: Because on the evening of that day I thought the result was decidedly in our favor, as it was. But, admitting that it was merely equally balanced, I think, and thought, that if the corps of General Porter, reputed one of the best, if not the best, in the service, consisting of between twenty and thirty regiments and some eight batteries, had been added to the efforts made by the others, the result would have been in our favor very decidedly.

COURT: When the Accused said to you that he could not go in

anywhere there without getting into a fight, did he or not appear to be averse to engaging the enemy?

McDowell: I cannot say that it made that impression on me, though, in giving my answer, I took the view that he did so imply, and made the remark; but I did not think he was averse to engaging the enemy. I mean by that, that that was not seriously a question with me, for when I left him I thought he was going to engage and would engage the enemy.

Court: Please indicate, as nearly as you can upon the map, the point on the Gainesville and Manassas road at which you left the Accused on the 29th of August, when you proceeded with your command to the battlefield, and state whether or not, in the military sense of the term, he was then in the presence of the enemy.

McDowell: I do not know that this map is altogether correct. It was made at my headquarters at Arlington; but, as far as I can recollect, the topographical engineer had much difficulty in locating some of these roads. I do not know that he has got them all down, or that he has them correctly laid down.

The witness reminisced for a while, finally recalling that Porter's Fifth Corps occupied perhaps three miles of the Manassas-Gainesville road. "A little in advance of the head of his column was where I left General Porter," he concluded. "I considered him then in the presence of the enemy."[9]

Court: When you left General Porter for the purpose of taking the Sudley Springs road, did you, or not, expect that he would attack the enemy as soon as he could reach them, and did you, or not, consider it his duty to do it?

McDowell: I have already said as much. I think; at least, I meant to say it.

Court: Had the Accused made a vigorous attack with his force on the right flank of the enemy at any time before the battle closed, would, or would not, in your opinion, the decisive result in favor of the Union army, of which you have spoken, have followed?

McDowell: I think it would.[10]

4

Reverdy Johnson resumed his cross-examination. "Do you know now," he asked McDowell, "or did you know when you left the Accused on the 29th of August, if Longstreet's corps had joined the enemy on the right, how far that would have extended their line to the right?"

"I do not know," the witness replied.

"Was there, between their right and the command of the Accused, any road over which he could have marched his command, in order to comply with the order of 4:30 P.M.?"

"I do not know that there was. I do not know that there was not."

"Do you know whether the order of 4:30 P.M. required the Accused, for the purpose of executing that order, to take with him his batteries?"

"As I said before, I recollect only the general import and purport of that order, which was to the effect that General Porter was to make an attack where I supposed he was going to make it when I left him."

"You have stated, if correctly understood, that the corps of the Accused was one of the best on the field, consisting of artillery about, as you supposed, of eight batteries of artillery, and that the effect of that corps, with those eight batteries, upon the right flank and rear of the enemy, would have changed the fortunes of the day. Do you mean to say now that the fortunes of the day would have been changed if he had made the attack without his batteries?"

"I believe it would."

"Will you look at that order, dated 4:30 P.M., August 29, and say whether that order did not require the Accused to use his batteries?"

"It so specifies: 'Keep heavy reserves, and use your batteries.' "

"Now, as a military man, will you say to the Court whether, if he had made an attack with his infantry and without his batteries, and had been defeated, he would not have been liable to the charge of having violated that order?"

A member of the Court objected.[11] Reverdy Johnson argued:

- That government witnesses had been asked repeatedly what their opinions were.
- That he proposed to show that the character of the country

which must have been traversed in order to carry out the order stated to have been given by General McDowell to the Accused on the 29th of August to turn the enemy's right flank and attack him in the rear, or the order of 4:30 P.M. of that day, was such that he could not have carried his artillery into action so as to comply with either of those orders.

- That at the time Porter received the order of 4:30 P.M. from General Pope, the enemy's right, by the junction of the force of Longstreet with the original right, was so extended that he could not have complied with that order in time to have made the attack contemplated by that order.
- That the enemy were in his immediate front, and that, if he had attempted to have executed that order, he might have been cut off.

These were, of course, the central issues of the entire trial, issues on which depended Fitz John Porter's innocence or guilt and his future as a member of the U.S. Army.

The Court was cleared. After some time, the Judge-Advocate announced that the witness shall not answer the question.

Johnson continued. "Will you state what, in your opinion, would have been the result of the battle of the 29th of August if the Accused had attempted to execute the order of 4:30 P.M., to attack the enemy on his right flank and in the rear, if he—the Accused—had been defeated?"

"To have defeated General Porter in that attack would have required a large force of the enemy, which would have relieved [Pope's] attack in front, and, I think, would have still resulted in a success to our side—to our army generally."

"Then, are we to understand you as saying that a failure of the attack contemplated by the order of 4:30 P.M., had it been made, would not have materially affected the fate of the day?"

"I have stated that, even if the attack had been made and had failed, it only could have failed by a very large force of the enemy attacking it, and that would so much have relieved the front as to have gained a success for our army generally."

No matter what approach Reverdy Johnson tried, Irvin McDowell always seemed to be there at the end to block him. After several more questions that led nowhere, he ended his cross-examination. But McDowell's ordeal was not quite over.

"In your own movements on the 29th of August," a member of the Court asked, "had you artillery, and did your artillery, if you had any, move with your other troops?"

"Yes, sir."

With what might have been an interesting colloquy just beginning, the Court adjourned until 11 A.M. on Monday next. General McDowell was again the witness; again he was questioned by members of the Court. But nothing came of that, and early on Day Fifteen the witness was dismissed.[12]

5

By this point, December 15, Judge-Advocate Holt had pretty well made his case. There remained fewer than a dozen prosecution witnesses to be called, most of them for the purpose of corroborating the testimony given by General Pope and other senior officers. Holt had benefited from all the resources the War Department could provide. All of the decisions regarding objections had been in his favor. Many of the questions asked by members of the Court had reflected pro-government bias. His witnesses had appeared well-coached, responding along the lines specified in the pamphlet Lieutenant Colonel Smith had prepared under Pope's direction before the trial opened.[13]

True, at times Reverdy Johnson had forced some of the officers he cross-examined to make embarrassing admissions and to answer unwelcome questions with "I do not recall" and its equivalents. These minor victories might have impressed a jury of impartial civilians; the nine generals comprising this court, however, were likely to ignore or even to admire government witnesses' employment of evasion and quibbling.

More serious had been Johnson's failures to follow-up inadvertent slips that had been made. For example, General Pope testified that he did not see cavalryman John Buford's message reporting the movement of Confederates through Gainesville at about 9:30 A.M. on August 29 until McDowell gave it to him at around 7:00 P.M. McDowell had been carrying that enormously important piece of paper around with him all afternoon. In the interim,

Pope—ignorant of the development Buford had reported—had thrown heavy forces into attacks against Jackson and sent the 4:30 order to Porter. Would he have done so if McDowell had forwarded Buford's message to Pope with reasonable promptness? Why did McDowell not do that? In the circumstances, was not *Irvin McDowell* the officer who should be on trial?[14]

Similarly, Johnson missed the opportunity to find out why Captain Douglass Pope swore that General Porter wrote a reply to the 4:30 order and gave it to him to take back to his uncle, yet the army commander professed to have no recollection of receiving it.[15] Porter's reply to the 4:30 order might well have ended the trial then and there—or, absent a credible explanation for Pope's inability to produce the message, the members of the Court would have had good reason to ask both witnesses some searching questions of their own.

Reverdy Johnson was successful, however, in a dispute with General Hunter, the Court's president, over procedure. In the winter of 1862, stenography was still new. Never before had it been used in a court-martial, but both Hunter and the Accused had accepted it at the outset. The innovation precluded much of the paper-shuffling, which consumed great gobs of time, so Johnson and his client were surprised on December 15 when Hunter proposed a return to the old system of preparing the record.

Why the proposal? And why right then, on Day Fifteen?

Fitz John Porter himself pointed out to the Court that he was not learned in the law and therefore unable to prepare all the forms and other documents required, which suggests that Hunter really intended to cripple Reverdy Johnson's and Charles Eames' ability to serve their client. As to the timing of Hunter's query, Holt's presentation of witnesses was fast coming to an end. The government had already enjoyed the benefits of stenography; reverting to *handschrift* would penalize the Accused's defense from then on.

During a closed-doors session the Court decided to stay with the new system. Apparently, Porter's desire to have the trial completed at the earliest possible time had been, for varying reasons, shared.[16]

Worth noting, also, was the fact that on December 15, 1862, Northerners were just beginning to comprehend the enormous cost of the whipping General Lee had inflicted two days earlier on Ambrose Burnside's Army of the Potomac at Fredericksburg. During only a few hours on that winter afternoon the Union had lost roughly 12,700 men in a series of frontal attacks that the Confederates defending Marye's Heights easily repelled, obliging Burnside to leave his dead and wounded on the frozen killing ground until the night of the trial's Day Fifteen.[17]

Coincidentally or not, Judge-Advocate Holt chose that day's session to read into the trial's records the texts of all the messages General Porter had sent back on August 27 and 28 to Burnside, who had then been at Falmouth, across the Rappahannock from Fredericksburg.[18] Prudently, Holt went on to obtain from witnesses who were telegraphers testimony that the transmissions had indeed occurred.[19] Reverdy Johnson objected. The purpose, said Holt, was "to show the animus of the Accused toward his commanding general."[20] Certainly, the Judge-Advocate was showing his animus toward Fitz John Porter.

CHAPTER EIGHT
Counterattack

DESPITE lawyers' and judges' declarations that trials are pure, structured searches for truth in which facts always trump emotions, inevitably these contests are flawed exercises simply because they are conducted by imperfect human beings. Indeed, the appellate process exists to identify errors made by the officers of the courts below who misbehaved and by witnesses whose lies, misleading statements, and other sins of commission or omission also polluted the trial record. Review of a lower court's findings may result in upholding, outright reversal, or remanding the case for retrial. Often, the losing side may file additional appeals all the way up to the Supreme Court of the United States; and in some instances, the justices have advised unsuccessful appellants to seek remedies in the Congress.

If the verdict went against Fitz John Porter in a civil court, such would be the path open to him. Reverdy Johnson could be content that his successes so far in causing Judge-Advocate Holt and the Court and equivocating witnesses to make mistakes would produce a badly flawed record, one establishing the basis for appeal to one higher court after another until the conviction was overturned.

But this proceeding was military. Findings of general courts-martial were subject to the approval of the President of the United States and of no one else.

Against all of this background, it was imperative that General Porter's defense be absolutely successful. In the present circumstances, however, that seemed increasingly unlikely. John Pope, Benjamin Roberts, and Thomas C. H. Smith had given Joseph Holt a reading of the battle of Second Bull Run that was plausible even though in many respects it stood history on its head. The quartet had had ample time in which to prepare. Edwin Stanton had given them a court dominated by officers who were beholden to him for one reason or another. Virtually all disputes has been settled in the government's favor.

There was more cause for discouragement: the success of efforts outside the courtroom to hamstring the defense. General Porter made his concern a matter of record near the end of Day Eighteen, December 22.

"I have a few remarks to make to the Court," he said, "before asking for a little time to enable me to enter upon my defense. I have made every effort possible to see my witnesses and to get in communication with them. I have failed in every instance.

"I have written to them. In some instances, my letters have reached them; in others, they have failed to do so. Their replies to me have reached me in only one instance.

"One of my own aides, whom I sent to the Army of the Potomac, has returned, but the letters that he sent to me some six or seven days since have not yet arrived. Those letters contain documentary evidence and information in relation to testimony that I desire to offer before this Court.

"I have also to add that the witnesses I desire to have summoned, with the exception, I think, of one or two now in town, have received no intimation whatever that they have been summoned. They are chiefly with the Army of the Potomac.

"In consequence of my inability to see my witnesses, my list is rather a large one, but I expect to be able to reduce it a great deal before the case is closed. The Court must not be surprised, however, at the large number of witnesses I have given the Judge-Advocate. I have done so merely because I have not had an opportunity of seeing or communicating with any of them.

"I have not yet been able to conclude my preparations to enter upon my defense. I therefore ask of the Court a delay until Wednesday morning next. From that time forth I expect to be able to push matters forward."[1]

Judge-Advocate Holt replied that the government had issued summonses for some of the witnesses desired by the Accused. It had, however, exercised its discretion in regard to others in active service, preferring to delay calling them from the field until they were actually needed in court. He said that he would make every effort now to have them sent for at once.[2]

Well and good; but Holt had said nothing about what had happened to all of those letters. Porter asked his friend Postmaster General Montgomery

Blair to look into the matter. Later, Blair reported that the interceptions had not taken place in his department. As to witnesses, only about half of those Porter needed would indeed be made available.[3] Such were the advantages the War Department bestowed upon the prosecution.

2

General Porter began his defense on Wednesday, December 24, Day Nineteen. In his opening statement to the Court it was hardly surprising that he continued to point out the adverse circumstances in which he and his counsel were placed.

"May it please the Court," he said. "Certain telegrams have been presented to this Court as evidence of a spirit by which it is supposed I was actuated toward my commanding officer, Major General John Pope, during the time covered by the charges against me. Isolated as are those telegrams from all reference to surrounding circumstances, the orders accompanying them, or to any explanations, it is manifest that their true meaning and spirit can be but very imperfectly perceived.

"In order that this Court, in its search for truth and desire to administer justice, may be fully enlightened on all the points of evidence, and understand, in all their bearings, the relations these telegrams have to the subjects of investigation, I desire to present in this, the opening of my defense, all the telegrams and messages in my possession, and all the orders of Major General Pope relating to the subject-matter of investigation, all of which I deem material evidence in my defense.

"I have reason to believe the government is in possession of all my telegrams, and the telegrams of those who were in communication with me. I have striven to obtain from officers all I sent out—I retained no copies of them—for the purpose of using them in my defense. I have secured only two of the originals. One is now in possession of the Court, remaining there because the one presented by the prosecution is an imperfect copy, a material concluding portion being omitted, doubtless by accident or inadvertence. The other I will furnish, as well as any others which I may become possessed of, or which the government will produce.

"I may be ignorant of what I have written, but whatever it may have been, I now unhesitatingly declare I will present in my defense any and all documents, if furnished me, which bear on the case. Whatever I may appear to have said in secret, I will here openly acknowledge and abide by. I have nothing to conceal."

What he wished the Court to bear in mind, Porter said, was that while he was on the way to join General Pope he was directly responsible to Generals Burnside and McClellan for all of his military acts. After reporting to General Pope, at Burnside's request he conveyed to him information tending to aid him in his operations and in securing his own forces on the line of the Rappahannock, which Porter had left unprotected by orders from General Pope.

"At the same time," Porter continued, "I was relying upon General Burnside for the only supplies which could keep alive my command. It will be seen that I was giving him information which I knew he was communicating to the government, tending to make him feel secure, and which caused me, for one reason, to wish to be recalled to operate over the Rappahannock upon the rear of the enemy, the only vulnerable point, in my judgment, in which the enemy could be struck.

"If the documents presented by the government show my feelings and disposition, so do these before, during, and after the actions, and constitute material evidence in my case. I ask the Court to maturely weigh and consider all this evidence, for evidence these documents must be, if the documents presented by the prosecution be evidence.

"I am now ready to go on with my case, reserving till the close of the whole evidence my entire defense."[4]

General Porter called Major General John G. Parke as the defense's first witness. "Will you state to the Court," he said, "the relations you bear officially to General Burnside, and your relations in regard to the telegram or telegrams and communications received from me during the march from Fredericksburg around to the Rappahannock."

"I was General Burnside's chief of staff, and the telegrams and messages passed through my hands, if not all of them, the greater portion of them."

"What opportunities did you have for ascertaining my opinions and feelings, and for observing my acts while at Fredericksburg and beyond?"

"I was with General Burnside from the time of the arrival of your troops up to the time of their departure, and while you were on the road to join General Pope. You showed energy, activity, and enterprise, and a desire to push your troops as rapidly as possible to the army of General Pope."

"Where was I during the time that I was staying at Fredericksburg?"

"Your headquarters were at our own headquarters, and we were constantly in communication."

"Do you know anything of the state of my health at that time?"

"Yes, sir; you were an invalid; but that did not thoroughly incapacitate you for the discharge of your duties."

"Did it seem to have any influence at all upon my activity?"

"I think not."

Porter said that he desired to have General Parke identify the telegrams to which he (the Accused) had referred in his opening, as they were mainly known to this witness.

Judge-Advocate Holt conceded that those telegrams bearing dates from August 27 through 29 were admissible as evidence, but he asked the Court to determine whether those bearing dates prior to those transactions should be received.

General Porter pointed out that telegrams presented by the prosecution earlier could be interpreted properly only in the light of information contained in those now offered. The telegrams presented by the prosecution were introduced to show his animus, Porter contended; in order to fully and properly ascertain that animus, the Court should have before them, not merely isolated telegrams, but also those sent just before and just after.

The Court considered the matter behind closed doors, then announced that the Accused's request was denied and Holt's position upheld. General Porter gave notice that he would file a protest at the next session, then resumed his examination of General Parke.

"Do you recollect the dispatch I now show you as one that I sent to General Burnside," he asked, handing the witness a paper dated Warrenton Junction, 4 P.M., August 27, 1862, an imperfect copy of which had been introduced by the prosecution.

"Yes, sir; I recognize it as one that was received from you."

"Do you recollect this portion of it: 'Don't let the alarm here disturb you. If you had a good force, you could go to Richmond. A force should at once be pushed out to Manassas, and open the road. Our provisions here are very scarce.' "

"Yes, sir; I recollect that distinctly."

Handing Parke another message, Porter asked, "Do you recognize this as one of the dispatches sent by me?

"I remember this dispatch."

General Porter then read the document, sent from Bristoe on August 28 at 9:30 that morning:

> My command will soon be up, and will at once go into position. Hooker drove Ewell some 3 miles, and Pope says McDowell intercepted Longstreet, so that without a long detour he cannot join Ewell, Jackson, and A. P. Hill, who are, or supposed to be, at Manassas. Ewell's train, he says, took the road to Gainesville, where McDowell is coming from. We shall be to-day as follows: I on right of railroad; Heintzelman on left; then Reno; then McDowell. He hopes to get Ewell, and push to Manassas to-day.
>
> I hope all goes well near Washington; I think there need be no cause of fear for us. I feel as if on my own way now, and thus far have kept my command and trains well up. More supplies than I supposed on hand have been brought, but none to spare, and we must make connection soon. I hope for the best, and my lucky star is always up about my birthday, the 31st, and I hope Mac's is up also. You will hear of us soon by way of Alexandria.[5]

"Do you know what this paragraph in the dispatch just read refers to: 'I feel as if on my own way now, and thus far have kept my command and trains well up?' "

"I presume it referred to the fact that from the time of your arrival at Falmouth, up to the time of your reporting to General Pope, you were under the orders of General Burnside, and that this was about the time that your command was transferred from General Burnside to General Pope."

"Was I at that time relying upon General Burnside for provisions, and getting them from him—the trains coming to me from General Burnside up to that time, and even after that time?"

"After your command left Falmouth, we sent you provisions as rapidly as we could get the wagons landed from the transports at Aquia, and pushed them on to you, until we were notified that it was not safe to send them without escort. As to dates, my memory is not sufficiently distinct to cover them."

"Do you know of any request, or any earnest desire expressed by General Burnside, or any other parties higher in authority, for information to be sent from my command?"

"Yes, sir. Dispatches were received from the President to the effect that communication with General Pope was cut off, and nothing was heard from him or of him, and that they had great anxiety to know what we knew of his command and situation."

"Do you know whether that was communicated to me or not?"

"I cannot say positively. It was natural that we should have communicated it, you being the channel of communication with General Pope's command."

"Do you know to what this expression refers, in the message from Warrenton Junction, dated 4 P.M., August 27: 'I would like also to be ordered to return to Fredericksburg, to push toward Hanover, or with a larger force to strike at Orange Court-House.' "

"You had communicated information to us regarding the position and strength of the enemy south of the Rappahannock. I presume that in this you suggest your wish to strike the enemy on his line of communication, as the matter was talked of and discussed before your leaving our headquarters at Falmouth."

"State if my dispatches of this character were sent to the President, or the commanding general here; and, if so, by whom?"

"Dispatches received from you were sent to the President and the General-in-Chief, in order to satisfy the anxiety for the command of General Pope, felt at that time both by the President and the General-in-Chief."

At this point, Reverdy Johnson asked General Parke: "From the knowledge that you had of the Accused, both before and whilst he was going to join General Pope's command, derived from his acts and his conversations, have you any reason to believe, or did you believe, that he would fail in obedience to General Pope, or in performing, to the best of his ability, the duty which he might be under after joining General Pope's command?"

"No, sir."

3

It was ironic at a minimum that Porter's telegrams to Burnside were taking front & center in his trial. Every soldier in the Courtroom had to recall that loyalties to outfits and often to certain commanders run inordinately deep, that all transfers are inherently upsetting and take an awful lot of getting used to, and that it is a solace to any writer to recognize these ancient verities in letters to kindred spirits. Moreover, it is almost a truism that the worse the initial impressions held by a transferee regarding his new commander may be, the stronger their bonds of respect tend to grow over time.

Why had the prosecution resorted to the drawing power of emotions? Had reliance on facts seemed inadequate less than twenty days into Porter's trial? Or was there another force working here, one that was malignant, submersed, yet moving the case inexorably toward Fitz John Porter's certain destruction?

However inadvertently, Fitz John Porter had given his enemies snake whips with which to lash him. Holt had made the Accused's alleged animus toward Pope, never concealed even well before Second Bull Run, available to compete for supremacy with matters of fact and opinion in prosecution witnesses' sworn testimony. And now the Court was denying Porter's request, thus further weakening a case already sadly disintegrating.

Reverdy Johnson understood this. But, absent eventual relief through the appellate process, about all that this able lawyer could hope to do was elicit from witnesses he had summoned—but might never get to interrogate—words capable of mitigating in the minds of the members of the Court the damage to Porter's case already done.

And by the way, how much damage had been inflicted on Fitz John Porter's morale after eighteen days of politically motivated attacks on his reputation? Providing a rare tangible indicator was a passage in a letter he wrote his wife on December 12, Day Thirteen:

> The feelings of the Court is such that I believe their minds were made up long since. The administration is resolved upon [dismissing me]. I have been informed that members of the Cabinet have used their influence on members of the Court. I intend to resign, even if found not guilty.[6]

Why the hell (any hardened veteran of combat would ask) should this battle-seasoned soldier *not* be attracted by the possibility of signing-out and going home to New Hampshire to build a new life raising—for example—pine Christmas trees on his native state's rugged hills?

Yet, offsetting such understandable outpourings of depression was General Porter's steadfast, ongoing support of Reverdy Johnson's and Charles Eames' efforts on his behalf. Habitually standing back by the wall in the Courtroom in the building on the corner of South Fourteenth Street and Pennsylvania Avenue in Washington, General Porter was, in a sense, the bastard at a family reunion. Rather than expose his counsel (who were officers of the Court) to criticism, however, Porter had gone front & center himself to suggest that persons unknown outside the Court were engaged in sabotage of his defense. And to emphasize the position he was taking, he had conducted General Parke's examination until the very last question, which he stepped aside so that Reverdy Johnson might ask: "Have you any reason to believe, or did you believe, that he would fail in obedience to General Pope, or in performing, to the best of his ability, the duty which he might be under after joining General Pope's command?" so that General Parke might answer, "No, sir."[7]

Johnson called the next five witnesses and examined them, drawing testimony that sharply contradicted that of Pope, DeKay, and McDowell regarding conditions on the night of August 27–28. While Captain George Monteith, General Porter's aide, was on the stand, Johnson moved. "Did you," he asked, "on the afternoon of the 29th, see a messenger from General Pope at General Porter's headquarters?"

"Yes, sir; Captain Pope."

"According to your recollection, what was the time when that messenger reached General Porter?"

"It was about sundown."[8]

Judge-Advocate Holt, in his cross-examination of Monteith, asked: "Are you able to recall with entire distinctness the hour at which you first saw Captain Pope, and do you know whether that was on his first or second arrival there?"

"I am not able to state distinctly the hour. It was very near sundown; either a little before or a little after; and it must have been the first time he came there, if he visited there twice, because General Porter was present."

"Why do you say that, because General Porter was present, it must necessarily have been Captain Pope's first visit there?"

"Because General Porter went to the front very soon after seeing Captain Pope."[9]

Another of General Porter's aides, Lieutenant Stephen M. Weld, was called, sworn, and examined by Johnson. After a question about the darkness of the night of August 27–28, Johnson asked, "Were you sent by General Porter, on the 29th of August last, to General Pope?"

This was new. Weld answered: "I started about 4 o'clock in the afternoon of the 29th, from the junction of the road that leads from Gainesville to Manassas Junction and the road that leads to Sudley Springs. I was sent with a message, not to General Pope, but to be delivered to either General McDowell or General King. I first received a written message, and then General Porter gave me a verbal message to the effect that General Morell would now be strongly engaged; that there was a large force in front of us; that large clouds of dust were seen there, and so on. I also glanced over the written message, and it was to the same effect, but went more minutely into details which I do not now remember."

"Did you see any one on your road to General Pope on that occasion?"

"Yes, sir. I saw General [John P.] Hatch, who told me that General King was sick, and not there, and that he commanded King's division. I then delivered the written message to General Hatch, and also gave him the verbal message. I asked him if he had any answer for General Porter. He said, 'Tell General Porter that we have whipped the enemy, and are driving them.'

"Just then quite a heavy fire of musketry broke out to our right and front. I then asked General Hatch if I should send that message to General Porter. He said, 'No; tell General Porter we have driven the enemy into the woods.' I then wrote that, and gave it to an orderly I had with me, and told him to deliver it to General Porter.

"I then asked General Hatch whether that would be sufficient, or whether I had better also deliver the message to General McDowell. He told me I had better deliver it to General McDowell, and he told me where he had last seen him. I went in the direction he indicated, and found General McDowell, who was just then leaving General Pope. I delivered the dispatch to him. He read it, and said, 'I am not the man; there is the man,' pointing to General Pope.

"I went up to General Pope, and delivered the message to him, both written and verbal. I asked him whether he had any answer for General Porter. He said, 'Tell General Porter we are having a hard fight.'

"Just then General Pope called General McDowell back. I asked him if that was all he had to send to General Porter, and he said, 'Yes.' He then said to General McDowell, 'The enemy are trying to turn our right; they have sent one or two brigades there, and I want you to send your division.' General McDowell, as far as I can remember, made some objection, but General Pope insisted upon having a division sent there.

"I then left General Pope, and went down to the road, and waited about five minutes to see if there would be anything else sent to General Porter. While waiting there, I wrote what General Pope had said, and sent it by an orderly to General Porter. It did not reach him then, for I met the orderly on my way back, and he told me that he could not find General Porter. I then delivered the message myself to General Porter."

"At what time did you get back?"

"I got back after sundown. I think it was about a quarter to 7 o'clock when I got back, as near as I can recollect."

"Did you see Captain Pope that evening, or do you know him?"

"I do not know him."

"Did you see that evening one who professed to be a messenger from General Pope?"

"Yes, sir."

"Was he there when you got back, or did he come afterward?"

"He came afterward."

"How long did General Porter remain there after that messenger reached him?"

"I think he remained about five minutes. He then mounted his horse, and went up in the direction of the front."

"Have you any recollection that you pointed out to the messenger to whom you have referred a road that he had better take returning?"

"I was told to show this messenger the direct road back to General Pope. I did show it to him, and described it, and even drew on a piece of paper the road I had taken, which I afterward found out was not the direct road; there was a little variation in it. He could not see the road; he did not seem to understand where the road was, where it crossed the railroad. Some one then told me that I better go and show him where the road was, and I went up to the railroad with him, and pointed out the road that I had taken."

"Was that messenger in officer's uniform?"

"Yes, sir."[10]

Cross-examination by Judge-Advocate Holt began with the question, "Will you look at this paper—the note from General Porter to Generals McDowell and King—and say whether you recognize it as the one you bore to General McDowell and General King on the occasion you have referred to?"

"I do not think that is the one. The one I took, General Pope put in his vest pocket."

"What enables you to remember the precise hour when you set out; did you look at your watch?"

"I looked at my watch. It was either five minutes of or five minutes past 4 o'clock, I am not certain which."

"Did you, or not, look at your watch when you were with General Pope and General McDowell, so as to enable you to speak as to the hour of that interview?"

"I do not remember of looking at it then."

"What hour do you suppose it to have been when you delivered this note to General Pope?"

"It was at least 5 o'clock."

"How long a time do you suppose you occupied in returning?"

"I think I was at least an hour and a half. I came back by a different road from what I went; and I did not go direct to General Porter, for he had told me that I would find him up to the front. I came out near Bethlehem Church, and went up to the front; and, not finding him there, I came back, and reached General Porter where I had left him.

"Was it dark then?"

"No, sir; it was not dark. I should call it dusk—between sunset and dark."

"Did you say that on your return you found there the messenger from General Pope?"

"No, sir; he was not there when I returned. He came there after I got back."

"How long after?"

"About fifteen minutes, according to my recollection."

"Was it dark when that messenger [departed]?"

"It was not dark, but it was pretty near it, for I remember that he could not see this road; I had to go out to the railroad and show it to him."

"You know nothing of his having been there before?"

"No, sir. I think that was the first time he had been there."

"What reason have you to believe that it was the first time?"

"Because I saw General Porter reading a note just after the messenger arrived there; and just after that I saw him writing a note, and then I saw him mount his horse and ride away toward the front, and I judged from that that the messenger had just arrived there with the order."

"You say you bore a verbal message back to General Porter, and also a written one?"

"All the messages I received were verbal. I wrote them down, and sent them back by orderlies. The first one from General Hatch reached General Porter by the orderly; the second did not."

"What was the first message?"

"It was from General Hatch, saying, 'We have driven the enemy into the woods.' "

"Can you remember the hour at which you sent off that message, and can you tell at what hour it probably reached General Porter?"

"I think I sent the one from General Hatch at from a quarter to ten minutes before 5 o'clock. It was before I saw General Pope. I do not know how long it took the orderly to get there. If he went directly back, I think he must have got there by a quarter to 6 o'clock."

"Was, or was not, the note which you bore to General McDowell and General King of the same import as the one that I showed you? If not, in what respects do they differ?"

"I do not remember anything in regard to going back to Manassas. In the note I carried, General Porter speaks of clouds of dust, as in the one showed me here. The note I carried began, 'Morell will soon be strongly engaged,' and that was also the verbal message that I took."

"Was, or was not, this after the engagement of General Morell with the rebel battery?"

"It was after."

"Were, or were not, the forces falling back at that time?"

"No, sir; they had halted."[11]

Day Nineteen, the first for the defense, Wednesday, December 24, ended with Stephen Weld's answer. The trial would resume on Friday, the day after Christmas of 1862.

4

Judge-Advocate General Joseph Holt opened Day Twenty by announcing that the Accused's protest regarding the admissibility of certain telegrams had been denied. The text of Porter's objection, however, would be incorporated in the trial's record—a concession dripping with irony, since if Porter were convicted there would be only one person beyond the members of the Court to whom it might be considered relevant: Abraham Lincoln.

But the opportunity to make the most of Day Twenty belonged to Reverdy Johnson, and he called as his first witness Lieutenant Colonel Frederick T. Locke, General Porter's chief of staff. As had been Johnson's practice, he began his examination by placing on the record the witness's recollection of the events during the events of the night of August 27–28. Locke's responses tracked those of General Porter's aides and contradicted prosecution witnesses, but one was particularly convincing. From the colloquy:

JOHNSON: Was the night very dark?

LOCKE: Extremely dark.

JOHNSON: Have you any recollection that you yourself got into difficulty in doing your own duty that night?

LOCKE: Yes, sir; I received a very severe injury, groping about in the darkness.

But Reverdy Johnson had moved Porter's defense a long way in his interrogation of the general's aides by sharpening the Court's focus on what had happened on Friday, and he sought to extend his gains by asking Locke, "Had you any conversation or conversations with General McDowell about the 29th of August?"

"In the afternoon of the 29th, I had."

"State what passed between you."

Joseph Holt interrupted to ask if any foundation had been laid for this question. Actually, none had been. But Johnson replied that according to his recollection, General McDowell had been questioned by him in reference to the conversation referred to. The judge-advocate said that, upon that statement by counsel for the Accused, he would not object.

Lawyering passed, Frederick Locke answered Johnson's question. "The circumstances occurred in this way," he began. "I was sent by General Porter with a message to General King. On finding General King, General McDowell was with him. I stated my message to General King, and General

McDowell answered, 'Give my compliments to General Porter, and say to him that I am going to the right, and will take General King with me. I think General Porter had better remain where he is; but, if it is necessary for him to fall back, he can do so upon my left.' "[12]

"What was the message you carried from General Porter to General King?"

"For him to remain where he was until further orders."

"Did you understand that General King was under the orders of General Porter?"

"I did."

"Did you deliver the message that General McDowell gave you for General Porter to the general?"

"Yes, sir."

"Do you recollect whether you saw General McDowell on that day, the 29th of August, before that time?"

"Yes, sir."

"Where did you see him?"

"On the ground where we had taken up our position, in the direction of Gainesville, and near the Manassas Gap Railroad."

"Was General Porter then forming his corps in line of battle?"

"Yes, sir."

"How far had he gone with that view?"

"He had made considerable progress in the disposition of his troops. A battery was in position, and the troops were being deployed. Skirmishers had been thrown out to the front."

"Did you hear anything said by General McDowell to General Porter at that time in relation to the location of his men, with a view to a battle? If you did, state what it was."

"Yes, sir. General McDowell said, 'Porter, you are out too far already; this is no place to fight a battle.' "

"How long did General McDowell remain with General Porter's command after he said that?"

"He remained some little time in private conversation with General Porter. They then mounted their horses, and rode off across the railroad to a woods upon our right of the road."

"After you delivered the message from General McDowell to General Porter, what did General Porter then do with his troops?"

"That portion of his command that he had sent off to the right was recalled, and he threw them a little back, so that they would be out of sight and protected from the enemy's fire."

"Was there any retreat at all?"

"No, sir."

"How long did his corps remain there?"

"Until the next morning, at daylight."

"Were the batteries in place?"

"Yes, sir."

Here, Johnson reverted to his opening subject. "Did you see any," he asked Locke, "and, if so, what, efforts made by General Porter to facilitate the march upon the 27th and 28th of August to Bristoe Station?"

"General Porter made great personal exertions to clear the way. He also had all his staff present with him upon that day; and he used all the cavalry that he had with him to assist in clearing the road, so that the troops could press on."

Another switch: "Have you any knowledge that Captain Pope arrived at General Porter's headquarters with an order?"

"I know that on the evening of the 29th of August a staff officer arrived from General Pope, who, I was afterward told, was Captain Pope."

"Were you present when that staff officer communicated with General Porter?"

"I was."

"What occurred?"

"He handed the general a note, which I afterward ascertained was an order for him to attack the enemy at once. General Porter very soon afterward ordered me to ride up to General Morell, and direct him to move forward and attack the enemy immediately, and to say that he would be up himself right after me."

"At what time was that message from General Pope delivered to General Porter?"

"Between sundown and dusk."

"How far was General Morell's division from General Porter's headquarters at that time?"

"About a mile and a half."

"Do you think you could point out upon the map the location of General Morell's force at that time?"

"Yes, sir." Colonel Locke did so.

"What was the position of the enemy in your front; or were they in your front?"

Locke indicated their position.

"Were you attached to General Porter's staff, and with him or his corps, the whole time he was under the command of General Pope?"

"Yes, sir."

"You have stated that you were with General Porter at the time General Porter joined the command of General Pope; did you witness the most of his conduct during that time, the management of his troops?"

"Yes, sir."

"Did he exhibit any indisposition to aid General Pope, or to do his entire duty?"

"He did not."[13]

Judge-Advocate Holt's cross-examination produced nothing new. Similarly, questions by members of the Court seemed designed merely to confirm their understandings of responses Colonel Locke had made during Johnson's examination.[14]

Captain A. P. Martin, an artilleryman, corroborated Locke's testimony, mainly regarding the conversation of McDowell and Porter on the morning of August 29. Next, Johnson called Major General George Morell, commander of one of Porter's divisions. By then, however, the hour was late. Johnson was questioning Morell about events during the night of August 27–28 when the Court adjourned.

Reverdy Johnson's examination of General Morell resumed the next morning, Day Twenty-One. "Now, to pass on to the 29th of August," Johnson began, "please state to the Court what orders were issued by General Porter on that day commencing at reveille, and what dispositions of your own command, and of others, were made by him during the day."[15]

This was a large order, and filling it obliged Morell to tell the Court a great deal that its members had heard before. If anything set his testimony apart, it was the authoritative manner in which he gave it.

Shortly before handing the witness over to the trial judge-advocate, Johnson asked Morell: "During the whole of the period now in question, say the last two weeks of the month of August, were you in frank and habitual intercourse with the Accused, and, therefore, cognizant of his plans, purposes, feelings, and doings?"

Morell replied: "I think I was. We were in daily intercourse during the retreat from James River, Harrison's Bar."

"Then, please state when, where, and how, if at all, to the best of your knowledge and judgment, the Accused ever failed during that period to exhibit all proper zeal and energy, first, to make junction, when ordered so to do, with the command of General Pope; and, second, to co-operate with that command in faithful duty against the enemy."

"I do not think that he ever failed to do so."[16]

5

Colonel George D. Ruggles, late chief of staff of the late Army of Virginia, was called by Johnson as a witness for the Accused. This may have surprised some observers, and if they interpreted it as evidence of some discord within the prosecution, they were correct.

Reverdy Johnson began by asking Ruggles to tell the Court what he recalled of a conversation on September 1 or 2 between Generals Pope and Porter "in relation to General Porter's conduct of the previous days."

"I was present at Fairfax Court-House, in a room in a private house there, where General Pope had his headquarters, on the morning of the 2d of September, 1862, Tuesday morning," Ruggles replied. "The several corps commanders had been sent for, General Porter among the rest. I was engaged at the time writing orders for the positions of troops. While I was writing these orders, General Porter and General Pope had a conversation, lasting about twenty minutes.

"Whilst studiously avoiding overhearing the conversation, I heard scraps enough of it to know that they were talking about the incidents of the few days previous. At the conclusion of the interview, General Pope and General Porter got up, and I heard General Pope say to General Porter that his explanations were satisfactory with the exception of the matter of the one brigade [which, Morell had explained, had gone astray to Centreville].

"I think [Pope] said 'entirely satisfactory,' though as to the word 'entirely' I cannot swear positively. I knew the matter of the one brigade meant Griffin's brigade, from my knowledge of what had happened at that time. I think General Porter replied; 'That can be easily explained,' though I am not positive about his answer."

"Did you afterward, and, if so, at what time, remind General Pope of that conversation?"

"My recollection is that I reminded him of that conversation on the 5th or 6th of September last."

Johnson needed a more precise answer. "Do you mean by that, that you reminded him that he had said to General Porter that he was satisfied with what he had done, with the exception you have stated?"

"My recollection is, that I reminded him that he had made that remark."

"What answer, if any, did General Pope make to you?"

"I do not remember that he made any answer."[17]

Joseph Holt hastened to repair the damage Colonel Ruggles' testimony might have done to his case. "You have stated that you only heard this conversation in scraps; that you studiously avoided hearing it. Can you repeat any of the portions of it except that which you have given in your testimony?"

Ruggles replied, "I cannot repeat any other portions of it, because it did not impress me particularly, except this one remark."

"Do you remember that, in the course of that conversation, a dispatch or letter was spoken of, which severely criticized the military conduct of General Pope, and which was said to have been sent by General Porter to General Burnside?"

"No, sir; I do not. I was on one side of the chimney, and General Pope and General Porter were sitting on a sofa on the other side of it. I did not see any dispatch, and do not remember of hearing any."

"Under what circumstances were you subsequently led to refer to your having overheard this conversation?"

"General Pope told me that he did not wish to appear as a witness against General Porter, but that he should summon me as the principal witness. I told him that I was not acquainted with all the circumstances of the case; that, though chief of staff, I had been employed as an aide-de-camp during much of the time and that orders had been issued by him that I knew nothing of.

"General Pope then said to me, 'You know that such orders were given?' I answered, 'Yes, sir.' He said, 'And you know that they were not carried out?' I answered that that was what I had been told; that that was my impression. He then said that that was sufficient, that he would have me summoned as the principal witness.

"Then, according to my recollection, I reminded him of this conversation. I felt that I was not sufficiently conversant with the case, and I immediately reported this conversation to the Adjutant-General of the Army, and to Colonel Kelton, the Assistant Adjutant-General at the headquarters of the army, and requested that General Pope might be summoned as a witness in the case. They both told me that he should be summoned, and both of them also told me to see Colonel Holt about it. I intended to, but before doing so I understood that the order for the trial had been suspended, and the impression was that there would be no trial. I therefore took no further action in the matter."

"You say that, according to your recollection, you reminded General Pope of that conversation at Fairfax Court-House. Is the Court to understand you that your recollection is entirely distinct; that you have full faith in its accuracy; that you have no doubt about your having made that reference?"

"I am not positive about it," Ruggles admitted. "That is simply my recollection. I would not wish to swear that I did remind him of that conversation, though it is my impression, my recollection that I did, when he told me that he should call me as the principal witness."

"What reply, if any, did General Pope make to your reminding him of that remark?"

"I do not recollect that he made any reply."

Holt asked, "Are your feelings toward General Pope kind and friendly?"

"I can hardly say that they are, from the treatment I received while upon his staff."

"Can you not answer that question more distinctly, and say whether, at this time, your feelings are friendly or hostile to General Pope?"

"I am on speaking terms with General Pope, but I would not like to serve with him as a staff officer. I would call upon him as a matter of respect, if he were in the city."

"Have you, or not, entertained the impression that you were badly treated by him in your official relations to him or otherwise?"

"I entertain, and I have entertained, the opinion that I was badly treated by him in both official and social relations. To explain that, I will say that there was considerable trouble between General Pope and several of his staff officers, and I was one of those. I thought several times that I was not treated as a gentleman should have been treated."[18]

General Ruggles' interrogation would continue on Monday, December 29, Day Twenty-Two, but not until the Court witnessed two displays of personal honor. First, after hearing the minutes of Friday's session read, General Morell offered a minor clarification of his testimony. Then George Ruggles stretched the upper limits of military courtesy when he said: "I should like to make an explanation in regard to the testimony I have given here. As to the trouble between General Pope and his staff officers, I would say that ill-feelings were entertained toward him by certain of his staff officers, myself among the number, in consequence of his treatment of us in our official relations. But subsequently, while at Fairfax Court-House, General Pope apologized to me for that treatment."[19]

Members of the Court wanted to know more from General Ruggles:

COURT: When did the conversation occur between General Pope and yourself, in which you think you referred to Pope's conversation with General Porter at Fairfax Court-House—after your return to Washington?

RUGGLES: It was after the army had been withdrawn to within the intrenchments around Washington.

COURT: Will you endeavor to recall, if you can remember, whether or not General Pope, in reply to your reference to the former conversation, stated that since his return to Washington he had had information communicated to him which had induced him to believe that the explanations which had been made to him by General Porter were not made in good faith?

RUGGLES: I do not recollect to have heard him say anything of the kind.

COURT: You think he made no reply at all?

RUGGLES: I think so. The only thing he ever said to me upon that subject was, that he thought that when they got his report in Washington it would make a big stir, or some commonplace expression of that kind, and that was not said at that time.

COURT: What are your feelings toward General Porter?

RUGGLES: They are not particularly friendly or unfriendly.

COURT: What was the opinion in regard to General Porter, if you know it, that was entertained by General Pope and the members of his staff preceding the 27th of August, when General Porter joined the command of General Pope?

RUGGLES: I do not know. I do not remember to have heard the subject referred to before that morning—the morning of the 27th of August.

COURT: What was said at that time in reference to General Porter?

RUGGLES: I cannot state definitely what was said; but I know that on the morning of the 27th of August, at Warrenton Junction, General Pope told me that his impression was that he would not receive much support from the command that was coming up from the James River, meaning the Army of the Potomac; and he conveyed to my mind the idea that he was not very favorably impressed with General Porter.

COURT: Did you receive yourself any unfavorable impression in regard to General Porter in consequence of conversations at General Pope's headquarters previous to the 27th of August?

RUGGLES: I was rather prejudiced against General Porter in consequence of what was heard at headquarters.

COURT: Will you state what those conversations were, what was said, and by whom said?

RUGGLES: I cannot state specifically what they were, but they were to the effect that, in the opinion of General Pope and his staff officers, General Porter was not giving a hearty support to General Pope. I heard that from General Pope and from some of his staff officers. I cannot specify the names of the staff officers.

COURT: Have you held any conversation with the Accused in reference to the subject of this trial since the last meeting of this Court?

RUGGLES: Yes, sir; on Saturday evening last.

COURT: Will you state what conversation you did hold with him on last Saturday?

RUGGLES: As I was going up town on Saturday evening, I stopped at General Porter's quarters, and told him that, instead of getting off that evening, or on Sunday, I should be detained until Monday; that the Judge-Advocate would, perhaps, ask me a few more questions. And I then told him that I was afraid the Court might think I was biased in his favor; that I desired to say to him that I was not particularly biased in his favor. I went on to make some explanation in regard to that, speaking of our serving together, and of my trial at West Point by a Court-martial of which he was a member. I said that, if necessary, I could state that I was not biased in his favor. I also mentioned that I desired to put the record straight, with regard to the difficulty between General Pope and myself, according to the explanation I have made here this morning.

COURT: Who requested you to remain until Monday?

RUGGLES: The Judge-Advocate of this Court.[20]

6

Reverdy Johnson's next witness on Day Twenty-Two, Brigadier General Charles Griffin, gave Fitz John Porter's defense an opportunity to refute the allegation that the Accused was responsible for Griffin's brigade having been in Centreville during the battle on August 30. Griffin testified that when the withdrawal from the position held on the 29th to join Pope's main force began at around sunrise on the 30th, he was following orders given him first by General Sykes and later by General Morell. When Griffin attempted to lead his brigade from Centreville to the line resisting the Confederates' drive, he said, his way was blocked by retreating Union troops. As had many other defense witnesses, Griffin swore that he had never seen or heard and indication of disloyalty on General Porter's part.[21]

Indeed, with the trial's duration having passed twenty days, the testimony was growing more and more repetitious. This was apparent on Day Twenty-Three, December 30, when Reverdy Johnson called and examined Brigadier General John F. Reynolds, Major George Hyland, and Brigadier General George Sykes.

Reynolds moved the case slightly by assuring the Court *from personal inspection* that the terrain that Porter would have encountered, had he attacked the Confederates on August 29, was nigh-impassible for troops unless they left their artillery behind.[22] The 4:30 order, of course, required Porter to "use your artillery." And when asked by Holt to point out on the Courtroom's map the place where he thought Porter's corps had been during most of August 29, Reynolds replied: "This map is very inaccurate, and as a military map is not worth much."[23] McDowell, under whose direction the Court's map had been made, had admitted as much during his response to a question asked by a member of the Court.[24]

If the map relied upon "is not worth much," Reverdy Johnson might have brought to the attention of the Court, how much credence does testimony related to it deserve?

George Sykes' answer to the often-asked question regarding General Porter's alleged animus toward John Pope ended with an interesting contribution:

> General Porter is an officer whose zeal is so well established that I hardly see the necessity of that question. I would like to add that General Porter's foresight, his providence for the wants of his command, and his attention to all the minutiae of his command are such and so great, that I have often thought that he relied or trusted too little to the capacity of his division commanders. *He seemed to do everything himself.*[25]

Judge-Advocate Holt's cross-examination included a colloquy that contained an echo of Sykes' characterization of Porter as a corps commander. Holt asked: "Do you know the officer who, on the 29th of August, bore to General Porter the [4:30] order?"

"I do not."

"Did General Porter make known to you the character of that order?"

"He did not."

"Did he read it in your presence?"

"Not that I know of."

"How long did you remain with General Porter on that occasion, after the receipt of this order?"

"I continued with him from that time all night."

"You had, then, as I understand you to say, no knowledge that a positive order had been given by General Pope on that afternoon for General Porter to attack the enemy on their right flank?"

"I had no such knowledge."[26]

If Fitz John Porter was indeed the kind of commander who "relied or trusted too little to the capacity of his division commanders," did it not follow that he would not consult Sykes, whose division was posted behind

Morell's brigades in the line of battle and whose continued presence at Fifth Corps headquarters was not clearly called for?

Hardly predictable, however, was what Major General Ambrose Burnside might add to the trial record on December 31, 1862, Day Twenty-Four, when Reverdy Johnson began his examination. Only two weeks before, at Fredericksburg, under this witness's command the Army of the Potomac had been nigh-wrecked, and had lost 12,600 men in attacking General Lee's impregnable defenses on Marye's Heights.[27] Since then, Burnside had been in discussions with Abraham Lincoln regarding overt efforts by certain of his subordinates to have him relieved. Defending his own conduct, then, not testifying, was the primary reason for his presence in Washington at the time.[28]

Apparently, Johnson felt it necessary to offset the issue of animus, which the prosecution had introduced even though General Porter was not on trial for that. Johnson asked the witness, "In August last, while the Accused, General Porter, was on his march to join the Army of Virginia, was he under your command, with orders from you to protect the line of the Rappahannock and its fords?"

"Yes, sir," General Burnside replied, "in connection with other orders."

"Did you, during that period, direct or request him to send you, by telegraph or otherwise, what information he could gain concerning the military situation in Virginia at that time?"

"I did."

"Did you receive such information from General Porter, from time to time, by telegraph?"

"I received from him frequent telegrams, as well as some verbal and written messages by orderlies."

"Did you regard the sending you such information, and the conclusions of the Accused thereupon, as an official act done by him in the performance of his duty, under your direction?"

"I did. The relations between General Porter and myself, in forwarding these troops, were such that I did not consider it necessary always for his language to be formal; and I did not consider it necessary for me always to give him a written order for any act I desired him to do. I was temporarily in command of that point, and the forces were forwarded through me, and all the officers knew very well that they were to receive their orders from me, and they were very considerate in carrying out their spirit, without there being much formality, because there was not much time for formality. Our communications may frequently have been somewhat informal, but they were in spirit entirely of an official nature."

"From your observation of General Porter's military conduct, and from your knowledge of him as an officer, what opinion have you formed of him touching his attention and fidelity to his duty and his zeal in its performance?"

"I have never seen anything to lead me to think that he was anything but a zealous, faithful, and loyal officer."[29]

Joseph Holt began his cross-examination by asking, "Will you state whether at the time these dispatches were received from General Porter—say, between the 26th and the 29th of August, inclusive—any of them excited in your mind the apprehension that General Porter might not be inclined to do his whole duty as a subordinate under the command of General Pope?"

"I received no such impression as that from the dispatches," Burnside responded. "I saw in General Porter's dispatches exactly what I heard expressed by a large portion of the officers with whom I happened to be in communication at the time—a very great lack of confidence in the management of the campaign. It was not confined to General Porter. I saw in his dispatches, and I told General Porter himself so, what may have been indiscreet language, but nothing that led me for one moment to feel that he would not do his whole duty.

"So much was I impressed with that, that I consulted my chief of staff on two or three occasions in reference to forwarding those telegrams, and we both decided—I certainly decided without any impression that there was anything expressed in them more than a lack of confidence—to send them, because they were the only means of communication with General Pope that we had. The President of the United States came to the telegraph office every morning at 7 o'clock, to request me to send him any information that I might have, and I did not feel myself authorized to withhold anything from him that would tend to give him a correct impression of what was doing on that line, and I sent the telegrams to General Halleck and to General McClellan—a copy to each."[30]

Members of the Court took up the questioning.

COURT: Was it from the dispatches you received from General Porter that you first learned, or formed the opinion, that he lacked confidence in the management of the campaign under General Pope?

BURNSIDE: I think not; I felt that he did not have confidence in him when he first started to join him; but, still, I cannot locate any time when I ever heard him say one word against General Pope.

COURT: Were the expressions of the officers you refer to, relating to the policy of the operations of the Army of Virginia, confined to officers belonging to the Army of the Potomac?

BURNSIDE: No, sir.

COURT: Did the doubts of those officers seem to relate to the general policy of the movement of the Army of Virginia toward the Rapidan or the Rappahannock Valley, or to the mode of its execution under General Pope?

BURNSIDE: I never heard any objection to the plan that made any impression upon me; but there was a strong distrust as to General Pope being able to carry out the plan.

COURT: Was, or not, the objection or distrust mentioned by you as existing among the officers who seemed to feel a want of confidence in General Pope, more in the nature of an exception to him as a man than to his capacity as a commanding general?

BURNSIDE: I think it was.

COURT: From what you know now, have you any reason to believe that the information given by General Porter in these telegrams as to the actual state of the army under General Pope was not correct?

BURNSIDE: I am myself quite satisfied that it was correct. But that opinion is merely one based upon the information I then received and what I have since heard.

COURT: You have spoken of the impression which you found a portion of the officers entertained of General Pope's capacity to carry on that campaign. Will you state whether, so far as you know, that impression was founded upon the character of the orders that he issued soon after taking command of the Army of Virginia?

BURNSIDE: I heard those orders very much ridiculed; but I do not think they had any special influence in the formation of the opinions of the officers who were acquainted with General Pope.

COURT: You have spoken of your estimate of the condition of things in the Army of Virginia in connection with the campaign of July and August last. Had you any opportunities of forming that estimate other than those furnished through the dispatches received from General Porter?

BURNSIDE: "Yes, sir."[31]

Following Ambrose Burnside as a defense witness was Brigadier General Daniel Butterfield, who commanded a brigade in General Sykes' division. His testimony was remarkable in that Butterfield refuted Benjamin Roberts' citation of the late Brigadier General Philip Kearny's alleged distrust of Fitz John Porter as a reason for Roberts' suspicion that Porter would "fail" General Pope.

Johnson asked, "Did you know General Philip Kearny?"

Butterfield replied, "I did, very well."

"Have you at any time had conversations with him in relation to General Porter as an officer?"

"Frequently. He always spoke in the highest terms of General Porter, both as a brave officer and a gentleman, and as a hard worker."[32]

Another contribution Butterfield made to Porter's defense was the believability that radiated from his answer to Johnson's question regarding what happened on the night of August 27 after Captain DeKay delivered the first of the orders that had led to the present Court-martial. General Butterfield's reply was long, yet it presented a picture of a man struggling to decide which claim on his duty was greater: the one the distant Pope had imposed, ignorant of conditions his messenger had encountered—or to his gallant, battle-seasoned men who were worn-out from following him from Harrison's Landing.

Daniel Butterfield testified:

> The order, I believe, was for General Porter to move his forces at 1 o'clock in the morning to Bristoe Station. He handed the order to General Morell or to General Sykes, who were present, and said there was a chance for a short nap, or something of that sort, indicating that there was but little time for preparation.

> General Sykes or General Morell, I do not remember which—one or both of them—spoke with regard to the fatigue our troops had endured, the darkness of the night, and the fact that, in their judgment, the troops would be of more service to start at a later hour than they would be to start at the hour named.
>
> In reply to these remarks, General Porter spoke rather decidedly, that there was the order; it must be obeyed; that those who gave the order knew whether the necessities of the case would warrant the exertions that had to be made to comply with it. I do not state that as his exact words, but as the substance of what he said.
>
> Captain DeKay, who brought the order, was then present, and was asked some questions about the road. He stated that it, was very dark, and that the road was full of teams. General Sykes, I think, suggested that it would be impossible for us to move at the hour named, if the road was full of teams; that they could not find the way. General Porter called two aides, and sent them off to investigate the condition of the road, and to ask General Pope to have the road cleared, so that we could move up.
>
> When we got outside, the darkness was so apparent (to use such an expression), and it seemed to be such a matter of impossibility to move, that General Porter said, "In consideration of all the circumstances, I will fix the hour at 3 o'clock instead of 1. You will be ready to move promptly." And I subsequently wrote an order, in General Porter's tent, for my command to be in line to march at 3 o'clock.[33]

Did this sound like the actions of an officer engaged in disobedience of an order and misbehavior in the presence of the enemy?

CHAPTER NINE

The Sour Scent of Perjury

HARDLY anyone in the courtroom could have known it on Friday, January 2, 1863, when Day Twenty-Five opened, but on the day before, the Union's high command had almost self-destructed.

Ambrose Burnside had appeared at the Executive Mansion early in the morning while President Lincoln was preparing for the New Year's Day reception and also a ceremony to sign the Emancipation Proclamation. Coping with his disaffected subordinates was Burnside's problem. Lincoln wrote a note to General-in-Chief Halleck in which he asked him to go down to Falmouth, the Army of the Potomac's headquarters, and settle the squabble.

Halleck, at the time busy telegraphing orders to everyone in sight westward to support Major General William Rosecrans' long delayed attack against Braxton Bragg's Confederates at Murfreesboro out in Tennessee, held correctly that the Lincolnian-proposed intervention at Falmouth would both undermine Burnside's command authority and shatter discipline throughout the rest of the Union's armies.

Neither Lincoln nor Secretary of War Edwin Stanton were remotely equipped by experience to comprehend the full implications of Halleck's finding. Without attempting to explain it, and recalling that Lincoln's note had been forwarded to him by Stanton, "Old Brains" interrupted his efforts to help Rosecrans for long enough to write Stanton:

> From my recent interview with the President and yourself, and from the President's letter of this morning, I am led to believe that

> there is a very important difference of opinion in regards to my relations toward generals commanding armies in the field, and that I cannot perform the duties of my present office satisfactorily at the same time to the President and to myself. I therefore respectfully request that I may be relieved from further duties as General-in-Chief.[1]

That done, Halleck returned his attention to the reports he was receiving from Rosecrans regarding the costly but indecisive battle he had fought on New Year's Eve. Lincoln withdrew the note he had sent Halleck, in part because no other officer was qualified to replace Old Brains.[2]

In the Commander-in-Chief's opinion, that is.

Back in the fall of 1861, Lincoln selected George McClellan to replace Winfield Scott as general-in-chief. Roughly four months later the disappointed President relieved the Young Napoleon. And in early November of 1862, frustrated by McClellan's sluggish conduct after Antietam, he had been obliged to relieve him again and to order him to await orders at Trenton, New Jersey.[3]

General Burnside's display of gross incompetence at Fredericksburg in mid-December caused outraged and saddened Northerners to demand his head and also those of Lincoln and Halleck. And to fill the need the Army of the Potomac had for a new commanding general, editorial writers throughout the Union had a nominee: George McClellan.[4]

Such was the background for the appearance in the Washington courtroom, on the day after the rupture of the Lincoln-Halleck relationship, of the man Fitz John Porter had habitually called Mac in his now-incriminating messages to Ambrose Burnside. Yet, embedded therein was another relevant story: the answer to the question, Whatever had happened to the McClellan-Porter relationship?

The paper trail originated back on December 12, 1862, when Little Mac wrote his wife from Washington:

> I have been summoned in Porter's case, but he will not be ready for me for some days. I am writing now in Porter's rooms. Fitz & I are the "great tabooed"—you would laugh to see how some officials fight shy in public, & then come to me privately to protest their devotion! It is too funny!

> I have not had a moment to myself & am more than ever tired of this wretched place. I hear that a battle is in progress on the Rappahannock—I fear the result will not be favorable & that Burnside will fail in his attempt.[5]

A week later, on December 19, General McClellan wrote "My dear old Fitz" from New York City and apparently arranged for the letter's delivery by hand. "Your notes arrived," he began. "I have not dared to reply to them by mail—so much do I distrust the honesty of certain surroundings."

Much of the letter pertained to telegrams and other documents that might be needed when Reverdy Johnson put him in the witness chair. Toward the end, though, he said: "I have no earthly doubt, Fitz, as to the result of your trial—you will come out brighter than ever & the wretched conspiracy against you will utterly fail." Then he answered an inquiry from his fellow "great tabooed":

> I did not reply to your questions about the members of the Court—1st because I did not believe I could get a letter to you unopened—2d because I really know but little of the members.
>
> Hunter I distrust. I never saw him—but he is an enemy of mine. [N. B.] Buford I knew in Illinois—he is a graduate [of West Point] & was a good man & a good friend of mine. Garfield I don't know at all.

McClellan concluded: "I will work with you, Fitz, to any extent—our cause is the same & we must crush these fellows." And he gave Porter some advice: "So long as I am here you had better enclose your letters (except when private hand can be availed of) to Dr. E. E. Marcy, 22 East 21st Street, New York City."[6]

In a cover letter (for enclosed documents) written the next day, December 20, General McClellan made some observations regarding the Union's situation:

> The monied men & the respectable men of this city are up in arms, their patience is exhausted & unless the Presdt comprehends the gravity of this situation I see great danger ahead.
>
> Burnside must have conducted his withdrawal [from Freder-

> icksburg's ghastly killing grounds, two nights after the Union disaster] very skillfully to have succeeded so well—poor fellow, how I pity him! I have defended him to the best of my ability.
>
> The sacrifice of Saturday was a useless one—nothing gained, not even honor. The future looks dark & threatening—alas for our poor country! I shudder, Fitz, when I think of those poor fellows of ours uselessly killed at Fredericksburg!

McClellan closed with a question: "When will you probably want me as a witness?"[7]

2

Before General McClellan was examined on Day Twenty-Five, January 2, 1863, Reverdy Johnson called Colonel E. G. Marshall, commander of a regiment in Morell's Division, to testify. "Where were you," counsel for the Accused asked, "on the afternoon of the 29th of August last?"

"I was on the road leading to Gainesville," Marshall replied, "the road from Manassas Junction."

"Specify the character of the duty you were performing that afternoon."

"About 1 o'clock I was detailed by General Porter to go with my regiment across an open country and a ravine to some timber that was facing our line of battle, and deploy skirmishers to find out the position of the enemy, and anything else that I could find out concerning them."

"State the position and force of the enemy in the immediate vicinity of General Porter's command, as far as you know it."

"Immediately after going there, my skirmishers were fired on by a body of dragoons, and shortly afterward there was a section of artillery which opened fire upon General Porter's command. Soon after that, perhaps about 2 o'clock, the head of a large column came to my front. They deployed their skirmishers and met mine, and about 3 o'clock drove my skirmishers into the edge of the timber. This force continued to come down all day, in fact until 1 o'clock at night. It was a very large force, and they were drawn up in line of battle as they came down.

"I reported the position of the enemy at different intervals to General Morell, my immediate commander. But at one time I deemed it so important that I did not dare to trust orderlies or others with messages, and

I went myself up to him, to confer concerning the enemy. This was about dusk. General Morell told me that he had just received orders from General Porter to attack the enemy—to commence the attack with four regiments. He seemed to be very much troubled concerning the order, and asked my advice, my opinion.

"I told him by all means not to attack; that it was certain destruction for us to do so; that I for one did not wish to go into that timber and attack the enemy. Their position was a very strong one, and they were certainly in force at that time twice as large as our own force—all of General Porter's corps. He had expressed to me the tenor of General Porter's order. I also deemed that we had executed the same with reference to the other part of the army—General Pope's army—by keeping this large body in place, and this was better than attacking them, because, if we had attacked them, I felt that it was certain destruction, as we would have had to move our line of battle across this ravine into this timber, and then, perhaps, our line of retreat would have been entirely cut off from General Pope's army.

"I may say that this army that came down in our front was a separate and distinct army of the enemy from that which we saw General Pope's army fighting with. About the same time, before I went to General Morell, I could hear and judge of the result of the fighting between the force of the enemy and General Pope's army. I could see General Pope's left and the enemy's right during the greater part of the day, about 2 miles off, perhaps more, diagonally to our front and to the right.

"The enemy set up their cheering, and appeared to be charging and driving us, so that not a man of my command but what was certain that General Pope's army was being driven from the field. In the different battles I have been in I have learned that there is no mistaking the enemy's yell when they are successful. It is different from that of our own men. Our men give three successive cheers, and in concert, but theirs is a cheering without any reference to regularity of form—a continual yelling.

"Afterward, at dark, I was sent for by General Porter, and questioned very stringently with reference to the enemy; and my remarks to him were the same as I am now making, and as I made to General Morell. I also stated in conversation that I felt that our right was very weak, and that the pickets should be increased, for there was danger of our being cut off entirely from General Pope's army; and I was given one regiment under my command to go to the right of me, and four companies of another regiment to go on the left of me, as pickets; and General Griffin was also ordered to place a strong force on my right, and to connect with me."

The length of Colonel Marshall's narrative obscured a point in the Accused's favor that had not been mentioned before: that by remaining in place, Porter was attracting and holding out of Pope's fight major elements of the arriving Confederate force. But Porter was being tried for not attacking, and Johnson's next question had to do with that: "The position and force of the enemy being as it was between 5 o'clock and dusk, and the position and force of General Porter being as it was at that time, was it possible, without the greatest danger, for General Porter to have made a movement to his right, to attempt to reach and attack Jackson on his right?"

Marshall replied: "No, sir; it was impossible to have done so. In the first place, it was impracticable to cross the country in that position during the day. Again, we would have been obliged to have whipped this very force in front of us, large as it was, to have got there, and it was very doubtful if we could have done it."

"They would have attacked you in flank if you had attempted that movement?"

"Yes, sir."

"Do you know that the order to attack, sent to General Morell from General Porter, was predicated upon the news which General Porter had received that the enemy was retiring?"

"General Morell told me that the news was that the enemy were retreating, and, says he, 'We know to the reverse; that they are not.' "[8]

Judge-Advocate Holt began his cross-examination of the witness by asking, "Did the force of which you speak seem to come from the direction of Thoroughfare Gap?"

"Yes, sir," Colonel Marshall responded. "Whilst the command was being got into line, prior to my going on this duty, my brigade was behind some others. General Porter had sent some dragoons of another regiment to the front, and my brigade was waiting in the road to get into position. I went to the left, and I could see a long line of dust; in fact, I saw two lines, one going along parallel to the mountains and the other one coming down through Gainesville, and it appeared to be close upon Gainesville at that time, perhaps this side of it; I cannot tell exactly, for I have never been to Gainesville; but the head of the column seemed to be about 5 miles off at that time."

"At what hour of the day was that?"

"It was 12 or half-past 12 o'clock. I joined my regiment and went on this duty at 1 o'clock. I should say the whole column of the enemy extended to Thoroughfare Gap. This column came down, and came rapidly to our front, as it appeared, along the Manassas Railroad. Their whole line seemed to be in the general direction of the railroad from Thoroughfare Gap down to our position. The other line of the enemy's left seemed to go to the left of the enemy's left that were fighting with General Pope. I was so close to the enemy that I could hear their officers give the command to wheel into line, and other commands that they gave, sometimes correcting their men."

"You spoke of another line of the enemy's forces that seemed to be proceeding in the direction of the battlefield. Did that line also appear to have come from the direction of Thoroughfare Gap?"

"They seemed to come through the same gap. The two lines joined together at a point just this side of the gap; where it was I do not know. It was a long distance off from our position. One line seemed to come directly down to the left of the enemy's extreme left, I should judge, and the other column came down to our front. There seemed to be two large armies."

"Did you make your estimate of the amount of that force principally from the extent of the line as indicated by the clouds of dust; or had you other means than that of judging?"

"My estimate was made mostly from the length of time in which they were coming down—there appeared to be artillery and infantry—and the time that we were attacked; and also what I had seen of the enemy's dust prior to going on this duty, and the length of their lines, as much as I could see of it, in our front."

"If the enemy had been in as large force as you suppose," Holt pressed, "double the force of General Porter's corps, do you not think they would have made an attack on you on the evening of the 29th of August, or would have prevented your withdrawing from there on the morning of the 30th?"

"I do not think they would have made an attack on the 29th. Our position was a very good one, and, if they had attacked, they would have had to move their line over toward us. But I think that, on the morning of the 30th, if we had remained there, they would certainly have attacked us."

"You withdrew in their immediate presence, did you not?"

"Yes, sir; my opinion on the 29th, while I was on that duty, was, that they desired to remain on the defensive, and have us attack them, feeling confident of their position."

"At what hour on that evening did you first receive the impression that the battle was going against General Pope?"

"Between 4 and 5 o'clock."

"Do you think that you communicated to General Morell, as fully as you now state it, your impressions as to the strength of the enemy in your front?"

"I think that I did. My object in going myself to confer with him was that he might get correct impressions; that a dispatch or a message by an orderly would not answer."[9]

Several members of the Court continued the examination of Colonel Marshall:

COURT: How large a force of the enemy did you see on that day with your own eyes?

MARSHALL: I cannot tell you. I could merely judge of their strength. It was a dense timber in which I was. We would get a view of the enemy first from one point through the timber and then from another. There was no place in which I could see their whole line. Their line of skirmishers was two regiments, at least, whereas mine was but one; and then, again, their troops appeared to be lying down behind this railroad.

COURT: Was the line of the enemy extended over the road which General Porter would have used in reaching the right flank of Jackson's forces?

MARSHALL: That road was blocked up by the enemy. There was no direct road to go over to General Pope's left, except by this road that the enemy already had.

COURT: Did the enemy in your front make a junction with the enemy in General Pope's front, according to your understanding?

MARSHALL: I do not think they did.

COURT: What space do you suppose there was between the two parts of the enemy's forces?

MARSHALL: They would naturally have made a connection with their dragoons; but their line of battle was not a continuous line.

Their line of battle in front of General Porter's command was separate and distinct from their line of battle in front of General Pope's command.

COURT: What was the space between their two lines of battle, should you think?

MARSHALL: I should judge it to be at least 2 miles.

COURT: From the position of the forces, both those of the enemy and our own, would the march of General Porter to reach the right flank of Jackson have been direct or circuitous?

MARSHALL: It would have been circuitous, through a broken country. If he had endeavored to go the most direct route, it would have been through a broken country. But I do not conceive that it was practicable for him to have gone that route. I think that, in order to have acted upon the enemy, he would have had to go back the same route we took the next morning in retreating.

COURT: Not practicable because of the character of the country, or the position of the enemy?

MARSHALL: Because of the broken country; it was rocky, and then a part of it was very heavily timbered; and it would have been impracticable to have carried artillery through there, besides being fired upon and met by this enemy in our front.

COURT: Did you go over that part of the country yourself?

MARSHALL: I could see it; I did not go over it.

COURT: What would have been the distance of the march if it had been made?

MARSHALL: He would have had to have gone perhaps a half a mile or more out of the way by going a little around to the right.

COURT: Was that route open, or was it obstructed, either by the nature of the country or by the enemy?

MARSHALL: It was obstructed by the nature of the country. Whether it was or not by the enemy, I do not know. I was told that their dragoons had taken some prisoners at that point, which we would have had to cross over. That point looked to me during the whole day to be a very dangerous one, and that night I so expressed myself, and requested that a strong force should be put in that direction to watch our right.

COURT: You have spoken of General Morell's division being drawn up in line of battle fronting the enemy. Will you please state, if you know, the relative position of the remainder of General Porter's corps to that force of General Morell, at the time they were drawn up in line of battle, and your command thrown forward as skirmishers?

MARSHALL: I was informed that they were directly in rear of us when I went on that duty.

COURT: Were they in line of battle?

MARSHALL: I do not know. I did not see them. I do not know anything about that. I was informed that they were close behind us. We were in the advance.

COURT: You have stated that General Porter's direct march toward Jackson's right was obstructed both by the character of the road and by the enemy.

MARSHALL: His direct march by the most direct route was obstructed; that was held by the enemy.

COURT: Was the circuitous route you have spoken of absolutely obstructed or not; was it a practicable route, in any sense?

MARSHALL: I do not think it was a practicable route in any sense, by day or night. I do not think there was any route left for General Porter to have acted upon except by going back again on the road to Manassas, and then joining our army.

COURT: What length of time would it have required to make that march, returning in the way you speak of?

MARSHALL: I cannot tell you the length of time. It would have taken several hours, perhaps about half a day, to have marched and got into position again, so as to have had any effect.

COURT: Was that the road taken by you on the 30th?

MARSHALL: Yes, sir.

COURT: Did it take a half a day then?

MARSHALL: I do not know how long it did take us. There was a data which I do not recollect. I would like to say here that I had been out on picket with my command from 1 o'clock on the afternoon of the 29th all that night, until the next morning. We had had nothing to eat until the next morning, and then I could get only a little hard bread, which I made my men carry on their shoulders until we could stop on the march somewhere for them to eat it. I did not feel like making any observations, but went right to the battlefield and into the fight.

COURT: Of the line of battle formed by the enemy opposed to General Porter's command between 5 o'clock and sundown, what portion of the enemy's troops were south of the Manassas Railroad?

MARSHALL: They were more along the railroad. The railroad came down close to us—off a little to the right of my skirmishers; so that, in advancing my skirmishers, my right came on to the railroad much sooner than my left.

COURT: Were any of the enemy's forces south of that road?

MARSHALL: They were along the railroad, but none this side of it except skirmishers. I met dragoons along the whole front, and particularly on this direct road; and then afterward their skirmishers came to my front, and extended in a longer line than I did, and drove me in.

COURT: Supposing the force of General Porter to have been extended from the point where General Morell's command was, down to Bethlehem Church, could not a large portion of them have moved along the Sudley Springs road to the battlefield within a much shorter period of time than you have named for the whole movement?

MARSHALL: By all means, much sooner than we would.

COURT: Do you know any reason why that road was not practicable for an advance on the 29th?

MARSHALL: I do not know any reason why it was not practicable.

COURT: Would such a separation of General Porter's corps on the 29th, by a part of it moving up the Sudley Springs road to the battlefield, have been an eminently dangerous military movement at that time, considering the position and force of the enemy in front?

MARSHALL: It would be unusual to separate parts of a corps, and particularly with such a large force of the enemy in our front. It would have left us very weak in our position in the advance. I understood that the part of the corps that was left behind by General Porter was left there as a support to us, to be used in any direction that he saw fit. It would have been unusual, and

I think it would have been criticized by General Porter's officers, to have sent them off in any other direction, leaving us alone with this large force of the enemy in our front.

COURT: Suppose the case of an order from General Pope to General Porter to make the movement to assault the right of Jackson's army, could that Sudley Springs road have been taken by any portion of General Porter's corps to accomplish that object?

MARSHALL: Yes, sir; it could have been taken; but it could not have been taken, when we got the order, in time to have met the enemy and done anything.

COURT: You mean done anything by daylight?

MARSHALL: Yes, sir; by daylight that day—to have done anything that day.[10]

3

Colonel Marshall's stay in the witness chair seemed to have been prolonged by the Judge-Advocate and members of the Court because of the importance of the events of August 29 and the prosecution questioners' frustration. Marshall's testimony and his refusal to concede that any portion of it needed modification had been impressive. No other defense witness had been able to offer so detailed or so convincing an account of operating so close to the arriving Confederates—and when members of the Court as well as Joseph Holt had proved unable to shake Marshall, supporters of Fitz John Porter in the courtroom must have been elated.

Next to be called, sworn, and examined by the Accused on Day Twenty-Five was Major General George B. McClellan—a witness for whom no rocking chair had been provided. Reverdy Johnson may have surprised some observers by opening his questioning by asking, "Have you any knowledge of any efforts made by General Porter for the purpose of removing his own command [from Harrison's Landing] in order to get to Aquia Creek and join General Pope?"

Little Mac's answer: "I have."

Reverdy Johnson: "State them, if you please."

"Immediately after the commencement of the movement for the evacuation of Harrison's Bar, General Porter was instructed to move his corps to the vicinity of Williamsburg, holding a position in front of it, to be able to support either wing of the army, if attacked. While there, he received information, through contrabands and intercepted letters, showing that the rebel troops in the vicinity of Richmond were moving upon General Pope.

"Immediately, without waiting for further orders from me, he moved his command with the utmost rapidity to Newport News, to embark it. And, while at Newport News, he used every effort to facilitate the embarkation of his command for Aquia Creek."

"Did he know that the object of that movement upon his part was to get as quickly as possible to the assistance of General Pope?"

"Yes."

"Will you look at this paper and say whether you recognize it."

McClellan read the words on the paper: *Please push off your troops without one moment's delay. The necessity is very pressing—a matter of life and death. What progress is made, and when will you be through? See me before you sail.*[11]

"Was that order executed by him to your satisfaction?"

"Entirely."

"You have stated, if I understood you, that the first movement which General Porter made for the purpose of getting to Newport News was without orders from you. Was it not contrary to orders at that time?"

"It was departing from the letter of the instructions I had given. I should say, in explanation of that, that General Porter sent me a telegram, one or perhaps two, stating that he would go by a certain hour if I did not forbid it. By some delay of the telegraph line, I did not receive those dispatches until after he had started; but I fully approved his course in doing as he did."

"Was the effect of that movement to expedite his arrival at Aquia Creek?"

"Very decidedly; at least one day, if not more."

"After he left Newport News with his command, where did you first see him?"

"At Aquia Creek."

"From what you saw of his conduct, or from anything that you may have heard from him, after he knew that he was to go to the assistance of General Pope, did he, in your opinion, do all that an energetic, and zealous, and patriotic officer could have done?"

"I think he did."

"Had you any reason, at any time, after he received notice that he was to go to the assistance of General Pope, to believe that he would fail General Pope, or the country, in the discharge of his duty?"

"None whatever."[12]

Here, Reverdy Johnson shifted to the subject of the telegrams Porter had sent Burnside. Had McClellan received any of them?

General McClellan answered: "I received several—the exact number I do not know, perhaps three or four, forwarded by General Burnside from Falmouth."

"To yourself?"

"The copies were addressed, I think, both to General Halleck and myself."

"Did you, from the telegrams that you so received, form the impression that General Porter would not be true to his duty to General Pope?"

"I did not."

Having established several times that McClellan could recall no occasion when Fitz John Porter had indicated any inclination to fail General Pope, Reverdy Johnson moved on to the telegram the witness sent Porter at Centreville on September 1, 1862, 5:30 P.M. "As you have stated that you never doubted that General Porter would be true to his duty to General Pope," Johnson asked, "how came you to send General Porter such a dispatch as that?"

"I sent it in accordance with the request of the President of the United States, who sent for me on that day, and told me that he had understood that there was an unkind feeling on the part of the Army of the Potomac toward General Pope, and requested me to use my personal influence to correct it by telegraphing either to General Porter or to any other of my friends there. I told him that I did not consider it necessary, but was perfectly willing to do it. I had no doubt, then, in my own mind, but that the Army of the Potomac, and all connected with it, would do their duty without there being any necessity for any action on my part."

"I understand you to say, then, that you sent the telegram to quiet the apprehensions of the President, and not to remove any apprehensions of your own?"

"Entirely so."[13]

Questions placed by the Judge-Advocate and the Court failed to advance the case. Neither did two other witnesses, although Assistant

Secretary of War John Tucker testified that at Old Point Comfort during Porter's movement to join Pope's army he "formed the opinion that he was most zealous and energetic in getting his troops on board of the various transports," that he saw no indications of disrespect toward General Pope, and that he reported favorably on Porter's conduct when he returned to Washington.[14] The other witness, Lieutenant George T. Ingham, an aide to General Sykes, identified Captain Douglass Pope—who was present in the courtroom—as the messenger who delivered the 4:30 order to General Porter and established the time of that event as "after sunset" on August 29.

4

Captain Pope's presence was an indication of Judge-Advocate Holt's concern over the dichotomy between the aide's contention that he had reached General Porter at or about 5:30 P.M. on August 29 and testimony such as that of Lieutenant Ingham and others to the effect that Pope had arrived after sunset. Bolstering Pope's account mattered; it would be embarrassing to the prosecution if the general's nephew were found to be lying, and everyone in the courtroom would agree with the Accused's assertion that an attack launched in the dark was bound to fail. Accordingly, shortly after Day Twenty-Seven opened the Judge-Advocate presented as a witness for the Court—the defense had rested—Charles Duffee.

Questions by members of the Court established that Duffee was no longer in the army but that in August he had been a cavalryman detailed as an orderly to Captain Pope. Duffee's interrogation continued:

COURT: Have you any recollection of having accompanied Captain Pope as his orderly on the 29th of August last, on the occasion of his bearing an order from General Pope to General Porter?

DUFFEE: I have.

COURT: Will you state all the circumstances connected with the transmission of that order?

DUFFEE: General Pope gave Captain Pope the order to carry to General Porter, and was telling him where he would find General Porter, when I spoke up, and told him that I knew the road myself; that I had traveled over it before. Thereupon he was satisfied for us to start with the order, which we did.

COURT: What was the hour at which you left?

DUFFEE: We started, as near as I can recollect, about half-past 4 o'clock, and went on at a pretty good gait until we came to General Porter's headquarters. Sometimes we were on a trot, sometimes on a walk, and sometimes on a canter, going about as fast as we thought our horses could travel.

COURT: State what happened on the way.

DUFFEE: We came across General McDowell, whom we expected to find at a certain place, and did find there. He told us exactly where we could find General Porter, and offered to send a guide with us. I said it was not necessary, as I knew the road myself. We went on until we came out on the Hay Market road, and there we found General Porter. Captain Pope delivered the order to him, and staid and talked some considerable length of time with him, I should judge from twenty minutes to half an hour, before we started to return. I should think, to the best of my judgment, that we occupied about an hour in going from General Pope's headquarters to where we found General Porter, which would make the hour of delivery about half-past 5 o'clock.

COURT: Will you state what General McDowell said? Did he see the order or not?

DUFFEE: He saw the order, and said that it was an important order.

COURT: Could you tell at about what place on the road you met General McDowell?

DUFFEE: We met General McDowell, I should think, not over 2 miles from General Pope's headquarters; not quite half way from there to General Porter's headquarters.

COURT: Did you return with Captain Pope?

DUFFEE: Yes, sir.

COURT: Was Captain Pope overtaken on his return and requested to go back to General Porter?

DUFFEE: He was met, as I understood, by another message, and went back with that.

COURT: Where were you in the mean time?

DUFFEE: At the time we were met by the other message, as I understood it, I had asked leave of Captain Pope to stop and get a drink of water at a well, and he sent an orderly to let me know that he was going back again, and I joined Captain Pope close to where the well was, and went back.

COURT: Have you any recollection of the appearance of the sun? Can you recall the hour by that? Or have you any impression as to the hour except that derived from the time that you supposed you occupied in riding from General Pope to General Porter?

DUFFEE: I do not think I particularly noticed the sun. I noticed the time more particularly when we started, in connection with the distance we had to go, and I said we would have to go in a hurry, or we would be in the night in getting back.

COURT: When did you start back from General Porter?

DUFFEE: I think we started back the first time about 6 o'clock, and, in stopping to get the water, I was detained a little time at the well. We did not stop long at General Porter's headquarters the second time, and I think it was between 6 and 7 o'clock—nearly 7 o'clock—when we started back the second time; it was getting dusk.

COURT:. Was it dark when you got back to General Pope's?

DUFFEE: Yes, sir; it was dark.

COURT: Did you stop on the way the second time you started back?

DUFFEE: We stopped at General McDowell's headquarters.

COURT: How long do you think you staid there?

DUFFEE: I reckon about 20 minutes. We found the headquarters pretty close together.

COURT: Did you stop anywhere else before you got back to General Pope?

DUFFEE: No, sir.

COURT: Was it fully dark when you got back to General Pope?

DUFFEE: Yes, sir; it was fully dark; some little time after dark. It was so dark that for a part of the road it was as much as I could do to distinguish the marks by which I knew the road.

COURT: Did you see the order delivered into the hands of General Porter?

DUFFEE: Yes, sir; I saw him take the order from Captain Pope.

COURT: Was he in his tent or out of doors?

DUFFEE: He was lying down under a shade tree when he took the order.

COURT: Did he change his position upon reading the order, or did he continue to lie down?

DUFFEE: I cannot state positively whether he rose to his feet or not, but at the time he was reading the order I noticed that he was lying in this position on the ground [describing him as lying resting on his elbow, his head upon his hand].

COURT: Did you leave him lying down on the ground when you came away?

DUFFEE: Yes, sir. Captain Pope also sat down, and they talked; had some little considerable conversation.

COURT: Was it after sundown when you left the second time?

DUFFEE: It could not have been far from sunset, but it was not dark.

COURT: The question is, was it after sundown?

DUFFEE: I could not state positively; it might have been after sundown; it was not far from sundown.

COURT: What was the distance from General Pope's headquarters to where you found General Porter?

DUFFEE: About 5 miles, as near as I could judge from traveling the road.

COURT: How much of the way did you gallop?

DUFFEE: That is more than I can tell you. We went as fast as we could from the nature of the road, and as we thought our horses could travel.

COURT: Do you remember whether you trotted, or walked, or galloped the most of the way?

DUFFEE: We had to go a great deal of the way quite slow, on account of the road being very bad—rough in places.

COURT: Did you gallop any at all?

DUFFEE: Yes, sir; we did. I recollect of galloping some. In other places we had to go quite slow.

COURT: Where was General Porter when you left the second time?

DUFFEE: That I could not state. I do not recollect of seeing General Porter the second time. I did not take notice.

COURT: Did you see anything of the enemy in passing from General Pope to General Porter, or on your return?

DUFFEE: No, sir; I did not. I heard firing on our right a part of the way going out and when we turned back. I still heard firing on our left as we came back.

COURT: Can you state the position of General Pope with respect to the right of the enemy commanded by Jackson?

DUFFEE: I should judge that General Pope was past the center of the enemy, toward the left of the enemy. The position of the troops on General Pope's left I could not exactly state.

COURT: Did you see about where the right of Jackson's force was at that time?

DUFFEE: All I judged about his right was from the firing, which I judged was not more than a mile and a half from where we started to where I heard the firing. I made inquiry of what troops were in there, and Captain Pope told me, but I have forgotten what they were.

COURT: How far was it from where you found General Porter, and where the dispatch was delivered to him, to the right of Jackson's army?

DUFFEE: To where I supposed Jackson's right was would be about three miles and a half, I should judge. I do not know that it was there, but that was where I heard the firing.

COURT: Where was General Porter?

DUFFEE: General Porter was on the Hay Market road, right where the road came out from the Bull Run battlefield, running from the stone house on the battlefield of Bull Run to Manassas Junction. It intersected with the Hay Market road right there at the railroad.

COURT: In what direction does the Hay Market road run? Is it the country road running from the railroad up to the old Bull Run battlefield?

DUFFEE: Yes, sir. It may be called the Gainesville road. I call it the Hay Market road.[15]

Next to question Charles Duffee was Reverdy Johnson. He asked the witness, "Are you a native of Virginia?"

"No, sir."

"How often had you been in that part of Virginia before?"

"I had been there some four or five times. I had traveled over the Bull Run battlefield and to Catlett's Station, and from there up through to the

Valley of Virginia. I was once down as far as Fredericksburg. I had been on several scouts through that part of the country."

"Are you a native of Ohio?"

"Yes, sir."

"At what point did you meet General McDowell when you were first going to General Porter?"

"He was on the road running from the stone house, on the Bull Run battlefield, out to what I call the Hay Market road, about 2 miles on the road from the stone house."

"What troops were with him, if any?"

"I did not notice any of the troops very close to him. There were a few orderlies with him. He appeared as if he had come from the right of the road as we were going out. I supposed that the troops that were in there were his own troops."

"I understand you to have stated that you went with Captain Pope, who was the bearer of the order, the entire distance between the headquarters of General Pope and where you found General Porter?"

"Yes, sir."

"Can you tell the Court how many roads you traveled, if you traveled more than one?"

"We left one road, that appeared to bear a little to our right, and turned a little to our left and went up around—I forget now whether it was a brick house or what it was—some kind of a farmhouse that had been kind of destroyed. In going across this distance, it appeared as if there had never been any main road through there. I had been shown the road before by a guide. In coming up to this farmhouse, we struck the road, and went right straight out to where we found General Porter."

"Then you traveled two roads?"

"It was either the road forked there or it was two roads, for the road that went across there seemed as if it was not much traveled."

"When you came to the fork that you speak of, what caused you to turn down the fork?"

"That was the road I had been shown before; I could not state exactly the time when, but it was at the time that General Shields marched through there. I passed over that road with a guide, and he told me that was a little nearer road to get out to the Hay Market road."

"By the Hay Market road are we to understand you as meaning the Gainesville road?"

"I call it the Hay Market road. It is the direct road we travel running from Manassas Junction to Hay Market, and so on up to Front Royal."

"Do you understand it to be also called the Gainesville road?"

"It may pass by that name; but I always call it the Hay Market road."

"How many roads, if more than one, did you take in returning?"

"We came back the same road."

"The second time as well as the first?"

"Yes, sir. When we first started back, we did not go as far as this house that I speak of, where the road made a turn around it."

Evidently, Reverdy Johnson wanted time in which to study Charles Duffee's testimony with assistance from a reliable map, for at some points it seemed at variance with that of Captain Pope. He left his examination of Duffee where it was for the day. Then Judge-Advocate Holt called as a government witness Brigadier General Rufus King, a member of the Court.

Holt developed testimony to the effect that King had not been with General McDowell during the afternoon of August 29 and that he had no recollection of seeing Porter's chief of staff, Colonel Locke, or of receiving a message Locke had testified he delivered to King and McDowell.

On cross-examination, Reverdy Johnson asked, "Were you unwell on that day?" King replied in the affirmative. He was known to suffer from epilepsy and to "drink" excessively.

Johnson asked King when he left the column on the 29th. "I rejoined the division about 8 o'clock of the evening of the 29th," the general said. He had not been responsive to the question but Johnson let that pass and asked, "Did you continue to be unwell on the 30th?" Answer: "I did."

"As you were so unwell during the 29th as to be unable to join your column during a greater part of the day, and also so unwell on the 30th, are you satisfied that you have a clear recollection of the events of the 29th?"

"I think I have."[16]

5

What had seemed minor points in earlier testimony had evolved into major ones by the afternoon of Day Twenty-Seven, or so it seemed when Joseph Holt recalled to the stand Brigadier General Benjamin S. Roberts,

John Pope's army's former inspector-general and the officer who had filed the charges against General Porter.

Most of the Judge-Advocate's questions dealt with the observations Roberts had made during the afternoon of August 29 of Confederate forces arriving and passing from Gainesville to their right, facing Porter, and others moving up the turnpike toward Pope's attacks against Stonewall Jackson and Centreville. General Roberts' answers to the questions Reverdy Johnson asked on cross-examination revealed that at no time had he been able to see Porter's position. But a member of the Court elicited an interesting response when Roberts was asked how many of the enemy were in front of Porter that afternoon: "I do not believe that there was any force in front of General Porter's command on that day, except a cavalry force in observation there with some light artillery."[17]

The parade of officers who had testified earlier continued on Day 28, January 6, 1863. However, after the minutes of the previous session had been approved, the Judge-Advocate read a letter to Major General Hunter, dated January 5, that had just been received from Secretary of War Edwin M. Stanton:

> The state of the service imperatively demands that the proceedings in the Court over which you are now presiding, having been pending more than four weeks, should be brought to a close without any unnecessary delay. You are, therefore, directed to sit without regard to hours, and close your proceedings as speedily as may be consistent with justice and the public service.[18]

Stanton's message was a clear directive to his political allies on the Court to accelerate Porter's conviction and sentencing. His text was as inaccurate as his intervention was improper: The Army of the Potomac was idle at Falmouth while its senior officers squabbled and Burnside pressed Lincoln to remove him, and out in Tennessee, William Rosecrans' army was resting in Murfreesboro after Braxton Bragg had abandoned it—and everyone in the North who could read a newspaper knew it.

Moreover, elsewhere in the building, on Day Twenty-Eight of Porter's trial by general court-martial, a court of inquiry had been looking into Radical Irvin McDowell's conduct for *thirty-six* working days—yet its president, Major General George Cadwalader, received no such message from Edwin Stanton, nor would he subsequently.[19]

In these circumstances, outrageously harmful to Fitz John Porter's case as clearly they were, Reverdy Johnson was powerless to protest. Judge-Advocate Holt hastened to move the prosecution effort forward as Stanton had directed by recalling Irvin McDowell.

Holt asked: "Will you state to the Court at what time and place you saw General King for the last time on the 29th of August last?"

General McDowell replied: "I do not recollect seeing General King on that day. I have been trying to recall to mind when I saw him, if did see him, on that day. I have asked of my staff officers, and tried to refresh my memory on that point, but I cannot recall to mind having met General King on the 29th of August last."

"After the interview which you had on the 29th of August with General Porter, of which you have spoken heretofore in your testimony, you stated that you turned down toward Bethlehem Church. Will you state whether you have any recollection of a staff officer from General Porter, bearing a message, while you were there, and if you made any reply?"

"I do not remember anything of the kind."

"Have you, or not, any recollection of having, after parting with General Porter on the 29th of August, sent back to him a message like this: 'Take my compliments to General Porter, and say to him that I think he better remain where he is,' or words to that effect?"

"I have no recollection of sending any such message."

"Have you, or not, any recollection of having said to General Porter, in your interview when you first met him on the 29th of August, that that was no place to fight a battle, that he was too far in advance?"

"I cannot recollect precisely what words passed between us at that time," McDowell reminded Holt. "I have no recollection of having said anything to the effect that it was not a good place to fight on. It was about as good a place, so far as topography was concerned, as any other in that part of the country. I think our conversation was chiefly upon the subject of not putting ourselves in a position to be unable to fulfill the requirements of the order about retiring behind Bull Run."

"Do you recollect at what hour you first met General Pope that evening on the battlefield, or near the battlefield?"

"I cannot tell the hour."

"Have you any recollection of a messenger from General Porter, bearing an order or message which he first offered to you, and which you directed him to hand to General Pope, alleged to be then in your presence?"

"I have not. There may have been, but I have no recollection of it."

"Have you been able to fix, from recollection, with any degree of certainty, the hour at which you met Captain Pope, or the messenger bearing the order from General Pope to General Porter, on the afternoon of the 29th of August?"

"I think I stated in my first examination here that I did not recollect the hour. If the time could be fixed when I saw General Pope, and how long I was occupied in bringing [one of my divisions] forward, then you can estimate that this took place somewhere on the road. That is all that I can tell. I got upon the battlefield some time before sundown; that I can state—that I arrived on the Henry House Hill sometime before sundown."

"As early as 6 o'clock, probably?"

"When I got on top of that hill, it must have been an hour at least before sunset."[20]

Was being examined something General McDowell found irritating beyond toleration, or had he been using his display of displeasure to emphasize to the Court the veracity of the testimony he had given back on Days Thirteen, Fourteen, and Fifteen? Whichever, Holt gave observers the chance to decide by turning the witness over to counsel for the Accused.

"Do I understand," Johnson asked, "you to say that you have no recollection of having met General King *at all* on the 29th of August last?"

McDowell, exasperated, asked if his answer to the first question in the examination of today might be read as his answer to the question now asked. Accordingly, it was read: "I do not recollect of seeing General King on that day. I have been trying to recall to mind when I saw him, if I did see him, on that day. I have asked of my staff officers, and tried to refresh my memory on that point, but I cannot recall to mind having met General King on the 29th of August last."

"There are some facts, perhaps, that will recall it to your recollection?"

"That may be."

"General King states that he saw you on the morning of the 29th of August."

"That may be."

"Have you any recollection of having dismounted at any time?"

"Most distinctly. It is always my rule, whenever I happen to go forward myself, to dismount and rest my horse, and that is a direction which I give to my staff, my escort, orderlies, and cavalry."

"Have you any recollection of having dismounted when you got to the neighborhood of Bethlehem Church, after you left General Porter, and if there was any officer with you at time near a fence?"

"I recollect distinctly having dismounted at the time referred to in the question, and that there were officers near me. I think it was under a tree. I have no recollection of a fence."

"Can you recollect the name of any general officer who was with you at that time?"

"I think General Bayard was with me, or came to see me, and I think I may have received visits from different officers of my command—perhaps General Patrick, perhaps General Gibbon. I am merely naming different officers who may have visited me, though I do not specially recollect of their coming near me or of my having seen them. I stopped at that place, and from that place sent out orders to get the corps on the Sudley Springs road, to the north. It was from that place that I sent the officers of my staff to get these different brigades and divisions on this road. But what officers may have come to see me, or may have been with me, for longer or shorter periods of time, I do not recollect. It was a matter that made no impression upon me at the time, for I was occupied with other matters of thought."

"Do you remember whether General King's division was there?"

"I do, most distinctly."

"His division being there, if the general was there, do you not think it probable he would have been with you on that occasion?"

"The general was not in command of his division during the whole of that day. But when he left the command of that division I do not know. If he had been there, it is more than likely I would have seen him."

"Do you recollect whether on that occasion you wore a blouse over your uniform?"

Irvin McDowell was famous throughout the army for wearing a conical straw hat on hot days and for other modifications.[21]

"Upon my word, I do not recollect."

"Are you in the habit of wearing it, on such occasions?"

"On what occasions?"

"During a battle or while traveling."

"That depends upon circumstances, whether I am cold or whether it is raining, &c. I sometimes do and sometimes do not. That is all the answer I can give."

"Can you recollect whether on that day you received any message or order at all from General Porter?"

"Yes, sir; I received messages from him on that day."

"Can you tell the Court particularly about any one of those messages?"

"I answered one of his messages in writing, but I have no copy of that note. I do not know whether I wrote it, or whether it was written by another, and signed by me. I think his notes were asking how the battle was going on, or what was the condition of things over with us, so far as I can recollect."

"Did you know at that time, or do you now know, Colonel Locke, who was General Porter's chief of staff?"

"I have been told that he is; and if he is the same person that I saw at General Porter's headquarters, at Upton's Hill, as his adjutant-general, I know him. I think I met him here to-day in the ante-chamber."

"Can you tell the Court if you have any recollection of having seen that officer at all on the 29th of August?"

"It is very likely I saw him; but if I did, it made no impression on my mind more than many other officers whom I saw."

"Have you any recollection that any one of the messages that you say General Porter sent you that day was borne by Colonel Locke?"

"Having said that I do not recollect seeing Colonel Locke at all during that day, of course that answers the question. What I meant when I said I might have seen that officer on that day, was simply this. There were many officers around General Porter, but I do not recollect that officer more than I do any of the others. I distinctly recollect seeing General Porter; that would very naturally make an impression on me. But who were around him, what officers were near him, I do not recollect."

"Have you any recollection of having been at or near General Pope's headquarters, with General Pope, on the afternoon of the 29th of August?"

"Yes, sir; afternoon, in one sense."

"About what time?"

"It was after the division had been ordered back to the Sudley Springs road, and north on that road toward the turnpike. It must have been somewhere in the vicinity of sundown that I first saw him. General Pope's headquarters, as I afterward learned, were some distance from where I met him; that is to say, several hundred yards, on a hill by a wood. I did not see him at those headquarters until after nightfall."

"Can you tell whether you met General Pope in the evening or afternoon of the 29th at a point near where his headquarters were on the morning of the 30th?"

"When I first met General Pope on the afternoon of the 29th, it was in the northwest angle made by the Sudley Springs road with the Warrenton turnpike, and near their intersection. General Pope's headquarters that night and the next day were in the northeast angle made by those two roads, and I judge some 300 or 400 yards from their intersection, in the edge of a wood, on the top of quite a high hill, on the north or left bank of Young's Branch."

"Do you remember who was with you when you met General Pope on the afternoon or the evening of the 29th?"

"I do not. I will mention one thing. I had a very large staff, and it is impossible for me to recollect who were with me at one time or another, unless there is something particular to call my attention to it."

Members of the Court had some questions:

COURT: From your knowledge of the condition of things on the 29th of August, was there any considerable force of the enemy in front of General Porter's corps, near the Manassas Railroad, on the south side of it?

MCDOWELL: I have no positive knowledge on that point; I have not supposed that there was, but I cannot support that supposition by any positive facts.

COURT: If there had been any such force in front of General Porter's corps and south of the railroad, do you think, from your knowledge of the ground, that would have prevented General Porter from obeying the order to attack the right wing of the main body of the enemy?

The Accused objected to the question, as not being in the nature of rebutting evidence. No member of the Court sustaining the objection, it was ordered that the question be answered.

MCDOWELL: I do not know where the right wing of the main body of the enemy was at that time. Such a force of the enemy, in such a position, would itself most likely have been the right wing of the enemy, so far as I can imagine the case. The distance from General Porter's head of column to the road at that time was not so great as to have enabled a large force of the enemy to be between them, and to be detached from the main body of the enemy.

COURT: At what time did you last see General Porter on the 29th?

MCDOWELL: I have stated, in my first examination, that I could not fix the time when I left General Porter to go back to the head of my own corps, near the Bethlehem Church, and I am not able to do so at this time. It was in the forenoon, at least.

COURT: Are you, or are you not, confident that you did not send a message on the 29th of August to General Porter that he better remain where he was?

MCDOWELL: I do not think I did.[22]

6

John Pope followed Irvin McDowell in the regular witness chair. Judge-Advocate Holt, perhaps recalling Edwin Stanton's admonition to hurry, used little preamble in placing his first question: "In your telegraphic dispatch of the 30th of August last, which has been read to the Court, giving to the Government an account of the battle of the 29th of August, you say that you fought with the combined forces of the enemy. Will you state what is the meaning of the word 'combined,' as used by you in that dispatch?"

"During the whole morning, and until late in the afternoon of the 29th," Pope replied, "the forces with which we were fighting, as I then understood and still understand, were the forces of Jackson, Ewell, and Hill; but before the battle closed on the 29th—I think at the time or about the time that the division of King was pushed to the front—a portion of the forces of Longstreet, leading, as I understood, the main portion of Lee's army, had gotten on to the field; how many I do not know. In that dispatch I merely meant to say, as I had previously reported to the War Department, that we had interposed between Jackson's forces and Longstreet's forces; that, on the 29th, the combined forces were those of Longstreet and Jackson."

"Have you any recollection of having received on the afternoon of the 29th, say about 5 o'clock, a written message from General Porter, which you retained?"

"I have no remembrance of that at all."

"Have you any recollection of having sent to him on that evening, about that hour, a verbal message by any of his officers?"

"I do not remember it."

"Do you remember about the hour that you first saw General McDowell on that afternoon?"

"I think it was about half-past 5 or between that and 6 o'clock in the afternoon."

"And at what point?"

"I had been visiting the left of our line in the front, and was returning to the point where I had established my headquarters, when I met General McDowell on the Warrenton pike, I think a little west of where the Sudley Springs road comes into the pike."

"Will you state what opportunity General Porter had, previous to and at the time the dispatches from him to General Burnside were written, to know the condition of the Army of Virginia, and was the information in regard to that army, as given in those dispatches, correct?"

The Accused objected to the question and was sustained, whereupon Judge-Advocate Holt turned the witness over to Reverdy Johnson.

"Have you any recollection," Johnson asked Pope, "that, having met General McDowell on the afternoon or evening of the 29th, you had any conversation with him as to the movements of any portion of his own command?"

"I think I had not. I do not remember. I think the orders that I gave to General McDowell I sent to him by aides. I had a moment's conversation with him on the road when I first met him, but I do not remember what it was about."

Answers such as that one were hardly worth recording, Johnson must have concluded, for he closed his examination at this point. Holt announced that the prosecution rested their case. Johnson asked permission to call two witnesses to testify to certain points in the rebutting evidence; the request was granted.

Lieutenant Colonel Frederick Locke, Porter's assistant adjutant general, was the first witness to be recalled. Reverdy Johnson asked: "When you received the message—to which you have testified—from General Porter for General King, were you at once impressed with the importance of that message—its special importance at that time?"

"I was."

"Why?"

"Because, first, I knew that General King was to operate with our corps that day; I knew that, because I had received the order to General Porter from General Pope in the morning, at the hands of General Gibbon, in which General Porter was directed to move toward Gainesville and take General King with him. General King being in the rear of our column, I presumed from his position, and thinking, from the operations that were going on, that we were going to have a fight, that he would be in reserve. Therefore, when General Porter gave me that message, I presumed that it was to hold General King where he was, so that he could act in cooperation with the rest of the command in case it was necessary."

"Did you then, at the time of receiving the message, expect that battle would probably be joined very soon?"

"Yes, sir."

"When you received from General McDowell the message to which you have testified, to the effect that he would carry General King with him, and that General Porter better remain where he was, did you or not regard that message from General McDowell as of still greater consequence and moment?"

"Yes, sir; it impressed me very strongly all the way up to the time that I gave it to General Porter."

"Did you make the best of your way to General Porter in haste to deliver the message to him?"

"Yes, sir."

"Do you recollect distinctly that your sense of the character of that message induced you to deliver it to General Porter in a particular manner?"

"Yes, sir; it did impress me in that way, so that I delivered it to him in an undertone of voice, as I thought it was for his ear alone."

"Did these facts to which you have testified impress both of these messages upon your memory indelibly?"

"Yes, sir. I have never forgotten the messages, or the incidents connected therewith."

"About that time, after the day was over, have you any recollection that you mentioned to any other officer or officers the having borne and delivered these messages, or either of them?"

"Toward the close of the day, when I was sent by General Porter to General Morell with the order for him to move forward his division and attack the enemy, on my way up to General Morell, I passed Colonel—now General—Warren. He asked me where I was going, and I told him. Said he, 'I will ride with you,' And I told him of the message which General McDowell had given to me to carry to General Porter the afternoon of that day. That I remember distinctly."

"Do you remember the precise spot where you met the two officers in whose presence you delivered the message from General Porter?"

"I think I do."

"Have you any doubt that you can indicate the spot exactly?"

"No, sir. I think if I was on the same ground, I could go right to it, or within a very short distance of it."

"And you could state to the Court the topographical details by which you could find it, could you not?"

"Yes, sir."

"At that time did you know General King, personally or by sight?"

"I had never seen General King, to my knowledge, before that day—that afternoon."

"Did you know General McDowell?"

"Very well."

"When you delivered the message from General Porter to the officer whom you met, did you first ask him if he was General King?"

"I did; because I did not know General King, and I wished to be sure."

"Do you remember distinctly that at that time the two officers were standing close to a fence, and that one of them was partially with his arm upon it?"

"They were standing close to a fence, on the right-hand side of the road going toward Manassas. General McDowell stood to the right of General King. As near as I can recollect, General King stood against the fence, with his arms in an easy manner."

"After delivering that message to the officer in question, did you, to the best of your recollection, see General King again until you saw him in this room?"

"I did not see General King, that I recollect, until I saw him the first day that he appeared in this room as a member of this Court. I came in the room, and he sat by this window here, and I recognized in him the officer I met on that day with General McDowell."

"Your attention having been directed to the message and its delivery, as you have stated, did you, at the time of delivering it to General King, notice a resemblance in personal appearance to any other officer, and was that resemblance recalled to your mind again when you saw General King in this room?"

"Yes, sir. General King always reminds me of General Seymour."

"Are you entirely positive, as much as you can be of any fact, that you did deliver to General Porter, on the afternoon of the 29th of August, words which purported to be a message from General McDowell, to the effect that General King was to be taken away, and that he—General Porter—was to remain there where he was?"

"I am positively certain of it."[23]

Locke's examination was continued by members of the Court, the first of which asked: "Did General King make any reply to your message?"

LOCKE: I think not in words. As near as I can recollect, General King deferred, by a motion of his hand or head, to General McDowell.

COURT: Was this message from General McDowell to General Porter an order, or in the nature of an order?

LOCKE: I considered it so.

COURT: Are you sure that when you saw either of those two officers alone, you could recognize General King from General Seymour?

LOCKE: Yes, sir; I know General Seymour intimately.[24]

Lieutenant Stephen Weld, Porter's aide, replaced Locke on the witness stand. Johnson reminded Weld that earlier he had testified that at about five o'clock on the afternoon of the 29th of August, he delivered to General Pope, in the presence of General McDowell, a message from General Porter. "State to the Court any facts, not already stated," said Johnson, "which make you certain that you are not mistaken in giving that testimony."

Weld replied: "After I left General Hatch on that day, and while going to General McDowell, I met Captain Haven, of General McDowell's staff.

I then went to General Pope, and after leaving him and going to the road, I looked toward our batteries, which were firing, and the sun shone right in my face, so that I could not see plainly at all.

"I remember that as distinctly as can be.

"And also I remember very plainly General Pope putting that message I gave him in his left-hand vest pocket. He was facing to the south, and General McDowell was facing about the opposite way. I am very positive about it, indeed. There was no one with General Pope then, except General McDowell."

"You know then, positively, the fact that when you delivered that message, the sun had not set?"

"I am as positive as I can be. I know it."

"State the spot where you delivered the message, as you recollect it, if you can describe it."

"It was north of what I supposed to be the Warrenton pike, and east of a road which I think is the Sudley Springs road; very near both roads. I would like to state that there might have been an orderly with General McDowell at that time; I am not positive about that."

"Are you entirely positive that, after your return to General Porter, you saw Captain Douglass Pope arrive?"

"No, sir; I cannot say that it was Captain Douglass Pope; I can only say that I am certain that a messenger from General Pope arrived."

"In other words, you are perfectly satisfied that your testimony on that point, as given earlier, is correct?"

"Yes, sir."

With Weld's strong affirmation his examination ended and the taking of testimony in this case was concluded.

How long would the Accused need to prepare his defense? Three days? Agreed.

Day Twenty-Eight ended; Fitz John Porter would "lay before the Court" his defense on Saturday morning, January 10, 1863.[25]

CHAPTER TEN

The Beginning of the Rest of the Accused's Life

WOULD Edwin McMasters Stanton have written the letter to General Hunter dated January 5 if he had foreseen that by the end of the very next day, both sides in the Fitz John Porter general court-martial would be resting their cases?

An interesting question, for it was not often that this crafty, deceitful man made a mistake. Moreover, by citing specious reasons Stanton had called attention to the irregularity of the action he had taken. Why this indication of impatience?

The trial had gone as Stanton may well have desired. Prosecutor Joseph Holt, his chosen instrument, had made a strong case. His War Department had been a cornucopia supplying any services Holt needed—including counsel on trial strategy, coaching of witnesses bordering on subornation of perjury, possibly even the interception of Porter's mail.

Had Reverdy Johnson been so successful in making Holt's most important witnesses (General Pope, McDowell, Roberts, mind-reader Smith, Captain Pope) uncomfortable under his persistent interrogation that the Court might not convict Porter? Certainly, the Accused's witnesses had been firm in giving testimony that was contrary to that of those that Holt had called, and they had remained definite in defending their assertions. For example, lowly Lieutenant Weld was arguably more convincing than Major Generals Pope and McDowell.

Such may well have been the musings of all concerned during the three days allotted the Accused for preparation of his defense. Each morning the Court met, then adjourned. Elsewhere in Washington General Porter,

Reverdy Johnson, and Charles Eames collaborated on a speech that would be the Accused's last opportunity to rebut the government's contentions and persuade the Court that he was not guilty of either charge or of any of the specifications.

2

The session on Saturday, January 10, 1863—Day Thirty-Two—began like any other with the approval of the minutes. From then onward, however, everything ran counter to Fitz John Porter's best interests.

The first sign of trouble was the calling of Reverdy Johnson to read to the Court the document marked "Defense of the Accused." This was most irregular; the defense was supposed to have the last word, so that response could be made to the Government's closing statement. Apparently, Judge-Advocate Holt thought it unnecessary for him to go beyond the points he had already placed in the record. In any event, Johnson was to open the proceeding. He read:

> Mr. President and Gentlemen: I stand before you, I trust, as a man who, up to the 27th of August last, was and desired to be of fair name and fame; a soldier held to be faithful, laborious, loyal, and trustworthy; prompt to honorable duty though involving personal peril, and having done some service which my country and my Government had seen fit generally to regard and to reward as meritorious. . . .

No, no! This was not General Porter addressing the Court, it was Reverdy Johnson—in fact, of course, but the words were his, the cadences those of a lawyer, the style florid. The impression made was all wrong. The effort was doomed from the outset.

"Defense of the Accused" was actually an extension of the operating fiction that Porter was conducting his own defense. The record so indicated; in print *Accused* asked questions, not *Mr. Johnson*. Ordinarily, that hardly mattered. Nor would harm have been done if the document were intended merely for use by someone reviewing the case. But applying the same technique to a speech text that works in written formats was a gross mistake. It is surprising that a lawyer of Reverdy Johnson's vast experience made it.

Even if General Porter himself had delivered the oration, one wonders if anyone in the courtroom could listen with a straight face to a soldier saying:

> Eminent and honorable men, fit in every way to be heard with respect, have come here before you, within the past few days, to bear upon their knowledge and their oath at least thus much of witness in my behalf and praise.
>
> Nor do I for a moment doubt that their words, so spoken: carried with them your belief. But in some sense such words were not needed to attest to you what I have been and what I was up to those two days of my life in August last, which this wicked accusation would have blackened if I had not crushed down its falsehood by my defense, even as you will, I do not doubt, in your finding, crush down its malice.

Or this:

> Your eminent official law adviser [Holt], who has conducted this prosecution calmly and fairly so far as on him depended, but with the vigilance and energy which his duty demanded, himself, in the recent past, when momentous events hinged on the great sway which in his high post he bore, has trusted me, and has felt that his trust was in nowise betrayed.

This was hogwash. Johnson's listeners must have been grateful when they heard him say, "But no more of this. I go on at once to answer these charges as they stand."

Porter/Johnson (or Johnson/Porter) need not have bothered. What followed was information by then familiar to everyone on the Court but recast in the prolix manner so dear to lawyers. For example, the passage beginning "The order set forth in the first specification to the first charge bears upon its face a plain purpose and meaning" consumed 703 words and concluded: "I now proceed to make such citations from the testimony before the Court as will fully establish all that I have stated."

Even in context, how many in the courtroom were likely to have comprehended what "Porter" was getting at when Johnson read:

> In addition to the unusual, if not unexampled, character of such a movement which appears from the testimony of the witness upon the point, it must be borne in mind that the adoption of such a course by me would have been in direct and palpable violation not only of the letter but of the whole spirit and meaning of the order which I was trying to execute.

Yet it could not have been carelessness on the part of Reverdy Johnson and Charles Eames that resulted in such turgid prose. It was far more likely that these lawyers had produced this document for lawyer Abraham Lincoln's eyes, that the Court's reaction to Johnson's reading of it was of little weight compared to the impact it might have on the President's thinking—especially if their client were convicted and Lincoln entered the case in his capacity as the only appellate authority.

Moreover, an hour or so into the "Defense of the Accused" the fog of words gave way to some straight-forward passages that suggested a contribution by Porter:

> That I could not at any time have literally obeyed the order of 4:30 P.M. of that day, by attacking the right of the enemy's forces which it directed and intended me to attack, namely, those under Jackson, is too clear to admit of dispute or doubt.
>
> What, then, remained for me to do in compliance with the general spirit and meaning of that order as a military movement of cooperation with the army of General Pope?
>
> Why, it was my duty to do just what I did do, as directed by General McDowell when he left me; that is, hold on to the strong position in which my front was posted, with my center and rear within close supporting distance, and thus hold in check before me the massing forces of the enemy, which, but for my presence there, would have closed up at once upon Jackson's right, crushed our forces in front of it, outflanked General Pope on his left, striking General McDowell on the Sudley Springs road . . . and this force surely doomed General Pope's whole army which was engaged that day to an inevitable and signal defeat, even though its efforts had been, if possible, more heroic and its courage more stubborn than they were.

> It was the presence and menacing aspect of my corps in its strong position before this separate enemy which alone prevented him from the overwhelming and decisive movement upon General Pope's hard-pressed left and upon General McDowell's column as he approached the battlefield.
>
> Thus I say, then, that I complied with the meaning and spirit of General Pope's order; and, when I received it, General Pope was in a position of peril which he did not suspect or imagine, but from which I could shield him so long as I could hold my position.

Here, finally, was the kind of emphatically and boldly put assertion—the proud, defiant statement of the seasoned combat soldier who, during the Seven Days, had amassed more experience than any other senior commander in facing Robert E. Lee—that could make the Court and everyone else in the room shake-off somnolence and strain to hear more.

There would be more, most of it near the end of the three-plus hours that delivering the speech required. There was vigor and audacity in passages such as these:

> But I will not tax the patience of the Court with further argument or protest against these details of accusation. I smite them, one and all—the charge and its three specifications—with the solid mass of evidence, which, as I conceive, has already beaten down the charge of disobedience to the order directing me to attack the enemy on his flank. That testimony shows my behavior before the enemy.
>
> Standing upon that testimony, I defy all accusation, and I challenge all proof, that it was misbehavior. I affirm that it was faithful, zealous effort, made according to my best judgment, then and there, to aid to the utmost, my country, her army, and her cause; and I further affirm that all the proof, and all reasonable judgment of it, show that by those efforts, mainly, was prevented a great and fearful addition to whatsoever of disaster or failure did then occur.
>
> ⁂
>
> What had happened in such a short interval to effect so wonderful a change in the mind and purpose of General Pope? He tells us plainly he had come to Washington, and here he had been

made to see my military conduct in a new light. His eyes were open here—that, I believe, is his very phrase—to many things that he had not rightly judged before; and now, on the 5th or 6th of September, he is hot in my pursuit. His eyes are opened!

What a confession is here! The commanding general of the Army of Virginia comes to Washington to have his eyes opened; to see aright in the light of alleged criminality my military acts, done under his orders, in the dark night of the 27th of August, at Warrenton Junction, or on the critical and anxious day of the 29th of August, on the road to Gainesville, or on the perilous ridge of battle, where it raged at the field of Bull Run, on the eventful day of the 30th.

⁂

Where are these mystical proofs of crime? Let them be produced! Are they the three or four telegraphic communications from me to General Burnside, which were introduced in evidence by the prosecution with my cordial assent, and which I would have introduced without hesitation, if the prosecution had not presented them? If these papers prove my guilt, or tend to prove it, or raise a reasonable suspicion of intention on my part to fail my commanding general, sacrifice the army of my country, and betray its cause, then let words and letters, in which such damning guilt is manifested, be set forth, so that all men may read my criminality with its doom.

⁂

And this brings me back again reluctantly to consider further the testimony and the action of General Pope in this matter. Believing, as it appears that he did, on the 5th or 6th of September last, that I had, by criminal conduct and intent, put his army and this capital into great peril, why did he not then exhibit charges against me?

Was it fit, if, after his eyes had been opened at Washington, he did at last see me as a man stained with the guilt which his subordinate, three months after, has undertaken in these charges to impute to me—was it fit for him, as a patriot or a soldier, or as my commanding officer, to stand by in silence and see me, for months afterward, invested with high and most responsible command?

> Does not the fact that he did thus so long stand silent, cover this whole accusation, to the judgment of all candid men, with the odious suspicion of being, at the best, a mere afterthought, if not something far more wicked and malignant? On page 52 [840] of the record of the session of this Court, on the 5th of December last, appears, in the testimony of General Pope on that day, the following statement:
>
> > *It was not until the campaign was closed, and I came to Washington City, on the 4th or 5th of September, that I was informed by the President of the United States that he had seen several dispatches or letters from General Porter to General Burnside, dated a day or two previous to these battles, which had occasioned him very grave apprehensions that General Porter would fail to do his duty. This communication of the President to me opened my eyes to many matters which I had before been loth to believe, and which I cannot bring myself now to believe.*[1]
>
> I invoke attention to the carefully measured, yet most sinister, language of this whole declaration, made by a man filling a high place in the service of his country, under the solemnity of an oath.

General Porter reminded the Court that the President subsequently entrusted the security of Washington to him and on September 12 restored him to command of the Fifth Corps for service in the battles of South Mountain and Antietam. He expressed his indignation that Pope would imply that the President could both share Pope's convictions that Porter was guilty and knowingly retain him in high command. "I exhort General Pope," said the Accused, "to find some other and better explanation for his so suddenly distempered mind than he has in his testimony above given, or that his subordinate officer, my accuser on this record, has been able in this trial to prove."[2] Porter continued:

> I come now to say a few words regarding the testimony of General McDowell. I shall speak of him as a witness with entire calmness and candor, because, though I speak with regret, I shall speak with no disrespect.
>
> His testimony, taken as a whole, has astonished me beyond

> measure. I feel that it has done me more harm and more wrong—I charitably hope unintentional wrong—than has been done to me by all the rest of the testimony of the prosecution put together.
>
> In saying this, I, of course, lay wholly out of view what I cannot but consider as the ravings of Lieutenant Colonel Smith about his fifteen minutes first and last interview with me on the morning of the 28th at Manassas, when he thinks that he saw in my face that I had a crime on my mind, and comes up here to encumber the record of this honorable Court with that and similar rubbish about my being a traitor.
>
> I return to the wholly different and broadly contrasted testimony of General McDowell. I remark with regret that General McDowell appears to have forgotten almost all that I remember of what took place between us on the 29th of August last, either face to face or by message, and that he seems clearly to remember some very important matters of which, after my best efforts, I can find no trace whatever, either in my memory or my action, or his action, or the communications direct or by message which on that day passed between us.

Much attention was given to controversy over exactly what the generals had—or had not—said to each other. Consider how favorably the following passage would have impressed the Court if Porter instead of Johnson had read it:

> General McDowell does not pretend to state or to remember any reply whatever made by me to him when, as he says, he gave me that order [to attack] and understood me to assent to it; but this Court well know, in view of all the proof upon this record, especially as given as to my position before the enemy, is the testimony of Marshall, Hyland, Stevenson, Morell, and Griffin—all speaking in just the same sense to the point, that if I had then received from McDowell such order to attack, it is utterly incredible and impossible that I could have received it with immediate and silent assent, and have permitted him to leave me without discussing it, and stating my objections to it. Still more utterly incredible and impossible is it, that if I had thus received

and assented to that order, and then failed to act in pursuance of any such direction, that I could possibly have abstained from sending to General McDowell, who was, for a long time afterward, as his own testimony shows, within a mile and a half of me, any notice or explanation whatsoever of my failure so to act.

Such a course would have been sheer insanity, utter craziness in me or in any other army corps commander in my position. Such conduct on my part would have resounded along the lines of the whole army. It would have been proclaimed forthwith at the headquarters of General Pope.

It would have been blazoned among these charges and specifications side by side with the order itself, and, if true, it ought to have made the words of exculpation which General Pope uttered to me at Fairfax Court-House on the 2d September, four days afterward, choke him as he spoke. But it is not true that General McDowell then, or at any time on that day, gave me any such order "to put my troops in there," or to do anything of the kind; and fortunate is it for General McDowell that it is not true, for if he had given me any such mandate, to thrust my corps in over that broken ground between Jackson's right and the separate enemy massing, in my front, the danger and disaster of such a movement would have been then and now upon his hands.

I am glad that I can say that General McDowell is utterly in error upon this point, and is in no way chargeable with such fatal military blunder. It is not alone that I am as clear as I can be as to any fact in my life that I received at that time no such order from him, but it is demonstrated in what I have said, as well as in what else stands proved in this record, that no such order to me could have been then by him given.[3]

3

Finally, Reverdy Johnson came to "Porter's" peroration. Much of it was in the florid style that prevailed elsewhere in the long document, but two passages were exceptions:

"If the charge had not assumed the solemn form that has been given to it, it would be received everywhere, where my whole conduct is known, as ludicrously false or the creation of a morbid or distempered brain.

"Without assuming to myself a purer patriotism than animates the soldiers of the Union, I say fearlessly that none, no, not one, loves our Union with a stronger, a holier love. There is nothing in the future, as there has been nothing in the past, that I would not do and gladly do to achieve its victory over its enemies and to bind up the wounds under which it now bleeds."

And finally:

"As far as one arm and the aspirations of one heart may be exerted to avert the dire calamity, mine will be used to the last moment of my life. I live now amidst whatever discouragements surround us, and through the gloom which they cause, cheered only by the anticipation that all will yet be well; that our Union will emerge from its present dangers even stronger for the trials through which it is passing; that it will be ours once more to be proud of and to glory in and again serve to light the world by the effulgence of its example; that it will become, as it was but recently, a monument of past renown and a pledge of future glory, and will so continue 'til time's last echo shall have ceased to sound.' "[4]

But the last words on Day Thirty-Two, January 10, 1863, were to be those addressed to the Court by Judge-Advocate Joseph Holt:

"I will simply remark that this case has been thoroughly and most patiently investigated. A continuous session of some forty-five days sufficiently attests this. Indeed, the greater part of the evidence touching the more important and the more severely contested points has, by re-examination and cross-examination, been again and again impressed upon your minds, so that I now feel entirely satisfied that it is completely comprehended and appreciated by you in all its bearings.

"Whatever, therefore, of inaccuracies of interpretation of testimony, and whatever of illogical deduction from it, may have found a place in the very elaborate defense of the Accused, which has been read, may be safely left for their correction to the recollection and judgment of the Court.

"To prepare a written reply, in keeping with the gravity of this proceeding, to the argument of the Accused, would require several days, thus involving a delay which it is most important to avoid. From this consideration, and from the urgent demand which exists for the services of members of this Court in other and more active fields of duty, it is felt that the public interests will be best subserved by asking, as I now do, that you will proceed at once to deliberate upon and determine the issues which are before you."[5]

4

Between two and three hours after Judge-Advocate Holt passed the case to the Court and its members began deliberating behind closed doors, the trial by general court-martial of Major General Fitz John Porter adjourned *sine die.*[6]

Several circumstances were unusual.

First, Holt's excuse for not rebutting Porter's closing statement was as transparent as Edwin Stanton's directive dated Monday, January 5 to end the proceedings instanter: Porter's enemies wanted him convicted and sentenced before Reverdy Johnson and Charles Eames found a witness who blew away Holt's case.

Second, Holt's claim—echoing Stanton's—that the generals on the Court were needed "in the field" invited ridicule.

Third, that a proceeding as long and complex and prominent as Porter's trial had been could be settled within less than three hours supported the suspicion that the members of the Court spent very little time in asking the Judge-Advocate to read back testimony to refresh their memories, or to advise them on points of law, or in debating controversial issues involved first in reaching a verdict on each of the eight specifications, and then on the two charges, and finally on the sentence.

Precisely what transpired during those few critical hours on that Saturday afternoon would never be known. Beyond the strict secrecy imposed on the deliberations' participants was the requirement that no disclosure of the Court's findings would be made until President Lincoln had reviewed the record and either approved the verdicts and sentence as imposed by the Court or modified it.

From late Saturday afternoon on, persons curious about the trial's outcome could only guess what it would prove to be. Understandably, the Accused and his counsel had nothing to say. Before and during the trial, however, two pamphlets prepared under General Pope's direction by Benjamin Roberts and Thomas C. H. Smith had been distributed in Washington, particularly to newspapermen and members of Congress. The first, *Pope's Campaign in Virginia*, was remarkable for the amount of misinformation it contained. Sometime before the verdict was announced, Roberts collected all but one of the outstanding copies; General Heintzelman had passed his copy on to Porter, who kept it. The next booklet, issued on or about December 22, 1862, by Pope, et al., was entitled *Proceedings of a General Court-Martial for the Trial of Maj. Gen. Fitz John Porter, U.S. Vols.* Drawn from the printed record up to December 22 when the prosecution's presentation ended, the booklet gave the erroneous impression that it was complete. Judge-Advocate Holt wrote Roberts on January 6, 1863, to ask for "a printed copy of the evidence for the government for each member of the court."[7] Such was the only source for speculating, and it was sheer pro-Pope propaganda.

By Monday, January 12, Abraham Lincoln knew that on Saturday General Porter had been found guilty of six of the eight specifications and of both charges and that—in David Hunter's words—"And the court do therefore sentence him, Maj. Gen. Fitz John Porter, of the United States Volunteers, to be cashiered, and to be forever disqualified from holding any office of trust or profit under the Government of the United States."[8] Promptly, the President wrote Judge-Advocate Holt and asked him "To revise [sic] the proceedings and to report fully upon any legal questions that may have arisen in them, and upon the bearing of the testimony in reference to the charges and specifications exhibited against the Accused, and upon which he was tried."[9]

General-in-Chief Halleck had been busy, and on the surface the trial was none of his business. But on Tuesday he wrote this cover note to Secretary of War Stanton: "In compliance with the Sixty-Fifth Article of War, these whole proceedings are transmitted to the Secretary of War to be sent to the President of the United States."[10] Had General Halleck suspected that the report Judge-Advocate Holt was preparing for the President might not tell the whole truth?

Halleck's reliance on the Articles of War to make Stanton responsible to see that Lincoln had access to the verbatim transcript reflected his pre-war experience as California's leading lawyer and his distrust of and contempt for politicians in general and of Joseph Holt in particular. General-in-Chief he might be, but this was all he could do to prevent the denial of justice to a distinguished brother officer.

At about the beginning of Porter's waiting period he received a letter from another brother officer, George McClellan, one written on January 8 apparently in response to two notes from the beleaguered Accused. Their contents and the mood in which Porter had been when he wrote them can be inferred from two of McClellan's fragments: "I shall be only too glad, Fitz, if my testimony has done you any good—your faithful service through so many long months should of itself have cleared you without the necessity of my opening my mouth." Earlier, he had advised: "Don't leave the service yet—be content to wait a while without a command & watch the boiling of the pot a little longer."[11]

5

Lawyers are usually meticulous in their choice of words, and also in reviewing outgoing letters and other documents put in final form by their clerks and secretaries. And Abraham Lincoln was an uncommonly able lawyer. Yet in his request to Joseph Holt on Monday, he had asked the trial judge-advocate to *revise* the proceedings. Had the President not meant *review* them?

Be that as it may, Joseph Holt's product was just about as complete a revision of the proceedings' record as the mind of man could concoct. At the very outset he diverted Lincoln's attention a country mile away from the mission the President had, however imprecisely, assigned him. Holt wrote:

> As the *animus* of the Accused toward his commanding general, in pursuing the line of conduct alleged against him, must largely affect the question of his criminality, and may furnish a safe and reliable light for your guidance in determining points otherwise left doubtful by the evidence, it is proper that it should, if possible, be ascertained before entering at large upon the review of the case, which you have instructed me to make.

In his very first sentence Holt was saying quite directly: If you are not already prejudiced against General Porter, read on and *I will make you prejudiced* despite the fact that he was not convicted of animus or even tried for his possible possession of it.

Holt's revision of Porter's participation in the Second Bull Run disaster began with the allegation that only when he was well along his way with his Fifth Corps from Harrison's Landing toward the Aquia Creek-Fredericksburg area did he learn that he was to serve under General Pope, and that from Falmouth onward he expressed in messages to General Burnside his lack of confidence in Pope. For the President's benefit he reproduced the incriminating telegrams.[12]

Lest Lincoln miss the point, prosecutor Holt abandoned his Presidentially assigned role of reviewer and argued:

> The precise import of these remarkable words, in their connection, cannot be mistaken, nor can it fail to be observed how harshly they jar upon the proprieties of military life. It may be safely affirmed that they express, on the part of the Accused, an intense scorn and contempt for the strategy and movements of the Army of Virginia, a weariness and disgust for his association with it, added to a bitter fling at his commanding general, as found in the extraordinary declaration that he had taken two divisions of his army as a "body guard" to Centreville.
>
> The words, as quoted, disclose also a looking by the Accused, not to General Pope, but to General McClellan as his guide, and a reliance upon his exertions and influence to relieve him from his connection with the Army of Virginia, and an expectation, if not a hope, that they would all soon arrive at Alexandria. This, it is true, would involve the discomfiture of that army, but it would also involve the discredit of its commander, and would restore the Accused to his former position under General McClellan.
>
> Such must have been the anticipation, and such certainly was the result.

"The testimony furnishes yet other indications of the *animus* of the Accused," Holt reported, highlighting the contentions of Roberts and Smith that they had warned Pope that Porter would "fail" him. After summarizing Roberts' testimony, Holt blended reporting and editorial comment in dealing with Smith's contributions to the case.

Well into his report, Judge-Advocate Holt had *not once* referred to proof or refutation of the charges and specifications which, presumably, were the functions of the trial that led ultimately to verdicts and sentencing. Yet, as if the record were nigh-irrelevant, the reviser continued to write in the reporterial-editorial manner with citations that were too vague to enable Lincoln to distinguish Holt's assertions from any witness' testimony:

> It was physically impossible for [Smith] to reproduce [Porter's] manner, the tone of voice, and the expression of the eye, and the play of the features, which may have so much influenced [Smith's] judgment; yet these often afford a language more to be relied on than that of the lips.
>
> [Smith] could not hold up before the Court, for its inspection and appreciation, the sneer of which he spoke; and yet we know that a sneer is as palpable to the mental as a smile is to the natural vision. It is a life-long experience that souls read each other, and that there are intercommunings of spirits, through instrumentalities which, while defying all human analysis, nevertheless completely command the homage of human faith.
>
> Great crimes, too, like great virtues, often reveal themselves to close observers of character and conduct as unmistakably as a flower garden announces its presence by the odors it breathes upon the air. The witness [Smith] may have misconceived this "look," but from the calamities likely to follow such an act of treachery, if, indeed, it was then contemplated, it must be admitted as altogether probable that the shadow of such a crime struggling into being would have made itself manifest.
>
> In view of the fearful perils which then menaced the Army of Virginia, to which they owed a common duty, is it not passing strange that during this interview the Accused uttered not to the witness one word of kindness or cordiality, of encouragement or determination in reference to the sanguinary conflict in which the morrow was to involve them with a common enemy?[13]

The assumption seemed to be that General Porter was really on trial for bad manners in the presence of a visitor.

6

"With this exhibition of the disposition of the Accused toward the service in which he was engaged," Holt wrote to the President, "I will proceed to review, as briefly as possible, the testimony in its bearing upon the charges and specifications of the record."[14]

Was that not what Abraham Lincoln was waiting for?

What followed was mostly a recitation of the Government's case against the Convicted. Only when it suited his purposes did Holt include testimony given by defense witnesses; even then, he cited only enough to refute. Otto Eisenschiml has summarized the effect of Holt's selectivity:

> Neither Porter nor his legal advisers knew that Holt's *Review* was being written, much less that it had gone to Lincoln, or they might well have wondered why the President, an experienced lawyer, did not see at a glance that he was not reading a digest of the trial but a brief of the prosecuting attorney. Would he not ask for a brief of the accused? But all that the record shows is that he received the *Review* on January 19, and signed the verdict two days later. It also has been established that the verbatim record of the proceedings [Halleck had sent Stanton for transmitting to Lincoln] had never left the War Department; even if it had, the President could hardly have perused it, hand-written as it was, in so short a time. Did not the very one-sidedness of the *Review* strike him as incongruous? Or did political considerations outweigh his proverbial sense of justice?[15]

The Radicals, Eisenschiml noted, "were demanding a simple uprooting of McClellan's tribe; did Lincoln decide to throw Porter to the wolves to appease them?"[16] He cited a number of mitigating circumstances, including the possibility that Lincoln resented "Porter's contempt for Pope and the indiscreet manner in which he had expressed it."[17] If so, then indeed Joseph Holt had done his work well in the opening passages of his *Review.*

Certainly, since the expensive humiliation General Lee had inflicted upon the Army of the Potomac at Fredericksburg back in mid-December, Lincoln's enemies had held the political high ground. "If there is a worse place than hell," Lincoln had declared, "I am in it."[18] Newspapers throughout the North agreed that there was where he belonged, overlooking twelve months of pressure on him to replace the Young Napoleon with "anybody" and Lincoln's own remorse over having put the confessed incompetent Burnside within range of General Lee's murderous firepower.

Theories abound, but the fact was that between January 19, when Holt's "review" of the case reached the President and January 21 when he made his decision, the document that he had requested drew much of his attention. Moreover, despite its many flaws Joseph Holt's product deserved respect. Considering its purpose—convincing Lincoln that Fitz John Porter was guilty and deserved to be cashiered—the closing paragraphs were particularly effective:

> There is one feature of the inaction of the Accused on the 29th which it is especially sorrowful to contemplate. How, unrestrained as he was, and with the cannonade of the battle in his ears, and its smoke and the dust of the gathering forces before his eyes, he could, for seven and a half or eight hours, resist the temptation to plunge into the combat, it is difficult to conceive.
>
> But this alone is not the saddest aspect in which his conduct presents itself. Colonel Marshall states that from the cheerings and peculiar yells of the enemy heard on the evening of the 29th, he and every man of his command believed that General Pope's army was being driven from the field. General Morell also says that from the sound of the artillery the battle seemed to be receding, which indicated that it was going against the Federal forces. The Accused, in his note to Generals McDowell and King, speaking of the enemy, says:
>
> > *As they appear to have driven our forces back, the firing of the enemy having advanced and ours retired, I have determined to withdraw to Manassas;*
>
> and, in further justification of this step, he adds:
>
> > *They [the Confederates he faced] have gathered artillery and cavalry and infantry, and the advancing masses of dust show the enemy coming in force.*
>
> In the afternoon, then, of the 29th, it is clear that the conviction was entertained by the Accused and his officers that our forces

were being driven before the enemy—a conviction which, in tones above even the roar of the artillery, should have appealed to his soldier's heart to rush to the rescue. But, heedless of the summons, he turned, not toward, but away from his struggling companions in arms, in the direction of Manassas.

Must we seek an explanation of this want of sympathy with the brave men who were doing battle that day in the feelings, as shown by his dispatches, which unhappily possessed him in reference to the Army of Virginia and its commanding general?

Toward the end of his *Review,* the author paid himself a compliment:

This case has been most patiently investigated. If, in war, and in the midst of active hostilities, any Government has ever devoted so long a period of time—some forty-five days—to the examination of a military charge, it has not come to my knowledge.

The Court was not only patient and just, but liberal, and in the end everything was received in evidence which could possibly tend to place the conduct of the Accused in its true light. It is not believed that there remains upon the record a single ruling of the court to which exception could be seriously taken.

The case is important, not only because of the gravity of the charges and the dignity of the officer arraigned, but also because of the fact that it involves a principle which lies at the very foundation of all discipline and of all efficiency in military operations—the principle of military obedience.

So vital to the military system is this subordination of will and action deemed, that it is secured by the most solemn of human sanctions. Each officer and soldier before entering the service swears that he "will observe and obey the orders of the officers appointed over him"; and it is from this, probably, that the offense of disobedience derives much of the depth and darkness of the criminality with which it is stamped by the Articles of War.

Obedience, indeed, is the very jewel of the soldier's life. It adorns him more, even, than laurels, which are so often plucked by unholy hands. The soldier who has given to the order of his superior officer a prompt, an earnest, a heartfelt support, has triumphed in the field of duty, even though he may have fallen on the field of arms.

The offenses for which the pleadings and testimony arraign the Accused are the very gravest that a soldier can possibly commit, being neither more nor less than the willful violation of the orders of his commanding general in the midst of momentous and perilous military movements, and the shameful abandonment of a struggling army which it was his solemn duty to support, in the very presence of the enemy, and under the very sound of his artillery.

The Court was careful to give to the Accused the benefit of all well-founded doubts that arose in their minds, in reference either to the fact of disobedience or in reference to the measure of criminality that prompted it, and hence they found him not guilty of the fourth and fifth specifications of first charge; and, in the same spirit, the fourth specification of second charge was withdrawn.

While, however, the Court felt that of crimes such as these no officer should be convicted but upon the clearest and most convincing proof of his guilt, they must also have felt that the honor of the profession of arms and the most enduring interests of our common Government and country imperatively demanded that there should be no acquittal when that proof had been made.

J. HOLT,
Judge-Advocate-General.[19]

After what he considered due deliberation, on January 21, 1863, the President signed this document:

The foregoing proceedings, findings, and sentence in the foregoing case of Maj. Gen. Fitz John Porter are approved and confirmed, and it ordered that the said Fitz John Porter be, and he hereby is, cashiered and dismissed from the service of the United States as a major-general of volunteers, and as colonel and brevet brigadier-general in the regular service of the United States, and forever disqualified from holding any office of trust or profit under the Government of the United States.

A. Lincoln.[20]

7

When Major General David Hunter cleared the courtroom on the afternoon of Saturday, January 10, Day Thirty-Two of the ordeal, the man referred to thousands of times since November 27, 1862, as "the Accused" entered a new phase of his life. A Limbo was not quite the right term for it; in fact there was no correct name for it.

Shakespeare's Ophelia was in a period of uncertain change similar to Porter's when she said to the King in *Hamlet,* "Lord, we know what we are, but know not what we may be."[21] Fitz John Porter knew who he had been, and still was—but who might he become, once Lincoln had concluded the only appellate review his kind of trial was entitled to receive?

Since right after First Bull Run in the summer of 1861 until six weeks or so after Antietam, General Porter led first a division and later the Fifth Corps. Within the Army of the Potomac he had enjoyed the additional distinction of being its controversial commander's most relied-upon subordinate, a circumstance that set him apart from generals such as "Bull" Sumner, Sam Heintzelman, and Erasmus Keyes. He and his first cousin, acting Rear Admiral David Dixon Porter, since September commander of the Mississippi River Squadron, were enhancing the reputation gained in three earlier wars of the Fighting Porters.[22]

Even so, Fitz John Porter had no power base of his own. When he was relieved in the same November order that cast George McClellan into oblivion, and then was placed under arrest without being advised of the cause, he discovered new meanings to the word loneliness. For a time he occupied himself with preparations for he knew not what. Then he achieved some stability when he formed the relationship with Reverdy Johnson and Charles Eames, and he acquired a new if undesired identity when he became known formally as the Accused.

From Day One of the trial onward, Porter was busy writing to potential defense witnesses, educating his counsel regarding the truth about Second Bull Run, and helping to identify flaws in Holt's prosecution. He was the central figure in the courtroom, yet day after day he stood over by the windows, saying nothing except to his counsel, listening—as cool as he had been when the balloon's rope broke, or when he fought off attacks thrown by R. E. Lee at Beaver Dam Creek, Boatswain's Swamp, and Malvern Hill during the Seven Days. Others in his peril might be excused for asking themselves *what if?* questions; Porter was obliged to concentrate on escaping conviction.

Anyone attending the sessions had to be struck by the utter unreality of what was happening, Here, perhaps the most successful general in the Union armies—certainly, the best of a miserably performing lot—was being tried by nine officers most of whose combat records to date varied between next to none and wretched. Daily testimony dealt with military matters, yet the unmistakable odor of politics in the courtroom's air was pervasive. The sight of smug John Pope in his Court-provided rocking chair and the sounds of his self-serving aspersions were enough to prove the point that politics ruled. Yet this was a serious undertaking—one that the dignified, ever-cool major general standing over by the windows knew might kill him.

How honest combat is, General Porter may have often thought. And after so many of the men in General Lee's army had tried their best to pack him off to Valhalla, how terrible it would be to die at the hands of men such as these sitting in judgment of him.

Then, early on the afternoon of Saturday, January 10, after General Porter and his counsel had finished presenting the closing statement of the Accused—and as they were waiting for Judge-Advocate Holt to begin the prosecution's response—abruptly, Court President Hunter ordered the room cleared and the doors closed so that the members might begin their deliberations. There would be no closing statement by Holt. Day Thirty-Two was the end of the trial—for Fitz John Porter, the end of the trail if he were found guilty.

When the courtroom doors opened after between two and three hours, all that anyone learned was that the Court had adjourned *sine die*, meaning that the members had reached a verdict and prescribed a sentence if the verdict was guilty and passed the case up to President Lincoln for his approval. How long his review would require and what its result might be, no one could even guess.

One thing, however, was clear. Fitz John Porter had entered what might be called the Ophelia phase: he knew all too well what he had been, but nothing at all about what he might become.

8

Every military academy worthy of its existence has always imposed strict discipline on its cadets in preparing them to cope with the most demanding of circumstances they are likely to encounter in battle. Not even West Point, however, had anticipated the peculiar situation Fitz John Porter, USMA 1845, faced as his post-trial phase opened.

The change was as drastic as Hunter's closing of the courtroom doors on Saturday afternoon had been abrupt. It was too late for Porter to fight any more but too soon to commit himself to any possible post-trial course of action.

Near term, he was scheduled to testify at Irvin McDowell's self-imposed court of inquiry. Reverdy Johnson was belatedly taking his seat in the Senate to which he had been elected by his fellow Marylanders before Day One of the Porter trial. Charles Eames was returning to his law practice. George McClellan, aided by his supporters among powerful businessmen in New York City, was busy working out his own salvation with diligence—but Mac had already advised Porter against leaving the army "while the pot is boiling."

Earlier, McClellan had remarked in a letter to Porter that around Washington they were known as "the great tabooed." Indeed, the Accused could hardly seek respite from his anxiety by leaving his rooms and going over to the Willard Hotel's bar. Which of the thirst quenchers he might encounter could be counted upon to abstain from asking awkward questions no one could answer? And which might be pro-prosecution sources of the next day's newspaper reports that tension had driven the despairing Accused to drink?

Actually, most reporters were speculating that Porter would be acquitted. Secretary of the Navy Gideon Welles made an entry in his diary to that effect; so did Lincoln's secretary, John Nicolay. In letters to his wife and his mother, Porter said that he had heard that the verdict would be favorable.[23] But in one to his wife toward the end of the waiting, he revealed some of his frustrations during the trial:

> Hattie, my dear, I was not allowed to consult my witnesses—and did not know till arraigned what I had to reply to; and I was astonished at the charges when presented, as I did not know of more than three persons whom I could call on to refute them. The enmity of the court was such that I at times had much difficulty in getting my questions accepted. Often I felt like giving up in

> disgust—and declaring that I saw no justice in the court or intention to permit justice or listen to it, but the thought of returning to you with the brand of traitor on my escutcheon stirred me to action.
>
> My counsel have been to me like parents. I do not begrudge their fee—$2000—because I am fighting a political persecution.[24]

On January 20, however, General Porter had one more chance to fight: he was called as a witness in the court of inquiry that had been looking into the conduct of Major General Irvin McDowell. This was an odd proceeding in that McDowell had caused it to be convened to clear him of allegations he had solicited. Also, he acted both as trial judge-advocate and in his own defense. Porter had no objection to testifying. His counsel had decided against his taking the chair during his own trial, so this might give him the opportunity to put information on a record that could enhance the public's opinion of him.

McDowell opened General Porter's examination by asking a number of questions regarding the events of August 29. Porter's answers were generally in line with testimony given by defense witnesses at sessions in the now-deserted courtroom down the hall. By adjournment on that Tuesday afternoon, the colloquy had moved McDowell's "case" not at all.[25]

An interesting incident marked the opening of Day Forty-Nine of McDowell's court of inquiry, Wednesday, January 21. On the day before, McDowell had asked this self-serving question: "Do you know of any matter or thing tending to show that General McDowell was treacherous, incompetent, unfaithful, or otherwise disqualified for the command of a division, corps, or department?"

Porter had replied: "I have no reason to know, and never had any reason to suspect, anything whatever of General McDowell which would tend in any way to disqualify him from holding either of such commands."[26]

That response had been more than a tad unequivocal. Accordingly, Day Forty-Nine's minutes contained this note:

> The witness stated that he answered one question propounded yesterday as considering it confined to General McDowell's ability and his faithfulness, and that the answer is not as general as he now finds the question requires. His further amendment is with ref-

> erence to General McDowell's integrity as a witness before the general court-martial of which General Porter was defendant.

After deliberation, the Court decided: "Evidence of General McDowell's integrity as a witness on any other trial cannot be received on this inquiry, nor does the question call for such testimony."[27]

McDowell's purpose, of course, was to obtain testimony confirming the accuracy of that he had given at Porter's court-martial. Most of the ground covered had to do with their conversations on August 29 and Porter's understanding of when he felt he was and was not under McDowell's orders. As on the day before, nothing of significance resulted.[28] And as it turned out, nothing new would have made any difference.

After Porter was dismissed from the court of inquiry that afternoon, he took a walk. In the lobby of the Willard Hotel he was approached by a reporter for the *New York Times*, a newspaper not friendly to Porter's side of the controversy. According to one account, the reporter asked if he had heard the news. What news? Porter inquired.

"From this moment on, General, you are dismissed from the service. Let me read you the President's decision."

That done, the reporter said, "Sorry, General," and disappeared into the crowd.[29]

Cashiered?

How could this be? Surely the *Times* reporter was wrong. But what if he was not? What could the Court have found in the trial's record to justify such a harsh sentence—indeed, how could they have found him guilty of *anything?*

Had it been those telegrams to Burnside? As soldiers themselves, the members of the Court ought to have recalled the countless times during their careers that they had lacked assurance that they were being ably led. And where in Army Regulations was it written that expressing innermost views was a crime—certainly one calling for *cashiering?*

Or had the nine judges been unduly inhibited by that order from Stanton to expedite the Accused's conviction because of public outrage over Burnside's performance at Fredericksburg in mid-December? Or by adverse reaction to Lincoln's Emancipation Proclamation, or to his management of the Union war effort to quell the rebellion?

And McClellan: Even as cashiering may have been the Court's way of protecting the reputations of John Pope and Irvin McDowell—certainly of Edwin Stanton and even Abraham Lincoln, and by the way those of the Court-martial's members—was this Draconian outcome not driven by Radical Republican frustration at not having been able to disgrace the Young Napoleon immediately after the Second Bull Run humiliation?

Worse, how much weight had lies in the trial record uttered under solemn oath contributed toward the verdict and sentence of cashiering? There had been so many of them! Yet the trial was over, its proceedings were locked in type, and in mid-January, 1863, there seemed no clear way of changing *anything*, ever.

Once back at his quarters, Porter wrote his wife: "I fear not the judgment of the court. I can proudly carry my head, and place my hand on my heart, and declare that I have never done anything for which my country has reason for regret."[30]

Now he knew what he would be: a warrior fighting to restore his reputation.

9

The *New York Herald* on January 22, 1863, may have been the first to break the story. "It is stated that," its account began, "notwithstanding the intimations that the findings of the Court in the Fitz John Porter case were favorable, the President, upon a review the findings of the Court and the testimony, has dismissed General Porter from the army." More:

> This decision, if it be true, is unexpected. It was believed that his vindication was complete, and the result is regarded more as another blow at General McClellan than a condemnation of Gen. Porter. The friends of Gen. McClellan are unfortunate, and they are stricken down for their friendship to him while the power that strikes can reach no nearer than the object of the blows.[31]

The *New York World*, where Porter's friend Manton Marble was editor, declared: "The conviction [belief] was universal that his innocence was established. The whole evidence is even more convincing than the brief reports were; yet, such is the spirit of things, which make partisan hatred take on the semblance at least of patriotic regret. The leading journals of the radicals exult."[32]

One of them, the *New York Times*, complained: "Porter ought not to have been let off with simply a dismissal and a disqualification from all future offices of trust or profit, but should have been shot to death. Impartial history will pronounce that to have been the only doom that could have expiated such guilt."[33]

Fitz John Porter's new task was to prove that all those who agreed with the *Times* were dreadfully wrong. But the painful Ophelia phase of his life had not quite ended. There remained his accepting the fact that many of his countrymen were treating him as though indeed he no longer existed, that his evolution into a fighter to restore his good name had never occurred and was of no consequence.

Only the reporter had informed him of Lincoln's action, and that disclosure on January 21 had been made during an accidental encounter. How had the reporter learned of this development? Secretary of War Stanton had control of the news of military matters, and presumably in this case, with delight he gave priority in its release to Radical newspapers such as the *Times* and Horace Greeley's *New York Tribune.* By the next day the news was being carried in newspapers throughout the North. Also on the 22d, the Adjutant General's Office in the War Department issued General Orders No. 18, which recited the authority for the trial, listed the charges and specifications, and closed with the verdicts, the sentence, and Lincoln's approval—but no one sent the Convicted a copy.[34] On the 23d, still ignored as if the sentence had been oblivion, his patience snapped. To the Adjutant General's Office he wrote:

> I now request to be informed officially whether I still am an officer of the U.S. Army and so under obligation to remain in this city, or whether I am a citizen and then at liberty to control my own movements.
>
> I trust the purpose of this request will not fail to be apparent to the proper authorities.[35]

Apparently to Edwin Stanton, of all authorities the most proper, Fitz John Porter was unworthy of further notice as a human being. Yet the

Cashiered had considerable symbolic value as a warning to all others who would dare oppose attempts by Stanton's political brethren to wrest control of the war from Abraham Lincoln.

Victory was Stanton's. He would celebrate it in two ways: rewarding the members of the Court who had destroyed Porter as directed, and using the powers of propaganda to make certain that if the Convicted were to be remembered at all, it would be only as a shameful traitor.

Hardly had the ink conveying A. Lincoln's signature dried on his approval of the Court's work on January 21 when Stanton began brightening the military futures of the nine men in various forms of need or trouble he had selected to sit in judgment of the Accused. Among the first was the Court's president, David Hunter, who was restored to being eligible for field command after having been relieved by Lincoln for usurpation of Presidential prerogatives regarding the emancipation of slaves. For Generals Slough, Prentiss, Casey, and Buford, Stanton removed the block he had imposed earlier on their promotions to the next higher grade. Generals King and Ricketts, both of whom ought not have been either appointed or accepted as members because of their own liability to discipline for poor performance at Second Bull Run, were excused from prosecution. Old Ethan Allan Hitchcock, who had done no harm, was assigned to duties such as administering prisoner exchanges. James A. Garfield was moved along in ways that would enhance his post-war career as a politician of the Radical persuasion.[36]

Ironically, all that John Pope received was a railroad ticket back to Minnesota even though he had done more than anyone else to cut Porter down.[37] Irvin McDowell fared no better despite the scent of perjury that clung to his testimony.

Next to Edwin Stanton himself, the hero of Third Bull Run was Joseph Holt. But he had not been standing in the pay line because he had received his fees in advance by having been appointed by Stanton as the army's judge-advocate general and also because his work was not done.

10

The text of Joseph Holt's blatantly misleading "revise" of the case—prepared at Lincoln's request during Fitz John Porter's "Ophelia" waiting period—enjoyed widespread circulation, first among members of the

Congress and soon afterward to all Radical newspapers and other shapers of Northerners' beliefs. To be certain that their "official" version would become the definitive edition, Stanton and Holt emblazoned on the booklet's cover this title:

PROCEEDINGS OF A GENERAL COURT-MARTIAL
For the Trial of
MAJ. GEN. FITZ JOHN PORTER
PRINTED BY THE PUBLIC PRINTER

PRINTED BY DIRECTION OF GENERAL ROBERTS AND COLONEL SMITH
OF POPE'S STAFF AND ASSENT OF COL. HOLT

Proceedings implied the presence of the complete trial record as the booklet's contents. In fact, testimony developed by counsel for the Accused, the closing statement by the defense, and almost everything but the substance of Holt's *Review* were *omitted.*[38]

The *Washington Daily Chronicle* Press reprinted Holt's *Review* in the spring of 1863. This edition bore the note, "Printed and circulated unofficially to the number of 40,000 by Judge Advocate General Holt."[39]

Understandably, Edwin Stanton's characteristically contemptible conduct infuriated Reverdy Johnson. All along Johnson had provided Fitz John Porter with encouragement as well as his best efforts as a lawyer. Now he went as far beyond his duties as a Senator as he could to refute the plethora of false and misleading impressions Holt's *Proceedings* had proliferated. In July he published his rebuttal, entitled:

REPLY OF HON. REVERDY JOHNSON TO THE PAPER WHICH JUDGE ADVOCATE HOLT FURNISHED TO THE PRESIDENT URGING GENERAL PORTER'S CONDEMNATION

and subtitled:

A BRAVE SOLDIER, A TRUE PATRIOT, A NOBLE MAN
DEFENDED AGAINST PARTISAN MALICE[40]

During Porter's trial, Johnson had paid tribute to the Court, treated Holt with courtesy, and exercised restraint in his objections—all normal practices in civilian courts. For having adhered to the code of gentlemen, he was criticized. But in his *Reply,* he allowed himself to write from the heart as well as from the head. His condemnations were harsh, sharp-pointed, and emphatic. He employed sarcasm, expressed outrage and scorn.

There had been no basis for the charges, Johnson argued. Anyone who could read would be satisfied that they were as malicious as they were false. "Never in the history of jurisprudence," he asserted, "civil, criminal, or military, was a judgment announced that so shocked and startled the sense of public justice."

Joseph Holt had introduced the extraneous issue of Porter's alleged animus at the outset in his *Review,* so Johnson did not hesitate to refer to the fact that Lieutenant Colonel Thomas C. H. Smith, John Pope's aide, had paid for the viciously anti-Porter pamphlet called *Pope's Campaign in Virginia, Its Policy and Results and the Relations of the Army of the Potomac to the Campaign, Exposed by a General Officer who Served at the Headquarters of the Army of Virginia From the First to the Last Day of the Campaign* that had been distributed to members of Congress before the trial. Afterward Smith, Johnson pointed out, had been promoted to brigadier general with date of rank November 29, 1862, four days after the trial began. Similarly, Johnson revealed, Benjamin Roberts—the author of the notorious pamphlet who had brought the charges against Porter—was assigned to a higher command but had since proved unable to meet its requirements and was remanded to General Pope's staff in Minnesota.

Reverdy Johnson reinforced his condemnation of the proceedings by referring to the hiring and rewarding of the members of the Court. He did not, however, attribute this outrage to the Radicals or refer to them by that name.

Fitz John Porter, Johnson continued, was among the thousands of Union army officers who agreed with the Congressional resolution of 1861 defining restoration of the Union as the war's purpose but had not accepted the abolitionists' recent drastic modification—hence, Porter's new role as an example of what can happen to generals who do not embrace certain partisan political beliefs.

"Porter was known to be a personal friend and admirer of McClellan,"

Johnson reminded his readers. "And this, in the view of the men referred to, seemed to be almost as great an offense as treason." Yet, if Porter had turned against McClellan, he would now be the favorite of the men who had denounced him.

Irvin McDowell did not escape Johnson's scrutiny. Using the record of the McDowell Court of Inquiry, he established enough instances of questionable conduct on McDowell's part during Second Bull Run to ask how he could have been honorably acquitted while Porter had been cashiered?

Similarly, why had Rufus King not been tried—instead, made a member of the Porter Court and allowed to testify against the Accused?

As to Porter's alleged animus, Johnson reviewed the open, studied insubordination displayed by certain generals in the Army of the Potomac after the slaughter inflicted by General Lee at Fredericksburg. Since Porter's trial ended, Commander-in-Chief Lincoln had been obliged to relieve Ambrose Burnside and a number of the dissidents and to give command of the recuperating army to Major General Joseph Hooker, who had been prominent in Burnside's overthrow and had been quoted as having called Lincoln an imbecile.[41] Had the animus shown Burnside not merited trials by courts-martial?

And then there was Abraham Lincoln. While being duly deferential, Johnson alternated between suggesting that the President had been negligent in relying on Holt's misleading *Review*, instead of reading the entire case, and offering the pressures of other matters as mitigating factors. Johnson's words:

> The President of all men must have experienced not only astonishment, but concern. He could not have but paused before approving such a sentence and asked himself how was it possible that Porter, the boast of the army, the recipient of honors he [Lincoln] had conferred upon him for distinguished services, should at once to have been so recreant to his past patriotism as to have committed acts to demand that he be cashiered.

Moving on, Reverdy Johnson exposed an error made at the end of the trial that Lincoln ought to have caught instead of allowing Joseph Holt's intentionally flawed *Review* to blindside him. Seasoned lawyer Lincoln could not have forgotten a trial rule that the defendant has the right to speak last. As it was, Holt's *Review* amounted to his closing argument; he had denied Porter the right to respond to it on the record by waiting until Hunter had closed the Court for deliberation to announce that he had waived presentation of his response to Porter's defense during open court because he was mindful of Secretary Stanton's letter admonishing all concerned to complete the trial as soon as possible.

So it was that the judge-advocate cleverly got the last word, and Johnson proceeded to expose many other sins of omission and commission that had been committed by the persecution during the trial's thirty-two working days. His concluding remarks, however, were more eloquent than accurate:

> The friends of Porter need fear no further concern for him. He was armed with the potent power of truth and the public judgment. And what shield against injustice is more invulnerable? It abides with the injured and consoles him in adversity.[42]

Very well, but Reverdy Johnson was missing something about his former client, the cool man who would now be a life-long friend—something absolutely vital: Fitz John Porter surely had been injured by the recent adversity but he most certainly did not want to be perceived—and pitied—as a victim.

He had been a fighter and a good one and he still was.

"I will lie me down and bleed a while," he might concede, being human, "then rise to fight again."

PART III: REMEMBERING THINGS PAST

CHAPTER ELEVEN

"IN THE MEANTIME, YOU SUFFER."

CITIZEN Porter got reacquainted with his wife and their three children during the spring of 1863. From their home on the corner of Fourth Avenue and East 14th Street in New York City he wrote a great many letters, some to potential employers, others to people who might help him clear his name. Never during his years in the army had supporting his family been a problem; now, while accepting financial help from his wife's aunt, he was discovering how little demand there was for cashiered professional soldiers.[1]

Publication of Reverdy Johnson's *Reply* to Holt's *Review* in July caused at least two senators to declare that it had changed their opinions, but in September the *Washington Daily Chronicle* began running a series of anti-Johnson articles. An excerpt:

> [Holt's *Review*] has dragged to the light a crime to which the past of this country offers no parallel—a crime whose history is written in the blood of a brave army, which was abandoned to its fate in its extremest need by one who was able to have rushed to its relief. . . . The wonder of military men who understand the atrocity of Porter's offense is not that he was condemned, but that his life was spared. The court-martial might well have sentenced him to death, and they forbore to do so, in all probability, only because they felt that, as a walking blasted monument of treachery he would be a warning to others more effective than any voice which could issue from the depths of his dishonored but perhaps forgotten grave.[2]

Later in 1863, a firm in Baltimore published *A Reply to the Hon. Reverdy Johnson's Attack on the Administration in the Case of Fitz John Porter, Convicted of Shameful Misbehavior Before the Enemy*. This was as much an attempt to intimidate Johnson as an assault on Porter. In Johnson's *Reply*, the pamphleteer contends, "We find that for some evil purpose Lincoln packed the Court, rewarded its members, and refused to examine the evidence but delegated that task to Holt, who distorted or concealed evidence."[3] Actually, Edwin Stanton had packed the Court and rewarded its members.

Initially, pamphleteering had been a continuation of Fitz John Porter's trial by other means. In these documents Holt and Johnson conveyed many of the things they had meant to say before the Court (Porter's animus) and restated other matters (Longstreet's presence) which they believed deserved greater emphasis. Such outpourings, however, passed the *who cares?* test with decreasing frequency during the months after A. Lincoln declared Citizen Porter a pariah.

Johnson's *Reply*, however, caused Edward Everett, president of Harvard, among the most distinguished men in the Union, to study the trial record and prepare a "Memorial" to the President urging a fresh review of Porter's case. Everett had been joined by a number of eminent Bostonians in forwarding the Memorial to Lincoln in August 1863, but the White House never acknowledged its receipt.[4]

Daniel Lord, a lawyer in New York, was another thinking person (Jefferson Davis' term for men he considered right-minded) who read the case and found Porter's conviction unwarranted. To Porter, Lord wrote:

> The truth is, a campaign had been lost. General Pope had been selected to conduct it. The Government needed a scapegoat and the populace a victim. In lighting on you, not only were those needs applied, but a threat and a blow were aimed at General McClellan.
>
> Still, your position is of extreme difficulty. Time alone can rectify the error, and in the meantime, you suffer. I hope that some useful occupation may present itself unto you which may enable you to rise above the effect of so bad a fortune.[5]

2

Lawyer Lord's hope was fulfilled early in 1864 when a group of Wall

Street financiers sent Citizen Porter to Denver to evaluate and ultimately to manage mining properties. This required a separation from his family that would last until August 1865. Along the way he had to overcome obstacles imposed by bad weather, unscrupulous competitors, adverse legislation, vandalism, even Indian raids. But it enabled him to put in place the cornerstone of a new reputation—one for getting all sorts of difficult things done successfully—and to benefit financially to an extent that enabled him and his family to settle in New Jersey in a new house on twenty acres near Morristown and a powerful friend, Theodore F. Randolph.[6]

Gone for nearly a year from Washington Citizen Porter may have been, but Edwin Stanton had not forgotten him. Shortly before the November 1864 presidential election, the panic-prone secretary of war summoned Major General Benjamin F. Butler to Washington to deal with confidential reports that a force of several thousand rebels was being formed to deliver the entire vote in New York City to Democrat candidate McClellan and that it would be led by Fitz John Porter.[7] Nothing of the sort could have happened with the target of Stanton's monomania in Colorado, of course, but Porter had long been established in Stanton's mind as a traitor and as such he could often be useful to the Radicals, absent though he might or might not be.

Conversely, while Fitz Porter had been demonstrating his ability to win battles of a new and different sort out in the West, his former comrades had ended the war east of the Rockies. By mid-1866 historians and journalists had access to Confederate records, including General Lee's *Report of the Operations of the Army of Northern Virginia.* And among the first corrective articles to appear was Alfred H. Guernsey's commentary in the *New York World* on July 2, 1866. Regarding the joint order and the equally controversial 4:30 order that Pope had sent Porter, Guernsey wrote:

> Both orders are based on the supposition that the "whole force" of the enemy under Longstreet was fully twenty-four hours distant; that Jackson's Corps was the only body to be encountered; and that the Union force consequently was nearly double that of the Confederates. [But] Longstreet had united with Jackson fully four hours before the 4:30 order was written and six hours before it was received, giving the Confederates a preponderance of three-to-two; the line of march prescribed to Porter would have brought him

> almost directly upon the rear Confederate center instead of upon its right flank and rear, as Pope presumed; and the execution of the 4:30 order would have involved the annihilation of Porter's corps, and could hardly have failed to result in the destruction of the entire union army. I shall show that Porter knew the essential facts of the case, that Pope did not, and that consequently he was fully justified in not complying with the order.[8]

Corroboration came from Longstreet himself in a letter to Porter:

> My command was ready to receive any attack after 11 o'clock A.M. and we all were particularly anxious to bring on the battle after 12 M.; General Lee more than the rest.
>
> My recollection of the ground on my right is that artillery could not be handled on it, and that infantry could not have been handled on it so as to make a formidable attack.
>
> If you had attacked any time after 12 M., it seems to me that we surely would have destroyed your army. That is, if you had attacked with less than twenty-five thousand men.[9]

Statements such as General Longstreet's increased the number of thinking men and led Massachusetts Senator Henry Wilson, earlier pro-Radical, to direct an appeal on Porter's behalf to President Andrew Johnson. On November 16, 1866, Wilson wrote: "I have been informed that new evidence has been discovered touching the case of Fitz John Porter. I cheerfully join with others in recommending the appointment of a commission, to consist of officers of acknowledged capacity and character, to examine the evidence and ascertain whether injustice has been done this officer."

This was remarkable for several reasons. Among the endorsers were Horace Greeley, publisher of the *New York Tribune,* the most pro-Radical newspaper in the country; Ohio Senator John Sherman, anti-Porter at the time of the trial; and Nathaniel P. Banks, earlier a favorite of the Radicals.[10] Also, for Wilson to have written such a letter to Andrew Johnson was recognition of a sort of how far from Radical domination Johnson had moved.

Porter might not have expected such a development because he was distracted or out in Colorado during the last half of the war and even in 1866 may not have caught up with many of the changes. At the time of his trial, the Radicals were applying heavy pressure on Lincoln. When Ambrose Burnside proved incapable of continuing as commander of the Army of the Potomac, the President replaced him with Radical-supported "Fighting Joe" Hooker—who was mauled by Generals Lee and Stonewall Jackson at Chancellorsville and had to be replaced just before Gettysburg by George Gordon Meade, a conservative who had been commanding Fifth Corps.

Union victories during 1863's second half and 1864 reduced Radical influence. Lincoln's reelection was another blow to the extreme faction, as were indications that he intended to bring on a peace "with malice toward none and charity for all." So bitter was Senator Ben Wade that three days before Lincoln was shot, he remarked, "By God, the sooner he is assassinated, the better!"[11] And soon after Andrew Johnson had been sworn in, Wade said, "Johnson, we have faith in you. By the gods, now there will be no trouble in running the government."[12]

Senator Wade was wrong. Johnson's policies regarding reconstruction turned out to be so close to those of Lincoln that "Congressional" Reconstruction, which would wreck the defeated South, prevailed. The armies commanded by General-in-Chief Grant, deployed on occupation duty, became the agents of Secretary of War Stanton and other Northerners bent on revenge.[13]

Such a situation surely was what lawyer Daniel Lord had in mind when he warned Porter, "Still, your position is of extreme difficulty. Time alone can rectify the error, and in the meantime, you suffer." True enough; but Fitz John Porter was incapable of sitting still and waiting for time to work its wonders. He was determined to fight, no matter how complex the problems facing him might prove. And he had seen enough of what Lord called extreme difficulty to comprehend where he stood and to perceive what he had to do.

He was a military man who had been convicted in a military court by other military men but his reputation could be restored only by civilians—more to the point, by politicians: a President willing to risk reversing a critical decision made by the martyred Lincoln, and majorities in both houses of Congress. No politician risked anything by condemning or ignoring him; none could expect any gain from supporting him. Yet, Senator Wilson had sent that letter to Andrew Johnson, and had been joined in doing so by men of the Radical political persuasion. How did this square with self-interest? What justified this exception?

First, honor. Fidelity to the rule of law. Love of Justice.

Second, self-assurance. Intellectual along with other aspects of personal independence. Courage enough to rebel.

Next, endurance. Resistance to the lure of compromise. Concentration on the longer term.

Pragmatism might be added to the list. Senator Wilson had asked President Johnson to take a simple action that was clearly within his power: "I cheerfully join with others in recommending the appointment of a commission, to consist of officers of acknowledged capacity and character, to examine the evidence and ascertain whether injustice has been done this officer." How could such a reasonable request be denied without suggesting that someone involved in Porter's conviction had something to hide?

The fate of Senator Wilson's appeal was instructive. Apparently, Andrew Johnson was more afraid of the political extremists than he was fond of justice.

3

In 1867 the bitter disputes between the President and the Congress over reconstruction policy caught Edwin Stanton in the crossfire. As secretary of war he had a duty to support Johnson and carry out his policies toward the former Confederacy, but politically he sided with his brethren of the Radical persuasion. On August 12, Johnson dismissed Stanton and replaced him with General Grant as secretary of war *ad interim* while Congress argued the question of whether Johnson had violated the Tenure of Office Act.[14] And with Stanton gone, Fitz John Porter began to think of making another appeal to Johnson.

Earlier in the year, General Lee had responded to a letter from Porter by answering six questions "in the order in which they are asked." Briefly, he confirmed Longstreet's account of the Confederate arrival on the morning of August 29 and expressed the opinion that had Porter attacked, he would have been repulsed. In closing, Lee noted that he had answered Porter's questions "for your own information." Accordingly, and with his customary sense of honor, Porter abstained from using the letter in the collection of fresh supporting materials he used in his submission.[15]

Johnson passed Porter's application to his attorney general, Henry Stanbery, for an opinion. Impatient, Porter called on the President in September. "Every private and public pressure upon him is being made," he wrote to Theodore Randolph afterward. "He still fears Stanton—so says his daughter, who has the most influence on him."[16] And following a visit with Acting Secretary of War Grant a week later, Porter wrote:

> If Grant is not a radical, I don't know who is. At all events he is now as much under Holt as any man can be. In my case, Holt has changed him, and now Grant tends to obstruct my chances. Yesterday he told me he would not confer with Holt, but today he recommends Holt's opinions be consulted by the Attorney General.[17]

Well, it was worth recalling that Grant was secretary of war *ad interim*, that Stanton might return at any time and reverse any action that had been taken favoring Porter. Even so, Grant gave Porter's appeal a qualified endorsement:

> Before any consideration should be given to the written application of Fitz John Porter for the reconsideration of the sentence of a court-martial it is manifestly hoped that he should demonstrate his ability to controvert by new evidence the testimony on which he was convicted. If injustice has been done him, every opportunity which the law allows should be given to Mr. Porter to expurgate himself. But no such testimony is presented with these papers, and until it shall be, no action in the matter is recommended.[18]

As Porter was scrambling to amass additional evidence of support, Grant was seeking opinions from Attorney General Stanbery regarding authority to try a second time a person whose case has been properly disposed, and if so, what preliminary proceedings are necessary. From the army's adjutant general came a ruling that no convicted officer can have a new trial and that no President can restore one to the army.

Such responses became academic, however, when the enhanced appeal Porter had submitted to the President disappeared somewhere between the White House and the attorney general's office. But even had Porter been able to reconstruct it with copies of the contents, the effort was doomed to failure when relations between Andrew Johnson and Congress deteriorated into the President's impeachment.[19]

Among other incidents along the way, Stanton returned and evicted Grant; Johnson suggested several other officers to succeed Stanton as secretary of war but the Radicals would have none of them. Finally, attorney William M. Evarts suggested the appointment of Major General John M. Schofield; he was confirmed in late April 1868, and Edwin Stanton departed with the thanks of the Congress.[20]

Years afterward, General Schofield wrote:

> When I was in the War Department in 1868, Porter came to me with the request that I would present his case to the President, and recommend that he be given a rehearing. I declined to do so, on the ground that, in my opinion, an impartial investigation and disposition of his case, whatever were its merits, could not be made until the passions and prejudices begotten by the war had subsided much further than they had done at that time.
>
> I told him that while I never permitted myself to form an opinion of any case without much more knowledge of it than I had of his, I presumed, from the finding of the court-martial, that he had at least been guilty of acting upon what he supposed to be his own better judgment under the circumstances he found to exist, instead in strict obedience to General Pope's orders.
>
> He said that that was not the case; that he had not even literally disobeyed orders; that in so far as he had acted on his own judgment, he had loyally done all that could be done to carry out General Pope's wishes; and that all he wanted was an opportunity to prove such to be the facts.
>
> I replied that if he could prove what he stated beyond question, he would of course have a case worthy of consideration—not otherwise. Nothing was said in respect to the facts or the evidence in contravention of the judgment of the court-martial which tried him.[21]

Nothing more was said, perhaps, because both men recognized that Andrew Johnson's enfeebled presidency was ending and that his successor,

Ulysses S. Grant, would surely want to select his own secretary of war. General Schofield went back to the army; Citizen Porter returned to Morristown to reflect upon his six years of seeming failures to accomplish anything and seek strength to rise and fight again.

4

In fact, Fitz John Porter had assembled so many letters from former Presidents, senior Confederate officers, eminent lawyers, educators, and other thinking men that his problem was fast becoming one of how to weave all of these assets into a new appeal that was unified, coherent, and emphatic. Unfortunately, the one that he submitted to President Grant in 1869 was badly organized, excessive in length, and so unconvincing that it was ignored.[22]

By that time Citizen Porter's financial condition needed immediate improvement. He had poured more than $20,000 into his struggle. All of his and Hattie's real estate had been mortgaged to the rooftops. Some solutions were offered—one, prompted no doubt by his classmate and predecessor in disgrace at the hands of the Radicals, Charles Stone, invited him to become Commander-in-Chief of the Egyptian Army—but acceptance smacked of retreat and he declined.[23]

Close to home was the opportunity to superintend the construction of a hospital for the insane at Morris Plains, New Jersey. It was to be the largest of its kind in the world and the budget was $3 million. Porter completed the project in a manner that pleased everyone concerned. In 1875 he served as head of New York City's Department of Public Works. Neighbor Theodore Randolph was elected a United States Senator from New Jersey in 1876 and he selected Porter to manage his coal and iron business. Later in the decade, Porter was appointed assistant receiver of the bankrupt Central Railroad of New Jersey.[24]

Concurrently, distinguished Northerners and former Confederate officers added their support, as did many of the veterans organizations. This was important as well as gratifying, for General Pope and his supporters in Congress were missing no opportunities to condemn Porter anew. Each time Porter filed an appeal, Pope wrote letters opposing favorable action in the bitterest terms; he even packaged and circulated his protests in pamphlet form. Ultra Radical Zachariah Chandler made a speech on February 21, 1870, in which he declared the Porter court-martial to have been the fairest and most just of any tribunal ever assembled. "I want to put this on the record for all time," he continued. "Let Fitz John Porter thank God that he yet lives. I told General Pope I had just one fault to find in the campaign, that he allowed Fitz John Porter to leave that battlefield alive!"

There was more, an untold story Chandler aimed at the reporters in the Senate's galleries:

> During the trial Porter said in the presence of my informant, who is a man most of you know, who is today in the employ of the Government, and whose word I would take as soon as I would take most men's. I will give his sworn testimony, taken down within two minutes after the utterance was made. Porter said, "I was not true to Pope, and there is no use denying it."[25]

Porter retaliated immediately with a twenty-page pamphlet. Near the end he wrote: "My reply to you, sir, is that the statement is FALSE in every particular. I certainly had no inducement to lose my senses pending my trial, and falsely assert what General Pope was forty-five days endeavoring to prove. Where was this reliable witness then? Why did he not testify to my confessed guilt?"[26]

Following up, Porter asked Senator Wilson for help in forcing Chandler to provide the informant's affidavit. Chandler refused.[27]

During the gaps in his employment Citizen Porter continued to assemble materials for his next appeal, which he submitted in 1874, two years after Grant was reelected. Porter's theory was that by then, this president had nothing more to fear from the Radicals.[28] That was only partially true. In recent years four of the most extreme Jacobins had died: Thaddeus Stevens in 1868, Edwin Stanton in 1871, Salmon Chase in 1873, Charles Sumner in 1874.[29] But Ben Wade and Zach Chandler survived and remained formidable. Fears of these adversaries and their disciples aside, Grant believed that Porter had been justly convicted, and he was not going to consider any more appeals.[30]

Accordingly, Fitz Porter was obliged to wait until early March of 1877 when another man replaced Grant.

5

All combat veterans revere luck. No matter how much they may have suffered from the bad kind, to have survived has so often seemed attributable only to luck that they are lost in wonder for the rest of their lives.

Much of the misfortune experienced by the Army of the Potomac under George McClellan's command had been the result of pressure applied on Abraham Lincoln by Senator Ben Wade to let Congressional Radicals direct the operations of the Union armies. John Pope's Army of Virginia was a by-product of that struggle—as was Second Bull Run—and, setting aside the excellence of the Army of Northern Virginia led by Generals Lee, Jackson, and Longstreet, so were the Union humiliations at Fredericksburg and Chancellorsville. Grant and Sherman owed nothing to Wade and his ilk when they took the surrenders of the surviving Confederates. But the Union's victory and Lincoln's assassination left Ben Wade in line to be President of the United States if the Radicals had succeeded in convicting impeached Andrew Johnson of high crimes and misdemeanors. In the Senate's trial Benjamin Wade missed the presidency by one vote—suggesting that the nation bequeathed to posterity by the Founders had also benefited by the presence of an enormous amount of luck.

Similarly, Fitz John Porter's luck had turned from good during the Seven Days to terrible after Fifth Corps joined Pope's Army of Virginia and it was hellish during and after the trial. Yet it changed slowly for the better when he came back from Colorado and settled next to property owned by Theodore Randolph, part businessman and part politician, who saw in Fitz Porter the fine qualities everyone had recognized in him before Second Bull Run. To Randolph, his neighbor was no victim whining over the cruelty of fickle Dame Fortune; he was a fighter, one worthy of more respect than ever because he had dared to stand up before the most powerful people in the government of the United States and seek the return of his good name. Porter had had scant help. He needed more. Randolph would provide as much as he could, not once but for as long as Porter's struggle took.

Another manifestation of luck was the outcome of the 1876 presidential election, at the time the closest, bitterest one in the nation's history. Democrat Porter had achieved nothing in thirteen years of trying to persuade three Republicans to grant a review of his case; now another one, Rutherford B. Hayes, had emerged as the victor, and this was hardly encouraging.

Theodore Randolph, however, was impressed by Hayes' reputation for independent thinking. In phasing out Reconstruction, for example, he defied the Radicals in Congress. Moreover, during the war Hayes had served as a regimental and temporarily as a brigade commander in forces led by John Charles Fremont in the Shenandoah Valley Campaign and later in John Pope's Army of Virginia; during Second Bull Run his outfit was in Nathaniel Banks' corps, which spent the battle guarding supply trains. Hayes then came under McClellan's command and was severely wounded at South Mountain, shortly before Antietam. He would be hit at least three more times. While serving under Philip Sheridan in his 1864 Shenandoah Campaign, he earned brevets for gallantry at Fisher's Hill and Cedar Creek. He was a major general at the war's end, although in all of his combat experiences he had been a colonel—hence closer to the hardest fighting.[31]

In December 1877, Senator Randolph paid a call on Rutherford Hayes. After two hours, during which the President referred frequently to the diary he had kept during the war, Randolph emerged convinced that Porter should send an appeal to Hayes as soon as possible. Toward the end of a letter to Porter, Randolph recalled that when he remarked that the

RUTHERFORD B. HAYES, PRESIDENT OF THE UNITED STATES, 1877–1881

After Porter's repeated appeals for presidential orders to review his conviction had been refused by Andrew Johnson and Ulysses Grant, Hayes—a four-times-wounded Ohio volunteer who attained the rank of brevet major general—reviewed the diary entries he had made during Second Bull Run and appointed a board of officers to reconsider Porter's case.

conviction had been intended as a blow to McClellan, the President had replied, "I think if Porter had had McClellan's place after the Seven Days or at Antietam, we should have won."[32]

Porter's appeal to Hayes dated March 9, 1878, evoked no immediate reaction. On April 13, Senator Randolph sent Porter a discouraging letter. "Every man in every department connected with the War Office has been openly hostile, or secretly indifferent," he reported. "A more merciless, cruel, and selfish crowd I do not think ever grew."[33]

A day earlier, however, Special Orders No. 78 had been issued. The text:

> In order that the President may be fully informed of the facts of the case of Fitz John Porter, late major-general of volunteers, and be enabled to act advisedly upon its application for relief in said case, a board is hereby convened, by order of the President, to examine, in connection with the record of the trial by court-martial of Major-General Porter, such new evidence relating to the merits of said case as is now on file in the War Department, together with such other evidence as may be presented to said board, and to report, with the reasons for their conclusion, what action, if any, in their opinion, justice requires should be taken on said application by the President.
>
> *Detail for the board:*
>
> Maj. Gen. J. M. Schofield.
> Brig. Gen. A. H. Terry.
> Col. G. W. Getty, Third Artillery.
> Maj. Asa B. Gardner, judge-advocate, recorder.
>
> The board will convene at West Point, N.Y., on the 20th day of June, 1878, and is authorized to adjourn from time to time, and to sit in such place as may be deemed expedient.
>
> By command of General Sherman.[34]

6

After so many years and all the disappointments, how much more generous to Fitz John Porter might Lady Luck have been? However, whatever the Schofield Board might report to President Hayes eventually, for it to have been given such a broad range of matters to investigate, review, and issue findings on was a mixed blessing from Fitz John Porter's point of view.

Authority to re-enter the proceedings of the November 1862–January 1863 court-martial was obviously an advantage, and so was the directive to consider all new evidence. But simply because the Schofield Board had been so amply empowered, its failure for any reason to recommend restoration of Fitz Porter's good name would foreclose any further attempts by him to vanquish his personal great white whale: his cashiering.

Specifying West Point as the initial site for the Board's work was altogether wise. Hardly a place on the North American continent could have been found that would differ as much from wartime Washington in both intellectual and physical environment than The Plain masking an outcropping of bedrock that forces the Hudson to change course downstream twice in only a few hundred yards as it flows southward to the Atlantic.

Fifteen years earlier, Fitz John Porter had been tried and disgraced in unseemly haste in that city on the Potomac in which politics vied for atmospheric supremacy with odors from a grossly inadequate sewage disposal ditch. Now, however, in this military monastery enclosed in and framed by the Hudson Highlands, fifty miles north of New York City and its newspapers' sensation-obsessed reporters and editorial writers, Schofield and his associates had a secure and serene setting and all of the authority and time they might crave.

However, Fitz John Porter had two reasons for wishing that some officer other than John Schofield would be sitting in judgment and heading the proceedings. After he returned from the Mexican War, then-Major Porter had been among the Military Academy's faculty detailed to serve on the court-martial of Cadet Schofield. The alleged offense was so minor, and the accused's culpability so doubtful, that eleven of the court's members favored clemency—but Porter had sided with George H. Thomas, another dissenter in advocating Schofield's dismissal.[35] Clemency had prevailed, but memories of critical moments in careers have a way of lingering—or so Fitz John Porter may have assumed in also recalling his unproductive meeting with Secretary of War Schofield in 1868. Porter's misgivings may have been groundless, though, for in his memoirs General Schofield recalled that in 1878 "I had no knowledge of [Porter's] case when the board of review, of which I was president, met . . . and I believe that neither of the other members of the board—Generals A. H. Terry and George W. Getty—was any better informed."[36]

Had General Sherman, or whoever selected those three officers, erred? Consider:

General Schofield was graduated from West Point in the Class of 1853. After two years of service in the artillery, he was called back to the Military Academy as an instructor in philosophy (physics). In 1860, on leave of absence, he was teaching at Washington University in St. Louis; for the next three years, all of his wartime assignments were west of the Mississippi. In 1864 he commanded the Army of the Ohio in Sherman's Atlanta Campaign, and late in that year his divisions fought a series of delaying actions that enabled Major General George H. Thomas to wreck Confederate General John B. Hood's army in the battle of Nashville. After the war, Schofield was sent on a secret mission to France to negotiate the withdrawal of French forces from Mexico. As noted, he was also briefly secretary of war during the confusion over the impeachment of Andrew Johnson. Since 1876, he had been superintendent of the United States Military Academy.[37]

Major General Alfred H. Terry, born in Connecticut and educated at Yale, practiced law until shortly after Fort Sumter. As colonel of a three-month regiment, he led his men at First Bull Run—then, after having been mustered out, he was reappointed colonel of a volunteer Connecticut regiment and commanded it and later larger units in operations along the Atlantic coast, including the capture of Port Royal and Hilton Head, the assaults on Battery Wagner near Charleston, and the seizure of Fort Pulaski, Georgia.

However, it had been Terry's misfortune to serve under the command of Major General Benjamin F. Butler, a notoriously incompetent "political" appointee. Late in the war, with Wilmington, North Carolina, the Confederacy's last Atlantic port, General-in-Chief Grant reluctantly permitted Butler to attempt the capture of Fort Fisher (at the entrance to the Cape Fear River) by filling a ship with 235 tons of high explosives, running it against the fort's masonry wall, and sending troops through the massive hole produced by the blast. This proved an embarrassing failure. Grant replaced Butler with Terry, who—ably supported by naval forces led by Rear Admiral David Dixon Porter—took the fort and Wilmington two weeks later.

During the war's last days, General Terry's X Corps was assigned to

Schofield's Army of the Ohio, then operating in North Carolina under the direction of W. T. Sherman. After the war, as a brigadier general in the regular army, Alfred Terry earned his pay leading troops fighting Indians. *Dictionary of American Biography* would describe him as "straight, vigorous, and active [with the supreme] ability to cooperate with superiors, equals, or subordinates."[38]

George Washington Getty's relatively low rank of colonel in 1878 was hardly a reflection of his performance as a soldier. At sixteen he entered West Point, graduating in 1840 and serving as an artillery officer during the Second Seminole War (ended 1842) and the Mexican War, later on the frontier.

Unlike either Schofield or Terry, Getty spent much of the Civil War in the Army of the Potomac and all of it in the East. As an artillerist, Getty's influence on events was mostly as a provider of fire when needed rather than as a mover and shaker of campaigns. Even so, he had served under Major General George B. McClellan—and had been in a position to watch him and also his "pet" Fitz John Porter—from the earliest weeks of the McClellan's Peninsula Campaign throughout the Seven Days. Getty and his batteries supported Porter's Fifth Corps at Gaines's Mills. Porter, an artilleryman during the Mexican War, had directed the placement of Getty's guns along the brow of Malvern Hill.

Getty's artillery was not committed to the support of Major General John Pope's Army of Virginia during Second Bull Run, but his men and guns were employed at Antietam, where Porter's Fifth Corps was held in reserve. General Porter had been arrested and was being tried back in Washington in mid-December when Getty's guns supported Major General Ambrose E. Burnside's costly attacks west of Fredericksburg that moved General Lee's Army of Northern Virginia not one inch.

Remaining with the Army of the Potomac, Getty was severely wounded in May 1864, during the fighting in the Wilderness. But he caught up with his outfit in the lines at Petersburg, south of Richmond, and when Confederate Jubal Early's troops threatened Washington in July, Getty's firepower was among the assets General-in-Chief Grant shipped northward to deflect that threat.

Just as General Schofield's presence in Missouri in 1860 had doomed him to remain in the West, George Getty's shifting to Virginia's Shenandoah Valley put him under the command of General Sheridan and kept him there throughout the destruction of Virginia's granary. By then, though, Getty was commanding a division and winning distinction for his conduct in the key battles.

In the spring of 1865, Getty's division was back in the trenches below Petersburg. On April 2, his men broke the Confederates' thin line—starting the chain of events that led within less than a week to the end of the war in the East at Appomattox Court House.[39]

Sherman may well have selected Schofield and Terry, knowing them as he did from the war years—in Schofield's case, from November 1861 when they served together in Missouri under Henry Halleck's command. George Getty was able to supply a quality that neither Sherman, Schofield, nor Terry possessed: first-hand experience in George McClellan's Army of the Potomac, in which Porter had been prominent. And Yale graduate Terry's presence on the Board precluded allegations that the investigation's outcome was preordained by the "elitist" West Point clique.

Indeed, there was no way of predicting the outcome: the Schofield Board would be proceeding without a precedent.

JOHN M. SCHOFIELD, MAJOR GENERAL, U.S. ARMY

Preferring troop duty, Schofield had tried to avoid becoming Superintendent of the United States Military Academy. Being appointed by President Hayes to preside over the reopening of the highly controversial Fitz John Porter case as an additional duty compounded his regret that he had failed. Even so, he and board members Alfred Terry and George Getty devoted more than six months to taking testimony from nearly 150 witnesses and providing President Hayes with their report and recommendations.

CHAPTER TWELVE

VIOLENCE RECOLLECTED IN TRANQUILITY

"THE DUTY of the board," General Schofield recalled in *Forty-Six Years in the Army*, "was very different from a court-martial appointed to try an original case." He continued:

> The accused had already been tried and convicted. He was not to have a new trial. He could not have any benefit whatever of any doubt that might exist after all the evidence, old and new, had been duly considered. He must prove his innocence positively, by absolutely convincing evidence, or else the original judgment of the court-martial must stand.[1]

Even so, to whom must Porter prove his innocence? The Schofield Board. And what was its mission? To render judgment, then report it to the President.

Actually, the work beginning in 1878 differed mainly from that done back in the winter of 1862–1863 in that the members of the Schofield Board had the benefit of hindsight—roughly fifteen years of it. They had witnessed the outcomes and consequences of many struggles that were far from resolved when Porter was being tried. For example, they knew that during the war the Radicals had fought with Lincoln over control of the war and lost, but that following his assassination they won control of Reconstruction and kept it; accordingly, it was not necessary for Porter to establish the facts that the Radicals had been influential in both the events leading to Major General John Pope's defeat at Second Bull Run and the conduct and outcome of his trial.

Moreover, by 1878, the literary outpouring known as the Great Remembering was only thirteen years old, but enough unit histories and memoirs and magazine articles had been published for students of the Late Unpleasantness to refine many of their earlier recollections of wartime events. Compilation of the *Official Records of the Union and Confederate Armies* was in progress, though the products of that massive undertaking were still years away from availability.[2] Some officers had released their copies of messages and reports to journalists and historians or used such materials in articles, raising questions regarding the mix of elucidation and reputation-protecting. Hindsight was becoming clearer and more abundant by the month, if not weekly.

In addition to making use of this expanding fund of information, sooner or later the Board would have to go through the transcripts of the Porter Court-Martial line-by-line with magnifying glasses. And there were all those pamphlets both sides had circulated during the past fifteen years, and sheaves of letters and magazine articles, newspapers' editorials, and Porter's previous appeals; each and every document would have to be examined, evaluated, and eventually assigned its proper place in the investigation's own record. There would come a time when witnesses would have to be summoned, but when? Generals Lee and Jackson were long dead, and so were Edwin Stanton and Henry Halleck. Which survivors of Second Bull Run should be called? Confederate General James Longstreet, of course; certainly, George McClellan.

Yes, what about McClellan, and his close relationship with Fitz John Porter? Had not inordinate loyalty to his controversial army commander been the tap root of Porter's difficulties? If so, might this constitute what Aristotle termed a hero's tragic flaw?

Perhaps, but while tragic flaws might be irrelevant legally, certainly it was understandable that any three humans investigating the conduct of another human would be curious about why dire things happened—and, inevitably, be curious about *relationships*.

But there were so many of them: Lincoln and the Radicals, Lincoln and his generals, the Radicals and Lincoln's generals, the relationships of all of them to Edwin Stanton—ultimately, in the crucible of a court-martial and its long aftermath, the relationships of the armies' generals to each other.

Complexity compounded!

And then there was the increasingly strong possibility that Second Bull

Run's outcome may have made it the most politically driven defeat the Union suffered during the entire war—a possible exception being Lincoln's personal direction of the attempts to trap Stonewall Jackson in the Shenandoah Valley in the spring of 1862. Of blunders made by Union generals during what victorious Confederates called Second Manassas there had been an abundance. Yet, in which of them had Radical influence been a factor, and how damaging had been the consequences? Was it even possible at a distance of sixteen years to separate politics from simple stupidity, professional incompetence, and the fog of war?

All things considered, might judging Porter this time around prove more demanding than the challenge the Petitioner faced?

2

Anyone who expected the convening of the Schofield Board to be exciting was bound to be disappointed. Only the location was impressive: the United States Military Academy.

The large room within the headquarters building in which the investigation would be conducted was Spartan. There was a table for the three members of the Board, another for the proceedings' recorder and his stenographer, and another for Fitz John Porter and his counsel. Benches along the walls were available for seating newspaper reporters or other aficianados of controversies who took the trouble to reach this remote place.[3]

Spectators on Day One, June 20, 1878, found their entertainment limited by the fact that of the presumed participants, only Generals Schofield and Getty were present and listening as Major Asa Bird Gardner read into the record the orders convening the Board.[4] Anticipating linkages of this inquiry's probable testimony to the official record of Porter's court-martial, General Schofield instructed Gardner to prod the army's adjutant general to provide the copy that had been requested but not yet received.[5]

When printed, that first day's progress would require only a hundred words in ten lines to describe. Yet the curiosity of any observer might well have been aroused by the presence of Major Gardner, and not someone of higher standing within the army's judge advocate general's branch, as the recorder for this investigation. Moreover, it was possible that anyone present who had been stationed at West Point would have been aware of certain awkward circumstances that had led to Gardner's assignment.

Asa Bird Gardner was a well-connected young lawyer who had been sent to West Point by the secretary of war four years earlier to teach jurisprudence to the cadets. By 1878, however, USMA's Superintendent Schofield had found Major Gardner's performance in the section rooms so deficient that he had blocked Congressional action to assure him a professorship. Scofield had mitigated the damage dismissal had done to lawyer Gardner's reputation by recommending his appointment to the inquiry's detail.[6] But in so doing, a knowledgeable benchwarmer may have wondered, might the general inadvertently have sowed dragon seed?

General Terry was away from West Point on public business on the next day, June 21.[7] Nothing was done beyond early adjournment, a decision that must have been welcomed on that Friday in the Hudson Valley's most delightful time of year. Monday, June 24, produced only the news that Fitz John Porter and his counsel would be present on the next day, Tuesday.[8]

Major Gardner opened Day Four by asking the Petitioner (as Porter was referred to in the record) to introduce Joseph H. Choate and Anson Maltby, both of New York, and John Christian Bullitt of Philadelphia, who were to represent him.

For Choate, in particular, to have taken the case elevated the importance of the investigation enormously. He was among the most distinguished and widely respected lawyers in the United States. Until recently he had believed that "nine eminent generals could not have found Porter guilty unless he had indeed committed some fearful crime." But Porter's confidence in the power of facts and Choate's study of the trial record changed his mind.

"It seemed to me an urgent public duty to enter into his defense," Choate said. "I say a public duty because, in my view, this is not General Porter's case alone; it is the case of the whole army—yes, it is the case of all the people of this country."[9] Accordingly, he accepted no compensation for his services.[10]

Earlier, Senator Randolph, Porter's friend and New Jersey neighbor, had retained Bullitt, who was a leading member of the Philadelphia bar. *Pro bono* like Choate, Bullitt would act as chief counsel, with Choate of counsel and handling most cross-examinations and Anson Maltby, also of counsel, preparing special materials.[11]

Indeed, after the introductions, Maltby began to offer what would be called Petitioner's Opening Statement. This document identified the issues that were to be raised and it also afforded a comprehensive review of the events leading up to Second Bull Run and developments during and after the battle as Porter recalled them, supported by texts of relevant messages and source citations. An idea of the extreme length and thoroughness of Maltby's product may be gained from the fact that he needed most of the next day's session in which to complete his presentation.[12]

That done, at 4:20 in the afternoon on Wednesday, June 26, Day Five, Choate proposed as the next step to have the record of Porter's court-martial read into the Board's proceedings. Thereafter, he said, "we expect to be ready" to introduce oral testimony.[13]

Whereupon the Recorder—as Major Gardner is referred to habitually in the investigation's minutes—raised the first of several interesting questions. After noting that there were no clear precedents for boards to operate given mandates such as President Hayes' to the present one, quite properly he asked, "What shall be the duty of the Recorder?"[14]

Was he to act on behalf of the government as a prosecutor, as had Joseph Holt in the 1862–1863 trial? Should he, as trial judge-advocates do, require all witnesses to testify under oath? Could he employ subpoenas in order to compel appearances? Would revelations made along the way qualify

JOSEPH CHOATE, LAWYER

Fitz John Porter's supporters had retained John Bullitt to represent him during the Schofield Board's hearings, but Choate volunteered to act as "of counsel" and Anson Maltby backed them up with research into the records and circumstances of the 1862–1863 court-martial. Choate, by 1878 long since a distinguished member of the bar, excelled in his ability to detect witnesses' lying and to force them to admit it.

as evidence, within the generally accepted meaning of that term?

Abruptly, Major General Schofield, superintendent of the Military Academy, was obliged to recognize that as President of the Board he was now *also* a judge presiding over a court destined to establish precedents rather than to find and follow them. He met the challenge directly. The Recorder would issue the oath to those who came as witnesses and he would act as counsel for the United States. And, turning to Choate, Schofield said that the Board would be glad to have the 1862–1863 trial record "and all other official papers relating to the case" read into the proceedings.[15]

These decisions shaped the investigation. Embedded within them, however, was a degree of latitude that the Recorder found excessive as to the calling of witnesses who had testified at Porter's trial. Only new evidence, counsel for the government held, should be admissible.[16]

From this dichotomy in opinions would flow a host of objections by the Recorder as the investigation progressed. And on each occasion, the quality of judgment rendered by the *de facto* court's involuntary judge, soldier John Schofield, would place his own reputation in jeopardy.

3

At the outset of the investigation's Day Six, Thursday, June 27, Major General John Pope made an appearance—of sorts. As far as Joseph Choate and Recorder Gardner could determine from an unsigned document forwarded from Washington to West Point, Pope had written the War Department to suggest that "Paymaster [Lieutenant Colonel Thomas C. H.] Smith" be subpoenaed by the Schofield Board.

Before beginning the morning's work, Choate asked the Board how the proposal should be treated—adding that the Petitioner had no objection to Pope's participation in the proceedings in any way. General Schofield said that the Board would take the matter under advisement.[17]

Everyone concerned would recall that John Pope was the surviving person most responsible for Porter having been tried back in 1862. His testimony had contributed heavily to the Petitioner's conviction and disgrace. Should the Schofield Board find in Porter's favor, the implication would be that John Pope was guilty of having done grievous wrong to a worthy and innocent brother officer and was, thereafter, himself to be considered deficient in personal honor.

During the years in which Fitz John Porter had been struggling to obtain precisely the fresh consideration of his case now in progress, General Pope had carried out his military assignments with competence bordering on eminence. And Choate had pointed out, "[the unsigned document] is to be treated respectfully as [it was] sent here by the War Department."[18] Army politics, too, the Schofield Board would have to consider.

Pope's name was mentioned time and again on Day Six during Choate's subsequent analysis and discussion of the charges and specifications brought against General Porter back in November 1862. Yet the Petitioner's attorney was merely offering the Board his interpretation or theory of the case. Given facts to be produced for the record, he said in effect, the Board would discern the difference between dangerous and damnable delusions spawned by wartime passions and documented and otherwise authenticated historic reality.[19]

Actually, Choate, Maltby, and Bullitt were reading into the investigation's record the text as well as the substance of Porter's trial. Along the way they provided comment and identified specific passages of the charges and specifications they urged the Board to concentrate attention upon. By so doing, Porter's advocates narrowed the span of relevant events and past and future testimony regarding them to the very heart of all this decades-long controversy: *obedience*.

Anson Maltby's diligence in preparing Choate and Bullitt was apparent in the extension of their presentation into Day Seven, Friday, June 28. At its conclusion, General Schofield recognized the need for time in which to convert words into print and for participants to bring witnesses from all over the restored Union to West Point. He adjourned the proceedings until Monday, July 8, 1878.[20]

Day Eight began with Joseph Choate reading into the record the statement General Porter had made in his defense near the close of his trial on January 10, 1863, and the review of the case Judge-Advocate General Joseph Holt prepared at President Lincoln's request dated January 12 and provided on January 19.[21] No board so reminded could possibly have missed counsel's point: Prosecutor Holt's failure to include anything regarding the defense in his report to Lincoln had been a major factor in what the President's approval of the verdict and sentence *only two days later* converted into a flagrant and long-lingering miscarriage of justice.

Correction, Choate seemed to suggest, should begin by isolating precisely those instances in which Porter either did or did not obey General Pope's orders and either did or did not misbehave in the presence of the enemy. As Maltby had foreshadowed, the critical events had been the march of Porter's divisions from Warrenton Junction to Bristoe Station on the night of August 27–28; the movement on the 29th up the Manassas-Gainesville road to the place near Dawkins' Branch where contact was made with the enemy, and subsequent developments; and on the 30th, Porter's attack against Jackson's troops defending the unfinished railroad embankment shortly before Confederate General Longstreet's powerful drive swept Pope's forces eastward across Bull Run to safety behind Centreville's fortifications.

Channeling information into the Night March, Dawkins' Branch, and Saturday Fighting categories would prove helpful. Yet a problem would remain.

Sequence of testimony given during Porter's trial in 1862 was determined mainly by day-to-day availability of witnesses. The spans and critical points of their experiences which were deemed relevant varied widely. And where maps were used to refresh participants' recollections and support the prosecution's case, Porter and Reverdy Johnson had no way of obtaining and producing maps challenging those supporting testimony regarding, for example, the time it took message-bearers sent by Pope to reach Porter.

Lest this fresh investigation be snakebit by the same flaw, on Day Eight Joseph Choate called as the Petitioner's first witness Gouverneur Kemble Warren, recently the maker of a new map of the battle area. Members of the Schofield Board needed no reminding of Warren's distinguished combat service throughout the war; arguably, he mitigated Joseph Hooker's defeat at Chancellorsville and facilitated George Meade's victory at Gettysburg. A native of Cold Spring, the village just north of West Point on the Hudson's east bank (and site of the foundry that produced Parrott guns), he was graduated from the Military Academy in 1850 second in his class and served in the corps of topographical engineers until Sumter. By the summer of 1862 he was commander of a brigade in George Sykes' Regulars within Fitz John Porter's Fifth Corps and a veteran of the Seven Days battles east of Richmond. Board members might well have remembered, also, Warren's having had to defend himself before a court of inquiry against charges of deficient performance during the battle at Five Forks, shortly before Appomattox.[22]

On Day Eight, however, all persons concerned with the future of Fitz John Porter's reputation needed agreement on the geographic and especially the topographic features of the battle area on which events such as the Night March and the face-off across Dawkins' Branch and many other alarums and excursions during Second Bull Run had occurred. Offering recent map-maker Warren as the Petitioner's first witness was confirmation of Joseph Choate's stature as a legal tactician. It was, moreover, notice to Recorder Gardner that he was deemed capable either of assisting in the search for truth or obstructing it.

John Bullitt opened the examination of Gouverneur Warren by taking him through the preparation of the new map, visible from an easel, to questions dealing with distances from one critical point to another. In Warren, Petitioner had a skilled cartographer testifying who had also been a participant in the events of August 29, 1862, near Dawkins' Branch. Bullitt made use of this double advantage.

"Was [this] forest or wood here [on the map] of a character to permit troops to move with artillery under ordinary circumstances? Could they have moved readily through it?"

"No prudent man, having anything at stake," replied Warren, "would march his men through there unless he had possession of the outskirts."[23]

After eliciting a description of the movements of Warren's brigade in the Dawkins' Branch area on that Friday, Bullitt returned to the issue of whether General Porter disobeyed orders by not moving through that batch of woods to assist Pope's forces engaged in a fierce fight with Stonewall Jackson's defenders of the unfinished railroad embankment near Groveton.

"Would it have been possible," Bullitt asked, "for you to have crossed over towards Groveton through the woods to the north of the Manassas Gap Railroad?" As a military movement, Warren responded, "it was impossible."[24]

But when Bullitt questioned Warren regarding events of Saturday, August 30—the day Porter attacked Jackson—Major Gardner objected. Had not the specification regarding that fight been withdrawn at the outset of the 1862 trial?

Joseph Choate addressed the Board: "I think as against the charge of hostile animus [v. Pope] of General Porter we are entitled to show what he did on the 30th." Gardner shot back: "I had rather not go into the details of the affair of the 30th. This was a subject thrown out by the Court, that specification having been withdrawn."

Choate replied: "I think it is very pertinent to our client's case."

Gardner's rebuttal: "I think there is no question that General Porter behaved gallantly on the succeeding day. . . . That charge was withdrawn; any evidence upon it will put upon me the labor of bringing out what there is, cumulative or otherwise, upon the other side, which I desire not to do."

John Bullitt, to the Board: "We suppose that that which really led to the finding of the court-martial was, that it was believed that General Porter's dislike of General Pope, or his want of confidence in him, or, as it was called, his disloyalty to him, was such that he was determined that he would not fight, and that he would do nothing to assist him. In that view it seems very important that we should be able to show that on the 30th it was [Porter's] corps which really sustained the heavy part of the battle that day."

Recorder Asa Bird Gardner: "I do not think we have a right to extend this investigation beyond the charges and specifications actually submitted originally to the court. If this is so extended it will be necessary to bring in all the witnesses, pro and con, to General Porter's conduct in that battle."

General Schofield was quick to render judgment. The Board would receive "any evidence bearing upon the question of General Porter's animus during the operations which were the basis of the charges against him."

ASA BIRD GARDNER, LAWYER, MAJOR, U.S. ARMY

Appointed by Schofield as the recorder of the Board's proceedings, Gardner took upon himself the role of a judge-advocate in a court-martial. As such, he vigorously contested everything favorable to Porter to the very end of the investigation.

Moreover, counsel for the Petitioner might "go beyond the limits of [August] 28th and 29th provided the examination is confined to matter bearing on the conduct of General Porter."[25]

Given questions regarding the Fifth Corps' attack on Saturday, August 30, Warren completely demolished the notion that Porter had devoted less than his best efforts in complying with Pope's orders. As Sykes' Regulars closed with the Confederates along the railroad embankment, he testified, "it was very apparent that the assaulting column had nothing but falling back as a consequence. As soon as this falling back took place . . . all this line of Jackson's advanced, and simultaneously with that Longstreet advanced south of the Warrenton Turnpike. . . .

"The advance of Jackson's line upon the regulars was very severe indeed," Warren continued. "But Hazlett's battery then came into very fine action; it was sufficient to break up the regularity of their line and make them seek cover, so they could not pour in any heavy fire upon the two regular brigades as they moved southeast. Consequently I held on to cover Hazlett until the last minute. My brigade was, really, unable to get away from there. They were nearly all killed. Hazlett's artillery escaped and moved back in good order."

Choate asked, "What was the general result on Porter's corps of the fight of the 30th?"

"Every part of it was really beaten and destroyed, except the regular brigades, and they suffered severely."

General Schofield had a question: "I understand you to say that your brigade was substantially destroyed?"

"Yes, sir. We held the front, and [Jackson's] line lapped us until we got a fire from behind."[26]

When direct examination of Gouverneur Warren resumed on the next day, the Ninth, July 9, 1878, Bullitt's questions had to do with events on Friday, August 29, near Dawkins' Branch. "Our movement forward was, as it were, suspended from the time [General Irvin McDowell] arrived," Warren recalled. "Nothing was done after he arrived except, as I said, the probable advance of our skirmish line. My impression is that General McDowell stopped our forward movement."[27]

Yet failure to attack the enemy beyond Dawkins' Branch was among the military crimes for which Porter had been convicted.

Bullitt then showed the witness a copy of the map, known as the "Pope Map," that had been used during the court-martial in 1862. "I show the position that is assigned on this map to General Porter," he said. "I ask if, on the 29th, at any time, General Porter or his force was in that position?"

"No, he was not," Warren replied. "It would be desirable to reproduce this map on the scale I have used to show how much it is out. There was certainly no such relation of Porter's corps to any troops that I know of on the other side, nor to any troops of ours."

"Does that map represent the position of the Confederate forces on the 29th?"

"That map is so erroneous that a proper answer cannot be given to the question. I cannot recognize these roads or places or any of the streams, as corresponding to the places they are on the map I have made, now before us."

Next, Bullitt read portions of testimony sworn to during the 1862 trial by Captain Douglass Pope in which General Pope's nephew and aide described the route he took on August 29 in carrying the "4:30 order" to Porter and asked Warren for comments, referring to the new map. After pointing out a number of locations Pope might have reached had he taken particular roads, Warren left the impression that the aide and the orderly riding with him must have covered a longer distance and have arrived at a materially later time than Pope had told the Court.[28]

Having established the basis for interrogating Irvin McDowell and Douglass Pope in due course concerning the joint order and the 4:30 order, Bullitt turned his line of questioning to the events of the night of August 27–28 and the circumstances of the march Porter's corps made from near Warrenton Junction to Bristoe Station.

"You saw General Porter on the night of the 27th at the time you have spoken of in his interview with Sykes and Morell," he reminded Warren. "Did he in that interview give any evidence, in what he said, or in his manner, of his desire to obey [General Pope's] order or to disobey?"

"The impression I got was, that he was very anxious to obey it literally, and that he yielded in the change to the earnest solicitation of those under him."

"Did you ever hear [Porter] say anything, or see him do any act, that led you to believe or infer that he was not disposed to sustain General Pope?"

"I never did. I think that he, in common with everybody in the Army of the Potomac, would have been as glad to see General Pope successful as any other man; that is, he was against anything that could be done to produce failure."[29]

4

Recorder Gardner's cross-examination of Gouverneur Kemble Warren was long, repetitious, and futile. Choate and Bullitt used re-direct opportunities to keep the Board's attention focused on the strong points in Warren's testimony. General Schofield asked questions that produced answers the Recorder could not have welcomed.[30]

Following Warren as a witness on Day Nine was James Longstreet. Joseph Choate led the former lieutenant general, Confederate States Army, through recollections of the movement of his divisions from west of Thoroughfare Gap southeastward to join General Jackson's forces during the early part of Friday, August 29, 1862. General Longstreet's answers to Choate's questions added detail and force to his earlier accounts, published soon after the Great Remembering began, which had declared that substantially all of his forces were in place northwest of Dawkins' Branch before noon on the day in question.[31] By contrast, General Pope had revealed in his joint order to McDowell and Porter, and had reiterated during Porter's trial, that he had not expected Longstreet to arrive until Saturday or even later.

Given Longstreet's awareness around noon on Friday that Union troops were present near Dawkins' Branch, Choate suggested: "Then your forces were in the positions which you have described before it was reported to you that the Federal force was advancing on the Gainesville road?"

"Yes, sir."

Choate's next question presupposed that Longstreet had been able to observe the battle area to his east and southeast. "Would it have been practicable for General Porter to have transferred his forces from your front, outside of that wood, up to join the Federal forces at Groveton?"

Failure to have done that was among the findings of the court that had convicted and disgraced Porter.

James Longstreet, the man General Lee had called "my old warhorse" after Antietam's first bloody day, replied: "It strikes me as a very hazardous move, one that could hardly be regarded as practicable under the circumstances. General Lee was very anxious for me to bring on a battle. Of course, I was anxious to meet his wishes. . . . I think we would have seized [Porter's shift toward Groveton] the very moment it occurred; it strikes me as a very hazardous move on that account."

"How would Porter's forces have fared, making that movement in front of your lines?"

"Well, I think we should have broken it up and we should have thrown everything we had right in pursuit; we had a good strong force of excellent troops, very anxious to get in and meet the wishes of General Lee and bring on the battle."

"Then," asked Choate, "do I understand that the presence of General Porter, where he was that day, held your force where it was and prevented an attack being made by it?"

"I don't know that it held us exactly, but it delayed us until the time passed for it. If we had had more time, I don't know but what we might have made the attack."

"But for that day it held you?"

"I think it checked our movement, retarded it so as to keep us there until too late."[32]

General Schofield it was, President of the Board, who asked Longstreet: "It has been said that if General Porter had attacked your force in front of him, it would have relieved Pope by drawing off strength from Jackson to meet it. Is that so?"

"I think not. We had ample force there to meet General Porter's attack on the right without calling on General Jackson at all."[33]

On cross-examination, Recorder Gardner wasted time by asking General Longstreet questions such as, "How far is it from Thoroughfare Gap to Gainesville?"[34] That, of course, was his right, and also evidence of his determination to be in fact as well as formal appointment counsel representing the United States.

Even so, enough time remained on Day Nine for Choate to call as a witness for the Petitioner Elisha G. Marshall, who had commanded troops within George Sykes' division of Regulars near Dawkins' Branch on August 29. Choate began his examination by asking him to describe the circumstances of his having given testimony during Porter's trial in 1862.

"I was very severely wounded at Fredericksburg, under Burnside, about twenty-five days before I was examined," Marshall began. "My condition was such that the Surgeon General would not allow my evidence to be taken. I considered that I was mortally wounded and would never be able to give any evidence before any court except the higher tribunal of God and Christ."

The court had met in Marshall's room. "Have you read recently," Choate asked, "the deposition that was then taken from you? Does it state all the facts that were in your knowledge at the time?"

"No, sir. I forgot to give other evidence with reference to the [Confederate] command on my extreme left."

So that the Board could consider this new information in perspective, Choate read a portion of Marshall's deposition from the 1862 trial record. Briefly, upon reaching Dawkins' Branch on August 29, General Porter had sent Marshall's regiment forward as skirmishers and to develop information. During the afternoon, Marshall sent reports back to General Morell that the Confederate forces to his front were large and increasing in strength. Toward dusk, Marshall learned that Porter had ordered Morell to attack, and that Morell objected. Marshall went back to Morell's headquarters. "I told him by all means not to attack; that it was certain destruction for us to do so." Later, Porter sent for Marshall, who repeated what he had told Morell.[35]

Porter had been found guilty of "shamefully" failing to attack and of retreating. The thrust of Marshall's testimony had been to the contrary. Now, by recalling that he had seen *additional* Confederate forces coming in on his left, he added weight to his belief that Porter had been correct in not attacking and that there was nothing shameful about it.

Also, when asked, "Was there any withdrawal or retreat on the part of General Porter that you know of?" Marshall replied: "No, sir; there was no withdrawal, no retreat. I got no order of that kind and no intimation of it from anybody."[36]

On the next day, July 10, John Bullitt opened Day Ten by calling Charles A. Johnson as a witness for the Petitioner and questioning him about the events of August 29 near Dawkins' Branch. "Was there anything in the nature of a retreat," Bullitt asked, "on the part of your forces that day from the point at which you say you deployed?"

"Nothing whatever," Johnson replied. Or on the part of other troops? "Nothing."

"You say positively that there was no retreat?"

"There was no retreat."

Recorder Gardner intervened. "I understand, then, that instead of allowing the witness to testify exactly as to the facts, counsel desires him to draw inferences from those facts."

"It is a little difficult for me to use language which shall exactly conform to the views of the Judge-Advocate," Bullitt responded. "If there are any better words to use I would be glad to have the Recorder suggest them. I suppose the witness knows what a retreat means as well as I do; it is a falling back to avoid meeting the enemy."

Joseph Choate joined the discussion. "How else can we prove a negative where simply an allegation has been made," he asked, "especially in view of the statement of Judge-Advocate Holt that there was a retreat? And we think we know that no such fact existed. We do not know any other way of proving it than to ask the question."

"I think the form of the question is unobjectionable," said General Schofield, "considering that the witness by his own testimony knows the meaning of the word retreat."

Major Gardner: "I respectfully suggest that the proper question to put to the witness is, what did he see and what did he do. Then whether there was a retreat or a falling back is for the Board to determine. When the witness is asked whether there was a retreat, it is left for him to say and not for the Board to determine from the facts elicited."

"The meaning of the word retreat is too well understood by military men to leave any room for doubt as to its proper use," Schofield declared. "Does the Recorder desire a formal decision of the Board on the subject?"

"No, sir."[37]

Bullitt moved on to questions regarding conditions on the night of August 27–28 and the march to Bristoe Station. Johnson recalled that his troops had been greatly fatigued when they arrived at Warrenton Station, supporting the position that Porter had ample cause for delaying the start of the movement to three o'clock the next morning from the one o'clock specified in General Pope's order.[38]

Johnson and two witnesses following him were among many called by both the Petitioner and the Recorder mainly to corroborate testimony given by others or to describe actions at points in the battle area other than in the Dawkins' Branch vicinity. John A. Judson had been a staff officer in Rufus King's division, and on Day Ten many of Choate's questions had to do with the fighting late on Thursday afternoon, August 28, when Stonewall

Jackson had attacked two of King's brigades as they moved toward Centreville along the Warrenton Turnpike. This triggered another of Recorder Gardner's interruptions.

"Before we go any further on this line of examination," he protested, "I should like to ask what relation this has to the charges under investigation in reference to General Porter?"

Good question. Choate's answer was not deemed satisfactory. "It seems to me," Gardner persisted, "that we are entering upon an investigation of the conduct of General Pope and General McDowell, rather than the conduct of General Porter on that day."

Choate's response: "General Porter has been convicted of lying still all day [on the 29th], from twelve o'clock until the receipt of the 4:30 order, when he knew that a furious battle was raging all the time between Pope's forces and the enemy. Is it not material and important for us to show that no such fact existed, and that there was no battle raging until the time that this witness has now reached? We suggest it is of the highest importance."

Predictably, Gardner disagreed. "I object to counsel going into an examination of the order of McDowell [for King to move to Centreville], and what was done the night before [the 29th] in the neighborhood of Groveton. . . . I do not think it is proper to investigate General Pope's and General McDowell's conduct, and the orders they gave, beyond the mere fact that there was an action, and what the character of the action was."

Choate replied: "Mister Bullitt suggests to me that the great point that was made [during the 1862–1863 trial] was that Porter's inaction on the Manassas and Gainesville road prevented the destruction or capture of Jackson by Pope's army; that it would have drawn off an immense body of men from the front of Pope's army, thereby enabling him to capture Jackson and 'bag the whole crowd,' as was his intent. . . . It is very important for us to show that General Pope and General McDowell at that time believed that the enemy was in full retreat, while the charges impute to General Porter a knowledge that our forces were being beaten."

"Let, then, the gentlemen subpoena these officers," the Recorder suggested.

"These officers have been fully examined," Choate replied, referring apparently to their testimony at the court-martial. "We prove our facts by our own witnesses."

General Schofield settled the dispute. "There can be no doubt of the propriety of the investigation proceeding in that direction," he declared, whereupon Choate led the witness through descriptions of his having been captured during the fighting near Jackson's line on the 29th by men in John Hood's division, an element of Longstreet's force, and also of the assistance Judson had given Gouverneur Warren recently in preparing the new map of the battle area.

Along the way, Choate had taken advantage of the latitude Schofield had given him to seek testimony regarding the conduct of Generals Pope and McDowell. It had already been established that late on Friday afternoon they had shared the belief that Jackson was retreating—hence, the 4:30 order to Porter, far over to their left, to attack. Had Brigadier General John P. Hatch, Judson's superior, found his superiors' judgment to be accurate?

"On the contrary. [The Confederates] were strongly posted, and were determinedly resisting us. [Hatch] directed me to ride back and tell General McDowell so, which I did. General McDowell said to me, 'What, does General Hatch hesitate? Tell him the enemy are in full retreat and to pursue him.' "[39]

Judson had obeyed, only—shortly thereafter on that evening—to become a prisoner of Hood's Texans who had poured southeastward from Thoroughfare Gap that morning well before noon.

5

A quick summary: By noon or thereabout on Day Ten, counsel for the Petitioner had elicited testimony from Charles Johnson that—contrary to the findings of the 1862–1863 court-martial—there had been no retreat by Fifth Corps forces on August 29 and also that on the morning of August 28 there had been good cause for General Porter to have ordered the march from Warrenton Junction to Bristoe Station to begin two hours later than General Pope had directed. John Judson had told the Board what he had seen and heard on the afternoon of the 29th that indicated errors in judgment on the part of both Pope and McDowell regarding Stonewall Jackson's behavior that led to Pope's issuance of the 4:30 order to Porter to attack Jackson's right and get in his rear.

Bullitt maintained the momentum of disclosures documenting gross miscarriage of justice by calling as a witness for the Petitioner John T. Leachman, a man capable not only of providing expert testimony but of sharpening the Board's focus on the circumstances regarding the 4:30 order—of all Pope's messages, perhaps the one that had been the most critical leading to the destruction of Fitz John Porter's reputation.

Leachman was a farmer who had lived within a mile or so of Groveton for fifty of his fifty-seven years. On August 28, 1862, as a patriotic son of Virginia he had been with Longstreet's forces west of Thoroughfare Gap standing by to act as a volunteer guide. Early the next morning Leachman proved helpful in expediting the movement of Confederate units into the positions General Porter's skirmishers were to encounter before noon on that Friday—a day before Pope had said, in his joint order to Porter and McDowell, that he expected Longstreet to arrive.

Fine, but in his testimony on Day Ten Leachman went well beyond confirming General Longstreet's recollections. In the recent past, the longtime Groveton resident had assisted Gouverneur Warren and his associates in preparing the new map before the Board of the battle area. In John Leachman, Bullitt had an expert witness who could and did testify as to terrain features—roads, streams, hills and ravines, woods, houses, even wells and springs—as he recalled they had existed in the high summer of 1862.[40]

For Leachman to have attested to the accuracy of the Warren Map was the least important of his contributions. And at times, Bullitt's leading of the witness to identify a series of locations on the map must have proved boring.

Yet there had been a point to counsel's thoroughness. It became apparent when Bullitt read to Leachman and the Board extracts from Captain Douglass Pope's testimony during the 1862–1863 trial in which the general commanding's aide had described the route he and an orderly had taken late on the afternoon of August 29 to deliver the 4:30 order to General Porter.

In 1862, the gravamen of Douglass Pope's recollections had been that he had reached Porter and presented the order early enough for the general to have complied with it. Counsel for the Accused, as Porter was referred to in the trial's record, had argued that in fact young Pope had not arrived until too near darkness for any combat operation to be launched. Members of the court had found in favor of the aide's version of events, as he had described them.

But what if Douglass Pope's memory had been, somehow, less than accurate? What if, in fact, *he had lied to protect his uncle's reputation*?

Adjournment time on Day Ten precluded Bullitt from exploring more possibilities. But soon after Day Eleven opened, with Leachman recalled and the Warren Map on the easel before the Board drawing as much attention, surely, as the human, Bullitt asked: "Will you state as nearly as you can what the character of the different roads was—and indicate them on the map—that you suppose Captain Pope traveled when carrying that message to General Porter, beginning where we suppose General Pope's headquarters was?"

Segment by segment, Leachman described the route. At times he provided details that left little to the listeners' imaginations: "Before you get to Gaskins', up by his house, and on until you get to Wheeler's house, opposite Wheeler's house, the road is comparatively smooth; but going down to Wheeler's gate, there is quite a hill where a horseman going in that direction, if he was at all a prudent man, would rein in and take it rather slower than he could have traveled along the other portion of the road."

"That is, from the rough part you have spoken of?"

"Yes. As soon as you pass Wheeler's gate he has a spring branch that runs out from his gate and makes on down this road. Water is in that road at any season of the year, whether it be wet or dry, and a horse will sink to his knees in crossing those places. About that point the stones crop out again, just before you get out to Smith's. . . ."[41]

With Leachman's statement of the conditions of the roads on the record, Bullitt asked: "Please say, from the experience you have had, and knowledge of those roads, how long, in your judgment, would it take a rider on a good horse, riding as rapidly as a man ought to do who is going upon a somewhat urgent mission—how long would it take him, traveling with prudence and proper regard for the safety of his horse and himself, and only so much of that—how long would it take him to ride over that road?"

"Assuming that the rider took the route that I have indicated here?"

"I mean from [Pope's headquarters] to Bethlehem Church."

"I don't think it could be done in under an hour and a half," said Leachman. "I wouldn't like to do it in less time."[42]

At the 1862 trial, Captain Pope had testified that the ride had taken about half an hour, from 4:30 P.M. to around 5:00 P.M.[43] Charles Duffee, the orderly who rode with him, had put the duration at "about an hour" and the distance covered at roughly five miles.[44] Names of both men were on the list of witnesses yet to be called.

6

Charles Marshall, who had been one of General Lee's four aides and the writer of the general's reports from March 1862 through the end of the war, followed John Leachman as a witness on Day Eleven, July 11, 1878. He was examined by Bullitt.

Generally, Marshall corroborated the testimony given by Longstreet and other former Confederates regarding the time on the morning on August 29 at which Longstreet's divisions moved into the positions northwest of Dawkins' Branch. Along the way, however, he described the actions the Army of Northern Virginia's commander took when told of a Federal force's presence on the right front. "General Lee was desirous to make an attack on the 29th," Marshall said, Longstreet was not, in part because of those troops on the far side of Dawkins' Branch.[45]

Next to testify was another former Confederate, Beverly H. Robertson, who had commanded a brigade of cavalry on August 29, 1862. After he had described the deployment of infantry units on the right end of Longstreet's line, Joseph Choate asked him: "Suppose that Federal force to have consisted of 10,000 troops, and that they had advanced over Dawkins' Branch and made an attack on your forces at any time from their arrival, what, in your judgment, would have been the result?"

"I think we would have repulsed them with 25,000 men; that was what we had."

What if the Federals had attempted to move to their right "so as to make a connection with the other Federal troops, up in the neighborhood of Groveton?"

"I think it would have been perfectly ruinous."

"Ruinous to you?"

"No, sir. To go to their right, they had to pass over a table land in front of artillery, in front of our troops. I think if it had been made, with no roads to facilitate the movement, that it would have been a very disastrous one. I think the results would have been fatal to them."

Choate wondered if an attack by that Federal force—Porter, of course—might have compelled "General Lee to withdraw the troops from in front of Pope's force."

"We didn't need any reinforcements for [throwing back] 10,000 troops," Robertson replied. "We had more than twice as many without drawing any from Jackson."

"You think it would not have forced the withdrawal of any troops from in front of Pope?"

"None at all."[46]

Yet all of the orders General Pope had sent Porter on August 29 had required the Fifth Corps' commander to take actions that Beverly Robertson had just shown to have been Union military disasters in the making.

Marsena R. Patrick, who had commanded a brigade in Rufus King's division, McDowell's corps, was called as a witness too late on Day Eleven to do more than confirm that road and other environmental conditions on the night of August 27–28 were such as to justify Porter's delay regarding the Fifth Corps' movement to Bristoe Station, General Pope's order to move out at one o'clock on that Thursday morning notwithstanding.[47]

Choate and Bullitt had been diligent in drawing testimony from all qualified witnesses regarding this proximate cause of Porter's disgrace. But their most intense scrutiny had shifted toward the events of August 29 near Dawkins' Branch, among which the court-martial had found cause to convict the Accused of misbehavior in the presence of the enemy. This became apparent as Choate resumed the examination of Patrick on Day Twelve, Friday, July 12, 1878.

Early on August 29, Pope had attached King's division to Porter's corps and ordered the force to march from Manassas Junction northwestward toward Gainesville. Patrick's brigade was following Sykes' division. He rode ahead, joining Porter and Morell.

"Did General Porter say anything indicating indisposition to support General Pope, or to do what he was sent to do?" Choate asked.

"No, sir," Patrick replied. "The difficulty that we were dreading was going into a country that we knew nothing about. . . . We spoke of our reaching positions just in time to get in at dark when we didn't know anything about the ground."

Some time after Patrick had returned to his brigade, he testified, "General McDowell came riding down, with his chief of staff, from the front. . . . He directed me to halt. He said, 'I am sorry'—or to that effect—

'that you are so fleet of foot. It turns out this time to your disadvantage. I have got to countermarch you. I want to take you over by another and a better route to the scene of yesterday's operations. . . . I am going to take you away from Porter.' [Then] 'Porter has gone as far as he can go,' or 'Porter is as far as he can go.' Something to that effect."[48]

Patrick's men saw action that afternoon and during the night against Jackson's troops near Groveton. Early on Saturday morning, when he warned Generals Pope and McDowell that "the wood was full of rebs," he was told, "You are mistaken. There is nobody in there of any consequence." Later, skirmishing prompted Patrick to make a second visit to the general commanding and McDowell. "O, these Dutchmen are always seeing the enemy," one of them said. "Now get off and get some coffee and you will feel better natured, and then go back and throw out your skirmishers and pursue them with your whole command, for we can't afford to let them escape. We have got to bag them."

Choate asked Patrick, "Who said that?"

"They both used the expression, but McDowell was the one who used it especially to me."

"Did you make any reply?"

"I think I asked him which side of the bag it will be."[49]

The Petitioner's next witness on Day Twelve was Fisher A. Baker, who had been a first lieutenant in a Massachusetts regiment, Morell's division. Bullitt drew from him the description of the night of August 27–28 as the darkest he had ever seen during his three years in the army. Most questions centered on the advance of Morell's division to Dawkins' Branch on the 29th and Baker's observation of skirmishing. But when Bullitt asked if there had been any retreat that day that Baker knew of, Gardner objected.

"Such a question has been propounded to a number of witnesses," he recalled. Indeed, he had protested on Day Ten when Charles Johnson had testified emphatically that there had been no retreat. General Schofield had found in favor of Joseph Choate's explanation. But this time, either the Recorder had forgotten the implied rebuke of two days ago or he was determined to renew the dispute for some other purpose.

John Bullitt responded: "I suppose one of the most important issues tried by the former court-martial, and that probably which had as much influence as any other, or more, upon the result of those proceedings, and that which had probably the greatest influence—and at least as much—

upon the mind of the President under the opinion given by the Judge-Advocate General, was precisely that which is involved in that which is now propounded to the witness.

"If the Board will recollect," he continued, "General Porter was charged and found guilty in having retreated before the enemy on that occasion. I think that is the exact word used. I suppose that there is no word that can convey what was to be charged against him more precisely, more accurately, than the word 'retreat.' I will now read from—"

General Schofield interrupted. "It is not necessary to hear argument," he said. "The only question is whether the witness understands the meaning of the word he uses when he employs the word 'retreat.' If he can be regarded as an expert who understands the meaning of the word, the question is certainly pertinent and proper. If the Recorder has any other ground for objection, we will hear it."

Gardner repeated his argument, rejected on Day Ten, that the witness can testify only as to facts and leave it to the Board to draw inferences. "On the original trial," he said, "witnesses were not asked, 'Did he retreat?' They were asked to say what he did, and what was done, and on that the court came to its conclusion. It is not a question for an expert to say whether there was a retreat or not. It is merely a question for the Board as one of law. . . .

"In an ordinary civil trial," Major Gardner pointed out, "under a charge of grand larceny, it is not proper to ask a witness 'Did you see the prisoner commit grand larceny?' although the witness may say he understands the meaning of the term 'grand larceny.' It would be transferring to the witness the power to say whether it was grand larceny or not, whereas he should be required to testify only to the facts and what he saw."

Then Gardner came to his peroration: "In this case it is for the Board to say whether there was a retreat or not. It is a question of law for the court."

General Schofield was not so persuaded. "The Recorder misunderstands the suggestion of the Board," he responded. "It is not a question for the witness to decide. It is only necessary to know if the witness understands the meaning of the word used. It is perfectly proper for the interrogation to take that form, 'Was there any movement in the nature of a retreat?' and if there was, to prove in what that movement consisted."

"That would be a leading question."

"It is perfectly competent for the counsel for the Petitioner to introduce testimony in that form now."[50]

Bullitt did so, establishing that Baker had been in retreats more than once and that on the 29th he had seen no movements in the nature of a retreat on the part of troops he had seen. After enabling Baker to describe the fighting on Saturday, August 30, as the "hottest" he had ever been in, Bullitt asked: "What was General Porter's conduct during that battle, as far as you had the opportunity to observe him personally?"

"He seemed to be exerting himself as much as it was possible for a man to exert himself."[51]

Last of the Petitioner's witnesses for Day Twelve, and indeed for the week, was Robert C. Buchanan, who had commanded the First Brigade of Sykes' Regulars. As was his practice, Bullitt opened by asking Buchanan to describe conditions on the night of August 27–28. It was so dark, the witness recalled, "that an aide-de-camp had to get down on his hands and knees to find the road."[52]

"Could you have made that march by leaving at one o'clock at night in any degree of order or having your men in any degree of condition after arriving at Bristoe?"

"I think not, on account of the difficulties we had when we did start. There was nothing to be gained by starting at one o'clock. That was the general impression of the brigade commanders."[53]

As had both examiners done so often before, Bullitt then took the witness to the events of August 29 near Dawkins' Branch. "Were you at all in front that day?" he asked.

"Yes, toward the latter part of the evening. I supposed we were going to make an attack. I saw General Porter ride off to the left of the road we were on into a little field. I think General Sykes was there with him. I rode up, and while there the enemy threw some two or three shells over by us. General Porter determined that there was no use whatever in trying to do anything with the force that was then opposed to us at that time. So I understood. At any rate we moved back."

"Was there any movement of your troops," Bullitt asked, "in the nature of a retreat upon that day, the 29th?"

Predictably, Major Gardner reacted: "I object to that as being a leading question."

That the Recorder was straining John Schofield's patience was evident in what he said next. "I think that objection has been covered by the previous decision."

"My previous objection was that it was improper. Now it is a leading question upon the direct examination."

"The counsel will proceed."

Bullitt did: "Was there any movement in the nature of a retreat of your troops upon that day?" he asked.

"Not only was there none, but the very idea was in itself absurd."

"Why?"

"Because there was nothing to produce it."[54]

Right there, John Bullitt might well have left his questioning of Buchanan. But he pressed on to the events of August 30, the Saturday during which Longstreet's attack wrecked John Pope's Army of Virginia.

"Did your men retire in good order?" Bullitt asked.

"I never saw a move on parade better."

"What was General Porter's conduct?"

"Always that of a zealous officer, thoroughly loyal to his cause, anxious to make it successful in every possible manner."

"Will you state what General Porter's manner in critical emergencies or under fire generally was? Was he an excitable man or a cool man?"

"I never saw him excited at any time; he was always perfectly cool on all occasions that I met him."[55]

CHAPTER THIRTEEN

INTERMINGLING OF SPIRITS

AFTER a long weekend, the Schofield Board's Day Thirteen—Tuesday, July 16, 1878, as before at West Point—began with John Bullitt eliciting from John Gibbon, who had commanded a brigade in Rufus King's division, a description of the fight along the Warrenton Turnpike late on Thursday afternoon, August 28. In effect, Bullitt was laying the groundwork for an incident that occurred the next morning, a conversation between Gibbon and John Pope that led to the issuance of the first order to General Porter to move toward Gainesville.

When Gibbon told Pope about the bitter stand-up battle Stonewall Jackson had initiated near Groveton, the general commanding "had not seemed to appreciate the importance of what I regarded as fatal, that is, the absence of [Union] troops from the Warrenton Turnpike between Jackson's position and Lee's main army [Longstreet]." A door, Gibbon had tried to warn Pope, had been left open.

"Why, we are pressing Jackson now," Pope had said, but then he had turned to Colonel George D. Ruggles, his chief of staff, and dictated instructions to Porter to take King's division and "Push forward up the Gainesville Road." Gibbon, riding a fresh horse and mindful of the admonition to "be expeditious, or we lose much," galloped to Manassas to deliver the order to Porter.[1]

General McDowell joined them and read the order. After a brief discussion with Porter, McDowell remained behind as Porter set his Fifth Corps in motion and Gibbon rode ahead to join Morell at the head of the column.[2]

As had become nigh-standard, Recorder Gardner's cross-examination of

Gibbon was unproductive at great expense of time—so much so that General Schofield asked the major to explain what he was trying to find out that was related to the case. Gardner's response led the President of the Board to warn him against introducing matters "foreign to the subject under investigation."

Choate and Bullitt assured Schofield that they had no objection to what the Recorder seemed so determined to do. Gardner pressed Schofield, who steadfastly ruled improper the questions the Recorder attempted to ask Gibbon.[3]

Blurred if not lost along the way were both references to whatever Gardner hoped to reveal and the relevance of much of Gibbon's testimony: such was the price the proceedings were having to pay for the major's manner of representing the United States. Moreover, it appeared that Choate and Bullitt were moving beyond events of the night of August 27–28 and the first causes of action against General Porter toward more intense scrutiny of the circumstances of the 29th near Dawkins' Branch in particular but *also* of how the orders Pope sent to Porter came into being.

While being examined by Joseph Choate, Ruggles—Pope's former chief of staff—testified that he had written substantially all of the messages General Pope had dictated for delivery to Porter. "It is so long ago," he added, "that my recollection is not certain."[4]

Choate was particularly interested in the 4:30 order. "Was '4:30 P.M.' at the top of the order written at the beginning," he asked, "before you had anything else on the paper?"

"I always put the hour down at the time I commenced an order," Ruggles replied, "It was taken from my watch."

Pope's former chief of staff could not recall how long it took the army commander to dictate the text or to refine it. Did he know at that time that Longstreet was up? No.[5]

Choate's interrogation of Ruggles was interrupted by adjournment for the night, but he picked it up promptly as Day Fourteen—Wednesday, July 17—began. How much time elapsed, he asked the witness, after the order was completed before the messenger left Pope's headquarters to deliver it?

"I have no definite means of knowing," Ruggles said, and he could not recall if he detailed an aide-de-camp, or if he did, which one.

"Captain Pope has testified," Choate told the witness, "that at the time he was sent off with the 4:30 P.M. order, that he was directed by you to go to a place which, if he had gone to it, would have brought him two or three miles in advance of General Porter. Is that your recollection of your understanding of Porter's probable position at the time the order was written and dispatched?"

"I do not remember detailing Captain Pope, and I do not remember giving him the direction to find General Porter," Ruggles answered. But if he did, he continued, Porter would have been supposed to be somewhere on the road from Manassas to Gainesville, toward Jackson's right.[6]

Abruptly, Choate changed his line of questioning. He established that Ruggles had been serving under General Pope since June 18, 1862, and that he was familiar with the address to the Army of Virginia that Pope had issued on July 18. Reacting quickly, Recorder Gardner demanded to know why the text was being admitted as evidence, given that Porter was not under Pope's command at the time.[7]

Joseph Choate obliged. "One great ground for the condemnation of General Porter," he said, "was his telegrams to General Burnside, which criticize and reflect on the conduct of General Pope, and it is important, as we think, for us to show what grounds there may have been for this criticism—whether it was right or proper for the criticism to be indulged in or not. Now, it does so happen that, in these much-complained-of telegrams to General Burnside, the allusions, among other things, to this address are perfectly clear, containing, as they do, direct and literal quotations from it. . . . Let me call special attention to one telegram which would seem to be a very severe reflection upon the commanding general. It is the one dated Warrenton, the 27th, in the afternoon."

Near the end of Choate's reading of the text, he placed emphasis on *our line of communications has taken care of itself in compliance with orders*. Then he explained: "Now, if we can show that the commanding general, in taking command of the army, had declared as his theory of war that the lines of communications must be left to take care of themselves, it breaks the force of this telegram, or of any conclusions against General Porter which may be drawn from it."

Gardner objected. "That could have been brought up at the original trial," he argued, "it being within the knowledge of the Accused."

General Schofield directed that the evidence be admitted, whereupon Choate read Pope's address into the record—and then made *another* abrupt change in his line of questioning.[8]

Back to events on the night of August 27–28 Choate turned, asking Ruggles, "Does your experience enable you to form a judgment as to the practicality of an army corps on such a dark night, with a road obstructed, starting from Warrenton Junction at 1 o'clock A.M. to reach Bristoe Station by daylight?"

"I don't think it could have been done."[9]

"Were you present at the meeting between General Pope and General Porter, when General Porter reported personally to General Pope?"

"I was." Ruggles recalled that Porter had "asked [Pope] the situation and what was proposed to be done, and the future of the campaign. General Pope was rather reserved in his manner; he was reticent and uncommunicative, as it seemed to me." Lest his own presence be inhibiting Pope, Ruggles left. Five or ten minutes later, Porter joined Ruggles outside the headquarters.

"What was General Porter's manner and appearance as he came out from General Pope?"

"His manner was serious; he seemed dejected; he seemed despondent."

"Prior to General Porter's reporting to General Pope," Choate asked, "had you had any conversation or heard any statements from General Pope about General Porter, or as to the probability of General Porter's supporting him or failing him?"

"It was before Porter reported and after we crossed the Rappahannock. He either said, 'Porter will fail me,' or 'Don't you think General Porter will fail me?' I think it was the latter."

"Did he state any facts or grounds?"

"I don't recollect; if he did, I don't remember."

"How did you receive it?"

"It came upon me, from my previous conception of General Porter's character, like a thunder-clap. I could not conceive of such a thing as General Porter failing anybody from what I knew of him, and I did not see how anybody else could get such an idea."

"You had previous knowledge of General Porter?"

"I had known him for eleven years."[10]

Next, Choate questioned Ruggles regarding a number of subjects—procedure for retaining copies of orders sent and acknowledging receipt of them, the state and discipline of wagon trains on the night of August 27–28, the condition of Pope's army as to food and supplies, the fighting on

August 29 and especially August 30. As to the latter, Choate asked: "How was General Porter conducting himself?"

"He seemed to be perfectly cool; he seemed to me to be doing his full duty."

"Did you know anything about a report by General Reynolds that day, the 30th, of the enemy turning your left?"

"I was at the headquarters at half-past two. General Reynolds came up in great haste and said to General Pope, 'The enemy is turning our left.' General Pope said, 'I guess not.' General Reynolds said, 'I thought the information of sufficient importance to bring it to you myself, and run the gauntlet of three rebel battalions, three rebel batteries, to bring you the information in person.' "

Ruggles added that Pope turned to John Buford and said, "You take your cavalry and see if the enemy is turning our left."[11]

Reynolds' division, the Board's members would recall, had formerly been a part of Porter's Fifth Corps.

To Choate's next question—"Did you write a dispatch to the government giving an account of that day's work?"—Ruggles replied that General Pope had dictated to him a message to General-in-Chief Henry W. Halleck. Choate's reading of the telegram into the record moved the Recorder to ask "the object of introducing that dispatch."

"I suppose," Choate responded, "that a report made by the commanding general at the close of a battle is part of the facts of that day, and that we are entitled to have it upon the record."

"Not necessarily. If it bears upon the conduct of General Porter, well and good. If not, I object to its being introduced."

"It is one of the plain facts of the history of that day," Choate countered, "of the battle in which General Porter was engaged. It makes no exception as to General Porter's movements, and is a certificate, so far as the Fifth Army Corps in concerned, of their very highest merit in the performances of that day."

"The Board," declared General Schofield, "can undoubtedly accept it as evidence on that point."[12]

Joseph Choate's examination of George Ruggles had covered a very broad span of subject matter. Along the way, the witness' answers had been generally favorable to the Petitioner—as had most of General Schofield's decisions when the Recorder had objected. Accordingly, when Major

Gardner's opportunity to cross-examine Ruggles arrived, his questions tended to contain a certain amount of bite.

For example: "Are you positive," he asked, "where General Porter's headquarters were at the time [Pope] dictated to you the 4:30 P.M. order?" Another: "Can you swear positively that you did not put the time on after you wrote the order, rather than before?"

"I don't think I ever dated an order after I had written it," Ruggles replied.

"My question is, can you swear positively?"

"I cannot say anything more than that I believe I did not make this one an exception in my practice."

"Then I understand that you cannot swear positively?"

"I cannot swear positively the exact minute that I made the figures '4:30 P.M.' any more than I believe it was 4:30 P.M. or a second or two afterward."

More badgering of this witness—or was it merely excessive diligence?—occurred a little later. "Do you know of the passage of a wagon train on [the Warrenton Junction-Bristoe Station] road that night [August 27–28]?" the Recorder asked Ruggles.

"Nothing except hearsay."

"Then you are not prepared to express an opinion as to whether an army corps could have marched after midnight from Warrenton Junction to Bristoe?"

"One possibly could have come along somehow. Straggling. Broken-up."

"If you don't know the character of the night after midnight, or do not know of the passage of a wagon train, you are not prepared to express an opinion as to whether an army corps could have marched from Warrenton Junction to Bristoe that night?"

"I have already stated my opinion on that subject."[13]

Once more: "Are you prepared to swear positively, in your opinion, that General Porter could not have moved at one o'clock with his corps?"

"I don't think I testified to that."

Choate intervened: "I didn't ask him any such question."

Ruggles: "I think the Recorder has put in my mouth the words I did not say."

Choate: "I asked his judgment as to whether it was practicable for an army corps to start from Warrenton Junction at one o'clock and reach Bristoe Station at daylight. He said he thought not."[14]

Gardner moved on. "What were your feelings toward General Pope?" he asked. "Were they kind and friendly?"

"They were fully so. . . . I have since sat at court-martials with General Pope; I have called upon him and he returned my call. He always called me into his room at recess, and he smoked my cigars and I smoked his cigars. I don't believe anybody could say there is any ill-feeling between General Pope and myself. I have the highest regard for General Pope's ability."[15]

During Choate's re-direct examination, however, Major Gardner's persistence did not flag. When Choate proposed to introduce three messages that Colonel Edmund Schriver, Irvin McDowell's chief of staff, had sent General Porter on August 30 as evidence, the Recorder asked if counsel proposed to prove that the orders had been delivered.

"The fact that these messages are in our possession," Choate pointed out, "is proof of their having been delivered."

"The question propounded to the counsel is, whether they were delivered to General Porter at that time."

"I think the burden," said Choate, "is upon anyone who questions their having been delivered on that day to show that they were not so delivered."

General Schofield settled the dispute by agreeing with Choate, whereupon the examination of George D. Ruggles reached its close.[16]

2

Time remained on Day Fourteen for several more witnesses to be called. Following Ruggles was William A. Newell, a longtime friend of the late Abraham Lincoln who had once called on the President to "make application to him in respect to the case of General Porter."

As night follows day, Major Gardner asked to be told the purpose of this examination. Choate's response led to a prolonged colloquy during which the fundamental purpose of the Schofield Board's investigation was called into question by the Recorder.

"We have brought Governor Newell here," Choate explained during the course of his extended reply, "not at all as the friend of General Porter, but as the friend of President Lincoln, to present a declaration that he [Newell] made in a somewhat formal manner afterward upon the subject of how his [Lincoln's] judgment had been made up."

Major Gardner was not persuaded. "I think," he said regarding Choate's point, "that we cannot inquire as to what President Lincoln said in an ordinary conversation after his act [approving Porter's condemnation] was completed. I believe that range of authority to be beyond our authority."

During the dispute between Porter's counsel and the one representing the government, nerves had been touched that must surely have made John Schofield wince. Because one president had acted in a specified way, did his successors have the right to do what only Rutherford Hayes had been bold enough to do: initiate proceedings that might overturn Lincoln's approval? Was President Hayes' power limited to pardoning Porter, instead of—if the Board's report to him eventually warranted—recommending legislation to restore his standing in the army and his good name?

Constitutional lawyers might have devoted years to contemplation of such controversial issues. But only three seasoned professional soldiers agreed during Day Fourteen that Newell's evidence was admissible for the purpose of placing "the present President of the United States in the same position as to information as to former action that the President who took the action [Lincoln] would possess if he were still living and President."

In the wake of the Choate-Gardner debate, Governor Newell's actual testimony must have seemed dull. Yet it was relatively brief and directly to the point:

> I stated to the President that I had called at the solicitation of friends of General Porter in our State [New Jersey] to say that in their judgment the finding of the recent court [1863] was very severe; that in view of new evidence being in possession of General Porter, we desired to have the case reopened in order that he might be reinstated or the sentence revoked.
>
> Mr. Lincoln stated that he had not been able to give that personal attention to the case which its merits required; that he had accepted the opinion of the Judge-Advocate General [Joseph Holt] and of the War Department [Edwin Stanton?] as the basis of his action; that if any new evidence exculpatory of General Porter could be introduced, he would be very glad to give him opportunity to have it presented; that he had had a high regard for

General Porter personally and as a soldier; and that he hoped that he would be able to vindicate himself in that way.

During cross-examination, Gardner asked Newell: "You don't know whether Lincoln had read the case himself?"

"I do not. I am under the impression from the manner of his conversation that he had not investigated it as a lawyer." And he added: "I recollect perfectly his expression at the time—I recollect that more than anything else—that if there was anything that could be brought out, he hoped it would be done."[17]

Petitioner's next witness on Day Fourteen was Frederick T. Locke, General Porter's chief of staff during Second Bull Run. Joseph Choate opened his examination by asking if he could recall any incident on the night of August 27 that gave an idea of its darkness.

"Between twelve and one o'clock," Locke replied, "in crossing from my private tent to my office tent it was so dark that I had to grope my way. I could not see my hand in front of my face, and in crossing from one tent to the other, a distance about as far as from here to that book case, I fell over a stump and severely injured myself."

"Were you there when Captain DeKay arrived with the order [to march at one o'clock to Bristoe Station]?"

"I was."

"Do you recollect what he said?"

"He said that he had been a long time in coming on account of the difficulty in getting over the road, the darkness of the night, and the road being so blocked with wagons. I know he grumbled a good deal about the trouble he had."

Locke testified that near three o'clock, when the leading brigade began its march toward Bristoe Station, "they had candles lit to find their way." Always up front during the march, he said, General Porter took a personal part "most actively."

"Do you know of any means by which that march could have been made more rapidly than it was?"

"I don't think that any human being, under the circumstances, could have done better. I was on some very troublesome marches during the war, falling back from Savage Station and White Oak Swamp [during the Seven Days], and that was holiday work to this."[18]

Locke testified that in less than ten minutes after Captain Pope arrived on August 29 near Bethlehem Church with the 4:30 order, General Porter had sent him forward to find General Morell and tell him to attack with his whole division. Also, Locke established the time as after sunset.

Had there been a retreat that day? "None at all," he replied. "Nothing to retreat for."[19]

Choate turned to some matters not developed earlier—beginning with General Porter's health at the time of Second Bull Run. It was very bad, Locke recalled, because of "great exertions that he had made in moving his command up the Peninsula to join General Pope." By the time they reached Aquia Creek, Porter was too sick to sit up. He was still "laboring under the effects of his complaint" on August 29, yet he was in the saddle for much of the day.

"What was General Porter's ordinary habit as to activity and vigilance in the performance of his duties?"

"Very active, very zealous, most indefatigable."

"How was it after he reported to General Pope? Was there any change in that respect?"

"No, sir. His conduct was equally zealous. He displayed great anxiety to push his troops up, and to carry out all the orders he received as far as he was able to do so."

"You have seen him under fire in critical emergencies?"

"I have."

"What is his ordinary appearance and habit?"

"I think he was one of the bravest and coolest men in action I ever saw."

"In the action on the 30th, did you observe him?"

"He conducted himself, I think, in a remarkably gallant manner. His coolness in some of the hottest fire I ever experienced was to me something marvelous."

"In the conversation you had from day to day, did you ever hear any suggestion on his part that indicated disinclination to support General Pope or to do what he could?"

"No, sir. On the contrary, his efforts were to push all the time. That was the burden of his directions to his subordinate commanders."[20]

Nearing the end of his examination of Locke, Choate said to the Board: "General Morell is still confined by sickness, and for fear that we may not be able to get him here I want to prove certain original orders that passed from

General Porter to General Morell by this witness. . . . The Board will understand that these, as we understand, are to be read in conjunction with the orders and messages of General Porter that were produced at the former trial and are in the record. These are those that subsequently came into his hands and are necessary to give a complete view of the day [August 29]."[21]

With the Board's permission, he read the following messages into the record:

> General Morell:
>
> Push over to the rear of Sigel and strike in his rear. If you reach a road up which King is moving and he has got ahead of you, let him pass, but see if you cannot give help to Sigel. If you find him retiring, move back towards Manassas, and should necessity require it, and you do not hear from me, push to Centreville. If you find the direct road filled, take the one via Union Mills, which is to the right as you return.
>
> F. J. Porter
> Major General
>
> Look to the point of the compass for Manassas.

> General: Colonel Marshall reports that two batteries have come down in the woods on our right towards the railroad, and two regiments of infantry on the road. If this be so it will be hot here in the morning.
>
> Geo. W. Morell
> Major General
>
> Indorsed as follows:
>
> Move the infantry and everything else behind the crest, and conceal the guns. We must hold that place and make it too hot for them. Come the same game over them they do over us, and get your men out of sight.
>
> F. J. Porter

> General Porter:
>
> I can move everything out of sight except Hazlett's battery. Griffin is supporting it, and is on its right, principally in the pine

bushes. The other batteries and brigades are retired out of sight. Is this what you mean by everything?

Geo. W. Morell
Major General

Indorsed as follows:

I think you can move Hazlitt's, or the most of it, and post him in the bushes with the others so as to deceive. I would get everything if possible in ambuscade. All goes well with the other troops.

F. J. Porter

General Morell:

Tell me what is passing quickly. If the enemy is coming hold to him, and I will come up. Put your men to repulse him.

F. J. Porter

General Morell:

Hold on if you can to your present place. What is passing?

F. J. Porter

General Morell:

The enemy must be in a much larger force than I can see; from the commands of the officers, I should judge a brigade. They are endeavoring to come in on our left, and have been advancing. Have also heard the noise on left as the movement of artillery. Their advance is quite close.

E. G. Marshall
Colonel, 3 NY

General Porter:

Colonel Marshall reports a movement in front of his left. I think we had better retire. No infantry is in sight, and I am continuing the movement. Stay where you are to aid me if necessary.

Morell

General Morell:

I have all within reach of you. I wish you to give the enemy a good shelling without wasting ammunition, and push at the same time a party over to see what is going on. We cannot retire while McDowell holds his own.

F. J. P.

General Morell:

Send down some good energetic men to General Pope at Centreville. Get hold of Colonel Beckwith and get some rations. Bring beef up to kill; we have nothing else; and get up enough to last two or three days.

F. J. Porter

Regarding these messages, which do not appear to have been available at the trial in 1862–1863, Locke was asked to verify the handwriting of Porter and Morell. He could not give the hours at which they were written or the sequence. Recorder was loath to admit them until authenticated by Morell. Over Recorder's protest, Schofield admitted them subject to corroboration.

3

Perhaps out of a superabundance of caution, John Bullitt opened his examination of George Monteith, formerly General Porter's aide-de-camp, by drawing from him detailed descriptions of the raw condition of the road and the chaotic spectacle of wagon-train traffic snarls that impeded the progress on the night of August 27–28. Could the march have been made sooner by starting—as ordered—at one o'clock? It could not have reached Bristoe Station at any earlier hour, Monteith replied, "retaining any sort of order, without scattering the troops, throwing them into perfect confusion, breaking up company as well as regimental organizations."[22]

Next, Bullitt asked the witness to recall being sent by General Porter, on August 28, with three other officers to obtain ammunition from the Fifth Corps ammunition train—then, alone, to ask Pope if he had any orders for Porter; then if Monteith had seen Porter with Lieutenant Colonel Smith that afternoon; and finally: "What was General Porter's manner just after this interview with Colonel Smith?"

"General Porter seemed vexed and disgusted with the manner and conduct of this officer," Monteith replied.

"Do you recollect his speaking of it?"

"Yes, that [Smith] treated him with insolence."

"You saw that officer afterwards?"

"At the trial in Washington."

"Now we come to the morning of the 29th," Bullitt began as he led Monteith through such events as the movement from Manassas to Dawkins' Branch and along the way Gibbon's delivery of an order from Pope to Porter and the interception of Porter by McDowell. "I heard no conversation between them," the former aide testified.

"How about when they parted?"

"McDowell rode a short distance, when General Porter turned his horse and asked him what he should do. General McDowell turned himself about a little and waved his hand and made no reply."[23]

Subsequently on Day Fourteen, Monteith confirmed earlier witnesses' testimony that Captain Pope had arrived with the 4:30 order "in the neighborhood of the close of the day . . . the shadow that was coming over us in the darkness. It was a growing shadow through the absence of the sun." There was no retreat that day, he said. And when Bullitt took Montieth to the events of Saturday, August 30, he elicited this recollection: "I have never seen anyone who was more self-possessed, more cool, or who bore himself in a more soldierly manner under fire than General Porter on that day."[24]

Predictably favorable had been the testimony of an aide who had been with Fitz John Porter since the summer of 1861, after the First Bull Run shattering when George McClellan had called upon his old friend to help him restore the combat effectiveness of what would become the Army of the Potomac. But what were spectators, and especially the members of the Board—and Asa Bird Gardner—to make of Bullitt's having drawn Monteith into one subject area, only to leave it dangling, not completely explored, and repeat the switching?[25]

But no clues were to emerge during the rest of Day Fourteen. Petitioner had no more witnesses to present for the time being. Recorder had a few on hand, but what he really wanted, he told the Board, was a thirty-day recess "in view of the necessity for taking some further action in the presentation of testimony."[26]

Joseph Choate leaned toward such an adjournment; he had taken Porter's case with the understanding that he might have to return his attention to the rest of his practice from time to time.[27] But he added wryly: "I think the Recorder ought not to ask and that the Board ought not to entertain the application, after he has examined all the witnesses that he knows of, for a long time in which he can explore the country for unknown witnesses."[28]

Whereupon John Schofield, who had heretofore confined his contributions to the record to occasional questions and as-needed rulings, made a comment. "The Petitioner," he said, "appears to have been 'exploring' a long time."[29]

Well, yes: since January 1863 when a court-martial rigged by politicians had destroyed his career and his reputation.

4

Day Fifteen, July 18, 1878, was Recorder Gardner's first opportunity to call and examine a witness in his own right. From the testimony of Hazard Stevens, his opening selection, however, it was difficult to discern what relevance to Porter the former captain's account of a fight on August 29 by the division commanded by his father had had.[30] John S. Slater, who followed Stevens, described Fifth Corps' movement to the vicinity of Dawkins' Branch on the morning of August 29. He heard General Porter tell Colonel E. G. Marshall to take his regiment forward as skirmishers, which added nothing to the proceedings. Choate, on cross-examination, brought out an account of the fighting on August 30 in which Slater was wounded and captured by Jackson's troops.[31]

Asa Bird Gardner may well have been embarrassed when he admitted that he had no more witnesses present for examination. Two had simply failed to arrive. He had told several others they would not be needed. He expected to have four the next day, a number of others later.

General Schofield recalled the recent discussion of an adjournment, and he asked the Recorder if he had "any other witnesses present whom he proposed to examine." Not today, Gardner replied.

Joseph Choate addressed the Board: "We understand that there is an important witness for the government who has been in attendance here, subpoenaed under the direction of the Secretary of War, and we suppose that the case ought to be exhausted, so far as it is now in the hands of the Recorder, before any adjournment—and that that gentleman should be examined before the adjournment if he is to be examined at all."

They were referring to Lieutenant Colonel T. C. H. Smith, but avoiding mentioning him by name in the record.

How soon could Gardner be prepared to introduce the witness whose name had been suggested, Schofield asked. "It depends a good deal," the Recorder said, "upon the answers that I may receive to such communications as I have sent which are pertinent to this investigation."

"There certainly can be no lack of preparation so far as that witness is concerned," Choate pointed out, "either on his part or on the part of the Recorder, because—as we have seen—they have been in constant consultation during the entire progress of this proceeding. I think that whatever light can be thrown upon the case by him, if any, should be shed while we are all here."

Whereupon, General Schofield declared an adjournment—but only until ten o'clock the next morning.[32]

Horace Bouton, who had been a captain in E. G. Marshall's regiment, opened Day Sixteen, July 19, 1878, by reciting the now-familiar events of Fifth Corps' advance to Dawkins' Branch on August 29. Up front with his troops as skirmishers, Bouton had heard Confederate officers and wagons moving during that night.[33]

Next to be called to testify that morning was Thomas C. H. Smith, the man whose name had not been deemed mentionable the day before. "In what capacity," the Recorder asked him, "were you acting during the month of August 1862?"

"I was acting as aide-de-camp upon General Pope's staff," Smith replied. "I had charge of all the cipher dispatches between the general and the government—all the confidential dispatches."

"Do you know of any address issued by General Pope on the 14th of July, 1862?"

"I saw the address before it was issued."

"Did you know the occasion of the issuance of that address?"

"Yes, sir."

Joseph Choate asked the Recorder to tell him the object of the question. "That address has been introduced for a purpose," Gardner argued, "and, as I understand it, that purpose is indirectly to reflect on General Pope."

"We disavow any reflection on General Pope. The grounds on which we asked to have the address admitted was that it explained certain passages in the telegrams of General Porter to General Burnside, which were regarded by the previous court as objectionable."

General Schofield reminded the Recorder that "assuming, as we are bound to do, the total absence of any purpose either to condemn or to approve the conduct of General Pope, the testimony cannot be introduced for the purposes of vindicating that address or his campaign." Major Gardner insisted that he had evidence to show that Pope had not meant to—in effect—insult the Army of the Potomac, "and that therefore these offensive expressions cannot be disposed of in the way that I understand the counsel to dispose of them."

Those disavowals of the intent to insult, Gardner had to concede, were made in newspapers which General Porter was presumed to have seen as readily as he did the address. "I do not see," said Schofield, "that there is any ground for that kind of testimony."[34]

Gardner then led Smith through a tedious description of a ride he made on the night of August 27–28. Choate found the narrative irrelevant and so stated. Again, the dispute centered on General Pope. After Smith voluntarily revised a statement, his examination resumed—only to run afoul of another problem cited by John Bullitt.

"We think that the examination of this witness should be conducted somewhat in the way that other witnesses have been examined," he told the Board. "We would like this witness to understand that he is not in the position of a judge-advocate, and that he must confine himself to his situation as a witness."

Schofield admonished Smith to answer questions "as they are propounded, as nearly as possible."[35]

Actually, Gardner's approach to interrogation was a proximate cause of the increasingly adversarial tone of the proceedings. Often, during cross-examinations, he had echoed questions Choate and Bullitt had already asked, as though he had been unprepared to move the case himself but wanted the record to show his diligence. Here, so far, the Recorder had wasted considerable time by dwelling on an incident—"transaction" was the term he and Smith were using—that appeared to have nothing to do with Fitz John Porter. Even when Gardner questioned Smith on several other matters, frequently the witness's answers were variations of "I don't recall."[36]

By contrast, Joseph Choate's cross-examination was focused from the onset. "Did you have anything to do with the preparation," he asked, "of the charges and specifications against General Porter upon which he was tried?"

"No, sir."

Quickly, Choate established that on November 29, 1862, as Porter's trial was beginning, Smith's name was submitted to Congress for confirmation as a brigadier general of volunteers; also, that in January of 1863 he verified the messages General Pope used in preparing his official report of the Army of Virginia's operations.[37]

"After the trial of General Porter," Choate asked, "did you know of the publication of a pamphlet containing what purported to be the proceedings of the court-martial?"

"I knew about that. I engaged the printing of that myself."

"At whose request?"

The Recorder interrupted to ask the purpose of the question. "My object," replied Choate, "is to show the bias of this witness."

In fact, counsel for the Petitioner drew admissions from Smith that he had been involved in the production and circulation of the pamphlet and that he had "very likely" paid for it. "If you did pay for it," Choate asked, "can you tell with whose money it was paid for?" No. "With General Pope's?" Smith said he didn't know.

Choate suggested that the pamphlet's object was to circulate evidence that "went to inculpate" General Porter. Smith replied that it was "to counteract the garbled accounts that had been put in the newspapers and the press" in the interest of the Accused in regard to the evidence.[38]

"What was the next publication in which you were concerned in regard to General Porter's case?"

"I don't remember."

It was, Choate forced Smith to concede, the report of General Pope to the Radical-dominated Joint Congressional Committee on the Conduct of the War. Indeed, Smith had prepared the four maps that were included in the document.

Choate's attempt to introduce three of Smith's maps into evidence triggered Major Gardner's objection and another exchange. Was this line of questioning allowable within the rules of cross-examination? Yes, Choate argued: "Part of the record stands as General Smith's opinion [at the 1862–1863 trial] that it was entirely practicable for General Porter to attack the flank and rear of Jackson as they understood it to be placed that afternoon, and that if he had done so the whole army of Jackson would have been destroyed. It is evidently upon that idea that the conviction proceeded, and very greatly in reliance upon the testimony of this witness. We have a right, in view of that, as this board has, to give all the weight to which his former evidence is entitled upon the record; to have his whole mind developed as far as possible."

There was merit in part of Gardner's response: "It seems to me an extraordinary proceeding to undertake to cross-examine [Smith] now in continuation of the court-martial proceeding of sixteen years ago."

Schofield declared that the question of admitting the maps could wait until the completion of Choate's cross-examination.[39] This was a decision that afforded the Recorder a few rare grains of comfort. Choate added a few more by changing the subject to events of the night of August 27–28. Try as he might, the distinguished counsel for the Petitioner was able to reveal only minor inconsistencies with the testimony Smith had given earlier that morning under Gardner's examination.[40]

Lawyers' convoluted games these were, a seasoned observer of the sessions might well have concluded. But to do so was to miss a critical point: These proceedings had not been initiated and were not being conducted to provide theater but to establish a record for use by politicians in settling or in squashing Fitz John Porter's case. And on Day Fifteen, no one present could have foreseen how vital the record's contents would be to the controversy's ultimate outcome years—not months—later.

Even so, arguments regarding the admissibility of Smith-drawn maps intensified in heat, and also complexity, until Choate drew from Smith the concession: "I thought that General Porter, at the time I gave my evidence, was further in the advance [on August 29] than he was." Thereupon, Choate said that he did not care about the other maps: "I will take that."[41]

Choate could afford magnanimity, for—as is true of all able lawyers—he knew the answers to the questions he asked witnesses before he put them into words. So it was with the next one he asked Thomas C. H. Smith: "Will you state what was the next publication in which you were concerned, or interested in procuring, in regard to General Porter's case, after the publication—which we have proved—of evidence for the prosecution?"

"I don't remember now making any publication."

"Or assist in making any?"

"No, sir."

"Nor in circulating any?"

"Nothing more than one or two copies. Whenever General Pope has made any of those publications there has been one for my use, and perhaps a couple more sent me."

A document issued by General Pope was shown to Smith, who said that he had called attention to errors in it—in particular, citations from Jackson's report as pertaining to attacks on August 29 as the ones actually thrown on the 30th.[42] Surely, Smith had not intended to leave lingering in the record the implication that his great friend and former superior had so egregiously warped the truth.

Choate pressed on. "Have you written a history of the campaign of General Pope in Virginia?"

"I have a large part of it written."

Major Gardner rose in protest. Choate allowed that there had been "a little disturbance in the order of proof." He added: "If [Smith], as a historian, has written an account of these transactions which severely inculpates General Porter, of course the reversal of that judgment, if it should be reversed, if General Porter should be declared innocent, would be quite disastrous to that history and would require a part of it, at least, to be rewritten; and we all know how averse historians are to being reversed, like anybody else."

Proceed, Schofield told Choate. But given Smith's assertion that—although his manuscript inculpated General Porter "very strongly" and reflected the views he had expressed at the 1862–1863 trial, he was leaving the project open pending further facts—counsel for the Petitioner turned his questioning into still another direction.[43]

"You testified at the former trial," Choate reminded the Recorder's witness, "as to an interview with General Porter on the afternoon of [August] the 28th?"

"Yes, sir."

"In which you discovered treason lurking within his eye?"

"That is your account of it."

"In the further course of your testimony, you stated that you had on several occasions made similar discoveries upon your first acquaintance with various persons. Can you specify those other cases?"

"I didn't state anything of the kind."

"Then I shall have to read to you what I mean."

"I spoke of it as a general fact in the knowledge of men, that you could occasionally, upon meeting a person even for the first time, see what he intends to do from his looks as well as from what he says."

Choate read from the trial record: "You say: 'I had one of those clear convictions that a man has a few times, perhaps, in his life as to the character and purposes of a person whom he sees for the first time.' "

"That is a very different thing from saying that I had such experience."

"You did not have such experience before, did you?"

"That is an irrelevant question."

"Did you refer to yourself as *the man* when you said: 'I had one of those clear convictions that a man has a few times, perhaps, in his life as to the character and purposes of a person whom he sees for the first time'?"

"No. I made it as a general observation in regard to men."

"Have you ever on any previous occasion in your life made any such discovery as to the character and purpose of a person whom you saw for the first time?"

"I say I do not regard that as a relevant or pertinent question. It does not grow out of my evidence. You have no right to ask me in regard to my experience in life."

Joseph Choate treated Smith's unresponsive response as an objection, though the Recorder had not. To the Board, and of course the record, he expressed an opinion that was more remarkable than most of his earlier ones in that Choate compressed into a minimum number of words the substance of the dispute:

> This gentleman was produced by the government as a witness before the court-martial, to prove that General Porter was a traitor, because when he visited him in his tent on the afternoon of the 28th of August he saw treason lurking in his eye. There are various forms in which he expresses it, but that is the most prominent one in which it was pressed upon the attention of President Lincoln by the Judge-Advocate [Holt].
>
> I differ from the witness entirely. I think it is quite pertinent for

> us to find out and probe the depths of his skill and the sources of such a clairvoyant discovery as that.
>
> If he [Smith] had had great experience before, and had made similar successful discoveries, it would add greatly to the weight of his testimony.

But if it had never happened before, Choate pointed out, "and if it should further appear that he didn't know any other man to whom it had ever happened before, it may tend to weaken the weight which this board would give his supposed discovery."

Understandably, Smith protested: "I do not wish the counsel to put words into my mouth!" But he made the mistake of continuing: "Nevertheless, I entirely appreciate the gentleman's ingenuity, and not the less because, like any other commodity, it is for sale at the market."

Was this another perception of intended depravity Smith had recognized, given his peculiar powers, but here regarding Joseph Choate?

"It seems to me," said the Recorder, "that the witness was quite proper in objecting to the question. There were able counsel to defend General Porter on the original trial, and he had opportunity to cross-examine at the time, and he pursued his cross-examination while the witness went on to speak as to the manner of General Porter." Gardner cited the passage in the trial record to which he was referring, then read:

> QUESTION: Can you state whether the disinclination to support General Pope, which you thought he manifested, was the result of his disgust with the immediate service in which he was then engaged, or of hostility to the commanding general, or upon what did it seem to rest?
>
> ANSWER: It seemed to me to rest on hostility. But I do not know that I could analyze the impression that was made upon me. I conveyed it to General Pope in the words that I have stated. I had one of those clear convictions that a man has a few times, perhaps, in his life as to the character and purposes of a person whom he sees for the first time. No man can express altogether how such an impression is gained from looks and manner, but it is clear.

"It seems to me," Gardner reiterated, "that the subject is exhausted."

Choate disagreed. "I want to call the attention of the board to what the Judge-Advocate said, presenting a little different view of it from what the Recorder takes. 'It is a life-long experience that souls read each other, and that there are intercommunings of spirits through instrumentalities which, while defying all human analysis, nevertheless completely command the homage of human faith.' That shows that he expected it to command the homage and faith of the President. I think I have a right to test the witness on this particular subject."

"But you have no right," said Smith, "to put words in my mouth."

General Schofield asked counsel for the Petitioner if this expected testimony was of any great importance. Choate replied: "I regard it of considerable importance, because we are dealing with three human minds and we do not know what effect this testimony as it stands on the record may have upon either or all three of them. It evidently had immense weight with the nine generals who constituted the former court, and, assuming that it might have weight with you, I want to test its foundation."

Not necessary, Schofield declared.[44]

"Then we may pass that by," Choate conceded. But he had one more question. "It appears in your testimony on the former trial," he told the witness, "that although you told General Pope, after you had spent some time talking with him, that you were certain Fitz John Porter was a traitor, you did not have that feeling at the time you left General Porter. You did not ride away from the Accused with that feeling. Now, what happened between the time you left General Porter and the time you told General Pope that led you to that feeling, or opinion, or conviction? What fact happened?"

In answering, Smith seemed to assume that some of his previous testimony was still fresh in the minds of those present—specifically, his description of his interview with General Porter on Thursday afternoon and the subsequent invitation to dinner that Porter had sent by a courier and which Smith had declined, citing the pressure he felt to return to General Pope and report the completion of his assignment to bring up the ammunition trains.

"The impression I gained when I received the invitation was that General Porter had sent for me in order to remedy a mistake he had made," Smith began, "but I do not think that that would have been at all sufficient to have made me use that expression." Then his recollection became more focused. "General Pope spoke in an overbearing way. He never liked to have any of his staff officers comment on any generals under his command. He snubbed me very decidedly when I made this remark in the way I say. He exclaimed, 'How can he fail me?' He said it in a very imperious way, as if my opinion was not worth anything in the matter. I was earnest, and I spoke then in an excited way in order to impress upon him my conviction."

"You say you did not have that feeling when you left General Porter. Did General Pope's snubbing you arouse that feeling in your heart?"

"Oh, no. What I mean is that it aroused me to use this strong expression. I felt the strength of my conviction when General Pope undertook to dispose of it in this way, and I spoke in that more decided manner."

"I am not asking you about your speaking," Choate told Gardner's witness. "You say in your former trial testimony that you did not ride away from Porter with that feeling. Now you say you did have that feeling."

"It was not aroused to the extent that I expressed there."

"Until after General Pope had snubbed you?"

"Until after he had treated my opinion about it in this way."

"Could you give the sequence of thought by which this feeling was aroused?"

"I presume no one can give such a sequence of thought. A man has a conviction on such a matter which is aroused by controversy with another person, and he then expresses it more decidedly."

Choate tried again: "Can you give the sequence of thought in your mind by which the feeling or conviction that General Porter was a traitor was aroused by the snubbing you got from General Pope?"

"I think after sixteen years I could hardly do that any more than was given at the trial."

"You say that the invitation to dinner affected your mind."

"Not to that extent. The feeling was aroused by the controversy with General Pope."

Choate, as had the witness earlier, assumed that the members of the Board and the Recorder would recall that then-Colonel Smith had testified in 1862 that he had told General Pope that "I was so certain that Fitz John Porter was a traitor that I would shoot him that night, so far as any crime before God was concerned, if the law would allow me to do it."[45] Hence his next question: "Were you armed when you were in the presence of General Porter?"

"Yes, sir. Belt pistols, saber and revolver at my saddle."

"Is it not true that the thought of shooting him for his treason did not occur to your mind until after General Pope snubbed you?"

"No, sir. I used that simply as a strong expression to show General Pope how clearly I had been impressed by General Porter's manner. It was an excited expression growing out of that discussion."[46]

During his re-direct, and to his credit, Recorder Gardner returned to the Smith/Choate colloquy. Referring to the admission of one of the Smith-drawn maps in evidence, he noted differences between the troop dispositions shown on his product and subsequent testimony. Would this change the opinion that Smith had given as a witness back in 1862?

"Yes. I expressed the opinion that General Porter could have attacked the right flank of the enemy in an hour with activity. I don't think he could have done it in two hours as I now understand it."[47]

For Thomas C. H. Smith, Day Sixteen—July 19, 1878—was over.

"We have now come to the question of adjournment," the Recorder told the Board. He mentioned a number of things that needed to be done during a recess, then said he did not believe that all of them could be attended to within thirty days; six weeks would be better, but sixty days would be more satisfactory.

General Schofield set Tuesday, September 10, 1878, as the date for the next session.[48]

CHAPTER FOURTEEN

Breaking Down Liars

Six weeks of recess had not been long enough for the government to finish printing the record of the sixteen days of sessions ended on July 19, Recorder Asa Bird Gardner reported as Day Seventeen, September 10, 1878, began. Reading the record could wait, General Schofield declared, whereupon Anson Maltby called as a witness for the Petitioner Alexander D. Payne, who had been a first lieutenant in the Black Horse Company in Jeb Stuart's Confederate cavalry.

Early in his testimony Payne described the movement on the morning of August 29, 1862, of General Lee and his staff from just west of Thoroughfare Gap down through Gainesville to the position James Longstreet's divisions were occupying southeast of the end of Stonewall Jackson's line. "When we got to Gainesville," Payne recalled, "General Lee sent to me to ride with him. As I was from that section of country, born and raised within 12 miles of Gainesville, his object was to question me about the country and the roads, directions and distances. I rode by General Lee's side until we came within sight of General Jackson's troops upon the pike."[1]

Maltby asked if Payne had been over that country recently. "Three or four times within the past six weeks," the witness replied. Was Payne familiar with the testimony given by Captain Douglass Pope and his orderly Charles Duffee regarding the route they took on August 29 to deliver the 4:30 order to General Porter? Payne was. Had he ridden over that ground? Yes. "How long did it take you?" On one occasion, 94 minutes; on another, 86 minutes—in either case, roughly twice as long as Pope and Duffee had recalled.[2]

Major Gardner pressed the witness at length regarding the possibility that conditions along the route might have changed materially since 1862. Referring to various roads shown on the Warren map, Payne pointed out instances of erosion and neglect as well as improvement. He also testified that the Warren map was correct.[3]

John Bullitt opened his examination of Walter Scott Davis by having the former first lieutenant and brigade staff officer describe the weather and road conditions on the night of August 27–28. It was, Davis recalled, "the darkest night I ever saw." He was up all night. At around three o'clock he was sent by his brigade commander to find out if General Sykes' units were moving. On the way, Davis said, he met General Porter. "It was so dark I could not see him, nor he see me. He spoke to me and I told him who I was."

Porter told Davis to tell General Sykes to move out at once. When Davis found him and relayed the order, Sykes replied: "Give my compliments to General Porter and tell him it is impossible to move the men out of these woods this dark night."[4]

Davis' recollections matched those of many other men who had been called by the Petitioner, but Choate, Maltby, and now Bullitt left nothing to chance. Similarly, Davis' description of the advance to Dawkins' Branch on August 29 contained details that were by then familiar.

Even so, his account became considerably more interesting when he recalled General McDowell's arrival. "He rode up to General Porter," Davis testified, "and said, 'Porter, you are too far out; move your troops back into these woods.' Then, in an undertone, he says, 'This is no place to fight a battle.' "

"You have used a gesture," Bullitt suggested.

"With his thumb that way," over the right shoulder, backward.

"What did General Porter do?"

"General Porter spoke to me and asked me to have the brigade moved back. I knew the anxiety of General Porter, and instead of going to my commander, Colonel Roberts, I went directly to the regiments."

"Is there any circumstance, connected with that, which impresses these facts upon your memory particularly?"

"Yes, sir. I first gave the order to the left regiment, then to the second in line; when I came to the third regiment, the First Michigan, commanded by Colonel Roberts, who was a very short man, standing down among his men—I did not see him; I passed by the First Michigan and went to the two regiments on the right; as I came back, the First Michigan was still standing there. I gave the command, 'First Michigan, right about!' when Colonel Roberts rose up, and says, 'Lieutenant Davis, if you have any orders for my regiment, please give them through me.' I says, 'I beg your pardon, Colonel; I never made that mistake before. I didn't see you.' All that day I tried to make friends with the colonel, but it seemed impossible to do so."

Reconciliation proved elusive. "The next day," Davis continued, "our commissary sergeant came up and said he was going back to Centreville, and if we had any letters he would take them along. Colonel Roberts borrowed an envelope and inclosed a letter to his wife. 'Gentlemen,' he said, 'I feel that this is the last letter I shall write.' Twenty minutes afterward I directed his body be taken off the field in a blanket."[5]

During August 29, Davis had acted as a combination scout and courier, making countless trips back and forth to the skirmishers and carrying messages. "Colonel Marshall was convinced that there was a strong force to our front," Davis said. "In going back to General Morell I met General Porter on the road and communicated that fact to him."

"What time was that?" Around mid-day.

Davis returned to the skirmishers. "I took two men and went forward crawling on hands and knees—within 300 yards of the enemy's line of battle—so near I could hear them giving orders. These men I took with me counted five guns very near the [Manassas-Gainesville] road. We tried and tried for a long time to see if we could count more, because we knew from the noise that there must have been more guns there."

"Did they seem to be in position to command the Manassas-Gainesville road?"

"Yes, sir."[6]

Considering the authenticity and resulting impact of Walter Davis' testimony, during cross-examination Major Gardner spent what must have seemed an inordinate amount of time attempting to find flaws in it. Eventually, it became apparent that six weeks of adjournment had diminished neither the Recorder's zeal in expressing objections nor Schofield's willingness to deny those that seemed to the Board—and counsel for the Petitioner—far-fetched.[7]

Francis S. Earle, formerly General Morell's adjutant, replaced Walter Davis as a witness for the Petitioner. After John Bullitt had elicited from

Earle confirmation of everything Davis and many others had said regarding conditions and events of the night of August 27–28, he drew corroboration of Irvin McDowell's statement on August 29, "Porter, you are too far out."[8]

Yet Francis Earle was prepared to go well beyond Davis' recollections. First, he recognized a dispatch that Marshall had sent Morell:

> The enemy must be in a much larger force than I can see; from the commands of the officers, I should judge a brigade. They are endeavoring to come in on our left, and have been advancing. Have also heard the noise on left as the movement of artillery. Their advance is quite close.[9]

Next, Bullitt asked Earle if he took any messages from General Morell to General Porter that day. Yes—one. The text: "Colonel Marshall reports a movement in front of his left. I think we had better retire. No infantry is in sight, and I am continuing the movement. Stay where you are to aid me if necessary."[10]

Bullitt asked: "Had you any conversation with General Porter when you took this dispatch?" Yes, Earle replied, and he reconstructed it:

> General Porter replied to me that he had just received advices from the right [the 4:30 order from Pope] that the enemy were retiring up the pike. I told him, from what we could see from our position, there was no indication of any such movement, but, on the contrary, we were satisfied that they were closing in on our front—so that we could not understand how they could be retiring up the pike, that there was no such indication. I also told the general that we were perfectly satisfied that they were Longstreet's men.
>
> General Porter said he was satisfied of that. Then he says, "Get on your horse and take this order back to General Morell" and he gave me an order. It was, "I wish you to push up two regiments."[11]

"State what occurred when you went back to Morell with this dispatch."

Earle replied: "The sun was just going down over the tops of the trees. He remarked to me that it was out of the question; he could not get over there before dark."[12]

"Did you see anything of Captain Pope?"

"No."[13]

Adjournment time precluded further examination of Francis Earle on Day Seventeen. Lurking in the record, however, was another message that Porter had sent Morell that afternoon before Douglass Pope had arrived with the 4:30 order from his uncle:

> I have all within reach of you. I wish you to give the enemy a good shelling without wasting ammunition, and *push at the same time a party over to see what is going on*. We cannot retire while McDowell holds his own.[14]

2

George Morell had been ill during the July series of sessions, but he had recovered enough by the Eighteenth Day, September 11, 1878, to be present at West Point. Even so, Joseph Choate informed the Board that since "General Morell was very fully examined on the occasion of the former trial, he is called now to identify dispatches."

Those messages, introduced in evidence on Day One, confirmed and buttressed the accounts of various witnesses regarding the events of the night of August 27–28 and all day and night near Dawkins' Branch on the 29th. Cumulatively, their effect was to demolish the allegations, in specifications to the second charge, that General Porter "did shamefully retreat from advancing forces of the enemy without any attempt to engage them . . . and without knowing the forces from which he shamefully retreated."[15]

In closing General Morell's examination, Joseph Choate asked him: "As an officer of education and experience in command of troops, did you have then, nor have you now, any doubt of the correctness of the situation, as reported to you, and as reported by you to General Porter on that day?"

"No, sir. None whatever."[16]

George Morell's division had led during the advance to Dawkins Branch on Friday, August 29, 1862, and so it was perhaps appropriate that George Sykes—Fitz John Porter's other division commander in his Fifth Corps—followed his former colleague as a witness for the Petitioner on Day Eighteen. Giving Joseph Choate a rest, John Bullitt examined Sykes.

Bullitt to the witness: "Did you receive any order that day [Friday, August 29] to retire to Manassas?"

"None whatever."

As able lawyers are wont to do, Bullitt put variations of the same key question to General Sykes. Each time, *none whatever* was the substance of Sykes' reply.

Much of Bullitt's subsequent questioning of Sykes was directed to events of Saturday, August 30, the day on which his division was nigh-wrecked by General Pope's having selected Porter's Fifth Corps to attack Stonewall Jackson's nigh-impregnable unfinished railroad embankment's defenses near Groveton. Toward the end of that long colloquy, Bullitt asked Sykes, "What was General Porter's conduct?"

Sykes replied: "It was all that a general officer's conduct should be. He was present everywhere his presence was needed. His conduct, as I have seen on many occasions, was always that of a cool, collected officer, full of foresight, care, and attention to all that matters of detail, and everything connected with his army."[17]

From the distance of more than a century, one wonders: After adjournment on that day, what was the mixture of pleasure and pain the three generals—Porter, Morell, and Sykes—must have shared if they spent more than a few hours on that fall afternoon on the terrace of Cozzen's Hotel on the bluff overlooking the Hudson and the foliage of the highlands that would soon be turning crimson and gold beyond it, holding a mini-reunion and recalling the best of times?

Cozzen's was the only place on the post where witnesses and others involved in the proceedings could stay, and the Recorder cited this limitation in recommending that the next series of sessions be held in New York. Counsel for the Petitioner preferred to keep West Point as the site. General Schofield made no decision, but in closing Day Eighteen he did grant an adjournment until October 1, 1878, so that Major Gardner might recruit more witnesses and otherwise prepare to "make my best endeavors to substantiate the original charges on which General Porter was tried and convicted."[18]

When the Board reconvened on Day Nineteen, October 1, the setting was the Army Building in New York City. Two witnesses were examined but neither moved the proceedings significantly.[19] The next session was held on Governor's Island in New York Harbor, which was to be the site of future ones during the fall. Major Gardner spent almost all of Day Twenty reading into the record his Opening Argument in rebuttal, a very long document in which he recited his objections to the case presented to date by the Petitioner and generally upheld the findings of the 1862–1863 court-martial.[20]

Day Twenty-One, October 3, 1878, opened with the Recorder objecting to the recall of Captain Douglass Pope as a witness. Bullitt had explained that "On the examination before the court-martial, Captain Pope gave certain testimony as to the delivery of what is known as the 4:30 P.M. order, and we wish now to introduce evidence for the purpose of showing statements which Captain Pope made subsequently and to give him the option of correcting his former testimony."

"This seems to be a most extraordinary proceeding," Gardner protested. "After a lapse of sixteen years a witness before a judicial tribunal, who underwent cross-examination at the hands of skillful and able counsel, it is now undertaken to recall before a board of three officers, without any judicial functions whatever, for the express purpose of continuing that cross-examination as to matters that are alleged to have occurred subsequent thereto."

Joseph Choate observed that "The only ground the Recorder states is the lapse of sixteen years, which certainly is no fault of ours. There has not been a day since he was informed of his sentence that General Porter has not been pressing for this rehearing and for opportunity to vindicate himself. As to the lack of functions of the Board, the Board is here to ascertain the truth. That is its whole province and duty."[21]

Once the Board had overruled Gardner's objection, John Bullitt asked Captain Pope a number of questions whose answers established the facts that he had been stationed in New Mexico during 1866 and 1867, that he had served with certain officers Bullitt named, and that in conversations he "probably" had mentioned in their presence his having carried the 4:30 P.M. order to General Porter. "Do you recollect," Bullitt asked, "that in the presence of those gentlemen that in going from General Pope's headquarters to General Porter carrying that order you had lost your way?"

"I have not any recollection of it."

"Do you recollect having said that you took about two hours to carry that order—that you were about two hours on the road?"

"No, sir. I am quite confident I never said that."

"Do you recollect having stated in any of those conversations the length of time that you did take?"

"I have no recollection of it. It is altogether probable that I did."

Bullitt asked a string of similar questions, in each citing details Pope might have provided: that he had gotten onto the wrong road, that he had seen a woman who had directed him onto a bridle-path, that emerging from some woods he had found himself almost upon a large body of rebel troops? Consistently, Captain Pope replied in the "I do not recall" mode. He continued to do so as Bullitt's questions cited instances in 1867 in which he may have been engaged in conversations with particular persons at specific times and places.

Toward the close of his examination, Bullitt gave the witness several opportunities to reconsider his responses. "Would you now state," he asked, "what you did say to any of these gentlemen, or in their presence, in reference to the trial and your delivering this order?"

"As to the conversation in detail," Pope replied, "of course I cannot give it. But I very likely gave them an account of the roads, and the position in which I found General Porter. But as to the conversation in detail, I have not the least recollection."

In wording his next question, Bullitt provided some wiggle-room: "Can you recollect that you stated *in substance* that it had taken you *probably* in the *neighborhood* of two hours to reach General Porter?"

"I am very confident I did not."

"You say that positively?"

"I am very confident—yes, I am quite positive I didn't say anything of that kind."

After three similar questions, which drew the same responses, Bullitt asked: "Have you any recollection whether you stated any time or not?"

"No, sir. It is altogether probable that I did, if there was any controversy about it. But my impression now is that there never was any discussion about it, and that my account was a running account of the whole battle."[22]

Edward Moale replaced Douglass Pope as a witness. Quickly, Bullitt established that Moale had been among the officers in New Mexico back in 1867 who had served with Pope and who was competent to answer a key question: "Did you ever hear [Pope] state the length of time it took him to reach General Porter?"

"I was very sure," Moale replied, "that I heard him say that it took him one or two hours, that he got lost on the road, and when he reached General Porter it was near dark. He did not say exactly two hours or two and a half, or two and three quarters or an hour or three quarters, but near or about that."

Did Moale recall Pope's having said anything about being confused during the 1862–1863 trial by Reverdy Johnson's questioning? "He asked me what the name of that cock-eyed old bugger was from my state," Moale replied. "I told him Reverdy Johnson. I recall that distinctly because Mr. Johnson's family had married into mine."[23]

Recorder Gardner opened his cross-examination by asking Moale directly: "What are your present relations with Captain Pope?"

"I hope," the witness replied, "the most friendly in the world."

Many of the Recorder's other questions having proved unproductive, he moved to ground John Bullitt had already plowed. "Nothing Pope said," he asked, "has impressed itself upon your mind except—what?"

"That while en route to General Porter with his order he got lost; that he got five or six miles on the wrong road, or something of that kind; that he got lost in delivering the order and he was about one or two hours in getting to him—I don't know whether it was over or under two hours—and when he reached General Porter it was near dark. I recollect that distinctly."[24]

On re-direct, Bullitt established that Moale had been indignant at being summoned, thus adding to that witness' credibility.[25] More was provided by Francis P. Jones, who had served with Moale and Pope in New Mexico in 1867. In general, Jones corroborated Moale's testimony.[26] That done, Bullitt recalled Douglass Pope.

"You have heard the evidence," he reminded Pope. "Is your memory refreshed?"

"It has not been refreshed by any statement made here."

Bullitt referred to statements Pope had made to the effect that Reverdy Johnson's questioning during the 1862–1863 trial had confused him. Pope confirmed that counsel for the Accused had seemed to be pressing him to testify that he had taken certain roads that amounted to a detour of enough miles to prolong his time en route to General Porter to "fully two hours."

Douglass Pope responded: "If I have ever mentioned two hours in connection with the delivery of the order, it was in connection with the examination of Mr. Johnson, that the route he attempted to make me take would have taken two hours to go over the distance."

So: If there was a problem here, Reverdy Johnson had created it? Such was the predicate of a number of questions Joseph Choate bombarded Pope with before he called the witness' attention to the trial record by reading his testimony—and then asking: "I wish you would point out now to the Board the questions which Mr. Johnson asked you?"

"I don't see them in the testimony."

"You found no such questions?"[27]

"I found no such question."

"Have you any recollection of any question that he may have put to you, or any answer that you made to him, that is not in the record?"

"I have not."

"Then, if there was anything said by Mr. Johnson when you were looking at the map, it was not a question to you, but some observation of his which escaped him?"

"I think it altogether likely."[28]

Thereafter on Day Twenty-One, Captain Pope was obliged to answer one question after another—some from Gardner, others from Choate or Bullitt or even Maltby—regarding the route he had taken between his uncle's headquarters and General Porter's in order to deliver the 4:30 P.M. order.[29] Spectators as well as the witness may well have grown weary, wondering why neither counsel for the Petitioner nor Gardner seemed to be doing anything beyond extending the length of the record.

After Pope's examination ended, the Recorder used the time remaining to take the testimony of two witnesses for the government who had been veterans of Second Bull Run. Relevance of their responses to Gardner's questions to the actions of General Porter seemed remote.[30] On the next day, Friday, October 4, 1878—Day Twenty-Two—counsel for the government called and questioned eight more witnesses whose contributions to the proceedings' progress were nigh impossible to discern.[31] But surely boredom must have been replaced by intense curiosity when Major Gardner began his direct examination of Charles Duffee, the orderly who had accompanied Captain Pope on the rides from General Pope's headquarters to wherever Fitz John Porter was found and back again late on the afternoon of August 29, 1862.[32]

An enormous amount of detail regarding those trips on horseback had recently been placed in the record by Douglass Pope's answers. Observers may well have wondered how much of it would be—or even *could* be—corroborated by Duffee's testimony. First, however, they were obliged to endure another reconstruction of the journey as Gardner led Duffee from waypoint to waypoint. But this time there was a difference: at the Recorder's direction, the witness had gone over the route on the previous Tuesday.

"On the former trial," Duffee said, "my testimony was that it took me about an hour" to ride with Captain Pope to deliver the 4:30 P.M. order. "It did not exceed an hour, and I think less. On examining the ground again I find it was not as far as I thought it was."

"How long are you prepared to swear now that it took you?"

"From three-quarters of an hour to an hour. I would not like to say three-quarters, but it would not exceed an hour."

"How do you fix the time?"

"By the gait we traveled and the distance we went."[33]

For a time after John Bullitt started his cross-examination it seemed that more repetition was in store. In answering an often-asked question, though, Duffee added: "I thought until I had gone on the ground that I had gone [down] that road."

"You thought until when?"

"Up to last Tuesday. I never had thought anything about that road until I was interviewed on the subject."

"When was that?"

"I was asked if I could go onto the battleground and tell the road, and I said I thought I could."

Again Bullitt pressed: "When was that?"

"I think it was about the latter part of August."

"By whom were you asked?"

"Colonel Smith."[34]

Might John Bullitt be operating on the theory that Charles Duffee's most recent ride had been for the purpose of establishing a credible reason for his reconfirming his testimony at the trial that he and Captain Pope had reached Porter and delivered the 4:30 P.M. order in less than an hour? If so, he succeeded in having Duffee identify a place called Five Forks where choices of roads were complex and questions at the trial regarding them had confused him. Thereafter, their colloquy—marked by nigh-constant reference to places on maps—became heated and confusing, in part because there were several maps being referenced.[35]

A degree of mystery had been introduced when Duffee, in the course of responding to a question regarding maps, mentioned having seen one during a meeting in Columbus, Ohio, in September—after Smith had contacted Duffee. That map was entered in evidence as the "Collins Map," which raised the question of who Collins may have been and how he had been involved.[36]

Yet Collins, and whether blue or red traces on one map or another correctly depicted the route, were merely surface indications of impressions forming as Day Twenty-One wore on. Embedded in Bullitt's questions were suspicions of felonies: perjury by Duffee and Douglass Pope, and of the subornation of perjury by Major Gardner, Thomas C. H. Smith, and possibly Major General John Pope.

So adroit was Bullitt's interrogation, however, that the Recorder could not object. Given the extraordinary nature of the Schofield Board's proceedings, of course, establishing grounds for future criminal prosecutions was hardly the point. Demolishing the charge and specifications that Fitz John Porter had disobeyed the 4:30 P.M. order, and in so doing had misbehaved before enemy, was counsel for the Petitioner's mission. And, inadvertently, Charles Duffee was helping John Bullitt accomplish it.

Referring to the meeting between Duffee and Collins in Columbus, Bullitt asked: "Did you not tell [Collins] that neither Captain Pope nor any other officer went with you?"

"I did. I didn't want him to know that Captain Pope was with me. I didn't care much about answering his questions. I was not under oath."

"You were not under oath, and therefore you did not feel bound to tell him the truth?"

"That is it exactly."

"Did you tell him that it was about six P.M. when you delivered to General Porter the order?"

"No, sir. [Collins] wanted me to say so but I wouldn't do it."

"You did not want to deceive him?"

"I had an object in not wanting to tell him about Captain Pope. I didn't want to be summoned."[37]

Returning to the aftermath of Captain Pope's delivery of the now-celebrated order, Bullitt established that a number of discrepancies existed in some of Duffee's replies regarding what he had told Collins regarding the return rides to General Pope's headquarters. Even so, with adjournment approaching, Captain Pope's former orderly was far from having been intimidated.

"What is your recollection of the truth of the time it took you?"

"About an hour."

"When you were disposed to change it this morning to less than an hour, why did you propose to change it to less than an hour?"

"I say now that it might be less than an hour."

"Then your change of opinion took place on Tuesday?"

"Yes, sir."

3

John Bullitt's cross-examination of Charles Duffee continued on Day Twenty-Three, Monday, October 7, 1878. At first the questions dealt with the places, going and returning, at which Duffee recalled meeting General McDowell—waypoints whose locations counsel for the Petitioner might want to test McDowell's recollection of later on. "It was quite dark," the witness recalled, when the second stop at the general's headquarters took place; campfires had been burning.[38]

Recorder Gardner, on re-direct, caused Duffee to shed a little more light on the mysterious Collins. Nothing had come of a request by Collins to talk to Duffee "eighteen months or maybe two years after the first trial," but long afterward a letter from Collins to Duffee and the promise of ten dollars to cover expenses led to the meeting in Columbus about which Duffee had testified earlier.

"What did Collins ask you?" Gardner said.

"He asked me the road, the point where General Porter's headquarters were, and what time I thought it took me to travel the distance, what time I started, and the time I got there. Says he, 'Can you recollect whether it was as late as half past six?' I told him no. Then he wanted to know if it was as late as six. I told him it was not; it was about half past four, or might have been a few minutes past that time, but it was half past four o'clock when we got there to General Porter."

Really? Gardner: "When you got there?"

"Half past five, I mean. He asked me a good many questions. He said all he wanted was a true statement."[39]

When Captain Pope replaced his former orderly as a witness on Day Twenty-Three, Joseph Choate had Pope draw the trace of his route to General Porter's headquarters on the "Douglass Pope map." Also, at Choate's request he marked the places where he recalled meeting General McDowell.[40]

Testimony given by Thomas F. McCoy, a witness called by the Recorder, was of slight relevance, but it was marked by another dispute among Gardner, counsel for Porter, and President of the Board Schofield. Arcane though some of the flare-ups seemed, they bordered on being as important to the outcome of Fitz John Porter's maximum and perhaps last attempt to gain back his good reputation as anything anyone had said during the proceedings since Day One, June 20. Absent precedents but also because of the political antecedents of the Porter case and President Hayes' considerable personal risks in launching the Schofield Board's investigation, it was essential that the Board's report reflect fidelity to due process of law.

Spectators in the room in headquarters on Governor's Island in New York's harbor who were concerned regarding principles may have listened with increasing concern as the Recorder asked McCoy, "Will you read the memoranda which you made as of [August] 29th?"

"Not in evidence," said Choate.

"I want to put his diary on record, as we did General Patrick's."

"Certainly witnesses cannot make diaries that will bind General Porter; they may refresh their recollection."

General Schofield: "The Board would like to know, after the witness has refreshed his recollection from the diary, what he is able to state as facts."

Gardner replied: "I think the witness has already testified to everything that the diary says; therefore, I propose to put the memorandum which he has made upon the record."

Choate objected. "I have never heard of such a form of testimony."

"The witness may refresh his recollection and then state the fact," Schofield directed. "That is the only evidence that is admissible. What purpose has the judge-advocate [sic] in introducing the memorandum itself? Does it contain anything more than a statement of facts which we could get orally?"

Gardner's answer was not responsive to the general's question; Schofield repeated it. "No," the Recorder said, "he has testified to all that is in the diary."

"Then you have all that is necessary."

"Then you rule it out?"

"We do."[41]

The government's next witness, W. L. Ormsby, recalled having seen General Porter during December 1862, "in his room in the city of Washington, in his residence."

"Were you accompanied by anybody?" Gardner asked. "If so, by whom?"

"By Mr. Lord, the official stenographer of the court-martial."

For what purpose had Ormsby and Lord gone to Porter's room? "Procuring some documents that had been offered in evidence that day, and which Mr. Lord desired for the official record, and which I desired to be used in my report for the *New York Times*, which I then represented."

"Do you recall any remarks made by General Porter?"

"I do. One made a strong impression on me at the time."

"What had it relation to?"

"His feeling toward General Pope and General McClellan."

"What was the remark?"

" 'I warn't loyal to Pope; I was loyal to McClellan.' "

"What did you at the time understand that the remark had reference to?

"That," Joseph Choate said, "I object to. His understanding of the matter is unimportant."

"On the contrary," argued Gardner, "if he knows what the conversation was about."

"He should certainly be permitted to give all the conversation that he recollects, but anything outside of that certainly cannot be drawn from the witness."

General Schofield suggested that the Recorder change the form of his question so as to elicit the facts. This led to Ormsby's answer: "It would be impossible for me to state another word of the conversation positively. My recollection is that it referred to the testimony that had been given that day, and concerning which General Porter seemed to be considerably excited. I have not the remotest recollection of what the testimony was, or what this document was, for which we went to his room."

Typically, when examining a witness Joseph Choate asked short, pointed questions designed to produce equally brief, precise answers. During his cross, Choate put one hundred and two questions to Ormsby. Some examples:

"Did General Porter say 'warn't'?"

"My recollection is distinctly that he said, 'I warn't.' "

Forty-four questions later, Choate revisited the subject:

"Are you sure that he said, 'I was not loyal?' "

" 'I warn't.' "

" 'I was loyal to General McClellan,' and that he said, 'I warn't loyal to General Pope?' "

"Yes, sir."

"Was he looking at anybody when he said this?"

"I think he was looking at Mr. Lord; I would not be positive."[42]

Among other bits of the story that emerged was that Ormsby and Lord agreed that they would not tell anyone about the incident. But had not Ormsby told Judge-Advocate General Holt about Porter's remark? "I have no recollection of so doing," the witness claimed, "although I have been informed that I did."[43]

General Schofield said to the witness, "I am not certain in what tone of voice you said General Porter used those words."

"I think it was an animated, excited tone."

"Can you use any other word as descriptive of the character of the tone of voice?"

"Earnest."

"As expressing any moral emotion?"

"It impressed me as indicative of strong feeling."

"I had rather have the manner of the tone than the impression which it may have had on you. For instance, was it a tone of humility, or repentance, or sorrow, or indignation?"

"Not repentance, certainly; not sorrow, certainly, nor do I know that indignation would be an appropriate term."

"Nor anger?"

"I do not think anger would be a good word; simply an *earnest* tone, indicative that he meant what he said—strong feeling."

John Bullitt suggested the term passionate. Someone asked if explanatory fit the case. Did Ormsby consider the remark to have been in the nature of a confession?

"You regarded it as an unguarded expression?"

"I did. Most decidedly."[44]

Choate wondered if the impression Porter conveyed to Ormsby might have been that he felt outraged by what had taken place at the court that day. "I cannot say that it was," the witness replied. "This was an explanation of his feeling towards the two men."[45]

4

Major Asa Bird Gardner called and examined six more witnesses before Day Twenty-Three ended.[46] None of them, however, did more than reconfirm testimony already given by others or add detail not clearly relevant. The proceedings having been inherently partly theatre, of course, the recent ventures of Schofield, W. L. Ormsby, Bullitt, and Choate into that mixture of semantics and psychology had been too refreshing for any act to follow without disappointment.

Even Fitz John Porter, the man whose innermost thoughts and moral values had been the subject of such animated, earnest, and unguarded speculation, must have found that digression diverting if not amusing. Not once from Day One through the Twenty-Third had he been directly involved in the proceedings in any manner worthy of mentioning in the record. Much had occurred that could have given him encouragement. But there had been too many times since 1863 when his hopes had been bubbles burst by Radical lawyer-politicians' pen-pricks, and if he was apprehensive as that Monday's session finally ended, it was certainly understandable.

On Day Twenty-Four, October 8, 1878, the Recorder's seven witnesses moved the investigation forward only in duration.[47] Day Twenty-Five was equally unproductive as six more of Gardner's witnesses came, testified, and departed.[48]

Perhaps this lack of progress was inevitable at this stage of the investigation, given the abundance of testimony recorded earlier and the four major subjects to which facts applied: events on the night of August 27–28, Fifth Corps' movement to Dawkins' Branch on the 29th and Porter's and Irvin McDowell's reactions to the "joint" order, circumstances related to Douglass Pope's delivery of the 4:30 P.M. order, and Porter's conduct on August 30. Of necessity, evidence had accumulated as witnesses had become available; there had not yet been much opportunity to sort it into categories. Yet there had been foreshadowings of fireworks as well as resolution of some of the issues that had been raised since Day One. And of all potential witnesses still to appear, only John Pope's arrival was more eagerly anticipated than that of Irvin McDowell.

CHAPTER FIFTEEN

"If you desire me to tell you how much harm I did, I cannot answer you."

MAJOR Gardner's examination of Major General Irvin McDowell began with a pointless question—"What troops constituted your corps on August 29?"—and for a time on October 15, 1878, it seemed that Day Twenty-Six would prove as dull as the two previous sessions had been. The Recorder did establish that McDowell had discovered Porter at Manassas Junction on that Friday morning.[1] And in the process, seasoned spectators may have noticed a tone of irritation in McDowell's responses, raising interest in whether the witness' reaction reflected resentment at being asked stupid questions or discomfort derived from having been drawn into these proceedings.

If Irvin McDowell had a chip on his shoulder the size and weight of a railroad tie, he had cause. For the Union defeats in both battles of Bull Run many considered him the scapegoat. Even the rear-echelon commands he had held during the rest of the war and thereafter had been attainable, in all probability, mainly as paybacks from the Radical Republicans (notably, Secretary of War Edwin Stanton). Yet no protection from the Recorder's subpoena had McDowell received, and now he faced more erosion of his reputation—a risk John Pope had so far managed to evade.

"While you were at Manassas Junction talking with General Porter," Major Gardner asked his witness, "what did you then know of any design of battle [for] that day?"

The reply: Only what had been in an order from General Pope to Porter that Porter had showed him, which was to move in the general direction of Gainesville and to take King's Division with him.[2]

The Recorder had just positioned McDowell and Porter near Dawkins' Branch when—in contrast to Joseph Choate's characteristic short questions—Gardner asked one that was long and convoluted; it was also, in Choate's opinion, a leading question to which he was obliged to object. Gardner restated it. Again, Choate objected.

"I infer from what has already fallen from the lips of the witness," said counsel for the Petitioner, "that the simple fact is that he does not recollect the conversation of sixteen years ago; but he has not said so, and certainly he should not be led in this manner as against us until he proves that he does not recollect what took place."

General Schofield asked McDowell if, at the present time, he recollected "anything in addition to or different from" his former testimony. "My memory," McDowell replied, "is no better now than it was sixteen years ago. I have no change whatsoever to make in the testimony I then gave."[3]

Rather a strong assertion for General McDowell to have made so early on Day Twenty-Six, acute observers may have noted. After several more of Choate's objections, however, Gardner's interrogation continued. "What had been the personal relations," the Recorder asked McDowell, "between you and General Porter?"

Joseph Choate may well have raised both his arms and waved both hands in the air. "I have never heard," he professed, "of a witness on the direct examination of the party that called him being allowed to fortify his evidence by any statements as to his personal relationships to anybody else, or his state of feeling. What he is to testify to is the facts occurring that day. Now: Of course the Board will recall that this is the witness by whose evidence chiefly General Porter was convicted."[4]

Gardner's response was rambling, concluding with a curious statement: "I think it is decidedly desirable that the animus of this witness, who was [Porter's] commanding officer at the time, should be made known to the Board."

Choate: "I should be very unwilling to believe that General McDowell had any animus except to speak the truth—either then or now. Whether he did or not must appear from the facts."[5]

The Recorder resumed his examination. "During that August campaign," he asked, "did the enemy capture any of your personal property?"

"None," the general replied.

"I ask the attention of the Board to the dispatch No. 19 of the Petitioner to General Burnside. 'The enemy captured all Pope's and other clothing, and from McDowell the same, including liquors.' "

Choate said to Gardner, "Don't you understand that a joke is a joke? Why do you wish to encumber this record?"

Ignoring Choate, Gardner asked McDowell: "Did you have in your baggage any liquors that were captured by the enemy, or otherwise?"

"Not to my knowledge."

Choate: "Or that were not captured."

McDowell: "Or that were not captured. I have been told that I gave a case of claret to General Porter, but I am certain that I did not have it to give to him; I should have done it with pleasure if I had."

Gardner to the witness: "You are not in the habit of drinking liquor, I believe."

"Is that the issue to be tried here?" Choate asked.

General Schofield thought not. "The judge-advocate," he declared, "will please bear in mind that this board and all the world know that there is probably no person who has read American history who does not know General McDowell's habits upon such matters. It is not proper to be put upon the record."[6]

So ended the Recorder's examination. Choate opened his cross-examination by asking, "With the exception of your own official reports, have you since Second Bull Run published or printed any statement in regard to the occurrences of that day?"

Before McDowell could reply, Gardner objected. Choate explained: "It may be that I shall be able to show that General McDowell has since that day printed and given currency to accounts of transactions that day which are at variance somewhat with his recollection of them as it stands upon his evidence [given at the trial]. I think I am clearly entitled to that."

McDowell conceded that on February 17, 1870, he had. "In the New York morning papers of the 15th instant, is a letter from Washington on the subject of the Fitz John Porter case, containing a criticism of General McClellan's, questioning the course taken by General McDowell in the battle of the 29th of [August], 1862. This paper forms part of a pamphlet printed last June for private circulation and has not been made public until now."[7]

After quoting McClellan to the effect that "the only opportunity of attacking with good chances of success and decisive results was early in the forenoon and with all the combined forces of McDowell and Porter," McDowell gave his reasons for rejecting McClellan's opinion.

"In that statement," Choate reminded McDowell, "referring to the time on the 29th of August when you and General Porter separated, you stated expressly that the separation took place 'before conflict was possible.' That is so, is it not? You stated, also, that there can be no question of the responsibility on either general for not making an attack before noon?"

"That is my recollection as to the time."

"Then, I understand you to say now that up to the time you left General Porter, he had made no mistake and had been guilty of no default or dereliction of duty?"

"I have not charged that he had."

Choate asked McDowell if he recalled a document entitled "A brief statement in the case of Fitz John Porter." Grudgingly, the general admitted that he may have received a copy from General Pope. "Did you take any part in the production of that document?"

After inspecting the copy handed to him, McDowell said, "I had printed extracts from the reports of Generals Stuart, Longstreet, and Jackson, and I see that those extracts are incorporated in that paper; to that extent, and to that extent only, was I in any way whatever concerned in that paper. I did not know of its production; I did not know it was to be produced."

"Do you know who was the author of it?"

"I do not know that I do."[8]

Choate asked that the document be placed in the record. The Recorder objected; the paper was not the witness' product.

"Did you aid in circulating copies of it in your possession to various persons?" Choate asked McDowell.

"Undoubtedly."

Gardner blocked every attempt Choate made to move the case with objections. Finally, again counsel for the Petitioner explained his intent. "Is [circulating] not a propagation of [McDowell's] views? And if we show that those views are entirely at variance with the facts, will it not have a bearing upon the weight to be given to the general's opinions which stand upon the record?"

Schofield found in favor of the Recorder. "It can only be regarded as showing what another man said upon the subject in controversy," he said.[9]

Choate turned to the extracts from Confederate generals' reports that

McDowell admitted he had made. "You printed a large edition?"

"Yes, sir."

"What did you do with it?"

"I sent them to my friends; I cannot tell to whom."

Questioning developed that the recipients included some members of Congress and General Pope. "When you sent it to him," Choate asked, "did you do it knowing that he was going to incorporate it in his brief statement?"

"How could I know?"

"I ask you."

"I could not know it. I could not know what was passing in his mind."

"Well, what was passing in your own mind?"

"I did not know whether he was going to have a brief statement or a long statement, or whether he was going to incorporate it or not. How could I know?"[10]

A copy of McDowell's contribution was admitted as evidence. Choate continued: "What portion of this document of yours is incorporated in General Pope's brief statement?"

"You can tell for yourself."

The Recorder: "Counsel assumes that that is *General Pope's* brief statement."

Choate responded with a reminder: "We proved that months ago by Lieutenant Colonel T. C. H. Smith, and it is in evidence and on the record. We have identified it as General Pope's now by General McDowell. It is the same document that was shown Colonel Smith, and he indicated what we had not known before, that those extracts from the reports of the rebel generals had originated from General McDowell."

The Recorder continued to object even after Choate read from the investigation's own record the pertinent portion of Smith's testimony. Wrangling between Gardner and Choate led Schofield to ask to see the "brief statement." Choate passed it to him, commenting: "Of course, it is a violent argument against General Porter by General Pope."

"I deny that it is an argument by General Pope," said the Recorder.

"General McDowell is as good a witness as we have got," Choate remarked, "and he says it was."

In the end, General Schofield allowed Choate to introduce Pope's "brief statement" as evidence.[11] With both McDowell's contributed extracts and the product in which Pope used them on record, counsel for the Petitioner were in a position to challenge the authenticity of the Confederate reports and the use McDowell made of General Jackson's report in particular.

At issue was whether McDowell had given the impression that certain passages referred to events of the 29th of August when in fact Jackson was describing action that occurred on the next day, Friday, August 30. Choate asked the witness: "These lines [in the heading] you furnished—'Operations of the 29th of August, second Bull Run'—now, did you intend in circulating this to circulate the report of these three rebel generals of the battle on the 29th of August, 1862?"

"At the time I made those extracts," McDowell replied, "I supposed they referred to that date."

"Do you not now know that what you printed and circulated as an extract from General Jackson's report of the battle on the 29th was in fact an extract from his report relating to the battle of the 30th?"

"It was afterwards claimed that it referred to the 30th. It seemed to me that General Jackson had mixed up the 29th and 30th, and that some parts might belong to one day and some parts might belong to the other."

"I speak of this part which you published as his report of the 29th. Do you not now know that it is actually his report of what took place on the 30th?"

"I do not now know any more than I knew then. I supposed it referred to the 29th. I heard afterwards that it referred to the 30th, and I supposed that he mixed the 29th and 30th together."

"Do you suppose so now?"

"I do. He made that report six or eight months after the occurrences. I think men very often mix up persons and occurrences after they have passed some time."

"You were an active participant in the events of both the 29th and 30th of August, were you not?"

"Yes, sir."

"Does not your personal knowledge of the events of those two days enable you to form a judgment as to whether that extract contained a truthful account of the 29th or the 30th, and which?"

McDowell's answer was not responsive. Choate repeated the question. "I have answered the question," the witness insisted.

"I submit to the Board," Choate stated, "that he has not."

Addressing General Schofield, McDowell reiterated his contention that Jackson had embedded confusion. When asked if he thought Jackson intended his report to refer to both days, he answered: "That is a question. What I think is a little too much of a psychological question for me to say."

Choate pressed: "Do not you know that it is actually an extract from his report given by him as a report of the transactions of the 30th?"

"I did not; if I did, I should never have published it as I did. If I made a mistake it certainly was a great mistake for me to suppose it was the 29th if it was the 30th."[12]

Here, Joseph Choate had in effect broken the witness. A less seasoned lawyer might have left it at that. But Choate stepped up his pressure on McDowell. "You [made your extract] and printed it," he said, "and circulated it supposing that General Jackson said that in reference to the battle of the 29th?"

"This is the seventh or eighth time I have told you so."

"That being so, I want to know whether, when you extracted it and printed it, you observed and read the next preceding sentence as follows:

> On the following day, the 30th, my command occupied the high ground, and the divisions the same relative positions to each other and in the field which they held the day before, forming the left wing of the army. General Longstreet's command formed the right wing, and a large quantity of artillery was posted upon a commanding eminence in the center.[13]

"Then comes your extract: 'After some desultory skirmishing and heavy cannonading' and so forth."

The Recorder objected; it had not yet appeared what Longstreet's opinion was. Choate easily disposed of the interruption, adding: "I ask the witness if he observed that the next preceding sentence says that on the following day, the 30th, such and such transactions took place."

"I did not observe that," Irvin McDowell admitted. "I am entirely satisfied that I was in error."

"Because you did not read the preceding sentence?"

"You are now asking me a little more than I am able to say. I cannot go back and say how I made the error which I acknowledge I have made. If you want something further on the subject I will say that I now see that I made a mistake at that time, and if you desire me to say so I will say that I am exceedingly sorry I made it."[14]

"No, I don't want that," said Choate. "Of course you are. What I want to ask is this: whether a publication made containing this extract as a basis of a report on or criticism of General Porter's conduct on the 29th was not calculated to do him great injustice?"

"It was not calculated to do him great injustice."

"Would it not have that effect?"

"I will not say that. But you can judge that for yourself. I told you that it was a mistake. I told you that I had apologized for making it. I do not know how much more you want. If you desire me to tell you how much harm it did I cannot answer you. I think that exhausts the whole question."

"If you will pardon me," said Choate, "I do not think it does."[15]

Counsel for the Petitioner went on to ask if McDowell had ever tried to correct his error—he had not—and there were several questions regarding communication between the witness and the Recorder prior to his appearance. Along the way, McDowell made a statement as curious as the one W. L. Ormsby testified that Fitz John Porter had uttered, "I warn't loyal to General Pope, I was loyal to General McClellan." Said the witness: "This whole campaign has been a nightmare to me."[16]

"In what sense?" Choate asked.

"Because right after it I was accused of being a drunkard and a traitor. I had the whole country howling after me from one end to the other. I was relieved from my command."

"And so it has been a nightmare to you ever since?"

"I will not say that. It was a subject that I kept clear of, except when it was thrust upon me."

"How was it 'thrust' upon you, when you printed and circulated those extracts from rebel archives?" He had felt compelled to respond to critics of his own performance, McDowell explained.[17]

Choate then questioned McDowell regarding the time and circumstances of his learning that Longstreet's forces had arrived and were facing Porter's near Dawkins' Branch. Actually, this was a continuation by Choate of efforts to link the general's misuse of the Confederates' reports to the damage done to Porter. Also, almost any additional admission of error would bring more into question the truth of McDowell's testimony during the long-ago trial.

As before, Major Gardner objected frequently and seldom with success. Aficianados of conflict who were present in the room may have noted that the persistence of Joseph Choate and the resistance of Irvin McDowell had relegated the Recorder almost to irrelevance.

Indeed, the witness complained to the Board: "The counsel tried to involve me in contradiction and inconsistency, when it all turns on that."[18]

Along the way, General McDowell had said: "Many things which I did not know when I was with General Porter came to my knowledge afterwards. I grew into the knowledge of the enemy's position since that time."

"You have learned a great deal of the history of that day since your former examination on the court-martial?"

"I think I have learned a great deal."[19]

2

So had the members of the Schofield Board thus far on Day Twenty-six. How much more, everyone present must have wondered, could Joseph Choate wring from McDowell?

Not much, if the congeniality of the next colloquy's opening was any indicator. "How long had you been with," Joseph Choate asked, "and under the command of, General Pope before the 29th of August, 1862?"

"What has this to do with the case?" Irvin McDowell countered.

"You have testified that on the 29th you had no knowledge in particular of the plans of General Pope."

"Now pardon me. You must give my language more nearly as I said it."

"I cannot recollect it," Choate conceded.

"Your memory seems to be bad, inasmuch as it is worse than my memory of sixteen years ago."

Choate repeated his question. And McDowell repeated his rejoinder. "I ask you what you want to know for. I am willing to tell you everything that bears on this case."

John Schofield must have given his nigh-bald head a good shake. "Questions that seem outside the of the subject," he admonished the unlikely exchangers of banter, "will not be allowed."[20]

Choate complied by asking McDowell a series of questions dealing with his relationship with John Pope, including a few that gave the former corps commander the opportunity to show his exercise of independent judgment. One of Choate's questions—"On or prior to the 28th, you stationed Ricketts' division at Thoroughfare Gap?"—caused an objection by the Recorder.

"We are traveling," he argued, "entirely out of the line of direct examination, which referred entirely to the 29th of August."

This led to an uncharacteristically long reply by Choate:

> It appears from General Porter's [opening] statement that he received from General McDowell certain general views of the situation and of the plan of the campaign at that time when they met on the morning of the 29th. General McDowell, with that statement evidently before him and with the purpose of contradicting it, has testified to show that he did not do so; that he could not have done so, because he didn't know.
>
> The Board heard just what his evidence was on that subject. I do not accept that evidence. I do not believe it is what the general, when his mind comes to be refreshed by questions, will be willing to let stand.
>
> I believe, on the contrary, that he did know—as he ought to have known, and as he ought not for one day to have retained his sword in that army without knowing—what was going on.
>
> General Porter has been convicted of causing the failure of a plan to "bag" Jackson's force, and it is attributed to his failure to make an attack on the 29th, and the witness' opinion went far to secure that verdict.
>
> Now, one idea that seems to have been demonstrated from the proofs already in is this: that the withdrawal of General Ricketts from Thoroughfare Gap, where he stood between Jackson and any possible reinforcements that might come to him, and the withdrawal of General King from Groveton on the night of the 28th, when he stood between General Jackson and any possible aid that might come to him from the direction of Thoroughfare Gap, had something to do with the failure to "bag" Jackson; that they wholly explain that failure, and that if General King had staid [sic] where he was and where he ought to have staid, and if General

> Ricketts had staid where he was and where he ought to have staid, possibly the consummation which was so much desired might have been accomplished.
>
> As bearing upon this important question, what General McDowell knew of the plans on the morning of the 29th is to the last degree material, and I have a right to show what he knew of the movements on the 28th, because as a military man it must be that he knew the situation on the morning of the 29th.

In his response, the Recorder argued that the Board should be concerned only with events of August 27 and 29, and exclude "transactions" on the 28th involving Generals Ricketts and King. Counsel for the Petitioner, he claimed, was attempting to broaden the scope of the proceedings to include the entire campaign. McDowell concurred, adding expressions of umbrage at Choate's allegation that he did not know what was going on and that he had erred in not keeping Ricketts and King in positions blocking Longstreet's advance to join Jackson.

"I have to say on behalf of General Porter," Choate responded, "and on behalf of the President for whom this Board acts, that you have a right to know the truth as far as bears on General Porter's guilt or innocence of the charges made against him. Here is a witness who knows a vast deal of the truth that is pertinent. And it has come to be pertinent by reason of his statement on the direct examination this morning of what knowledge he had on the morning of the 29th."

"Pardon me," said McDowell, "that is not so."

Choate: "Well, I have the floor now. I say that, as a soldier, and a distinguished soldier, General McDowell, knowing what took place and being a participant in the actions of the 28th, did necessarily have knowledge on the 29th of the situation and of the plans. This is what I propose to show by this witness and by this question [Did McDowell station Ricketts at Thoroughfare Gap?]. The Board has already declared that it is pertinent to the inquiry. What right has this witness to interpose? What property has he in the events of those days that he may raise a question of personal comfort or of personal annoyance—"

"No, sir!"

"—that it should stand between us and the truth? We have a right to our vindication if the truth will vindicate us, and this is a part of it. I cannot believe the Board will for a moment entertain the idea of allowing General McDowell the right to stand between us and the facts of the case, and the right to set up a property in the events of those days as belonging to himself."

"I deny that absolutely," McDowell insisted. "I say here that all that question has been gone into. It is all in testimony, and you can get hold of it if you want it. I do not propose to go into it a second time."

Rephrase the question, Major Gardner suggested. John Bullitt entered the discussion—which grew more heated as it continued, in part because of the Recorder's objections. General Schofield's attempt to get the case moving again ran afoul of Choate, who declared: "I do not think I should be asked to put the examination in the hands of a witness whose hostility has been shown."

"I deny that there is any hostility on the part of the witness," said Gardner.

"Then why did he get angry?"

"I have not been angry today," McDowell maintained. "You have not seen me angry."

Finally, Schofield ruled in Choate's favor. Questioning resumed. So did the Recorder's objections. But McDowell's answers and his cooperative attitude seemed to reflect acceptance of the Board's decision.[21]

Among other information Choate developed was the story of how McDowell got lost during the night of August 28 and was out of communication until early the next morning.[22] With that embarrassment passed, Choate drew from the general a description of his movements during the early hours of the 29th and of his visit later that morning to Porter near Dawkins' Branch.[23]

Curiously, Choate did not make much of the fact that by noontime both generals had received the "joint order" from General Pope and that clearly McDowell was in command. Such was the situation, though the record did not show it.

Choate's questions were aimed toward establishing what orders or instructions McDowell had given Porter before he left to lead King's Division from near Bethlehem Church northward to join the "main" units of Pope's Army of Virginia opposite Jackson's unfinished railroad embankment north of the Warrenton Turnpike. At the trial, of course, McDowell had testified to the effect that Porter had "shamefully" failed to carry out his order to attack and, therefore, had denied Pope's forces the opportunity to "bag" Jackson's divisions.[24]

But *had* McDowell in fact used his position and the joint order's force on August 29's forenoon, before leaving, to tell his subordinate Porter *clearly* what he wanted him to do?

To find out, Choate asked a number of questions leading to this one: "Was it your idea that when you should get around by the Sudley Springs road and have placed King, or King and Ricketts, on the left of Reynolds, that you would find yourself near Porter's troops to the right of where you left him?"

"I did not say I should expect to find them near, because that was a question of topography," McDowell replied. "All of it was that I expected Porter to be over on the left and to operate there from where he was, and I would go and join the main force. Whether General Porter would connect immediately with this force after it had been joined by my corps, I could not say."

"Did you not expect, in pursuance of the suggestion you made to him on leaving, that while you were occupied in taking King's troops, or King's and Ricketts' divisions around to place them on the left of Reynolds, [Porter] would be occupied in extending his troops to the right?"

"It was more his extending to the right than his going in the direction of Gainesville."

"Did you not suppose that he would use the time while you were going around in doing that?"

"No, sir. I expected him to go and attack that force the dust of which I saw above the trees."[25]

A spectator might well have been tempted to shout, *"Which was it, General? Extend or attack?"*

Surely, Joseph Choate recognized the opportunity to abash the witness by asking that unanswerable question. But he restrained himself, continuing instead to bring into testimony whatever had been going on in the mind of Irvin McDowell.

"You did not think that General Porter would stretch out his force to the right to connect with you and Ricketts?"

"The point was, I expected him to go over in that direction. You forget that I was not commanding the whole Army of Virginia."

"I understood you to say a moment ago that the idea was that you should have a jointed and not a disjointed army, and that when you got to the left of Reynolds with King and Ricketts, Porter should be in conjunction with you."

"I thought he would be in a position to do that."

"How long did you think it would take him?"

"I did not make any calculation. How could I tell you, when it involved resistance by the other side?"

"Did you think he could be doing it while you were going around with King and Ricketts on the Sudley Springs road to get on the left of Reynolds?"

"I would have thought so."

"Did you then anticipate that it would be six o'clock before that force would be around to a place to be engaged in a fight?"

"I don't know that it has been established that it would take until six o'clock."

"Did your troops do any fighting before six o'clock?"

"I do not know that they did."[26]

Choate referred to testimony McDowell had given at the trial to the effect that the distance between General Porter's deployment near Dawkins' Branch and the Warrenton Turnpike had not been great enough for a large body of Confederate troops to oppose him. He drew from the witness the admission that the distance had actually been greater than he had recalled in 1862, and also that he had assumed that the enemy force facing Porter was no larger than the number of regiments Union cavalryman John Buford had counted passing through Gainesville at around 9:30 on the morning of August 29.

"Suppose that you had known that instead of being only that amount of rebel troops between Gainesville and Groveton," Choate said to McDowell, "there were two or three times as many. Would that have altered your judgment of what it was expedient for General Porter to do?"

"I think at this late hour of the day it is hardly worth while to go into a military criticism of what might have been done. I will concede it might have been better if I had not taken those troops over to the right, but I don't think so. You are getting into a general criticism or general view of military matters."

"I am not. I am asking you a question to which I want an answer." Choate repeated the question.

"It might have done so," McDowell granted.[27]

Shifting the pressure but not easing it, Choate asked, "After you left General Porter, who was to judge of the considerations that should govern his conduct?"

"After I left General Porter I took my troops away from him and ceased to have any control over him."

This was not responsive. Choate repeated the question.

"When I got away from him you will please drop all questions as far as General Porter was concerned."

"Before you took King away, did you know whether Colonel Marshall had been sent forward with a regiment of skirmishers beyond Dawkins' Branch, who had come in close contact with a large body of rebel skirmishers?"

"I did not know there was a Colonel Marshall."

"Did you know that certain rebel scouts had been captured and brought to General Porter, who reported that the forces in front of him were Longstreet's army?"

"I did not. I was not told so by anybody, if it was so."

"Then if, after you took King away there was not only a large army of rebels, twice as large as you thought, between Gainesville and Groveton, but actual information of its being there was brought in the way I have said to General Porter, would you not consider that he was then bound to act on his own discretion, without regard to the suggestion or direction you had given on leaving him?"

"I do not think it is competent for the counsel to bring me here as an expert, before these gentlemen, to tell them what deductions they are to make upon any condition of things, actual or supposed. What I did at the time was upon certain information and belief. If that was wrong, if the suppositions under which I acted were not well taken, if there was no battle, if this, that, and the other were not so, this Board will find that out. But if the things were as you suppose them, a certain supposed state of affairs, it is for this Board to determine that. You tell me to suppose so-and-so, and that *that* is not for me to say. I am here as a witness to tell you facts. I do not want you to put opinions or make me answer suppositious questions, nor examine me on military operations that I do not know to have existed, and on certain matters that I do not know to have taken place."

Joseph Choate addressed his reply to the Board, going well beyond McDowell's objection:

> The disadvantage that we labor under, if the general is to be permitted to have his own way, is this; that the record stands before you; you are bound to give it your attention and consideration, and a very important feature in it, and one without which I undertake to say General Porter never would have been convicted by the former Board, was the opinions, the very emphatic opinions, given by General Pope and General McDowell, this witness, to the effect that he should have attacked between the time when General McDowell left him and five o'clock, say; and that his failure to do so made the difference between the result as it was and the possible capture of the whole rebel army, which was hoped for.
>
> Now, that is before you, and you have got to give it your consideration. General Pope has conceded the whole matter by sending word to the Board that in spite of the changed condition of facts he has not a word to say. General McDowell has come here to testify, and being here, we claim that nothing could be clearer than that we have a right to ask him or have him say whether, on this changed state of facts which is proved before the Board, the opinion that he then [at the trial] gave would stand the same.

Choate read from the trial record:

> QUESTION: What would probably been the effect upon the fortunes of that battle if between five and six o'clock in the afternoon General Porter, with his whole force, had thrown himself upon the right wing of the enemy, as directed in this order of 4:30 P.M. of the 29th of August, which has been read to you?
>
> ANSWER: This is a mere opinion that you ask?
>
> QUESTION: Yes, sir.
>
> ANSWER: I think it would have been decisive in our favor.

And Choate concluded: "Judge-Advocate General Holt in his review stakes his case upon the integrity of the opinion of General McDowell, and of course it had immense weight, as it was entitled to have, with President Lincoln."[28]

"I think the gentleman's want of military experience has probably led him into a little error in the direction in which he is questioning," Major Gardner's response began, and his condescending tone prevailed until his close: he did not think the facts involved in the question had been developed during the direct examination.

"Is it possible," Choate asked, "that we are to stand on such a quibble as that?"

That quibble caused the investigation to stall while its movers and shakers wrestled once again to another decision by Schofield that Choate's question should be answered. Still McDowell resisted and Choate persisted: "I have asked the witness whether General Porter was then to act on his own discretion," he reiterated, "without regard to the suggestions or direction General McDowell had given him."

"I think," the witness finally allowed, "that my separating and going away from him would not have relieved him from the operations of that order, and he should have carried it out [unless it was countermanded] or that execution of it became impossible."

"Don't you think that when you left Porter he was left to the unrestrained operations of General Pope's joint order?"

"No, sir. It was modified by me. It is for the Board to decide."

If Porter had determined that the force in front of him was twice the size of his own, should he have attacked? McDowell: "He should have found out the force."

Having done that, should he have attacked? "He should have made some tentative operations. But to do nothing whatever certainly would not be complying with the order."

"Now I ask you," said Choate, "if after making efforts necessary for the purpose, he had ascertained that there was a force there double his own, after you left him and took King away, do you say that he should have attacked?"

"He should have made an attack, yes."

"He should have made an attack just as you ordered it?"

"My order was, I confess to you, a very vague one. It was made to a person whose zeal and activity and energy I had every knowledge of. I did not pretend to give him any particular instructions or directions that he should skirmish, or shell, or charge, or anything of the sort; I merely indicated the direction in which his troops should be applied. Further than that I did not think and would not think now if I had the thing to go over again to direct."

"You did not construe it as an order given by you to an inferior general?"

"Certainly I did."

"What did you mean by giving orders that were 'vague' and merely an indication?"

"I meant just what I said. General Porter commanded a corps. I did not tell him to deploy so many troops or to do this, that or the other. All I did was give line to his operations."

"You meant that, with the indication you gave him, he should act on his own discretion?"

"Yes; but he should act."

"Now I come back to the question I put to you before. If, after acting, Porter ascertained the presence of a rebel force in front of him twice as great as his own, twice as great as you on leaving him had supposed it to be, he should have brought on a general fight with them?"

"He should not have brought on so general a fight as to have thrown the whole of his force headlong upon this supposed double force of the enemy."

"What sort of a fight should he have brought on?"[29]

McDowell, not waiting for the uncharacteristically sluggish Recorder to do it, objected. Schofield sustained it. Choate pressed on.

3

Proceedings does not make this clear—it was only a record, not an explication—but in fact, Joseph Choate had slowly, carefully, skillfully moved the case into a zone where he could show, through Irvin McDowell's generally hostile testimony, how far toward compliance General Porter's conduct had been with both John Pope's complex "joint" order and his peremptory 4:30 P.M. order. Choate was building upon additions to the investigation's record made earlier by witnesses called by both sides who had recollected what they had seen and heard and done during those August days in 1862's high summer. Backed by Anson Maltby's familiarity with the text of the 1862–1863 trial record, Choate was in the position every trial lawyer envies, of being able to set traps rather than to beware of them.

Put simply, Fitz John Porter had been found guilty of disobeying both whatever orders he had been given by Irvin McDowell under the terms of the joint order but also of the peremptory one General Pope had sent him late in the afternoon when it appeared that Porter had not performed as McDowell had directed in the middle of the day. So far during Day Twenty-Six of this investigation, Choate had given the Schofield Board ample reason to treat Irvin McDowell's testimony as a country boy does his first taste of beer: with long teeth. Also, counsel for the Petitioner had spread the mantle of doubt over Captain Douglass Pope's assurances that he had delivered the 4:30 P.M. order in time for General Porter to have executed it.

Much had been done, yet much remained.

Continuing to question Irvin McDowell regarding the events of the afternoon of August 29, 1862, Joseph Choate asked: "Would it not make a difference in your opinion, as to the probable result of an attack by General Porter, whether the rebel force in front of him was confined to the troops mentioned in Buford's dispatch, or was an army twice as great?"

"You will understand that that attack there, at least as it was propounded to me for an opinion, was to be an attack in conjunction with the attack made along the Warrenton Turnpike, or with the force that was confronting what was known of Jackson's force. Even if there were a superior force opposed to General Porter, he should have attacked that superior force; he would have withdrawn the enemy from and relieved the front of another part of the line."[30]

General Longstreet had testified, months earlier, that had Porter attacked, there would have been no need to draw troops from Jackson, but Choate merely commented: "You seem very zealous in this examination to argue this case against General Porter. Are you aware of such feeling?"

"I am arguing against you."

"Not against General Porter?"

"No, I don't think of General Porter. It is this: I want to keep myself clear from what you seem disposed to add to what I say."[31]

Choate moved on. "Three dispatches from General Porter to yourself have been read here by the Recorder," he reminded McDowell. "You, I suppose, furnished them?"

"I was called upon by the Board to do so, and I furnished them to him."

"How long have you had them?"

"About sixteen years."

"Have you had them ever since you received them from General Porter that day?"

"I suppose so. I didn't know I had them. I found them when I went through my old papers."

"Will you tell me why they were not produced on the trial of General Porter by court-martial?"

"I was not aware that I had them."

"Did not you think it your duty, in giving testimony against a brother officer, to make an examination of the dispatches you had received from him in order that full justice should be done him?"

"At the time I was before the court I did not know that I had these dispatches. If you want to imply that I suppressed these dispatches, I say to you I could as well suppress them now as then."

"You were asked this question at the trial: 'Can you recollect whether on that day you received any message or order at all from General Porter?' And you replied: 'Yes, sir. I received messages from him that day.' Question: 'Can you tell the court particularly about any of those messages?' You answered, 'I answered one of his messages in writing, but I have no copy of that note. I do not know whether I wrote it or whether it was written by another and signed by me. I think his notes were asking how the battle was going on, or what was the condition of things with us, so far as I can recollect.'[32] Now, as you state that you had a fixed habit of preserving all official papers that you received, did you not regard it as your duty, when the question was put to you so pointedly during the trial of General Porter, to look for those dispatches, that the truth might be known?"

"I have answered your question once before. I had no memory of having received those dispatches at the time of General Porter's trial. I wish I had had those dispatches then. They would have established a point."

"You need not argue."

"You imply that I suppressed those dispatches. There is an implication of that in your question which I wish to resent."

"You will answer first and then resent," said Choate, and he repeated the question. McDowell repeated his claim that he had no memory regarding the messages and also his wish that "I had produced them at the time, because they established a point I should like very much to have established."

"Against General Porter?"

"In my favor. This dispatch—'I failed to get Morell over to you'—I should liked [sic] to have had that point come up on the trial."

Choate tried twice more to get McDowell to answer the question regarding his duty to produce the messages and his habit of retaining papers. The only result was the addition to the witness' litany that he might have given the dispatches to General Pope. That hardly mattered, for Choate was ready to establish a point of his own.

"Did you know," he asked, "upon that trial, that it was claimed by the government that what was called Pope's 4:30 P.M. order, which you happened to read, was received by him about five o'clock?"

"I don't know what time it was received."

"Did you know at that time what the claim was that was made?"

"I don't know."

"Don't you know that you were called as a witness, as a link in the chain, to prove that the order was received by Porter as early as five o'clock?"

"Don't you know that I said I didn't know what time it was given to me, therefore I could not tell."

The Recorder protested: "I think the witness is entitled to the protection of the Board. I have very strenuously put myself on the record against the continuance of a cross-examination that was had thoroughly sixteen years ago."

Gardner was ignored; Choate continued. "Did you not know that the question that was being investigated by the court-martial and deemed important was, what time General Porter received the 4:30 P.M. order?"

"I have been told so."

"You knew it, then?"

"Yes, sir."

"Did you know that one of the dispatches that you did not produce, namely, one dated August 29, 6 P.M., showed upon its face that at that hour General Porter could not possibly have received the 4:30 P.M. order?"

"As I told you before, I did not know I had that dispatch in my possession. I did not know what time that dispatch which you have just read came into my hands."

"I did not ask you whether you had it in your possession or whether it came into your hands, but did you know?"

"I tell you I did not know at the time you speak of. When I was before the court I was not aware that that dispatch was in my possession."

"You had received it on the 29th?"

"Yes, sir."

"It was dated 6 P.M.?"

"You are now asking me as if at the time I could imagine that sixteen years afterwards we would have this investigation. It never came into my mind at the time that paper came to me that anything was coming out against General Porter. That paper was received, I think, after General Pope had sent orders to General Porter to come over. My mind was never fixed on this question. You are now asking me as if I knew we were going to have this investigation."

"I am not."

"I tell you I did not know of that order being in my possession. I tell you and the court that at the time I received it I did not take into consideration the date of 6 P.M. It was not a thing that to me had any consequence."

"Then, as I understand you, you were not aware that this dispatch, if introduced, would have demonstrated that at the time it was written, 6 P.M., he could not possibly have received General Pope's 4:30 P.M. order?"

"I tell you I had no knowledge at the time I was in the court of that paper. That answers your question."

"Did you transmit General Porter's dispatches—the three which you have produced—to General Pope?"

"I think I received them after night-fall; whether I showed them to General Pope I don't recollect."

"They did not have any effect upon your movements that day?"

"No, sir."

"When did you receive the dispatch from him about his purpose to retire to Manassas—was it also after the day was over?

"My impression is, it was."

"Then that had no effect on anybody's movements?"

"I don't know that it had."[33]

Texts of the three missing messages:

Genl McDowell: The firing on my right has so far retired that, as I cannot advance, and have failed to get over to you except by the route taken by King, I shall withdraw to Manassas. If you have anything to communicate please do so. I have sent many messengers to you and Sigel and get nothing.

[signed FJP]

An artillery duel is going on now—been skirmishing for a long time.

Genl McDowell or King: I have been wandering over the woods and failed to get a communication to you. Tell how matters go with you. The enemy is in strong force in front of me, and I wish to know your designs for tonight. If left to me I shall have to retire for food and water, which I cannot get here. How goes the battle? It seems to go to our rear. The enemy are getting to our left.

[Signed FJP]

Genl McDowell: Failed in getting Morell over to you. After wandering about the woods for a time I withdrew him, and while doing so artillery opened on us. My scouts could not get through. Each one found the enemy between us, and I believe some have been captured. Infantry are also in front. I am trying to get a battery but have not succeeded as yet. From the masses of dust on our left, and from reports of scouts, think the enemy are moving largely in that way. Please communicate the way this messenger came. I have no cavalry or messengers now. Please let me know your designs; whether you retire or not. I cannot get water and am out of provisions. Have lost a few men from infantry fighting.

[Signed FJP]

Aug. 29—6 P.M.

4

Day Twenty-Seven, October 11, 1878, must have seemed placid to everyone present at the session on Governor's Island compared with its predecessor, even though Joseph Choate's cross-examination of Irvin McDowell was resuming. After only a few questions the witness had conceded that he and Porter had agreed, during their conversation near Dawkins' Branch late on the morning of August 29, that their forces should comply with General Pope's admonition in his "joint" order not to advance so far that they would be unable to get back behind Bull Run that night.[34] But when Choate drew McDowell into whether he told Porter to put his troops in "here" or "there," that October 1878 morning's calm was shattered.[35]

Disturbing the peace had been the question of how long McDowell had expected it would take Porter to attack the force in front of him. Choate asked: "Will you state why you thought then that it would have taken him an hour?"

"Because then what was in front of us," replied McDowell, "that dust cloud above the trees, indicated that so far as we could see they were not so far off, that if he pushed on with his troops he would in an hour's time have been met with some resistance from the enemy."

"In that hour, or hour and a half, whatever it was, your purpose was to be going around with your troops on the Sudley Springs road to General Reynolds?"

"Yes—but I wish to say right here that this judgment of mine was not only concurred in but anticipated by the Petitioner himself. He says that it was at his suggestion that I should do his very thing."

"Do you recollect whose suggestion it was?"

"He says it was his own."

"Do you recollect whose suggestion it was?"

"I do not, because I intended to do it."

"When you left General Porter, did you expect that within an hour he would be engaged with the enemy?"

"Yes, sir."

"Did you expect that by the end of that time to get your force well around and connect with Reynolds?"

"I hoped to do so."

"Then as you left General Porter, I understand your plan was one of cooperation?"

"We were all cooperating toward the same point."

"But you did not expect Porter should become engaged with the enemy until you should get around to the left of Reynolds?"

"I did not make any such calculation. I have said nothing of the kind."

"You said something very near it."

"You want to make me say what he would be doing at a certain time and where I should be."

"Well, the record will show what you did say. Did you intend that Porter should get into a general engagement with the enemy while you were removed from the scene, back on the Sudley road so as to be out of all possibility of rendering him immediate assistance?"

"I do not want the question put in that way—"

"That is the one I want you to answer."

"—because you are putting words in my mouth, and putting plans in my head that were not suggested there."

"Then you can merely say that it was not the case."[36]

McDowell ignored the distinguished lawyer's freely offered advice. Instead, he reiterated that he assumed that a corps commander as able and experienced as Porter needed no specific direction. "As to saying that I did not want him to do any fighting until I got around to a certain place," he added, "I made no such calculations."

"You did not expect that Porter should become engaged with the enemy," Choate probed again, "until you should get around to the left of Reynolds?"

"Yes, I did."

"Are you aware that within two hours after you left General Porter there was no fighting anywhere along the line except artillery dueling?"

"I am not."

"Do you know of any fighting between twelve and two o'clock that day anywhere?"

McDowell's lengthy, vague reply was unresponsive to Choate's yes-or-no question. Counsel for the Petitioner tried again: "Was it your expectation that General Porter with the force with which you left him should, during the next two hours, *alone* of the Federal troops, engage the rebel army?"

"It was not my expectation that he alone should do it. It was my expectation that he should do it; whether alone or not is another question."

Choate asked it: "Who else did you expect would at the same time become engaged with the enemy?"

"I expected the troops that were then engaged according to the sound of this firing that we heard."

"Do you say that there were then any troops engaged except an exchange of artillery shots?"

"I did not know what the nature of the contest was, because I was too far off, but we heard the contest going on at that time."

"Where was it that you were too far off to know the nature of the contest that was going on, when you talked with General Porter?"

"From that place to Bethlehem Church."

"Then Porter was also too far off to know?"

"Too far off to know whether there was a contest of musketry going on on the right."[37]

"Do you know that General Pope came on the field at one o'clock and gave positive orders that at that time there should be no fighting?"

"I do not."

"Do you know that he so testified at the former trial?"

"I do not. Or if he did, I have forgotten it."

"On page 86 of your former examination is the following. Question: 'Was or not the battle raging at the time?' Answer. 'The battle was raging on our right.' Will you please state what battle was then raging as then known to you, or as since ascertained?"

"The battle that was 'raging,' as the term seems to have been used, referred to the firing which we heard in the direction of Groveton."

"Did you hear any infantry firing at that time?"

"I do not think I did. I cannot recall at this day whether I did or not."

"To your present recollection you heard nothing but artillery shots?"

"But artillery; never mind the 'shots.' "

"Did you expect General Porter to engage the rebel army when all along the rest of the line there was nothing but artillery engaged?"

"I did not at all give any instructions to General Porter as to what should be the nature of the attack that he was going to make. That was not a matter that came into my mind."

Recorder Gardner objected. "The counsel assumes something that has not been shown by the witness."

"If anything has been shown," said Choate, "it is that between twelve and two o'clock there was no infantry fighting anywhere along the line. Now, what I want to know from this witness is whether, under those circumstances, and when he left General Porter, he expected General Porter should do that alone."

Gardner protested: "The gentleman assumes something I do not admit—that there was no fighting or musketry firing between twelve and two and no battle."

Choate: "I appeal to the recollection of the Board."

Schofield: "The question may be based upon the hypothesis of what the evidence is."

McDowell: "I was not expecting General Porter to engage the rebel army, meaning thereby the whole force under General Lee, if he commanded the whole force."

"Well," said Choate, "for 'army' substitute 'troops.' "

"Engage with the enemy."

"Engage with the enemy?"

"Yes, I did."

"You expected him to engage with the enemy alone?"

"I did not say alone."

"The question calls for an answer on that."

The Recorder remarked: "Now the Board can see the point of my objection."

General Schofield suggested that the question be rephrased. Choate complied, and McDowell answered: "He would not be engaging the enemy alone if the rest of the line were engaged with artillery. You seem to think artillery is of no consequence."

"What kind of an engagement did you expect him to enter into while no other but artillery fighting was going on along the rest of the line?"

"As I have tried to make myself understood on several occasions, the nature of the particular kind of contest which he was to engage in was not a matter which I ventured to impose upon him. As a distinguished and zealous officer, with his corps under his command, I did not venture to do anything more than indicate the place where I thought he was to apply that force. Whether he was to skirmish or have a very deep line, or extended one, was a question I did not go into at all, or think of going into."

"Then a skirmish line would have answered your expectations when you left General Porter, if in his discretion that was more advisable?"

"It would depend upon the nature of the skirmish, how it was done, how vigorously carried out, whether the circumstances required it and it only. It depends upon a great many things that you must make a great many suppositions about before I can give an intelligent answer. If you want to know a general principle, I believe it is laid down by military writers that a body of men should be in a condition to offer battle or decline it; whether the main body shall be advanced or retire on the reserve, and many other positions, all of which are conditions upon which battles are determined."

"And determined upon the discretion of the corps commander?"

"Yes, provided he acted energetically."

"Provided he acted according to the best of his discretion as a soldier?"

"Yes, sir."[38]

Joseph Choate's cross-examination continued for a while, and Major Gardner had some follow-up questions. General Schofield probed McDowell regarding discussion of the joint order during the late morning of the 29th, but their colloquy produced nothing of significance—or so it seemed, in the wake of two days of remarkable testimony by the most important witness to appear so far.[39]

CHAPTER SIXTEEN

THE RECORDER SELF-DESTRUCTS

MAJOR Asa Bird Gardner had been calling and examining witnesses for the government since Day Nineteen, October 1, but as Day Twenty-Eight, October 12, opened, surely it must have seemed to most observers that the results were not what the Recorder had intended. Cross-examinations by John Bullitt and especially by Joseph Choate had caused Gardner so much anguish that on several occasions he had suggested that they claim persons he had produced and question them as witnesses for the Petitioner.

Because the Schofield Board's investigation was establishing precedents rather than following them, however, it may have been something of a leap for Gardner to have put so much effort into the judge-advocate's role as (among others) counsel for the government, as prosecutor, especially in view of Joseph Holt's obvious success back in 1862–1863. Also, after Choate's demolition of Irvin McDowell's credibility, the Recorder might have been forgiven for reverting to his basic obligations: advising the Board on questions of law, and performing administrative duties.

Gardner had followed McDowell's devastation by Choate on Day Twenty-Seven by calling nine witnesses whose testimonies moved the case not an inch in any direction. Counsel for the government's first witness on Day Twenty-Eight was former Confederate Lieutenant General Jubal A. Early. He gave a lengthy description of the movement of Longstreet's divisions from west of Thoroughfare Gap to the junction with Jackson on the morning of August 29, in the process reconfirming evidence given earlier suggesting that reports reaching General Porter that a strong force opposed him beyond Dawkins' Branch had been true. Moreover, Early recalled that two of his regiments had been sent to block a Yankee threat on the Confederate right (Porter's corps) while the rest of Longstreet's units were arriving.[1]

Much of Early's testimony was counterproductive from Gardner's point of view because "Old Jube" took full advantage of each question the Recorder put to him to tell the Confederate side of the story, as though he knew that neither Choate nor Bullitt were likely to interrupt his pro-Porter narratives with objections.[2] By contrast, soon after Choate's cross-examination began, the Recorder protested vehemently the admission of a letter Early had written in Porter's favor in 1874. After verifying the authenticity of the document he had been shown, Early told the Board: "This paper contains in substance the statement that I have made now, with the exception that in that report I said to General Porter that if he had attempted to advance at any time after I got to that position on the morning [of August 29], that he would have had great difficulty in getting to General Jackson's right; and if he had attempted it in the afternoon, it would have been impossible, for he would have had to go through Longstreet's whole command."[3]

Whereupon, Major Gardner declared: "Now the Board see [sic] the result of allowing such testimony over my objection."

Schofield responded: "It is the statement of facts in the paper that will be accepted as evidence. The opinion of the witness is immaterial."

"The Board fails to see the point."

"The Board does not fail to see the point. The objection of the Recorder will be noted."[4]

Toward the end of General Early's testimony, Choate asked him: "Your recollection of the hours of these various days, is it precise?"

Early replied: "I cannot undertake to say that. I recollect events very well, but unless the time was of great importance, I cannot recollect it. If I was ordered to do a thing at a particular hour of course I noted it. But when I had not the direction of movements and only had to obey orders of my superiors, I never thought it proper to make notes of the time; it was enough for me to obey the orders."[5]

Asa Gardner's diligence continued to exceed his prudence. Following Jubal Early as witnesses for the government were eight Union veterans of Second Bull Run who confirmed details of testimony given earlier by others or contributed nothing material at all.[6]

However, the Recorder's final witness for Day Twenty-Eight provided some wry relief from tension aggravated by tedium. Former Sergeant John Bond recalled that while he was at Manassas on the afternoon of August 29, he had a conversation with a major general who asked him how the battle was going up near Groveton; Bond had just returned from delivering rations to units in Franz Sigel's corps.

After that conversation ended, Bond said, he asked some soldiers who had witnessed it who that general was. One of them told him it was General Porter.

"Had you ever seen General Porter before?" Joseph Choate asked.

"No, sir."

"Have you ever seen him since?"

"Not that I know of. That gentleman there looks a good deal like him, but he didn't wear any whiskers, only a mustache."

"Then if General Porter wore a full beard at that time, you got hold of the wrong man?"

"He didn't have a full beard, I don't think."[7]

Major Gardner's luck failed to improve on the following Monday, October 14, Day Twenty-Nine. At first a witness who had been a surgeon in a Fifth Corps unit had testified to overhearing General Porter say, "Tell Morell to halt his division, I don't give a damn if we never get there" during the march to Bristoe Station on the morning of August 28. But Joseph Choate's adroit, often ruthless cross-examination exposed the man as a fool.

"You did not know that General Porter had already reported to General Pope that morning," Choate asked, "and had been ordered to remain at Bristoe with the rest of his troops that day?"

"No, sir."

"And you do not know it now?"

"No, I don't know a word about it now. And I don't want to, either."[8]

The Recorder's next witness was Robert T. Lincoln, who testified regarding a conversation he had with his father in the White House during the winter break in his studies at Harvard in early 1863. "He gave me some account of the case as it presented itself to him," Lincoln recalled, "and either read to me or quoted to me, I don't recollect which, a note written by General Porter, as I recollect, to General McDowell. I never saw the note until this morning, so I give my recollection of it. General Porter wrote to General McDowell that he judged by the sounds of the firing that our troops were beaten, and that he should therefore withdraw his corps from the field. That is my recollection of the contents of the note as given to me then. My father was exceedingly urgent or strong in his condemnation."

Gardner asked, "As to the spirit of that note, what did he say?"

"I recollect one distinct remark that he made," Robert Lincoln replied, "but at what period in the conversation I do not now recollect. He said that the case would have justified, in his opinion, the sentence of death."

Joseph Choate found this disturbing, but it was General Schofield who asked Lincoln if he knew whether or not his father had personally examined the record of the court-martial. No, Lincoln said, adding: "My impression was then, and my recollection is now, that he considered himself very familiar with the case, and I now recollect that his language was strong in condemnation of that letter. I recollect that very distinctly."[9]

Choate asked Lincoln: "Did you infer from your father's language that he believed that General Porter did what was intimated in that letter as his intention—that is, to withdraw?"

"I should say yes."

"Did you understand that it was upon the assumption that General Porter was guilty of that which the court had found him guilty, that a sentence of death would have been proper?"

"My understanding was that from his knowledge of the case derived in some way from the matters before him—whether the record or the review of General Holt I do not know—that he had satisfied his own mind that the sentence of the court was too mild; that was his feeling."[10]

"Do you know whether the review of Judge-Advocate General Holt was before him?"

"I do not."

"Did you read the report?"

"No, sir."

"Have you at any time read any of the papers?"

"I never, until this morning, read a single paper in the case. Then I read this letter and nothing else."[11]

After Lincoln, the Recorder examined fifteen more witnesses for the government before Day Twenty-nine ended. In the process, nothing significant was developed.[12] Gardner presented five more veterans of Second Bull Run on Day Thirty, October 15. Although they included former Major Generals Franz Sigel and Joseph Hooker, the only testimony that advanced the government's case came from Basil T. Bowers, formerly a second lieutenant of artillery.[13]

Gardner's first series of questions drew a description of Bowers' services on August 29, which amounted to more repetition of trivia. Then the Recorder asked, "Do you recollect seeing General Porter on the 31st? If so, where?"

"I recollect seeing General Porter," Bowers replied, "on the Sunday after the battle."

"Where?"

"To the right of the village of Centreville, looking to the south or southwest. At his headquarters."

"How did it happen that you were at his headquarters? What military cause had taken you there?"

"By direction of our commander, I had started out to look for a place to water our horses. I got inside of General Porter's lines and came up to an officer, a lieutenant-colonel. He asked me where I was going. I told him—I had no insignia of rank upon me—that we had been having a pretty hard time of it, and no chance to change clothing since the 18th of August. He appeared to disbelieve my statement. He took me to General Porter's headquarters. I was directed to stay there—there was a slight guard around headquarters—and while remaining there, under arrest as I considered myself, I saw General Porter."

"Did you hear any conversation on the part of General Porter?"

"I heard a gentleman that they called General Porter say to the officers, who I took to be of his staff, something like, 'General Pope is coming through this command shortly, and I don't wish any honors or courtesies shown to him, and I want my troops to be informed of my desire.' Thereupon these officers left his headquarters tent, and shortly afterward came back. Some twenty minutes or half an hour after that time, General Pope came through, and no attention was paid to him."

"How long did you remain at these headquarters?"

"Until some time—perhaps half-past four o'clock—when General Milford came up. I called to him, and told him I was under arrest, and by some means he had me released, and I took my horse and started off to rejoin my command."

In cross-examining Bowers, John Bullitt extracted the story of his life as well as his military record, which was unusual in that he had entered and left the service on several occasions, he had acted as a scout for General Milford and others, he had been arrested and released a number of times, and on one occasion he had been held in the Union prisoner of war camp known as Camp Chase.

"In view of the character of the cross-examination of Mr. Bowers," said the Recorder, "I desire to send to Washington and bring from the files there and put upon record the official copies of the letters that were written with reference to his imprisonment at Camp Chase, [letters] by General Milford and others."[14]

So ended Day Thirty. On the following one, the Recorder called William Blair Lord, the "Shorthand writer" who—according to W. L. Ormsby's testimony—had gone to General Porter's quarters in Washington in December 1862, during the trial, to obtain some document.

Having established that Lord was the reporter assigned by Judge-Advocate Holt to record the testimony at Porter's trial, Gardner asked the witness to state what he recalled regarding the interview on December 15, 1862.

"I had been directed by the Judge-Advocate of the Court to proceed to the rooms of General Porter and to look for some telegrams that had been introduced into evidence that day, and that had been mislaid in some way. While there looking over some papers General Porter made the remark, 'I was not loyal to General Pope; there is no denying that.' "

"Do you recall anything else that he said in that connection?"

"I cannot say that I do, and I doubt if I should recall that now but for the peculiarity of the circumstance, and the fact that I made a record of it myself a few days afterwards otherwise, I think it likely I would have forgotten it."

On cross-examination, John Bullitt asked Lord: "How did you happen to take Mr. Ormsby with you to General Porter's when you were going on an errand from the Judge-Advocate?"

"I did not take him with me; he was corresponding [sic] for the *New York Times*, and said that he wanted to see some of these same telegrams that I was looking for and would go along; I did not ask him to go with me."

"You did not feel that it was at all improper for you, being an officer of that court-martial, to take a man who was not an officer, who had nothing to do with the court-martial, with you to General Porter's private quarters?"

The Recorder objected; Schofield declared the question admissible.

"I did not take him along with me," Lord insisted. "I felt that I had no right to prevent his going."

"You said that you made a record of the remark a few days afterward."

"I did, in a letter to my wife."

Lord was unable to recollect where Porter had been in the room, whether he was sitting or standing, or to whom he spoke. "It was a soliloquy," he said, "a remark made to himself."

"Apparently under excitement, or not?"

"Somewhat so. My impression was from the ending of the day's proceedings in court there was still some excitement remaining."

"Was it said apparently with passion and resentment?"

"That I could not say. It was more an impulsive remark."

"Did you and Mr. Ormsby regard that as a remark made by him which imposed upon you under the circumstances any confidence not to speak of it?"

"I hardly gather the drift of your question."

"I want to know whether you understood, from the position in which you were placed at that time by General Porter, that it would be an improper thing for you and Mr. Ormsby to mention it to others or not."

"I recollect making some remark to Mr. Ormsby that under the circumstances—that being in General Porter's private room—I thought it would be well that we said nothing about it."

"Did you say nothing about it?"

"I did not. Except in the letter to my wife I mentioned it to no one until after the court-martial proceedings were terminated."

Bullitt gave the witness so many opportunities to modify that reply that it became apparent that counsel for the Petitioner had information or evidence to the contrary. Lord, however, was adamant—insisting even that all testimony had been taken by the close of the proceedings on January 6, 1863. First, Bullitt presented Lord with a copy of a letter Judge Holt had written the witness on May 21, 1871:

> My remembrance of the trial of Fitz John Porter, of which you were reporter, has been within a few days revived by a notice which has appeared in the public prints to the effect that the officers of the Army of the Potomac, recently assembled in convention at Boston, had forwarded a petition to the President urging him to review the proceedings of that trial, to relieve General Porter from the effects of that sentence pronounced upon his rank and reputation.

> During the trial, some time in the latter part of December, I think, you came to me, I being Judge-Advocate of the court, stating that as a matter of conscience you felt bound to communicate to me a certain confession or reference made by General Porter a few days before in reference to the leading charge, that of disobedience to orders, on which he was then being tried. I listened to it and deemed it most important, and told you I did not believe it would be necessary to introduce it in evidence, as I anticipated that the proof of his guilt would be complete without it. In that anticipation I was not disappointed. No use was therefore made of the confession.
>
> I write now to ask that you may be so good as to—[15]

"Do you recollect, in your reply, whether you referred to the statement or not that this was during the trial, or that you corrected the apparent mistake into which Judge Holt had fallen?"

"I think I made no reference to it in my answer."

"I will ask you to state whether you did not furnish a copy of that letter from Judge Holt to yourself to some one?"

"Not that I am aware of."

"Do you recollect giving a copy of a letter of [W. L.] Ormsby to you, dated May 22, 1870, to any one?"

"I do not."

"In order to refresh your memory, did you furnish this correspondence to General Pope?"

"I do not recollect."

"Give us your best recollection as to the time with reference to the publication of the finding of the court-martial that you mentioned the remark to Judge Holt; was it before or after that?"

"I could not tell you."

"But you are sure that it was not while any evidence was still being taken?"

"I am sure of it."

Bullitt moved on. "You have stated that you made no affidavit of those words at any time until the present."

"That is my recollection."

"Do you know Senator Chandler, of Michigan?"

"I do."

"Do you recollect the speech which Mr. Chandler made on the 21st of February, 1870, in the Senate, in reference to General Porter's case?"

"I recollect the substance of it."

"Do you recollect this language in that speech which I now read to you?

> There is one other point to which I wish to allude, During this very trial, during the very pendency of the trial, Fitz John Porter said in the presence of my informant, who is a man whom most of you know, who is to-day in the employment of Congress, whose word I would take as soon as I would most men's—though I told him I would not use his name, I will give you his sworn testimony, taken down within two minutes after the utterance was made, that Fitz John Porter said in his presence, "I was not true to Pope, there is no use of denying it."[16]

"Was it true or not that within two minutes after you heard General Porter use the expression which you attribute to him, that those words were reduced to writing in your sworn testimony?"

"That is not correct; it is a mistake."

"Well, Mr. Chandler, in making such a statement, in the Senate, was stating what you knew to be incorrect?"

Major Gardner objected. "What has Mr. Chandler to do with this matter? We have had enough of a dragnet here in reference to outside parties. It is an improper question."

General Schofield: "The objection is overruled."

Bullitt continued: "Did you not know at the time that Mr. Chandler made that speech that you were the person referred to by him in that speech?"

"I knew I was the person referred to."

"Did you go to Mr. Chandler to correct that?"

"I did."

"Did he correct it, that you know of?"

"Not that I am aware of."

"Did you not make any affidavit at all?"

"I did not."

"You never asked Mr. Chandler to correct it in the Senate?"

"I told Mr. Chandler that he was mistaken."

"Did you ask him to make a correction in the Senate?"

"I did not."

"Did you ever ask anyone else to make such a correction?"

"I did not. Why should I?"[17]

"It seems to me if I knew a remark was attributed to me which had done such a gross injustice to somebody, I should be very apt to try to correct it."

A few questions later, Bullitt returned to the Holt letter. "Do you recollect having seen Judge Holt in Washington in the month of May, 1871," he asked Lord, "just before this correspondence between him and yourself took place? I see that his letter to you is dated May 27 and the reply is dated May 30."

"I do not recollect; but while he was holding the office of Judge-Advocate General I was in the habit from time to time of calling to see him, having known him for many years."

"Do you recollect whether or not this correspondence was the result of a conversation that you and he had immediately preceding?"

"I do not."[18]

An objection by the Recorder gave John Bullitt the opportunity to cite all of the inconsistencies revealed in his cross-examination of Lord. On redirect, Gardner did what he could to repair the damage.

"You have stated that the feelings which had actuated you, you expressed at the time you wrote that letter to your wife. It was not called for by the counsel for the Petitioner. I will call for it."

"Shall I read?"

"Just that part and no more."

> I have been a little bothered about General Fitz John Porter. I had to go to his room on Monday to get some papers that belonged to the court that he had had to copy. One of the reporters of the *New York Times* was along with me. While in the room, after some conversation, General Porter made the remark, "Well, I wasn't loyal to Pope; there is no denying that." Now, that is really the charge against him before the court-martial—that he did not do his duty as an officer before the enemy, and that he did not act rightly

> towards General Pope, his commanding officer. General Porter said what he did in the privacy of his own room; without thinking of the effect of his words. After thinking it over, I have concluded it better not to say anything about it now, though I would not promise as much for that newspaper correspondent.[19]

Finally, Asa Gardner asked Lord: "Do you know whether or not some one may not have heard the same language at some other time, or an affidavit made on the subject and communicated it to Senator Chandler?"

"I know nothing about that."[20]

2

At the end of Day Thirty-One neither side had any more witnesses to present. On Day Thirty-Two, October 17, 1878, the Recorder added to the record some excerpts from the record of the court of inquiry convened in 1862–1863 to deal with allegations regarding General McDowell.[21]

After a lengthy dispute between John Bullitt and the Recorder regarding the admissibility of certain reports in part or whole, Bullitt requested that General Pope be brought before the Board.

Gardner objected; Choate explained that Pope ought to be given the opportunity to change his prior testimony, given the new evidence produced during the present investigation. "The Board is outside the law," the Recorder argued. "It has no legal power to summon or compel the attendance of witnesses, and consequently no military order, I venture to say, has any validity to compel the attendance of any military man before it, unless he chooses to come. The gentlemen are entirely in error when they bring up, time after time, this question as to the power of this Board. It is merely an advisory Board."

Joseph Choate replied: "If it is true, as the Recorder says, that [General Pope] cannot stand or be expected to stand a cross-examination upon his former testimony, in view of what has since transpired, it is obvious that justice demands that he appear here. I do not think there is any question about the power of the government to get him here. General Pope is a servant of the government, in its employ to-day, and upon the order of the President, or the Secretary of War, he must come. Whether he can be compelled to testify when he gets here is another question. The horse can be brought to the water, but if he should refuse to drink, why, the world may conclude that it is a case of military hydrophobia, and that credence is not to be placed upon the evidence as it stands."

General Schofield said that an invitation would be sent to General Pope. "Will the Board apprise General Pope," the Recorder inquired, "that it is for the purpose of having his cross-examination of sixteen years ago continued?"

"No."[22]

Subsequently, Gardner called and examined six witnesses whose testimonies added nothing significant to the record.[23] Bullitt called Stephen H. Weld, formerly Porter's aide, who stated emphatically that Porter never ordered anyone to refrain from giving General Pope honors at Centreville on September 2, or at any other time. More contradiction of allegations made on Day Thirty by Basil T. Bowers came from Alexander S. Webb, who had served on General Porter's staff, and Frederick Locke.[24]

Day Thirty-Three, October 24, 1878, opened with the announcement by General Terry that General Schofield was ill and he adjourned the session until the following Monday. However, the Recorder presented a reply he had received from General Pope to a telegram Schofield had sent him. Pope said, in effect, subpoena me as a witness either for the government or the Petitioner. To volunteer, he stated, "would be to place myself in a position not only false, but in every respect extraordinary and unknown to the laws or to the practice of the civil and military tribunals of the country." This language had the smell of the Recorder's lamp upon it.[25]

By Monday, October 28, it was apparent that the work of taking testimony was nearing its end. Spring had turned to summer and now the year was well into the fall, yet on Day Thirty-Four the Petitioner had one more witness who could and did add something new to the record. He was O. D. Greene, formerly assistant adjutant of the Sixth Corps—William Franklin's, in the Army of the Potomac—and on September 2, 1862, he had just reached Centreville.

John Bullitt asked Greene, "Did you see General Pope and General Porter together, and if so, how often and where?" Twice, Greene recalled, the second time at Fairfax Court-House.

"Do you know what the occasion of these meetings between them was?" Not exactly; Greene was too far away to overhear conversations, but he assumed that Pope was conferring with Porter, Franklin, and his own corps commanders regarding what to do. "What were the apparent relations between General Pope and General Porter," Bullitt asked, "during those conferences?" The Recorder objected; Bullitt revised his question.

"General Pope was giving General Porter instructions," Greene recalled, "nobody within six or eight or ten steps of them; the tone of voice was an ordinary one, and people at the distance I was could have heard a detached word without hearing the conversation. The tone and manner were all perfectly perceptible, and I never had the slightest doubt that the relations between them were perfectly friendly; in fact, I was impressed by the appearance of both. I thought—I did not doubt—that General Pope was relying very largely upon General Porter."

On cross-examination, the Recorder asked: "What was there particularly about the manner of General Pope that impressed you with the belief that he was relying very largely upon General Porter?"

"General Pope looked to me as if he had been exceedingly tired physically and mentally. I had never seen him before, and looked at him very intently. He produced an impression upon me of a man who had gone through an enormous mental and physical struggle; that he was completely fagged out; that here was a man [Porter] that he could count upon and rely upon."

And Porter's manner? "He was remarkably zealous and earnest; perfectly respectful, and seemed to be desirous of receiving the exact instructions of General Pope. I can hardly command words to give fully my exact impressions, but it struck me as being a remarkable interview, that on the one side was a man who was counting upon the loyal and capable support of the other, a competent lieutenant; and on the other side the appearance of General Porter impressed me as being a man who was capable of giving such support, and that he was desirous of giving it."

On re-direct Joseph Choate asked: "Did anything occur shortly after that day that aided in impressing this interview on your memory?"

"Yes. General Porter's corps brought up the rear of the army as we marched from Fairfax Court-House to Washington."

Late in both the year and the investigation's Day Thirty-Four surely was, Asa Bird Gardner was as zealous as ever in objecting: "What is the object of that?"

Choate: "To see how this remarkably vivid impression was made upon his mind."

"That is for me to do on cross-examination."

"Suppose this officer happened to hear a day or two afterwards that General Pope had made charges against General Porter; it may explain how it is."

Witness Greene volunteered: "Finding that General Porter had the position of honor, the rear guard, it confirmed the impression produced upon my mind at the interview, that General Pope was relying upon him."[26]

3

On Day Thirty-Five, October 29, procuring General Pope as a witness took precedence over all else. Also, from the outset it was clear that General Schofield, Major Gardner, and the distant department commander in Fort Leavenworth, Kansas, were singing from different songs in the hymnal.

Reducing complexity requires some blackboarding:

Date:	*From:*	*To:*	*Action:*
10/17	Schofield	Pope	Invitation
10/18	Schofield	Pope	Please set date
10/21	Pope	Gardner in New York	Covering Reply
10/21	Pope	Schofield in New York	"Subpoena me!"
10/21	Pope	Schofield at USMA	"Subpoena me!"
10/21	Schofield	Pope	Here one is
10/21	Schofield	Pope	Be here on 10/24
10/23	Schofield	Pope	When will you come?
10/24	Pope	Schofield at USMA	(See Below)

"I have received instructions from the Secretary of War," Pope informed Schofield, "to remain here [at Fort Leavenworth] until further advices are sent me."[27]

Clearly, Fitz John Porter's quest for justice seemed to have degenerated into hide-and-seek. But John Schofield was not of a mind to leave this aspect of the case where it had stalled. On Day Thirty-Five, October 29, he revealed not only what he had done subsequently but how he judged the performance of the Recorder in the premises.

Recalling Pope's message concerning his instructions from the Secretary of War, the Board's president said: "The same day, the 24th, a dispatch was received from the Secretary of War; it was replied to that day by me from West Point, briefly, which occasioned the secret session on the following day, at the Sturtevant House; at which time a formal response was made to the dispatch from the Secretary of War, of a confidential character, not proper to be made public at this time, but in that report to the Secretary of War were embraced the views of the Petitioner's counsel as expressed upon their motion here, the replies of the Recorder thereto, and the views of the Board. In consequence of that correspondence this telegram was sent [on October 27] by the Secretary of War to General Pope:

> After full deliberation the President declines to order you either to appear or not to appear as a witness before the Advisory Board in the case of Fitz-John [sic] Porter; and says you will determine for yourself what action to take, and advise General Schofield promptly by telegraph of your decision.[28]

"I have received no response from General Pope," John Schofield continued, "but the Recorder has just now handed me one from General Pope to him on that subject. I am informed that, some days ago, a dispatch was also received from General Pope, and read here in public, embracing the first part of this correspondence which I have just read, but not the second."

John Schofield's absence due to illness on Day Thirty-Three, October 24, was a proximate cause of confusion. He had been at West Point while on Governor's Island in New York Harbor the Recorder had been reporting the receipt of Pope's "subpoena me!" reply to the Board's invitation.

Schofield continued: "Of course we do not know what confidential relation may exist between General Pope and the Recorder, which may have justified him in furnishing the Recorder with copies of the correspondence between the Board, through its president, and General Pope; therefore, no opinions are to be expressed here on that subject."

Here, Asa Bird Gardner may well have relaxed.

"But the reading of that correspondence in public," General Schofield pointed out, "whether before the Board or not, without the knowledge of the Board, was of course inadmissible; and the reading of any communication of an official character, when the Board was not present for the transaction of business, there being only one member present, was of course unauthorized and improper; and so much of that day's record as relates to that subject will of course be stricken out. The Judge-Advocate is now at liberty to read the communication received from General Pope if he pleases to do so."

"Before I do so," Gardner replied, "the remarks which the president has made make it necessary that I should explain."

"Whatever reply the Recorder has to make," Schofield told him, "may be submitted in writing to the Board."

Asa Bird Gardner was an officer, a major, yet he was no soldier—otherwise, he would have realized that having drawn a rebuke from a superior, he was compounding his error by continuing the colloquy. "What I have done as Recorder has been done in the open Board and in a respectful and courteous manner," he insisted. "I have never at any time done differently. I protest against this attempt to characterize my action as improper, and I shall take the liberty of bringing it to the notice of the President of the United States directly."[29]

Fitz John Porter must surely have realized that after all the weeks and months and perhaps millions of words of testimony by more than a hundred witnesses, after all the encouragement he had derived from the skillful efforts of Joseph Choate and John Bullitt to wring the truth from Irvin McDowell and so many others after sixteen years, after all of his hopes that vindication was at long last attainable—after all these things, this dispute between Gardner and Schofield might easily degenerate into the scrapping of everything achieved to date. Worse, there was nothing that he, or his learned counsel, could do to prevent such a catastrophe.

Gardner had insulted Major General Schofield, the President of the Board and superintendent of the United States Military Academy, and the other members of the Board of Officers—distinguished veterans of combat during the War of the Rebellion—appointed by President Hayes. Apart from his apparent refusal to obey a lawful order from a superior, ironically an offense for which Porter had been convicted and cashiered, Gardner's behavior had been that of an arrogant fool unworthy of the trust that Generals Schofield, Terry, and Getty had reposed in him. And, sadly, the Recorder's hubris had brought the proceedings of the Schofield Board to the most critical point in its existence.

Admirable though it often is for a man to defend his actions and statements and beliefs in controversies where differences between right and wrong are obscured, in this instance the Board would have been fully justified in relieving Major Gardner as Recorder and even in bringing charges against him for conduct unbecoming an officer; here, the military equivalent of contempt of court. Moreover, this dispute was merely the most recent—and suddenly, the most important—one in a chain of clashes over his objections that amounted to a pattern of practice on the Recorder's part.

When echoes of Asa Bird Gardner's childish threat to tell Rutherford Hayes on John Schofield had faded, all ears must have strained to hear the president of the Board's response. It was: "It will, of course, come to the attention of the President."

General Schofield continued: "We have no objection to the Recorder making his protest against this mode of treating the subject. That must end whatever explanation he may have to make as between him and the Board."

"I wish to know whether that is the opinion of the president of the Board, that criticism which is attempted to be made upon my performance of my official duty," the Recorder responded, "or whether it is the opinion of the full Board."

"That is not a pertinent question."

"It is."[30]

Again, the intolerable was challenging the unyielding. Hearts must certainly have raced. Was this to be the end?

John Schofield sent everyone but Terry, Getty, and the Recorder outside beyond closed doors. All those excluded were left to wonder if there was anything else that Fitz John Porter could ever possibly do to recover his good name if—as seemed likely—inside the nigh-emptied room, Asa Bird Gardner was destroying the Schofield Board's investigation in order to protect his own reputation.

When Day Thirty-Five's proceedings resumed, the Recorder said, "After a free consultation with the members if the Board, I think that I am better informed of the situation in this matter." He and General Schofield had not been aware of each other's actions. "While I am always ready to stand up for my individual rights when I think they have been infringed upon," he continued, "yet I always feel it my duty to acknowledge, when I have done anything hastily, however good my motives might have been, that probably on more mature reflection I would have done differently."

Conciliation was reflected in General Schofield's response. "Of course the president of the Board takes great pleasure in assuring the Recorder as well as all present that he had no thought of impugning his motives," he said. "The Recorder may now read, if he desires, the dispatch which he received this morning from General Pope."

That message was to the effect that, shielded by the President and the secretary of war from subpoena, his decision not to appear still stood. As transparent as the exchange of assurances by the Recorder and Schofield had been, however, was Pope's final sentence: "If the Board require any information in my power to give on any points brought out by this investigation, I will cheerfully give it either by sworn replies to written interrogatories, or if the Board deem it necessary by appearing in person for this purpose, on due notification to that effect."[31]

General Schofield asked if counsel for the Petitioner had any remarks to make. John Bullitt did. After reiterating the now-familiar point that John Pope should welcome the opportunity to correct his former testimony, he urged the Board to continue its efforts to produce him as a witness. Gardner, predictably, disagreed.

For the second time on Day Thirty-Five, the Board cleared the room. Even the Recorder was excluded from deliberations regarding the problem Pope's response had presented. When the session resumed, General Schofield announced that in the circumstances "General Pope's presence here would be of no service to the Board and would be a waste of time," and that as "the Board has exhausted its powers to compel attendance without conditions, they therefore think it inexpedient to take any further action in the matter."[32]

Bullitt seemed to have anticipated such an outcome. "Then the Board will be so kind," he said, "as to oblige us by allowing time enough to reflect upon the documentary evidence which we may wish to offer in view of the absence of General Pope."

Absolutely inadmissible, Gardner argued—entirely and completely inadmissible.

"This Board will observe," Bullitt countered, "that we are in the position of having a witness who was the most important of all witnesses issuing documentary evidence which shows that he was utterly mistaken in the statements which he had made before the court-martial. If he were here on the witness-stand we should most confidently rely upon making him either admit that he had fallen into those errors or mistakes, or be placed in that other position that his own declarations would show that not one word which he uttered was to be relied upon. Now, we are unable to obtain him; he stands in Leavenworth, a thousand miles beyond the reach, apparently, of any power to bring him here before this Board. He chooses to place himself in the position of a man who once has sought the condemnation of an officer under him, and who, when that officer is seeking again to have justice done him, is not willing to meet that issue. Under these circumstances, we feel that this Board may very properly apply rules with reference to the evidence which do not ordinarily pertain to the rules which, if I am not mistaken, will be found to meet exigencies of just this character."

Counsel for the Petitioner was indeed mistaken, or so the Recorder maintained. "Have not the Board," he asked, "time and time again since they began this case, seen the counsel apply the very strictest rules of evidence at common law in criminal cases to me and insist that those rules should govern? And now they turn around and say that any rules the Board may choose to adopt shall apply and be used? I do not think the Board should give them any more time. Let us come to a conclusion."[33]

General Schofield granted Gardner's suggestion—but only to adjourn for the day.

4

Actually, the Schofield Board's investigation was much nearer to conclusion than the Recorder may have imagined. On Day Thirty-Six, October 30, 1878, John Bullitt submitted and the Board admitted a number of the documents Gardner had hoped to keep out of the record; General Terry read a memorandum explaining the Board's finding. "Then," said the Recorder, "the record will show that my objection to the admission of this class of testimony is overruled?"

Schofield: "Certainly."[34]

Several witnesses were unable to appear at Governor's Island. Their testimony would be taken later in Baltimore.[35] With those exceptions, the submission of evidence came to an end.

"Nothing remains to be done," General Schofield noted, "but to fix the time when the counsel and Recorder may be ready for argument." During an informal discussion he proposed a sequence that called for counsel for the Petitioner to make the concluding argument.

"I think it hardly fair to me if these gentlemen are all to speak," Gardner complained. "I have had to take alone the laboring oar for the government. Let them all speak and then let me have the close. I have to go over all this record alone; I have quadruple the labor that they have; they can divide the case between themselves, and one take one branch and the other another branch. Therefore I ask, not only from the fact that I am alone, but because I am the government representative—made so by your ruling—that I have the closing word."

Schofield's reply: "We are very sorry to do anything which the Recorder thinks will be any obstacle in the way of his doing all that can possibly be done in the line of his duty. But we have considered that matter, and cannot fail to recognize the principle that in this kind of a case the counsel for the Petitioner have the right to the closing argument."

"I dislike to protest as much as I have in this case," replied Gardner, "but I will enter a protest on the record against the ruling that does not give me the closing argument."

General Schofield observed that the Recorder was not likely to be sustained. "As the counsel for the Petitioner admit, the burden of positive proof is upon them, and they must make their case affirmatively; they are not on the defensive. In accordance with that state of facts, and the principle based upon it, we think that they must be entitled to the closing argument. We will now adjourn until Wednesday, December 18, 1878, at 11 o'clock A.M., to meet at West Point."

The Recorder had not exhausted his supply of objections. "I hope," he said, "the Board will continue to meet here at Governor's Island, not only on the ground of economy, but of convenience to me in making the argument which I have to make in reply."

"We came here somewhat at the convenience of the Recorder," Schofield reminded him, "and we now think he ought to come up there. We believe that we can make him comfortable."[36]

5

The Schofield Board's sessions resumed at West Point on January 2, 1879—Day Thirty-Seven, as the proceedings' record counted them, nearly seven months from the outset in the lives of the participants. A train bearing a witness for the government was delayed, so Asa Bird Gardner used the scrap of time to introduce some documents.

Counsel for the Petitioner raised no questions of substance until the Recorder attempted to introduce the letter Secretary of War Edwin Stanton wrote to General-in-Chief Henry W. Halleck on August 28, 1862, demanding answers to questions regarding Major General George McClellan's compliance with orders to expedite the arrival of his Army of the Potomac's forces to augment those—Porter's and Heintzelman's—already operating under John Pope's control within his Army of Virginia.[37]

"This is something new," protested Joseph Choate. "What inquiries the secretary of war may have been setting on foot on the 28th of August, which is prior to the principal events involved in this inquiry, seems very far out of the present case."

Indeed it was. Earlier, the Recorder had fought fang and claw to exclude from the record any inputs suggesting that Major General John Pope's controversial conduct of Second Bull Run was relevant. Focus, he had insisted, had to be fixed sharply upon the instances in which Fitz John Porter had shamelessly betrayed his general commanding.

Now, however, Choate was challenging Asa Gardner to explain his sudden enlargement of the Porter case's frame to include what Halleck had sought to avoid as "the quarrels of Stanton and McClellan" and the struggles of the Radical Republicans in Congress and the President's cabinet to wrest prosecution of the war from Abraham Lincoln.[38]

"I desire to have the whole history of this transaction," the Recorder declared, "placed before this Board, and have a record for the historian of the future. [History] also shows that the Petitioner was criticizing General Pope for his movements when General Pope was acting according to a regular and well-sustained plan."[39]

Choate's response: "We certainly have nothing to do with the 'historian of the future,' unless the Recorder refers to Colonel Smith, who has placed himself in that attitude."[40]

Distinguished counsel for the Petitioner might well have replied otherwise. If the Recorder really wanted to (in effect) incorporate the "entire" history of Second Bull Run, he had to be prepared to deal with controversial issues such as the extent to which, back in 1862 and 1863, General Porter's court-martial had been rigged by Stanton as agent for the Radical Republicans in Congress and the press. Moreover, by involving General McClellan in the proceedings, Gardner was inviting the resurrection of the bitter disputes between the Jacobins and Lincoln that may well have led to McClellan's Army of the Potomac's humiliating confinement at Harrison's Landing following its bungled scourging by General Lee's forces during the Seven Days.

John Schofield was having none of that. "It will be ascertained by referring to the record," he stated, "that early in these proceedings the decision of the Board was announced that we could go into the plans and conduct of the Second Bull Run Campaign only so far as might be necessary to determine the action of the Petitioner in accordance with those plans, or under any orders that he might have received. Any evidence clearly not bearing on the points at issue we must necessarily exclude under our duty to all concerned as well as to the Petitioner."[41]

Even so, the Recorder attempted to introduce various documents of doubtful relevance. Choate and Bullitt protested, with mixed results.[42]

Next, Archelaus Dyer was called and examined by the Recorder. Dyer had been a cavalryman who was serving as an orderly assigned to General Pope's headquarters. On August 29, 1862, he had accompanied Captain Douglass Pope and Charles Duffee on the mission to deliver the 4:30 P.M. order to General Porter.

Gardner's purpose in examining Dyer seemed to be to corroborate the testimonies of Pope and Duffee, particularly to the effect that the ride from General Pope's headquarters to Porter's had taken three-quarters of an hour, or slightly more or less. Dyer also described the route and waypoints, such as Bethlehem Church. During his cross-examination, John Bullitt pressed the witness to provide more detail regarding the structures he recalled having seen on his ride. Bullitt also extracted Dyer's recollection that Captain Pope did not encounter General McDowell on the way back from delivery of the 4:30 P.M. order.

Some excerpts:

Bullitt: "Do you know what Bethlehem Church is?"

Dyer: "I never was right at Bethlehem Church."

"Do you know whether there was any building there or not?"

"I saw a church; I saw it at a distance."

"Had the church a spire?"

"It did."

"How tall a spire?"

"I could not say."[43]

As to Douglass Pope's stop at McDowell's headquarters on the way back, according to Pope a necessity in order to find General Pope's headquarters in the dark, Bullitt asked Dyer three times if he could recollect such an incident. "No, sir," he replied repeatedly. "I have no recollection."[44]

In effect, the Recorder had shot himself in the foot by calling Dyer: able lawyers never expose their witnesses to hostile questions to which they do not already know the answers.

Whereupon Gardner recalled Charles Duffee, apparently for the purpose of allowing him to make minor corrections in his prior testimony. That done, the Recorder asked Duffee an interesting question: "In going down this road along Chinn's Branch, did either of you lead?"

Duffee replied: "Mr. Dyer led most of the time. I could not recollect, and do not to-day recollect Mr. Dyer being with me only from his knowledge of the road. When we first started from [General Pope's headquarters] I tried to lead him off the road to test him whether he was along or not."

Apparently, John Bullitt restrained himself from seizing the opportunity to exploit Charles Duffee's just-revealed vulnerability. "Never mind," the record shows he said, then he asked the Recorder: "Have you closed your case?"

Gardner: "I have."[45]

William L. B. Wheeler was recalled and examined by Anson Maltby. "Did Bethlehem Church have a spire on it," Maltby asked, "on the 29th of August, 1862?"

"It never has had since I have known it."

"How long have you known it?"

"Since I was eight years old. I went to school there in 1834."[46]

Maltby led Wheeler through a number of other questions regarding landmarks that had been mentioned in testimony given by Captain Pope, Duffee, Dyer, and others—along the way, citing facts that brought into serious question the veracity of the Recorder's witnesses.[47] Following Wheeler were William P. Hereford and John T. Leachman, both long-time residents of the Groveton vicinity.

"I do not recollect whether you testified about Bethlehem Church on your former examination," Maltby admitted.

"I did not," Leachman replied.

"Did Bethlehem Church ever have a spire on it?"

"No, sir."

"Or a belfry?"

"No, sir. My brother was minister of that church for a number of years. Long prior to the war it had begun to give way. The walls cracked from ceiling to foundation on both sides. It got in such bad condition that the congregation was afraid to meet in it lest the church should tumble down."

"What was its condition in 1862?"

"Entirely down."[48]

6

Day Thirty-Eight, January 3, 1879, began with the examination of George H. Gordon by Joseph Choate. Since Gordon had served in the Army of Virginia corps commanded by Major General Nathaniel P. Banks, a unit that had been so nearly wrecked by Stonewall Jackson at Cedar Mountain that General Pope had relegated it merely to guarding trains near Warrenton during Second Bull Run, nothing of significance resulted from his testimony.[49]

Another witness called by counsel for the Petitioner had not arrived, so Choate turned to the task of introducing documentary evidence—mostly letters General Pope had written to President Ulysses S. Grant and Secretary of War William M. Belknap in 1867 and 1869 opposing the petitions Fitz John Porter had filed seeking reconsideration of his conviction and cashiering. Predictably, strong objections on the part of the Recorder intensified as Choate moved on to communications from General Pope to persons such as General-in-Chief William T. Sherman bearing dates in 1878 just preceding and during the Schofield Board's investigation.

Both in sum and substance, John Pope was attempting to distance himself from the embarrassing damage done to the government's case against Porter by the admissions of error made by Irvin McDowell. But try vehemently and frequently though he did, the Recorder failed to prevent the Board from accepting all of the documents.[50]

Day Thirty-Eight was also the beginning of closing arguments. Although this was a sign that the end of the long string of sessions was in sight, the three Board members—anticipating inordinate amounts of quotation from the records of two trials and the testimony of almost a hundred and fifty witnesses—could hardly have relished the prospect of hearing all that Anson Maltby, Recorder Asa Bird Gardner, and Joseph Choate had to say. Spectators, as well, surely dreaded being kept in suspense while the orators droned on and on, delaying the Board from reaching a decision.[51] What more need be said, besides whether the three generals found in favor of Fitz John Porter?

CHAPTER SEVENTEEN

The Casting of Pearls Before Swine

On Day Forty-Four, Joseph Choate ended his closing argument. The members of the Schofield Board took up the case. Once again, Fitz John Porter entered a Limbo-like existence. Were the forty-four sessions since last June going to produce nothing but the awesome realization that he had been given his last chance, and had lost?

Like Sisyphus, Porter had raised the rock to the top of the mountain and he was trapped in the uncertain moment, watching to see whether the stone would remain still or plummet again. Might this latest trip upward be his last, might the Board find in his favor? It was far easier to imagine why they would not. Back near the end of Johnson's administration—how many years ago was that?—General Schofield had made it clear that he believed him guilty of at least acting on what be believed his own better judgment under the circumstances he found to exist, instead of in strict obedience to Pope's orders. Might Getty and Terry have felt the same way?

Month after month of intense listening must surely have impressed upon the Petitioner over and over how horribly complex his case was simply in its military aspects—never mind its political and even personal components. Often it had seemed as though base emotions had driven everything during his trial back in 1862 and 1863, with truth and honor and decency shoved aside and ignored. Had those three soldiers Rutherford Hayes had appointed been capable of determining right from wrong in such a maelstrom of conflicting forces? Could any three men discern the truth?

The process, however, was far from over. Uncertainty, Fitz John Porter could handle. How often had he survived it since those ten dark days and nights in the "Ophelia" phase long ago? But *despair*—could he handle *it*?

2

On Day Forty-Five, January 13, 1879, only the members of the Board met, presumably to discuss the steps required to complete the investigation. No minutes were kept. The Board adjourned to meet at the call of the president.[1]

"When the evidence was all in," General Schofield wrote long afterward, "the members of the Board separated for several weeks to let each examine all the evidence and reach his own conclusion, to be presented in form at the next meeting of the Board. I believe I devoted more earnest work to the examination and analysis than I had ever done to any one thing before in my life. I tried in succession every possible combination of the established facts, in the effort to find some one consistent with the theory that Porter had been guilty of disobedience, as charged, or of any other military offense. But I could not find one."[2]

Neither, apparently, could Terry nor Getty. There would be no dissenting reports.

Not until Wednesday, March 12, 1878, did Day Forty-Six take place—in the Army Building in New York City, not at West Point. General Schofield announced that if the Recorder or counsel for the Petitioner had any further business to submit to the Board before the final adjournment of the public sessions, the Board would receive them.

Anson Maltby said that some messages had been discovered since the last session and asked that they be added to the record even though they had no importance as evidence. Predictably, the Recorder objected; he was overruled.

Maltby told the Board that there were "some matters between the Recorder and myself upon which there is not a perfect understanding. I think it is a misunderstanding on his part which on showing him parts of the record will be cleared up."

"We will, then," said Schofield, "close our public sessions, congratulating both counsel and the Recorder upon the very complete manner in which they have presented the case in all its bearings. We will proceed to make up our report and submit it to the President without delay."[3]

Not a word leaked out regarding the findings the members of the Board had reached.

Days Forty-Seven through Fifty were work sessions for the Board, with the main effort on placing the report in final form. On Day Fifty-One, Tuesday, March 18, the Board considered letters from John Bullitt and the Recorder regarding their inability to settle a procedural matter. But it was of no consequence. According to the minutes, "as there was no business requiring the further attendance of the Recorder, he withdrew, and the Board continued its deliberations until 1 P.M., when it adjourned to meet at the call of the President of the Board, after having prepared the following report, viz:[4]

NEW YORK CITY, March 19, 1879.

To the honorable the SECRETARY OF WAR,
Washington, D.C.:

SIR: We, the Board of Officers appointed by order of the President to examine the evidence in the case of Fitz John Porter, late major general of volunteers, and to report, with the reasons for our conclusions, what action (if any), in our opinion, justice requires should be taken by the President on the application for relief in that case, have the honor to make the following report.

The Recorder has been directed to forward to the Adjutant-General of the Army the printed record of our proceeding, including all the evidence examined and the arguments of counsel on either side.

We have made a very thorough examination of all the evidence presented and bearing in any manner upon the merits of the case. The Recorder has, under instructions from the Board, sought with great diligence for evidence in addition to that presented by the Petitioner, especially such as might appear to have a bearing adverse to the claims urged by him.

Due care has been exercised not to inquire into the military operations of the Army of Virginia, or the conduct of officers thereof, any further than has seemed necessary to a full and fair elucidation of the subject submitted to us for investigation. On the other hand, we have not hesitated to examine fully into all the facts, accurate knowledge of which seemed to us to be necessary to the formation of a correct judgment upon the merits of the case, and to the determination of the action which justice requires should be taken by the President on the Petitioner's application for relief.

We have had the benefit of the testimony of a large number of officers of the late Confederate Army, a kind of testimony which was not available at the time of General Porter's trial by court-martial. We have also availed ourselves of the testimony of many officers and soldiers of the Union forces who were present on the battlefield, and of much documentary evidence, to throw additional light upon points not made perfectly clear in the record of evidence taken before the court-martial; and we have had the use of accurate maps of the battlefield of Manassas, constructed from recent actual surveys made, under the direction of the Chief of Engineers, by a distinguished officer of that corps, who was himself a participant in that battle. Without such a map neither the testimony upon which General Porter was convicted nor the additional testimony submitted to this board could have been correctly understood.

The evidence which we have thus been able to examine, in addition to that which was before the court-martial, has placed beyond question many important facts which were before the subjects of dispute, and in respect to some of which radically erroneous opinions were entertained by General Porter's accusers, and doubtless by the court-martial that pronounced him guilty.

The result has been, as we believe, to establish beyond reasonable doubt all the facts essential to the formation of a correct judgment upon the merits of the case of Fitz John Porter. We are thus enabled to report, with entire unanimity, and without doubt in our own minds, with the reasons for our conclusions, what action, in our opinion, justice required should be taken by the President on the Petitioner's application for relief. . . .[5]

In our opinion justice requires at his hands such action as may be necessary to annul and set aside the findings and sentence of the court-martial in the case of Maj. Gen. Fitz John Porter, and to restore him to the positions of which that sentence deprived him—

such restoration to take effect from the date of his dismissal from the service.

Very respectfully, your obedient servants,
J. M. SCHOFIELD,
Major-General U. S. Army.
ALFRED H. TERRY,
Brigadier-General U. S. Army.
GEO. W. GETTY,
Brevet Major-General, U. S. Army,
Colonel Third Artillery.[6]

3

So—for the time being, at least—Fitz John Porter's Sisyphean rock would remain atop the mountain. Newspapers of every political persuasion praised the Board's work and Porter's persistence; even the Radical *New York Tribune* declared that "The [Board's] unanimity leaves little doubt that the President will restore General Porter to the position he held at the time of his unjust dismissal."[7]

Not likely. Awareness of changing trends in Republican politics had died with *Tribune* editor Horace Greeley in 1872, evidently, for in 1879 James A. Garfield, who had been a Stanton-placed member of the court-martial that convicted Porter, was a rising star while his fellow Ohioan President Rutherford Hayes was concluding that one term would be enough for him. Whatever the cause, Hayes' reaction to the Schofield Board's strong recommendations was to refer it to the Congress without comments or recommendations of his own, closing his message of transmittal with this excuse:

> As I am without powers in the absence of legislation to act upon the recommendation of the report further than by submitting the same to Congress, the proceeedings and conclusions of the Board are transmitted for the information of Congress, and such action as in your wisdom shall seem expedient and just.[8]

"All the good opinion I had of this man," mourned Senator Randolph, "has been done away with by his cowardice. He is destitute of moral courage." Perhaps. Rutherford Hayes was, after all, a product of Ohio politics and therefore akin in *weltanschauung* to such ultra-Radical Republicans as Benjamin Franklin Wade, Salmon Chase, Edwin Stanton (born in Steubenville), Irvin McDowell, and James A. Garfield. In 1877, with Wade fading from public life, Porter had predicted that Hayes "would be ruled by Zach Chandler." And Porter had been dismayed that April when Hayes appointed Thomas C. H. Smith to a prominent position in the Treasury Department.[9]

The simple fact was, by casting the Schofield Report—the purely military product Hayes had asked for and received—into the miasmal swamp known as Congress, he had sent Porter's Sisyphean boulder tumbling down the mountainside and made politics the particular form of gravity that he must overcome in raising it again.

Irony compounded! Only Rutherford Hayes had given Fitz John Porter the chance to convince a board of officers of his innocence—yet in the end, what one person except Benjamin Roberts, John Pope's stooge who filed the original charges against Porter, had ever done as much to damage Porter as Hayes?

Fitz John Porter had proved able to cope with two military tribunals whose proceedings were devoted to reaching judgments based on facts pertaining to incidents that occurred during Second Bull Run. While politics had everything to do with the bringing and outcome of Porter's original trial, its sequel was remarkable for the extent the Board restrained the Recorder, Major Asa Bird Gardner, from introducing politics into that undertaking. And absent that corrupting element, at long last military truth emerged—only to be submerged deep in the muck of Congressional politics from which there was no escape short of abandoning the sixteen-year struggle to restore a soldier's good name.

Very briefly, the first effort to obtain legislation giving the President authority to give any sort of relief at all to Fitz John Porter was introduced in the House of Representatives on December 15, 1879, six months after the Schofield Board's Report had been issued.

Six and a half years pass.

On August 7, 1886, Colonel Porter asked to be placed on the retired list following his reappointment to that rank two days earlier and the approval in early July 1886 by President Grover Cleveland of an act of Congress permitting Porter's return to the United States Army after the better part of a quarter-century of enduring the direst disgrace to which a surviving soldier can be condemned.

Why did it take six and a half years from the nationally acclaimed Schofield Board Report's acceptance for Congress to do what Rutherford Hayes failed to recommend?

Politics. Nothing but politics.

Hope glimmered in December of 1880 after the Senate, led by Porter's steadfast friend and neighbor Theodore Randolph, passed a bill in his favor. But Porter's opponents in the House blocked a vote on a similar measure. By February 17, 1881, it was clear that the bill would die before Congress quit in March.[10]

Late in February of that year Porter wrote Joseph Choate that he had no hope of anything being done by Congress. To General Schofield he denounced "the timidity of the democrats [sic]—together with deception of some if not treachery—united with the determined opposition of the Republicans to the case being up—destroys all hope."[11] Understandably, his health broke.[12]

Yet this rise and fall had been instructive as well as agonizingly disappointing.

Representative Garfield, urged on by John Pope, had succeeded in inducing General-in-Chief William T. Sherman to order Major Asa B. Gardner to Washington to help bring potentially damning aspects embedded in the testimony given before the Schofield Board to the attention of House members who were not yet true believers in Porter's guilt. Garfield saw to it that every Republican member of Congress and newspaper reporters nationwide received a copy of Gardner's closing argument before the Schofield Board.[13] At Garfield's direction, the Recorder was also able to shape the thinking of unpersuaded senators and to add to the impact of General Grant's vehement anti-Porter influence on Illinois Senator John A. Logan, during the war and afterward a close associate of Grant.[14]

Logan had proved to be the most vicious, vituperative enemy of Porter and he would remain so. His acquired animosity was expressed conspicuously in a four-day speech on March 2, 3, 4, and 5 of 1880, consisting of absolutely nothing but recitation of anti-Porter matters long since revealed in one forum or newspaper or another.[15] At appropriate points during the harangue General Sherman and Garfield had held up the map that Logan was using to illustrate his points.[16] Yes, Logan wanted Porter to fail in his quest for recovery of his reputation. But the senator was apparently eager to use his defamation of Porter to attract veterans' votes in the coming elections.

Now, recollect: Did anyone involved in the Schofield Board investigation except the Petitioner have anything at all to gain from their participation? No. Did anyone involved in Porter's first trial have anything to gain? Great God, yes—virtually all the members of the Court and the Radical faction of the Republican Party. Finally, here: What did members of Congress opposing justice for Porter have to gain? Votes. Reelection. Power. Advancement. Dominance.

4

James A. Garfield was inaugurated President of the United States on March 4, 1881, shot on July 2, and died on September 19. Crime had removed a formidable enemy, but his successor, Chester A. Arthur, had retained Garfield's cabinet. In it sat Robert Lincoln as secretary of war and Benjamin H. Brewster, attorney general. Lincoln, of course, had testified for the Government during the Schofield Board's investigation. The reasons for his animus against Porter were obvious. Brewster, for his part, held that once a man had been convicted by a properly conducted court-martial and the sentence had been approved and was being carried out, there was no appeal and the President could do no more than use his power to pardon if he chose to do so.

While Porter was recovering from illness during the spring, he decided to change his tactics. Working through friends was getting him nowhere; what if he went to work on his enemies? Accordingly, he wrote Senator Logan to ask for an interview. Logan's reply: "I think it is doubtful if we could agree upon any point in your case—which I examined most carefully and without any malice toward you, but upon the merits of the case."[17]

At about the same time, Porter made similar attempts to reestablish contact with General Grant. By the end of October they had set a date for a meeting in New York City. There would be three of them, each for one hour, during which Porter furnished Grant with many documents and letters. Also, General Terry had written Grant to express his shame at having once formed a fixed opinion, only to learn while sitting on the Schofield Board that he had been in error.[18]

On December 9, Grant wrote Porter that while he had not entirely finished his restudy of the case, it appeared that "from what I have read, I believe I have heretofore done you an injustice, both in thought and speech, and if of the same opinion when through the examination of your case, I will regard it a most solemn obligation on my part to correct the wrong so far as I have any responsibility for it."[19] Later in the month, he sent Porter a copy of the letter he had written to President Arthur. In part, Grant had said: "The reading of the whole of this record has thoroughly convinced me that for these nineteen years I have been doing a gallant and efficient soldier a very great injustice in thought, and sometimes in speech. I feel it incumbent upon me now to do whatever lies within my power to remove from him and from his family the stain upon his good name."[20]

General Grant's sense of duty and honor sparkled in his reversal; this act ranks high among his finest. "What I would ask in General Porter's behalf from you," he added, "is that you give the subject the same study I have given it."[21]

But he had cast this eminently reasonable appeal before a politician who did not respond but—if he had—surely would have agreed with what Logan had told Porter: "There is no possibility of my ever changing my mind on the subject."[22] And if pressed, Arthur could drape himself in Attorney General Brewster's opinion to the effect that a President's powers were limited to pardoning Porter or anyone so situated.

Grant lived up to his pledge. Anticipating Rhode Island Senator Ambrose Burnside's continuing opposition to Porter's struggle—"Poor Burn," as McClellan had referred to him, pressed hard by Jacobin Ben Wade's Committee on the Conduct of the War after his appalling performance at Fredericksburg, had experienced miraculous conversion to Radical Republicanism after Porter's conviction—Grant wrote Senator J. D. Cameron of Pennsylvania: "If every man in the army had been punished who had expressed lack of confidence in his superior officer, many of the best soldiers would have been punished. Even as amiable people as Logan and myself would have been apt to have made very uncomplimentary remarks."[23]

While rejoicing over Grant's gratifying evidence of support, Porter decided that he ought to apply to President Arthur for the pardon in his power to grant. This Porter did in mid-April 1882. On May 4, Arthur granted him remission of the continuing penalty.[24]

His next movement began on May 5 when he sent a new appeal to Congress, which was referred to the Senate Committee on Military Affairs. Only Logan objected to approval of the bill favorable to Porter.[25]

Months passed. Nothing happened. Finally, General Grant brought Porter's case back front and center by writing an article, "An Undeserved Stigma," that was published in the *North American Review* magazine's December issue. In going over the heads of Chester Arthur and the luggards in Congress and taking Porter's case to the American people, Grant admitted:

> I had a double interest in the case because as General of the Army, when I might have been instrumental in having justice done to General Porter, and later as President, I labored under the firm conviction that he was guilty. Having become better informed, I at once gave, as I have continued to give, every earnest effort to impress the minds of my countrymen with the justice of this case, and to secure from our government the restitution due to General Fitz John Porter.[26]

Grant even specified the form he thought it should take:

> General Porter should be declared by Congress to have been convicted on mistaken testimony, and, therefore, to have never been out of the army. This would make him a major general of volunteers until the date of his muster out, after which he should be continued as a colonel of infantry, and brevet brigadier general of the U.S. Army.[27]

But a former President is a toothless tiger, or so Grant would learn as his political enemies gleefully reminded him of his many unequivocal condemnations of Porter during the years before he read the full record of the Schofield Board's investigation. The hard fact was that an appalling number of his former constituents and their current representatives and senators in Congress truly believed that the court-martial had been correct in convicting Fitz John Porter in 1863 and that he had been living on borrowed time ever since.

Such was the lingering appeal of the archaic notion that for every disaster, there must be a scapegoat.

5

Senator Logan, General Grant's former subordinate, observed the ending of 1882 and the advent of a new year by delivering a speech that began on December 29 and ended on January 3, 1883. For all its dismaying duration, in the course of all those days, all that the Appellant's implacable enemy did was to recite all of the chapters and verses of the volumes of anti-Porter vituperation and vilification theretofore uttered. When challenged at one point, Logan replied: "The effort to vindicate Porter at the expense of the reputations of such men as General Garfield, General Hunter, and their associates, and to cloud the reputation of Abraham Lincoln, who approved the findings, can not succeed. This is asking too much, even though it be asked by such a man as Grant."[28]

Logan was correct in pointing out that the decades-long controversy was about reputations. Why else had Fitz John Porter fought so long and so hard to have his restored? And why except to save his own from stain had Grant reversed his opinion?

George F. Hoar of Massachusetts countered Logan. Was every new trial granted by a court an insult to the original court? he asked. Was a difference in judgment a reproach to the person with whom one differed?

"It is not an easy thing for a Republican, a partisan," Hoar continued, "to incur the condemnation of his political friends, but I thank God that after doing the best to discover what my duty requires, He has given me the grace to perform it. I believe that if Abraham Lincoln sat in this seat today and could read the testimony, changing so materially the situation, his vote, with his kind heart, with his sound sense, and the fearless independence in doing right, would be cast as I mean to cast my own."[29]

The Senate voted 33 to 27 in favor of the Porter bill.

When the House took up the measure a month later a number of speakers on either side tried to introduce fresh points. Former Lieutenant General Joseph Wheeler of Alabama said of John Pope, men in high places always found a victim when they needed one, together with a court subservient to their purposes, and witnesses quick and apt with the testimony necessary to convict him. This was as close as anyone had dared to come to charging the Radical Republicans with the crime. The Confederate cavalryman once known as the "War Child" closed with these moving words: "My object is to add my feeble note toward the establishment of truth, the vindication of honor, and the upholding of the sublime principles of justice."[30]

Then, for the second time, Congress quit before a vote could be taken in the House.

Fitz John Porter and his Sisyphean stone were back at the mountain's base. Associates were worried about his health but it was his great friend Theodore Randolph who died, in November 1883. William J. Sewell had succeeded Randolph in the Senate and he reintroduced legislation to reinstate Porter when Congress reconvened in December.[31]

The House passed a pro-Porter bill on February 1, 1884, by a vote of 184 to 78. On March 13 the Senate for the third time gave its approval by 36 to 25. Not until June 17, however, did the bill emerge from a conference committee for President Arthur's signature.[32] Had Fitz John Porter reached the top of the mountain for the final time?

Robert Lincoln and Benjamin Brewster were still in Arthur's cabinet and their minds had not changed. On June 23, Brewster provided the President with an opinion in which he reiterated his objections: "The decision of a court-martial is irrevocable. . . . Congress cannot encroach on the authority of the Executive. . . ." And on July 2, 1884, Chester A. Arthur vetoed the Porter bill. The next day the House voted to override but the Senate deadlocked.[33]

Porter's rock would remain at the bottom of the mountain until after November, or whenever someone else moved into the Executive Mansion. Joseph Choate, John Bullitt, and Anson Maltby responded in October 1884 with their *Review of the Opinion of the Attorney-General* and Porter's supporters in Congress pushed through a resolution requiring Arthur to furnish a copy of Porter's latest appeal—a 300-page document that would be waiting for incoming members in December 1885.[34]

The struggle would continue. Meanwhile, Porter was serving as New York City's Police Commissioner—a position he accepted in the fall of 1884. This enabled him to escape utter financial ruin. His term would extend at least until 1888.[35]

Grover Cleveland, a Democrat, was elected President in November 1885. Democrats controlled the House, but the Senate remained Republican. For the fourth time since the Schofield Board issued its report in 1879, Congress went through committee procedures and engaged in debate. By early 1886 almost everything pro and con had been said that could be said. On February 16, the House bill in Porter's favor was passed by 171 to 113.

In the Senate, John Logan continued his strong opposition despite Grant's example. Logan had been the Republicans' candidate for vice-president. Defeat removed pandering to the soldier vote as the Senator's motive, leaving sheer hatred of Porter. This was confirmed when Logan offered an amendment calling for all Union officers who had lost an arm or leg or vision during Second Bull Run to be placed on the retired list. His explanation: "It is only placing men who did fight and were honorably discharged on a level with a man who did not fight and was dishonorably discharged."[36]

On June 25, 1886, the Porter bill was passed by the Senate 30 to 17.[37] Now everything depended on Grover Cleveland. Once again Porter's boulder was trembling on the brink.

New York City's police commissioner was at his desk on July 1 when someone handed him an envelope containing a simple message: *Cleveland had signed the bill.*[38]

6

The struggle had ended twenty-three years after Fitz John Porter had considered his conviction as justice delayed and started his long fight for restoration of his reputation. To the extent that he was from August 7, 1886, onward a colonel with date of rank May 14, 1861, on the retired list, he had attained his objective. Years earlier he had dropped restitution of back pay from his goals in order to make recovery of his good name more attainable. Now he was being congratulated from coast to coast, south to north. With a pension of $3,375 per annum he would have no financial problem even after he was no longer police commissioner.[39]

Yet in this case justice by two decades delayed had really amounted to justice denied. General Porter had been charged, tried, convicted, and cashiered unjustly by people of the Radical Republican persuasion who themselves went to their graves unpunished for their excessive zeal in any way.

Embedded in this long study, however, are examples of heroism by persons other than the Accused, the Convicted, the Petitioner, and the Victor: the members of his family, his neighbor Theodore Randolph, his counsel Messrs. Reverdy Johnson and Charles Eames, and Joseph Choate, John Bullitt, and Anson Maltby—the Board, John Schofield, Alfred Terry, and George Getty—the Confederate veterans who with the men of Porter's Fifth Corps came to his defense and so many more. None of them benefited materially; all gained in honor, none more, possibly than Ulysses S. Grant.

Too little time remained for Colonel Porter to gain much enjoyment from his good name's restoration. He died on May 22, 1901, at his home in Morristown, New Jersey.[40] All of his adult life had been shaped by his fidelity to duty, honor, and his love of country—especially, to honor.

Whence cometh such others?

Epilogue — 2003

What in the story of Fitz John Porter's struggle should we consider still pertinent, upwards of twelve decades after it ended?

His experience demonstrates that it is possible for a person wronged by government to obtain correction, given willingness to fight and the endurance to keep fighting until justice—however delayed—is done.

In a larger sense, however, the wrong done to General Porter calls attention to what can happen to any citizen when the judiciary and legislative processes become politicized to the extent his court-martial was contaminated and his vindication was delayed. Yet the evil was done not by some amorphous force, but by men afflicted with power madness: *character counts.*

That General Porter was persecuted as a proxy for his unreachable superior, George McClellan, seems to suggest his own failure to heed President George Washington's admonition to avoid endangering entanglements, or Voltaire's to tend your own garden—and for that he can be blamed. As all soldiers should, Porter heeded the call of duty and honor. But he ought to have given more thought to how Charles Stone's loyalty to McClellan had led to utterly undeserved punishment and disgrace, just as in every age prudence lies in recognizing the pitfalls lurking in all relationships.

Finally, Fitz John Porter's ordeal reminds us of the fragility of reputations and of the nigh-impossibility of removing tarnish from them. Would we remember him at all had he not fought so hard and so long to recover his good name, and won?

But we do remember him, and in so doing we recognize anew the values William Faulkner said were essential to any story worth telling: *Courage and honor and hope and pride and compassion and pity and sacrifice and endurance which have been the glory of our past.*

Appendix I

Prominent Radicals

[Chapter One / Note 23]

"The easiest way to identify radicalism," wrote historian Hans L. Trefousse, "is to determine which leaders constituted its core."[1] These included Ohio's Ben Wade, Michigan's Zachariah Chandler, and Massachusetts' Charles Sumner in the Senate; George W. Julian of Indiana, Thaddeus Stevens of Pennsylvania, and Owen Lovejoy of Illinois in the House of Representatives; Horace Greeley, editor of the *New York Tribune*; and Salmon P. Chase of Ohio, Secretary of the Treasury in Lincoln' cabinet.

Both Wade and Chandler were born on New England farms, which may have had something to do with traces of Puritanism that remained evident in their conduct after they had settled in the "Old Northwest"[2] and later emerged as national figures. Massachusetts-born Wade, the tenth of eleven children, had little formal schooling but his mother, the daughter of a minister, instilled in him a love of books that—after having been a teacher, a laborer, a cattle drover, and a medical student—enabled him to become a lawyer. Having to make his own way on the Ohio frontier shaped him in other ways, as Professor Trefousse has pointed out:

> That life was a struggle between right and wrong was clear to him, and those who opposed him were obviously not merely obstinate or mistaken, but often downright evil. There could be no compromise on fundamentals; for to yield on matters of substance would be to yield to sin. Wade always lived up to this belief.[3]

Wade entered the United States Senate in 1851 and quickly became known as an opponent of slavery. When some remark by Wade caused a Southern senator to challenge him to a duel, he specified that it would be fought with squirrel rifles at twenty paces with a white paper the size of a dollar pinned over each combatant's heart. That ended the matter, and added meaning to Wade's nickname: "Bluff Ben."[4]

In the Senate, wrote T. Harry Williams, Wade's striking figure commanded immediate attention:

> He was of average height, but squarely built, heavy, and slightly stooped. His long white hair fell straight back from a good forehead. His complexion was clear and dark, his eyes small, jet-black, staring. His jaw protruded aggressively, and his upper lip doubled at the corners over the lower, giving his face a ferocious appearance.[5]

Bluff Ben's zeal encompassed a number of controversial issues other than abolition. Professor Trefousse noted:

> Having experienced poverty himself, he hated exploitation, whether of Negroes or whites, men or women, and all his life he affirmed his belief that the aim of government was the protection of the weak from the strong. In keeping with this conviction, he championed the Negro, fought for the abolition of imprisonment for debt, interested himself in the protection of individual investors in corporations, advocated free land for settlers, demanded a fair deal for the laboring man, and supported woman suffrage. Moreover, once he made a cause his own, he tended to fight for it to the bitter end.[6]

Zachariah Chandler, born in New Hampshire, settled in Detroit and became wealthy as a merchant and investor in real estate before winning control of the Republican party in Michigan. In the Senate he and Wade were kindred spirits, although Chandler's interests included internal improvements (rivers and harbors), particularly in the Old Northwest. He has been described as a "coarse and determined fighter as well as a shrewd organizer," and also as a "radical's radical."[7]

Differing sharply from Wade and Chandler in many respects other than dedication to the abolition of slavery was Charles Sumner—tall, extremely handsome, educated at Harvard and later a teacher of law at his alma mater, in the Senate a polished and much-admired orator. On one occasion, however, Sumner's remarks had the unintended effect of enraging a colleague from South Carolina who struck him senseless with a cane.

Sumner's constituency, wrote James G. Blaine, "was not merely the State of Massachusetts, but the radical and progressive Republicans of the entire country."[8]

Hans Trefousse praised Pennsylvanian Thaddeus Stevens as "the very incarnation of the radical cause:"

> His New England origin, his indominable will, his singlemindedness of purpose—all added up to qualities of leadership which he was quick to employ to best advantage. Many observers have described his sardonic face with its dark blue and dull-looking eyes, overhanging brows, thin stern lips, and an ill-fitting dark-brown wig. Because of a clubfoot, he walked with a limp, but his physical infirmity was belied by the vigor with which he attacked the problems of congressional management. . . . His devotion to the Negro was boundless, and he soon became the most influential radical in the lower House.[9]

George Washington Julian served one term in Congress from his native Indiana in 1849–1851, only to be defeated for his anti-slavery views, but he returned in 1861. Of Quaker parentage, self-educated, he usually took a more advanced stand on controversial issues than his more circumspect colleagues; T. Harry Williams saw Julian as "fiery, sincere, intellectual, a crusader for unpopular causes."[10]

In contrast to Bluff Ben Wade, who acquired eloquence in the use of profanity as a laborer on the Erie Canal, and Zach Chandler, whose fondness for whiskey extended to the employment of it to buy political support, Owen Lovejoy of Illinois was a Congregationalist minister before and during his service in Congress. When Maine-born Lovejoy's abolitionist brother was murdered, he vowed never to abandon the fight to eradicate slavery—and he kept that vow.[11]

Horace Greeley, editor of the powerful, widely read *New York Tribune*, provided the inestimable service to his fellow Radicals in Congress of disseminating their speeches and his own always-favorable reports of their activities. Otherwise, his ideological brethren in Washington might well have been condemned to preaching to each other, with their earnest outpourings finding ink only in the mind-numbing columns of the in-house *Congressional Globe*.[12]

Salmon P. Chase was the first of the Radicals to serve in Lincoln's cabinet.[13] Governor Chase, who had recently been elected to the Senate from Ohio, had been reluctant to accept. But Jacobin friends applied pressure. Wrote one: "We want a 'Radical' . . . in the Cabinet to stand by and stiffen up the President."[14]

Indeed, *stiffening-up Abraham Lincoln* is perhaps the most succinct way anyone could have put the Radicals' immediate course of action. Lincoln would have been a target for Jacobin opposition in any case; he was not only conservative, but *too* conservative. To them, his tendency to explore every conceivable way of eradicating slavery short of outright abolition indicated weakness. His search for compromise enraged them, committed as they were to an absolute solution. Defenders of the Radicals, however, argue that the end, the abolition of slavery in general but especially in the South, justified the extreme means they employed—including, in particular, abuse of the awesome powers of government.[15]

In retrospect, the Radicals seem to have craved the perpetuation of their political power more than the eradication of slavery. Often, statements by Senator Wade, chairman of the Joint Congressional Committee on the Conduct of the War, defined Radical objectives. For example, on April 16, 1865—the day after Abraham Lincoln died—when members of the committee called on the new president, Wade declared: "Johnson, we have faith in you. By the gods, there will be no trouble now in running the government."[16]

Abraham Lincoln had called for a peace "with malice toward none and charity for all." At the war's outset and afterward, Jefferson Davis had insisted, "All we want is to be let alone."[17] With Lincoln dead and the rebellion quelled, the Radical-dominated postwar Congresses imposed on the late Confederacy a brutal Reconstruction characterized by malice toward all Southerners and charity for none.[18]

Contemporary historians tend toward neutrality regarding the Radicals. They were not as malignant a force as some have charged (the current consensus seems to hold) but they did not achieve as much toward social justice as their modern admirers claim; the truth, we are assured, lies somewhere in between.

APPENDIX II
MEMBERS OF THE PORTER COURT-MARTIAL

David Hunter

[Chapter 4 / Note 48]

Born in Washington, where his father was a chaplain in the navy, Hunter was graduated from West Point in 1822. For six years beginning in 1836 he was in business in Chicago. Reentering the army in 1842 as a paymaster, he served in that capacity during the Mexican War.[1] In February 1861, still a paymaster, Major Hunter volunteered to join Colonel Edwin V. Sumner and Captain John Pope as a military escort of President-Elect Lincoln on his trip from Springfield, Illinois to his inauguration in Washington. At Buffalo, New York, Hunter suffered a dislocated shoulder while protecting Lincoln from his overly enthusiastic admirers and was unable to continue the journey.[2]

Once in the capital, he was placed in charge of 100 "gentlemen volunteers" guarding the White House. From May until First Bull Run, by then a brigadier general, Hunter commanded a division in Irvin McDowell's army. Early in that fight's opening clash he forgot his proper duties. While helping an artillery battery get into firing position he was badly wounded—leaving his brigades confused and leaderless.[3] Lack of training was cited afterward as the main reason for the poor performance of his troops.[4]

Hunter's recovery and availability may well have been the reasons for his selection by Lincoln in October 1861 to relieve—temporarily—Major General Fremont at St. Louis. "The Pathfinder" had given the President a number of good reasons to guillotine him, but Fremont's deserved beheading was certain to ignite a Union-wide firestorm of ultra-Radical outrage.

En route from San Francisco via Nicaragua was Henry Halleck, the man most likely to succeed in cleansing The Pathfinder's Augean stables in

Missouri. However, an interim appointee was needed and Hunter, who was of Fremont's political persuasion, could be counted upon to minimize the political damage to the administration.[5] Indeed, sacking the Radicals' hero infuriated the Jacobin press lords and lawgivers anyway, but Hunter had performed as directed and was promoted to major general and given command of operations in then-quiet Kansas.[6]

An entry in the *Dictionary of American Biography* gives a summary of General Hunter's next service:

> In March, 1862 he assumed command of the Department of the South. Fort Pulaski, Georgia, was at once besieged , and after heavy bombardment surrendered on April 11. The next day Hunter issued an order liberating the slaves which had fallen into Federal hands, and on May 9 followed it by another order liberating all slaves in his department.
>
> Applauded by abolitionists, this move caused uneasiness in the border states and excitement in Congress, and on May 19 the President issued a proclamation annulling the order on the ground that [as in Fremont's case back in November] it exceeded the General's authority.
>
> Hunter had also sanctioned the raising of a negro [sic] regiment (the 1st South Carolina), and in that action was upheld by Congress. The Confederate States proclaimed him a felon, and ordered his execution if captured.
>
> He now attempted to take Charleston, but lost the battle of Secessionville on June 16 and was forced to suspend further operations. When he left his department on leave to seek more active duty, he was employed as president of courts martial. . . .[7]

Actually, General Hunter's Radical activism was nothing new. Moreover, even before he took command of the Department of the South, he and Edwin Stanton had been kindred spirits. "Please let me have my way on the subject of slavery," Hunter wrote the new secretary of war on January 29, 1862, from Fort Leavenworth. "The Admiration will not be responsible. I alone will bear the blame; you can censure me, arrest me, dismiss me, hang me if you will, but permit me to make my mark in such a way as to be remembered by friend and foe." Stanton later enhanced his reputation for duplicity by claiming that he had known nothing about Hunter's proclamation, that he had no intimation that the general was planning any such violations of Lincoln's policies.[8]

❋ ❋ ❋

Silas Casey

[Chapter Four / Note 51]

A soldier's soldier since his graduation from West Point in 1826, as an infantryman Silas Casey served in the five-year Seminole War in Florida. During Winfield Scott's advance from Vera Cruz to Mexico City, Captain Casey was in virtually all of the major battles; at Chapultepec, where he led a force that made the decisive break through the Mexican defenses, he was wounded seriously—but the causeway was then open to Belen Garita, where artilleryman Fitz John Porter won his second brevet for gallantry.[9]

Between wars Casey was stationed in the Department of the Pacific, where he wrote books on infantry tactics that were to be swept up avidly after Fort Sumter. When he was ordered east in 1861 he was promoted to brigadier general and given command of a division in McClellan's Army of the Potomac. In the battle of Fair Oaks, east of Richmond, on May 31, however, his fortunes changed. "The enemy attacked on Saturday & Sunday with great ferocity & determination," McClellan wrote his wife on June 2. "Their first attack alone was successful—Casey's Division broke & ran—losing most of their guns & camp."[10]

On the day before, the army commander had sent Stanton a flash report in which he had included these remarks: "Casey's division, which was in first line, gave way unaccountably and discreditably. This caused a temporary confusion, during which some guns and baggage were lost."[11]

Evidently, the Secretary of War—who controlled the telegraph network, hence releases of information to the press—leaked this indication of McClellan's vulnerability. In any event, even the *New York Herald,* a newspaper favorable to McClellan and therefore far less likely than the Radical *Tribune* to publicize lapses by anyone commanded by the Young Napoleon, applied the lash to General Casey, as this fragment of a correspondent's dispatch published on June 4 confirms:

> The bravery of our troops, with few exceptions, was unsurpassed. One brigade of Casey's division was an exception. During the fight on Saturday they became demoralized, and retreated. . . . Through the conduct of Gen. Casey's division, we were terribly cut up and lost considerable ground.[12]

"Bull" Sumner was a step ahead of Casey in expressing outrage, his complaint being that McClellan had not given him sufficient credit for preventing the destruction of two Army of the Potomac corps. On the day the offending article appeared, the general commanding assured Sumner that "My telegraphic dispatch to Secretary of War in regard to battle of Fair Oaks is uncorrectly printed in the *Herald* in several particulars."[13] As to Casey, Little Mac had Assistant Adjutant-General Colburn write Sumner:

> General McClellan directs me to say that it is difficult for him to decide what was the exact conduct of Casey's division during the fight. The report of the corps commander differs from the information that the general had before received.
>
> The general desires that you give him as soon as possible, in a few words, the position and condition of Casey's troops when you came onto the field, mentioning any that you believe to have acted creditably and those who did not.
>
> It is the general's impression that that division should be broken up, and such portions of it as are not completely demoralized transferred to other divisions. Before doing this, however, he wishes for your statements in the case, to enable him to do justice to all concerned. Your statements will be considered purely confidential, and will only be used to assist the general in deciding what to do, so that no one shall be treated unjustly.[14]

Concurrently, Brigadier General Henry M. Naglee, one of Casey's brigade commanders, sent this succinct message to Assistant Adjutant-General Williams:

> I would respectfully request that the commanding general shall appoint a proper board of officers to investigate and report upon certain charges made against Casey's division, that the truth may be

> known concerning their conduct and that of others engaged in the affair at the Seven Pines on May 31 and June 1 and 2.

This request bore two endorsements. Casey's:

> Approved and respectfully submitted.
>
> I feel confident that the general commanding could not have been possessed of the whole truth with regard to the affair of the 31st ultimo. or he would not have made the remark he did about my division.
>
> I feel that injustice has been done.

And that of Brigadier General Erasmus D. Keyes, commanding Fourth Corps:

> I approve the within application of Brigadier-General Naglee and the above indorsement of Brigadier-General Casey, and respectfully request that a board of officers be named as desired.[15]

On the next day, June 5, General McClellan telegraphed Stanton that his dispatch sent on June 1 had been incorrectly published in the newspapers. He enclosed a "correct" copy in which Sumner received praise. However, it still contained the slur: "With the exception of Casey's division, our men have behaved splendidly."[16]

General Casey defended himself and the conduct of his troops in a letter to McClellan's chief of staff (and father-in-law) Brigadier General Randolph Marcy. Toward the end, he wrote: "From an examination afterward of my field of battle, from the number of graves, and the number of killed and wounded still on the ground, I am of opinion that no division on that day or the next killed and wounded more of the enemy than mine. You can well imagine that I feel much aggrieved by the remarks of the general commanding."[17]

Adjutant-General Williams wrote Keyes on June 5 that "a board of officers of high rank cannot conveniently be summoned now" but that it would be done as soon as "the exigencies of the service" might permit. Meanwhile, the inspector general would investigate.[18]

Justice dallied proved to be justice denied. On June 23, a paragraph in

Special Orders No. 189 seemed to close the case: "Brig. Gen. Silas Casey will proceed without delay to the White House [Virginia] and take charge of that important depot, including the protection of the railway and telegraphic communications between that point and the Army of the Potomac. All the troops at the White House and upon the railway will be so disposed of by General Casey as best to insure the safety of our supplies and their prompt and secure transmission to the army."[19]

To an infantry commander who measured success in terms of how many Confederates his men killed and wounded, being relegated to the rear echelon was deep disgrace, indeed. But within a week General Lee's army was driving Porter's Fifth Corps eastward and McClellan was forced to abandon the White House base. Accordingly, Casey's success would be measured by how many tons of supplies he managed to ship to the new base on the James River, compared with the volume he was obliged to burn lest the rebels capture them.

How General Casey reached McClellan's refuge at Harrison's Landing is not clear. Once there, according to Otto Eisenschiml, "Casey appeared at headquarters with an appointment from Stanton, endorsed by Lincoln. He was to be put in command of the Pennsylvania Reserves, one of Porter's crack divisions. Porter demurred at Stanton's interference, and wrote a letter to the adjutant general in which he did not mince words."[20] The text of the message, dated July 4 (three days after Malvern Hill), addressed to Lorenzo Thomas at the War Department, that was signed by McClellan's adjutant general, S. Williams:

> General Casey has reported here to me from the White House. I have no command which can be given him with a beneficial result to the public service. I have great respect for the military information and character of General Casey, but his health and years do not fit him for the active command of troops serving under the circumstances under which this army has now to make its way. I have therefore been compelled, reluctantly, to order him to repair to Washington.[21]

Hence General Casey's availability to serve on the Porter Court martial—and his attractiveness to Edwin Stanton, for in this seasoned fighter he had an officer who had both understandable cause to resent bitterly his treatment by McClellan and an opportunity to exact revenge on Little Mac's pet, Fitz John Porter.

✵ ✵ ✵

N. P. Buford

[Chapter Four / Note 52]

Brigadier General Napoleon Bonaparte Buford was in the Washington area recuperating from sunstroke suffered while participating in the second battle of Corinth, Mississippi, fought on October 4, 1862. His rank reflected his having been graduated from West Point in 1827, his having studied law at Harvard, his assistant professorship of Natural and Experimental Philosophy at the military academy in the mid-1830s, and his service in the Island No. 10 campaign under John Pope.[22]

Absent any record of Buford's having crossed trails with either George McClellan or Fitz John Porter, or of his political beliefs, Otto Eisenschiml forged a link between the general and the Radicals:

> Porter referred to him in unflattering terms. "[Buford] was friendly to me up to a certain day—when Secretary [of the Treasury] Chase visited him and convinced him that [my] conviction was a necessity to the government. The next morning [Buford's] wife told me not to consider him a friend.
>
> "General John Buford . . . told me the next day that his brother had confessed to him that Secretary Chase had been to see him to convince him of the necessity of my conviction."[23]

Napoleon Buford's gallant half-brother cavalry leader John was usually right. Moreover, if Salmon Chase was second to Edwin Stanton within Lincoln's cabinet in terms of power, he was first in Radical zeal.

✵ ✵ ✵

B. M. Prentiss

[Chapter Four / Note 53]

Brigadier General Benjamin N. Prentiss happened to be in Washington and within Stanton's reach because he had only recently been released from the Confederates' Libby Prison in Richmond. Prentiss had won residence in that notoriously unpleasant place by holding a desperately contested perimeter later dubbed the Hornet's Nest during the battle of Shiloh until, after six hours, he was forced to surrender.[24]

Other than the color of his uniform, Prentiss had nothing much in common with his fellow members of the Porter Court-martial. He was neither a West Pointer nor openly a Radical. Moreover, having been a prisoner of war from early April to October, in November he was in the unenviable position of having to catch up on what had happened during his captivity involving the Accused: Yorktown, the Seven Days, Second Bull Run, Antietam.

Prentiss' enforced ignorance appears to have been the only reason, apart from his availability and rank, that Stanton might have had for making him a member of the Porter detail.

❋ ❋ ❋

J. P. Slough

[Chapter Four / Note 54]

W. W. Morris' successor on the court-martial detail,, John P. Slough (pronounced *slow*), was an unsuccessful Colorado politician whose moment of military glory came in a battle he had been ordered not to fight: Glorieta Pass, in New Mexico. Transferred to the east, he was assigned to Franz Sigel's corps in the Shenandoah Valley and very briefly to John Pope's Army of Virginia, but there are no indications that he held a command or participated in Second Bull Run. From October onward, Slough was military governor of Alexandria—hence, available for court-martial duty.[25]

According to Eisenschiml, Slough was dependent upon Stanton to send his promotion to brigadier to the Senate for confirmation. "Slough's own officers in Colorado had doubted his loyalty," Eisenschiml wrote. "Reports to that effect probably had reached Stanton." His behavior as a member of the court, then, would determine his future status in the army.[26]

Rufus King and James B. Ricketts

[Chapter Four / Note 55]

Both Rufus King and James B. Ricketts were born in New York City, both were graduates of West Point, both were brigadier generals who commanded divisions during Second Bull Run, both were in Washington for reasons of health, and both were listed among the witnesses General McDowell intended to call in his defense during the Court of Inquiry taking place down the hall from the Porter court-martial in the same building, on the corner of Pennsylvania Avenue and Fourteenth Street.

At forty-eight, King was three years older than Ricketts. Unlike career soldier and Mexican War veteran Ricketts, King had spent most of the years since his graduation as a civilian, notably as an educator in Wisconsin.[27]

Both generals emerged from Second Bull Run facing questions regarding their conduct under fire. Ricketts had been criticized for having failed to prevent Longstreet's wing of the Army of Northern Virginia from advancing through Thoroughfare Gap and joining Jackson. He had not been relieved, however, and he remained in command of his division until September 17 when he was seriously wounded during the battle of Antietam.

King's predicament was more complex. Brigadier General John Gibbon's Iron Brigade, which King had organized, and Brigadier General Abner Doubleday's troops, were drawn by Jackson into a fierce fight late in the day on August 28 while moving eastward on the Warrenton Turnpike. At the time, King was suffering from one of his occasional bouts with epilepsy; it was also alleged that he was drunk. Either way, he not only could not function but failed to place anyone else in command of his division. Late that night, absent orders from McDowell or Pope, he moved his brigades to Manassas Junction instead of (as Pope had expected) standing fast where Gibbon and Doubleday had fought. Also, for a time on August

29, King's division had been assigned to Porter's Fifth Corps.[28]

Against such a background, it could be argued that Stanton used these officers' precarious situations to extort judgments unfavorable to Porter.

James A. Garfield

[Chapter Four / Note 57]

James A. Garfield, half ultra-Radical Republican Senator B. F. Wade's age, had many other things in common with him—including the transcending of hard times while growing up and the absorbing of Northeastern Ohio's abhorrence of slavery and inclination to look first to federal government for solutions to economic and social problems.

Garfield was just entering a political career as a state senator when Fort Sumter drew him into uniform. Although he had no military experience, he was elected colonel of his regiment; intense study of books and manuals, together with his skills as a teacher, enabled him to lead a brigade effectively in several minor engagements. He participated in General Halleck's Corinth Campaign, after which bad health ended his career as a line officer and led to his transfer to Washington.[29]

Former Ohio Governor, now Secretary of the Treasury Salmon Chase extended the right hand of Radical fellowship to Garfield. "Mutual friends reported to Porter," wrote Otto Eisenschiml, "that Chase had told Garfield, 'Great things are expected from you on the court.' Chase and Pope were close friends, which made the meaning of the admonition obvious."[30]

Joseph P. Holt

[Chapter Four / Note 60]

Holt, fifty-five, a native of Kentucky, a lawyer since he was twenty-one, had acquired wealth as well as prominence—enough to take only cases that interested him. He had also edited a newspaper, he was renowned as a speaker, and despite his anti-slavery pro-Union views he was a power in Kentucky's Democratic party. In the 1856 election he supported James Buchanan, who rewarded Holt by calling him to Washington where he served first as commissioner of patents, later as postmaster general.[31]

Lincoln's election in 1860 and South Carolina's moves toward secession called into question the retention of men from Southern states in Buchanan's cabinet. By December, for other reasons, the President had replaced Lewis Cass as secretary of state by moving Attorney General Jeremiah S. Black into that post; *replace me with my old friend Edwin Stanton*, Black advised, and Buchanan complied. Not much later, Secretary of War John B. Floyd, a Virginian, was suspected of official actions bordering on treason. He was forced to resign. Buchanan replaced him with Joseph Holt.

Quickly, kindred spirits Black, Stanton, and Holt formed a triumvirate that—supported by General-in-Chief Winfield Scott—instilled enough backbone in Buchanan to avoid catastrophic mistakes in dealing with secession, the creation of the Confederacy, and the Fort Sumter crisis until Abraham Lincoln's inauguration on March 4, 1861.[32]

Holt's successor as secretary of war, Simon Cameron, the Pennsylvania politician Radical Thaddeus Stevens had correctly described as a man who would not steal a hot stove, proved enough of a disaster to cause Lincoln to exile him almost to Siberia: to Russia as ambassador. Salmon Chase, surely recalling with gratitude the day-to-day reports of developments within Buchanan's cabinet Attorney General Edwin Stanton had passed secretly to Radical Republicans, overlooked the Ohio native's Democrat affiliations and vigorously supported him to replace Cameron.[33]

The only alternative to Stanton advanced had been Joseph Holt. His advocates were mostly Californians who understandably had been embittered by then-Attorney General Black's designated federal prosecutor Stanton's ruthlessness in litigation involving claims over land ownership resulting from the Treaty of Guadalupe Hidalgo that had ended the Mexican War.[34] But Lincoln—impressed, no doubt, by Democrat Stanton's strong support from ultra-Radical Republicans such as Ben Wade and Zach Chandler—set aside War Democrat Joseph Holt's previous though brief experience as a secretary of war and selected Stanton.[35]

Corruption had proliferated within Simon Cameron's War Department. Among Stanton's earliest objectives was correction of the abuses regarding contracts with suppliers. This task he assigned to his former associate in Buchanan's cabinet, Joseph Holt.[36]

And so it was that—as in the cases of the real army officers appointed to be members of the Porter court-martial—Colonel Joseph Holt's availability and kindred spiritship with Edwin Stanton placed him in a position to manage the destruction of Major General Fitz John Porter.

Appendix III
Concerning the Trial

Charges and Specifications

[Chapter Five / Note 8]

CHARGE 1st.—Violation of the Ninth Article of War
[Disobedience of Orders].

Specification 1st.—In this, that the said Maj. Gen. Fitz John Porter, of the volunteers of the United States, having received a lawful order, on or about the 27th August, 1862, while at or near Warrenton Junction, in Virginia, from Maj. Gen. John Pope, his superior and commanding officer, in the following figures and letters, to wit:

HEADQUARTERS ARMY OF VIRGINIA,
Bristoe Station, August 27, 1862—6:30 P.M.

Maj. Gen. F. J. PORTER, Warrenton Junction:

GENERAL: The major-general commanding directs that you start at 1 o'clock to-night, and come forward with your whole corps, or such part of it as is with you, so as to be here by daylight to-morrow morning. Hooker has had a very severe action with the enemy, with a loss of about 300 killed and wounded. The enemy has been driven back, but is retiring along the railroad. We must drive him from Manassas, and clear the country between that place and Gainesville, where McDowell is. If Morell has not joined you, send word to him to push forward immediately; also send word to Banks to hurry forward with all speed, to take your place at Warrenton Junction. It is necessary, on all accounts, that you should be here by daylight. I send an officer with this dispatch, who will conduct you to this place. Be sure to send word to Banks, who is on the road from Fayetteville, probably in the direction of Bealeton. Say to Banks, also, that he had best run back the railroad trains to this side of Cedar Run. If he is not with you, write him to that effect.

By command of Major-General Pope:

GEO. D. RUGGLES,
Colonel and Chief of Staff.

P. S.—If Banks is not at Warrenton Junction, leave a regiment of infantry and two pieces of artillery as a guard till he comes up, with instructions to follow you immediately. If Banks is not at the junction, instruct Colonel Clary to run the train back to this side of Cedar Run, and post a regiment and section of artillery with it.

By command of Major-General Pope:

GEO. D. RUGGLES,
Colonel and Chief of Staff

Did then and there **disobey the said order, being at the time in the face of the enemy**. This at or near Warrenton, in the State of Virginia, on or about the 28th of August, 1862.

Specification 2d.—In this, that the said Maj. Gen. Fitz John Porter, being in front of the enemy, at Manassas, Va., on or about the morning of August 29, 1862, did receive from Maj. Gen. John Pope, his superior and commanding officer, a lawful order, in the following letters and figures, to wit:

HEADQUARTERS ARMY OF VIRGINIA,
Centreville, August 29, 1862.

Generals McDOWELL and PORTER:

You will please move forward with your joint commands toward Gainesville. I sent General Porter written orders to that effect an hour and a half ago. Heint-zelman, Sigel, and Reno are moving on the Warrenton turnpike, and must now be not far from Gainesville. I desire that, as soon as communication is established between this force and your own, the whole command shall halt. It may be necessary to fall back behind Bull Run, at Centreville, to-night. I presume it will be so on account of our supplies. I have sent no orders of any description to Ricketts, and none to interfere in any way with the movements of McDowell's troops, except what I sent by his aide-de-camp last night, which were to hold his position on the Warrenton pike until the troops from here should fall on the enemy's flank and rear. I do not even know Ricketts' position, as I have not been able to find out where General McDowell was until a late hour this morning. General McDowell will take immediate steps to communicate with General Ricketts, and instruct him to join the other divisions of his corps as soon as practicable. If any considerable advantages are to be gained by departing from this order, it will not be strictly carried out. One thing must be held in view: that the troops must occupy a position from which they can reach Bull Run to-night or by morning. The indications are that the whole force of the enemy is moving in this direction at a pace that will bring them here by to-morrow night or the next day. My own headquarters will for the present be with Heintzelman's corps, or at this place.

JOHN POPE,
Major-General, Commanding

Which order the said Major-General Porter did then and there **disobey**. This at or near Manassas, in the State of Virginia, on or about the 29th of August, 1862.

Specification 3d.—In this, that the said Maj. Gen. Fitz John Porter, having been in front of the enemy during the battle of Manassas, on Friday, the 29th of August, 1862, did on that day receive from Maj. Gen. John Pope, his superior and commanding officer, a lawful order, in the following letters and figures, to wit:

HEADQUARTERS IN THE FIELD,
August 29, 1862—4:30 P.M.

Major-General PORTER:

Your line of march brings you in on the enemy's right flank. I desire you to push forward into action at once on the enemy's flank, and, if possible, on his rear, keeping your right in communication with General Reynolds. The enemy is massed in the woods in front of us, but can be shelled out as soon as you engage their flank. Keep heavy reserves, and use your batteries, keeping well closed to your right all the time. In case you are obliged to fall back, do so to your right and rear, so as to keep you in close communication with the right wing.

JOHN POPE,
Major-General, Commanding

Which said order the said Major-General Porter did then and there **disobey, and did fail to push forward his forces into action either on the enemy's flank or rear, and in all other respects did fail to obey** said order. This at or hear Manassas, in the State of Virginia, on or about the 29th of August, 1862.

Specification 4th.—In that the said Maj. Gen. Fitz John Porter, being at or near Manassas Junction, on the night of the 29th August, 1862, did receive from Maj. Gen. John Pope, his superior and commanding officer, a lawful order, in figures and words as follows, to wit:

HEADQUARTERS ARMY OF VIRGINIA,
In the Field, near Bull Run, August 29, 1862—8.50 P.M.

Maj. Gen. F. J. PORTER:

GENERAL: Immediately upon receipt of this order, the precise hour of receiving which you will acknowledge, you will march your command to the field of battle of to-day, and report to me in person for orders. You are to understand that you are expected to comply strictly with this order, and to be present on the field within three hours after its reception, or after daybreak to-morrow morning.

JOHN POPE,
Major-General, Commanding

And the said Maj. Gen. Fitz John Porter did then and there **disobey** the said order, and did permit one of the brigades of his command to march to Centreville—out of the way of the field of battle—and there to remain during the entire day of Saturday, the 30th of August. This at or near Manassas Station, in the State of Virginia, on the 29th and 30th days of August, 1862.

Specification 5th.—In this, that the said Maj. Gen. Fitz John Porter, being at or near Manassas Station, in the State of Virginia., on the night of the 29th August, 1862, and having received from his superior commanding officer, Maj. Gen. John Pope, the lawful order set forth in specification fourth to this charge, did then and there **disobey** the same, and did permit one other brigade attached to his command—being the brigade commanded by Brig. Gen. A. S. Piatt—to march to Centreville, and did thereby greatly delay the arrival of the said General Piatt's brigade on the field of battle of Manassas, on Saturday, the 30th August, 1862. This at or near Manassas, in the State of Virginia, on or about the 29th day of August, 1862.

B. S. ROBERTS,
Brigadier-General of Volunteers and
Inspector-General of Pope's Army.

CHARGE 2d.—Violation of the Fifty-second Article of War
[Misbehavior in the Presence of the Enemy].

Specification 1st.—In this, that the said Maj. Gen. Fitz John Porter, during the battle of Manassas, on Friday, the 29th August, 1862, and while within sight of the field and in full hearing of its artillery, did receive from Maj. Gen. John Pope, his superior and commanding officer, a lawful order to attack the enemy, in the following figures and letters, to wit:

HEADQUARTERS IN THE FIELD,
August 29, 1862—4:30 P.M.

Major-General PORTER:

Your line of march brings you in on the enemy's right flank. I desire you to push forward into action at once on the enemy s flank, and, if possible, on his rear, keeping your right in communication with General Reynolds. The enemy is massed in the woods in front of us, but can be shelled out as soon as you engage their flank. Keep heavy reserves, and use your batteries, keeping well closed to your right all the time. In case you are obliged to fall back, do so to your right and rear, so as to keep you in close communication with the right wing.

JOHN POPE,
Major-General, Commanding

Which said order the said Major-General Porter did then and there

shamefully disobey, and did retreat from advancing forces of the enemy without any attempt to engage them, or to aid the troops who were already fighting greatly superior numbers, and were relying on the flank attack he was thus ordered to make to secure a decisive victory, and to capture the enemy's army, a result which must have followed from said flank attack, had it been made by the said General Porter in compliance with the said order, which he so shamefully disobeyed. This at or near Manassas, in the State of Virginia, on or about the 29th of August, 1862.

Specification 2d.—In this, that the said Maj. Gen. Fitz John Porter, being with his army corps, on Friday, the 29th August, 1862, between Manassas Station and the field of a battle then pending between the forces of the United States and those of the rebels, and within sound of the guns and in the presence of the enemy, and knowing that a severe action of great consequence was being fought, and that the aid of his corps was greatly needed, did **fail all day to bring it on to the field, and did shamefully fall back and retreat from the advance of the enemy, without any attempt to give them battle, and without knowing the forces from which he shamefully retreated.** This near Manassas Station, in the State of Virginia, on the 29th of August, 1862.

Specification 3d.—In that the said Maj. Gen. Fitz John Porter, being with his army corps near the field of battle of Manassas, on the 29th August, 1862, while a severe action was being fought by the troops of Major-General Pope's command, and being in the belief that the troops of the said General Pope were sustaining defeat and retiring from the field, did **shamefully fail to go to the aid of the said troops and general, and did shamefully retreat away and fall back with his army to the Manassas Junction, and leave to the disasters of a presumed defeat the said army, and did fail, by any attempt, to attack the enemy, to aid in averting the misfortunes of a disaster that would have endangered the safety of the capital of the country.** This at or near Manassas Station, in the State of Virginia, on the 29th day of August, 1862.

Specification 4th.—In this, that the said Maj. Gen. Fitz John Porter, on the field of battle of Manassas, on Saturday, the 30th August, 1862, having received a lawful order from his superior officer and commanding general,

Maj. Gen. John Pope, to engage the enemy's lines and to carry a position near their center, and to take an annoying battery there posted did **proceed in the execution of that order with unnecessary slowness, and, by delays, give the enemy opportunities to watch and know his movements and to prepare to meet his attack; and did finally so feebly fall upon the enemy's lines as to make little or no impression on the same, and did fall back and draw away his forces unnecessarily, and without making any of the great personal efforts to rally his troops or to keep their lines, or to inspire his troops to meet the sacrifices and to make the resistance demanded by the importance of his position, and the momentous consequences and disasters of a retreat at so critical a juncture of the day.**

B. S. ROBERTS,
Brigadier-General Volunteers and
Inspector-General Pope' s Army.[1]

GENERAL POPE'S REPLY REGARDING ISSUANCE OF ORDERS ON AUGUST 27–29, 1862

[Chapter Five / Note 19]

HOLT: Will you state what orders, if any, you gave to General Porter, on the 29th of August, in reference to the movements of himself and his men, and the grounds upon which those orders were based?

POPE: In answer to that question, it will, perhaps, be necessary for me to state, at least partially, the condition of things on the afternoon of the 28th, and during the night of the 28th and 29th of August, for the reason that the information from the front, upon which the dispositions of the army were made, varied at different periods of the day and night, and it was not until toward daylight in the morning of the 29th that I became thoroughly satisfied of the position of the enemy, and of the necessary movements of troops to be made in consequence.

The orders that I gave to General Porter on the 29th of August, as I remember them, were four. One of them was dated in the night, I think; I do not remember the time. That order, I think, required him, in consequence of information we had received of the concentration of the enemy's forces beyond Centreville, to move upon Centreville. But about daylight in the morning, I sent General Porter an order to take his own army corps, which was then at Manassas Junction, and which by my order had been re-enforced by the brigade of General Piatt—which had come up there in the command of General Sturgis and King's division of McDowell's corps, which had withdrawn to Manassas Junction, or to that vicinity, during the night of the 28th—and move forward in the direction of Gainesville.

An hour and a half later I received a note from General McDowell, whom I had not been able to find until that hour in the morning, requesting that King's division of his corps be not turned over to General Porter, but that he be allowed to conduct it himself. I then sent a joint order to Generals Porter and McDowell, directed to them at Manassas Junction, specifying in detail the movement that I wished to be made by the troops under their command—the withdrawal of King's division, of McDowell's corps, which, during the greater part of the night, I had understood to be on the Warrenton turnpike, and west of the troops under Jackson. [King's] withdrawal to Manassas Junction, I feared, had left open Jackson's retreat in the direction of Thoroughfare Gap, to which point the main portion of the army of Lee was then tending to re-enforce him.

I did not desire to pursue Jackson beyond the town of Gainesville, as we could not have done so on account of the want of supplies—rations for the men and forage for the horses. My order to Generals Porter and McDowell is, therefore, worded that they shall pursue the route to Gainesville until they effect a junction with the forces that are marching upon Gainesville from Centreville—the forces under Heintzelman, Sigel, and Reno; and that when that junction was formed (as I expected it would have been very near to Gainesville), the whole command should halt, it being, as I stated before, not feasible with my command in the condition it was in, on account of supplies, to pursue Jackson's forces farther.

During the whole morning the forces under Sigel and Heintzelman had kept up a skirmishing with the rear of Jackson's forces, they retiring in the direction of Gainesville. They were brought to a stand at the little town of Groveton, about 8 miles, I think, from Centreville, and perhaps 5 or 6 miles from Gainesville. When I rode on to the field of battle, which was about noon (having been delayed at Centreville), I found that the troops had been sharply engaged, and were still confronting each other. General Sigel reported to me that he needed re-enforcements in the front; that his line was weak, and that his troops required to be withdrawn from the action. I told him (as I did General Heintzelman, who was present on the ground) that I only wished them to maintain their positions, as the corps of McDowell and Porter were then on the march from Manassas Junction toward the enemy's right flank, and ought, in a very short time, to be in such position as to fall upon that portion of his line. I desired them, therefore, only to maintain the positions they occupied.

We waited for the arrival of Generals McDowell and Porter. At 4 o'clock, or some little after that time (perhaps at half-past 4 in the afternoon), finding that neither McDowell nor Porter had made their appearance on the field, I sent an order to General Porter, informing him, generally, of the condition of things on the field, and stating to him that I desired him to push forward and attack the enemy in flank, and, if possible, in rear, without any delay. This order was sent to General Porter about half-past 4 in the afternoon.

Finding that General Porter did not comply with this order, and receiving a dispatch which he sent to Generals McDowell and King, stating to them that he was about to fall back, or was falling back, to Manassas Junction, and that he did so because he saw clouds of dust, showing that, in his judgment, the enemy was advancing on the road he was occupying, and stating that it appeared to him, from the fire of the battle that he had been listening to, that our forces were retreating and the enemy advancing, and he had determined to fall back to Manassas Junction, and recommended Generals McDowell and King to send back their trains also—receiving this note, purporting to be from General Porter to Generals McDowell and King, I sent an order to General Porter, directing him, immediately upon the receipt of the order, to march his whole command to the field of battle, and to report to me in person for orders, stating to him that I expected him to comply strictly with that order. I put it in such form (perhaps not entirely courteous) because I had understood General Porter, upon two several occasions, to have disobeyed the orders that I had sent him.

These are all the orders that I issued on that day and night to General Porter. I will state, in addition to what 1 have already said, that the first of these orders to which I have referred, being subsequently superseded, is not perhaps referred to here. I will also state that the corps of Sigel, Heintzelman, and Reno were formed in line of battle across the Warrenton turnpike, facing to the west, and near the little town of Groveton, or at it, almost at the point where the road from Manassas Junction to Sudley Springs—the Sudley Springs road, I think it is called—crosses Warrenton turnpike a little in advance of that road.[2]

General Pope's Reasons For Not Acting Against Porter on September 2, 1862

[Chapter Five / Note 28]

On the night of the 29th of August, when I found that General Porter did not make his appearance upon the field, and when I had received the dispatch which he wrote to Generals McDowell and King, stating that he was about to fall back to Manassas Junction, I determined to arrest him, and had, I think, commenced to dictate the order for that purpose. I was persuaded not to do so by several officers who were about me at the time, and changed the order into the one that appears in one of the specifications of these charges.

I now remember a portion of that conversation at Fairfax Court-House which I could not recall yesterday, and which I will repeat here. I said to General Porter that I had received information from friends of mine in Washington that he had written letters or sent dispatches to General Burnside, dated before he had joined me, which criticized my conduct, my military capacity, and the campaign which I was conducting, very severely, and which exhibited an exceedingly unkind spirit. I asked General Porter whether he did not consider it unfair and unjust to me for him to have written such a letter before he had seen me; before he knew the orders under which I was acting; before he knew the condition of the army and the disposition of it, or of the army of the enemy; before, in fact, he knew anything about the plan of campaign, as far as I was concerned; whether he did not consider it unfair and unjust to me to have written such a letter, as he was on the point of joining me.

He seemed surprised that his letter had become known, and stated to me that it was a private letter of his to General Burnside, which he had never intended to go further than General Burnside; that General Kearny had expressed opinions opposite to his own on the subject of the campaign, and that, therefore, both sides of the question would now be heard. He expressed his regret to me that he had written the letter, under the circumstances, without knowing the facts; said that he was sorry he had done so.

After this remark, I told General Porter I was satisfied that in writing this letter he had not intended to hold back from any proper co-operation with me; that it was merely an expression of his private opinion, in a private letter to another officer. Although I considered that it was unfair and unjust to have written such a letter, yet I was satisfied when he said he thought it was not right. And I said to General Porter that I thought I would not push the matter against him further, or did not propose to take any further action in the matter of his conduct previously in the campaign.

I said so at Fairfax Court-House, because I did not at that time believe that General Porter deliberately and of purpose had withheld his command from the assistance of the army engaged in that battle. I am a frank, open man, and slow to entertain suspicions of so grave a character against an officer. Although I had been warned by several officers a day or two previously that he would fail me, I did not believe so at Fairfax Court-House.

General Porter could not have believed—I am sure I had no idea that he believed—when I stated that I did not design to take any further action against him, that I meant to say that I did not design, in my official reports of the operations of the army, to set forth all the facts as they had transpired on the field. This is all I have yet done. I have not preferred charges against him. I have merely set forth the facts in my official reports, which embrace the operations of everybody else connected with that army, as well as of General Porter.

It was not until the campaign was closed, and I came to Washington City, on the 4th or 5th of September, that I was informed by the President of the United States that he had seen several dispatches or letters from General Porter to General Burnside, dated a day or two previous to these battles, which had occasioned him very grave apprehensions that General Porter would fail to do his duty.

This communication of the President to me opened my eyes to many matters which I had before been loth to believe, and which I cannot bring myself now to believe.

I will now proceed to answer the preface to this question which has been put to me. The question is prefaced by a representation that I have here given certain testimony and made certain statements which I have not made, and which will not be found upon the records of this court. Why the question is put in that shape, when the record is before the court and before the counsel for the Accused, I am not able to say. Certainly no such statements as those have been made by me.

The reason why I did not put these charges against General Porter, and why I told him, at Fairfax Court-House, that I thought I should take no further action, was, that I did not then believe that General Porter's conduct was deliberate and of purpose, but I was inclined to think that his action or want of action there was the result of mistake or blundering rather than of intention. But I never for a moment had an idea of withholding from the knowledge of the Government a full detail of facts, which, as every member of this court must know, every officer commanding an army is required to give in his official report concerning every important transaction that takes place in his command.

I will say to the court that I have answered this question, and only should have answered it, in consequence of the manner in which the protest of the Accused was presented to the court, which protest sought to present me in a false light. I answer it with reluctance, and I respectfully submit to the court that that sort of questions are not relevant to this case, and I would say to them respectfully that I shall decline, unless they insist upon it, to answer any such questions in future."[3]

Appendix IV
Benjamin S. Roberts and Philip Kearny

[Chapter Six / Notes 8 & 16]

Roberts, fifty-two at the time of the trial, was graduated from West Point in 1835. Although he stood 53d in class of 56, he was by no means a "goat." After four years of service with dragoons on the frontier—during the last two of which he may well have crossed trails with Phil Kearny many times—he was chief engineer of a railroad in upstate New York, the state's chief geologist, builder of a railroad in Russia from St. Petersburg to Moscow, and a lawyer in Iowa. During the Mexican War he won the brevet of lieutenant colonel for gallantry while serving with a militia mounted rifles unit. He remained in the army after that war ended. Before becoming Pope's inspector general, he had taken part in the fighting in New Mexico.[1]

Pressed by Reverdy Johnson, Roberts said that the officer he had been reluctant to name had been Philip Kearny, killed in action at Chantilly on September 1.[2] Absent the possibility of corroboration, the weight of this testimony then depended upon the quality of the prior relationship of Kearny and Roberts as it would most likely to have been evaluated by the members of the court—given *their own* recollection of the two generals' reputations.

Long afterward, historians would nigh-instinctively resort to semi-Homeric epithets such as "gallant Phil Kearny" or "old soldier's old soldier Phil Kearny" when narrating the many incidents in which he earned distinction as a warrior. This had not been his family's intention, however; despite young Philip's desire for a military life, his wealthy maternal grandfather had lost too many sons and directed him to Columbia College instead of West Point. Despite the million dollars his grandfather left him, though, in 1837 he obtained a commission as a second lieutenant in the 2d United States Dragoons and not long afterward he was sent to France to study that nation's cavalry tactics. Student though he was, he saw action at

Algiers while serving with the Chasseurs d'Afrique. His next fight was in Mexico, where he was an aide to General-in-Chief Winfield Scott but lost an arm at Churubusco. Europe's wars attracted Kearny again in 1859 when he won the French Legion of Honor for gallantry in Napoleon III's Imperial Guard during the Italian War battle of Solferino.[3]

Fort Sumter brought Phil Kearny to the command of a New Jersey brigade in an Army of the Potomac division led by William Franklin, a favorite of the Young Napoleon. Despite his uniform's empty sleeve, during George McClellan's Peninsula Campaign he rose to division command and major general rank.[4] But at the end of the Seven Days, as nightfall stopped the slaughter of General Lee's Confederates on the northern slopes of Malvern Hill, given the order to withdraw to refuge at Harrison's Landing he had announced to members of his staff:

> I, Philip Kearny, an old soldier, enter my solemn protest against this order to retreat. We ought instead of retreating to follow up the enemy and take Richmond. And in full view of the responsibility for such a declaration, I say to you all, such an order can only be prompted by cowardice or treason.[5]

Kearny's fury was directed toward McClellan, of course, but the officer who had marshaled the Union forces there and directed the victory was also the enforcer of the army commander's detested order: Little Mac's other pet, Fitz John Porter.

Such was the reputation of soldier's soldier Phil Kearny. "He was an old particular friend of mine," Roberts had told the court, "[one] that I had served with a great many years."[6] Indeed, he was well qualified to judge performances of men such as Kearny.

Appendix V
General Griffin's Testimony

[Chapter Eight / Note 21]

Reverdy Johnson began his examination of Brigadier General Charles Griffin by asking: "Do you know of the receipt of any orders by General Porter from General Pope to attack the enemy on that afternoon?"

"I do not," Griffin replied.

"Do you know of any orders having been given by General Porter on that day to attack the enemy?"

"I know that General Morell [Griffin's commanding officer] received one somewhere near sundown; it may have been a little before or a little after."

"What then took place?"

"We had started back toward Manassas Junction when this order came down the road. The order was carried by an orderly, and was stopped by Colonel Warren, who read it. We faced our command about immediately, and started back. I rode ahead to General Morell, who had received the order, and asked him if he was going to attack. He replied, in substance, 'No, it is too late; and this order has been given under a wrong impression.' I do not know but that, in justice, I ought to state what the substance of that order was. 'That the enemy are retiring or retreating; attack and pursue him vigorously.' That is as nearly as I recollect it, the substance of it. General Morell said to me, 'Colonel Marshall, who commands the pickets in front, states that the enemy are receiving re-enforcements.' "

A member of the court objected to the witness stating what others had said; he desired him to confine his testimony to what he knew of his own knowledge. Counsel for the Accused wanted to know if the latter part of the answer already given by the witness would be allowed to remain upon the record. After the usual door-closing, Judge-Advocate Holt announced that the witness could proceed with his testimony.

"Do you know that the enemy were, in point of fact, retiring at the time you saw General Morell?"

"I feel very positive that he was not retiring just at dark."

"Did your command spend the night in the place they then occupied, or very near it?"

"Yes, sir."

"About what hour the next morning, August 30, did you commence to move?"

"Just as day was beginning to break."

"What did you know of the direction you were to take?"

"I understood from the staff officer that brought me the order that the division was to follow General Sykes."

"Please state now, as briefly as possible, what route you took, and how it happened that you reached Centreville."

"We went back the same road we came down from Manassas Junction. I went with my command to Centreville, by direction of my commanding officer, General Morell, who accompanied me."

"Do you know what route General Sykes took?"

"I do not, except from hearsay."

"In proceeding, as you did, toward Centreville, did you, or not, suppose that you were following on after General Sykes?"

"I supposed we would find the entire corps at Centreville when we arrived there."

"Did you see any other forces belonging to General Porter's corps on the way?"

"Near Manassas Junction we passed General Sturgis, with Piatt's brigade. He said that he had been directed to follow Sykes, and wanted to know which way he had gone."

"Did you take the road which you did take in the belief that it was the road that Sykes had taken, or that it would lead you to the same place where Sykes had gone?"

"I took the road, believing that we would all meet at Centreville. I have reasons to believe that General Sykes took another road."

"What reasons had you at the time for thinking that he had taken a different road?"

"As we were going up the road, a man with his hat and coat off stood by the side of the road, and said, 'The regulars—Martindale's and Butterfield's brigades—went this road.' That is the only reason I had to believe that they took a different road."

"Were you present at the headquarters of General Porter on the evening of the 27th of August?"

"No, sir."

Reverdy Johnson turned the witness over to Judge-Advocate Holt, who began his examination by asking:

"Did I understand you correctly as stating that you do not know why the detention until two hours after daylight occurred on the morning of the 28th of August?"

"As I stated before, I know that some of the carriages of the artillery got stuck in a little stream, and, after I had halted, General Morell directed me to remain until I got further orders."

"You have mentioned various obstacles to the passage of artillery over that road as you passed over it on the morning of the 28th of August. Do you know whether General Porter knew of the existence of those obstacles on the evening of the 27th of August?"

"I do not."

"Did General Porter make known to you and to the other generals of his corps the urgent reasons assigned by General Pope for his corps to be at Bristoe Station by daylight on the morning of the 28th?"

"He did not make them known to me. I do not know what he made known to his other officers."

"Did you, on the 29th, make a reconnaissance to the front, or order one to be made, to ascertain the force of the enemy that opened their artillery upon your troops?"

"Not after the artillery opened, that I know of. Before that we had whole regiment to the front as skirmishers. We took three mounted prisoners, I know."

"Do you believe you had in front of you any considerable force of the enemy?"

"Yes, sir; I believe that in the course of the day we had the larger part of Lee's army."

"Immediately in front of you, I mean. I do not mean in the remote distance."

"According to my recollection and impression at the time, they formed a line a little obliquely to our front, extending back to Thoroughfare Gap. They were coming from Thoroughfare Gap toward us."

"You mean by that to say that in the course of the day they passed by you in your front; not that they passed in their march, and put themselves in position for action."

"I mean that heavy bodies of troops were passing from Thoroughfare Gap down toward our front all day long—that is, that they passed. Some of them may have been 3 miles, some of them may have been 5 miles, and some of them may not have been over 2,000 yards from us."

"Do you not know that the field of the battle of the 29th was some 2 miles to your right, and did you not hear firing in that direction all day?"

"On the 29th I heard no firing whatever, except artillery at a long distance. That is, I can call to mind no other firing. In the evening, a little after dark, there were some very heavy volleys of musketry, the enemy evidently driving our troops right before them. That musketry was to our right and front, I should say 2 miles, may be not so far; may be farther. I should have stated, when I stated that I heard no other firing but artillery, that in the morning we had some skirmish firing."

"You spoke of having returned from the movement you made to your right, in consequence of obstacles that you encountered. What was the character of those obstacles, and what efforts did you make to overcome them?"

"I led off my column. We ran up into some little thick pine bushes. We halted there. The next order I got was to move back again. Some one reported that we could not get through. I made no reconnaissance whatever myself."

"What road did General Sturgis, with General Piatt's brigade, take from Manassas, when that general inquired of you what road General Sykes had taken?"

"They followed immediately in the rear of the brigade that I commanded."

"Why did you not follow General Sykes, if such were your orders?"

"That morning, before leaving the position we had occupied all night, I was directed to bring up the rear. I threw out pickets of my brigade, and relieved all the others, and after the other commands were in motion, as reported to me by General Morell, I recalled my pickets, and got in motion as soon as possible. The other commands must have had a half an hour the start of me. We never overtook them at all; never got in sight of them."

"How far was your front from the Gainesville and Centreville pike, do you suppose?"

"I do not know."

"Do you know whether General Sturgis and General Piatt, with their forces, reached the field, and took part in the action of the 30th of August?"

"I do not."

"Did you, or not, on your march that morning, hear the guns of that battle?"

"No, sir; we heard them after we arrived at Centreville."

"Not until then?"

"No, sir; I should think we heard them about 4 o'clock in the afternoon, at Centreville."

"Did you, or not, hear General Porter, at any time during the 27th, 28th, 29th, and 30th of August, criticize General Pope's military conduct, or his capacity for generalship, unfavorably? If so, will you state the substance of such criticism?"

"I never did. I never heard him, to my recollection, mention General Pope's name but once. On the 29th of August, General Porter said, 'My orders are very conflicting. I first receive them from this officer, and then from that officer; officers whom I do not know and have never seen, and they are brought to me by orderlies. I have written General Pope a note, requesting of him hereafter to send all his orders to me in writing.' That is the only time that I recollect of ever hearing General Porter mention General Pope's name. As I have stated before, when he read that communication to his generals, he stated that it was from General Pope. In reference to any transactions between himself and General Pope, I never heard him speak of him but that once, at the time I have mentioned."[1]

Appendix VI
Closing Arguments

[Chapter Sixteen / Note 51]

In several respects, opposing lawyers' closing arguments provide a valuable service. These carefully crafted statements are helpful to judges and juries in that they summarize facts incorporated in testimony and evidence that are often complex and easily overlooked. Also, these orations place advocates' most persuasive points in a logical sequence that leads to the conclusion (or verdict) each seeks to achieve. Closing statements also give litigants the opportunity to add personal, even emotional, appeals to supplement the possibly mind-numbing stream of facts.

A measure of this ritual's importance can be gained by recalling Judge-Advocate General Joseph Holt's failure to make a closing argument at the end of General Porter's court-martial in January 1863. This put the Accused and his counsel at a distinct, possibly critical disadvantage. Absent the prescribed opportunity to hear the summation of the government's case, Reverdy Johnson was unable to counter Holt's assertions with Porter's responses. Worse, in the "review" Holt wrote for President Lincoln, Holt inserted what he had declined to say in court and left out the closing statement Johnson *had* presented on Porter's behalf.

Against that background, mindful of the prominent role of earlier concluding arguments as texts for pamphlets and widespread publication in newspapers, Joseph Choate, John Bullitt, and Anson Maltby made certain that Recorder Asa Bird Gardner could not engage in similar chicanery at the close of the Schofield Board's investigation. Over Major Gardner's vigorous protests, General Schofield set the sequence of presentations. Maltby and Bullitt would be followed by the Recorder, and Choate would have the last word.

2

Anson Maltby began his argument for the Petitioner late on Day Thirty-Eight, January 3, 1879. His opening remarks, coming as they did immediately after the long series of acrimonious squabbles between the Recorder and Maltby's associates, were candid yet conciliatory: "It is a matter of congratulation to us all that after this inquest has dragged its slow length along since the 20th of last June, after one hundred and forty-two witnesses have been examined, of whom we have introduced not more than forty-three, and after thirty-seven sessions, we are now near the period when our labors shall be at an end."[1]

Months earlier, Maltby had used the Army of the Potomac's involuntary presence at Harrison's Landing as the starting point for the Petitioner's Opening Statement. Now, however, he took the arrival of General Porter's Fifth Corps at Warrenton Junction on August 27, 1862, as the beginning incident. Drawing from several layers of information available to him—reports of the battle, the 1862–1863 court-martial's record, claims and counter-claims following Porter's conviction, and now the record of the Schofield Board's investigation—Maltby could and did weave a fascinating narrative. The pattern was simple: we thought thus-and-so was true because that was what the court-martial found, but now we know that such was not the case; instead, this-and-that happened.

Maltby's fund of reversals in matters of fact was so large that his presentation of them extended into Day Thirty-Nine and indeed required all of it. But counsel for the Petitioner added style and conviction and enthusiasm and occasional ridicule and sarcasm to his exposure of wrongdoing. A sample of Maltby's argument:

> General Porter, in thinking that Longstreet had arrived with a large force to oppose him, was perfectly right and the court-martial, in finding that he did not, was perfectly wrong. At the trial the following was shown:
>
> - Lieutenant Stevenson judged 12,000 or 15,000 of the enemy were present. Judge-Advocate General Holt criticized this young man as being inexperienced in war and therefore unable to tell anything about it. But in the light of all these

facts [Confederates' testimony before the Schofield Board] Stevenson was right. His testimony was disregarded.

- General Buford's evidence that 14,000 men had passed through Gainesville at a quarter before nine was disregarded.
- Major Hyland's estimate that 10,000 men, "probably a larger force than we had," was opposing General Porter, was disregarded.
- Colonel E. G. Marshall's estimate that the enemy's force was twice as large as all of General Porter's corps was disregarded. All these opinions, founded upon personal observation, were disregarded by that court and by that Judge-Advocate [Holt], to adopt the opinion of that distantly placed though "intelligent and reliable witness" General Roberts, who never saw General Porter's front at all, and who thought there might have been a slight force of cavalry opposing him.[2]

Maltby went on to rip apart General Pope's understanding of the situation as it was reflected in seven passages he quoted from the court-martial record.[3] He also tore into another of Fitz John Porter's detractors: Irvin McDowell.[4] And while quoting from the testimony of General Roberts, Maltby interrupted himself to observe: "Now, this is delicious—" and then continued to read.[5]

Anson Maltby concluded his second day of argument in relatively few words. "The government," he reminded the Board, "has summoned a hundred witnesses without proving General Porter's guilt. Every person that could be reached has been summoned, and—save his chief enemy—they have all given their testimony. I confidently hope that you will be able to give the verdict back to the President and to the people of the United States that Major General Fitz John Porter is not guilty, and never was so, and that his actions and intentions were upon the former trial, and ever since have been, misunderstood."[6]

3

Curiosity as Day Forty, Monday, January 6, 1879, opened centered on how John Bullitt could avoid repetition in offering his portion of the Porter side's closing argument. Bullitt provided a clue by restating the charges Porter had faced in six sentences using plain language. More to the point, he began by using Judge-Advocate General Joseph Holt's review of the court-martial, prepared at President Lincoln's request and delivered to him on January 19, 1862, as the primary object of his analysis of errors the government had made.

Judge Holt's review had been denounced immediately after the trial by Reverdy Johnson, Porter's attorney, because it was nothing more than a restatement of the government's case and included not a word regarding the evidence and arguments to the contrary presented during the trial by the Accused. The nigh-forgotten document afforded Bullitt with a surprise asset, one that now enabled him to employ an approach that was quite different from Maltby's.

Bullitt began by showing how and where Judge Holt cited excerpts of testimony to the effect that conditions along the road from Warrenton Junction to Bristoe Station and weather (e.g., darkness) on the night of August 27–28, 1862, made it feasible for General Porter to have obeyed Pope's order to the letter, where those same witnesses had in fact described elsewhere in their testimony circumstances that *supported* the Accused's actual decisions and actions.[7] The details were familiar but Bullitt's documented exposure of Holt's malicious intellectual and procedural dishonesty must have caused the members of the Board to listen with growing curiosity.

Counsel for the Petitioner maintained the generals' interest as he moved to the second of the restated charges, the one based on Pope's "joint order" to McDowell and Porter dated August 29, 1862. Here, Bullitt substituted that vague directive for Holt's incomplete and misleading "review" as the target for his incisive remarks.

General Pope, Bullitt explained, had required his two subordinates to do several impossible things within a narrow time frame and then had granted them absolution if reality prevailed. Worse, Pope had revealed his own ignorance and confusion by stating on that Friday morning that Longstreet's wing of General Lee's divided army would not arrive before "tomorrow night or the next day."[8]

Here, it was *delicious*—Maltby's term—that Bullitt could point out to the Board the many absurdities embedded within the joint order without fear of rebuttal by its author, General Pope, who had successfully resisted all attempts to bring him to Governor's Island or West Point. Excruciatingly painful to the temporarily silenced Recorder, this ironic result must have been.

Yet John Bullitt left ridicule behind and linked the joint order to Irvin McDowell's contention in his trial testimony that he had ordered Porter to attack on August 29 and also to the studied slanting of Judge Holt's "review," the only document known to have caused Abraham Lincoln to approve Fitz John Porter's conviction and cashiering. "These charges and specifications," Bullitt observed in passing, "were evidently prepared by somebody who intended to throw a drag-net around General Porter and cover all of his actions on August 29."[9]

Bullitt directed much of his heaviest fire at Irvin McDowell. "Let me call the attention of the Board," he said, "to the influence which his testimony must have had with the court-martial, by showing you the influence that it had with the Judge-Advocate. He gave a prominence to that alleged order [to attack], and put it forward as the thing of all others which chiefly condemned General Porter."[10]

Counsel for the Petitioner returned to this contention later: "So far as General Pope and General Roberts and Colonel Smith were concerned," he suggested, "they were giving but opinions; they knew little of the actual facts; they took their facts mainly from what General McDowell told them. It was surmise or speculation or hearsay with them, but with General McDowell it was knowledge."[11]

John Bullitt's concluding remarks included an entirely new notion—that the court-martial did not sentence Porter to be shot because they harbored "a slight suspicion" that they had convicted the wrong man. He followed that assertion by reminding the Board of the temper of the time when the mistakes were made: "We think that the circumstances under which the trial took place and the influences that were then operating, the influences that made the minds of men inflamed, made them ready to receive extravagant statements, made them susceptible to influences, to prejudices, to bias—influences from which no man can be free. Now the trial record, from beginning to end, shows the influences of which I have been speaking. While the results were produced in the main by the stories of Generals McDowell and Pope, yet those stories had a degree of inconsistency and contradiction about them which, if they had been analyzed as they can be now, it would have been seen how unreliable and contradictory they were."[12]

It was the Board's duty, he declared, to vindicate General Porter, to "restore his name to that page of history which, thus far, since 1862 has been a blank; to restore it there with the purity and integrity and the honor for which he exerted himself as a soldier, and which he has always endeavored to maintain as a man."[13]

4

Asa Bird Gardner, of course, did not concur with John Bullitt's recommend-ation or the support for it that Anson Maltby had provided. To explain why took the Recorder from early on Day Forty-One, Wednesday, January 8, 1879, until the Forty-Third, January 10, and 238 pages of 541 of the *Proceedings*' Volume II.

Gardner opened with a semi-scholarly review of the Schofield Board's nigh-unique standing within the entirety of judicial bodies.[14] How the Board operated regarding established rules for admitting or rejecting proffered evidence was of great concern to him, he recalled, adding: "This Board saw very plainly that if evidence—so-called—was to be received by it as to the *merits*, someone must cross-examine and present rebuttal evidence, if any there was"—hence, his acquisition of the additional duty of acting as counsel for the government.[15]

Major Gardner's argument was organized as a series of topics beginning with *Jurisdiction of the General Court-Martial.*[16] Next came *Composition of the General Court-Martial.*[17] In *Condition of Affairs Just Prior to the First Charge* he quoted at length from General Pope's testimony before the Joint Congressional Committee on the Conduct of the War regarding the Army of Virginia's operations leading up to August 27, 1862; the Radical-dominated committee, chaired by Senator Ben Wade of Ohio, was friendly to Pope.[18] As the title implies, *1st Charge, 1st Specification* included Gardner's review of General Porter's actions during the night of August 27–28 that led to the allegations. In this section, the Recorder argued: "General Pope need not have given any reason whatever why he desired the Petitioner to march at 1 A.M. or why he desired him to be at Bristoe at daylight. His courtesy was thrown away, but the fact that he did go fully into his reasons for issuing the order took from the Petitioner any possible opportunity for exercising *any discretion whatever as to literal compliance.*"[19]

Gardner's practice was to make an assertion and back it up by liberal quotation from either the trial record or the *Proceedings* of the Schofield Board or both. Often his extracts of questions and answers were of such great length that soon a listener was likely to have forgotten the point the Recorder was attempting to make. It was as though Gardner equated masses of words with power, or that he was inordinately desirous of providing ample context; either way, the effect was deadening. And even if his intent had included enabling the Radicals in Congress to find a super abundance of rich material for use in denying Porter relief later on, the sheer bulk of his product was likely to prove counterproductive.

As the Recorder's closing argument was nearing its end on Day Forty-three, January 10, 1879, Gardner's tone shifted from prosecutorial to one tinged with contempt. "Next to be considered," he said, "is the method of procedure of this Petitioner, and in this connection it is to be noted:

> First, that he did not hesitate to avail himself of the libels of his former senior counsel [Reverdy Johnson] against the court that tried him; against the witnesses who gave evidence against him; against the Judge-Advocate General [Joseph Holt] who reviewed his case; and indirectly against President Lincoln himself.
>
> Second, that he sought before this Board to continue a cross-examination, voluntarily concluded by him sixteen years ago, of several who were witnesses before his court-martial, for the purpose of throwing doubt upon their statements on direct examination, when it was not possible that, after the lapse of so much time, any witness could recall vividly all the circumstances then in his recollection upon which he based his statements of facts.
>
> The history of jurisprudence will be searched in vain for such another like procedure.
>
> Third, his conduct toward Major Generals McDowell and Pope.[20]

As to McDowell: Inadvertently or not, Gardner linked the general to the Congressional Radicals and generals of their political persuasion such as notoriously incompetent John Charles Fremont and Nathaniel P. Banks.

Counsel for the government also attempted to apply plaster to Irvin McDowell's admission that he had misrepresented in anti-Porter publications the date of combat action Stonewall Jackson had reported pertaining to August 30th as having occurred on the 29th.

After suggesting that if Porter had attacked on the 29th, "as was his duty," the Recorder told the Board, "probably those attacks [on the 30th] would not have taken place."[21] Every soldier in the room and Fitz John Porter's lawyers could agree: Fifth Corps would have been wrecked on Friday instead of Saturday and General Lee would have ignored Longstreet's misgivings and sent his Army of Northern Virginia charging behind Pope's forces facing Jackson, cutting them off to die on the vine by crossing undefended Bull Run and seizing Centreville and the supplies the Yankees needed but then would never reach.

The Recorder was—in boxing terms—swinging from the floor, as though he considered what any newspaper reporters present might use in their submissions for tomorrow's and subsequent days' editions more important, somehow, than the integrity and persuasiveness of his protracted argument.

But having given the gentlemen of the press exactly the kind of statement they craved, he hurried toward the end of the closing argument he had commenced on Day Forty-One, two long days earlier. Members of the Board and everyone else must have breathed sighs of relief as they heard him say: "The conduct of this Petitioner in the eventful days of the August campaign of 1862 has now been reviewed."

Gardner continued: "I have now concluded the duty put upon me, a duty among the most disagreeable in all my professional experience. In performing it, I have felt that the honor of the service required every exertion on my part to ascertain the facts, so that the President, the historian, and the public might read this case and know it had been as fully investigated as possible, in the absence of any judicial or quasi-judicial power in the Board."[22]

5

"If the Board please," Joseph Choate said as Day Forty-Four began, "I will—as briefly as I can—conclude the argument on behalf of the Petitioner, and reply, so far as it may seem necessary, to what has been presented on the part of the government. I say 'as briefly as I may' for I have been reminded of the advice that was given by Dr. Breckenridge to a class to whom he was lecturing on the subject of the efficacy of prayer, as compared with its length, when he said, 'Young gentlemen, I beg you to remember that the Lord knows something.'"[23]

Choate continued:

> I am going to argue the case upon the assumption that this Board knows something of the evidence which has been taken, and which they have been engaged in receiving and examining for a period of six months, and especially something of the laws of war and of the rules of military conduct. We, who represent General Porter, pretend to know very little of the latter subject, and confide entirely in the ample knowledge of the whole subject which this Board possesses.[24]

However, replying to the Recorder's exhausting closing argument, and to the gratuitous insult embedded in the concluding sentence—Gardner's questioning of the Board's legitimacy—could not be done briefly. Neither could Choate assume that any board, despite its wealth of knowledge, would recall testimony and documents introduced during the better part of forty sessions spanning half a year. Counsel for the Petitioner blended sarcasm and ridicule with compliance with ritual as he moved deeper into his response to Gardner:

> At the outset, I wish to express our obligations to the learned Recorder for the diligence which he has manifested in searching for and procuring evidence supposed to be adverse to the cause of General Porter. A large part of it consists, in my view, of matter which we never could have found by any search or power on our part. He has gone further than the mere gathering of facts. Every rumor, every suspicion; yes, I may say, every piece of scandal detrimental to the interest or conduct of General Porter has now been presented before you. Everything that could possibly be thrown into the balance against him has been thrown in.[25]

Soon Choate turned to a topic headed "Powers and Duties of the

Board." He recalled that "the learned Recorder, from motives that I cannot understand, and from a view of the case that he has not disclosed, has studiously undertaken to belittle the functions of this Board. Ah, he says, it is to be regretted that this Board has no judicial functions."

Choate asked: "What object could tempt him to impute to it insignificance? I had always thought that the highest function of judicial bodies, the highest and grandest, was the ascertainment of truth; and when it takes the shape of the ascertainment of the truth of a point in history, which involves the good name not only of a gallant soldier, but of a great army, and a great nation, human justice can attain to nothing higher. And so it did seem to me that this reflection upon the Board of which he is a constituent member was wholly uncalled for."[26]

Major Gardner had also expressed regret that the Board had no power to summon witnesses or to compel their attendance, and this drew more scorn from Joseph Choate:

> Well, who has been hurt by that? Who has not come that was wanted by us or by the Board? One man, and one man only. There is one big fish who had escaped from the meshes of this judicial net, the great general who stands behind the prosecution, holding up its arms. But is it for the learned Recorder, especially in view of the tender and confidential relations which seem to have existed between himself and General Pope, to regret that this Board has not had the power to bring him across the continent, and to place him a reluctant witness upon the stand, and have the truth drawn out of him as by the forceps of the dentist? Considering the defiant attitude in which that gentleman stands to this case, and to this Board, I think that the suggestion is cool, even for West Point in the month of January.[27]

Major Gardner must have been relieved when Choate passed on to comment on "Circumstances Under Which Porter Was Tried Before." Here, Choate reviewed the Union's naive initial assumption that the rebellion could be quelled in a short time and at little cost, the disillusionment caused by Irvin McDowell's whipping at First Bull Run and then by Union defeats during the Seven Days and at Second Bull Run and in mid-December at Fredericksburg, and the ensuing demand for a scapegoat. "There are times," he reminded the Board, "when the administration of justice in the face of this subtle, far-reaching, irresistible popular power becomes wholly impossible. And this court-martial sat in times and under circumstances that were not favorable to the administration of justice."[28]

In making those remarks, and also those anent his next topic, "The Composition of the Court-Martial," Joseph Choate alluded occasionally to political disputes but never referred to the Radical Republicans as a faction or individuals as having been adherents of that group. In fact, as has been noted earlier, the attempts by the Jacobins to wrest control of the war were not only material but central to any consideration of that period's history.

Choate's omission may have been justified by the fact that although by 1879 the Radicals' power had peaked and was now declining, a recommendation from President Hayes for the restoration of Fitz John Porter's good name might require favorable action by both houses of Congress—in which enough Jacobins remained to cause trouble. Beyond not wanting to borrow difficulties, Choate seems to have recognized also that it was unnecessary to go into extreme detail.

However, by shifting the blame from Secretary of War Edwin Stanton for the exclusively Radical and Radical-influenced membership of the Court to General-in-Chief Halleck, counsel for the Petitioner may have been misled by a technicality. Halleck signed the order calling for the general court-martial of General Porter and appointing the members. Although nominally a Democrat, "Old Brains" despised politics; the rigging was unquestionably the work of Stanton, Halleck's superior, and therefore beyond the general-in-chief's power to oppose.[29] So Reverdy Johnson and other defenders of Porter understood in 1862 and 1863, as their post-trial writings reflected.

"Why do I cite all this?" Choate asked as he neared the end of his exposure of the errors committed in the selection and appointment of members of the court. "Because the Recorder said that the judgment of that court-martial was right, and must be accepted by you. I think we see now that it was impossible for those nine men, all of them, to act as judges. That could not be. They might sit there and record their votes, but it was impossible for them all—in the nature of things, according to the laws of the human mind—to be judges."[30]

Choate also recalled Asa Gardner's assertion that "it took a great many days to get in the evidence" and noted that it had taken President of the

Court David Hunter only five days to complete the conviction and sentencing of Fitz John Porter after he received this message dated January 5, 1863, from Stanton:

> The state of the service imperatively demands that the proceedings in the court over which you are now presiding, having been pending more than four weeks, should be brought to a close without any unnecessary delay. You are therefore directed to sit, without regard to hours, and close your proceedings as speedily as may be consistent with justice to the public service.[31]

"It was not," Choate pointed out, "justice to the accused, but justice to the public service that the Secretary appealed to as the final motive for a hasty decision of the case." He recalled exactly how unseemly the court's haste had been in convicting and sentencing the accused. "Was that a condition of things favorable to the administration of justice?" he asked, and then he wondered how the members of the Board would react if the sitting secretary of war thought it so important for them to return to their units that he sent such a message to General Schofield.

"I should think," he said, "that you, after all you know about this case, would deem it necessary to deliberate after the arguments were concluded, and to compare the evidence with the arguments to see whether on either side they were specious and fallacious or sound and based on the truth. You would not say, 'Why, I must be off to St. Paul on the morning train,' and 'I must be off to Fortress Monroe to-night,' and 'I must return to my neglected cadets.' But you would say, 'Let us look into this thing; there is a man's life at stake; the fame of an officer of the Army is involved.' If you did receive an order such as Stanton's to Hunter, you would refuse to decide the case without a chance for deliberation."[32]

Summing up the many problems Choate had with the 1862–1863 court-martial, he said: "It does seem to me that there are circumstances surrounding the history of that court-martial which make it only fair for us to say—and even the learned Recorder will not term it libelous—that it was asking more than human judgment, and more than human nature was master of, for them to pass judicially upon the case."[33]

Choate kept his argument advancing topic by topic, documented with quotations from testimony and illustrated with various maps. As Day Forty-

Four wore on he felt confident enough regarding the effectiveness of his points to tell the Board: "So much has been said already on the subject of the 4:30 P.M. order on the 29th that I am only called upon to answer what the Recorder has said about it."

That was, Choate recalled, that there was no new evidence before the Board, and that the case is not changed from the attitude which it held on the former trial.

"*No new evidence?*" Choate must have shouted.

> "What do you say to the evidence of General Ruggles, the man who wrote that order, the man whose unfailing habit it was to date each message first thing, before John Pope began dictating? The very foundation of Captain Pope's evidence entirely falls out of the case, specifically, his connection between 4:30 as the time of the beginning of the order and 4:30 as the time of its delivery to Captain Pope. Now, when the Recorder says there is not any new evidence in the case, he must have forgotten that."[34]

Had Major Gardner also forgotten the testimony of Captain Randel, Choate wondered, who had sworn that he saw Pope deliver the order at sundown—not 6:30, not 5 o'clock, or 5:30? Or the recollections of Captain Moale and Lieutenant Jones regarding the story Captain Pope had told out in New Mexico, the one in which he admitted he had gotten lost?[35]

"What, then, is the fair conclusion from all the testimony as it stands?" Choate asked. "Is it not that the testimony of Douglass Pope and of Duffee on the former trial ought not to have been credited, and that now it cannot be credited, in the least?"[36]

Choate also recalled "the production here of a third party, a second orderly, one Dyer, who pretends to have accompanied Captain Pope and Orderly Duffee on that expedition. But Duffee does not recollect his presence; if you can accept Duffee's testimony, it is that Dyer was not there, and the most convincing proof that he was not there is what Dyer says himself." Dyer it was who claimed to have seen a steeple on a church that had never had one and a house that was not built until after the battle. "Now, we are known by the company we keep," Choate observed, "and when you find these three witnesses now brought, standing together, Douglass Pope, Duffee, and Dyer, what remains to sustain the ground of this prosecution on their evidence and accusation? It seems to me that they will all tumble out of the case together."[37]

Answering only what the Recorder had said about the 4:30 order may well have been Joseph Choate's intention, but he went beyond it to remind the Board of the recently introduced copy of an order General Porter had written at 6:00 P.M. to "McDowell or Pope." In the text, after describing his situation, Porter had stated: "Please let me know your designs"—which he would not have needed to write had he seen the contents of the 4:30 order before sundown.[38] That point made, Choate continued:

> I accept the military authority that has been brought into the case, to the effect that it was impracticable then to make an attack. General McDowell said on the former trial that [Porter] might have made an attack within an hour after receiving the order. McDowell confessed, on the present examination, that he knew he was wrong about this, confessed that Porter's position was in fact not so far advanced as he had supposed. Colonel Smith, who before testified—to the destruction of General Porter—that that attack might have been made within an hour, concurring with the opinion given by McDowell, now comes and frankly states that it would have taken not less than two hours.[39]

Supposing that Captain Pope had delivered the 4:30 order at six o'clock and that Smith's revised opinion was valid, for Porter to have attacked at eight o'clock would have been a "military absurdity," Choate suggested—and there he left that branch of the case.[40] Indeed, his next topic was sharply different.

"Having acquitted General Porter of all that can possibly be charged against him under the head of disobedience," he said, "now comes the question of whether he was guilty of the highest crimes charged upon him in the specifications under the second charge—imputing to him shameful treachery and misconduct in the face of the enemy, running away when he knew that a battle was raging on his right in which the rest of the forces were engaged, by which even the capital of the country itself was involved in danger, and moving off without the least effort, or lying still upon his arms all day without the least effort to assist."[41]

Although Choate had described Porter's jeopardy in the harshest words, conviction of the charge of misbehavior in the presence of the enemy had done more damage to the general's reputation than anything else. It was for this that Abraham Lincoln was said to have told his son Robert that Porter ought to have been shot. Radical Senator Zachariah Chandler had been of the same opinion. Short of agreeing that the extreme penalty had been justified, Ulysses Grant had been unable to bring himself around to giving any consideration to a Petitioner convicted of such a crime. Even Joseph Choate had confessed that for more than fifteen years he had believed Porter guilty of "something heinous and derogatory to his character as a soldier."[42]

Accordingly, if the second charge could be refuted more completely than the first, Fitz John Porter's vindication would be all the more impressive. Fortunately for all concerned, Choate's disposals of topics such as the 4:30 order and the events near Dawkins' Branch on August 29 had been so thorough, and there was so much overlap among certain specifications, that he could concentrate on demolishing the allegation that Porter had retreated on that afternoon.

During the past six months a number of witnesses had testified emphatically that there had been no retreat, or anything resembling a retreat, that day. Twice in the text of the joint order, General Pope had provided grounds for Porter to withdraw from his Dawkins' Branch lines: first, the admonition to avoid getting too far out to preclude return to Bull Run or behind it, either to be resupplied or because the Confederates might combine before sometime on Saturday in front of Centreville, and second, permission to depart from the order if any considerable advantages were to be gained. There was no need to prolong the proceedings by returning to all that or even by reciting relevant portions in the present record. So what did Choate do?

With his argument nearing its end, he based its main weight on Porter's *intent* as it was reflected in his actions and the texts of *all* of his orders that afternoon. Absent a single reply to any of the messages the Fifth Corps' commander had sent to his superiors after McDowell had acknowledged his cry, "What shall I do?" with merely a wave as he began his ride to find King's division, Choate was obliged to revisit his position that Porter would have committed a grievous error had he attacked that afternoon. Withdrawal—not retreat—became an option available to Porter when changes in perceived location of battle sounds from the direction of Groveton suggested that Pope's units were initiating a pull-back toward Bull Run and

Centreville, possibly as foreshadowed in the joint order. Accordingly, for a time on that Friday afternoon his actions and orders had reflected his intent to conform with imagined rearward movements of Pope's army's other elements. Then, as soon as fresh information arrived, General Porter had ordered Sykes to move back up the road toward the enemy and to prepare to join Morell's division in an attack.

Said Choate:

> We know now that if [Porter] had sacrificed his whole corps in the blunder of an attack, it would not have afforded any relief to Pope's army. There is a demonstration of this, as it seems to me, in this case that the whole world would be content with, in confirmation of Longstreet's testimony that it was Porter's presence there that prevented an attack by Lee that day.
>
> What happened next day when Porter was withdrawn by the orders of General Pope from this position? What is the evidence? What is the irresistible conclusion from the proofs as to what happened on the 30th?
>
> Why, that it was only Porter holding on to where he was against every threat and every doubt that prevented on the 29th the slaughter that was consummated on the 30th.
>
> What could have justified Porter in withdrawing his force from there on the morning of the 30th but the positive [peremptory] orders of General Pope, who still remained, or claimed to have remained, in absolute ignorance of the intervening [Longstreet] situation?[43]

And there was another thing, Choate said: "The court-martial believed, and it was so sworn, that there was a battle raging all day in Porter's plain sight and hearing. Well, was there? You know all about that now. The Recorder called a host of witnesses to prove that there was a battle. It has enabled us to develop exactly the situation." He continued:

> There was not a battle raging with continuous fury from daylight to dark on August 29, as Pope, in his dispatch of the next morning, asserted. There was a series of successive spurts, as Heintzelman said; there were skirmishes all along the line from just below the Warrenton pike up to Sudley Springs and Sudley Church.

> Was there no battle? Why, yes; there were lots of them. Every regiment, apparently, and every brigade, had a battle of its own. But they were no more connected than if one had been in Maine and another in Florida, and the rest in interlying states.
>
> There was no support of one attack by another attack. Let me read what General Schurz said upon that subject. He was there; he was engaged in it. Heintzelman says there were successive spurts. General Schurz says:
>
>> If all those forces, instead of being frittered away in isolated efforts, had co-operated with each other at any one moment after a common plan, the result of the day would have been far greater than the mere retaking and occupation of the ground we had already taken and retaken in the morning, and which, in the afternoon, was for a short time at least lost again.[44]

Choate reminded the Board of testimony reiterating the sheer impossibility of Porter's having seen or heard any of the spurts of fighting on the Florida, much less the Maine, segments of Pope's line. This was quickly done, permitting him to proceed from establishing Fitz John Porter's innocence of misbehavior in the presence of the enemy to exposing the facts suggesting that his superiors were guilty of obstructing justice.[45]

"There is not a rag left," said Joseph Choate, "of the government's case against General Porter. Yet, something remains. General Pope and General McDowell have placed themselves in such a position before this Board that you must utterly reject their opinions when given adversely to General Porter."[46]

McDowell had been mistaken, Choate recalled, first in allowing the testimony he had given during the court-martial to be misconstrued and then "this time he claimed that he didn't mean any such thing." But there was more: "bias and hostility from some cause, I don't know what, to General Porter." Choate cited McDowell's publication in 1870 of the document opposing Porter's petition in which McDowell gave the impression that—according to Jackson's report—certain events that occurred on August 30 had taken place on the day before.

"If it had stopped there," Choate noted, "it would have been bad enough. But what more have we? Why, when that came out, Colonel

Smith—who seems to be a deluded but a reasonably truthful witness—at once protested that this was not true. Well, the question was raised, and it became a public, bruited, agitated question among military men. What happened?

"I should suppose that the first instinct of a soldier in such a case would have been to find out if he had made a mistake or not. It would have been the first impulse of anybody outside of the Army, and it seems to me that it would be of every man in the Army. Well, now, what did General McDowell do?

"Knowing that the question was agitated, and that he was suspected of having made this mistake, to the great damage of his brother soldier who was suffering under this undeserved ignominy, what did he do? He did nothing. He let it go uncorrected. Why?

"Now, do not let me do General McDowell any injustice. I read from the record: 'I did not think it my province to do it.'

"It cannot be that he wants fair play for General Porter. It cannot be that any opinion that he expressed ought to be for one moment considered."[47]

Joseph Choate's remarks regarding Irvin McDowell would prove gentle compared with those he proceeded to make anent the general commanding the Army of Virginia during Bull Run, John Pope. His opinion, Choate began, "so much relied upon by the prosecution, is now the only one remaining—but it has been abandoned by his contemptuous refusal to come before this Board and support it."

Exhibited upon the record, Choate declared, "is a deadly hostility to General Porter, and a confession by Pope of personal interest in the question of Porter's guilt or innocence. And there is something more exhibited. He has a most peculiar congenital defect: I mean, his way—constitutional with him and peculiar to him—of looking at things and stating things—his method of stating the 'truth,' if that is the proper word. He will tell the biggest kind of a 'truth,' that is out of all relations, not only with all truths known to other people, but with his own truths as he has seen them and stated them the day before. Now, if that be so, his opinion certainly ought not to be regarded as of any great force."[48]

Choate recalled the affliction known as color blindness. "It is a natural, inherent, constitutional defect. But it seems to me that there is such a thing as blindness toward the truth, and inability to recognize the existing relations of things. That seems to be the infirmity of General Pope."[49]

On September 2, Choate reminded the Board, at Centreville in the presence of Generals Webb, Green, and William F. "Baldy" Smith, Pope's manner toward Porter had been entirely cordial. "But as to this natural infirmity of his," Choate continued, "I want to call attention to certain written statements." These were messages to General-in-Chief Halleck, the first sent at 5:00 A.M. on Saturday, describing the action on the day before, the 29th: "We fought a terrific battle here yesterday with the combined forces of the enemy, which lasted with continuous fury from daylight until after dark, by which time the enemy was driven from the field, which we now occupy."[50]

Choate's comment: "If he did not know anything of the presence of Longstreet, it is a very curious thing to find here a statement that he had been fighting against the combined forces of the enemy; and if he knew that, as he swore upon the court-martial, he came upon the field about twelve or one, and practically put a stop to the hostilities until about four, it is a very remarkable thing that on the next morning he saw the truth to be in this way: 'We fought a terrific battle yesterday with the *combined forces* of the enemy, which lasted with continuous fury from *daylight until after dark*.' "

Next, Choate reminded the Board that General Porter's Fifth Corps was ordered, under McDowell, to make an attack with the assurance that Jackson's forces were flying and were in full retreat. "Well, they made an assault," Choate said. "They were almost cut to pieces. Blood flowed like water. Thousands of brave men perished." Yet in the account General Pope gave in a message to General Halleck that same night, Saturday, August 30, at 9:45 P.M., from Centreville, he stated that the Confederates attacked "early to-day" and that "we held our ground firmly until 6 P.M., when the enemy, massing very heavy forces on the left, forced back that wing almost half a mile. At dark we held that position." There was more, including: "We have lost nothing, neither guns nor wagons."

General Ruggles, Pope's aide-de-camp, testified that he had attempted to correct the army commander. "I saw some guns lost," he said he told Pope. "I saw some wagons lost. You are mistaken, are you not?" And Pope had replied: "Well, write it. We have lost nothing, neither guns nor wagons."[51]

Referring to Pope's report of September 3, Choate said, "That is one of the most remarkable manifestations of this peculiarity of General Pope that I have ever found." He cited a passage in which two orders were mentioned, orders that "nobody else had ever heard of. Can you conceive of a general who has commanded three or four days before, and had issued these written orders which we have been considering here, that he should state it in this way, unless he was suffering from the disease which I have imputed to him?"[52]

Pope's official report dated January 27, 1863, withheld until all of the evidence had been received by the Porter trial, was another rich source of John Pope's misstatements. "Think of this," said Choate to the Board. "Months after the events he still insists that the main army of Lee came through Thoroughfare Gap on the night of the 29th and the morning of the 30th to get on the field." And he called attention to a particularly malicious "truth," that Porter's attack on the 30th had been neither vigorous nor persistent, and that his troops soon retired in considerable confusion.

"Certainly the mind that penned that sentence," said Choate, "knowing and seeing what he did of Porter's conduct and the conduct of his Fifth Army Corps on the 30th, is suffering from some serious perturbation. Now, the report to the Committee on the Conduct of the War made by General Pope has another startling 'truth.' It is one that shows his hostility to Porter. His claim of the authorship of the prosecution, and his claim for reward from the administration for having successfully carried it through, show, as I think, his infinite bias against Porter."[53]

"Enough, Counselor," John Schofield may have felt like pleading, but Joseph Choate went on with his documentation of Pope's "malady." He offered other examples detrimental to General Porter in the letter to President Grant in 1870, in Pope's "Brief statement of the Case," and the letter he wrote General Sherman on October 23, 1878.[54] But he was nearing the end of his argument.

Having established General Pope's animus against the Petitioner, Choate took up the topic "The Animus of General Porter." It was almost immaterial, he said, because it was now clear that Fitz John Porter had done his whole duty regardless of his distrust of "General Pope's ability to conduct a great campaign."[55]

Even so, Choate placed each of Porter's statements in common-sense perspective—just as he had in truly grave matters such as the joint order and the 4:30 order. One after another in demolishing the noxious notions that Porter had harbored intent to be disloyal to John Pope, Choate also applied principles that lifted specific bits of trivia from their origins to the level of precedents to be avoided widely in the future. Among the ways in which he introduced principles and suggested conclusions were these:

- Has it ever been known, in any country, that subordinate generals might not send criticisms to headquarters, even upon the conduct of a campaign by their immediate commander? In what country has it not been permitted? Why, the theory of the infallibility of the Pope, to question which is heresy, is now for the first time sought to be applied to military matters: They set up the infallibility of *this* Pope and that all questioning of it is treason. That will not do.[56]
- Porter's allusions in those telegrams were all true, all perfectly justifiable—although the discreetness of sending them or making some of those remarks, knowing what General Pope is, might possibly be questioned.[57]
- Pope brought criticism upon himself from many sources by publishing the bombastic address to the Army of Virginia on July 14, 1862, in which he presumed by innuendo to criticize General McClellan.[58]

But perhaps the most scathing language Joseph Choate devoted to refuting Porter's alleged animus toward Pope came near the end of his closing argument. After quoting from a letter to Ambrose Burnside in which Porter had said, "The strategy [here] is magnificent, and tactics in inverse proportion. I would like to be ordered to return to Fredericksburg, to push toward Hanover, or, with a larger force, to push towards Orange Court-House" Choate said:

> What does that mean? I have heard military men say that, even in the then-wretched situation, a wise expedient [would have been] to strike behind Lee, at his lines of communication, and compel his instantaneous retreat. If that had been done, all this useless slaughter of the 29th and 30th would have been avoided. That was

> Porter's suggestion, of which they complained. That was his idea of getting away and doing something: of dealing an effectual blow at the enemy, with whom they were all contending.[59]

Joseph Choate, able as he was, failed to make one more significant point. On the afternoon of August 27, as Porter was expressing that wish (actually suggesting a Union military action) in his letter to Burnside, not far up the Orange & Alex-andria Railroad at Manassas Junction, Jackson's troops were joyously and thoroughly looting John Pope's supply base. Stonewall was *doing* what Porter was showing he knew *could* change the situation drastically and perhaps critically. Choate did refer to Jackson's raid, but in a different context: that it was a response to Pope's statement in his July 14 harangue that he was going to "look before and not behind" at his base of supplies, because "disaster and shame lurk in the rear."[60]

Yet there was this offset: "The President thanked General Porter personally for those very telegrams," Choate reminded the Board, "on the battlefield at Antietam where he met him."[61]

All that remained were disposal of the petty "scandals" that the Recorder had made much of—Lord's and Ormsby's recollection of Porter's alleged "I was not loyal to General Pope" outburst, for example—and Joseph Choate's peroration:

> And now, if the Board please, enough has been said.
>
> The fate of the Petitioner is in your hands. His sufferings under this sentence for the past sixteen years have been peculiar, unlike those that any other general or soldier have ever sustained. I do not propose to depict them; they cannot be exaggerated by any language. Only eminent soldiers, such as compose this Board, can fully realize and appreciate them.
>
> But General Porter is not the only person who stands awaiting your judgment. Not only he, but his family and his comrades in arms, that glorious Fifth Army Corps which never yet has met without affirming their faith in his innocence, the whole Army as I believe and every faithful man who has ever been connected with it stands expecting and hoping for the restoration of his good name and fame—because it is not his good name and fame only that is concerned, but the Army's and the country's. . . .

> We think that the time has come at last for this gross wrong to the Petitioner to be righted.
>
> He has looked for it hopefully and faithfully for the last sixteen years. He has looked for it because he was sure of his innocence, because he had absolute faith in his cause, faith in his country, faith in justice, faith in God.
>
> The question now is whether God and justice and country shall all forsake him.
>
> We have no fears.

Joseph Choate concluded: "It seems to me that time and place are both propitious for his vindication. In ten days more will be the anniversary of his humiliation. Here at West Point where his military life began is where his star should be restored to its true and native luster, and so in his name and the name of his brave army corps which he commanded, in the name of the Army which he did his best to honor, in the name of truth insulted and of justice outraged, we demand for the Petitioner full and complete reparation."[62]

Appendix VII

Text of the Schofield Board Report

[Chapter Seventeen / Note 5]

NEW YORK CITY, *March 19, 1879.*

To the honorable the SECRETARY OF WAR,
Washington, D.C.:

SIR: We, the Board of Officers appointed by order of the President to examine the evidence in the case of Fitz John Porter, late major general of volunteers, and to report, with the reasons for our conclusions, what action (if any), in our opinion, justice requires should be taken by the President on the application for relief in that case, have the honor to make the following report.

The Recorder has been directed to forward to the Adjutant-General of the Army the printed record of our proceeding, including all the evidence examined and the arguments of counsel on either side.

We have made a very thorough examination of all the evidence presented and bearing in any manner upon the merits of the case. The Recorder has, under instructions from the Board, sought with great diligence for evidence in addition to that presented by the Petitioner, especially such as might appear to have a bearing adverse to the claims urged by him.

Due care has been exercised not to inquire into the military operations of the Army of Virginia, or the conduct of officers thereof, any further than has seemed necessary to a full and fair elucidation of the subject submitted to us for investigation. On the other hand, we have not hesitated to examine fully into all the facts, accurate knowledge of which seemed to us to be necessary to the formation of a correct judgment upon the merits of the case, and to the determination of the action which justice requires should be taken by the President on the Petitioner's application for relief.

We have had the benefit of the testimony of a large number of officers of the late Confederate Army, a kind of testimony which was not available at the time of General Porter's trial by court-martial. We have also availed ourselves of the testimony of many officers and soldiers of the Union forces who were present on the battlefield, and of much documentary evidence, to throw additional light upon points not made perfectly clear in the record of evidence taken before the court-martial; and we have had the use of accurate maps of the battlefield of Manassas, constructed from recent actual surveys made, under the direction of the Chief of Engineers, by a distinguished officer of that corps, who was himself a participant in that battle. Without such a map neither the testimony upon which General Porter was convicted nor the additional testimony submitted to this board could have been correctly understood.

The evidence which we have thus been able to examine, in addition to that which was before the court-martial, has placed beyond question many important facts which were before the subjects of dispute, and in respect to some of which radically erroneous opinions were entertained by General Porter's accusers, and doubtless by the court-martial that pronounced him guilty.

The result has been, as we believe, to establish beyond reasonable doubt all the facts essential to the formation of a correct judgment upon the merits of the case of Fitz John Porter. We are thus enabled to report, with entire unanimity, and without doubt in our own minds, with the reasons for our conclusions, what action, in our opinion, justice required should be taken by the President on the Petitioner's application for relief.

The evidence presents itself under several distinct heads, viz:

First. The imperfect, and in some respects erroneous, statements of facts, due to the partial and incorrect knowledge in possession of witnesses at the time of the court-martial, and the extremely inaccurate maps and erroneous locations of troops thereon, by which erroneous statements were made to convey still more erroneous impressions.

Second. The opinions and inferences of prominent officers based upon this imperfect knowledge.

Third. The far more complete and accurate statements of facts now made by a large number of eye-witnesses from both the contending forces.

Fourth. The accurate maps of the field of operations and the exact positions of troops thereon at different periods of time, by which statements otherwise contradictory or irreconcilable are shown to be harmonious, and opposing opinions are shown to have been based upon different views of the same military situation; and,

Finally, The conflicting testimony relative to plans of operations, interpretation of orders, motives of action, and relative degrees of responsibility for unfortunate results.

A careful consideration of all the material facts now fully established, in com-bination with the conflicting or inconclusive testimony last above referred to, gives rise to several diverse theories respecting the whole subject with which General Porter's case is inseparably connected. These diverse views of the subject necessarily involve in a greater or less degree the acts, motives, and responsibilities of others as well as those of the Petitioner.

We have considered, with great care and labor, and with our best ability, each and all of these phases in which the subject can be and has been presented, and we find that all these possible views of the subject, when examined in the light of the facts which are fully established by undisputed testimony, lead inevitably to one and the same conclusion in respect to the guilt or innocence of Fitz John Porter of the specific charges upon which he was tried and pronounced guilty by the court-martial.

Therefore, while exposing General Porter's conduct to the test of the highest degree of responsibility which recognized military principles attached to the command he held under the circumstances in which he was placed, and the orders which he had received, we are able to take that view of the whole subject which seems to involve in the least possible degree any question as to the acts, motives, or responsibility of others.

We will now proceed to give, as concisely as we are able to do, a narrative of the events which gave rise to the charges against Maj. Gen. Fitz John Porter, omitting the multitude of interesting but unessential details and all facts having no necessary bearing upon his case, and limiting ourselves to a plain statement of the essential facts of the case which have been established, as we believe, by positive proof.

While the Army of the Potomac was withdrawing from its position on the James River in August, 1862, the Army of Virginia, under Major-General Pope, was ordered to hold the line of the Rappahannock, and to stand on the defensive until all the forces could be united behind that river. General Pope was given to understand that, when this concentration was effected, Major-General Halleck, the General-in-Chief, was to take the field in command of the combined armies. On the other hand, it appears that Major-General McClellan, then commanding the Army of the Potomac, was given to understand that he was to direct the operations of all the forces in Virginia, as soon as they should be united.

It appears that General Pope was notified on the 25th of August that an active campaign was soon to be commenced, without waiting for a union of all the forces, and under some commander other than either of those before named. But this information appears to have been of a secret character, afterward suppressed, and not made known to General McClellan and his subordinates until five days later, when the order appeared from the War Department, depriving McClellan of the command of all his troops then between the Potomac and the Rappahannock, although leaving him in nominal command of the Army of the Potomac.

Thus General Porter, who joined General Pope's army about that time, was left under the impression, which all had previously shared, that the operations of the army were to continue of a defensive character until all the forces should be united and proper preparations made for the commencement of an offensive campaign under a general designated by the President to command the combined armies.

But just then the Confederate general, Jackson, with three divisions of infantry, one of cavalry, and some artillery, commenced his movement to turn the Union right through Thoroughfare Gap, which Gap he passed on the 26th, and that night struck the rear of the Union army at Bristoe and Manassas Junction. The next morning, August 27, the Union army changed front to the rear, and was ordered to move on Gainesville, Greenwich, and Warrenton Junction.

General Porter, with his two divisions of the Fifth Corps, arrived at Warrenton Junction on the 27th, and there reported in person to General Pope. That afternoon Hooker's division was engaged with the enemy at Bristoe Station; McDowell and Sigel were moving on Gainesville, and Heintzelman and Reno on Greenwich. Banks was covering the rear below Warrenton Junction and guarding the trains in their movement toward Manassas Junction.

Porter was at first ordered to move toward Greenwich upon the arrival of Banks at Warrenton Junction but after Hooker's engagement at Bristoe the following order was sent him, and he received it at 9:50 P.M.:

HEADQUARTERS ARMY OF VIRGINIA,
Bristoe Station, August 27, 1862—6:30 P.M.

Maj. Gen. F. J. PORTER, *Warrenton Junction*:

The major-general commanding directs that you start at 1 o'clock to-night and come forward with your whole corps, or such part of it as is with you, so as to be here by daylight to-morrow morning.

Hooker has had a very severe action with the enemy, with a loss of about 300 killed and wounded. The enemy has been driven back, but is retiring along the railroad. We must drive him from Manassas, and clear the country between that place and Gainesville, where McDowell is.

If Morell has not Joined you, send him word to push forward immediately; also send word to Banks to hurry forward with all speed to take your place at Warrenton Junction.

It is necessary on all accounts that you should be here by daylight. I send an officer with this dispatch who will conduct you to this place. Be sure to send word to Banks, who is on the road from Fayetteville, probably in the direction of Bealeton. Say to Banks, also, that he had best run back the railroad trains to this side of Cedar Run. If he is not with you, write him to that effect.

By command of General Pope:

GEORGE D. RUGGLES,
Colonel and Chief of Staff.

P. S. If Banks is not at Warrenton Junction, leave a regiment of infantry and two pieces of artillery as a guard till he comes up, with instructions to follow you immediately upon his doing so. If Banks is not at the Junction, instruct Colonel Clary to run the trains back to this side of Cedar Run, and post a regiment and a section of artillery with it.

By command of General Pope:

GEORGE D. RUGGLES,
Colonel and Chief of Staff.

This order plainly contemplated an aggressive movement against the enemy early on the 28th, and required the presence of General Porter's corps at Bristoe Station as early as possible in the morning, to take part in the pursuit of and attack upon the enemy. The order did not indicate any anticipation of defensive action at Bristoe, but, on the contrary, it indicated continuous, active, and aggressive operations during the entire day of the 28th, to drive the enemy from Manassas and clear the country. Hence the troops must arrive at Bristoe in condition for such service.

The evidence clearly shows that General Porter evinced an earnest desire to comply literally with the terms of the order, and that he held a consultation with his division commanders, some of his brigade commanders, and his staff officers on the subject. One of his divisions had arrived in camp late in the evening, after a long march, and was much fatigued. If the troops marched at 1 o'clock, none of them could have much sleep before starting, and, even if they could arrive at Bristoe by or soon after daylight, they must be in poor condition for a vigorous pursuit of the enemy, who was already some distance beyond Bristoe.

But this was not regarded by General Porter as sufficient reason for hesitating to make the attempt to comply literally with the order. He still urged, against the advice of his division commanders, the necessity of implicit obedience.

Then further consideration of the subject disclosed the fact that the road was filled with army trains, which had been pressing in that direction all day and as late at night as they could move, until the way had become completely blocked with wagons. The trains of the army moving back from the line of the Rappahannock had been ordered to take that road to the number of "two or three thousand." In the language of one of the most intelligent witnesses, the mass of wagons blocked together at places in the road was "like a lot of ice that jams in on the shore." The night had become very dark, or, as testified by most of the witnesses, excessively dark. It would have been difficult to march troops upon a plain and unobstructed road. It was a manifest physical impossibility to march over that road that night or to remove the obstructions in the darkness of the night.

When this situation was made evident, General Porter reluctantly consented to delay the movement two hours, or until 3 o'clock. At that hour the march was commenced, but it was found that no appreciable progress could be made before daylight. Nothing was gained, or could have been gained, by the attempt to move before the dawn of day. It would have been wiser to have delayed the attempt to move until 4 o'clock.

A vigorous and persistent effort to make that march, commencing at 1 o'clock, could only have resulted in greatly fatiguing the troops and throwing them into disorder, from which they could not have been extricated until long after daylight, without making any material progress, and would thus have caused the corps to arrive at Bristoe at a later hour and in a miserable condition.

Abundant experience in situations similar to that above described leaves no room for doubt what General Porter's duty was. He exercised only the very ordinary discretion of a corps commander, which it was his plain duty to exercise, in delaying the march until 3 o'clock, and in his attempt to move at that time instead of at 4 o'clock he showed only too anxious a desire to comply with the letter of his orders.

If the order had contemplated, as has been represented, an attack by the enemy at dawn of day, then it would have been Porter's duty to start promptly, not at 1 o'clock, but at the moment he received the order, so as to have brought at least some fragments of his infantry to Bristoe in time to aid in repelling that attack. That was the most that he could have done in any event, even by starting the moment the order was received, and then his troops would have been in no condition for any aggressive movement that day.

General Porter reached Bristoe Station as soon as practicable with his corps on the morning of the 28th, and there remained, under orders from his superior commander, until the morning of the 29th, taking no part in the operations of the 28th.

During the morning of the 28th McDowell sent Ricketts' division of his corps to Thoroughfare Gap to resist the advance of re-enforcements from the main body of Lee's army then known to be marching to join Jackson. Banks was at Warrenton Junction and Porter at Bristoe. The rest of the army moved from Gainesville, Greenwich, and Bristoe on Manassas Junction to attack Jackson at that place; but that general withdrew his forces during the night of the 27th and morning of the 28th toward Sudley and Groveton. He was followed by Heintzelman and Reno, via Centreville, and McDowell and Sigel, after having marched some distance toward Manassas, were ordered to direct their march toward Centreville.

In this movement toward Centreville King's division of McDowell's corps struck the right of Jackson's force late in the afternoon, just north of the Warrenton turnpike, a mile west of Groveton. A sharp contest ensued, lasting until some time after dark, when King still held his ground on the turnpike. Reynolds was then near the right of King, Sigel on his right near the stone house, Heintzelman and Reno near Centreville; Ricketts, who had been sent in the morning to Thoroughfare Gap, was disputing with Longstreet the passage of the Gap.

Thus it was still hoped to strike Jackson a decisive blow on the morning of the 29th before re-enforcements could reach him. In the meantime the Confederate general had taken up a favorable position a little to the north and west of Groveton and Sudley. Under these conditions General Porter, who was still at Bristoe Station, received, at 6 A.M., the following order from General Pope:

> HEADQUARTERS ARMY OF VIRGINIA,
> *Near Bull Run, August 29, 1862—3 A.M.*
>
> Major-General PORTER:
>
> McDowell has intercepted the retreat of Jackson. Sigel is immediately on the right of McDowell. Kearny and Hooker march to attack the enemy's rear at early dawn. Major-General Pope directs you to move upon Centreville at the first dawn of day with your whole command, leaving your trains to follow. It is very important that you should be here at a very early hour in the morning. A severe engagement is likely to take place, and your presence is necessary.
>
> GEORGE D. RUGGLES,
> *Colonel and Chief of Staff.*

Under this order General Porter marched promptly with his corps toward Centreville. He had passed Manassas Junction with the head of his column when he was halted by counter-orders, issued in consequence of a grave change which had occurred in the situation since the night before.

King had withdrawn from his position near Jackson's right, on the Warrenton turnpike, and had fallen back to Manassas Junction. Ricketts had fallen back in the night from Thoroughfare Gap to Gainesville, and thence, in consequence of the movement of King, had retired to Bristoe Station.

Thus the way had been left open for the retreat of Jackson to Thoroughfare Gap or for the advance of Longstreet from that point, and ample time had elapsed for them to effect a junction, either at the Gap or near Groveton, before a force could again be interposed to prevent it. The opportunity to attack Jackson's detached force with superior numbers had passed beyond the possibility of recall.

As soon as the withdrawal of King became known to General Pope he hastily sent a verbal message to General Porter to retrace his steps and move toward Gainesville, and soon followed this message with the following order, which was received by General Porter about 9:30 A.M.:

> HEADQUARTERS ARMY OF VIRGINIA,
> *Centreville, August 29, 1862.*
>
> Push forward with your corps and King's division, which you will take with you, upon Gainesville. I am following the enemy down the Warrenton turnpike. Be expeditious or we will lose much.
>
> JOHN POPE,
> *Major-General, Commanding.*

Under these orders Porter advanced promptly with his corps, followed by King's division, on the direct road from Manassas Junction toward Gainesville, having knowledge of the military situation as above described.

General Porter had met General McDowell near Manassas Junction, and they had conversed with each other relative to this order, placing King's division under Porter's command. McDowell claims that it was conceded that he might go forward and command the whole force under the Sixty-second Article of War, but he desired to reunite all the divisions of his corps on that part of the field where Reynolds then was. Hence he wrote to Pope on this subject, awaited his orders, and did not exercise any command over Porter's corps until after the receipt of further orders from Pope.

When, about 11:30 o'clock, the head of Porter's column arrived at Dawkins' Branch, about 3 ½ miles from Gainesville and 9 ½ miles from Thoroughfare Gap, he met the enemy's cavalry advance, and captured some of Longstreet's scouts. The clouds of dust in his front and to his right, and extending back toward Thoroughfare Gap, showed the enemy coming in force, and already arriving on the field in his front.

Morell's division was at once deployed; Sykes closed up in support, King's division following. A regiment was sent forward across the creek as skirmishers, and Butterfield's brigade was started across the creek to the front, and somewhat to the right, with orders to seize, in advance of the enemy, if possible, the commanding ground on the opposite ridge, about a mile distant. Morell's division, with Sykes' in support, was ready to advance at once to the support of Butterfield.

At this stage of Porter's operations, some time between 11:30 and 12 o'clock, McDowell, in person, arrived on the field and arrested the movement Porter was making, saying to him, in the hearing of several officers, "Porter, you are too far out. This is no place to fight a battle," or words to that effect.

McDowell had received a few minutes before a dispatch from Buford, informing him that seventeen regiments of infantry, a battery, and some cavalry had passed through Gainesville at 8.45 o'clock, and moved down the Centreville road toward Groveton, and hence must have been on the field in front of Sigel and Reynolds at least two hours.

The dust in Porter's immediate front and extending across toward Groveton, as well as back toward Gainesville, showed that large forces of the enemy, in addition to those reported by Buford, were already on the field. The latest information from the Confederate army showed the whole force of the enemy within reach of Gainesville by noon on the 29th. McDowell's troops (Ricketts' division and some cavalry) had delayed Longstreet's advance at Thoroughfare Gap from about noon until dark on the previous day, 28th. Hence Lee's column had had eighteen hours by the morning of the 29th to close up in mass near the Gap, and seven hours that morning in which to march 8 miles and form line on the field of battle.

Jackson, who had been supposed anxious to retreat, and for whom the way had been left open, had not retreated, but was still holding his position of the previous evening, as if confident of adequate re-enforcements. Sigel's pursuit had been checked, where it started that morning, at Groveton.

It was certain that the head of column of Lee's main army had arrived on the field in front of Groveton at least two hours in advance of the arrival of the head of column of Porter's and McDowell's corps at Dawkins' Branch, and it was so nearly certain that the main body of Lee's army was already on the field and in line of battle as to absolutely require corresponding action.

This was Porter's impression at the time, and he conveyed it to McDowell by words and gesture that left no doubt in the mind of the latter that he (Porter) believed the enemy was in force in his immediate front.

In contrast to this evident preparation of the enemy for battle only Porter's 9,000 or 10,000 men were ready for action of the 35,000 men then composing the left wing of the Union army.

Banks' corps, 10,000, was still at Bristoe without orders to move beyond that point. Ricketts' division, 8,000, was near Bristoe, under orders to move to the front, but his men were so worn-out by constant marching, night and day, that they could not possibly be got to the field even for defensive action that day. King's division, 7,000, was just in rear of Porter, but was so fatigued as to be unfit for offensive action, and hardly able to march.

Thus this long column, stretching back from Dawkins' Branch by way of Manassas Junction to and even beyond Bristoe, had struck the right wing of the Confederate army in line of battle, while a gap of nearly 2 miles remained in the Union line between Porter and Reynolds, who was on the left of Sigel, near Groveton.

The accompanying map, marked board map No. 1, illustrates the positions of the Union troops at noon of August 29, and the probable positions of the Confederate troops at the same time, as indicated by the information then in possession of the Union generals. This map is not intended to show the actual positions of the troops at that time, but to correctly interpret the information upon which the Union generals then acted.

This was the military situation on the Union left and Confederate right of the field when McDowell arrested Porter's advance, and Porter's operations under the direct orders from Pope heretofore mentioned ceased, and, under new orders just received, Porter became subordinate to McDowell.

Not only had the effort to destroy Jackson before he could be reenforced totally failed, but the Confederate army was on the field and in line, while the Union army was not. The time to resume defensive action, awaiting the concentration of the army, had not only arrived, but had been too long postponed.

On his way to the front McDowell had received the following order from General Pope, addressed jointly to him and Porter, and Porter had received a copy of the same order a moment before McDowell's arrival:

HEADQUARTERS ARMY OF Virginia,
Centreville, August 29, 1862.

Generals McDOWELL and PORTER:

You will please move forward with your joint commands toward Gainesville. I sent General Porter written orders to that effect an hour and a half ago. Heintzelman, Sigel, and Reno are moving on the Warrenton turnpike, and must now be not far from Gainesville. I desire that as soon as communication is established between this force and your own the whole command shall halt. It may be necessary to fall back behind Bull Run, at Centreville, to-night. I presume it will be so on account of our supplies. I have sent no orders of any description to Ricketts, and none to interfere in any way with the movements of McDowell's troops, except what I sent by his aide-de-camp last night, which were to hold his position on the Warrenton pike until the troops from here should fall upon the enemy's flank and rear. I do not even know Ricketts' position, as I have not been able to find out where General McDowell was until a late hour this morning. General McDowell will take immediate steps to communicate with General Ricketts, and instruct him to rejoin the other divisions of his corps as soon as practicable. If any considerable advantages are to be gained by departing from this order it will not be strictly carried out. One thing must be had in view, that the troops must occupy a position from which they can reach Bull Run to-night or by morning. The indications are that the whole force of the enemy is moving in this direction at a pace that will bring them here by to-morrow night or next day. My own headquarters will be for the present with Heintzelman's corps or at this place.

JOHN POPE,
Major-General, Commanding.

This order and the Sixty-second Article of War made it the duty of McDowell to command the combined corps so long as they should continue to act together and General Pope should be absent from the field. In this interpretation of the law Generals McDowell and Porter agreed, and upon it they acted at the time. Upon McDowell devolved the responsibility of modifying the joint order as its terms authorized and as the military situation seemed imperatively to require.

The terms of the order contemplating that communication should be established with the troops on the other road, or, as General McDowell interpreted it, that line should be formed in connection with those troops, that the whole command should then halt, and that the troops must not go beyond a point from which they could reach Bull Run by that night or the next morning, and the military situation, as it then appeared to them, was briefly discussed by the two generals.

The situation was exceedingly critical. If the enemy should attack, as he seemed about ready to do, Porter's two divisions, about 9,000 men, were all the force then ready to stand between Lee's main army, just arrived on the field, and McDowell's long and weary column, or the left flank of Pope's army near Groveton. McDowell was "excessively anxious" to get King's division over on the left of Reynolds, who then occupied with his small division that exposed flank; and he quickly decided that "considerable advantages" were "to be gained" by departing from the terms of the joint order, so far as to make no attempt to go farther toward Gainesville, and to at once form line with the troops then engaged near Groveton; and this departure from the strict letter of the joint order was evidently required by the military situation as it then appeared and as it did actually exist.

After this brief consultation the two generals rode together through the woods to the right about three-quarters of a mile toward Groveton, and made a personal examination of the ground. As soon as this was done, McDowell decided not to take the troops through these woods, but to separate his own corps from Porter's, take King's division (Ricketts following) around the woods by the Sudley Springs road, and thus put them in beyond the woods and on the left of Reynolds.

McDowell then left Porter very hurriedly, announcing his decision, as he testified, by the words, "You put your force in here, and I will take mine up the Sudley Springs road on the left of the troops engaged at that point against the enemy," or words to that effect. Even these few words, we are satisfied, Porter did not hear or did not understand, for he called, as McDowell rode away, "What shall I do?" and McDowell gave no audible answer, but only a wave of the hand. In this state of uncertainty, according to the testimony of one of General Porter's staff officers, Porter sent a message to King's division to ascertain positively if that division was ordered away by McDowell, and, if not, to give proper orders for its action with his corps, and a reply was returned by McDowell himself that he was going to the right and should take that division with him; that Porter had better stay where he was, and, if necessary to fall back, he could do so on McDowell's left.

This testimony has given rise to much controversy; but, in our opinion, the question whether that message was or was not sent is unimportant. If it was sent, it did not differ in substance from the instructions which General McDowell testifies he had previously given to General Porter, "You put your force in here," &c. Neither could be construed as directing what Porter's action should be, but only as deciding that he should continue on that line while McDowell would take his own troops to another part of the field.

There appears to have been an understanding, derived either from previous conversation or from the terms of the joint order, that when McDowell did get King's division on the other side of the woods Morell's division on the right of Porter's corps should make such connection or establish such communication with that of King as might be practicable through the woods. None of them then knew how wide was that belt of woods, nor what was its character beyond where they had reconnoitered, nor whether the ground beyond was in possession of the enemy.

When the two generals had started to take that ride to the right Morell's troops had been ordered to follow them, and Griffin's brigade had led off after its pickets had been called in. After McDowell took his departure this movement was continued for some time and until Griffin had crossed the railroad and reached a point near half way across the belt of woods and where the forest became dense. There the movement was arrested. This movement might have meant an attempt to stretch out Morell's line through the woods so as to connect with King's on the right or a completion of the deployment for an attack upon the enemy in front. General Porter explained it as intended for an immediate attack upon the enemy if he found he could keep King in support, and that he only desisted upon being informed that King was going away. But the attack would have been a rash one under the circumstances even with King's support. Soon after this scouts were sent on through the woods to look for King, Reynolds, Sigel, or some body of Union troops in the direction where artillery firing was heard.

Presently Griffin was withdrawn to the south side of the railroad. The enemy's artillery opened on his troops during this latter movement and was replied to by one of Morell's batteries, but few shots being fired on either side. Then Morell's division was put in defensive order to hold the ground then occupied and under cover from the enemy's artillery. The scouts sent through the woods ran upon the enemy's pickets and were driven back. This effort to get scouts through the woods was repeated from time to time until late in the afternoon, but every effort failed. The scouts were all driven back or captured. As it turned out, this resulted from the fact that King's division did not get up on the right of the woods at all. That division reached a point some distance in the rear of its position in the line about 4:30 P.M., and then, after some marching and counter-marching, was sent northward to the Warrenton pike. Thus the gap in the line which McDowell's troops were to occupy remained open all the afternoon and the margin of the timber remained in possession of the enemy's pickets.

These failures to connect or to communicate directly along the front were reported by Porter to McDowell by way of the Sudley Springs road, on which McDowell had gone. The reports were made in at least four different written dispatches, which have been preserved. The hour was named in only one, apparently the latest, sent at 6 o'clock in the evening. Two reports—one about 4 o'clock and the other about 6:30 P.M.—were sent to General Pope direct. Both of these were received by him, but have not been preserved.

About the time General McDowell arrived on the field at Porter's position, and for an hour or two thereafter, a heavy artillery combat was going on between the Union batteries near Groveton and the Confederate artillery. During this artillery combat, and until 5 o'clock P.M., there was no infantry engagement, except skirmishing and some short and sharp contests between small portions of the opposing forces, and until 6:30 P.M. no musketry was audible to any one in Porter's corps.

On the Confederate side, as it now appears, Porter's display of troops—-three brigades in line—-in the early part of the afternoon had given rise to the expectation of an attack on their right. This having been reported to General Longstreet, that commander sent his reserve division (Wilcox's) from his extreme left, just north of the Warrenton turnpike, to his extreme right, on the Manassas and Gainesville road. Wilcox reached this latter position about 4 o'clock P.M., and Porter having before that time withdrawn his troops under cover, some troops from the Confederate right (D. R. Jones') were pushed to the front in the woods occupied by Porter's skirmishers, apparently to reconnoiter. This movement gave rise to the impression among Porter's officer's (Morell's division) that the enemy was about to attack about 5 P.M.

General Pope having arrived some time after noon on the field in the rear of Groveton, and General McDowell's column approaching that part of the field by the Manassas and Sudley road, an attack was ordered upon the enemy's extreme left near Sudley, and a written order was sent, dated 4:30 P.M., to Porter to attack the enemy's right, and, if possible, his rear. After some time had elapsed, General Pope ordered McDowell, with King's division and other troops, to pursue up the Warrenton turnpike the enemy, who, thus to be assailed upon both flanks, would be compelled to retreat.

The attack on Jackson's left was begun by Kearny about 5 P.M.; but the order to Porter was not delivered in time. The messenger did not find General Porter until sunset. Thus at 5 o'clock, nothing having occurred to suggest to General Porter any change in the plan indicated in the joint order to retire behind Bull Run, instead of giving battle that day, the sound of artillery near Sudley, so much apparently to the rear of Groveton, suggested to Porter, who was then at Bethlehem Church, that Sigel was retiring or perhaps being driven back, and that his artillery was then in a new position near the Sudley Springs road.

If it was true that Sigel was being driven back the military situation was extremely perilous, and Porter must instantly do what he could to avert disaster. His order to Morell, which must have been issued at that instant, shows what he proposed to do. It is as follows, viz:

> General MORELL:
>
> Push over to the aid of Sigel and strike in his rear. If you reach a road up which King is moving, and he has got ahead of you, let him pass; but see if you cannot give help to Sigel. If you find him retiring, move back toward Manassas, and, should necessity require it, and you do not hear from me, push to Centreville. If you find the direct road filled, take the one via Union Mills, which is to the right as you return.
>
> F. J. PORTER,
> *Major-General.*
>
> Look to the points of the compass for Manassas.
>
> F. J. PORTER.

This movement would have left Porter with Sykes alone to hold the Manassas road and cover the retreat of Ricketts' worn-out troops, who then were stretched along the road for 4 or 5 miles both toward Sudley and back toward Manassas Junction, while Morell should cover the retreat of the center of the army. But now, before Morell had time to commence this movement, came a report from him that the enemy was coming down in force to attack both his front and flank. Porter might in a few minutes have to meet the attack of 20,000 men. The purpose to cover the retreat of Sigel must needs be abandoned. Hence Porter dispatched to Morell:

General MORELL:
Hold on, if you can, to your present place. What is passing?
F. J. PORTER.

Again:

General MORELL:
Tell me what is passing quickly. If the enemy is coming, hold to him and I will come up. Post your men to repulse him.
F. J. PORTER,
Major-General.

And again, in reply to advice from Morell that they had better retire, &c.:

We cannot retire while McDowell holds on.

Notwithstanding contradictory testimony, we believe it was at this time that Porter ordered Piatt's brigade, of Sturgis' command, about 800 men, to move back to Manassas Junction and take up a defensive position to cover the expected retreat.

General Porter reported to General McDowell his views and intentions in the following dispatches:

Generals McDOWELL and KING:
I found it impossible to communicate by crossing the woods to Groveton. The enemy are in great force on this road, and as they

appear to have driven our forces back, the fire of the enemy having advanced and ours retired, I have determined to withdraw to Manassas. I have attempted to communicate with McDowell and Sigel, but my messengers have run into the enemy. They have gathered artillery and cavalry and infantry, and the advancing masses of dust show the enemy coming in force. I am now going to the head of the column to see what is passing and how affairs are going, and I will communicate with you. Had you not better send your train back?

F. J. PORTER,
Major-General.

General McDOWELL or KING:

I have been wandering over the woods and failed to get a communication to you. Tell how matters go with you. The enemy is in strong force in front of me, and I wish to know your designs for to-night. If left to me, I shall have to retire for food and water, which I cannot get here. How goes the battle? It seems to go to our rear. The enemy are getting to our left.

F. J. PORTER,
Major-General Volunteers.

General McDOWELL:
The firing on my right has so far retired that, as I cannot advance and have failed to get over to you except by the route taken by King, I shall withdraw to Manassas. If you have anything to communicate, please do so. I have sent many messengers to you and General Sigel and get nothing.

F. J. PORTER,
Major-general.

An artillery duel is going on now; been skirmishing for a long time.

F. J. P.

General McDOWELL:

Failed in getting Morell over to you. After wandering about the woods for a time I withdrew him, and while doing so artillery opened upon us. My scouts could not get through. Each one found the enemy between us, and I believe some have been captured. Infantry are also in front. I am trying to get a battery, but have not succeeded as yet. From the masses of dust on our left and from reports of scouts think the enemy are moving largely in that way. Please communicate the way this messenger came. I have no cavalry or messengers now. Please let me know your designs, whether you retire or not. I cannot get water and am out of provisions. Have lost a few men from infantry firing.

F. J. PORTER,
Major-General Volunteers.

AUGUST 29, 6 P.M.

But Porter soon found the sounds of artillery had deceived him. The renewal of the firing toward Groveton showed that Pope's troops were still there. Piatt's brigade was then recalled, and no further preparations for retreat were made.

Next came to Porter about 5:30 o'clock a report from the right that the enemy was in full retreat and heavy sounds of musketry soon after showed that serious work had commenced near Groveton. Porter ordered Morell to make a strong reconnaissance to learn the truth. Morell, knowing the report must be false, at least as to the enemy in his front, prepared to support this reconnaissance with his whole division. While this preparation was being made came the long-delayed order, dated 4:30 P.M., to attack the enemy in flank or rear:

HEADQUARTERS IN THE FIELD,
August 29—4:30 P.M.

Major-General PORTER:

Your line of march brings you in on the enemy's right flank. I desire you to push forward into action at once on the enemy's flank, and, if possible, on his rear, keeping your right in communication with General Reynolds. The enemy is massed in the woods in front of us, but can be shelled out as soon as you engage their flank. Keep heavy reserves and use your batteries, keeping well closed to your right all the time In case you are obliged to fall back, do so to your right and rear, so as to keep you in close communication with the right wing.

JOHN POPE,
Major-General, Commanding.

This order, though dated at 4:30 P.M., was not received by Porter, at Bethlehem Church, before 6:30 P.M. The evidence before the court-martial tending to show that Porter received the "'4:30" order in time to execute it is found in the testimony of the officer who carried the order, and of one of the orderlies who accompanied him. Neither of these two witnesses appears to have carried a watch, and their several statements of the time when the order was delivered were based on estimates of the time occupied by them in riding from General Pope's headquarters to the place where they found General Porter. One of them at least knew from an inspection of the order that it was dated at 4:30; he, and probably both of them, therefore assumed that it was then that they started to deliver it, and adding to that hour the estimated time occupied by them, they severally fixed the hour of delivery. It is now proved by the testimony of the officer who wrote the dispatch that "4:30" was not the hour when the messenger started, but was the hour when he began to write the dispatch, and consequently that it was after that hour that the officer started to deliver it.

It is also shown that these messengers did not and could not, if other parts of their own testimony are true, have traveled over the route which they supposed they had taken. Moreover, it was proved by unquestionable testimony that since the court-martial trial one of these witnesses had made statements and admissions inconsistent with and contradictory of his former testimony, and the other witness confessed before us that recently he had deliberately made false statements in regard to the route taken while carrying the dispatch. We have therefore felt compelled to lay the testimony of these witnesses out of the case. An attempt was made to support these witnesses by the testimony of another person, who, as it was alleged, also accompanied, as an orderly, the officer charged with the dispatch, but his testimony was so completely broken down by cross-examination that we regard it as entitled to no weight whatever.

On the other hand, the testimony of General Sykes, Lieutenant-Colonel Locke, Captain Montieth, Lieutenant Ingham, and Lieutenant

Weld before the court-martial that the order in question was not delivered until about sundown, either a little before or a little after that hour, has now been supported by a new and entirely independent witness, Captain Randel, and has been singularly confirmed by the production, for the first time, of the dispatch from Porter to McDowell, dated 6 P.M., the terms of which utterly forbid the supposition that at that time Porter had received the order.

The moment this order was received Porter sent his chief of staff, Colonel Locke, to General Morell, with orders to make the attack at once. He then wrote and sent a reply to Pope, and immediately rode to the front. On his arrival there Morell had about completed his preparations for the attack under the previous order to make a reconnaissance, but darkness had already come on. It was evidently impossible to accomplish any good that night, for, even if Morell might have begun the attack before dark, Sykes could not have been got into line after the order was received. The contest at Groveton had already so far spent its force as to derive no possible aid from Morell's attack. The order was based upon conditions manifestly erroneous and directed what was impossible to be done. To push Morell's division against the enemy in the dark would have been in no sense obedience to that order. Porter wisely ordered the preparations to cease, and the troops were put into position to pass the night, picketing in all directions, for Porter had but a few mounted men, and the enemy had 2,500 cavalry near his flank.

About this time, when darkness had come on, the rear of McDowell's column of weary troops was passing by the rear of Porter's column, still several miles from their destined place on the field. The Union army was not even yet ready for battle.

The accompanying maps, marked board maps, Nos. 2 and 3, exhibit substantially the military situation at the time the 4:30 P.M. order was issued, and that which was then understood by General Pope to exist, as explained to the court-martial upon the trial of General Porter.

We believe this plain and simple narrative of the events of the 29th of August clearly shows the true character of General Porter's conduct during that time. We are unable to find in that conduct anything subject to criticism, much less deserving of censure or condemnation.

Porter's duty that afternoon was too plain and simple to admit of discussion. It was to hold his position and cover the deployment of McDowell's troops until the latter, or some of them, should get into line; then to connect with them as far as might be necessary and practicable, and then, in the absence of further orders, to act in concert with those troops and others to the right.

If King's division had come up on the right, as was expected, and had advanced to attack, Porter would have known it instantly, and thus could have joined in the movement.

If the main army retired, as indicated in the joint order, it was Porter's duty to retire also, after having held his ground long enough to protect its left flank and to cover the retreat of Ricketts' troops.

Porter did for a moment entertain the purpose of trying to give aid to Sigel, who was supposed to be retiring before McDowell had got King's division up to his support. That was the nearest to making a mistake that Porter came that afternoon. But it soon enough became evident that such a purpose must be abandoned; Porter had quite his full share of responsibility where he was.

The preparations made for retreat were the ordinary soldierly dispositions to enable him to do promptly what he had good reason to expect he might be required to do at any moment and must do at nightfall.

He made frequent reports to his superiors, stating what he had done and what he had been unable to do; what his situation was in respect to the enemy in his front and the strength of the enemy there; what his impressions were from the sounds of action toward his right; how he had failed thus far to get any communications from any commander in the main army, or any orders from General Pope, asking McDowell, who was nearest to him, for such information and his (McDowell's) designs for the night; sending an aide-de-camp to General Pope for orders and receiving no reply, not even information that the 4:30 order had been sent to him; and, finally, informing his superiors that if left to himself, without orders, he would have to retire at night for food and water, which he could not get where he was. These reports were sent not only frequently, but early enough to insure the receipt of orders from Pope or correct information from McDowell, if they had any to send him, before it would be time for him to withdraw. All these dispatches were sent in the latter part of the afternoon. They all indicated a purpose to retire only after being assured that the main army was retiring, and then to cover the retreat of the army as far as possible, or to withdraw after night-fall, as the joint order had indicated, if no further orders or information of General Pope's plans could be obtained.

There is no indication in any of those dispatches, when fairly construed, nor in anything which Porter did or said, of any intention to withdraw until after dark, unless compelled to do so by the retreat of the main army; and even then he was compelled to hold on until McDowell's troops could get out of the way, and that was not until after dark, for Ricketts' division was on the road in Porter's rear all the afternoon.

It is perfectly clear that Porter had no thought whatever of retreating from the enemy, or of withdrawing because of the enemy in his front; for when the enemy was reported advancing as if to attack his orders were: "If the enemy is coming, hold to him." "Post your troops to repulse him." "We cannot retire while McDowell holds on."

It appears to have been assumed in the condemnation of General Porter's conduct that he had some order to attack or some information of aggressive plans on the part of General Pope, or some intimation, suggestion, or direction to that effect from General McDowell, or that there was such a battle going on within his hearing, or something else in the military situation that required him to attack the enemy without orders before receiving the 4:30 P.M. order at sunset. All this was the exact reverse of the truth. General Pope's last order, General McDowell's directions while he was with General Porter, the military situation as then known to both Porter and McDowell, and the movement McDowell had decided to make to get his own troops into line of battle and the state of the action on the right of the field, all combined to absolutely forbid any attack by Porter during that entire afternoon until he received Pope's order at sunset, and even that order could not possibly have been given if the situation had been correctly understood. An attack by him would have been a violation of the spirit of his orders and a criminal blunder, leading to inevitable disaster. In short, he had no choice as a faithful soldier but to do substantially what he did do.

The range of our investigation has not enabled us to ascertain the source of the great error which was committed in the testimony before General Porter's court-martial respecting the time of arrival of the main body of Lee's army on the field of Manassas. But the information which was in possession of the Union officers at noon of the 29th of August, and afterward published in their official reports, together with the testimony before the court-martial, affords clear, explicit, and convincing proof that the main body of that army must have been there on the field at that time.

The recent testimony of Confederate officers hardly adds anything to the conclusiveness of that proof, but rather diminishes its force, by showing that one division (Anderson's) did not arrive until the next morning; while the information in their possession at that time required the Union officers to assume that that division as well as the others had arrived on the 29th. Yet General Porter's conduct was adjudged upon the assumption that not more than one division under Longstreet had arrived on the field and that Porter had no considerable force in his front.

The fact is that Longstreet, with four divisions of full 25,000 men, was there on the field before Porter arrived with his two divisions of 9,000 men; that the Confederate General-in-Chief was there in person at least two or three hours before the commander of the Army of Virginia himself arrived on the field, and that Porter with his two divisions saved the Army of Virginia that day from the disaster naturally due to the enemy's earlier preparation for battle.

If the 4:30 order had been promptly delivered a very grave responsibility would have devolved upon General Porter. The order was based upon conditions which were essentially erroneous and upon expectations which could not possibly be realized.

It required an attack upon the enemy's flank or rear, which could not be made, and that the attacking force keep closed on Reynolds, who was far to the right and beyond reach. Yet it would have been too late to correct the error and have the order modified. That order appeared to be part of a general plan. It must be executed promptly or not at all.

If Porter had made not the impossible attack which was ordered, but a direct attack upon the enemy's right wing, would he have been blameless for the fruitless sacrifice of his troops? We believe not. It is a well-established military maxim that a corps commander is not justifiable in making an apparently hopeless attack in obedience to an order from a superior who is not on the spot, and who is evidently in error in respect to the essential conditions upon which the order is based. The duty of the corps commander in such a case is to make not a real attack, but a strong demonstration, so as to prevent the enemy in his front from sending re-enforcements to other parts of his line.

This is all that Porter would have been justifiable in doing even if he had received the 4:30 order at 5 o'clock; and such a demonstration, or even a real attack made after 5 o'clock by Porter alone, could have had no beneficial effect whatever upon the general result. It would not have diminished in the least the resistance offered to the attacks made at other points that afternoon. The display of troops made by Porter earlier in the afternoon had all the desired and all possible beneficial effect. It caused Longstreet's reserve division to be sent to his extreme right in front of Porter's position. There that division remained until about 6 o'clock—too late for it to take any effective part in the operations at other points of the line.

A powerful and well-sustained attack by the combined forces of Porter's corps and King's division upon the enemy's right wing, if it had been commenced early in the afternoon, might have drawn to that part of the field so large a part of Longstreet's force as to have given Pope some chance of success against Jackson; but an attack by Porter alone could have been but an ineffective blow, destructive only to the force that made it, and, followed by a counter-attack, disastrous to the Union army. Such an attack, under such circumstances, would have been not only a great blunder, but, on the part of an intelligent officer, it would have been a great crime.

What General Porter actually did do, although his situation was by no means free from embarrassment and anxiety at the time, now seems to have been only the simple, necessary action which an intelligent soldier had no choice but to take. It is not possible that any court-martial could have condemned such conduct if it had been correctly understood. On the contrary, that conduct was obedient, subordinate, faithful, and judicious. It saved the Union army from disaster on the 29th of August.

This ends the transactions upon which were based the charges of which General Porter was pronounced guilty; but some account of the part taken by him and his corps in the events of the following day, August 30, which gave rise to a charge which was withdrawn, is necessary to a full understanding of the merits of the case.

At 3 A.M. of the 30th General Porter received the following order, and in compliance with it promptly withdrew from his position in presence of the enemy and marched rapidly by the Sudley road to the center of the battlefield, where he reported to General Pope for orders:

HEADQUARTERS ARMY OF VIRGINIA,
In the Field, near Bull Run, August 29, 1862—8.50 P.M.

Maj. Gen. F. J. PORTER:

Immediately upon receipt of this order, the precise hour of receiving which you will acknowledge, you will march your command to the field of battle of to-day and report to me in person for orders. You are to understand that you are expected to comply strictly with this order, and to be present on the field within three hours after its reception, or after daybreak to-morrow morning.

JOHN POPE,
Major-General, Commanding.

(Received August 30, 3:30 A.M.)

At first sight it would appear that in this prompt and unhesitating movement under this order General Porter committed a grave fault. He was already on the field of battle, confronting the enemy in force, and holding a position of vital importance to the security of Pope's army; while the latter appeared from the order to be wholly in the dark respecting these all-important facts. It is true the order was most positive, imperative, and also distrustful in its terms. But those very terms served to show only the more forcibly that the order was based upon a total misapprehension of the essential facts, without which misapprehension it would not seem possible that such an order could have been issued. The well-established military rule is that such an order must never be obeyed until the commander who gave it has been informed of his error and given an opportunity to correct it; but, upon close examination, the opposite view of Porter's conduct under this order appears to be the just one.

Porter had repeatedly reported to McDowell the presence of the enemy in large force in his front. Presumably these reports had gone to Pope, as one of them had in fact. Porter had also sent an aide-de-camp with a written message to Pope about 4 P.M., and had sent a written reply to the 4:30 P.M. order after 6:30 P.M. These last two dispatches have not been preserved by General Pope, and hence their contents are not known to us; but we are bound to presume that they reported the situation as Porter then knew it, and as he had frequently reported it to McDowell, and the last of these dispatches, in reply to the 4:30 P.M. order, was later than the latest of those in which Porter had spoken of any intention to fall back. Hence Porter had already given to his superior all the information which it was possible for him to give, and nothing remained for him but to obey the order. This movement of Porter's corps on the morning of the 30th was the beginning of the unfortunate operation of that day. This corps, which had been protecting the left flank of Pope's army, was withdrawn from its important position, leaving the left wing and flank exposed to attack by greatly superior force of the enemy, brought to the center of the field and then ordered "in pursuit of the enemy":

> August 30, 1862—-12 m.
> *HEADQUARTERS, NEAR GROVETON.*
>
> The following forces will be immediately thrown forward in pursuit of the enemy and press him vigorously during the whole day. Major-General McDowell is assigned to the command of the pursuit; Major-General Porter's corps will push forward on the Warrenton turnpike, followed by the divisions of Brigadier-Generals King and Reynolds. The division of Brigadier-General Ricketts will pursue the Hay Market road, followed by the corps of Major-General Heintzelman. The necessary cavalry will be assigned to these columns by Major-General McDowell, to whom regular and frequent reports will be made. The general headquarters will be somewhere on the Warrenton turnpike.
>
> By command of Major-General Pope:
>
> GEORGE D. RUGGLES,
> *Colonel and Chief of Staff.*

> HEADQUARTERS THIRD CORPS, *ARMY OF VIRGINIA,*
> *August 30, 1862.*
>
> Major-General PORTER:
>
> Major-General McDowell, being charged with the advanced forces ordered to pursue the enemy, directs me to inform you that your corps will be followed immediately by King's division, supported by Reynolds. Heintzelman, with his corps, preceded by Ricketts' division, will move on your right, on the road from Sudley

Springs to Hay Market. He is instructed to throw out skirmishers to the left, which is desirable you should join with your right. General McDowell's headquarters will be at the head of Reynolds' division, on the Warrenton road. Organize a strong advance to precede your command, and push on rapidly in pursuit of the enemy until you come in contact with him. Report frequently. Bayard's brigade will be ordered to report to you; push it well to the left as you advance.

Very respectfully, your obedient servant,

ED. SCHRIVER,
Colonel and Chief of Staff.

These orders led to an attack upon the Confederate left wing, Jackson's command, made mainly by Butterfield's and Barnes' brigades, of Morell's division, and by Sykes' division, which is described as follows by the Confederate generals:

[EXTRACT FROM GENERAL LEE'S REPORT OF OPERATIONS OF THE ARMY OF NORTHERN VIRGINIA, BATTLE OF MANASSAS.]

HEADQUARTERS ARMY OF NORTHERN VIRGINIA,
March 6, 1863.

SIR: * * * About 3 P.M. the enemy, having massed his troops in front of General Jackson, advanced against his position in strong force. His front line pushed forward until engaged at close quarters by Jackson's troops, when its progress was checked, and a fierce and bloody struggle ensued. A second and third line, of great strength, moved up to support the first, but in doing so came within easy range of a position a little in advance of Longstreet's left. He immediately ordered up two batteries, and two others being thrown forward about the same time by Col. S. D. Lee, under their well-directed and destructive fire the supporting lines were broken and fell back in confusion. Their repeated efforts to rally were unavailing, and Jackson's troops, being thus relieved from the pressure of overwhelming numbers, began to press steadily forward, driving the enemy before them. He retreated in confusion, suffering severely from our artillery, which advanced as he retired. General Longstreet, anticipating the order for a general advance, now threw his whole command against the Federal center and left. * * *

I have the honor to be, very respectfully, your obedient servant,

R. E. LEE,

General S. COOPER,
Adjutant and Inspector General,
Richmond, Va.

[EXTRACT FROM THE REPORT OF GENERAL JAMES LONGSTREET, OCTOBER 10, 1862.]

* * * During the day Col. S. D. Lee, with his reserve artillery placed in the position occupied the day previous by Colonel Walton, engaged the enemy in a very severe artillery combat. The result was, as the day previous, a success. At 3:30 o'clock in the afternoon I rode to the front for the purpose of completing arrangements for making a diversion in favor of a flank movement then under contemplation. Just after reaching my front line I received a message for re-enforcements for General Jackson, who was said to be severely pressed. From an eminence near by one portion of the enemy's masses attacking General Jackson were immediately within my view and in easy range of batteries in that position. It gave me an advantage that I had not expected to have, and I made haste to use it. Two batteries were ordered for the purpose, and one placed in position immediately and opened. Just as this fire began I received a message from the commanding general informing me of General Jackson's condition and his wants. As it was evident that the attack against General Jackson could not be continued ten minutes under the fire of these batteries, I made no movement with my troops.

[EXTRACT FROM THE REPORT OF GENERAL JACKSON OF OPERATIONS FROM AUGUST 15 TO SEPTEMBER 5, 1862.]

HEADQUARTERS SECOND CORPS,
ARMY OF NORTHERN VIRGINIA,
April 27, 1863.

GENERAL: After some desultory skirmishing and heavy cannonading during the day the Federal infantry, about 4 o'clock in the evening, moved from under cover of the wood and advanced in several lines, first engaging the right, but soon extending its attack to the center and left. In a few moments our entire line was engaged a fierce and sanguinary struggle with the enemy. As one line was repulsed another took its place and pressed forward as if determined, by force of numbers and fury of assault, to drive us from our positions. So impetuous and well sustained were these onsets as to induce me to send to the commanding general for re-enforcements; but the timely and gallant advance of General Longstreet on the right relieved my troops from the pressure of overwhelming numbers, and gave to these brave men the chances of a more equal conflict. As Longstreet pressed upon the right the Federal advance was checked, and soon a general advance of my whole line was ordered.

T. J. JACKSON,
Lieutenant-General

Brig. Gen. R. H. CHILTON,
Acting Assistant Adjutant-General, Headquarters Department A. N. V.

As Longstreet's army pressed forward to strike Pope's exposed left wing and flank, Warren, with his little brigade, sprang into the gap and breasted the storm until but a handful of his brave men were left alive. Then Sykes, with his disciplined brigades, and Reynolds, with his gallant Pennsylvania Reserves, seized the commanding ground in rear, and, like a rock, withstood the advance of the victorious enemy and saved the Union army from rout.

Thus did this gallant corps nobly and amply vindicate the character of their trusted chief, and demonstrate to all the world that "disobedience of orders" and "misbehavior in the presence of the enemy" are crimes which could not possibly find place in the head or heart of him who thus commanded that corps.

These events of the 30th of August were excluded from the evidence before the court-martial that tried General Porter; but justice requires that they should be mentioned here as having an important bearing upon the question of animus, which was so strongly dwelt upon in the review of Porter's case by the Judge-Advocate-General.

The foregoing is the simple history of the part taken by Porter and his corps in the events which gave rise to the following charges and specifications, findings and sentence, and executive action.

❋ ❋ ❋

These charges and specifications certainly bear no discernible resemblance to the facts of the case as now established. Yet it has been our duty to carefully compare with these facts the views entertained by the court-martial, as shown in the findings and in the review of the case which was prepared for the information of the President by the Judge-Advocate-General who had conducted the prosecution, and tends to clearly perceive every error into which the court-martial was led. We trust it is not necessary for us to submit in detail the results of this comparison, and that it will be sufficient for us to point out the fundamental errors, and to say that all the essential facts in every instance stand out in clear and absolute contrast to those supposed facts upon which General Porter was adjudged guilty.

The fundamental errors upon which the conviction of General Porter depended may be summed up in few words. It was maintained, and apparently established to the satisfaction of the court-martial, that only about one-half of the Confederate Army was on the field of Manassas on the 29th of August, while General Lee, with the other half, was still beyond the Bull Run Mountains; that General Pope's army, exclusive of Porter's corps, was engaged in a severe and nearly equal contest with the enemy, and only needed the aid of a flank attack which Porter was expected to make to insure the defeat and destruction or capture of the Confederate force in their front under General Jackson; that McDowell and Porter, with their joint forces, Porter's leading, had advanced toward Gainesville until the head of their column had reached a point near the Warrenton turnpike, where they found a division of Confederate troops, "seventeen regiments," which Buford had counted as they passed through Gainesville, marching along the road across Porter's front, and going toward the field of battle at Groveton; that

McDowell ordered Porter to at once attack that column thus moving to join Jackson, or the flank and rear of the line if they had formed in line, while he would take his own troops by the Sudley Springs road and throw them upon the enemy's center near Groveton; that Porter, McDowell having then separated from him, disobeyed that order to attack, allowed that division of the enemy's troops to pass him unmolested, and then fell back and retreated toward Manassas Junction; that Porter then remained in the rear all the afternoon, listening to the sounds of battle and coolly contemplating a presumed defeat of his comrades on the center and right of the field; that this division of the enemy having passed Porter's column and formed on the right of Jackson's line, near Groveton, an order was sent to Porter to attack the right flank or rear of the enemy's line, upon which his own line of march must bring him, but that he had willfully disobeyed, and made no attempt to execute that order; that in this way was lost the opportunity to destroy Jackson's detached force before the other wing of General Lee's army could join it, and that this junction having been effected during the night of the 29th, the defeat of General Pope's army on the 30th thus resulted from General Porter's neglect and disobedience.

Now, in contrast to these fundamental errors, the following all-important facts are fully established:

As Porter was advancing toward Gainesville, and while yet nearly 4 miles from that place and more than 2 miles from the nearest point of the Warrenton turnpike, he met the right wing of the Confederate army, 25,000 strong, which had arrived on the field that morning and was already in line of battle. Not being at that moment quite fully informed of the enemy's movements, and being then under orders from Pope to push rapidly toward Gainesville, Porter was pressing forward to attack the enemy in his front, when McDowell arrived on the field with later information of the enemy, and later and very different orders from Pope, assumed the command, and arrested Porter's advance. This latter information left no room for doubt that the main body of Lee's army was already on the field and far in advance of Pope's army in preparation for battle. General McDowell promptly decided not to attempt to go farther to the front, but to deploy his column so as to form line in connection with General Pope's right wing, which was then engaged with Jackson. To do this General McDowell separated his corps entirely from General Porter's, and thus relinquished the command

and all right to the command of Porter's corps. McDowell did not give Porter any order to attack, nor did he give him any order whatever to govern his action after their separation.

It does not appear from the testimony that he conveyed to General Porter in any way the erroneous view of the military situation which was afterward maintained before the court-martial, nor that he suggested to General Porter any expectation that he would make an attack. On the contrary the testimony of all the witnesses as to what was actually said and done; the information which McDowell and Porter then had respecting the enemy, and the movement which McDowell decided to make, and did make, with his own troops, prove conclusively that there was left no room for doubt in Porter's mind that his duty was to stand on the defensive and hold his position until McDowell's movement could be completed. It would have indicated a great error of military judgment to have done or ordered the contrary, in the situation as then fully known to both McDowell and Porter.

General Pope appears from his orders and from his testimony to have been at that time wholly ignorant of the true situation. He had disapproved of the sending of Ricketts to Thoroughfare Gap to meet Longstreet on the 28th, believing that the main body of Lee's army could not reach the field of Manassas before the night of the 30th. Hence he sent the order to Porter dated 4:30 P.M., to attack Jackson's right flank or rear. Fortunately that order did not reach Porter until about sunset—too late for any attack to be made. Any attack which Porter could have made at any time that afternoon must necessarily have been fruitless of any good result. Porter's faithful, subordinate, and intelligent conduct that afternoon saved the Union army from the defeat which would otherwise have resulted that day from the enemy's more speedy concentration. The only seriously critical period of that campaign, viz, between 11 A.M. and sunset of August 29, was thus safely passed. Porter had understood and appreciated the military situation, and, so far as he had acted upon his own judgment, his action had been wise and judicious. For the disaster of the succeeding day he was in no degree responsible. Whoever else may have been responsible, it did not flow from any action or inaction of his.

The judgment of the court-martial upon General Porter's conduct was evidently based upon greatly erroneous impressions, not only respecting what that conduct really was and the orders under which he was acting, but also respecting all the circumstances under which he acted. Especially was this true in respect to the character of the battle of the 29th of August. That battle consisted of a number of sharp and gallant combats between small portions of the opposing forces. Those combats were of short duration and were separated by long intervals of simple skirmishing and artillery duels. Until after 6 o'clock only a small part of the troops on either side were engaged at any time during the afternoon. Then, about sunset, one additional division on each side was engaged near Groveton. The musketry of that last contest and the yells of the Confederate troops about dark were distinctly heard by the officers of Porter's corps; but at no other time during all that afternoon was the volume of musketry such that it could be heard at the position of Porter's troops. No sound but that of artillery was heard by them during all those hours when Porter was understood by the court-martial to have been listening to the sounds of a furious battle raging immediately to his right. And those sounds of artillery were by no means such as to indicate a general battle.

The reports of the 29th and those of the 30th of August have somehow been strangely confounded with each other. Even the Confederate reports have, since the termination of the war, been similarly misconstrued. Those of the 30th have been misquoted as referring to the 29th, thus to prove that a furious battle was going on while Porter was comparatively inactive on the 29th. The fierce and gallant struggle of his own troops on the 30th has thus been used to sustain the original error under which he was condemned. General Porter was, in effect, condemned for not having taken any part in his own battle. Such was the error upon which General Porter was pronounced guilty of the most shameful crime known among soldiers. We believe not one among all the gallant soldiers on that bloody field was less deserving of such condemnation than he.

The evidence of bad animus in Porter's case ceases to be material in view of the evidence of his soldierly and faithful conduct. But it is our duty to say that the indiscreet and unkind terms in which General Porter expressed his distrust of the capacity of his superior commander cannot be defended. And to that indiscretion was due, in very great measure, the misinterpretation of both his motives and his conduct and his consequent condemnation.

Having thus given the reasons for our conclusions, we have the honor to report, in accordance with the President's order, that in our opinion justice requires at his hands such action as may be necessary to annul and set aside the findings and sentence of the court-martial in the case of Maj. Gen. Fitz John Porter, and to restore him to the positions of which that sentence deprived him—such restoration to take effect from the date of his dismissal from the service.

Very respectfully, your obedient servants,

J. M. SCHOFIELD,
Major-General U. S. Army.
ALFRED H. TERRY,
Brigadier-General U.S. S. Army.
GEO. W. GETTY,
Brevet Major-General, U. S. Army,
Colonel Third Artillery.[1]

Endnotes

Preface

1. Kenneth P. Williams, *Lincoln Finds a General*, II, 788.
2. Fletcher Pratt, *Stanton: Lincoln's Secretary of War*, 482–483.
3. Stephen W. Sears, *Controversaries & Commanders: Dispatches from the Army of the Potomac*, 71, quoting Allan Nevins, *The War for the Union: War Becomes Revolution*, 1862–1863, 400.
4. Sears, 64, citing R. E. Lee interview, February 19, 1870, William Allen Papers, Southern Historical Society, University of North Carolina.

Prologue

1. *War of the Rebellion: Official Records of the Union and Confederate Armies*, Series I, 16, / Volume XII, Part 2, 512.
2. Otto Eisenschiml, *The Celebrated Case of Fitz John Porter*, 188–191.
3. Ibid., 211.
4. O.R., 16, / XII, Part 2, 512.

Chapter One

1. Otto Eisenschiml, *The Celebrated Case of Fitz John Porter*, 18–20; Patricia L. Faust, editor, *Historical Times Encyclopedia of the Civil War*, 594–595.
2. Association of Graduates, *Register of Graduates and Former Cadets of the United States Military Academy*, 269–270.
3. K. Jack Bauer, *The Mexican War, 1846–1848*, 318–319.
4. Eisenschiml, 20.
5. Ibid., 21; Sears, *George B. McClellan: The Young Napoleon*, 30.
6. Eisenschiml, 21; Sears, *George B. McClellan*, 36–41.
7. Sears, *George B. McClellan*, 43–49.
8. Eisenschiml, 21.
9. Ibid., 22; *War of the Rebellion: Official Records of the Union and Confederate Armies*, Series I, 1 / Volume I, 70–72. 22.
10. Eisenschiml, 2*3; O.R.*, 1 / I, / 534, 587–588.
11. Eisenschiml, 22–25.
12. Sears, *George B. McClellan*, 66–67.
13. Eisenschiml, 24–25.
14. Ibid., 24.
15. Ibid., 24–25.
16. Ibid., 25.
17. Ibid., 26–27.
18. Curt Anders, *Hearts in Conflict: A One-Volume History of the Civil War*, 47–49.
19. Shelby Foote, *The Civil War*, I, 82–83; Margaret Leech, *Reveille in Washington*, 100–101.
20. David Herbert Donald, *Lincoln*, 307.
21. Kenneth P. Williams, *Lincoln Finds a General*, I, 104.
22. Stephen W. Sears, *The Civil War Papers of George B. McClellan*, 70.
23. Eisenschiml, 27.
24. See Appendix I, Prominent Radicals.

25. Hans L. Trefousse. *The Radical Republicans: Lincoln's Vanguard for Social Justice*, 168.
26. T. Harry Williams, *Lincoln and the Radicals*, 10.
27. Ibid., 13
28. T. Harry Williams, 15–16; Trefousse, *The Radical Republicans*, 23.
29. For accounts of Ball's Bluff, see Byron Farwell, *Ball's Bluff: A Small Battle and its Long Shadow*, and Kim Bernard Holien, *Battle at Ball's Bluff.*
30. Bruce Tap, *Over Lincoln's Shoulder: The Committee on the Conduct of the War*, 38–80.
31. Charles Winslow Elliott, *Winfield Scott: The Soldier and the Man*, 730–738.
32. Foote, I, 108–110.
33. Sears, *George B. McClellan*, 147–167.
34. Foote, I, 253.
35. George B. McClellan, *McClellan's Own Story*, 165.
36. Ibid., 164–165.
37. T. Harry Williams, 125–132.
38. Sears, *Civil War Papers*, 230.
39. *O.R.*, 12 / XI, Part 1, 15. Emphasis supplied.
40. Clifford Dowdey, *The Seven Days*, 40–42.
41. McClellan, 309–310.
42. *New York Herald*, April 16, 1862.
43. Dowdey, 84–127.
44. Foote, I, 465.

Chapter Two

1. Stephen W. Sears, *The Civil War Papers of George B. McClellan*, 250.
2. *War of the Rebellion: Official Records of the Union and Confederate Armies*, Series I, Volume 12, / XI, Part 1, 43.
3. Ibid., 47.
4. Ibid., 89–93.
5. Sears, *Civil War Papers*, 297–298.
6. *O.R.*, 12, / XI, Part 1, 48; Sears, *Civil War Papers*, 299. Emphasis supplied.
7. David Herbert Donald, *Lincoln*, 357; Stephen W. Sears, *George B. McClellan: The Young Napoleon*, 203, citing Marble Papers, Library of Congress.
8. Sears, *Civil War Papers*, 304; *George B. McClellan*, 204.
9. *O.R.*, 12, / XI, Part 1, 48.
10. Donald, 361; Patricia L. Faust, editor, *Historical Times Encyclopedia of the Civil War*, 593.
11. See Hans L. Trefousse, *The Radical Republicans: Lincoln's Vanguard for Social Justice*, 198; T. Harry Williams, *Lincoln and the Radicals*, 142; *New York Tribune*, June 27, 1862.
12. *O.R.*, 18, / XII, Part 3, 435.
13. Clifford Dowdey, *The Seven Days*, 148–157.
14. *O.R.*, 12, / XI, Part 1, 50.
15. Ibid., 13, / XI, Part 2, 221–222.
16. This account of the battle of Mechanicsville is based mainly on Dowdey, 168–192. See also Stephen W. Sears, *To the Gates of Richmond: The Peninsula Campaign*, 195–209.
17. *O.R.*, 13, / XI, Part 2, 224.
18. Otto Eisenschiml, *The Celebrated Case of Fitz John Porter*, 36.
19. Dowdey, 210–224; Sears, *To the Gates of Richmond*, 210–248.
20. Dowdey, 227.
21. *O.R.*, 14, / XI, Part 3, 264.
22. Ibid.
23. Ibid., 264–265.
24. Ibid., 265.

25. Ibid.
26. Sears, *Civil War Papers*, 321n.
27. Ibid., 321.
28. Dowdey, 219–241.
29. Gary Gallagher, editor, *Fighting For the Confederacy: The Personal Recollections of General Edward Porter Alexander*, 103.
30. *O.R.*, 14, / XI, Part 3, 266.
31. Sears, *Civil War Papers*, 322.
32. Ibid.
33. Sears, *George B. McClellan*, 211.
34. Eisenschiml, 38; Dowdey, 242–245.
35. *O.R.*, 12, / XI, Part 1, 61.
36. Shelby Foote, *The Civil War*, I, 491–492; Sears, *To the Gates of Richmond*, 249–277.
37. Foote, I, 492–508.
38. Dowdey, 325–326.
39. Sears, *To the Gates of Richmond*, 308–336; Foote, I, 513
40. Foote, I, 509.
41. Sears, *George B. McClellan*, 219–221.
42. Ibid., 222.
43. Foote, I, 514.
44. *O.R.*, 12, / XI, Part 1, 70.
45. Foote, I, 514–515.
46. Sears, *Civil War Papers*, 341–342; *O.R.*, 16, / XII, Part 2, 1111.
47. Sears, *Civil War Papers*, 342.
48. Margaret Leech, *Reveille in Washington*, 175.
49. For the text, see *O.R.*, 12, / XI, Part 1, 73–74.
50. Earl Schenck Miers, editor, *Lincoln Day by Day, 1861–1865*, 126–127; Donald, 359–360.
51. Miers, 127.
52. Sears, *Civil War Papers*, 348.
53. Ibid.
54. For the background of this development, see Curt Anders, *Henry Halleck's War: A Fresh Look at Lincoln's General-In-Chief*, 136–144.
55. Peter Cozzens and Robert I. Girardi, editors, *The Military Memoirs of General John Pope*, 119. Emphasis supplied.
56. *O.R.*, 18, / XII, Part 3, 474–475.
57. J. G. Randall, *Lincoln the President*, II, 99–100, 100n; Henry Gabler, *The Fitz John Porter Case: Politics and Military Justice*, 53–54. According to Gabler, Porter wrote the letter to J. C. G. Kennedy, who passed it along to Secretary of State William H. Seward who gave it to Lincoln, Stanton, and Pope.
58. Clifford Dowdey, *Lee*, 279.
59. Sears, *Civil War Papers*, 365
60. Ibid., 366n.
61. Ibid., 368.
62. Ibid., 374.
63. Ibid.
64. Ibid., 380–381.
65. Ibid., 381.
66. *O.R.*, 12, / XI, Part 1, 80–84.
67. Sears, *Civil War Papers*, 388.

Chapter Three

1. *War of the Rebellion: Official Records of the Union and Confederate Armies*, Series I, 18, / Volume XII, Part 3, 435.
2. Ibid., 12, / XI, Part 1, 82–84.
3. Curt Anders, *Henry Halleck's War: A Fresh Look at Lincoln's Controversial General-in-Chief*, 164.
4. Ibid., 168; *O.R.*, 17, / XII, Part 3, 547.
5. For an account of the battle, see Robert K. Krick, "Cedar Mountain," in Frances H. Kennedy, editor, *The Civil War Battlefield Guide*, 70–73.

Slaughter Mountain, the fight's alternate name, probably refers to ownership of the site by a member of that distinguished Virginia family.

6. For the armies' opening moves, see John J. Hennessy, *Return to Bull Run: The Campaign and Battle of Second Manassas*, 1–80.
7. Stephen W. Sears, *The Civil War Papers of George B. McClellan*, 389.
8. Ibid., 393.
9. *O.R.*, 12, / XI, Part 1, 89.
10. Ibid., 90–91.
11. Sears, *Civil War Papers*, 406.
12. Ibid., 407.
13. Ibid., 408–409.
14. Ibid., 410.
15. *O.R.*, 14, / XI, Part 3, 359–360.
16. Peter Cozzens and Robert I. Girardi, *The Military Memoirs of General John Pope*, 130–131.
17. Accounts of Jackson's destruction of the Yankees' supply depot abound; see any biography of Jackson.
18. G. F. R. Henderson, *Stonewall Jackson*, 436.
19. Herman Haupt, *Reminiscences*, 75.
20. John Pope, "The Second Battle of Bull Run," in Robert U. Johnson and Clarence C. Buel, editors, *Battles and Leaders of the Civil War*, II, 462.
21. Ibid., 462–463.
22. *O.R.*, 16, / XII, Part 2, 70–71.
23. *O.R.*, 18, / XII, Part 3. 699.
24. Ibid., 700.
25. Haupt, 73; Kenneth P. Williams, *Lincoln Finds a General*, I, 255.
26. *O.R.*, 16,/XII, Part 2, 71–72.
27. Pope, 466.
28. Hennessey, 143–144.
29. *O.R.*, 16, / XII, Part 2, 72.
30. Haupt, 75.
31. *O.R.*, 18, / XII, Part 3, 706.
32. Ibid.
33. Ibid., 709.
34. Ibid.
35. Ibid., 710.
36. Ibid., 732–733.
37. Hennessey, 143–145.
38. Excellent accounts of the fighting on August 28 are to be found in Hennessey, 138–193, and David G. Martin, *The Second Bull Run Campaign*, 133–154.
39. Hennessey, 190–192.
40. Pope, 470.
41. Hennessey, 194.
42. *O.R.*, 16, / XII, Part 2, 74–75.
43. Hennessey, 195.
44. Ibid.
45. *O.R.*, 18, / XII, Part 3, 733.
46. Ibid., 15, / XII, Part 1, 243, 245.
47. Ibid., 243.
48. Hennessey, 198–199.
49. This statement presupposes that Pope had in mind bagging Jackson, and nothing more, by ordering Porter to Gainesville.
50. Hennessey, 224–226.
51. *O.R.*, 12, / XI, Part 1, 97–98.
52. Anders, 214.
53. *O.R.*, 12, / XI, Part 1, 98.
54. Ibid.
55. Sears, *Civil War Papers*, 417.
56. *O.R.*, 18, / XII, Part 3, 730.
57. Ibid., 16, / XII, Part 2, 76.
58. Hennessey, 232.
59. Ibid., 232–234, 514 note 29.
60. *O.R.*, 15, / XII, Part 1, 242.
61. Martin, 173–177.
62. Hennessey, 235–236.

63. Ibid., 236.
64. Good accounts of the fighting near Groveton on August 29 may be found in Hennessey, 200–286, and Martin, 159–168.
65. Hennessey, 287–288.
66. Ibid., 268.
67. *O.R.*, 17, / XII, Part 2 Supplement, 826.
68. Hennessey, 306.
69. Otto Eisenschiml, *The Celebrated Case of Fitz John Porter*, 61.
70. Hennessey, 306.
71. Hennessy, 306, provides these details: To Pope, this latest dispatch from Porter validated all of his suspicions about Porter and others of the McClellan cabal. Porter was playing sabotage. His words seemed to be the wailings of a traitor. He had his orders. Why did he not obey? Pope flew into a rage. "I'll arrest him!" he stormed, and started dictating a searing note to Porter. But before Pope could finish, McDowell intervened and, according to Chief of Staff Ruggles, "remonstrated strongly" with Pope. Offering a defense of Porter calculated to salvage only the moment and not the man, McDowell argued that Porter acted not only out of disloyalty; he was just "incompetent."
72. *O.R.*, 16, / XII, Part 2, 18.
73. Eisenschiml, 63.
74. *O.R.*, 16, / XII, Part 2, 17.
75. Ibid., 15–16.
76. Hennessey, 310.
77. Ibid., 311–312.
78 Ibid., 312.
79. Ibid.
80. Ibid., 313–315.
81. *O.R.*, 18, I XII, Part 3, 739–741.
82. Anders, 217–228.
83. Allan Nevins, *The War for the Union*, II, 182–183.
84. Hennessey, 332.
85. Ibid., 328–329.
86. Ibid., 332–361.
87. Ibid., 362–471; Martin, 203–249.
88. *O.R.*, 16, I XII, Part 2, 78.
89. Ibid.
90. Ibid., 78–79.

Chapter Four

1. *War of the Rebellion: Official Records of the Union and Confederate Armies*, Series I, 18, / Volume XII, Part 4, 764–765.
2. *O.R.*, 16, / XII, Part 2, 82–83.
3. Ibid., 12, / XI, Part 1, 104–105.
4. Ibid., 18, / XII, Part 3, 796–797.
5. Douglas Southall Freeman, *R. E. Lee*, II, 348–351.
6. *O.R.*, 18, / XII, Part 3, 797
7. Hans L. Trefousse, *The Radical Republicans: Lincoln's Vanguard for Social Justice*, 200.
8. T. Harry Williams, *Lincoln and the Radicals*, 178–179.
9. Ibid., 178.
10. *O.R.*, 16, / XII, Part 2, 19
11. Ibid., 15–16.
12. John J. Hennessey, *Return to Bull Run: The Campaign and Battle of Second Manassas*, 464–465.
13. *O.R.*, 28, / XIX, Part 2, 169.
14. Ibid., 183.
15. Ibid.
16. Ibid., 182.
17. Ibid.

18. Ibid., 189–190.

19. Stephen W. Sears, *The Civil war Papers of George B. McClellan*, 436–437, 436n.

20. Otto Eisenschiml, *The Celebrated Case of Fitz John Porter*, 67.

21. *O.R.*, 28, / XIX, Part 2, 253.

22. Ibid.

23. Wrote historian Kenneth P. Williams in *Lincoln Finds a General,* II, 448:

> McClellan's plan certainly paid high tribute to John Pope, for the initial heavy work was allotted to the old Army of Virginia, of which Porter—who was to sit the battle out—had spoken when he first came to it. Hooker had McDowell's old corps, Mansfield had that of Banks, and most of Burnside's troops had been under Pope. McClellan's old commanders of the Peninsula—Sumner, Franklin, and Porter—were to have supporting or reserve roles. McClellan had an excellent opportunity to remove the cloud, which had hung over Porter since Second Bull Run, and it looks as if he may have had that general deliver the final thrust that would win the battle.

24. *O.R.*, 28, / XIX, Part 2, 312.

25. Stephen W. Sears, *Landscape Turned Red*, 246–247.

26. Sears, *Landscape Turned Red*, 276–285; Douglas Southall Freeman, *Lee's Lieutenants,* II, 220–221; Freeman, *R. E. Lee*, II, 398–401.

27. K. P. Williams, II, 456.

28. Sears, *Landscape Turned Red*, 287–288, 290–292.

29. K. P. Williams, II, 458.

30. Sears, *Civil War Papers*, 469.

31. Eisenschiml, 68.

32. Shelby Foote, *The Civil War*, I, 749.

33. McClellan's biographer Stephen Sears has described the result:

> The dispatch opened a thirty-day war of words between McClellan and Washington. Unwilling either to obey the order and make the best of the situation or to resign in protest against it, McClellan generated one excuse after another to delay his movement. Nothing so clearly reveals his design than the fact that while Lincoln and Halleck pressed him almost daily to march, he was playing host to his wife and his year-old daughter and his mother-in-law in a farmhouse near his camp in Pleasant Valley, where they remained in domestic tranquillity for nearly two weeks. . . . A frustrated General Halleck would tell a friend that there was an immobility about the Army of the Army of the Potomac that exceeded belief: "It requires the lever of Archimedes to move this inert mass. I have tried my best, but without success." Sears, George B, McClellan: *The Young Napoleon*, 332.

34. *O.R.*, 27, / XIX, Part 1, 13–14; Curt Anders, *Henry Hallecks' War: A Fresh Look at Lincoln's Controversial General-in-Chief*, 309–312.

35. *O.R.*, 28, / XIX, Part 2, 464.

36. Ibid., 545.

37. Ibid., 18, / XII, Part 3, 817–823.

38. Ibid., 22, / XVI, Part 1, 6–67: Mark M. Boatner, III, *The Civil War Dictionary*, 96–97.
39. *O.R.*, 18, / XII, Part 3, 817–823.
40. ***General Porter to General Thomas, September 10, 1862:***

    I have reason to believe that charges have been made by Maj. Gen. John Pope against my official conduct during the portion of the campaign in Northeast Virginia in which the corps I have the honor to command was serving under his orders.

    Justice to my brave command and to the army, justice to those who have honored me with their confidence and with command, and justice to the country would seem to require an investigation of these charges, and in justice to me I ask that a thorough examination into their truth or falsity and all attending circumstances may be made at an early hour.

    I would have preferred this request at an earlier day had anything tangible been in my possession and had not Major-General Pope informed me at Fairfax Court-House that he had no cause to complain of me during the period I was under his command.

    I am more urgent for an early consideration of my case since Major General Pope is himself a witness in my favor and since many of the general officers now in this vicinity are also essential witnesses.

Porter to Thomas, September 11, 1862:

I have to-day, to my surprise, seen in the New York newspapers Maj. Gen. John Pope's official report of the recent battle at Bull Run.

Having thus been apprised of the charges made against me by General Pope (of which charges I had before received intimation), I have only now to urge an early investigation of them, and would therefore earnestly request that this investigation may take place as soon as the interests of the service may permit, in order that I may prove the falsity of the charges and of the inferences drawn from them in that report. *O.R.*, 16, / XII, Part 2, 506.

41. T. Harry Williams, 176.
42. Ibid., 179–180.
43. *O.R.*, 18, / XII, Part 3, 820–823.
44. Peter Cozzens, *General John Pope: A Life For the Nation*, 213–214.
45. Eisenschiml, 73–74.
46. *O.R.*, 16, / XII, Part 2, 506–507.
47. Ibid., 17, / XII, Part 2 Supplement, 821. Peter Cozzens, in *General John Pope: A Life For the Nation*, 214, suggests that General-in-Chief Halleck "did [Pope] one better" by issuing Special Orders No. 362 and appointing the members of the court. As is noted below in the text, it seems highly unlikely that Halleck had anything to do with the selection of members of the court.
48. See Appendix II: David Hunter.
49. Eisenschiml, 170; Boatner, 418–419.
50. Foote, I, 266–267; Patricia L. Faust, editor, *Historical Times Encyclopedia of the Civil War*, 363.
51. See Appendix II: Silas Casey.
52. See Appendix II: N. P. Buford.

53. See Appendix II: B. M. Prentiss.
54. See Appendix II: J. M. Slough.
55. See Appendix II: Rufus King and James B. Ricketts.
56. Eisenschiml, 170.
57. See Appendix II: James A. Garfield.
58. Cozzens, 218–219.
59. Eisenschiml, 81.
60. See Appendix II: Joseph Holt.

Chapter 5

1. *Dictionary of American Biography*, V, 112–113.
2. Ibid., 113.
3. Otto Eisenschiml, *The Celebrated Case of Fitz John Porter*, 77.
4. *DAB,* III, 502–503.
5. *War of the Rebellion: Official Records of the Union and Confederate Armies*, Series I, 17, / XII, Part 2, Supplement, 821.
6. Ibid., 822.
7. Ibid., 822–823.
8. See Appendix III: Charges and Specifications, *O.R.*, 17, / XII, Part 2 Supplement, 824–827.
9. Ibid., 823.
10. Ibid., 824.
11. Ibid , 828–829.
12. Ibid., 828.
13. Ibid., 827.
14. Ibid., 828.
15. Ibid., 829.
16. *Army Regulations* opens with this simple sentence: "The first duty of the soldier is to obey." When charged with any violation, West Point cadets are taught to reply, "No excuse, sir!" Provisions exist for explaining how the offense occurred, and often they lead to reduction or elimination of penalties imposed initially. But anyone who dares claim that any military mission was impossible as the reason for non-obedience has next to no chance of prevailing, given precedents reflecting extreme and heartlifting devotion to duty such as Ilium, Masada, Balaklava, the Alamo, and more recently, Fredericksburg, Gettysburg, and Cold Harbor, and closer to our time, Passchendaele and Bataan and Chosin Reservoir.
17. Eisenschiml, 82.
18. *O.R.*, 17, / XII, Part 2, Supplement, 829–830.
19. Ibid., 831.
20. See Appendix III: Pope's Reply Regarding the Orders he Issued
21. *O.R.*, 17, / XII, Part 2, Supplement, 831–832.
22. Ibid., 836.
23. Ibid., 837.
24. Ibid., 838–839.
25. Ibid., 839–840.
26. A possible translation from the legalese:

    General Pope has attributed the disasters of the army under his command to the failure of General Porter to obey all or some of his orders. Pope has also stated that he thought such orders might have been obeyed.

    Since, so far as the prosecution has gone, it is upon Pope's evidence that the prosecution is trying to convince the court that disobedience occurred, the accused is advised by his counsel that the question just ruled out by the court is not only relevant and legal but most material, in order to show that the recollection of the witness is not to be relied upon; and that Pope has charged the accused with disobedience.

It was General Pope's duty not only NOT to doubt whether he would take any action in relation to the matter, but to report the same as a grave offense on the part of the accused. Pope's doubts are facts not only admissible but material evidence that—at the time to which the question relates—Pope did not believe there had been any such disobedience on the part of the accused.

Therefore, we respectfully request to have this protest entered on the proceedings of the court against the exclusion of the question referred to.

27. *O.R.*, 17, / XII, Part 2, Supplement, 839.
28. Peter Cozzens, *General John Pope: A Life for the Nation*, 221.
29. See Appendix III: Pope's Reasons For Not Acting Against Porter on September 2, 1862.
30. *O.R.*, 17, / XII, Part 2, Supplement, 840.
31. Ibid., 841.
32. Ibid., 847.
33. Ibid., 848.
34. Ibid.
35. Ibid., 849.
36. Ibid., 850.
37. Ibid., 851.
38. Ibid., 852.
39. Ibid., 853.
40. Ibid., 854.
41. Ibid.
42. Cozzens, 221.

Chapter Six

1. *War of the Rebellion: Official Records of the Union and Confederate Armies*, Series I, Volume 17, / XII, Part 2 Supplement, 856.
2. Ibid., 857.
3. Peter Cozzens, *General John Pope: A Life for the Nation*, 222–223.
4. *O.R.*, 17, / XII, Part 2 Supplement, 861.
5. Ibid., 862.
6. Ibid., 863.
7. Ibid., 864.
8. See Appendix IV, Benjamin S. Roberts.
9. *O.R.*, 17, / XII, Part 2 Supplement, 865.
10. Ibid., 867.
11. Ibid., 868.
12. Ibid.
13. Ibid., 869.
14. Ibid., 870.
15. Ibid., 871.
16. See Appendix IV, Philip Kearny.
17. *O.R.*, 17, / XII, Part 2 Supplement, 872.
18. Ibid., 874.
19. Ibid. The text:

Generals McDowell and King:

I find it impossible to communicate by crossing the roads to Groveton. The enemy are in strong force on this road, and as they appear to have driven our forces back, the firing of the enemy having advanced and ours retired, I have determined to withdraw to Manassas. I have attempted to communicate with McDowell and Sigel, but my messengers have run into the enemy. They [the enemy] have gathered artillery and infantry and cavalry, and the advancing masses of dust show the enemy coming in force. I am now going forward to the head of the column to see what is passing and how affairs are going. Had you not better send your trains back? I will communicate with you.

20. *O.R.*, 17, / XII, Part 2 Supplement, 875–888. For the Porter–Abbott colloquy, see Ibid., 887–888.
21. Otto Eisenschiml, *The Celebrated Case of Fitz John Porter*, 253–254, 282.
22. *O.R.*, 17, / XII, Part 2 Supplement, 889.
23. Ibid., 890.
24. Ibid., 891.
25. Ibid.
26. Ibid., 892. A missed opportunity? Apparently, Reverdy Johnson had forgotten or was not aware that the pursuit following General Halleck's capture of Corinth was commanded by Major General Pope. See Curt Anders, *Henry Halleck's War: A Fresh Look at Lincoln's Controversial General-in-Chief*, 120–121.
27. *O.R.*, 17, / XII, Part 2 Supplement, 893.
28. Ibid., 894.
29. Ibid., 898.
30. Ibid., 899.
31. Ibid.
32. Mark M. Boatner, III, *The Civil War Dictionary*, 774.

Chapter Seven

1. *War of the Rebellion: Official Records of the Union and Confederate Armies*, Series I, Volume 17, / XII, Part 2 Supplement, 902–904.
2. Ibid., 904.
3. Ibid.
4. Ibid., 905.
5. Ibid., 907.
6. Ibid., 909.
7. Ibid., 910.
8. Ibid., 911.
9. Ibid., 914.
10. Ibid., 915.
11. Ibid.
12. Ibid., 916.
13. Otto Eisenschiml, *The Celebrated Case of Fitz John Porter*, 92; Peter Cozzens, *General John Pope: A Life for the Nation*, 213–214.
14. Eisenschiml, 89–90.
15. Ibid., 92; *O.R.*, 17, / XII, Part 2 Supplement, 877.
16. *O.R.*, 17, / XII, Part 2 Supplement, 920–921.
17. Mark M. Boatner, III, *The Civil War Dictionary*, 313.
18. *O.R.*, 17, / XII, Part 2 Supplement, 918–926.
19. Ibid., 923.
20. Ibid., 924.

Chapter Eight

1. *War of the Rebellion: Official Records of the Union and Confederate Armies*, Series I, Volume 17, / XII, Part 2 Supplement, 936.
2. Ibid.
3. Otto Eisenschiml, *The Celebrated Case of Fitz John Porter*, 106–107.
4. *O.R.*, 17, / XII, Part 2 Supplement, 936–937.
5. Ibid., 939.
6. Eisenschiml, 105.

7. *O.R.*, 17, / XII, Part 2 Supplement, 937–940.
8. Ibid., 947.
9. Ibid., 948–949.
10. Ibid., 949–951.
11. Ibid., 951–953
12. Ibid., 954–956.
13. Ibid., 956–958.
14. Ibid., 959–962.
15. Ibid., 968.
16. Ibid., 968–971.
17. Ibid., 975–977.
18. Ibid., 977–978.
19. Ibid., 979–980.
20. Ibid., 980–981.
21. Ibid., 982–980. See Appendix V, General Griffin's Testimony.
22. Ibid., 992–995.
23. Ibid., 994–995.
24. Ibid., 914.
25. Ibid., 999. Italics supplied.
26. Ibid., 999–1000.
27. A. Wilson Greene, "Fredericksburg," in Frances H. Kennedy, editor, *The Civil War Battlefield Guide*, 97–103.
28. For an account of Burnside's plight and the Union high command's disarray before New Year's Day 1863, see Curt Anders, *Henry Halleck's War: A Fresh Look at Lincoln's Controversial General-in-Chief*, 321–356.
29. *O.R.*, 17, / XII, Part 2 Supplement, 1002–1003.
30. Ibid., 1003.
31. Ibid., 1003–1007.
32. Ibid., 1009.
33. Ibid., 1007

Chapter Nine

1. Curt Anders, *Henry Halleck's War: A Fresh Look at Lincoln's Controversial General-in-Chief*, 357–372.
2. Ibid., 366–367.
3. Stephen W. Sears, *George B. McClellan: The Young Napoleon*, 318–343.
4. Ibid., 348–349.
5. Stephen W. Sears, *The Civil War Papers of George B. McClellan*, 530.
6. Ibid., 532.
7. Ibid., 533.
8. *O.R.*, 17, / XII, Part 2 Supplement, 1011–1012.
9. Ibid., 1013–1014.
10. Ibid., 1013–1015.
11. Ibid., 1017.
12. Ibid., 1018.
13. Ibid., 1017–1019.
14. Ibid., 1020.
15. Ibid., 1032–1034.
16. Ibid., 1034–1037.
17. Ibid., 1037–1040.
18. Ibid., 1041.
19. Otto Eisenschiml, 154–155; *O.R.*, 15, / XII, Part 1, 36.
20. *O.R.*, 17, / XII, Part 2 Supplement, 1041–1042.
21. John J. Hennessy, *Return to Bull Run: The Campaign and Battle of Second Manassas*, 466.
22. *O.R.*, 17, / XII, Part 2 Supplement, 1042–1046.
23. Ibid., 1046–1048.
24. Ibid., 1048.
25. Ibid., 1049.

Chapter Ten

1. *The War of the Rebellion: Official Records of the Union and Confederate Armies*, Series I, Volume 17, / XII, Part 2 Supplement, 1104.

2. Ibid., 1105–1106.
3. Ibid., 1106–1110.
4. Ibid., 1110–1112.
5. Ibid., 1051.
6. Ibid.
7. Henry Gabler, *The Fitz John Porter Case: Politucs and Military Justice*, 306–307. Gabler says the originals are in the Porter Papers in the Library of Congress.
8. *O.R.*, 17, / XII, Part 2 Supplement, 1051.
9. Ibid., 1113.
10. Ibid., 1052.
11. Stephen W. Sears, *The Civil War Papers of George B. McClellan*, 534–535.
12. *O.R.*, 17, / XII, Part 2 Supplement, 1112–1113.
13. Ibid., 1115–1116.
14. Ibid., 1116.
15. Otto Eisenschiml, *The Celebrated Case of Fitz John Porter*, 166–167.
16. Ibid., 167.
17. Ibid., 167–168.
18. Allan Nevins, *The War for the Union*, II, 352–354; J. G. Randall, *Lincoln the President*, II, 242–243.
19. *O.R.*, 17, / XII, Part 2 Supplement, 1116–1133.
20. Ibid., 1052.
21. William Shakespeare, *Hamlet, Prince of Denmark*, Act IV, Scene V.
22. Mark M. Boatner III, *The Civil War Dictionary*, 661
23. Eisenschiml, 16.
24. Ibid., 176–177.
25. *O.R.*, 15, / XII, Part 1, 241–244.
26. Ibid., 243.
27. Ibid., 246.
28. Ibid., 246–249.
29. Eisenschiml, 16–17, 171; Gabler, 288. Eisenschiml said the reporter was from the *New York Tribune*, Gabler *The Times.*
30. Eisenschiml, 177.
31. *New York Herald*, January 22, 1863.
32. Eisenschiml, 169.
33. Ibid.
34. *O.R.*, 16, / XII, Part 2, 508–512.
35. Eisenschiml, 169.
36. Ibid., 170–171.
37. Peter Cozzens, *General John Pope: A Life For the Nation*, 226.
38. Eisenschiml, 173.
39. Ibid., 174–175.
40. Ibid., 179.
41. Curt Anders, *Henry Halleck's War: A Fresh Look at Lincoln's Controversial General-in-Chief*, 357–375, for Hooker's replacement of Burnside..
42. Eisenschiml, 179–183 as to the contents of Johnson's *Reply.*

Chapter Eleven

1. Otto Eisenschiml, *The Celebrated Case of Fitz John Porter*, 177–184.
2. Ibid., 184.
3. Ibid., 185–186.
4. Ibid., 186–187.
5. Ibid., 187.
6. Ibid., 188–191.
7. Ibid., 191–192.
8. Ibid., 193–194.
9. Ibid., 194–195.
10. Ibid., 195.
11. Philip Van Doren Stern, *An End to Valor*, 305.
12. Hans L. Trefousse, *The Radical Republicans: Lincoln's Vanguard for Social Justice*, 308.

13. Anyone who blames the Radical Republicans in post-war Congresses for the severity, duration, and cruelty of the Reconstruction Era strikes a hornets nest of criticism. For perspective, see Michael Les Benedict, *The Fruits of Victory: Alternatives in Restoring the Union, 1865–1877.*
14. Fletcher Pratt, *Stanton: Lincoln's Secretary of War*, 442–450.
15. Eisenschiml, 196.
16. Ibid., 196–197.
17. Ibid., 197.
18. Ibid., 197–198.
19. Ibid., 198–200. Gabler discovered the documents in the Andrew Johnson Papers in the Library of Congress. Gabler, 343.
20. Pratt, 450–453.
21. John M. Schofield, *Forty-Six Years in the Army*, 460–461.
22. Eisenschiml, 200–205.
23. Ibid., 207. Stone was senior military advisor to the Khedive of Egypt
24. Ibid., 207, 210–211.
25. Ibid., 206.
26. Ibid., 206–207.
27. Ibid., 207.
28. Ibid.
29. Trefousse, 464–465.
30. Eisenschiml, 207–209.
31. Mark M. Boatner, *The Civil War Dictionary*, 389; Patricia L. Faust, editor, *Historical Times Encyclopedia of the Civil War*, 353.
32. Eisenschiml, 212–213.
33. Eisenschiml, 212–213.
34. *O.R.*, 16, / XII, Part 2, 513.
35. Schofield, 241–242.
36. Ibid., 461.
37. Faust, 661; Boatner, 726–727.
38. Faust, 748–749; Boatner, 831.
39. Faust, 305; Boatner, 329–330.

Chapter Twelve

1. John M. Schofield, *Forty-Six Years in the Army*, 461.
2. Alan and Barbara Aimone, *A User's Guide to the Official Records of the American Civil War*, in its entirety.
3. Otto Eisenschiml, *The Celebrated Case of Fitz John Porter*, 217.
4. *Proceedings and Report of the Board of Army Officers in the Case of Fitz John Porter*, Volume I, 1, hereinafter referred to as *Proceedings.*
5. Ibid.
6. Eisenschiml, 216.
7. *Proceedings*, I, 2.
8. Ibid.
9. Eisenschiml, 215, citing *Proceedings*, II, 1, 576.
10. Ibid.
11. Ibid., 215–216.
12. *Proceedings*, I, 2–3. Petitioner's Opening Statement begins on page III and ends on LXIII, much of it in fine print.
13. Ibid., 3.
14. Ibid., 4.
15. Ibid., 4–6.
16. Eisenschiml, 217.
17. *Proceedings*, I, 6–7.
18. Ibid.
19. Ibid., 7–12.
20. Ibid., 12–14.
21. Ibid., 14–15.
22. Patricia L. Faust, editor, *Historical Times Encyclopedia of the Civil War*, 803.
23. *Proceedings*, I, 17.
24. Ibid., 21.

25. Ibid., 22–23.
26. Ibid., 24.
27. Ibid., 26.
28. Ibid., 27–29.
29. Ibid., 29–31.
30. Ibid., 32–55.
31. Ibid., 57–63.
32. Ibid., 63–64.
33. Ibid., 64–66.
34. Ibid., 66–72.
35. Ibid., 74–75, For Marshall's deposition, see *War of the Rebellion: Official Records of the Union and Confederate Armies*, Series I, 17, / Volume XII, Part 2 Supplement, 1011–1016.
36. *Proceedings*, I, 79.
37. Ibid., 83–85.
38. Ibid., 86.
39. Ibid., 102–113.
40. Ibid., 119–131.
41. Ibid., 132–134.
42. Ibid., 136.
43. *O.R.*, 17, / XII, Part 2 Supplement, 878.
44. Ibid., 1031, 1033.
45. *Proceedings*, I, 161.
46. Ibid., 173–181.
47. Ibid., 181–186.
48. Ibid., 188–189.
49. Ibid., 193–194.
50. Ibid., 203–209.
51. Ibid., 209–211.
52. Ibid., 214.
53. Ibid.
54. Ibid., 216.
55. Ibid., 218.

Chapter Thirteen

1. *Proceedings and Report of the Board of Army Officers in the case of Fitz John Porter*, Volume I, 244, 251.
2. Ibid., 245.
3. Ibid., 256–258.
4. Ibid., 271–273.
5. Ibid., 276.
6. Ibid., 276–277.
7. Ibid., 277–278.
8. Ibid., 278–279.
9. Ibid., 279.
10. Ibid., 279–281.
11. Ibid., 281–284.
12. Ibid., 284.
13. Ibid., 286–287.
14. Ibid., 288.
15. Ibid., 289.
16. Ibid., 290–291.
17. Ibid., 291–295.
18. Ibid., 295–296.
19. Ibid., 297–300.
20. Ibid., 300.
21. Ibid., 301, 304.
22. Ibid., 308.
23. Ibid., 308–311.
24. Ibid., 311–315.
25. Ibid., 316–318.
26. Ibid., 318.
27. Henry Gabler, *The Fitz John Porter Case: Politics and Military Justice*, 385–386.
28. *Proceedings*, I, 318.
29. Ibid.
30. Ibid., 319–324.
31. Ibid., 324–328.
32. Ibid., 328–330.
33. Ibid., 330–334.
34. Ibid., 334–336.
35. Ibid., 336–340.
36. Ibid., 342–343.
37. Ibid., 343–345.

38. Ibid., 345–347.
39. Ibid., 347–349.
40. Ibid., 349–353.
41. Ibid., 353–360.
42. Ibid., 360–361.
43. Ibid., 361.
44. Ibid., 361–363.
45. *War of the Rebellion: Official Records of the Union and Confederate Armies*, Series I, Volume 17, / XII, Part 2 supplement, 889.
46. *Proceedings*, I, 363–365.
47. Ibid., 365–366.
48. Ibid., 371–372.

Chapter Fourteen

1. *Proceedings and Report of the Board of Army Officers in the Case of Fitz John Porter*, Volume I, 373–375.
2. Ibid., 376–379.
3. Ibid., 379–385.
4. Ibid., 389–390.
5. Ibid., 390–392.
6. Ibid., 392–393.
7. Ibid., 395–408.
8. Ibid., 409–410.
9. Ibid., 303.
10. Ibid.
11. Ibid., 410–412.
12. Ibid., 412.
13. Ibid.
14. Ibid., 304. Emphasis supplied. Later, Porter would be criticized for not patrolling aggressively.
15. Ibid., 419–440; *War of the Rebellion: Official Records of the Union and Confederate Armies*, Series I, Volume 17, / XII, Part 2 Supplement, 827.
16. *Proceedings*, I, 440.
17. Ibid., 440–442.
18. Ibid., 447–448.
19. Ibid., 449–464.
20. Ibid., 464–547.
21. Ibid., 551.
22. Ibid., 551–555.
23. Ibid., 555–557.
24. Ibid., 557–558.
25. Ibid., 559.
26. Ibid., 560–562.
27. Ibid., 562–563.
28. Ibid., 563–564.
29. Ibid., 564–579.
30. Ibid., 579–587.
31. Ibid., 587–615.
32. Ibid., 615.
33. Ibid., 615–617.
34. Ibid., 617–618.
35. Ibid., 618–623.
36. Ibid., 622–623.
37. Ibid., 623–627.
38. Ibid., 629–633.
39. Ibid., 633–637.
40. Ibid., 637–639.
41. Ibid., 640–642.
42. Ibid., 653, 656.
43. Ibid., 654.
44. Ibid., 657–658.
45. Ibid., 660.
46. Ibid., 660–680.
47. Ibid., 680–717.
48. Ibid., 717–742.

Chapter Fifteen

1. *Proceedings and report of the Board of Army Officers in the case of Fitz John Porter*, Volume I, 742–743.
2. Ibid., 744.
3. Ibid., 744–745.
4. Ibid., 745–747.

5. Ibid., 747.
6. Ibid., 748.
7. Ibid., 749–750.
8. Ibid., 751.
9. Ibid., 751–753.
10. Ibid., 753.
11. Ibid., 753–757. The "Brief" Statement requires six pages in fine print in the *Proceedings*, 757–763.
12. Ibid., 764–765.
13. Ibid., 767.
14. Ibid.
15. Ibid., 767–768.
16. Ibid., 768–771.
17. Ibid., 771–773.
18. Ibid., 777.
19. Ibid., 775.
20. Ibid., 778.
21. Ibid., 778–785.
22. Ibid., 785–786.
23. Ibid., 786–791.
24. *War of the Rebellion: Official Records of the Union and Confederate Armies*, Series I, Volume 17, / XII, Part 2 Supplement, 902–915.
25. *Proceedings*, I, 791–795.
26. Ibid., 795–796.
27. Ibid., 798–799.
28. Ibid., 799–800. The quoted passage is from *War of the Rebellion: Official Records of the Union and Confederate Armies*, Series I, Volume 17, / XII, Part 2 Supplement, 906.
29. *Proceedings*, I, 795–803.
30. Ibid., 804.
31. Ibid., 805.
32. Ibid., 805–806. The quoted passage is from *War of the Rebellion: Official Records of the Union and Confederate Armies*, Series I, Volume 17, / XII, Part 2 Supplement, 1044.
33. Ibid., 806–809.
34. Ibid., 811–812.
35. Ibid., 812–813.
36. Ibid., 813–815.
37. Ibid., 815–816.
38. Ibid., 816–817.
39. Ibid., 817–832.

Chapter Sixteen

1. *Proceedings and Report of the Board of Officers in the Case of Fitz John Porter*, Volume I, 848–849.
2. Ibid., 849–853.
3. Ibid., 854–855.
4. Ibid., 855–856.
5. Ibid., 857.
6. Ibid., 857–881.
7. Ibid., 881–886.
8. Ibid., 889–900.
9. Ibid., 900–903.
10. Ibid., 903–904.
11. Ibid., 904.
12. Ibid., 904–939.
13. Ibid., 939–952.
14. Ibid., 952–966.
15. Ibid., 971–973.
16. Ibid., 973–976.
17. Ibid., 976–978.
18. Ibid., 978–979.
19. Ibid., 979–980.
20. Ibid., 980.
21. Ibid., 980–1011.
22. *Proceedings and Report of the Board of Officers in the Case of Fitz John Porter*, Volume II, 1020–1022.
23. Ibid., 1022–1034, 1045–1093.
24. Ibid., 1035–1044.
25. Ibid., 1093–1094.
26. Ibid., 1098–1102.

27. Ibid., 1093–1094, 1102–1104.
28. Ibid., 1104–1105.
29. Ibid., 1105.
30. Ibid., 1106.
31. Ibid., 1106–1107.
32. Ibid., 1107–1110.
33. Ibid., 1110–1113.
34. Ibid., 1113–1133.
35. Ibid., 1134–1157.
36. Ibid., 1133–1134.
37. Ibid, 1160–1167; as to the Stanton directive to Halleck, see Curt Anders, *Henry Halleck's War: A Fresh Look at Lincoln's Controversial General-in-Chief*, 210, 225–228.
38. Anders, in many subsequent documented passages covering these disputes.
39. *Proceedings and Report of the Board of Officers in the Case of Fitz John Porter*, Volume II, 1170.
40. Ibid., 1171.
41. Ibid.
42. Ibid., 1171–1177.
43. Ibid., 1190.
44. Ibid., 1189.
45. Ibid., 1193.
46. Ibid., 1194.
47. Ibid., 1194–1198.
48. Ibid., 1198–1204.
49. Ibid., 1208–1214.
50. Ibid., 1208–1240.
51. See Appendix VI, Closing Arguments.

Chapter Seventeen

1. *Proceedings and Report of the Board of Officers in the Case of Fitz John Porter*, Volume II, 1782.
2. John M. Schofield, *Forty-Six Years in the Army*, 461–462.
3. *Proceedings*, II, 1782–1787.
4. Ibid., 1787–1801. The report begins on 1801 and ends on 1825. Exhibits continue to 1869, errata.
5. See Appendix VII, Schofield Board's Report, for full text.
6. *War of the Rebellion: Official Records of the Union and Confederate Armies*, Series I, Volume 16, / XII, Part 2, 512–535.
7. Otto Eisenschiml, *The Celebrated Case of Fitz John Porter*, 252.
8. Ibid., 255.
9. Henry Gabler, *The Fitz John Porter Case: Politics and Military Justice*, 371–372.
10. Ibid., 434; Eisenschiml, 256–266 for the 1880–81 session.
11. Gabler,434–435.
12. Eisenschiml, 267.
13. Gabler, 428.
14. Ibid., 429.
15. Eisenschiml, 260.
16. Gabler, 431.
17. Eisenschiml, 267.
18. Ibid., 267–268; Gabler, 436.
19. Gabler, 436–437.
20. Ibid., 437.
21. Eisenschiml, 268.
22. Gabler, 436.
23. Eisenschiml, 268–269.
24. Ibid., 269–270.
25. Ibid., 270.
26. Ibid., 272–273.
27. Ibid., 273.
28. Ibid., 277–278.
29. Ibid., 279–280.
30. Ibid., 282–285.
31. Ibid., 285–288.
32. Ibid., 288–295.

33. Ibid., 296.
34. Ibid., 297.
35. Ibid., 297–299.
36. Ibid., 300–303.
37. Ibid., 303.
38. Ibid., 303–304; Gabler, 466.
39. Eisenschiml, 305.
40. Gabler, 472.

APPENDICES

I

1. Hans L. Trefousse, *The Radical Republicans*, 5.
2. Generally, the states of Ohio, Indiana, Illinois, Michigan, Wisconsin, and Minnesota.
3. Hans L. Trefousse, *Benjamin Franklin Wade: Radical Republican From Ohio*, 19.
4. T. Harry Williams, Lincoln and the Radicals, 66.
5. Ibid., 66–67.
6. Trefousse, *Benjamin Franklin Wade*, 26–27.
7. Trefousse, *The Radical Republicans*, 5; Patricia L. Faust, editor, *Historical Times Encyclopedia of the Civil War*, 129.
8. Trefousse, *The Radical Republicans*, 5–6; Faust, 732.
9. Trefousse, *The Radical Republicans*, 12–13.
10. Faust, 406; Williams, 70.
11. Trefousse, *The Radical Republicans*, 14.
12. For more on Greeley, see Faust, 322.
13. The second would be Edwin M. Stanton, in January 1862.
14. Trefousse, *The Radical Republicans*, 148.
15. See Charles Adams, *When in the Course of Human Events,* in its entirity for an indictment of Radical behavior.
16. Trefousse, *The Radical Republicans*, 308. On April 12, 1865, two days before Lincoln was shot, Wade is said to have said: "By God, the sooner he is assasinated, the better." See Trefousse, *Benjamin Franklin Wade*, 246; Philip Van Doren Stern, *An End to Valor*, 305. However, the Radicals had nothing to do with Lincoln's assassination.
17. W. A. Swanberg, *First Blood,* 229: see also Emory M. Thomas, *The Confederate Nation.*
18. See Eric Foner, *Reconstruction: America's Unfinished Revolution,1863–1877*, in its entirety, and also in its entirity, Michael Les Benedict, *The Fruits of Victory: Alternatives in Restoring the Union, 1865–1877.*

II

1. *Dictionary of American Biography*, V, 400.
2. Ibid.; David Herbert Donald, Lincoln, 273–274.
3. Kenneth P. Williams, *Lincoln Finds a General*, I, 93.
4. *DAB,* 400.
5. For circumstances leading to Fremont's relief, see Curt Anders, *Henry Halleck's War: A fresh Look at Lincoln's Controversial General-in-Chief*, 30–39; for Hunter's execution of his mission, see Shelby Foote, *The Civil War*, I, 97–99.
6. Mark M. Boatner, *The Civil War Dictionary*, 418–419; *DAB*, V, 400.
7. *DAB*, V, 400–401. See also, Hans L.

Trefousse, *The Radical Republicans: Lincoln's Vanguard for Racial Justice*, 213–216.

8. Benjamin P. Thomas and Harold M. Hyman, *Stanton: Lincoln's Secretary of War*, 233–239; Hunter to Stanton is on 236.

As to Silas Casey:

9. Faust, 118–119; *DAB,* II, 560; K. Jack Bauer, *The Mexican War 1846–1848*, 311–319; Boatner, 131.
10. Stephen W. Sears, *The Civil War Papers of George B. McClellan*, 287.
11. *O.R.*, 12, / XII, Part 1, 749.
12. *New York Herald*, June 4, 1862.
13. *War of the Rebellion: Official Records of the Union and Confederate Armies*, Series I, Volume 12, / XII, Part 1, 750.
14. Ibid.
15. Ibid., 750–751.
16. Ibid., 751–752.
17. Ibid., 752.
18. Ibid., 752–753.
19. Ibid., 14, / XII, Part 3, 248.
20. Eisenschiml, 78. Eisenschiml did not cite a source for the assertion that Casey was armed with "an appointment from Stanton, endorsed by Lincoln." Also, in suggesting that Casey should have disqualified himself because he resented Porter's rejection, he completely overlooked Casey's causes for being hostile to McClellan.
21. *O.R.*, 14, / XII, Part 3, 298.

As to N. B. Buford:

22. *DAB*, II, 244–245; Boatner, 97–98.
23. Eisenschiml, 80.

As to B. M. Prentiss:

24. Faust, 600–601; Boatner, 667; *DAB*, VIII, 188. For Prentiss' gallantry at Shiloh, see Foote, I, 324–345.

Ast to Slough:

25. Boatner, 706; Faust, 692–693.
26. Eisenschiml, 80–81.

As to King and Ricketts:

27. Faust, 418; Boatner, 463; *DAB*, V, 400 as to King; Faust, 633–634; Boatner, 699–700; *DAB*, VIII, 587 as to Ricketts.
28. These actions are described, with source citations, in Chapter Three.

As to Garfield:

29. *DAB*, III, 145–146; Faust, 299; Boatner, 323–324.
30. Eisenschiml, 80.

As to Holt:

31. Faust, 366; *DAB*, V, 181–183.
32. Thomas and Hyman, 88–117.
33. Ibid., 135–140.
34. Ibid., 139–141. Major General Henry W. Halleck, a Californian accused without substantiation by Stanton of perjury in the course of the land claims litigation, supported fellow Democrat Holt.
35. Ibid., 139–142.
36. Ibid., 156.

III

1. *O.R*, 17, / XII, Part 2 Supplement, 824–827. Emphasis supplied.
2. Ibid., 831–832.
3. Ibid., 840–841.

IV

1. Patricia L. Faust, editor, *Historical Times Encyclopedia of the Civil War*, 636.

2. *O.R.*, 17, / XII, Part 2 Supplement, 872.
3. Faust, 408.
4. Ibid., 408–409.
5. Shelby Foote, *The Civil War*, I, 514–515.
6. *O.R.*, 17, / XII, Part2 Supplement, 873.

V

1. *O.R.*, 17, / XII, Part 2 Supplement, 985–990.

VI

1. *Proceedings and Report of the Board of Officers in the Case of Fitz John Porter*, Volume II, 1241.
2. Ibid., 1312.
3. Ibid., 1312–1314.
4. Ibid., 1313–1314.
5. Ibid., 1314.
6. Ibid., 1368.
7. Ibid., 1369–1380.
8. Ibid., 1381–1387.
9. Ibid., 1387–1401.
10. Ibid., 1401–1404.
11. Ibid., 1411.
12. Ibid., 1427–1428.
13. Ibid., 1429.
14. Ibid., 1439–1440.
15. Ibid., 1440.
16. Ibid., 1450–1453.
17. Ibid., 1453–1455.
18. Ibid., 1455–1458.
19. Ibid., 1455–1465; the quotation is on 1461.
20. Ibid., 1661.
21. Ibid., 1662–1663.
22. Ibid., 1672.
23. Ibid., 1679.
24. Ibid.
25. Ibid., 1679–1680.
26. Ibid., 1683.
27. Ibid.
28. Ibid., 1688–1693.
29. Curt Anders, *Henry Halleck's War: A Fresh Look at Lincoln's Controversial General-in-Chief*, 325–340. At the time of the order, Halleck was too immersed in dealing with problems presented by Burnside, Grant, Banks, Rosecrans, and others to have engaged in court–martial members' selection. See also Eisenschiml, 74–75, 77–81, 169–171.
30. *Proceedings*, II, 1693.
31. Ibid., 1693.
32. Ibid., 1694.
33. Ibid.
34. Ibid., 1748–1749.
35. Ibid., 1749–1750.
36. Ibid., 1750.
37. Ibid., 1750–1751.
38. Ibid., 1751–1753.
39. Ibid., 1753.
40. Ibid.
41. Ibid., 1754.
42. Ibid., 1681 as to Choate.
43. Ibid., 1758.
44. Ibid., 1758–1759.
45. Ibid., 1761.
46. Ibid.
47. Ibid., 1761–1763.
48. Ibid., 1763.
49. Ibid., 1764.
50. Ibid.
51. Ibid.
52. Ibid., 1764–1765.
53. Ibid., 1765–1766.
54. Ibid., 1766–1770.

55. Ibid., 1770.
56. Ibid., 1771.
57. Ibid.
58. Ibid., 1771–1776.
59. Ibid., 1778.
60. Ibid.
61. Ibid., 1778–1780.
62. Ibid., 1780–1782.

VII

1. *O.R.*, 16, / XII, Part 2, 512–535.

Bibliography

Adams, Charles. *When in the Course of Human Events: Arguing the Case for Southern Secession.* Lanham, MD: Bowman & Littlefield, 2000.

Aimone, Alan C. and Barbara A. *A User's Guide to the Official Records of the American Civil War.* Shippensburg, PA: White Mane Publishing Co., 1993.

Anders, Curt. *Hearts in Conflict: A One-volume History of the Civil War.* New York: Barnes & Noble, 1999.

——. *Henry Halleck's War: A Fresh Look at Lincoln's Controversial General-in-Chief.* Zionsville, IN: Guild Press of Indiana, 1999.

Association of Graduates, USMA. *Register of Graduates of the United States Military Academy.* West Point, NY: 1999.

Bauer, K. Jack. *The Mexican War.* New York: Macmillan, 1974.

Benedict, Michael Les. *The Fruits of Victory: Alternatives in Restoring the Union, 1865–1877.* Philadelphia: J. B. Lippincott Company, 1975.

Boatner, Mark M. III. *The Civil War Dictionary.* New York: McKay, 1959.

Cozzens, Peter. *General John Pope: A Life for the Nation.* Urbana, IL: University of Illinois Press, 2000.

——, and Robert I. Girardi, editors. *The Military Memoirs of General John Pope.* Chapel Hill, NC: University of North Carolina Press, 1998.

Donald, David Herbert. *Lincoln.* New York: Simon & Schuster, 1995.

Dowdey, Clifford. *The Seven Days: The Emergence of Lee.* Lincoln, NB: University of Nebraska Press, 1993.

Eisenschiml, Otto. *The Celebrated Case of Fitz John Porter.* Indianapolis, IN: Bobbs-Merrill, 1950.

Elliott, Charles Winslow. *Winfield Scott: The Soldier and the Man.* New York: Macmillan, 1937.

Farwell, Byron. *Ball's Bluff: A Small Battle and its Long Shadow.* McLean, VA: EPM Publications, 1990.

Faust, Patricia L., editor. *Historical Times Encyclopedia of the Civil War.* New York: Harper & Row, 1986.

Foner, Eric. *Reconstruction: America's Unfinished Revolution, 1863-1877.* New York: Harper & Row, 1988.

Foote, Shelby. *The Civil War.* 3 vols. New York: Random House, 1958, 1963, 1974.

Bibliography

Freeman, Douglas Southall. *Lee's Lieutenants.* 3 vols. New York: Scribner's, 1942.

——. *R. E. Lee.* 4 vols. New York: Scribner's, 1934.

Gabler, Henry. *The Fitz John Porter Case: Politics and Military Justice.* New York: Unpublished Dissertation, City College of New York, 1979.

Gallagher, Gary, editor. *Fighting For the Confederacy: The Personal Recollections of General Edward Porter Alexander.* Chapel Hill, NC: University of North Carolina Press, 1989.

Haupt, Herman. *Reminiscences.* Milwaukee, WI: Wright & Joy, 1901.

Henderson, G. F. R. *Stonewall Jackson and the American Civil War.* New York: McKay, 1961.

Hennessey, John J. *Return to Bull Run: The Campaign and Battle of Second Manassas.* Norman, OK: University of Oklahoma Press, 1993.

Holien, Kim Bernard. *Battle at Ball's Bluff.* Orange, VA: Moss Publications, 1985.

Kennedy, Frances H., editor. *The Civil War Battlefield Guide.* Boston: Houghton Mifflin, 1990.

Leech, Margaret. *Reveille in Washington.* New York: Harper, 1941.

Long, E. B. and Barbara Long. *The Civil War Day-by-Day.* Garden City, NY: Doubleday, 1971.

Malone, Dumas, editor. *Dictionary of American Biography.* New York: Charles Scribner's Sons, 1934.

Martin, David G. *The Second Bull Run Campaign.* Conshohocken, PA: Combined Books, 1997.

McClellan, George B. *McClellan's Own Story.* New York: Charles L. Webster & Company, 1887.

Miers, Earl Schenk. *Lincoln Day-by-Day.* Dayton, OH: Morningside, 1991.

Nevins, Allan. *The War For the Union.* 4 vols. New York: Scribner's, 1959-1971.

New York Herald.

New York Tribune.

Pope, John, in Robert U. Johnson and Clarence C. Buel, editors. *Battles and Leaders of the Civil War.* 4 vols. New York: Century, 1887-1888.

Pratt, Fletcher. *Stanton: Lincoln's Secretary of War.* New York: W. W. Norton, 1953.

Proceedings and Report of the Board of Officers in the Case of Fitz John Porter. 2 vols. Washington, DC: Government Printing Office, 1879.

Randall, J. G. *Lincoln the President.* 4 vols. New York: Dodd, Mead, 1945–1953.

Schofield, John M. *Forty-Six Years in the Army.* Norman, OK: University of Oklahoma Press, 1998.

Sears, Stephen W. *Controversies & Commanders: Dispatches From the Army of the Potomac.* Boston and New York: Houghton Mifflin, 1992.

——. *George B. McClellan: The Young Napoleon.* New York: Ticknor & Fields, 1988.

——. *Landscape Turned Red: The Battle of Antietam.* New York: Ticknor & Fields, 1983.

——. *The Civil War Papers of George B. McClellan.* New York: Ticknor & Fields, 1989.

——. *To the Gates of Richmond: The Peninsula Campaign.* Lincoln, NB: University of Nebraska Press, 1992.

Stern, Philip Van Doren. *An End to Valor.* Boston: Houghton Mifflin, 1958.

Swanberg, W. A. *First Blood.* New York: Scribner's, 1957.

Tap, Bruce. *Over Lincoln's Shoulder: The Committee on the Conduct of the War.* Lawrence, KS: University Press of Kansas, 1998.

Thomas, Benjamin P. and Harold Hyman. *Stanton: The Life and Times of Lincoln's Secretary of War.* New York: Knopf, 1962.

Thomas, Emory M. *The Confederate Nation.* New York: Harper & Row, 1979.

Trefousse, Hans L. *Benjamin Franklin Wade: Radical Republican From Ohio.* New York: Knopf, 1963.

——. *The Radical Republicans: Lincoln's Vanguards for Social Justice.* New York: Knopf, 1969.

War of the Rebellion: Official Records of the Union and Confederate Armies. 70 vols. in 128. Washington, DC: Government Printing Office, 1880-1902.

——. *The Civil War CD-ROM.* Zionsville, IN: Guild Press of Indiana, 2000.

Williams, Kenneth P. *Lincoln Finds a General.* 5 vols. New York: Macmillan, 1949–1959.

Williams, T. Harry. *Lincoln and the Radicals.* Madison, WI: University of Wisconsin Press, 1965.

Index

Index

Index